Correctional Counseling and Treatment

Fourth Edition

Correctional Counseling and Treatment

Fourth Edition

Peter C. Kratcoski
Kent State University

WAVELAND

PRESS, INC.

Prospect Heights, Illinois

For information about this book, write or call:

Waveland Press, Inc.
P.O. Box 400
Prospect Heights, Illinois 60070
(847) 634-0081
www.waveland.com

This book is dedicated to the memory of my brother,
John E. Kratcoski

Contents

Preface

Correctional Counseling and Treatment, Fourth Edition, is designed to provide information on a number of treatment techniques currently being used in American corrections and to describe and demonstrate the applicability of these techniques in correctional settings. No attempt was made to include every counseling and treatment method currently in use. Rather, the selections in this book concentrate on the most widely used techniques, those that can be applied to juveniles and adults in both institutional and community settings.

The scope and purposes of correctional treatment today and the methods of evaluating correctional treatment are considered in Section 1. The role of treatment and counseling in corrections today is also considered. The trend in recent years toward determinate sentencing and retributive justice seemed for a time to reduce the importance of treatment and counseling in corrections. However, the "lock them up" correctional policies resulted in prisons becoming so overcrowded that other solutions had to be sought. This had the latent effect of stimulating the development of new, innovative approaches in community corrections and a growth in the tried and trustworthy older approaches to community correction. New programs, often labeled "intermediate sanctions" emphasize "enhanced" supervision and mandatory involvement in treatment programs. Although the strongest emphasis of these programs is on supervision of the offender, their treatment goals are also apparent.

When the effectiveness of various treatment techniques is evaluated, the question of the *purpose* of correctional treatment becomes highly important. Prevention of recidivism or demonstrated low levels of recidivism among those who were involved in specific treatment programs have always received high priority in evaluations of program success or failure. However, many staff members who administer correctional treatment programs maintain that the goals of correctional treatment must be more broadly defined and that successful treatment should be measured not only in terms of lack of recidivism, but also by such factors as improved mental health, ability to perform adequately in a work situation, successful adjustment in the community, and appropriate handling of interpersonal relationships.

Section II of this book describes career opportunities in corrections today and the characteristics and unique problems of people involved in corrections work.

The current emphasis on crime prevention and on concern for the needs of the victims of crime is reflected in the articles presented in Section III. Requiring that convicted offenders give restitution to victims, engage in community service, or participate in various types of treatment programs are examples of the "restorative justice" approach to correctional treatment described in this section. Diversion programs, such as mediation, are also considered.

In Section IV, "Classification for Correctional Treatment," the many facets of an offender's background (age, sex, family history, offense record, results of psychological and educational testing, physical health, presentence investigation, and reports by social and correctional workers) that may have a bearing on the type of treatment chosen are explored. Various classification systems developed, implemented, and evaluated by experts in the field are described. Attention is also given to multi-offender cases.

Sections V, VI, VII, and VIII are devoted to detailed descriptions and explanations of the tools and techniques used by those involved in providing correctional counseling and treatment. Those include interviewing techniques, anger management programming, crisis intervention, reality therapy and responsibility training, behavior management, and group counseling.

Section IX, "Special Areas of Correctional Treatment," focuses on the problems and unique situations that arise when counselors are working with retarded or mentally ill offenders, sex offenders, substance abusers, or older inmates. The selections provide many practical suggestions for working with such problem clients and describe programs that have been applied effectively.

Section X, "Correctional Treatment: Past, Present, and Future," summarizes the successes and problems of correctional treatment and highlights innovations in correctional supervision and administration, including the use of electronic monitors, privatization of correctional services, development of prison industries, educational programs in prisons, home confinement, and shock incarceration (the "boot camp" approach).

No attempt is made here to discuss the relative merits of various counseling and treatment techniques or to compare the effectiveness of community and institutional programs. Instead, the techniques are presented in such a manner that they can be applied in either type of correctional setting, with juvenile or adult offenders, or adapted to deal with adjustment problems of members of the "normal" (noncriminal) population.

Counseling and treatment techniques cannot be considered without reference to those who apply them. Several selections in this book report the efforts, frustrations, styles, reactions, and learning experiences of correctional personnel engaged in treatment.

Presentation of the wide range of correctional counseling and treatment techniques described here would not have been possible without the gracious cooperation and assistance of the many contributing authors and their publishers. In addition, the encouragement and support of Neil Rowe and Carol Rowe of Waveland Press and Jeni Ogilvie, Associate Editor, Waveland Press, helped make this book a reality. The numerous suggestions for improvements made by many professional colleagues were invaluable in developing a fourth edition that I hope will be useful to those in the corrections field.

Introduction

The Scope and Purposes of Correctional Treatment

This book is designed to present and describe some of the counseling and treatment techniques that are available to assist correctional workers toward accomplishing the goals they have established for their work. These goals are broadly defined as (1) to assist the offender in establishing a lifestyle that is personally satisfying and conforms to the rules and regulations of society and (2) to protect the community from harmful activity by offenders placed under correctional workers' supervision. These dual demands of correctional work—to provide assistance, counseling, and treatment and, at the same time, to act in a manner that will minimize the offender's threat to the community— are present for correctional workers who serve as youth counselors, guards, probation officers, juvenile aftercare supervisors, parole officers, social workers, psychologists, or coordinators of educational or employment programs.

In the view of many, correctional counseling and treatment is associated with employment by a government agency (federal, state or local) that has the responsibility to control offenders. While this description is accurate for the majority of individuals who work with delinquent and criminal offenders, there has been a significant trend in recent years toward contracting correctional or counseling services with private agencies or corporations. As a result, many of the professionals who work with offenders have credentials in fields other than criminal justice and corrections, including psychology, rehabilitation counseling, education, sociology, and social work. Occupations that involve some contact with offenders through counseling or treatment activity also include parole officer, child welfare caseworker, recreation leader,

1

social group worker, academic teacher, vocational instructor, correctional counselor, and psychiatrist.

Traditionally, the correctional worker's role was viewed as one of supportive assistance and surveillance-supervision. The correctional worker had to balance these two facets of the role and decide whether allowing certain behavior to occur was in the best interests of the offender and the residents of the community.

In the nearly twenty years since the first edition of *Correctional Counseling and Treatment* appeared, the goals of corrections have not changed appreciably, but the methods used and the emphasis on certain elements of corrections have undergone considerable alteration. The influence of Martinson's research finding that "nothing works in correctional treatment," coupled with an increase in the crime rate and related legislative changes, resulted in a decrease in interest in providing resources for community-based correctional programs and an increased emphasis on institutionalization of offenders. Those placed in secure, long-term correctional facilities were not always offered the wide variety of correctional treatment options formerly available. The correctional facilities became more punishment, "just deserts" oriented, with correctional treatment frequently not viewed as an integral aspect of inmate life. The prison overcrowding that resulted from these policies created a situation in which correctional administrators and legislators were forced to consider and again provide alternatives to institutionalization for some offenders.

In the late 1990s and into the 2000s, a renewal of interest in community corrections and correctional treatment modalities occurred, with emphasis on close supervision and surveillance of those allowed to remain in the community instead of being institutionalized. The types of programs regarded as correctional treatment now include a variety of intermediate sanctions, such as shock incarceration (boot camps), electronic monitoring, mandated substance abuse counseling/treatment, and activities provided at community corrections treatment centers. In addition, there is renewed interest in diversion, manifested in the advent of legislation that allows deferred prosecution for offenses; drug courts, which require that participants receive mandated treatment for their substance abuse problems; and the use of mediation as a means of diverting minor criminal offenders out of the criminal justice system. As a result of these changes in emphasis, the term "correctional treatment" must be viewed in a much broader context than in the past.

Today, the roles of correctional workers, particularly those who work in community settings, have become more complex. The expertise needed to provide the types of counseling, therapy, or treatment appropriate for certain offenders may be beyond the scope of a single professional's training. For example, offenders who have problems with alcohol or drug abuse, sexual deviance, mental retardation, or violent behavior may require widely divergent types of counseling and therapy. Thus, a very important function of correctional counseling today is assessment, classification, and referral activity. In many instances, a correctional counselor must be aware of the possibilities for referral and make decisions as to the most appropriate therapy, rather than attempt to personally provide specialized types of counseling to the offenders. The ambiguities and pressures associated with such decision making are documented and discussed by various authors in this book.

Defining Correctional Treatment

When correctional treatment is discussed, terms such as humanitarian reform, corrections, rehabilitation, and treatment are often used interchangeably, creating some confusion as to just what correctional treatment involves. Also at issue is the part played by incarceration and mandatory supervision in the correctional treatment process.

Humanitarian reforms are usually thought of in terms of what directly benefits and affects the physical welfare of the offender. Such initial modifications of the penal system as elimination of long periods of solitary confinement, flogging, or bread-and-water diets obviously fall within this definition, as do more contemporary changes that provide recreational facilities for inmates and allow prisoners to wear personal clothing rather than uniforms. Such liberal practices as allowing attendance at college classes outside the institution and weekend home visits for selected prisoners have caused some critics to observe that humanitarian reforms have gone too far and that the "country club" atmosphere of many institutions has minimized or virtually eliminated the impact of incarceration as punishment. Such thinking ignores or downplays the importance of personal motivation as an important factor in correctional treatment.

As implied in the word itself, "corrections" means to change a condition that is considered to be undesirable or has been a mistake and to bring things back to a state that is considered desirable or appropriate. In the correctional process, measures are taken to change the behavior of the offender to that which conforms with the standards and laws of the society. Corrections involves care, custody, and supervision of convicted offenders who have been sentenced or whose sentences have been suspended. The correctional process can occur in a federal or state correctional institution; as part of parole from such an institution; in a local jail or workhouse; or as part of probation at the federal, state, or local level. With the advent of diversion, pretrial intervention, deferred prosecution, and similar types of programs, it is logical to say that corrections has an opportunity to occur at any stage within the criminal justice process after a contact has been made between the offender and a law enforcement official.

The primary goal of corrections is to change the offensive behavior of the offender to a behavior that is designated appropriate by the laws of society. Before the eighteenth century, punishment was considered the central ingredient of corrections in European countries; thus, the dispensation of justice involved some form of physical torture or mutilation, banishment, or enslavement in galleys or on work farms. Prisons were used almost exclusively for those awaiting trial and for political prisoners. It wasn't until the eighteenth century that Cesare Beccaria (1738–1794) proposed the *pleasure-pain principle*—that is, that punishments should only be severe enough to deter offenders from repeating their unacceptable behavior (Sutherland, 1974:50).

At the same time, Jeremy Bentham (1748–1832) expounded his theory of utilitarianism in England. Both Beccaria and Bentham assumed that, given a free choice, a reasonable person would choose to avoid behavior for which he was sure to be punished. Bentham envisioned the prison as a correctional institution, located within the community, where citizens who had chosen to violate the law would be punished, while others would view it as a daily reminder of the penalties for violation of the law (Reid, 1976:106). The idea that the punishment should "fit the crime" became an accepted part of correctional practice, and various types of prisons and workhouses were built for the express purpose of being correctional centers or "houses of correction."

In the above context "correction" did not include rehabilitation as a key component. As time passed it became apparent that punishment alone did not guarantee a reduction in the criminal behavior of offenders, and there was gradual acceptance of the notion that those who eventually would be returned to society must be given some guidance and opportunities that would lead them toward a socially acceptable future lifestyle. Thus, while present-day "corrections" is not synonymous with "rehabilitation," it is very closely linked to it. Rehabilitation activity is set in motion when an individual comes to the attention of the correctional system after conviction. Such rehabilitation is involuntary in the sense that the offender has not actually sought it, but is rather required to undergo certain therapies, engage in counseling, or follow specified courses of action.

According to Allen (1964), the theoretical basis of rehabilitation is a complex of ideas that assumes human behavior to be a product of antecedent causes which are in turn part of the physical-social environment. This idea also presupposes that, given knowledge of the causes of human behavior, it is possible to scientifically control human behavior. Measures designed to treat the convicted offender should therefore serve a therapeutic function and should effect changes in his or her behavior that will be in his own best interests.

The notion of correctional rehabilitation as a return to a point in an individual's development when his or her behavior was satisfactory has been challenged by those who have observed that many offenders never experience anything in their lives resembling satisfactory adjustment, and that such persons are candidates for "habilitation" rather than rehabilitation. "Habilitation" here would refer to familiarity with and adjustment to normal society and the holding of values in line with the norms and laws of the community. Correctional work concerned with "habilitation" could well involve attack on the causes of an individual's poor adjustment to society (family problems, unemployment, lack of education) in addition to guidance toward acceptable behavior.

Correctional treatment, then, can be defined as any planned and monitored program of activity that has the goal of rehabilitating or "habilitating" the offender so that he or she will avoid criminal activity in the future.

The Effectiveness of Correctional Treatment

In *Correctional Counseling and Treatment*, Fourth Edition, we will explore the many ways in which correctional treatment may be attempted and note points of disagreement, controversy, or even diametric opposition in the approaches advocated.

No individual type of treatment has proved to be a panacea for reducing criminal activity. During the past twenty years, a debate has raged regarding the possibility that correctional treatment may be ineffective in reducing recidivism (additional criminal behavior) by those who receive it. If this is true, should correctional treatment attempts be abandoned, or is lack of recidivism by offenders the only factor to be considered in assessing treatment success? Is partially successful adjustment of the offender to his or her social environment justification for providing correctional treatment, even if some recidivism does occur? We must also consider another question that has gained considerable attention in recent years—is the application of correctional treatment better or more' effective in changing offenders' behavior than doing nothing at all? If the answer is negative, should we revert to a punishment-centered correctional philosophy?

Punishment vs. Treatment

In *We Are the Living Proof*, Fogel (1975) noted that two camps developed in regard to the advisability of undertaking rehabilitative correctional treatment with all types of offenders. One side, disillusioned by revelations of the inadequacy of policies in criminal justice and corrections, and buttressed in its arguments by high crime rates, citizens' fear of crime, and the apparent ineffectiveness of correctional treatment in preventing recidivism, advocated a very punitive, severe sentencing approach. The opposite camp had not given up on the possibilities of effective correctional rehabilitative treatment, but contended that the failure of correctional policies and programs was linked to inadequate resources, poorly trained personnel, political interference, and the existence of huge, brutalizing and dehumanizing prisons, which were schools for crime. This group was convinced that, with improvements in these areas, attempts at rehabilitative correctional treatment could still be successful.

Between these two points of view, Fogel saw an approach that would place renewed emphasis on an offender's responsibility and accountability for his or her actions, coupled with an emphasis on rehabilitative treatment that is *available* but not *mandatory*. Fogel termed this the "justice model for corrections." In this model, "justice as fairness should be the goal of all attempts at corrections, and all agencies of criminal law should perform their assigned tasks with offenders lawfully." Fogel addressed the area of the offender's responsibility for his or her actions and noted that restitution might often be substituted for harsh punishment, depending on the nature of the offense. He suggested an alternative to indeterminate sentences. In their place, Fogel advocated a return to "flat time," a set length of time in prison, which could be shortened only by good time (lawful behavior) credit, not by participation in any sort of treatment program.

This justice model, which emphasizes responsibility under the law, could reasonably be applied in programs outside institutions, including probation, parole, and community residential programs.

Many states and the federal prison system were quick to accept the assumption underlying the "justice model" and proceeded to adopt determinate sentencing policies for all convicted offenders (Champion, 1990:123) Other states, while not totally eliminating indeterminate sentencing, instituted measures that tended to reduce the emphasis given to the treatment and rehabilitation of convicted offenders and increased measures to deal more harshly with them (see Moore and Miethe, 1987; and Hamm, 1987).

The enthusiasm for the "justice model" waned somewhat as a result of the increasing evidence that determinate sentencing did not produce the anticipated results. For example, Wakefield (1985), who surveyed sentencing reforms for forty-four states, found that, rather than being treated more harshly by being given longer sentences, the lengths of the sentences given to drug traffickers were actually shorter than they were before the sentence reforms were instituted.

It is also apparent that treatment programs for convicted offenders did not disappear. As the evidence accumulated that much criminal activity is directly or indirectly related to such factors as substance abuse, illiteracy, mental illness or unemployment, which must be addressed if there is any hope of the offender becoming a productive person, the number and variety of treatment strategies actually increased. While the "justice model" proposes a "no right to treatment" policy and maintains that convicted offenders under local, state or federal supervision either in institutions or in the community should not be required to become involved in treatment programs, in practice correctional agencies have not abandoned treatment.

In some instances, the nature of the programs has changed. Many of these programs, such as "boot camp" training, may appear to be punishment rather than treatment oriented. However, they are well-thought-out projects which are geared toward making the offender accept responsibility and become disciplined and self-reliant. No one says treatment has to be pleasurable. The definition of treatment has also been expanded, so that work and educational programs are now encompassed under the treatment label. Many states and the U.S. Bureau of Prisons require prisoners to work, if they are physically able, or to go to school, if they are illiterate. Some forms of treatment are not only provided but are mandatory in these jurisdictions.

Thus, in most community or institutional corrections situations, the matter of choosing or rejecting treatment is not even debatable. Juvenile corrections continues to provide a range of counseling, education, vocational development and treatment services. On the adult level, those on probation, parole, or in community rehabilitation facilities discover that involvement in substance abuse counseling, employment counseling, or family therapy is likely to be required as a condition of placement in this status. Even those serving determinate sentences may elect or are required to take part in correctional counseling or treatment programs. Correctional counseling and treatment continue to be vital aspects of correctional work.

References

Allen, Francis A. 1964. "Legal Values and the Rehabilitative Ideal," in *The Borderland of Criminal Justice*. Chicago: University of Chicago Press, 1964.

Champion, Dean J. 1990. *Probation and Parole in the United States*. New York: Macmillan Publishing Co.

Fogel, David. 1975. *We Are the Living Proof*. Cincinnati: Anderson Publishing.

Hamm, Mark. 1987. "Determinate Sentencing in Indiana: An Analysis of the Impact of the Justice Model," Unpublished paper presented at the American Society of Criminology meeting, Montreal, Canada.

Moore, Charles A. and Terance D. Miethe. 1987. "Can Sentencing Reform Work? A Four-Year Evaluation of Determinate Sentencing in Minnesota."

Unpublished paper presented at the American Society of Criminology meeting, Montreal, Canada.

Reid, Sue Titus. 1976. *Crime and Criminology.* Hinsdale, IL: Dryden Press.

Sutherland, Edwin H. and Donald R. Cressey. 1974. *Criminology.* Philadelphia: Lippincott.

Wakefield, Penny. 1985. "The Sentencing Process: Redefining Objectives," in *State Laws and Procedures Affecting Drug Trafficking Control,* J. Bentevoglio, ed. Washington, DC: National Governors' Association.

Section *I*

Evaluation of Correctional Treatment

In this era of tightening state and federal budgets and emphasis on cost efficiency and fiscal accountability, any treatment program extensive enough to seek state or federal funding must contain some provision for evaluation. Statistical reports, which concentrate on numbers of clients served, hours worked by staff, estimates of the number of community members affected directly or indirectly by the program, and recidivism rates of the clients are familiar to those involved in correctional treatment. It has become very important to examine whether a certain type of treatment works as well as or better than another type and whether clients given a specific mode of therapy or supervision are likely to adjust in the community and remain offense-free more frequently than those given another type of treatment or no treatment at all.

Producing a meaningful and effective evaluation of any type of treatment program is beset with problems. It is difficult and often impractical to establish control groups with which those receiving treatment can be meaningfully compared and there is concern about the ethics of giving treatment to some offenders and withholding it from others for the sole purpose of comparative research. The short length of time between the initiation of the program and the required evaluation report frequently makes it difficult to establish comparative experimental and control groups. The ideals of random placement of those treated in experimental or control groups, or even matching of offender

9

populations according to age, number of prior offenses, or background characteristics must frequently give way to less meaningful comparisons. For example, the current residents of a halfway house that has a new job-training or employment-education program may be compared with those who resided in the house before the program began, with regard to their ability to get and hold jobs. In such an instance, changes in economic conditions within the community between the two time periods may be so extreme that the results coming from such a comparison may be questionable.

Evaluation may also be colored by the personal biases or characteristics of the evaluators. Internal evaluations, that is, those completed by the administrators of the programs, are particularly prone to this type of problem, since those in charge are anxious to show that the program is succeeding and that they are doing a good job. Outside consultants may also lean toward showing that the program is successful, since payment for their services in the future obviously hinges upon refunding and continuing the program. The subjects of a treatment program may also behave in such a way as to color its results. If, for example, subjects are aware that they are involved in a new or experimental program, they may do everything in their power to make sure it appears to succeed—or may sabotage it, if they dislike the demands made upon them.

A problem in developing the research design to evaluate a program is the formulation of a definition of "success." The indicator chosen most often to measure the success of correctional treatment is the amount or rate of recidivism (new offenses). Even on this point evaluation cannot be precise, because recidivism statistics are available only for those offenders who have been arrested and do not necessarily include all of the unlawful behavior that has occurred following correctional treatment. The level of supervision given to those who complete treatment is an important consideration in the amount of recidivism reported, particularly if violations tabulated as "new offenses" are probation or parole violations.

Also, the length of time covered by recidivism measurements has a bearing on the effectiveness evaluation. For example, the Highfields experiment in guided group interaction was declared a success because the recidivism rates one year after its completion were much lower for the experimental group than for a comparison group. After two years had passed, however, the variations in levels of recidivism between the two groups were greatly reduced.

If measures other than recidivism rates are used for purposes of evaluation, the problem of bias by the evaluators increases. Such instruments as personal adjustment checklists and case reports by probation or parole officers, which report the offender's readjustment to the community or degree of effort put forth in working on solutions to his or her problems, are obviously colored by the reporter's reaction to the offender. Even when a program has been judged to be successful by what appear to be objective evaluators and firm criteria, the reasons for its success may lie in the dedication or ability of the program's directors or workers or in certain ethnic or environmental characteristics of those being treated, and the likelihood of attaining the same level of success in other settings may be low.

The matters of correctional treatment and the possibilities for rehabilitation of offenders came under scrutiny in the 1970s when Robert Martinson, a sociology professor, wrote a series of articles in *The New Republic* which described and commented on his extensive examination of correctional treatment programs in English-speaking countries in the years 1945 through 1967. While the evidence presented in these articles was grounded in empirical research and eventually published in the book, *The Effectiveness of Correctional Treatment* (1975), by Douglas Lipton, Robert Martinson, and Judith Wilks, their conclusion that "with few and isolated exceptions, the rehabilitative efforts that have been reported so far have no appreciable effect on recidivism" (Martinson, 1974:25) aroused a furor in correctional circles. Those who felt that the criminal justice system had gone too far in terms of protecting the rights and interests of offenders at the expense of the victims of crime seized upon the study's conclusion, simplified it to contend that "nothing works" to change the behavior of criminals, and used this contention as the basis for calls to abandon the efforts to rehabilitate and to focus on harsher punishments.

It is true that Martinson painted a gloomy picture of the possibilities for rehabilitation success. In his article, "What Works?—Questions and Answers about Prison Reform" (1974), he reported the specific types of programs which he had evaluated and found lacking in success in preventing recidivism. The types included academic education, social skill development, vocational education, individual counseling, group counseling, and even milieu therapy, which used every element of the inmate's environment as part of the treatment modality. After reviewing many community treatment programs administered in halfway houses or as part of probation or parole activity, the author stated: "In some, even in the case of treatment programs administered outside penal institutions, we simply cannot say that this treatment in itself has an appreciable effect on offender behavior" (Martinson, 1974:50–51). On the basis of his examination of more than 200 programs of correctional treatment involving hundreds of thousands of offenders, Martinson stated that, although instances of success or partial success were noted, no pattern emerged to indicate that any method of treatment was effective in reducing recidivism (1974:54).

There is no doubt that *The Effectiveness of Correctional Treatment*, popularly known as "The Martinson Report," had a strong impact. The trends away from probation and toward sentencing to institutions, calls for determinate sentences, and shifts in emphasis in many correctional programs to punishment rather than rehabilitation closely followed circulation of the view that "nothing works"—or that very little can be done to change the behavior or offense patterns of juveniles or adults who have been involved in offenses serious enough to warrant their formal handling by the justice system.

Stuart Adams, in a review and critique of Martinson's research. observed that academicians as well as administrators and politicians may cloud the real issues and findings with rhetoric. He noted that before *The Effectiveness of Correctional Treatment* (the book which detailed the research) appeared, Martinson's articles in *The New Republic* and his appearance on the television program *60 Minutes* created a good deal of public interest in his findings. Efforts to capsulize them for popular consumption resulted in their simplification into what might be termed the "Nothing Works Doctrine," which became a rallying point for those interested in changing the focus and direction of correctional policy.

When Adams (1976) systematically compared the evaluations of specific programs cited in *The Effectiveness of Correctional Treatment* with evaluations of the same programs by other researchers, he found considerable variations in the conclusions reached regarding the effectiveness of the programs. For example, Palmer reported that 40% of the 231 program evaluations in *The Effectiveness of Correctional Treatment* showed at least partial positive results and termed them "partially or fully successful," while Martinson characterized the same programs as "few and isolated" instances of success. In addition, Adams concluded that the key factor in programs that achieved some success was the change agent—the rare individual who could inspire, goad, coax, frighten, or bully an offender enough to make him or her want to change.

Martinson continued to explore the degree of success of correctional treatment programs. In the article, "New Findings, New Views: A Note of Caution Regarding Sentencing Reform," he reported the results of additional research, which included not only evaluative research studies that matched control groups with the experimental groups receiving treatment, but also studies that reported on the progress of sentenced offenders. Believing that the term "recidivism" was a confusing one, Martinson (1979) systematically compared the evaluations of specific studies, with "reprocessing" defined as "subjecting an offender to further arrest, conviction, or imprisonment." Based on his new information, from 555 studies, Martinson retreated from his earlier conclusion that "with few and isolated exceptions, the rehabilitative effects that have been reported so far have no appreciable effect on recidivism." Instead, he declared that some programs were beneficial, others were neutral (had no impact), and still others were detrimental. He identified the key factor in the success of treatment programs as the "conditions under which the program is delivered."

Gendreau and Ross (1987) reviewed the research pertaining to offender rehabilitation for the period of 1981 through 1987. They assessed the literature that pertained to the effectiveness of a wide variety of treatment programs. They concluded that the "nothing works" statement on the effectiveness of treatment programs was fallacious. They also discovered that many innovative approaches being used in correctional treatment showed great promise. Some of these approaches were not being used during the period when Lipton, Martinson, and Wilks conducted their research.

Gendreau and Ross (1987:395) summarized their findings by stating: "It is downright ridiculous to say 'Nothing works.' This review attests that much is going on to indicate that offender rehabilitation has been, can be, and will be achieved. The principles underlying effective rehabilitation generalize across far too many intervention strategies and offender samples to be dismissed as trivial."

Palmer (1994) reviewed the debate sparked by Martinson's findings and concluded that two quite divergent points of view regarding the effectiveness of correctional treatment emerged in the late 1980s. Those who belonged to the "skeptical" camp concluded either that rehabilitation should be given a minor role because it held little promise or that the research into its effectiveness or the implementation of rehabilitation programs was so flawed that we do not know if it can work. In contrast, Palmer's "sanguine" camp maintained that some programs have been shown to work with certain offenders, even though many or most offenders will not be positively affected. The specific approach and external conditions were viewed as the key factors which dictated whether offenders would respond positively, neutrally, or negatively to treatment programs. Palmer identified intensive applications of "multiple modality" approaches, which combined various types of counseling according to the needs, interests, and limitations of individual offenders, as areas where both camps agreed efforts should be concentrated.

In selection 1, "Evaluating Interventions With Violent Offenders: A Guide for Practitioners and Policy Makers," Van Voorhis, Cullen, and Applegate note that evaluations of correctional programs are often not very useful in planning or policy making. Many program evaluations projects are poorly designed, and thus they do not yield valid or useful information. Other projects lack the appropriate financial and/or organizational support that is needed by the researchers to complete a quality evaluation. In the article, the authors offer several suggestions on how practitioners and policy makers can eliminate some of the impediments to conducting successful program evaluations. If these recommendations are followed, the evaluations of programs should be better and more useful for future planning.

In selection 2, "Evaluating Intensive Supervision Probation/Parole: Results of a Nationwide Experiment," Petersilia and Turner report some very recent findings relating to the use of intensive supervision for probationers and parolees. Intensive supervision has been hailed as a very important innovation for the rehabilitation of offenders for various reasons, including the fact that it is much less expensive than institutionalization and, since it is considered a substitute for incarceration, it helps relieve the current serious prison overcrowding problem.

The researchers discovered that those under intensive supervision are likely to be charged with more technical violations than those who receive traditional styles of supervision. However, compared to those supervised in other manners, intensively supervised offenders received more treatment in the forms of drug and alcohol counseling and employment counseling and participated in more community service and restitution programs. Involvement in the treatment components of intensive supervision correlated with a reduction in recidivism in some of the programs studied.

While the debate over the effectiveness of correctional treatment has not resulted in the total demise of treatment programs, it has had the positive effect of making those responsible for administering correctional treatment more selective in the types of treatment offered. The faddishness which was associated with earlier choices of treatment, with many techniques used experimentally because they appeared to offer novel approaches, has disappeared. Administrators and program directors now have to reach some degree of conviction that a treatment technique has long-term merit before it is instituted. Most treatment programs, particularly those that receive outside funding, have an evaluation component built in and must demonstrate that positive results are occurring.

In the final analysis, the resurgence of correctional treatment programs, which began in the 1990s and will certainly continue well into the twenty-first century, is the result of the "prison overcrowding" dilemma rather than any strong conviction that correctional treatment works. A positive outcome of the debate over the effectiveness of treatment is the stipulation that correctional treatment programs that are government funded must be evaluated. The sophistication of the research designs and the thoroughness of the evaluation process, which in most cases is completed by an independent, disinterested evaluator, is likely to make it much easier to separate those treatment programs that have merit and are effective from those that are deficient and should be discarded.

References

Adams, Stuart. 1976. "Evaluation: A Way Out of Rhetoric," in Robert Martinson, Ted Palmer, and Stuart Adams, *Rehabilitation, Recidivism, and Research.* Washington, DC: National Council on Crime and Delinquency: 75–91.

Gendreau, Paul and Robert R. Ross. 1987. "Revivification of Rehabilitation: Evidence from the 1980s," *Justice Quarterly,* Vol. 4, No. 3 (September): 349–408.

Martinson, Robert. 1974. "What Works? Questions and Answers about Prison Reform," *Public Interest* (Spring): 25–54.

Martinson, Robert 1979. "New Findings, New Views: A Note of Caution Regarding Sentencing Reform," *Hofstra Law Review,* Vol. 7, No. 2 (Winter): 243–58.

Palmer, Ted. 1994. "The 'Effectiveness' Issue Today: An Overview," in Peter C. Kratcoski, *Correctional Counseling and Treatment,* 3rd ed. Prospect Heights, IL: Waveland Press:15–30.

1

Evaluating Interventions
with Violent Offenders
A Guide for Practitioners and Policymakers

Patricia Van Voorhis, Francis T. Cullen, and Brandon Applegate

Growing frustration with the Nation's high rate of violence has prompted a sustained movement to "get tough" with violent offenders. Policies ranging from mandatory minimum sentences to "three strikes and you're out" promise to increase both the number of dangerous offenders who will be incarcerated and the duration of their time behind bars. In reality, however, many violent offenders will receive community-based sanctions, particularly during the early years of their criminal careers. And even if imprisoned, many will return to society.

Indeed, increased use of incapacitative and deterrent approaches is at best a partial solution to violent crime. Although prison typically is warranted for other reasons, the factors associated with violent behavior are not likely to be affected by after-the-fact prison terms (Gendreau & Little, 1993; Quinsey & Walker, 1994). Clearly, correctional agencies continue to be challenged to implement treatment programs that can be targeted to violence.

Unfortunately, a "knowledge gap" exists on the details of prevention and treatment programs that might be most effective with violent offenders. To date, important steps have been made in understanding the principles of effective correctional treatment programs; we also

Source: *Federal Probation*, 59(2) (June 1995): 17–27.

have learned a good deal about what types of programs "work" (Andrews, Zinger, Hoge, Bonta, Gendreau, & Cullen, 1990; Gendreau & Ross, 1987; Lipsey, 1988; Palmer, 1992). Yet, existing "meta-analyses" of evaluations of treatment programs, which identify program factors that are important in reducing recidivism, do not cite many studies specifically targeted to violent offenders (see Andrews et al., 1990b; Gendreau & Ross, 1987; Lipsey, 1988; Palmer, 1992; Whitehead & Lab, 1989).

It is noteworthy that a recent National Academy of Sciences Panel on the Understanding and Control of Violence confirms the continuing knowledge gap in the treatment of violent offenders and underscores the need for more effective evaluations of existing programs (Roth & Reiss, 1993). The panel has issued important conclusions:

a. Findings of program evaluations are not yet conclusive enough to warrant a national commitment to any single strategy.

b. Strategies aimed at predisposing risk factors, even when they are effective, require time to demonstrate that they will work.

c. While some strategies will doubtless prove more effective than others, the diversity of violent events guarantees that no single strategy will prevent more than a small fraction of them.

d. Violence control policy should be committed to small investments in the testing of many small-scale but sustained problem-solving initiatives—each initiative focused on a specific source of violence.

The panel has recommended, further, that each treatment initiative should involve five steps:

a. Diagnose the problem, using criminological and epidemiological techniques to document its importance and identify risk factors that suggest a preventive strategy.

b. Develop prototypes of several tactics for strategy implementation that show promise based on theory, research findings, or experience.

c. Compare the effectiveness of the alternative tactics through rigorous evaluations that use randomized assignment wherever feasible.

d. Refine the tactic for implementation using the evaluation findings as the basis.

e. Replicate the evaluation and refinement steps to sharpen the effectiveness of the interventions and adapt them to local community characteristics.

Past research confirms the panel's wisdom. Most of what we have learned has come from small, well-controlled studies, rather than from large-scale initiatives. We often neglect to replicate the most successful programs, and we often fail to create a clear prototype that will facilitate replication. The paucity of evaluation research, and the failure to replicate successful strategies, embodies the tragedy of many social programming endeavors: Most of what we know to be effective is not currently in practice; many of the seemingly good ideas which constitute current practice have not been or are not being tested.

Closing the knowledge gap on what works with violent offenders, thus, will depend on the development and *effective evaluation* of programs within a variety of settings. Yet, conducting effective evaluations often is viewed as a time-consuming and frustrating challenge to administrators and practitioners.

We approach this challenge from the growing realization that most of the impediments to conducting a useful evaluation occur far in advance of the program evaluation during the design phase of a program. And many of these design problems then adversely affect the evaluation and its findings. Design flaws may even affect *whether* the program can be evaluated.

The intent of this article is to discuss the interrelationship between program design and program evaluations. We review a number of program issues that become impediments to conducting sound evaluations of correctional interventions. We then offer numerous suggestions. Ultimately, we hope to put forward reasonable programmatic and evaluation directions which will then increase the likelihood of finding positive evaluation results. We do not address those activities that the evaluators are either solely responsible for or can execute with minimal input from the staff. These include development of a research design and comparison groups,[1] data analysis, and report preparation. The issues put forward in the sections below, however, are of more primary importance because technical expertise is of little value otherwise.

Impediments to Conducting Successful Program Evaluations

Unfortunately, in the field of corrections, it is the rare evaluation that is not doomed far before the first data collection form is completed. As the following sections detail, evaluation impediments begin in the environment of the program being tested and emerge from the manner in which the program is designed. At key points, administrators and program staff may be setting themselves up for unnecessary program disappointments.

Problems within the Program Climate

Perhaps one of the first questions we might ask is: Is it safe for staff and administration to evaluate their program? One does not have to look far to observe that evaluation results have been misused to undermine the continued existence of correctional interventions. Evaluation results are extremely vulnerable to political interests and are often misinterpreted. They are too frequently conducted with the understanding that negative evaluation results will sound the final bell for a program. Indeed, at one point in our recent history, misinterpreted evaluations placed the entire goal of rehabilitation in jeopardy and resulted in severe fiscal cuts to state and Federal treatment budgets (e.g., see accounts of the Martinson [1974] "nothing works" debacle as detailed in Cullen & Gilbert, 1982). Small wonder that program staff may not want to cooperate with evaluation research. A more constructive approach is sorely needed.

Evaluation efforts are also sometimes marred by a lack of financial and organizational support. This occurs in many ways. Agency administrators may not be willing to endorse or might withdraw support from the research design, compromising the integrity of the comparison group or the random assignment procedures in the middle of the research. Staff may not be able to break free from ongoing responsibilities to meet in planning or evaluation sessions. Finally, there may be insufficient financial resources to conduct the research. In such situations, programs may want rapidly assembled results that can be shown to their stakeholders (e.g., referral sources, funders, and political constituencies). And while they may be able to produce an evaluation quickly, the result may be an evaluation that: a) is based upon remote measures of program success, b) cannot be used to learn much of anything about effective programming, and c) is even *more* likely, by virtue of the program and evaluation design flaws, to portray the program as a failure.

Perhaps the most important issue concerns how well the program has been planned by the administrators and staff and how well program staff are then able to articulate various program components to evaluators. As a recent panel on Violence Prevention for Young Adolescents observed, evaluations must be planned at the earliest stages of program design (Wilson-Brewer, Cohen, O'Donnell, & Goodman, 1991). Here, the mindset of a good evaluation and the mindset of good program planning are strikingly similar. The program that cannot describe the population it serves, or is not delivering a clear process of treatment, or is not targeting the treatment to a cause of the problem being treated, usually will not succeed. Beyond that, it usually should not be evaluated because evaluation results will be highly misleading.

In response, the "evaluability assessment" has become an increasingly popular practice among government agencies contemplating funding a substantial evaluation of an experimental initiative (Rossi & Freeman, 1989). An evaluability assessment involves an external consultant's examination of a program's plan. A decision against evaluating the program is often made in instances where program staff and planners cannot identify several key questions: Who are our clients and what problem characteristics are we treating? What intervention fits our client problems? Why did we choose this particular intervention?[2] What are our goals and objectives? What intervention fits these goals and objectives? How will we know when we have implemented this intervention according to design? How will we know whether this intervention was effective?

Often, corrections is pressured to use a less rigorous planning process. Daily, atheoretical "magic bullets" are put forward by the media and by politicians; such pressures drive policy and intervention designs (Palmer, 1992). The proposed panacea often prescribes an intervention that: a) does not target a cause of crime; b) has already been found to be ineffective (e.g., boot camps without a treatment component); c) has no theoretical reason for working (e.g., yelling at boot camp participants); or d) defies everything that we know about crime and its effective treatment. As a result, most of what we know about effective interventions is not currently in practice; an emerging knowledge base that shows great consistency across authors and studies is virtually being ignored (see Andrews et al., 1990b; Andrews & Bonta, 1994; Gendreau & Ross, 1987; Lipsey, 1988; Palmer, 1992; Van Voorhis, 1987). The following sections expand upon these issues.

Who Are We Treating?

The identification of key client characteristics is important for two reasons. First, in order to successfully treat a client for violence or aggression, we must point (or target) our program services to some individual trait/problems or environmental factors that are known to predispose individuals to violence. It is not overly difficult to identify the risk factors for aggression and violence, for we probably know far more about the causes of aggression and violence than we know about their treatment. Aggressive behavior is typically the result of an interaction between personal characteristics and situational factors (Goldstein & Keller, 1987; Quinsey & Walker, 1994). In a valuable summary of the causes of violence, the National Advisory Panel accounts for both macro social (e.g., poverty, physical structure of a neighborhood) and micro social (e.g., community and family disorganization, bystander activity) correlates of violence. These are portrayed as interacting with numerous psychosocial and biological factors (Roth & Reiss, 1993). Equally instructive is a causal sequence of events shown in the work of Arnold Goldstein and his associates at Syracuse University (see Goldstein & Keller, 1987), where the authors identify perceptual and cognitive patterns, coping skills, contingencies, and values as ideal targets for intervention.

The second set of individual characteristics speaks to clients' amenability to treatment. Even when targeting our services to those clients at risk of violence/aggression, additional factors such as motivation, personality, and intelligence will affect a client's success in the program, regardless of whether or not they are correlates of violence.

As will be seen shortly, knowledge of the second set of individual characteristics (treatment amenability factors) affects both the plans for service delivery and the evaluation. Program staff will need to facilitate offenders who are likely to have difficulties in the program, while evaluators should want to consider these factors in their analyses of the evaluation results.[3] Andrews and Bonta (1994) include these characteristics under their "responsivity principle," while Warren (1983) and Palmer (1978, 1984, 1992) incorporated them earlier under the notion of differential treatment or "matching." A program that is conducting very little diagnostic and assessment work or is not screening for specific risk factors is likely to be making poor decisions about what specific aspect of violent behavior might be addressed by the program. Programmatic decisions about risk and responsivity factors should be related to the services the program delivers, its criteria for program admission, and the assessments it conducts at admission.

When we do not accommodate program interventions to offender risk and amenability factors, the following are the most likely outcomes:

a. A good program fails because it is targeted to individuals who cannot benefit from the program.

b. A good program works with some and not with others. Our successes are canceled out by our failures. The program looks bad when it really *did* work with some offenders.

c. The program was a true failure because planners did not provide a service which targeted a factor that is related to violence.

Did We Choose and Implement an Effective Intervention?

When evaluators, program personnel, planners, and others are not able to articulate the type of treatments or services delivered by a program, we refer to the programmatic services as a "black box." We do not, in other words, know what is in the box. In fact, it is not uncommon to observe evaluations with outcome data (e.g., recidivism measures or improvements on test scores) but no clear indication of what the program did to achieve these results. In such situations we know what the program accomplished, but we do not know what it did!

The seriousness of this problem is underscored by a view to the earlier history of evaluation research and correctional treatment. As the term suggests, some of our earlier published evaluations showed outcomes, but they failed to note whether the program was able to do what it was designed to do. Moreover, some programs provided results, but perhaps *never had* a clear intervention model. Thus, it is entirely possible that many of the failures of correctional treatment were not failures of a program but rather programs that never occurred.

There are several ways in which a program "might not occur":

a. The program is not grounded in the knowledge base of the discipline and therefore is not utilizing program strategies that are either empirically or theoretically sound.

b. The program has chosen a strong program design but is not *operating* according to the design or the clinical dimensions of an intervention (e.g., a social learning program which does not incorporate principles of good role modeling).

c. There is a lack of specificity in the program's design; we are delivering some global treatment, e.g., counseling, case management, job skills (which can mean different things to different staff), rather than an explicit treatment process that is known to be effective.

d. Staff members do not understand the intervention. They do not wish to cooperate, or they do not have or do not follow a treatment manual.

e. The organizational and political climate is too confusing and is not conducive to successful implementation.

f. Budget cuts create a situation where we are asked to do the impossible—keep the program without the funds.

g. The "dosage" is inadequate. It may be a good intervention, but the amount of time the client participates in the program is insufficient.

h. Clients did not or could not attend.

i. The program is too turbulent, undergoing several changes during the evaluation. Evaluators do not know what they tested.

j. Evaluators fail to measure various components of service delivery (e.g., contact hours, attendance, content analysis). The evaluation puts forward assumptions about whether or not the services were delivered.

The most tragic outcome of such events occurs when an evaluation creates the impression that "nothing worked" when, in fact, "nothing happened." The importance of adequate program implementation was recently illustrated poignantly by the Violent Juvenile Offender Project. The project had been implemented in four sites but only showed success in two. The factor that differentiated success from failure was the *quality* of program implementation, which th   l meticulously (Fagan, 1990).

There are other problems with neglectful int situations where we cannot make program adju because we don't know what the program did.

Important
for essay/PP

Will We Know If We Have Succeeded?

The answer to this question involves constructing measures of program success. Very often "success" is measured by using general measures of recidivism, such as revocation, rearrest, or reconviction.[4] However, while recidivism, especially for new violent offenses, is an important measure of program success, programs should not ignore a second type of measure linked to intermediate objectives. These depict whether or not our program affected a risk factor for aggression/violence. In answering the earlier question, "who are we treating?," we might have indicated that we were treating some "cause" of aggression (e.g., poor conflict management skills). In this case, an intermediate objective would address improvement in conflict management skills. Usually we would measure attainment of this objective just before each client's release from the program.

Unfortunately, the importance of intermediate objectives and measures of their attainment are often overlooked, particularly in programs for violent offenders (Wilson-Brewer, Cohen, O'Donnell, & Goodman, 1991). In doing so, two problems are created. First, the program ignores an important measure of treatment integrity. And stakeholders are entitled to ask, "Why isn't the program addressing aggressive behavior?" In contrast, an obvious way to show that the program *had* targeted aggression and *had* delivered an effective intervention would be to show that it affected risk factors related to aggression.

Second, the program ignores another function of these measures; if properly chosen, they tap dynamic risk factors. Dynamic risk measures offer extremely important information to programs because the research shows us that improvement on dynamic risk factors is typically as predictive or *more* predictive of post-program success than are more traditional risk assessment instruments (Andrews & Bonta, 1994).

The task of obtaining the more distal outcome or "success" measures of recidivism is more complicated, particularly with respect to violence or aggression (see Goldstein & Keller, 1983; Monahan & Steadman, 1994). And each type of measure has its own source of measurement error. Medical and psychological interventions, for example, often use analogue measures which pose problems of external validity (i.e., a subject's aggressive response to a hypothetical situation may not translate into actual aggression). Self-report measures may be marred by behavioral and temporal specificity, social desirability, response bias, attribution styles, and motivation. There is also a tendency to pick up minor forms of aggression, rather than more serious behaviors. Staff observational measures, which are very efficiently obtained in institutional settings, may reflect subject reactivity to the observer or staff biases. Measures of overt violent behavior (official measures) may result in high amounts of undetected behavior and low base rates (Monahan & Steadman, 1994; Van Voorhis, 1994a). Finally, each measure is likely to tap a different component of aggression, ranging from overt aggression to aggressive attitudes to aggressive tendencies.

In contrast to the measures of intermediate objectives and recidivism, program completion rates, client satisfaction surveys, or number of clients served are *not* measures of program success. Although they serve *some* purpose in the larger scheme of program accountability, these measures do not answer *any* questions about "what works" in the treatment of the violent offender.

Suggestions for Improving Program Evaluation and Planning

Improving the Organizational Climate

Any improvements in the organizational support for evaluation research must effect positive change on two fronts: the organization's perspective on the evaluation and the staff's skill in planning and developing programs. With respect to the former, some improvements have already occurred, largely in response to increased pressures on agencies for accountability from funding sources. Indeed, there are good reasons for conducting an evaluation. We might cite, for example, the American Correctional Association's accreditation criteria which, while not requiring research, nevertheless offer additional credit for participation in evaluations or other types of research. In another sense, an evaluation, if properly conducted, *can* help a program improve its planning and effectiveness. In doing so, an evaluation can engage staff in a constructive share of the planning. Staff involvement in planning and program articulation can be a source of staff motivation. In support of this notion, one of the characteristics of an effective program is the absence of top-down planning and the presence of staff involvement in program design (Andrews & Kiessling, 1980; Cullen & Gendreau, 1992; Gendreau, in press).

We can expect substantial improvements in the climate of a program evaluation by simply rejecting the "win-lose" perspective on evaluation research, which sees programs as either "working" or "not working." If the evaluation study is comprehensive enough, it will produce more information than whether the program worked. It may, for example, identify specific program components or services that failed (rather than the entire program); it may show us that the program worked for some types of offenders but not for others; it may tell us whether the program achieved a proper service "dosage." If none of these components of the program are measured in the evaluation, these crucial questions will not be answered. When they are assessed, however, the evaluation may become an important source of feedback, thus leading to program adjustments rather than to program obliteration (Rossi & Freeman, 1989).

We might also create a fairer climate for the program by promoting more widescale appreciation for realistic standards of success. Indeed, more conservative researchers tell us that the most we can hope for, with the most effective program designs and implementation, is a 20 percent improvement in recidivism rates for an experimental group over a comparison group (see Lipsey, 1988; Palmer, 1992), perhaps 40 to 50 percent among the most optimistic reviewers (see Andrews & Bonta, 1994; Gendreau, in press). While some have argued that these figures indicate failure rather than success (see Lab & Whitehead, 1990; Martinson, 1974), even the conservative 20 percent success rate translates into impressive cost benefits (Gendreau & Ross, 1987; Lipsey, 1984). More importantly, the 20 percent success figure for treatment is the best we have because alternative policies of incapacitation and deterrence don't come close to this figure (see Irwin & Austin, 1994; Roth & Reiss, 1993), and often the deterrent or "get tough" strategies find higher recidivism in the experimental programs than in the comparison groups (Gendreau & Ross, 1987).

A Model for Program Planning

Even when organizational considerations are addressed successfully, sound planning must become a structural component of programming at both administrative and staff levels of responsibility. Much of what we have addressed in this article comes together in the diagram shown in figure 1, which also depicts the relationship between the program design and the evaluation design.

Figure 1

The Interrelationship between Planning and Evaluation Tasks

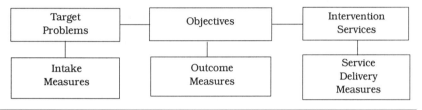

The program begins with a thorough understanding of the target problems and the characteristics of individuals who need to be served in order to address these problems. Program selection/screening criteria follow from this understanding. At the same time, the evaluation staff designs and uses intake data collection forms that tap the selection criteria, any relevant assessment data, and routine demographic and social background factors.

Given the staff members' understanding of the problem and their client base, the program identifies objectives that it can reasonably meet within its current resources. There will be intermediate objectives, depicting what the program accomplishes, and long-term objectives, such as a post-program reduction in recidivism. The evaluation staff helps the program to identify measures or data that must be collected in order to assess attainment of these objectives. Often change in one of the intake assessment measures will be one such measure, e.g., improvements on the Buss-Durkey Hostility Inventory.

Finally, when the program designs its service delivery strategies (e.g., a skills development program), the evaluation staff helps the program to devise methods for determining whether the service was administered according to design and how much time clients spent in the program (dosage). These factors will be assessed through service delivery measures.

Simply put, there must be a systematic planning process which evidences a logical interrelationship between the components identified above. Services, for example, should "fit" the objectives of the program. Most importantly, the planning process should be grounded in the literature pertaining to what works as well as the psychological and criminological theories of what caused the problem behaviors to begin with.

We offer some suggestions keeping to such a planning model:

a. Greater interaction between case management and counseling staff and evaluators and planners as a part of an overall planning/evaluation model. Creating a climate where staff members work from a base of: 1) What is the problem?; 2) Who are our clients?; 3) What are our objectives?; 4) What intervention will achieve these objectives?; and 5) How will we know when we have achieved our objectives?

b. Consider evaluation and planning skills in the hiring of staff members, even those who are not hired for research purposes. Many undergraduate programs in social sciences require relevant course work. Consider inservice training for current staff members who have not been so trained.

c. Fit evaluation instruments to organizational and structural demands. Data collection efforts need not go against the natural case processing flow of a program.

d. Finally, it perhaps goes without saying that correctional administrations cannot view evaluation research as an "add on." Such orientations can result in failure to support the integrity of the treatments and the evaluations. Evaluations, in such cases, usually find that the program didn't work.

Improving Our Knowledge of Who and What We Are Treating

Figure 1 indicates a box for "target problems." This is where any programmatic intervention begins. Objectives, the choice of interventions, and ultimately measures of success all relate back to the problem(s) we are addressing. If we do not know what the problem is, it is impossible to plan clear objectives, interventions, and outcome measures. Clearly, most programs for aggressive individuals should plan for some level of client assessment.

Goldstein and Keller (1987), for example, provide clear but intensive examples of program planning that moves from a clear assessment of the problem to interventions that fit each problem. The authors assess adult clients on each of the types of target problems that they address and give examples of psychological tests and inventories that fit each target problem: 1) for measuring arousal-heightening interpretations, the Anger Inventory (Novoco, 1975) or the Reaction Inventory (Evans & Strangeland, 1971), 2) for assessing heightened affective arousal, the Buss-Durkee Hostility Index (Buss & Durkee, 1957) or marital conflict measures (Filsinger, 1983), 3) for malcommunication, the Conflict Tactics Scale (Straus, 1979), 4) for deficiencies in social skills, the Social Performance Survey Schedule (Lowe & Cautela, 1978) or the Conflict Resolution Inventory (Hartwig et al., 1980), and 5) for assessing antisocial values, the Psychopathy Checklist (Hare et al., 1992) or the Sociomoral Reflections Measure (Gibbs & Widaman, 1982).[5]

From there, the authors proceed to link specific interventions to each problem area. For example, they recommend that clients known to have distorted perceptions of what is a provocative event receive Anger Control Training (see also Novaco, 1976). Likewise, clients with deficiencies in social skills should engage in skills training, etc.

For those who view Goldstein's approach as an overly elaborate model, a more straightforward method is found in Andrews' notion of the "criminogenic need" (Andrews, Bonta, & Hoge, 1990a; Andrews & Bonta, 1994). Many programs have been introduced to needs assessment instruments that supplement the current risk assessment forms (e.g., see NIC, 1982). However, the standard needs assessment often neglects close attention to the "criminogenic need," which involves identifying that risk factor which is linked to a particular offender's criminal actions. For programs for the aggressive offender, this could involve a checklist of aggressive risk factors incorporated into a routine intake interview and staff discussions of the criminogenic needs at team meetings and staffings.

We might also consider the use of certain assessment instruments to make determinations about program "responsivity" that allow us to identify which type of offender was most successful in the intervention. For these purposes, consider instruments listed by Goldstein and Keller (1987); a personality typology (e.g., the Jesness Inventory (Jesness & Wedge, 1983), Quay's behavioral categories (Quay & Parsons, 1972; Quay, 1983; Quay, 1984), or the Megargee MMPI-Based Taxonomy of Adult Offenders]; or a theoretically based risk assessment instrument such as the Level of Supervision Inventory (which also addresses criminogenic needs) (Andrews, 1982).

In sum, we mentioned that programs have two purposes in understanding their target population: 1) targeting the services to specific client risk factors and 2) the "responsivity principle," ensuring that even the service that logically fits a client's need also fits his or her abilities, motivation levels, and personality considerations (Andrews et al., 1990a; Goldstein & Keller, 1983; Palmer, 1978; Warren et al., 1966). More careful attention to both is likely to greatly improve program and evaluation results.

Improving Treatment Integrity

Problems related to treatment integrity occur in two ways. The first problem occurs when a program is unwilling or unable to operate from the knowledge base of the discipline. Asking the question, "Where did the idea for our intervention come from?," would be extremely important. With growing knowledge about what works, it makes little sense to follow a hunch. Thus, before asking whether a program *does* work, we must ask whether there is any reason why it *should* work. Programs grounded in a theoretical model (theory of crime) or found in previous controlled evaluations to be effective really *should* work, so we at least should start at that point.

Even when adopting a sound program design, it would be easy to fail to communicate a clear picture of the clinical or procedural components to the staff who must administer it. To address this concern, written *treatment manuals* would appear to be essential documents in efforts to improve the consistency of service delivery models within programs as well as across them (Gendreau, in press). A good treatment manual would provide a "how to" description of the intervention model; it should not be written to serve the dual purpose of a program's promotional brochure.

The fact that programs seldom develop and use treatment manuals may be partly the responsibility of the research and scholarly community who has written the evaluation studies over the years. Seldom are program accounts written in a manner that facilitates replication and the development of a treatment manual. The few exceptions include, but are not limited to, Palmer's and Warren's accounts of the Community Treatment Project (see Palmer, forthcoming; Warren et al., 1966; Warren, 1983); Vicky Agee's Closed Adolescent Treatment Program (Agee, 1979) and the Paint Creek Youth Center (Agee, 1987); Fabiano, Robinson, & Porporino's (1991) work on Cognitive Skills Training Programs; Don Andrews' accounts of effective social learning approaches (Andrews & Bonta, 1994). Arnold Goldstein's treatments for aggression (Goldstein & Keller, 1987) and Novocos Anger Control Training (1975) have already been mentioned.

In order to assess the second problem, whether a program is being administered according to design, a fairly straightforward process may be followed. This task involves determining the data elements needed in order to assess program integrity. Some of the more common data needs at this point are:

a. Attendance lists and case management logs to collect valuable information on dosage.

b. Surveys of clients and staff in order to determine the extent to which key program components were adhered to. A skills development program, for example, might survey for whether skills were actually modeled.

c. Intake assessments relevant to the nature of the aggression dynamic (e.g., anger management) could be re-administered immediately following the completion of an intervention. Use of alternative test forms is preferred.[6]

d. Intermediate program objectives should lead to evaluation variables or measures of program integrity. They can only do this if they are written in a specific manner. Such clear objectives also reduce program confusion and conflict and facilitate successful program implementation.

Less common measures of program integrity should also be considered. For programs that operate from a more complex clinical model, most forms of family therapy, for example (Van Voorhis, Braswell, & Morrow, 1992), clinical observation or content analysis would be very important. A discussion among family members lacks the clinical dimension of some of the family therapy models known to be effective with some offenders.

Existing assessments of program characteristics are also useful. The Correctional Program Assessment Inventory (CPAI) (Gendreau & Andrews, 1994), for example, offers a measure of program integrity and other characteristics. A unique contribution of the CPAI is that it asks program staff members where the idea for their interventions originated (from theory or research). It also makes note of whether a treatment manual is in use.

Improving Measures of Program Effectiveness

A program for violent offenders will ultimately be held to the goal of reducing violent and/or aggressive behavior, but this can be shown by measuring attainment of intermediate objectives (e.g., improvement in conflict management skills) or by measuring future aggressive behaviors or violent crimes (i.e., long-term objectives)—or by both (see figure 1). While the most convincing outcomes pertain to follow-up recidivism for new aggressive offenses, it is surprising, nevertheless, to observe programs neglecting the importance of measuring the attainment of intermediate objectives.

Indeed, full attention to whether intermediate objectives had been achieved is more likely to show a well-designed program in a favorable light than not. This occurs because: 1) programs often are more likely to show success on the intermediate objectives than on long-term, post-program measures because, in most instances, the latter are affected by factors that are outside of the program's control (Quinsey & Walker, 1994); 2) measurement problems are more likely with the long-term recidivism measures than with measures relevant to intermediate objectives[7]; 3) the attainment of intermediate objectives can be used as both measures of program effectiveness *and* a measure of treatment integrity; 4) some measures can also be viewed as "dynamic risk factors" which are predictors of recidivism (Andrews & Bonta, 1994); and 5) we may compare recidivism figures for those who succeeded in the program (scored well on the intermediate objective) to those who did not (scored poorly). It is surprising how often evaluation results are presented in an undifferentiated format, allowing the program's failures to cancel out its successes (Palmer, 1978).

What constitutes a measure of an intermediate objective? Any objective developed by a program should be stated in quantifiable (measurable) terms in order to guide the selection or the design of an appropriate measure. Particularly with programs targeted for aggressive offenders, attainment on an intermediate objective will often be improvement on one of the intake assessment tests (e.g., anger management, Buss-Durkey Hostility Inventory). If it fits the objective, an existing measure is preferred because, usually, reliability and validity have been established by previous research.

It is important to stress that the evaluator's success in selecting or developing the measures will depend upon the program's statement of a quantifiable objective. Vague objectives cause measurement problems as well as programmatic confusion.

None of the preceding discussion should negate the importance of recidivism measures and the question of whether or not the program had impact upon future violent crimes. Possible sources of data on client recidivism include self-reports, arrests, and, for those who have been institutionalized, official disciplinary citations for aggressive incidents and staff evaluation. Because each measure is likely to have a unique type of measurement error, the best response may be to use multiple measures of aggression (Farrington & Tarling, 1985). The most accurate picture may be in the combination of results, tempered by our knowledge of potential sources of measurement error (Van Voorhis, 1994b).

Conclusion

We began this article by underscoring the need for additional evaluation research pertaining to "what works" in the treatment of violent offenders. Citing the National Academy of Sciences Panel on the Understanding and Control of Violence and others, we recognized a strong need for small initiatives for dealing with the violent offender; those experiments *must be* adequately tested and replicated. Indeed, our society's fear of violent crime should be accompanied by social outrage over the fact that most of what is known to work is not currently in practice; and in many instances, little to no interest is being shown for whether current practices are working.

In addressing this problem, we have attempted to show that many evaluation problems begin while the program is being designed. Conversely, the evaluation should be planned at the same time the program is designed; at that point, any program component which is not amenable to research is also likely to be unclear in programmatic ways and probably needs to be further articulated.

In many respects, our comments need not be limited to the violent offender, but are pertinent to other offender treatment programs or for that matter to evaluations of most social programs. This is true for the structure of our suggestions but not necessarily for their specific content. As for the structure of program planning and evaluation, figure 1, and many of the comments pertinent to it, represent a standard model for the social sciences. But we are less comfortable asserting that specific assessments and strategies for violent offenders can be extended to other offender groups. We are especially not ready to agree with the suggestion that violent offenders and other high-risk offenders always can be treated in the same groups (e.g., Gendreau, in press; Quinsey & Walker, 1994); with so few tests of programs specifically targeted to aggression and violence, such assertions appear to be premature. In fact, aggression and violence have some unique risk factors which are not at work in other forms of criminal behavior.

In addition to hampering the development of knowledge, many programs appear to be hurting themselves by not following a sound program and evaluation plan and by conducting evaluations too haphazardly. This occurs in many ways. First, in agreement with Palmer (1978), we suspect that many evaluations showing no treatment effect have, instead, masked the treatment effect. That is, many programs have worked with some offenders and not others, but with no way of subdividing the research sample into subgroups that account for different levels of responsivity, we produce successes which are canceled by our failures. Second, many program evaluations have not fully utilized the results that have maximum chance of showing success (e.g., attainment of intermediate objectives); or they produce evaluation measures which do not fit program services and clients. Third, when program disorganization results in staff members working in different directions or when we are uncertain about the characteristics of program clients, we will probably have insignificant results. Statistical tests are designed to reject all but those events which are most likely to be related, and random events are not related! Moreover, invalid measures attenuate research findings. Fourth, many failures have resulted from treatment of factors such as self-esteem, which are not necessarily a cause (or correlate) of aggression. Finally, well-supported theories of violence and aggression, and the few extant evaluation studies of effective programs that can point us to programs that work, are not used as guides for program development. We hope we have shown that all of these unfortunate shortcomings can be addressed during the planning phases of the program.

Notes ·

[1] Comparison groups, particularly those that utilize random assignment of clients to experimental and comparison groups, are essential if the evaluation is to contribute to the knowledge base. Once external evaluation services have been contracted for, however, it is the evaluator's responsibility to design the research itself—staff may be asked to see only that the design is adhered to and may be given instructions as to how to adhere to a specific assignment process.

[2] A crucial concern here is for whether the choice of interventions reflects prevailing knowledge about effective programming, or if the intervention was selected for some other reason.

[3] How, for example, do results differ for the two groups of individuals, those amenable to the program and those who were not?

[4] An adequate program evaluation would compare the recidivism measures of an experimental group to a randomly assigned or matched comparison group of participants who did not receive the program services being tested. Given the difficulty of conducting such a "controlled" study, many evaluations compare post-program successes to pre-program measures or provide only a post-program figure. The latter tells us very little about whether or not the program succeeded. Indeed, it is widely accepted that only controlled studies will produce a contribution to our understanding of the treatment of aggression.

[5] These do not exhaust all of the assessments suggested by Goldstein and Keller (1987). The book also contains a list of assessments that would be suitable for children. Moreover, the authors identify a number of suggestions for designing interviews and surveys pertinent to these problem dimensions.

[6] The change in the assessment measure (from intake to program completion) measures attainment of an intermediate objective, but it could be as a dynamic risk factor (Andrews & Bonta, 1994) for its impact on the long-term objective of reducing recidivism.

[7] This is because evaluators have more control over the creation of measures for intermediate objectives and their administration. In contrast, official measures of new offenses (e.g., police data) are likely to have some problems with both validity and low base rates (Monahan, 1981). Moreover, researchers are experiencing increasing difficulties securing access to the national data bases for criminal records.

References

Agee, V. (1979). *Treatment of the violent, incorrigible adolescent.* Lexington, MA: Lexington Books.

Agee, V. (1987). *The treatment program: Paint Creek Youth Center.* Unpublished manuscript obtained from Paint Creek Youth Center, Bainbridge, OH.

Andrews, D. (1982). *The Level of Supervision Inventory (LSI).* Toronto: Ontario Ministry of Correctional Services.

Andrews, D., & Bonta, J. (1994). *The psychology of criminal conduct.* Cincinnati, OH: Anderson Press.

Andrews, D., Bonta, J., & Hoge, R. (1990a). Classification for effective rehabilitation: Rediscovering psychology. *Criminal Justice and Behavior, 17*, 19–52.

Andrews, D., & Kiessling, J. (1980). Program structure and effective correctional practices: A summary of the CAVIC research. In R. Ross & P. Gendreau (Eds.), *Effective correctional treatment* (pp. 441–463). Toronto: Butterworth.

Andrews, D., Zinger, I., Hoge, R., Bonta, J., Gendreau, R. & Cullen, F (1990b). Does correctional treatment work? A psychologically informed meta-analysis. *Criminology, 28,* 369–404.

Buss, A., & Durkee, A. (1957). An inventory for assessing different kinds of hostility. *Journal of Consulting and Clinical Psychology, 21,* 343–349, cited in Goldstein & Keller (1987).

Cohen, S., & Wilson-Brewer, R. (1990). *Violence prevention for young adolescents: The state of the art of program evaluation.* Presentation for the conference, "Violence Prevention for Young Adolescents," Washington, DC.

Cullen, F., & Gendreau, P. (1992). The effectiveness of correctional rehabilitation and treatment. In D. Lester, M. Braswell, & P. Voorhis (Eds.), *Correctional counseling* (pp. 227–242). Cincinnati, OH: Anderson Press.

Cullen, F., & Gilbert, X. (1982). *Reaffirming rehabilitation.* Cincinnati, OH: Anderson Press.

Evans, D., & Strangeland, M. (1971). Development of the reaction inventory to measure anger. *Psychological Reports, 29,* 412–414 cited in Goldstein & Keller (1987).

Fabiano, E., Robinson, D., & Porporino, F (1991). *A preliminary assessment of the cognitive skills training program: A component of living skills programming: Program description, research findings and implementation strategy.* Ottawa: Correctional Service of Canada.

Fagan, J. (1990). Treatment and reintegration of violent juvenile offenders: Experimental results. *Justice Quarterly, 7,* 233–263.

Farrington, D., & Tarling, R. (1985). Criminological prediction: introduction. In D. Farrington & R. Tarling (Eds.), *Prediction criminology* (pp. 2–33). Albany, NY: SUNY Press.

Filsinger, E. (Ed.). (1983). *Marriage and family assessment.* Beverly Hills, CA: Sage, cited in Goldstein & Keller (1987).

Gendreau, P. (in press). *The principles of effective intervention with offenders.* In A. Harland (Ed.), *Choosing correctional options that work: Defining the demand and evaluating the supply.* Thousand Oaks, CA: Sage.

Gendreau, P., & Andrews, D. (1994). *Correctional program assessment inventory* (4th ed.). St. John, New Brunswick: University of New Brunswick.

Gendreau, P., & Little, T. (1993). *A meta-analysis of the effectiveness of sanctions on offender recidivism.* Unpublished manuscript, Department of Psychology, University of New Brunswick, St John.

Gendreau, P., & Ross, R. (1987). Revivification of rehabilitation: Evidence from the 1980s. *Justice Quarterly, 4,* 349–408.

Gibbs, J., & Wideman, F. (1982). *Social intelligence.* Englewood Cliffs, NJ: Prentice Hall, cited in Goldstein & Keller (1987).

Goldstein, A., & Keller, H. (1983). Aggression prevention and control. In A. Goldstein & L. Krasner (Eds.), *Prevention and control of aggression* (pp. 338–350). New York: Pergamon Press.

Goldstein, A., & Keller, H. (1987). *Aggressive behavior: Assessment and intervention.* New York: Pergamon Press.

Hare, R. D., Forth, A., & Strachan, K. (1992). Psychopathy and crime across the lifespan. In R. D. Peters, R. McMahon, & V Quinsey (Eds.), *Aggression and violence throughout the lifespan* (pp. 285–300). Newbury Park, CA. Sage.

Hartwig, W., Dickson, A., & Anderson, H. (1980). Conflict resolution inventory: Factor analytic data. *Psychological Reports, 46,* 1009–1010.

Irwin, J., & Austin, J. (1994). *It's about time: America's imprisonment binge.* Belmont, CA: Wadsworth Publishing Co.

Jesness, C., & Wedge, R. (1983). *Classifying offenders: The Jesness inventory classification system.* Sacramento: California Youth Authority.

Lab, S., & Whitehead, J. (1990). From "nothing works" to "the appropriate works": The latest stop on the search for the secular grail. *Criminology, 28,* 405–417.

Lipsey, M. (1984). Is delinquency prevention a cost-effective strategy? A California perspective. *Journal of Research in Crime and Delinquency, 21,* 279–302.

Lipsey, M. (1991). Juvenile delinquency treatment. A meta-analytic inquiry into the viability of effects. In T. Cook, H. Cooper, D. Corday, H. Hartment, L. Hedges, R. Light, T. Louis, & F. Mosteller (Eds.), *Meta-analysis for explanation: A casebook.* New York: Russell Sage Foundation.

Lowe, M., & Cautela, J. (1978). A self-report measure of social skills. *Behavior Therapy, 9,* 535–544, cited in Goldstein & Keller (1987).

Martinson, R. (1974). What works?—Questions and answers about prison reform. *The Public Interest, 34,* 22–54.

Megargee, E. (1972). Standardized reports of work performance inmate adjustment for use in correctional settings. *Correctional Psychologist, 5,* 48–64.

Megargee, E., & Bohn, M. (1979). *Classifying criminal offenders: A new system based on the MMPI.* Beverly Hills, CA: Sage.

Monahan, J. (1981). *Predicting violent behavior and assessment of clinical techniques.* Beverly Hills, CA: Sage.

Monahan, J., & Steadman, H. (1994). Toward a rejuvenation of risk assessment research. In J. Monahan & H. Steadman (Eds.), *Violence and mental disorder* (pp. 1–17). Chicago: University of Chicago Press.

National Institute of Corrections (NIC). (1982). *Classification: Principles, models, and guidelines.* Washington, DC: U.S. Department of Justice.

Novoco, R. (1975). Anger control: *The development and evaluation of an experimental treatment.* Lexington, MA: Lexington Books.

Palmer, T. (1978). *Correctional intervention and research: Current issues and future prospects.* Lexington, MA: Lexington Books.

Palmer, T. (1984). Treatment and the role of classification: A review of the basics. *Crime and Delinquency, 12,* 133–152.

Palmer, T. (1992). *The re-emergence of correctional intervention,* Newbury Park, CA: Sage.

Palmer, T. (forthcoming). *Individualized intervention with young multiple offenders: The California community treatment project.* Hamden, CT: Garland Press.

Quay, H. (1983). *Technical manual for the Behavioral Classifications System for Adult Offenders.* Washington, DC: U.S. Department of Justice.

Quay, H. (1984). *Managing adult inmates: Classification for housing and program assignments.* College Park, MD: American Correctional Association.

Quay, H., & Parsons, L. (1972). *The differential behavioral classification of the juvenile offender.* Washington, DC: Department of Justice.

Quinsey, V., & Walker, W. (1994). Dealing with dangerousness: Community risk management strategies with violent offenders. In R. D. Peters, R. McMahon, & V. Quinsey (Eds.), *Aggression and violence throughout the lifespan* (pp. 244–262). Newbury Park: Sage.

Rossi, R., & Freeman, H. (1989). *Evaluation: A systematic approach.* Newbury Park, CA: Sage.

Roth, J., & Reiss, A. (1993). *Understanding and preventing violence.* Washington, DC: National Academy Press.

Straus, M. (1979). Measuring intrafamily conflict and violence: The Conflict Tactics (CT) Scales. *Journal of Marriage and the Family, 41*, 75–88, cited in Goldstein & Keller (1987).

Van Voorhis, P. (1987). Correctional effectiveness: The high cost of ignoring success. *Federal Probation, 51*, 56–62.

Van Voorhis, P. (1994a). *Psychological classification of the adult male prison inmate.* Albany, NY: SUNY Press.

Van Voorhis, P. (1994b). Measuring prison disciplinary problems: A multiple indicators approach to understanding the prison experience. *Justice Quarterly, 11*, 679–709.

Van Voorhis, P., Braswell, M., & Morrow, B. (1992). Family therapy. In D. Lester, M. Braswell, & P. Van Voorhis (Eds.), *Correctional Counseling* (pp. 155–174). Cincinnati, OH: Anderson Press.

Warren, M., & the Staff of the Community Treatment Project. (1966). Interpersonal maturity level classification: Diagnosis and treatment of low, middle, and high maturity delinquents. Sacramento, CA: California Youth Authority.

Warren, M. (1983). *Applications of interpersonal maturity theory to offender populations.* In W. Laufer & J. Day (Eds.), *Personality theory, moral development, and criminal behavior* (pp. 23–50). Lexington, MA: Lexington Books.

Whitehead, J., & Lab, S. (1989). A meta-analysis of juvenile correctional treatment. *Journal of Research in Crime and Delinquency, 26*, 276–295.

Wilson-Brewer, R., Cohen, S., O'Donnell, L., & Goodman, F. (1991). *Violence prevention for young adolescents: A survey of the state of the art.* Paper presented by the Educational Development Center, Inc. for the conference, "Violence Prevention for Young Adolescents," Washington, DC, July 12–13, 1990, by the Carnegie Corporation of New York.

2

Evaluating Intensive Supervision Probation/Parole
Results of a Nationwide Experiment

Joan Petersilia and Susan Turner

Sentencing practices in this country suggest that offenses can be divided into two categories. When the crime is relatively serious, offenders are put behind bars; when it is less so, they are put on probation, often with only perfunctory supervision. This two-fold division disregards the range of severity in crime, and as a result, sentencing can err in one direction or another: either it is too harsh, incarcerating people whose crimes are not serious enough to warrant a sanction this severe, or too lenient, putting on probation people whose crimes call for more severe punishment. This need for more flexible alternatives—punishments that in harshness fall between prison and probation—led many States to experiment with intermediate sanctions, such as intensive supervision probation/parole (ISP).[1]

Intensive supervision probation/parole is a form of release into the community that emphasizes close monitoring of convicted offenders and imposes rigorous conditions on that release. Most ISP's call for:

- Some combination of multiple weekly contacts with a supervising officer.
- Random and unannounced drug testing.
- Stringent enforcement of probation/parole conditions.

Source: *National Institute of Justice: Research in Brief*, U.S. Department of Justice, May 1993: 1–11.

- A requirement to participate in relevant treatment, hold a job, and perhaps perform community service.

Interest in ISP's has been generated in part by the increased proportion of serious offenders among the probation population, a group whose needs and problems may not be effectively addressed by routine probation. Another reason for interest in ISP's is the greater flexibility in sentencing options that they permit. They are better able than the traditional alternatives—prison or probation—to fit the punishment to the crime.

The Problem

The population on probation is a particular focus of ISP's. This population has been growing, increasing 5 to 7 percent each year from 1985 to 1990. At the end of 1990, two-thirds of all people who were under correctional supervision were on probation.[2] More importantly, the type of offender on probation has also changed. More of the current probation population consists of people convicted of felonies than misdemeanors.[3]

As a sentencing option, routine probation was neither intended nor structured to handle this type of offender. One reason is that felons are not good risks for routine probation. A recent report by the Bureau of Justice Statistics revealed that 43 percent of felons on State probation were rearrested for another felony within 3 years.[4] This threat to public safety underscores the need for sentencing alternatives. Moreover, the need is even greater in view of budget cuts at probation agencies.

At the other extreme, reliance on imprisonment has limitations. Prison populations have tripled since 1975. States have responded to the increased need with enormous investments in prison construction. Yet the level of violent crime is now substantially higher than it was a decade ago, indicating that the prospect of imprisonment has not had the deterrent effect that investment in prisons hoped to buy.[5] It has also meant that 36 States are currently operating all or part of their correctional systems under court orders or consent decrees to reduce crowding.[6]

The Rationale for ISP's

Since neither prison nor routine probation can fully respond to the current situation, ISP's have increasingly been viewed as an alternative. Indeed, these programs have been hailed by many as

---

Types of ISP's

ISP's are usually classified as prison diversion, enhanced probation, and enhanced parole. Each has a different goal.

Diversion is commonly referred to as a "front door" program because its goal is to limit the number of offenders entering prison. Prison diversion programs generally identify lower risk, incoming inmates to participate in an ISP in the community as a substitute for a prison term.

Enhancement programs generally select already sentenced probationers and parolees and subject them to closer supervision in the community than regular probation or parole. People placed in ISP enhanced probation or enhanced parole programs show evidence of failure under routine supervision or have committed offenses generally deemed to be too serious for supervision on routine caseloads.

---

the most promising criminal justice innovation in decades. Between 1980 and 1990 every State adopted some form of ISP for adult offenders.[7] The Federal system has not been as aggressive as the States in ISP experiments, although there are a few programs in selected districts.

A growing number of jurisdictions have come to believe that by providing increased supervision of serious offenders in the community, ISP's can both relieve prison crowding and lessen the risks to public safety that such offenders pose—and all at a cost savings. In addition to these practical considerations, many believe ISP's should be adopted as a matter of principle, to meet the need for greater latitude in sentencing and to achieve the sentencing objective of just deserts.

The practical argument is the one advanced most often. ISP's are believed to be cost-effective, either in the short run or the long run. Prison-diversion programs (see "Types of ISP's") are thought to be able to reduce corrections costs because they presumably cost less than prison. Probation-enhancement programs are believed to prevent crime because the close surveillance they provide should deter recidivism. With lower recidivism, the need for imprisonment is also reduced, since fewer offenders will be reprocessed by the system.

Assumptions about the effect of ISP's on crime control involve comparisons of various types of sanctions. Prison is assumed to provide the strongest, and routine supervision the weakest, crime control. ISP's are a middle ground, with more control than routine supervision but less control than prison. Theoretically, offenders in ISP programs are deterred from committing crimes because they are under surveillance, and they are constrained from committing crimes because the conditions of the program limit their opportunities.

Initial Reactions to ISP's

Some of the enthusiasm for ISP's was generated by early reports from programs like that of the Georgia Department of Corrections, which seemed to bear out many of the assumptions and to produce a number of benefits.[8] Many ISP programs claimed to have saved at least $10,000 a year for each offender who otherwise would have been sentenced to prison.[9] Participants in the Georgia program, which served as the model for programs adopted elsewhere, had low recidivism, maintained employment, made restitution, and paid a monthly supervision fee.

In other places where ISP's were adopted, evaluations produced mixed results, with some sites reporting cost savings (Illinois and New Jersey, for example), while others did not (such as Massachusetts and Wisconsin); and some reporting reduced recidivism (Iowa, for example), while others did not (such as Ohio and Wisconsin).

The ambiguous results of these programs indicate that assumptions about the ability of ISP's to produce practical results—relieve prison crowding, lower costs, and control crime—may not have been well-founded. Reservations have been raised by independent agencies (such as the U.S. General Accounting Office), as well as by a number of scholars, including proponents of the ISP concept.[10] It appears not that the ISP's themselves have failed, but that the objectives set for them may have been overly ambitious, raising expectations they have been unable to meet.

The evidence seems better able to support the argument based on principle. That is, because ISP's are more punitive than routine probation and parole and because they provide for greater surveillance, they may be able to achieve the goal of permitting needed flexibility in sentencing.

The Demonstration Project

To test the relative effectiveness of ISP's and traditional sanctions, NIJ evaluated a demonstration project sponsored by the Bureau of Justice Assistance (BJA). The demonstration, which involved 14 programs in 9 States, ran from 1986 to 1991 and involved about

Exhibit 1. The 14 Demonstration/ Evaluation Sites

Contra Costa County, California

Los Angeles County, California

Seattle, Washington

Ventura County, California

Atlanta, Georgia

Macon, Georgia

Waycross, Georgia

Santa Fe, New Mexico

Des Moines, Iowa

Winchester, Virginia

Dallas, Texas

Houston, Texas

Marion County, Oregon

Milwaukee, Wisconsin

2,000 offenders. NIJ commissioned the RAND Corporation to evaluate the programs in a project supported by the Institute as well as BJA.

The participating jurisdictions (see exhibit 1) were asked to design an ISP program and were given wide latitude in doing so. Only two sites (Marion County, Oregon, and Milwaukee, Wisconsin) selected prison diversion programs, in which lower risk offenders who would have entered prison were diverted into the community. All others chose either probation enhancement or parole enhancement programs for the more serious offenders who were then under community supervision.

The offenders whom the jurisdictions chose to target had to meet only two criteria: they had to be adults and they could not be currently convicted of a violent crime. Once these criteria were met, the jurisdictions were free to focus on whatever type of offender population they wished: probationers and/or parolees, people currently in jail, or people who were prison bound.

They were also free to tailor their programs to meet local needs. For example, several sites designed their programs specifically for drug offenders. However, for a variety of reasons, the agencies were unable to place many offenders in drug, alcohol, or other such treatment programs. Thus, the ISP's evaluated were not primarily service and treatment programs, but rather were oriented more toward surveillance and supervision. (See "Study Methods.")

Effectiveness of ISP's

The demonstration was intended to answer the question of how participation in an ISP affected offenders' subsequent criminal behavior (that is, its effect on recidivism). The evaluation was intended to bring to light information about cost-effectiveness and extent of offender participation in counseling, work, and training programs. The effect of ISP's on prison crowding was not a study

Study Methods[11]

Program Design

All jurisdictions selected by the Bureau of Justice Assistance for participation in the demonstration and evaluation were asked to design and implement an ISP program that was to be funded for 18 to 24 months. The jurisdictions also were required to receive training and technical assistance, both provided by outside consultants.[12] In addition, they took part in the independent evaluation, which required their gathering data about the program.

The population studied consisted of approximately 2,000 adult offenders who were not currently convicted of a violent crime (homicide, rape, robbery, and assault). The vast majority of the offenders were men in their late 20s and early 30s, and most had long criminal records. In other respects, sites varied. Some, for example, chose offenders with more serious prison records than others. The nature of their offenses varied, as did their racial composition. The proportion of offenders in Dallas had served a prison term, while for Contra Costa the figure was only 5 percent.

Because each site was allowed to design its own ISP, no two programs were identical. They adopted whatever components of the general ISP model they wished (such as random urine testing, curfews, electronic monitoring, and treatment referrals).

Close supervision of offenders was one of the few required program components. It consisted of weekly contacts with the officers, unscheduled drug testing, and stricter enforcement of probation/parole conditions.

Random Assignment

The study was conducted as a randomized experiment. Indeed, the study may well be the largest randomized experiment in corrections ever undertaken in the United States. At each site, along with the experimental group, a control group of offenders was set up to serve as a comparison. The offenders in the control group were not part of the program but instead were given a different sanction (either prison or routine probation or parole, for example).[13] After the jurisdictions selected the pool of offenders they deemed eligible for ISP programs, the researchers assigned them randomly to one or the other of the two groups.

Having a control group with which to compare findings ensured that the results were the product of the manipulated variables of the ISP program rather than of differences among the offenders in the two groups. Previous ISP evaluations lacked matching comparison groups.

Data Collection

For each offender, in both the experimental and the control groups, data collection forms were completed by the participating agency in the respective jurisdictions. A *background assessment* recorded demographic information, prior criminal record, drug dependence status, and similar information. The other forms—*6- and 12-month reviews*—recorded probation and parole services received, participation in treatment and work programs, and recidivism during the 1-year followup. Also recorded on this form were the number of drug tests ordered and taken, the types of drugs for which the offender tested positive, and the sanction imposed.

Measuring Program Effects

Separate calculations were devised for estimating costs and for measuring program implementation, the effect of the ISP's on recidivism, and the effect on social adjustment (percentage of offenders who attended counseling, participated in training, were employed, and the like).

aim, but it has been a major policy interest in all ISP programs. The participating sites had their own objectives and interests. Most wanted to learn whether ISP's are an effective intermediate sanction, in which probation and parole conditions are monitored and enforced more credibly.

Overall, the results revealed what *cannot* be expected of ISP's as much as what *can* be. Most notably, they suggest that the assumptions about the ability of ISP's to meet certain practical goals—reduce prison crowding, save money, and decrease recidivism—may not have been well-founded and that jurisdictions interested in adopting ISP's should define their goals carefully. Other study findings indicate that ISP's were most successful as an intermediate punishment, in providing closer supervision of offenders and in offering a range of sentencing options between prison and routine probation and parole.

The programs were effective as surveillance.   The ISP programs were designed to be much more stringent than routine supervision, and in every site they delivered more contacts and monitoring than did the routine supervision provided in the control groups. Most of the ISP's were significantly higher than the control programs in number of face-to-face contacts with supervisors, telephone and collateral contacts, law enforcement checks, employment monitoring, and drug and alcohol testing. (See exhibit 2 for findings on contacts and drug tests.)

The data reveal no straightforward relationship between contact levels and recidivism; that is, it is not clear whether the surveillance aspect of the ISP had a positive effect on offenders' subsequent behavior. For example, although the average number of face-to-face

Exhibit 2.   **Number of Monthly Face-to-Face Contacts and Drug Tests During 1-Year Followup**

| | Face-to Face Contacts | | Drug Tests | |
	ISP	Controls	ISP	Controls
Contra Costa County, California	2.7	0.5*	1.7	0.2*
Los Angeles County, California	4.1	0.6*	0.5	0.2*
Seattle, Washington	3.4	0.8*	0.4	0.1*
Ventura County, California	7.4	3.0*	2.7	1.3*
Atlanta, Georgia	12.5	14.9	4.8	4.9
Macon, Georgia	16.1	17.7	5.8	3.7*
Waycross, Georgia	22.8	22.4	14.2	1.6*
Santa Fe, New Mexico	10.6	2.8*	2.9	1.1*
Des Moines, Iowa	5.8	3.8*	2.8	1.0*
Winchester, Virginia	8.1	1.9*	1.5	0.4*
Dallas, Texas	3.3	1.5*	0.1	0.0*
Houston, Texas	4.0	1.9*	0.7	0.0*
Marion County, Oregon**	12.2	n/a	2.2	n/a
Milwaukee, Wisconsin	8.8	n/a	0.7	n/a
AVERAGE	5.8 [a]	1.6 [b]	1.4 [a]	0.2 [b]

* Indicates that ISP and control are significantly different, p <.05.

** Based on 6-month followup only.

[a] Weighted average of ISP in all sites.
[b] Weighted average of routine probation in Contra Costa, Los Angeles, Seattle; routine probation/parole in Santa Fe, Des Moines, Winchester; routine parole in Dallas and Houston.

contacts in Seattle was 3.4 per month and the average in Macon was much higher at 16.1, the percentage of ISP offenders arrested at both sites was about the same—46 percent in Seattle and 42 percent in Macon.

This finding must, however, be qualified by the nature of the data. The ISP programs were "packages" of contacts and services, and for this reason it is difficult to distinguish the specific effect of individual components of a package (such as contact level, drug testing, and electronic monitoring) on recidivism.

The programs were effective as intermediate sanctions. In a sense, this issue is the same as the preceding one if more frequent contacts and drug testing are viewed as punishment. Most of the ISP's had significantly higher levels of the features that curtail freedom.[14] Both coercion and enforced diminution of freedom were higher for most ISP's than for the control group when measured by the criminal justice system response to offenders' technical violations.[15] In fact, the response to this type of violation gives ISP's their greatest punitive value. The rate of technical violations was high, making the resultant coercion and diminution of freedom experienced by the offenders an added punitive sanction as well as creating a public safety benefit.

The General Accounting Office, in its report on intermediate punishments, noted that if judged by a standard of zero risk, all ISP programs fail to protect public safety.[16] However, what most of these programs try to achieve is a more stringent punishment for at least some of the serious offenders who now receive only nominal supervision. Judged by that criterion, virtually all of the sites succeeded. It is also possible that the closer surveillance imposed on ISP participants may increase the probability that they are caught for a larger percentage of the crimes they commit.

To test this effect, researchers conducted interviews with ISP participants in the Contra Costa site to discuss their perceptions of the harshness of the program. The interview findings confirmed that these offenders viewed the likelihood of their being caught for probation violations to be higher than for offenders who were on routine probation. They felt this to be particularly true when the violations involved drugs. In addition, the ISP offenders believed they would be treated more harshly for most types of violations than would their counterparts who were on routine supervision.

Evidence also suggests that some offenders may view ISP's as even more punitive and restrictive of freedom than prison. Among offenders at the Oregon site, 25 percent who were eligible for prison diversion chose not to participate. The reason may be that Oregon's crowded prisons made it unlikely that anyone sentenced to a year would serve the full term, while offenders assigned to ISP's could be certain of a full year of surveillance in the program. As prisons become more crowded and length of sentence served decreases, ISP's may come to seem increasingly punitive to offenders.

The Effect on Recidivism

The major recidivism outcome measures were officially recorded arrests and technical violations. On these measures, the ISP programs were not as successful as on others.

ISP participants were not subsequently arrested less often, did not have a longer time to failure, and were not arrested for less serious offenses than control group members. The findings reveal that in 11 of the 14 sites, arrest rates during the 1-year followup were in fact higher for ISP participants than for the control group (although not significantly so). At the end of the 1-year period, about 37 percent of the ISP participants and 33 percent of control offenders had been arrested. (See exhibit 3.)

These findings should be interpreted with caution, because officially recorded recidivism may not be as accurate an indicator of an individual's criminality as it is a measure of the impact of the ISP program on the criminal justice system. That is, officially recorded recidivism measures enforcement—the system's ability to detect crime and act on it (through arrests).

As noted earlier, with an ISP program, surveillance may be so stringent as to increase the probability that crimes (and technical violations) will be detected and an arrest made. In this way ISP's may increase officially recorded recidivism. Thus, it may be that an ISP offender is committing the same number or fewer crimes than someone on routine supervision, who has a lower probability of being arrested for them. The ISP offender, whose behavior is more closely monitored, may be caught in the enforcement net, while the offender on routine probation or parole may escape it.

Effect of technical violations.   If technical violations are interpreted as another measure of recidivism, the findings are also less positive for the ISP's than the controls. An average of 65 percent of the ISP clients had a technical violation compared with 38 percent for the controls. (See exhibit 3). However, technical violations can be interpreted as effects of the program itself rather than as evidence of criminal activity or recidivism. For one thing, the view of technical violations as a proxy for crime commission is only an assumption. Non-compliant behavior such as disregarding curfews, using alcohol and drugs, and missing treatment sessions may not necessarily signal that the ISP participant is going to commit "new" or "real" crimes.

To test the hypothesis that revoking offenders for technical violations prevents arrests for new crimes, the researchers examined the ISP programs in California and Texas. They computed correlations between number of arrests and number of technical violations and found few statistically significant relationships. In other words, offenders who committed technical violations were no more likely to be arrested for new crimes than those who did not commit them. Moreover, when convictions for arrests during the 1-year followup were examined for all sites, the researchers found no difference in the rates of the ISP offenders and the control group.

ISP's were consistently associated with higher rates of technical violations because of the closer supervision given to those in the programs. If stringent conditions are imposed and people's behavior is monitored, they have more opportunities for violations and for being found out than if there are few conditions and few contacts. For example, the requirement of frequent drug testing alone is virtually guaranteed to generate a large number of technical violations. Few of the sites had many low-risk[17] offenders. The higher the risk, the more likely that offenders are involved with drugs. At most of the sites, drug-related technical violations accounted for a large proportion of all technical violations. Offenders under routine supervision were not subjected to such close scrutiny and would not therefore have had as many opportunities to commit technical violations of the conditions of their probation or parole.

Effect of type of ISP program. Because only 2 of the 14 sites implemented prison diversion programs and their programs experienced difficulties, the research remains inconclusive regarding the ability of this type of ISP to relieve prison crowding. (See "The Experience of the Prison Diversion Programs.")

The findings for parole and probation enhancement ISP's suggest that commitments to prison and jail may actually increase under the program. The reason is the large number of technical violations, which lead to a higher percentage of ISP offenders than controls being recommitted to jail and prison. At a minimum, ISP programs attempt to increase the credibility of community-based sanctions by making certain that the conditions ordered by the court, including those considered "technical" in nature, are monitored, enforced, and if violated, punished by imprisonment. Depending on how severely ISP staff and their respective courts choose to treat ISP infractions, commitments to prison and jails may rise precipitously.

Exhibit 3. **Offender Recidivism During 1-Year Followup**

	Percentage of Offenders With Any Arrest		Percentage of Offender With Technical Violations		Percentage of Offenders Returned to Prison	
	ISP	Controls	ISP	Controls	ISP	Controls
Contra Costa County, California	29	27	64	41*	2	4
Los Angeles County, California	32	30	61	57	26	22
Seattle, Washington	46	36	73	48*	6	5
Ventura County, California	32	53*	70	73	23	28
Atlanta, Georgia	12	04	65	46	23	4
Macon, Georgia	42	38	100	96	8	21
Waycross, Georgia	12	15	38	31	4	0
Santa Fe, New Mexico	48	28	69	62	14	17
Des Moines, Iowa	24	29	59	55	39	23
Winchester, Virginia	25	12	64	36*	14	8
Dallas, Texas	39	30	20	13	28	17
Houston, Texas	44	40	81	33*	35	20*
Marion County, Oregon	33	50	92	58	50	25
Milwaukee, Wisconsin	58	03*	92	17*	35	3*
AVERAGE	37 [a]	33 [b]	65 [a]	38 [b]	24	15

* Indicates that ISP and control are significantly different, p <.05.

[a] Weighted average of ISP in all sites.
[b] Weighted average of routine probation in Contra Costa, Los Angeles, Seattle; routine probation/parole in Santa Fe, Des Moines, Winchester; routine parole in Dallas and Houston.

The Experience of the Prison Diversion Programs

Prison diversion programs in this study did not provide data on the effect of ISP's on prison crowding. Of the two participating sites that implemented prison diversion programs in the demonstration, one had too few eligible offenders to yield usable results. In the other, the use of randomization was overridden by the jurisdiction, thereby foiling its purpose. The selection process at these two sites therefore makes it impossible to state with certainty the effect of ISP's in reducing prison crowding.

The experience of the two sites (Marion County, Oregon, and Milwaukee, Wisconsin) does reveal a number of insights into the issues jurisdictions face when making decisions about selecting convicted offenders for diversion into the community.

Marion County, Oregon

Marion County set eligibility requirements so stringent that few offenders could qualify for the prison diversion ISP. The study's mandated criterion of excluding offenders currently convicted of violent crimes was extended to exclude offenders with any prior record of violence. Examination of the Marion County data revealed that, in addition, a large percent of potential participants who had current burglary convictions were rejected. Although this offense is considered nonviolent, evidently Marion County did not wish to place burglars into ISP programs.

The three criteria—exclusion of violent offenders, people with any history of violence, and convicted burglars—shrank the pool of eligibles considerably. Furthermore, the local Marion County judge imposed the requirement of informed consent from the offender, producing a sample too small to yield statistically reliable results.

Milwaukee, Wisconsin

In Milwaukee, judges and probation/parole officers overrode the researchers' random assignment of offenders into the experimental and control groups. Milwaukee initially had two pools of eligibles: "front-end" cases consisting of high-risk offenders newly convicted of nonviolent felonies, and "back-end" cases consisting of probation or parole violators who were facing revocation. Regardless of the random designation made by the researchers, most front-end cases were sentenced to prison rather than diversion to an ISP. Of the back-end cases, more than half were sent to routine probation or parole.

That only two sites chose prison diversion suggests the level of concern on the part of the criminal justice system about the risks involved in sending convicted offenders into the community. Further evidence of this concern is the response of these two sites in placing additional restrictions on program implementation.[18]

Data from the Houston site illustrate this point. The Houston ISP was a parole-enhancement program that targeted people under supervision who had a high probability of returning to prison. ISP participants were not arrested for new crimes more often than the controls (who were on routine parole), but were returned to prison more frequently for more technical violations. Fully 81 percent of the ISP offenders had technical violations, compared with 33 percent of offenders in the control group. As a result, five times as many ISP offenders were returned to prison for technical violations as those on routine supervision (21 percent versus 4 percent), and at the end of the 1-year followup, about 30 percent of ISP participants were in prison, compared with only 18 percent of the control group.[19]

Thus, in Houston, putting people on ISP added more offenders to the prison population than did routine parole. This is interpreted as an effect of the ISP program itself—which tends to generate more technical violations—rather than the result of differences between the ISP experimental and control groups. Any other differences were eliminated through random assignment of offenders to both groups.

Cost Benefits

Are ISP's a cost-saving alternative? Like other questions about ISP's, this too has an ambiguous answer—one that depends on what is being compared to what. Compared with routine probation, ISP's are more costly because they are highly labor intensive. Because supervision is intensive, ISP's require lower caseloads—typically 25 offenders per supervisor or team of supervisors. An increase of only 100 offenders in an ISP would call for hiring and training 4 to 8 new employees.

If the cost of ISP's is compared to that of imprisonment, the opposite is true. Virtually no one would question the claim that it is more expensive to keep an offender in prison than on probation. The costs per day for imprisonment are much higher per offender than the costs per day for an ISP. Obviously, ISP's cost less than building new prisons.

Length of time under each sanction also has to be taken into consideration when comparing costs of prison and ISP's. The average cost per year per imprisoned offender is $12,000 and per ISP offender only $4,000. However, if the ISP offender would have otherwise served time in prison (had he or she not been placed in an ISP) for a period of only 3 months, the cost would be $3,000—less than the $4,000 it costs for 1 year of an ISP program. In addition, some of the ISP participants spent part of the followup year incarcerated rather than in the ISP program, thus eliminating part of the cost savings of diversion from prison.

Again, it should be kept in mind in interpreting these findings that the ISP programs resulted in more incarcerations and consequently higher costs than routine probation/parole because of the higher number of technical violations. Across the 12 probation/parole enhancement programs, high violation and incarceration rates for ISP offenders drove up the estimated costs, which averaged $7,200 per offender for the year, compared with about $4,700 for the control group on routine supervision.

Results for Treatment

Treatment and service components in the ISP's included drug and alcohol counseling, employment, community service, and payment of restitution. On many of these measures, ISP offenders participated more than did control group members (see exhibit 4); and participation in such programs was found to be correlated with a reduction in recidivism in at least some sites.

When figures from all sites are examined, they reveal that participation in counseling was not high in either the experimental or control groups, but it was higher for ISP offenders. Forty-five percent of ISP offenders received some counseling during the followup period, compared with 22 percent of the controls.

Overall figures indicate that more than half of the ISP participants were employed compared with 43 percent of the offenders who were on routine supervision. In 4 of the 14 sites (Contra Costa, Los Angeles, Seattle, and Winchester), ISP offenders were significantly more likely than controls to be employed.

Participation in community service varied considerably by site. The highest rate (more than two-thirds of offenders) was reported in the three Georgia sites, where community service has historically played a major role in the ISP design. In seven of the ISP programs, 10 percent or fewer offenders participated in community service, and at no site did ISP offenders participate significantly more often than routine supervision offenders.

Although restitution was paid by only a small minority of offenders, the rate was higher among ISP offenders than those on routine supervision (12 percent and 3 percent, respectively, paid some restitution).

Analysis of the programs in California and Texas revealed a relationship between treatment participation and recidivism. A summary score was created for each offender, with one point

Exhibit 4. **Representative Program Participation**

	Percentage of Offenders in Any Counseling During 1-Year Followup		Percentage of Offenders With Any Paid Employment During 1-Year Followup	
	ISP	Controls	ISP	Controls
Contra Costa County, California	39	14*	41	26*
Los Angeles County, California	16*	02	45	18*
Seattle, Washington	42	14*	31	08*
Ventura County, California	78	76	80	79
Atlanta, Georgia	48	48	54	65
Macon, Georgia	65	50	85	71
Waycross, Georgia	100	88	92	96
Santa Fe, New Mexico	100	59*	86	79
Des Moines, Iowa	59	41*	76	70
Winchester, Virginia	32	12	89	56*
Dallas, Texas	04	02	37	33
Houston, Texas	55	32*	61	61
Marion County, Oregon	50	n/a	33	n/a
Milwaukee, Wisconsin	54	n/a	54	n/a
AVERAGE	45 [a]	22 [b]	56 [a]	43 [b]

* Indicates that ISP and control are significantly different, $p < .05$.

[a] Weighted average of all sites.
[b] Weighted average of routine probation in Contra Costa, Los Angeles, Seattle; routine probation/parole in Santa Fe, Des Moines, Winchester; routine parole in Dallas and Houston.

assigned for participation in any of four treatment or service programs. Analysis revealed that higher levels of program participation were associated with a 10- to 20-percent reduction in recidivism. However, because offenders were not randomly assigned to participate in these activities within the experimental and control groups, it is not possible to determine whether the lower recidivism was the effect of the treatment or of selection bias. In other words, the positive outcomes may be a function not of the treatment but of the type of offender who entered the treatment program. Nevertheless, the results are consistent with literature showing positive outcomes of treatment.

The ISP programs in the demonstration project were by design oriented more toward surveillance than treatment, with funds used largely for staff salaries rather than for treatment service. Sites had to rely on existing treatment programs, which in some communities were quite minimal. This raises the issue of whether participation in treatment would have been higher had more resources been allocated to it.

Policy Implications

Jurisdictions that wish to adopt ISP's might want to revise the model represented in the demonstration to create a better "fit" with their particular needs.

Making controls more stringent. ISP contact levels were greater than with routine supervision, but it might be argued that the programs were not "intensive" enough. It appears that more stringent conditions could be required of ISP's. In the demonstration, ISP contact of any type amounted, on average, to a total of less than 2 hours per month per offender (assuming that 20 minutes, on average, was spent per face-to-face contact). The same is true of drug testing—the average for all sites was just over two tests per month. If the amount of time spent in contacts were greater (that is, if conditions were tougher), the result might be less recidivism. Jurisdictions would have to decide how much more restrictive the conditions should be and would have to weigh possible benefits against the probable higher cost.

Increasing treatment. Jurisdictions might want to strengthen the treatment component of ISP's in hopes of a positive behavioral effect that would lower recidivism. As stated earlier, at the California and Texas sites the recidivism of offenders who received any counseling (for drugs or alcohol), held jobs, paid restitution, and did community service was 10 to 20 percent lower than those who did not.

Overall outcomes might have been even more positive had a greater proportion of the offenders participated in treatment.[20] Participation in drug treatment, in particular, might have had a high payoff. In all the sites, about half the offenders were judged drug dependent by their probation or parole officers. Yet ISP staff often reported difficulties obtaining drug treatment for these people, and at some sites a large percentage of all offenders in need of drug treatment went untreated.[21] It comes as no surprise, therefore, that about one-third of all new arrests were drug-related. A high priority for future research would be evaluation of ISP programs in which treatment plays a major role.[22]

Deemphasizing technical violations.   Jurisdictions might want to reexamine the assumption of technical violations as a proxy for criminal behavior. Offenders who commit this type of violation constitute a considerable proportion of the prison population. On any given day, about 20 percent of new admissions nationwide consist of parole or probation violators, and the resultant crowding means early release for other offenders.

The experience of the State of Washington in rethinking parole and probation revocations is instructive. There, the State legislature, responding to the heavy flow of technical violations attendant on stringent parole and probation conditions, set new rules. The rules require conditions be set according to the specific offense and the particular offender's past criminal behavior; they effectively bar the imposition of conditions affecting all offenders. In addition, the new rules state that prison cannot be used as a sanction for technical violations; the maximum sentence is 60 days in jail.[24]

No empirical studies have been performed yet, but Washington officials believe that as a result of the new rules, revocations for technical violations have decreased while arrest rates for new crimes have remained roughly the same.[25] If Washington is successful, it may mean that jurisdictions will have more prison space for really serious offenders and therefore increase public safety by decreasing the number of people sent to prison for technical violations of parole and probation.

Handling costs.   When considering the issue of affordability, jurisdictions need to keep in mind its relation to program goals. The more constraints a program imposes and/or the more it is service- and treatment-oriented, the higher will be the cost. In Ventura and Houston, for example, stringent conditions and rigorous response to technical violations drove up costs. On the other hand, future evaluations might reveal that the return on investment in programs with these types of emphasis may be lower recidivism.

Judging outcomes.   In assessing the success of ISP's (and deciding whether to invest further in them), jurisdictions need to use the same criterion for deciding whether a program is affordable; that is, does it achieve the goals set? One of the study's strongest implications is that jurisdictions need to establish very clearly their intentions for the ISP's they develop and structure the programs accordingly. If jurisdictions are interested primarily in imposing intermediate sanctions, even if the result is not lower recidivism, that goal should be made clear. Otherwise, the public may interpret the recidivism rates as an indication of program failure.

If jurisdictions are primarily interested in reducing recidivism, prison crowding, and system costs, ISP programs as currently structured may not meet all their expectations. These more "practical" objectives were set on the basis of overly ambitious assumptions and on the early results of a few programs that received a great deal of attention and perhaps unwarranted enthusiasm. The findings of this evaluation provide further evidence that surveillance-oriented ISP's will have difficulty in fully achieving these objectives.

If jurisdictions target objectives based more on intermediate sanctions principles, ISP's hold promise. By setting this type of objective, they may be able to impose more stringent controls on offenders than are possible without probation and parole, and they may achieve greater flexibility in sentencing decisions by punishments that more closely fit the crimes committed. Developing an array of sentencing options is an important and necessary first step to creating a more comprehensive and graduated sentencing structure. This goal alone can provide the justification for continued development of ISP and other intermediate sanctions.

Is prison diversion viable?.   The evaluation findings indicate that prison diversion and, by extension, reduction of prison crowding, is particularly difficult to implement. This difficulty is reflected in the decision by only 2 of the 14 sites to adopt this type of program. The criteria these two jurisdictions used to assign offenders to the programs also suggest a measure of reluctance. (See "The Experience of the Prison Diversion Programs.") The experience with prison diversion in this study indicates that the criminal justice system and the general public do not at present seem receptive to this type of ISP. A targeted public and judicial education campaign would be required to overcome that reluctance.

Future Research

The major issue for further research is determining whether ISP, a concept that may be sound in theory, might be structured and implemented differently to produce better results. The experience of the California sites suggests, for example, that certain program components could be manipulated. At these sites, a higher level of offender participation in treatment and service programs was associated with lower recidivism. In Ventura, which had the highest levels of surveillance, arrest rates were lower than among the controls. A revised ISP model could answer these and other questions:

- Would ISP's reduce recidivism if resources were sufficient to obtain treatment drug offenders need?
- Would more intensive surveillance lower recidivism?
- Would more selective conditions of parole and probation lower revocation rates?
- What combination of surveillance and treatment would produce the best results?

The study findings indicate a number of additional areas for research:

The potential of ISP as prison diversion.   The limited number of study sites selecting this option and their restrictions on the programs indicate major concerns about ISP for prison diversion. Researchers may want to examine the nature of the potential pool of eligibles, document the most commonly utilized criteria for ISP eligibility, and depending on the criteria, simulate the prison population that would qualify.

Testing of different offender populations.   The ISP model in this study was tested primarily on drug-involved offenders who had committed serious crimes. Studies have shown that the more experienced the offenders, the lower they rate the risk of being caught and confined.[26] For this reason, models using a population of less serious offenders might result in greater deterrence.

The effects of different ISP components.   The random assignment in this study permitted testing the effect of the entire ISP "package," but made it impossible to test the effect of a particular program component. By extension, it was not possible to determine how changing a component might change the effects. Future research could be designed specifically to test the incremental impact of various ISP conditions (such as drug testing and drug and alcohol treatment) on offender behavior.

Effectiveness over time.   Recent research indicates that a 1-year followup, the time period on which the evaluation of outcomes was based, may not be long enough.[27] Future research might focus on whether longer followup might ultimately result in behavioral differences between ISP offenders and controls.

Technical violations and criminal behavior.   The study revealed that technical violations resulted in many recommitments to prison and jail. As noted earlier, the view that such recommitments prevent crime may be only an assumption. The policy significance of technical violations suggests that research is needed in a number of areas:

- Empirical evidence of the relationship of technical violations to criminal behavior.
- The types of technical conditions currently imposed at sentencing.
- How technical conditions are used by community corrections to manage offenders, encourage rehabilitation, and protect the community.
- Trends in the growth of the technical violator population and the effect on jails and prisons.
- Innovative programs, policies, and statutes that have emerged to deal with technical violators.

Appropriate outcome measures.   Recidivism is a key outcome used in evaluating all types of interventions, and because success in rehabilitation has been far from complete, it is almost the only measure used in corrections.

In reaffirming its commitment to ISP and to its focus on rehabilitation, the American Probation and Parole Association issued a position paper that identifies behavioral change, not recidivism, as the appropriate outcome measure. Such change includes negotiation skills, managing emotions, and enhanced values and attitude shifts.

Given the centrality of recidivism to research and practice, it is essential to examine its appropriateness as a measure for certain interventions. For some programs, recidivism may be one of many measures, but perhaps not the primary one.

These are not the only issues for a future criminal justice research agenda, but they are currently the most pressing for research on the future of intensive supervision probation and parole.

Notes

[1] The results of NIJ-sponsored research into four major types of intermediate sanctions are summarized in Gowdy, Voncile B., *Intermediate Sanctions*. Research in Brief. Washington, DC: U.S. Department of Justice, National Institute of Justice, 1993.

[2] Bureau of Justice Statistics, *Probation and Parole 1990*. Bulletin. Washington, DC: U.S. Department of Justice, Bureau of Justice Statistics, November 1991.

[3] The figure for felonies is 48 percent, and for misdemeanors, it is 31 percent, according to Bureau of Justice Statistics, *Correctional Populations in the United States, 1990*. Washington, DC: U.S. Department of Justice, Bureau of Justice Statistics, July 1992.

[4] Langan, Patrick A., and Mark A. Cuniff. *Recidivism of Felons on Probation, 1986–89*. Special Report. Washington, DC: U.S. Department of Justice, Bureau of Justice Statistics, February 1992.

[5] A discussion of recent findings about the rise in the rate of violent crime despite the increase in the number of people incarcerated is presented in the National Research Council's *Understanding and Preventing Violence*, ed. Albert J. Reiss, Jr., and Jeffrey A. Roth, Washington, DC: National Academy Press, 1993: 292–294.

[6] Macguire, Kathleen, and Timothy J. Flanagan, eds. *Sourcebook of Criminal Justice Statistics—1991*. Washington, DC: U.S. Department of Justice, Bureau of Justice Statistics, 1992.

[7] General Accounting Office. *Intermediate Sanctions: Their Impacts on Prison Crowding, Costs, and Recidivism Are Still Unclear*. Gaithersburg, Maryland: General Accounting Office, 1990.

[8] For descriptions of the Georgia program, see Erwin, Billie S. "Turning Up the Heat on Probationers in Georgia." *Federal Probation*, vol. 50 (1986):2. See also: Petersilia, Joan. *Expanding Options for Criminal Sentencing*. Santa Monica, CA: RAND Corporation, 1987. Byrne, James M., Arthur J. Lurigio, and Christopher Baird. "The Effectiveness of the New Intensive Supervision Programs." *Research in Corrections*, vol. 2 (1989). The results of a National Institute of Justice evaluation of the program are presented in Erwin, Billie S., and Lawrence A. Bennett. *New Dimensions in Probation: Georgia's Experience With Intensive Probation Supervision (IPS)*. Research in Brief. Washington, DC: U.S. Department of Justice, National Institute of Justice, January 1987.

[9] Byrne, Lurigio, and Baird, "The Effectiveness of the New Intensive Supervision Programs."

[10] General Accounting Office, *Intermediate Sanctions*. See also Morris, Norval, and Michael Tonry. *Between Prison and Probation: Intermediate Punishments in a Rational Sentencing System*. New York: Oxford University Press, 1990.

[11] For more information on the experiences of the site in implementing the experiments, see Petersilia, Joan. "Implementing Randomized Experiments: Lessons for BJA's Intensive Supervision Project." *Evaluation Review*, vol. 13, 5.

[12] The training component was directed by Rutgers University, the technical assistance by the National Council on Crime and Delinquency.

[13] In the Georgia and Ventura sites, the control programs were another form of intensive supervision. References to all ISP's mean all 14 experimental programs. References to ISP enhancement programs mean all experimental ISP's except Milwaukee and Marion, which adopted prison diversion programs. References to routine supervision probation and parole mean the control programs in eight sites: Contra Costa, Los Angeles, Seattle, Santa Fe, Des Moines, Winchester, Dallas, and Houston.

[14] This meets the definition of effective sentencing proposed by Morris and Tonry. It involves "the curtailment of freedom either behind walls or in the community, large measures of coercion, and enforced diminutions of freedom." (*Between Prison and Probation*)

[15] A violation that does not consist of committing a crime or is not prosecuted as such is usually called a technical violation. It is behavior forbidden by the court order granting probation or parole but not forbidden by legal statute. Examples

are failure to observe curfew, abstain from alcohol, or attend treatment sessions.
[16] General Accounting Office, *Intermediate Sanctions.*
[17] The risk score was constructed from the following variables: drug treatment needs, age at first or current conviction, previous probation terms, previous probation and parole revocations, previous felony convictions, and type of current offense.
[18] NIJ has provided support to RAND to evaluate a prison diversion program in Minnesota that promises to furnish more reliable evidence on the impact of this type of sanction.
[19] Turner, Susan, and Joan Petersilia. "Focusing on High-Risk Parolees: An Experiment to Reduce Commitments to the Texas Department of Corrections." *Journal of Research in Criminology and Delinquency,* vol. 29, 1 (1992):34–61.
[20] Some recent literature gives credibility to this notion. See Anglin, M. Douglas, and Yih-Ing Hser. "Treatment of Drug Abuse." In *Crime and Justice: An Annual Review of Research, Volume 13: Drugs and Crime.* ed. Michael Tonry and James Q. Wilson. Chicago: University of Chicago Press, 1990; and Paul Gendreau and D. A. Andrews. "Tertiary Prevention: What the Meta-Analyses of the Offender Treatment Literature Tell Us About 'What Works.'" *Canadian Journal of Criminology,* vol. 32 (1990):173–184.
[21] For a more complete presentation of this finding, see Petersilia, Joan, Susan Turner, and Elizabeth Piper Deschenes. "Intensive Supervision Programs for Drug Offenders." In J. Byrne, A. Lurigio, and J. Petersilia. *Smart Sentencing: The Emergence of Intermediate Sanctions.* Newbury Park, CA: Sage Publications, 1992.
[22] NIJ is providing RAND with support for a randomized field experiment, currently being conducted in Maricopa County, Arizona, that will test the impact on probationers of different levels of treatment.
[23] Petersilia, Joan, and Susan Turner. "Reducing Prison Admissions: The Potential of Intermediate Sanctions," *The Journal of State Government,* vol. 62 (1989):2.
[24] Washington State Sentencing Guidelines Commission. *Preliminary Evaluation of Washington State's Sentencing Reform Act.* Olympia, WA: Washington State Sentencing Guidelines Commission, 1983.
[25] Greene, Richard. "Who's Punishing Whom?" *Forbes,* vol. 121, 6 (1988):132–133.
[26] Paternoster, R. "The Deterrent Effect of the Perceived Certainty and Severity of Punishment: A Review of the Evidence and Issues." *Justice Quarterly,* 4 (1987).
[27] Anglin, M. D. and W. H. McGlothlin. "Outcomes of Narcotic Addict Treatment in California." In *Drug Abuse Treatment Evaluation: Strategies, Progress, and Prospect,* ed. F. M. Tims and J. P. Ludford. National Institute on Drug Abuse Research Monograph No. 51. Rockville, MD: U.S. Department of Health and Human Services, National Institute on Drug Abuse, 1984.

Section *II*

Correctional Personnel
Past, Present, and Future

The field of corrections offers a wide range of career opportunities, including administrative and supervisory positions in institutions or agencies, work as a practitioner, or activity in program development, evaluation, research, and teaching. In *Career Planning in Criminal Justice* (DeLucia and Doyle, 1994:73–86), job titles given as career opportunities in corrections include: correctional treatment specialist, corrections counselor, corrections officer, juvenile justice counselor, parole officer, pre-release program correctional counselor, pre-release program employment counselor, recreation counselor, academic teacher, HIV caseworker specialist, education counselor, substance abuse specialist, classification and treatment director, management coordinator, inmate records coordinator, correctional facilities specialist, prisoner classification interviewer, and penologist.

There are three broad categories of correctional personnel: administrators and supervisory personnel, treatment personnel, and line staff. In the past, these corrections positions were predominantly filled by Caucasian males, but the proportion of women and members of minority group members in these posts has increased substantially in recent years. The U.S. Bureau of the Census lists corrections as one of the ten fastest growing occupations in America. During the 1990s, corrections employment enjoyed an annual growth rate of nearly 8 percent. More than half a million employees work in institutional corrections. This includes state prisons, federal prisons, the local jails, and juvenile corrections facilities. Female and minority state prison employment is increasing at a faster rate than the rate of increase for such employment for white males (Blair and Kratcoski, 1996:123).

Administrators tend to have the longest terms of employment in the corrections field. They may have obtained their present positions by political appointment, civil service examination, or advancement through the ranks. The managerial style of an administrator may be the result of personal experience or philosophy; acquaintance with styles of administration apparently being used successfully elsewhere; or pressures to adopt current emphases or fads in correctional organization and/or treatment in vogue on federal, state, or local levels. As the range of activity covered by corrections has expanded, administrators have been called upon to demonstrate management skills in institutional management, prerelease and work release program planning, residential community-based treatment, juvenile institutional and residential treatment, innovative pretrial diversion programs, probation, parole, juvenile aftercare, and various types of adult and juvenile diversion activity. They also must be prepared to deal with prisoner rights issues, disturbances within institutions, and close monitoring of institutional activity by civil libertarians and other interest groups.

Treatment personnel are employed in correctional work both within secure institutional settings and in community settings. In the community, they will be employed by either private or public agencies. Treatment staff members are considered to be professionals and ordinarily hold at least the baccalaureate degree. A large proportion of them have master's degrees, and a specialized doctorate and/or a medical degree is required for some treatment positions. The majority of treatment personnel work in community corrections rather than in institutional corrections, and they hold such positions as probation and parole officers, juvenile aftercare officers, furlough or work release supervisors, educational program supervisors, substance abuse counselors or restitution supervisors. The treatment staff located within institutional settings may be psychiatrists, psychologists, social workers, teachers or counselors of various types.

The majority of persons employed in corrections are line officers. In institutions, these include corrections officers, youth development counselors and youth leaders. In community corrections, line officers may be restitution or community service supervisors, house parents employed at community treatment centers, and those supervising adults or youths placed on home detention or electronic monitoring. In the institution and in the community, the line officer's role involves both providing supervision and maintaining security.

In the past, those involved in corrections work, particularly line officers, rarely chose this profession but entered it by chance after service in the military or because of the need for a secure job. The location of large institutions in rural areas allowed the entry into corrections work of poorly trained and lowly motivated personnel, chiefly because better qualified persons were not available. However, The credentials of current corrections officers are more impressive. They are better educated, more highly motivated, and more career oriented than in the past. A survey by the American Correctional Association (1997) revealed that new corrections officers are better educated and trained than their predecessors, younger, and more representative of the general population in terms of sex and racial and ethnic origins.

Corrections officers have the highest level of direct interaction with offenders and bear chief responsibility for the orderly operation of the institution. Their operational styles vary, but there is frequently a sense of "accommodation" between successful correctional officers and inmates, which benefits both.

Higher Education Preparation for a Corrections Career

Specific academic programs in corrections were not available until the 1960s. Before that time, students drawn to the general area of correctional work were likely to major in sociology, social work, or psychology. There were few textbooks dealing specifically with corrections, and those available took a non-theoretical, technical approach to the subject.

A major factor in the delay in the emergence of corrections as a field of study was the fact that the image of what constitutes corrections was not well defined. In the eyes of the public, corrections was equated with institutional work in prisons or jails.

It was not until the 1960s, when increased federal funding created many new programs in law enforcement and corrections, that varied career opportunities in criminal justice appeared.

In the turbulent 1960s. inner city disturbances, campus unrest, public fear of crime, revelations of abuses and primitive conditions in institutions, and demands by prisoners for better conditions and recognition of their rights led to legislation which provided funds for expansion of existing programs in criminal justice and the creation of many new programs. The Law Enforcement Assistance Administration, which provided colleges and universities with curriculum development grants for programs in law enforcement and corrections and gave students training grants and tuition loans, supplied a powerful economic incentive for institutions of higher learning to become involved. Many new programs were hastily formulated to take advantage of the available federal funding. In 1960, only 26 colleges and universities in the United States offered full-time programs in any law enforcement-related field. However, by 1970, the Law Enforcement Education Directory listed 292 institutions which offered 340 different programs, and many other colleges and universities offered a specialization in some type of law enforcement-related field within their sociology or political science departments, making the actual number of existing programs much higher (Tenney, 1971).

As new higher education programs in criminal justice and corrections developed, the tendency was to create separate departments of criminal justice or law enforcement rather than develop them as specializations within existing departments of sociology or social science. Since the available sociological solutions called for broad changes in the political and economic systems of the community and the country that would require years of effort to implement, there was a movement to create new departments and programs which emphasized training in social control skills. In addition, many of the social science and sociology programs were not designed or prepared to provide the types of field experience and direct training for employment which were now viewed as important. The new departments and programs that were created tended to rely heavily on part-time faculty members who were employed in the field and could offer the students practical advice and the benefit of their expertise.

During the 1980s, many of the hastily designed programs that emphasized training were eliminated. Most of these were located in community colleges or were two-year programs within large colleges or universities that were heavily dependent upon federal subsidies. When funding for the Law Enforcement Assistance Administration was severely reduced and eventually eliminated, these institutions were unable to attract students for the programs or to continue to support them, and they were eventually dropped. Other programs survived and became part of independent departments of criminal justice. By 1980, 816 institutions of higher education were offering crime-related programs. This included 1,209 associate-level programs, 589 baccalaureate programs, and 222 graduate programs (Myren, 1980:23).

In 1991, *Anderson's Directory of Criminal Justice Education* (Nemeth, 1991:iii) reported that 1,041 educational institutions offered one or more criminal justice degrees. This was a 10.5 percent increase in the number offering such degrees since the 1986–87 directory was published.

The current emphasis on criminal justice education is on the types of programs which Tenney characterized as "professional," which stress a strong interdisciplinary curriculum and frequently include courses in professional ethics and in research methods and statistics.

Correctional Personnel and the Changing Philosophical Climate in Corrections

To understand the specific duties and functions of correctional workers, the political and social climate of the times must be considered. The distinct boundaries separating management, treatment and line personnel gradually became blurred as new philosophies of corrections were adopted. With the advent of the "just deserts" philosophy and a more punitive approach to corrections, manifested in the adoption of determinate sentencing, new strategies to correct were introduced. Those working in all categories of corrections were expected to assume certain responsibilities that were different from those previously assigned to them. Administrators needed more interpersonal relations skills and treatment personnel had to focus more on control matters, while the emphasis for corrections officers fluctuated between custody and treatment. The unit management concept, adopted by the federal prisons system and many state systems, was based on the assumption that staff, supervisors, treatment and corrections officers will work as a management team and assist each other in the completion of all of the tasks assigned to the team. The mandatory involvement of inmates in counseling and other types of treatment programs, which formerly served as the cornerstone of the rehabilitation philosophy, was generally replaced with voluntary involvement, or a "take it or leave it" approach. In institutional corrections, increased emphasis was placed on making the institutions safe and secure for everyone who lived and worked in the facilities. This is not to say that such programs as vocational training, basic education and counseling were abandoned. They were still available, but now internal security became a higher priority.

Many officers, particularly those who were college educated and had internalized a more professional concept of their roles as correctional officers, experienced frustration or role strain when these changes occurred. Hepburn and Knepper (1993:318), in referencing Cressey's work on human service correctional officers, noted that:

> When officers are called on to serve the treatment needs of the facility, they are expected to form personal relationships with prisoners, to display helping behaviors, and to exercise professional judgment and flexibility in performing their job and enforcing discipline. Yet, custody and control remain their primary duties and the custodial needs of the facility require impersonal relationships, full enforcement of rules. and controlling behaviors.

Hepburn and Knepper (1993) completed a survey of corrections officers employed by the Arizona Department of Corrections. The state uses a two-track career model for corrections officers. In the correctional custody track, the officers' duties are predominantly custodial and rule-enforcing, while those designated correctional program officers are expected to assist inmates in problem solving, provide counseling, and in general be more supportive of the inmates' needs than are the custody track officers (320). The authors found that the human service oriented correctional program officers were significantly more satisfied with their jobs and experienced less role strain than the correctional custody officers (331).

Kratcoski and Blair (1999) surveyed officers in seven state correctional facilities in Ohio that represented a cross-section of maximum to medium security levels. Women and minority officers were well represented in the sample, and officers from institutions located in both urban and rural areas were included. When asked to rank rehabilitation, incapacitation, deterrence, and retribution according to their opinions of what should be the goals of imprisonment, less than one-fourth of the corrections officers surveyed considered rehabilitation to be the primary or first goal of imprisonment. In responses to other items, the officers strongly supported the custodial functions of the corrections officer position. Nearly half of them stated that rehabilitation of prisoners has proven to be a failure, and just does not work. However, more than half of the officers stated that rehabilitation is an important function of incarceration and that "the only effective and humane cure to the crime problem in America is to make a strong effort to rehabilitate offenders"(8). The research revealed an ambivalence among officers toward their role. Although the majority of the officers saw a need for rehabilitation and treatment of the offenders, they did not view themselves as having an important role to play in this process. Approximately one-third of the officers agreed with the statement that "I would support expanding the rehabilitation programs with criminals that are now being undertaken in our prisons"(8).

Community corrections has also been affected by the trend toward a more punitive approach. In community corrections, this was manifested by the introduction of intermediate sanctions. The U.S. Department of Justice (1990) referred to intermediate sanctions as types of punishments that fall between probation and incarceration (3). These new sanctions include shock incarceration (boot camps), electronic monitoring, home detention, and intensive supervision probation. They emphasize enhancing the level of supervision of offenders who are allowed to remain in the community. The intermediate sanction options were developed as a response to prison overcrowding, to allow convicted offenders who would ordinarily have been institutionalized to remain in the community. Because these offenders have committed more serious offenses than those ordinarily given community supervision, the concern for community safety is heightened, and this is reflected in the nature of the sanctions. Pearson (1987) contended that intensive supervision programs place as much emphasis on punishing and controlling the offender as on rehabilitation. Corrections personnel employed as probation and parole officers, surveillance officers, or as counselors in community treatment centers must be more cognizant of the control facet of their role when working with such offenders.

Development of Specialists in Community Corrections

The intermediate sanctions concept implies that those convicted offenders who are allowed to remain in the community rather than being sent to prison will be given "enhanced" supervision and treatment. In contrast to inmates housed in federal or state correctional institutions in which their involvement in rehabilitative programs is optional, those offenders given intermediate community sanctions must complete the treatment programs prescribed by the sentencing judges.

The diverse needs of the community sanctioned offenders necessitate that a wide range of community treatment services be available. Most of the actual treatment services are provided through private agencies. However, correctional personnel working in community settings must become more specialized in order to have knowledge of the types of treatment offenders under their supervision should receive and how to access these services. For example, Abadinsky (1997:381) delineates categories of probationers and parolees who are supervised by specialized probation and parole officers. These include drug-abusing offenders, alcohol-abusing offenders, dangerous felony offenders, gifted offenders, mentally ill offenders, retarded offenders, and young offenders. He also notes that specialized units in probation have been developed for those convicted of driving while intoxicated. New York State Parole has trained officers to specifically work with parolees who have contracted AIDS. In some states, specialized units have been developed to supervise sex offenders and older offenders.

Various specialists are also found in the U.S. Probation and Pretrial Service. The substance-abuse specialist, working in U.S. Probation, is responsible for brokering services by making referrals to drug treatment agencies. Most probation officers are not therapists, and they do not have the time or the expertise to provide direct treatment services. Read (1997:25) mentions that "the underlying challenge for the district—and often the responsibility of the substance-abuse specialist—is to award a contract or package of contracts to vendors who will service unique needs of the offender population." The services provided may include cognitive therapy, reality therapy, group and individual counseling, family treatment, day treatment programs, and education programs. The substance abuse specialist also maintains the contracts with the private service providers and assures that they are in compliance with these contracts. In addition, these specialists provide training for line officers who work directly with probationers and serve as consultants to sentencing judges on difficult drug-related cases. Mental health specialists have also been developed within U.S. Probation. These officers are trained to provide services to probationers with mental disorders of varying degrees of severity. According to Freitas (1997:33), "some of the most common disorders among offenders are depression, bipolar mood disorder, post-traumatic stress disorder, adjustment disorders, anxiety disorders, narcissistic personality disorder, and antisocial personality disorder." The mental health probation officer specialist supervises a diverse group of offenders. Many of them have substance-abuse problems in addition to their mental health difficulties, and the specialist must decide on appropriate treatments, make the needed referrals, and work to assure that the offender does not endanger the safety of the community. Locating service providers and obtaining the services constitute a formidable challenge for the mental health specialist. U.S. probation officers often work hand in hand with drug-abuse specialists. Monitoring the contracts with private agencies is also a major duty of the mental health specialist.

Another duty of these officers is providing employment counseling and referral services. Since employment is vital to successful reintegration into the community, many federal probation and pretrial service districts use employment specialists to assist offenders in finding and maintaining meaningful employment. Rahill-Beuler and Trait Kretzer (1997:36) note:

> Now, more than ever, helping offenders find jobs requires a proactive approach. Employment specialists must have broad knowledge of community agencies that offer more than conventional job placement. They must develop resource manuals and information to help the general officer staff with delivering employment services. They most be prepared to make referrals to a variety of educational programs, specific vocational training, and colleges.

Trends in Juvenile Corrections

The trend toward more punitive handling has also touched juvenile corrections. Feld (1990) noted that the juvenile courts have become more punishment and just deserts oriented during the past 20 years. Bazemore and Feder (1997:108) found that most of the judges included in their survey of Florida juvenile court judges supported a punitive orientation toward juvenile corrections and used the rationales of specific deterrence and retribution to justify their punitive orientation. The authors concluded that "judges are in step with the prevailing support for an increased emphasis on punishment in the juvenile justice system." Many states discarded indeterminate dispositions for juveniles and moved to determinate dispositions. In fact, some states have ceased to use the term "disposition" in describing the outcome of juvenile cases and now call this "sentencing." In addition, facilities formerly termed "youth development facilities" or "training schools" are now designated "juvenile correctional institutions." Mandatory treatment for juveniles in correctional facilities has not been abandoned, but the notion that juvenile delinquents need to be punished has become more and more accepted by political policy makers, the juvenile court judges who sentenced under these policies, and the administrators who enforced them. The increased number of aggressive youths with emotional and substance-abuse problems now found in the juvenile inmate population makes close supervision and security a strong concern in these overcrowded facilities. This emphasis on control definitely affects the overall atmosphere in the institutions and makes it more difficult to provide effective education and treatment programs. The intermediate sanctions applied to adult offenders are also used for serious juveniles released for community supervision. As with adults, both supervision and service provision are enhanced, but control is an overriding concern.

Career Opportunities in Corrections

The field of corrections is broad enough to allow for a large number of persons with varying educational backgrounds, interests, and skills to carve out satisfying careers. There are opportunities to work in the community and in institutions, and to deal with adults and juveniles through various agencies and widely different types of interaction. While the majority of careers in corrections involve direct contact with offenders in a supervisory or counseling role, there are also positions in administration, training, research, evaluation, and education.

The need for correctional personnel also extends to the private sector. An ever increasing portion of needed correctional services, including institutional care, is being provided by nonpublic agencies. Although the private sector has been involved in providing correctional services for many years, more recently private firms have even extended their services to financing, building, and operating correctional institutions. Federal, state, and local governments have developed contracts with private correctional service providers, and the opportunities for employment in private corrections have expanded considerably.

Most of the individuals who pursue careers in corrections eventually move into administrative and supervisory positions. In the past, those who held such positions were predominantly holders of the Master of Social Work degree, and this degree was considered the highest needed to move into the more responsible and better paying positions. This dominance of the administrative levels of institutions and agencies by social workers has gradually eroded, and those who hold M.A.s or Ph.D.s in criminal justice, corrections, or applied sociology are now being given equal consideration for administrative positions.

Once an individual reaches an administrative or specialized position, the opportunities to advance or to make a parallel move into another agency increase. The management and supervisory skills needed to be effective in administering the juvenile court system, for example, are quite comparable to those needed to administer a county mental health facility. Once a certain level of administrative expertise is developed, it is quite common for persons to transfer from one correctional or social service agency to another.

The job opportunities which require the use of skills of research design, evaluation, procedures, and statistics are increasing in the field of corrections. Most of the agencies are required to submit various types of periodic statistical reports and to complete records on their operations. In addition, even the smaller agencies have computerized their records and office procedures. The skills needed to fill these positions do not necessarily have to be obtained in a corrections degree program. Since much of the research and theoretical development in corrections and criminal justice has emanated from sociology, political science, and psychology departments, graduates of a variety of academic programs who have an aptitude for research and some experience with statistics and the use of computers can fit into these positions. However, those with degrees in corrections have an advantage because of their familiarity with the criminal justice process, the terms used in statistical reports, and the legal facets of criminal justice and corrections work. In addition, they are likely to have completed internships which further familiarized them with the types of reports involved and the legal and criminal justice terminology used.

In selection 3, "The Correctional Worker Concept," Hambrick describes the position the Federal Bureau of Prisons has established in regard to correctional practices and security. The Bureau operates under the correctional worker concept; that is, all staff members, including wardens and treatment and medical personnel, are designated as "correctional workers" and have some responsibility for the security of the institution and the security of inmates.

Selection 4, "Reflections on the Education Factor in the Correction Officer Role," by Blair and Kratcoski, is based on information obtained from corrections officers and administrators working in state facilities.

It was found that it is difficult to differentiate a specific type of education that best prepares a person for work in a correctional institution, and that no form of formal education is comparable to the knowledge obtained through "on-the-job" experience. Also, corrections officers must develop a wide range of skills, including those that pertain to working with a culturally diverse population, if they are to be effective in their work.

In selection 5, "A New Look at Officers' Role Ambiguity," Cheek and Miller contend that the role ambiguity for corrections officers is not primarily caused by the conflict between the role of custodian and that of rehabilitator. Instead, it results from situations in which the corrections officers must make management decisions and use discretion in rule enforcement without having the written authority and training to do so. Although they are responsible for administering the rules and regulations pertaining to their work posts, they have no voice in formulating these policies and regulations. The authors contend that the job requirements for the corrections officers fit the model of a manager.

Selection 6, "Burnout: Avoiding the Consequences of On-The-Job Stress," by Morris describes some stressful features of correctional work which also occur in other occupations, and differentiates others from those that are specifically related to corrections work. Stress management strategies for corrections workers and their families are presented.

References

Abadinsky, Howard. 1997. *Probation and Parole*, 6th edition. Upper Saddle River, NJ: Prentice Hall.

American Correctional Association, 1997. *ACA Correctional Officers' Resource Guide*. Laurel, MD: American Correctional Association.

Bazemore, Gordon and Lynette Feder. 1997. "Judges in the Punitive Juvenile Court: Organizational, Career and Ideological Influences on Sanctioning Orientation," *Justice Quarterly*, Vol. 14, No. 1 (March): 87–114.

Blair, Robert B. and Peter C. Kratcoski. 1996. "Career Opportunities for Correctional Officers," *Encyclopedia of American Prisons*. New York: Garland Publishing, 122–126.

DeLucia, Robert C. and Thomas J. Doyle. 1994. *Career Planning in Criminal Justice*. Cincinnati, OH: Anderson Publishing Company.

Feld, Barry. 1990. "The Punitive Juvenile Court and the Quality of Procedural Justice: Disjunctions Between Rhetoric and Reality," *Crime and Delinquency*, Vol. 36:443–464.

Freitas, Sheralynn. 1997. "Mentally Disordered Offenders: Who Are They? What Are Their Needs?" *Federal Probation*, Vol. 61, No.1 (March): 33–35.

Hepburn, John R. and Paul E. Knepper. 1993. "Correctional Officers as Human Services Workers: The Effect on Job Satisfaction," *Justice Quarterly*, Vol.

10, No. 2 (June): 315–337.

Kratcoski, Peter C. and Robert B. Blair. 1999. "Correctional Officers' Views on the Goals of Incarceration," unpublished manuscript.

Myren, Richard A. 1980. "Criminology and Criminal Justice: Definitions, Trends and the Future," in *Two Views of Criminology and Criminal Justice: Definitions, Trends and the Future*, 23–38. Washington, DC: U.S. Department of Justice.

Nemeth, Charles P. 1991. *Anderson's 1991 Directory of Criminal Justice Education*. Cincinnati, OH: Anderson Publishing Company.

Pearson, F. S. 1987. *Research on New Jersey's Intensive Supervision Program*. New Brunswick, NJ: Administrative Office of the Courts.

Rahill-Beuler, Colleen and Kathleen Trait Kretzer. 1997. "Helping Offenders Find Employment," *Federal Probation*, Vol. 61, No. 1 (March): 35–37.

Read, Edward M. 1997. "Challenging Addiction: The Substance Abuse Specialist," *Federal Probation*, Vol. 61, No. 1 (March): 25–28.

Tenney, Charles W., Jr. 1971. *Higher Education Programs in Law Enforcement and Criminal Justice*. Washington, DC: U.S. Government Printing Office.

U.S. Department of Justice. 1990. *Survey of Intermediate Sanctions*. Washington, DC: U.S. Government Printing Office.

3

The Correctional Worker Concept
Being Connected in the '90s

Margaret Hambrick

Connectedness. It's a word you'll hear more and more frequently in the '90s. When people are connected, good things seem to happen. They feel good about themselves and what they do.

In any workplace, being connected can mean having a say in what goes on through strategic planning or some other planning process, receiving support from co-workers, knowing there is a system to provide assistance when you need it, having a sense of common purpose, or sharing a common knowledge base. In the correctional workplace, fostering this sense of connectedness is vital to the success of the institution and individual workers.

How do we achieve this connectedness among a large number of staff, where turnover fills the ranks with inexperience and where education ranges from advanced degrees to GEDs?

In the Federal Bureau of Prisons, security is everybody's business. All job delineations include basic correctional practices and security. We say that we are "correctional workers" first and whatever else we are second.

The Federal system has operated under the correctional worker concept for nearly 20 years. Walk into a living unit in any Federal prison, and you are likely to wonder where all the staff are. The answer: they are throughout the facility, and not just in correctional officer uniform.

In contrast to many State and local correctional systems, the Federal Bureau of Prisons staffs its facilities with only one class of personnel.

Source: *Federal Prisons Journal*, 2(4) (Winter 1992):11–14.

All Bureau of Prisons staff are correctional workers first. Everyone understands that specialty roles are assumed after the security needs of the institution are met.

In one institution, the word spread like wildfire—the warden had written a "shot"—a report on an incident involving a rule violation by an inmate. Not only one, but two! And busted contraband on the food cart going to a housing unit! Writing a shot was not something executives usually did. It certainly made the point—security was everybody's business.

As correctional workers, all staff, including the warden, take responsibility for the security of the institution and supervision of inmates. If the unit officer—or any other staff member—needs emergency assistance, all available staff respond. Department heads leave a meeting, caseworkers leave their desks, construction and maintenance personnel leave their projects—all respond to help the officer and perform any necessary correctional tasks. If a physician comes across an inmate who is out of bounds, the physician assumes responsibility for the inmate, escorts that individual to the appropriate area, and writes disciplinary reports, without assistance from the correctional officer staff.

Many visitors to the Los Angeles Metropolitan Detention Center when I was warden there remarked on the staffing patterns, particularly that of the housing units, where correctional officers supervise up to 134 inmates. They typically asked, "Is this officer alone in here with all these inmates?" The officer would answer, "I'm by myself but not alone."

The Bureau of Prisons' supervision system has evolved over the past 2 decades, originating with management's goal of establishing a centralized training center and a standardized training model. Previously, the Bureau had operated using the traditional program/custody division—and with the resulting byproduct, a sometimes problematic "we/they" philosophy. In the early 1970s, however, the Bureau began to provide the same training for all staff, reinforcing the philosophy that we are all correctional workers first.

All staff are given the same basic correctional training—2 weeks of institution familiarization at the local institution and 3 weeks of Introduction to Correctional Techniques at the Federal Law Enforcement Training Center in Glynco, Georgia. All new employees, from the correctional officer and secretary to the doctor, lawyer, or psychologist, start their careers from the same frame of reference.

There are many reasons for training all staff as correctional workers:

- When all staff know the emergency routines, it multiplies the numbers available to assist. Staff in the immediate area—caseworkers, psychologists, or counselors—may be the first on the scene if an officer calls for help. All inmates can count, even the most disturbed ones. Many situations are defused by the mere appearance of numbers of staff trained in security procedures. Huge inmates have been heard to mutter "too many" and hold out their hands to be cuffed.

- All staff are more conscious of security issues in their own areas, knowing that they too must respond if something goes wrong. It provides additional incentives to check the security of doors and windows and account for inmates if all staff know that they will be called out in the middle of the night if there is an escape—not just correctional officers.

One of my "fond" memories is of spending all night on an escape post near a railroad track with another institution department head. We didn't personally catch the inmate, but we learned a lot about each other and our respective departments.

Allowing a knife to be made in the metal shop becomes more serious when that shop supervisor knows he or she may have to respond to an inmate fight on the yard.

- It eliminates the "we/they" attitude among staff that implies some may be too important to participate in the unpleasant business of dealing with a disruptive inmate.

Education and position, as well as the formal organizational structure, can create hierarchies in institutions. Having common correctional responsibilities is a great leveler. In the black jumpsuits of a BOP Special Operations Response Team, everyone looks alike; the skills needed to quell the disturbance have nothing to do with education or rank.

- It provides more career flexibility, allowing staff to move back and forth between disciplines and into management. There are no separate career tracks for custodial or "professional" personnel.

Staff in upper management need a good grounding in basic correctional practices, which the Bureau's current training philosophy provides. In the Federal system, staff may work in several disciplines on their way up. Someone may start off as a correctional officer, move into case management, possibly back into custody as a supervisor, and then into Federal Prison Industries on the way to becoming an associate warden or warden. If he or she feels unsuited for a certain kind of work, there are always other options.

- It keeps inmates from looking at staff as "good guys" vs. "bad guys," depending on whether they are responsible for enforcing the rules.

Inmates always try to play staff off against each other. An understanding of the correctional basics helps staff sort out the truth. If you've worked the officer's post as part of your training, you are more likely to know what really goes on and less likely to fall for a story.

I recently stepped up beside the officer doing shakedowns of the inmates as they left the noon meal and helped him check coats. The inmate's response was, "Hey, I got shook down by the warden."

When I discuss institution familiarization training with new employees, they often mention time spent on such correctional posts as their favorite part of the training. Those who may have had an unconscious bias against others who were going into custodial positions have new respect for their co-workers.

- It creates team spirit among staff to know they all have the same training, regardless of position.

I really enjoy talking to staff just back from "basic training" at Glynco. They are confident and excited and ready to go to work. They have made friends in other parts of the country and have a sense of connectedness with the entire system.

A recent, failed escape attempt at the Federal Correctional Institution in Lexington, Kentucky, was a good example of team spirit. In this instance, the day shift, consisting largely of specialty workers, was held over to help search the entire institution. Everyone pitched in. From searching remote corners of the compound to preparing and serving the evening meal, they all did what was asked of them. The next day several staff commented that they had enjoyed the challenge; they felt they were all part of the team.

- The staff complement can be more effective when program staff are available for emergencies.

As you can imagine from the above example, it was a tremendous help to have all the staff available to search for the inmates who were attempting to escape. In emergency situations, the available, trained staff is multiplied many times when all have been trained to respond first as "correctional workers."

In the event of a disturbance or riot, all staff can be counted on to help. Staff from all disciplines can be deployed for temporary duty, primarily to serve as correctional officers. Since each has been trained and then refreshed annually on weapons and other basic security procedures, we are confident of their ability to perform, even under the most difficult conditions.

During last year's budget crisis in the Federal Government, institutions were faced with the possibility of furloughing one-third of their work force. Our ability to reassign any staff member into a direct security post meant the basic functions of the institutions would continue even though we would be critically short of staff.

Make no mistake, it is more expensive to train all staff in all aspects of correctional procedures rather than just selected categories. But the long-term cost-efficiencies of this approach definitely outweigh the initial investment in comprehensive training.

The correctional worker system works well for the Bureau of Prisons. It complements the philosophy of direct supervision—operationally keeping staff in immediate, regular interaction with inmates—and creates a positive spirit and cooperative atmosphere among staff that improve the work environment. It also offers administrators a crucial management tool by increasing their options in an emergency.

This approach may become even more important in the '90s. The staff we hire will be a part of a society that values "connectedness" and will work best in organizations that offer it. With our growth rate, we will need every advantage we can get.

We will also be promoting staff into positions of responsibility much sooner than in the past, and with correspondingly less experience. They will need all the support they can get from the whole correctional team. The correctional worker concept fosters this teamwork, so that correctional officers are "by themselves, but never alone."

4

Reflections on the Education Factor in the Correction Officer Role

Robert B. Blair
Peter C. Kratcoski

Introduction

Much of the literature on the educational achievements of correction officers is less than complimentary (Davidson, 1974; Toch, 1978). If one were to take at face value the assertions of some authors, being a dim-witted Neanderthal is a prerequisite for employment as a correction officer. Jacobs' (1978) classic study of officers working in nine correctional facilities in Illinois revealed that most guards were not attracted to correctional work because of a desire to dominate or punish people, but because they were looking for a job with security, and the prison was conveniently located near their place of residence. When the correctional officers were asked why they chose this occupation, 57% stated that they "just needed a job" (187). In fact, 41% reported that they were unemployed at the time they specifically "aspired to become a guard" (187). Crouch and Marquart (1980) point out that in the past, most of the people found working as correction officers did not plan on corrections work as a life career, but rather drifted into it when they reached a "turning point" in their lives. Examples of such turning

This article first appeared in *Correctional Counseling and Treatment*, Third Edition. All rights reserved.

points included leaving the military, becoming dissatisfied with other employment, being laid off or fired from another job, or relocating to a town near a correctional institution.

In the past, most guards received on-the-job training, which was generally completed under the direction of one or several veteran officers and which involved trial-and-error experiences. A new guard was quickly made aware of what was expected of him or her. The experienced guards let new guards know subtly or directly that loyalty toward other officers was demanded and that prison administrators were not likely to be competent or trustworthy. The only way to learn one's job was from the instruction given by the other guards. A small minority of the personnel employed in correctional facilities were college educated, but these generally worked in administration, personnel, or in the specialized areas of social and psychological services. For example, Jacobs (1978) found that slightly more than half of the guards had a high school diploma or equivalent, while only 11 guards in the entire state of Illinois at the time of the study had a four-year college education (187).

In contrast, many, if not the majority of correction officers recruited in recent years, actually chose this type of employment and prepared for it through formal college-level education. Formal education for those working in the corrections field received a tremendous boost with the Report of the National Advisory Commission on Criminal Justice Standards and Goals, in which it was recommended that "each unified state correctional system should insure that proper incentives are provided for participation in higher education programs" (1973: 490). In the 1970s and 1980s, thousands took advantage of Law Enforcement Assistance Administration grants by attending colleges and universities that developed educational programs in corrections. Perhaps most of these students expected to be employed in supervisory or counseling-type positions within the correctional facilities, but a large number of them began their careers as correction officers. The correction officer occupation ranks among the top growth occupations in the U.S. (Benton, 1988; Silvestri and Lukasiewicz, 1989). The number of students enrolled in criminal justice programs has continued to increase, and one can predict that the correction officer ranks will continue to be filled by college graduates and that they will eventually take over the administrative positions. In the 1990s, Blair and Kratcoski (1992) found a wide variation in the educational levels of correctional officers, with 27% having a bachelor's degree or above, 67% having a high school diploma or its equivalent, and only 6% having completed less than a high school education (8).

It has been suggested that a college educated person who has developed a degree of professionalism is not likely to be very satisfied working as a correction officer, since the expectations of the role tend to demand that the officer be authoritarian, rigid, obedient, and punitive, whereas the concept of professionalism implies having a degree of personal autonomy in decision making, dedication to service, and self-regulation. It has also been suggested that learning about correctional work in a classroom has little relevance to the actual job performance, since there is a wide gap separating the theory pertaining to correctional work and the actual practice of such work.

There are numerous studies that include education as a variable in their research designs, but the findings of the research on the importance of education in correctional work are not definitive. One reason for this may be that education is often one of many variables involved in the analyses rather than being the primary focus of the studies.

Most of the earlier research work on correction officers or guards (Clemmer, 1940; Giallombardo, 1966; Jacobs, 1978) tended to portray the correction officer as having completed a limited amount of formal education. Duffee (1972) noted that the conventional training program for correction officers, which is based on the university classroom lecture model, is not likely to be effective in preparing persons for work in correctional institutions, and Jurik et al. (1987) suggested that the attainment of high levels of education by correction officers led to alienation within the institution, since correction officers did not have an opportunity to perform in the manner in which they were prepared.

No relationship was found between correction officers' levels of education and their attitudes toward punitiveness (Crouch and Alpert, 1982) or between levels of education and the correction officers' beliefs about the rehabilitative potential of prisons (Shamir and Drory, 1981). Likewise, neither Jurik (1985) nor Kassebaum, Ward and Wilner (1964) found a relationship between correction officers' education levels and their attitudes toward inmates. Poole and Regoli (1980) reported that education was inversely related to a custody orientation by correction officers. Blair and Kratcoski (1992) found a weak, but non-significant, correlation between education and the professionalism scores of correction officers.

Qualitative Research Methods

The data for this study were derived from interviews with the corrections officers that included a self-completion questionnaire. Completed responses were received from 274 officers employed in nine state prisons in Pennsylvania. A systematic random sampling design was used to select officers employed in the nine prisons. Care was taken to select subjects from rosters for each eight-hour shift in the nine state facilities. Only one officer refused to complete the interview process and the one-hour questionnaire. The interviews were conducted as part of a participant observation field study that took place over a 12-month time period. The questionnaire included the usual demographic data (age, gender, education, years of experience, and rank) as well as various questions pertaining to their attitudes on the use of authority and punishment, their orientation toward their work, levels of professionalism and alienation, and correctional policy orientations.

Although all of the correction officers included in this study completed questionnaires and were also interviewed, and considerable quantitative information was collected and analyzed, this chapter focuses primarily on the information gleaned from the responses of the officers to the questions posed during the interviews. We interviewed several hundred officers and supervisors over a period of one year. We were attempting to understand how education is interpreted by staff members with different backgrounds and how the context of the work environment shapes attitudes and behavior patterns of staff in state correctional facilities.

One of the most obvious problems of conducting research in prisons concerns the amount of autonomy outside researchers can be granted in prison settings. Access to officers and inmates is often controlled and carefully monitored by shift supervisors; the time allotted for most interviews is, therefore, usually restricted. Moreover, the location and opportunities for observing officer behaviors do not usually permit the recording of data that lead to "thick description." Fortunately this was not the case in this study. The researchers were given a free reign to come and go at their convenience and to spend as much time with the inmates and COs as they wished, as long as it did not interfere with the activities and duties of those being interviewed. We learned in the early stages of fieldwork to pay attention to what officers have to say, but to also observe and record the emotional intensity of their response. The qualitative methodological approach we used included a long interview and intensive structured observations. Many of the facilities were visited several times before interviewing started. As operationalized in the fieldwork, we gathered information that pertained to cultural factors and personal qualities that come into play when officers supervise and interact with inmates and other staff members. Along with the disciplining, counting, and locking, we also observed and recorded the quality of the exchanges, the humor, the hostility, and the compassion.

Qualitative Research Findings

On one level, we discovered that officers adopt a defensive posture toward formal education; they view education as possibly dysfunctional for many of their duties; appropriate education for the officer role is conceptualized in terms of hands-on training, and the most effective teachers are thought to be experienced officers or supervisors who work side by side with the officers and who serve as their mentors. The interview and observation data are rich with evidence that documents this generalization.

When asked to define the knowledge needed to perform their job, the officers discussed security functions and emphasized the importance of structural or institutional variables for shaping role performance. One officer's comment is typical of the responses we recorded in all nine institutions: "A college diploma carries no guarantee that you'll make it on the inside." In fact, many officers view a college education as a potential liability, a preparation for, what one supervisor referred to as, "trained incapacity." A lieutenant explains how education might work against an officer:

> The inmates resent the newer officers more than they used to. The average inmate has an education level of eighth grade to high school, and the new officer who has an education tries to show it, and to really communicate you have to get down to their level. (Interview by R. Blair with a lieutenant)

An experienced officer was asked to comment on the increasing numbers of entry-level officers with advanced degrees. He concluded his observations with the following comment: "The CO today is better educated test-wise but not street-wise. It takes a long time to become street-wise, and you should always be picking up stuff [on the job]. . . ."

The officer force as a group tends not to make direct connections between formal education and on-the-job functioning. Many officers view the process of learning the CO role as being caught rather than taught. Hence, the representative comments of officers in two separate institutions who addressed the issue of the utility of pre-institutional training for new recruits:

> They require you to spend four weeks at the Academy, but it's hard to prepare an officer for [his local state prison] by going down there [to the Academy]. It was too much like the classroom

thing. There's not much in the way of practice or hands-on type of training.

It's [the CO role] like working around people who speak French. When you have to speak it, you begin to pick it up. . . . (Interview by R. Blair with several correction officers)

Supervisory staff also see more value in on-the-job training than they do in other forms of education. A captain with 28 years of experience commented on the evolving role of the correction officer. His comments reflect the emerging concessions being made to education, but suggest the importance of grounding an education for corrections in the local institution of the CO.

The biggest and most recent change is the overcrowding and added responsibilities. We have had little increase in staff. The actual duties that officers are asked to do have tripled, and if you're going to triple the duties, you should at least double the manpower! Over the past twenty years the COs have come to see their jobs as a career, and now it's evolved into a highly scientific career-type job and the only way to learn it is on the floor. If you could work a guy a half-day, and then send him to school too, then [education] would have a very valuable impact. It's the "in thing" to go the training Academy, but it just doesn't mean that much. (Interview by R. Blair with a captain)

Finally, supervisors of a military-type organization, whose primary function is to lock up offenders against their will, tend almost naturally to expect officers to acquire fundamental skills related to security. Training supervisors tend to see the base information for the role as shaped by technical security skills that are more effectively learned by on-the-job training than through formal education. A number of the supervisors emphasized the need for officers to have good communication skills, but most typical of all responses we recorded are views that reflect the following comment that argues for the primacy of security "training."

It's mostly a matter of socializing [the new officers], and there is not enough information on security techniques. So I worked on training on the job for officers, and designed it for places where the need was maximal, such as in the use of weapons, corridor duty, cell search and packing [of inmate belongings]. (Interviewed by R. Blair with a lieutenant)

These quotations were selected for their value as typical statements of the correctional staff who were asked questions related to the role of education for the CO. The overwhelming weight of the evidence in our data support the generalization that correction officers as a group nurture a skeptical attitude regarding the usefulness of formal education for performing the correction officer role.

What are we to make of these reflections on education? If these are the only results that we could report, we would add little to what we already know about the education factor in the CO role. We decided, therefore, that limiting our study to data gathered through one-shot survey interviews would not do justice to the complexity of the issues. We also reasoned that terminating the study after the first wave of standard interviews would constitute a premature closure of inquiry on an important topic that warrants more intensive investigation. The purpose in adapting the field design followed in the research was to acquire data that capture the subtlety, complexity, and varied aspects of the CO role and, in the same way that quantitative researchers use an elaboration model to check for spuriousness, we attempted to specify the conditions under which our first set of findings might vary. Specifically, we were searching for "counterfactuals" in the data that suggest diversity of views regarding education. Increasingly there is recognition that correction officers are a diverse group and that their roles involve a flexibility that permits qualities to come into play that reflect, among other things, their unique cultures, backgrounds and the type of correctional facility in which they are employed. The discussion that follows focuses on three questions that represent variables that account for a richer and more in-depth understanding of the education facts than those revealed in our initial findings. The second round of interviews was completed for the purpose of answering the following questions:

1. Do unique characteristics of individual correctional institutions influence the way officers and supervisors think about the importance of education?
2. What are the variables that account for differences in opinions on the relevance of formal education for the officer role?
3. What evidence is there that the CO role would benefit from efforts to upgrade education requirements?

Regarding the first question of institutional characteristics, we begin the discussion by challenging what is frequently a common assertion: a prison is a prison. Prisons vary, we discovered, and their unique locales, employment practices, and histories all contribute to diversity in the orientations and performance styles of their COs and supervisors. One institution studied, which we will refer to as Valleyview, is known throughout the state as a prison that is "tight" on security; officers in Valleyview are proud of their roles, and their children might come about as close as any to voicing an unfamiliar aspiration: "I want to be a CO when I grow up." Morale is high among staff and there is a good working relationship between the correction officers' union and management. The prison is perceived by inmates as a "no bullshit operation," and despite the complaints of "redneck" behavior from a few officers, several of the dozen or so inmates we interviewed expressed appreciation for the relative safety they enjoy in an institution that "belongs to the guards." Officers tend to have a "we" versus "they" view in regard to the other prisons in the state, and they often stated that the "system" is "sending us all the bad apples." Of course this feeling was also pervasive among staff in the other state prisons, but the isolation of Valleyview accentuates the distrust of outside change; directives that disrupt traditional authority patterns, regardless of their sources of origin, are usually interpreted as meddling by outsiders.

Part of the success of "running a good shop" like Valleyview, argues one officer, can be explained by the prison's strategic role as a major source of employment in the area. Community attitudes toward the prison are so positive that local leaders petitioned the state to locate and build a second prison in the Valleyview area. A cohesive officer force is one of the consequences of these unique geographical and employment patterns, as suggested in one of our interviews.

> At _____ we help officers. There are lots of relatives working together in here. We have 31 sets of brothers in the institution and aunts and cousins too. The community is so small that everyone knows everyone here, and in some way or another everybody socializes together. Ninety percent hunt and fish and shop and boat together and are closely related through blood or friendship. There are fifteen officers I went to high school with who are working in here. There's a thing here of evaluating officers. Even the poorest officer in here would get some backing [by other officers].

The superintendent of Valleyview had considerable formal education in corrections and had attended college at a time when the treatment and rehabilitation of inmates were given a great deal of emphasis. We were interested in the way a superintendent with a counseling background would articulate the types of skills a correction officer needs to be effective. His statement reaffirmed the statements of the correction officers on this matter. Security concerns at Valleyview take precedence over all other matters, but an officer's knowledge must extend far beyond the mechanical aspects of the job.

> Officers are becoming more professional. The professional carries himself with pride and dignity. He treats his peers as well

as inmates with respect; he respects his superiors. He respects the chain of command, the hierarchy of authority, and there's more of that here than anyplace else in the state. He understands how the institution functions, and he understands his role in relation to the roles of other people in the institution. The guy knows the rules and regulations, and he knows how to deal with inmates without being a hard nose about rules and regulations. He can reason with them and talk them out of situations. He also has basic skills in first aid and CPR; he has basic safety skills; he knows how to conduct a security search—he's good at it, thorough—and knows how to handle security equipment, whether it's handcuffs, shackles, weapons, whatever it might be. That's professionalism. (Interview by R. Blair with an anonymous superintendent)

The superintendent traced the development of large numbers of professional officers in his institution to legitimated authority. The communal ties that cut across ranks, position, and job categories provide the cement that reinforces a security-oriented chain of command.

This institution has been here for a hundred years. It has grown up and the community has grown with it. This is the only [prison] I've ever seen where people aspire to a career in corrections. I mean actually grow up and say they want to work in corrections, and you have grandfathers, fathers, and sons working in this institution. Employees come back to visit the facility after they retire. When you walk through the institution and talk to people in any department here, they treat it and talk about it like it's theirs, and it is. They have a vested interest in it; it's their own. They carry themselves more professionally. Any time we send a couple of our officers for training and officers show up from other institutions in the state, everybody from staff training and development comment; they say, "Look at the officer from _____; they even look better, they carry themselves better." (Interview by R. Blair with anonymous superintendent)

These sets of comments contrast sharply with those offered by another superintendent whose major labor supply includes graduates from a state university criminology program. Reflecting upon the ingredients that make up professionalism in the officer force, he responded as follows:

We are a profession. We have a formal training program . . . you have to have a background [education] and you have to learn a philosophy; you have to learn goals; you have to learn procedures.

You have individuals who are what we would call a "professional officer." He has to make the grade by taking the test, and so you have the whole business of selection. He starts out with formal training and then has on-the-job training. If I had to compare it with a similar profession, I would say the nursing profession. Another comparison would be with law or lawyers, [but at a time when] lawyers did not bother going to law schools and did their clerkships, and then were able to pass the boards. To some extent we're doing the same thing because the training is the equivalent of a clerkship, and passing the bar is in effect too when you move into a particular status after you've been around awhile. . . . (Interview by R. Blair, with an anonymous superintendent)

Of course more information is needed about the superintendents and their institutions, but the results are suggestive of possible ways that personal orientations interact with institutional milieus in shaping understanding and interpretations of the education factor. Returning to the Valleyview example, we also discovered that education was never really a significant factor in hiring or promotion. A strong nepotism in employment practices that favored "who you know" over "what you know" indirectly contributed to a strong communal system that minimized the importance of education. For an institution that has always socialized its officer force through on-the-job training, it is understandable that there would be resistance among officers to Academy training and to other state directives that attempted to implement court-mandated changes. It is understandable, therefore, that officers naturally resisted changes in promotion policies that gave an added edge to officers with formal educational backgrounds. Officers who had accumulated considerable seniority were very negative toward the new state regulation which required the completion of a written test in addition to a specified number of years experience for those seeking promotion to a higher rank. This change was interpreted as unfair and as a violation of local traditions. A block sergeant shared his personal reactions to the indirect effects that education had on the promotion system.

A man with two years [experience] can be academically inclined, and can take tests and beat out the others, yet never be able to run a block; yet they're the guys who are going to get the high score. A older guy, even with the five points extra that they give veterans, may not have a chance. Now they [Bureau promotion policy] are calling for a minimum time of five years before you are eligible for promotion. In the beginning, when they made these changes, maybe I was jealous, but it affected me to see a younger officer with education move ahead. Later I could see

it, but it took me eight years to make sergeant and yet it only
took him seven years to make lieutenant. But now he's got both,
the education and the experience, and now it's OK. He carries
a great deal of respect and he is a potential captain. (Interview
by R. Blair with a correction officer)

The sergeant's comment is particularly poignant, because in
addition to its typicality, it illustrates the fact that even the "old
timers" were beginning to accept the importance of education as
a major change in the way their roles are defined. The point is,
different interpretations of education do not just happen in a
vacuum; they reflect combinations of institutional and individual
variables working together.

Another source of diversity in thinking about the role of education
is represented in the court-mandated hiring of minorities and
women as correction officers. As the superintendent of Valleyview
suggested, his prison "lags behind most other institutions" in hiring
minority COs. The few minority officers who work at Valleyview
were interviewed, and they expressed concerns about practices in
Valleyview that reflect their definition of the situation. A minority
officer with two years of experience offered these comments.

There is a black versus redneck thing in here. In this county
most of the black people live in _____, and yet they hire their
people from _____ where there are no blacks. With the black
[inmate] population growing in here, it's like sending the pope
to talk to a bunch of Jews. I never see these people [other officers]
on the outside. They don't get enough race training at the
Academy, and they don't recruit blacks. There is a lot of
nepotism here too. There are [racist] jokes all the time. When
they come at me with them I just play the dozens with them,
and they can't take that. All they want to do is talk about
hunting and fishing and their four-wheel drives, and if they kick,
it's on somebody else. (Interview by R. Blair with a black
correction officer)

The "good-old-boy network" at Valleyview is viewed by minority
officers as impervious to change. Implied in the following assessment of conditions at Valleyview, as voiced by a minority officer
with 10 years experience, is an argument for changing employment
patterns at Valleyview as well as upgrading education requisites.

They don't recruit right. You have to deal with them [prospective
minority employees], you have to go to their community and
get them. They screen us out. They put in their friends and
relatives. There is so much nepotism here! When we were on
A ward we ran it well, and we weren't big guys either; we ran
it well because we're from the same community as the inmates.
You need streetwise people in here.

> If you're looking for black officers you got to put it in the paper, take the job information to colleges and to programs where there are blacks. If they really want to get some good officers, why don't they go to the south? Go to the colleges in the south! You get coal region guys here who can't talk to a black man. It's a communication barrier and it takes 5 years to learn their lingo. (Interview by R. Blair with a black correction officer)

The data we collected from interviews with approximately 50 minority officers contain numerous appeals for COs to have specialized educational experiences that would better equip them for working with a growing minority inmate population. Nearly every one of the minority officers cited specific academic subjects, such as "race and ethnic relations," or "what it's like to live in a ghetto" as requisite courses for white correction officers who interact with nonwhite inmates.

Still another source of diversity in thinking about the relevance of education for the CO role comes from the increasing number of female officers in male prisons. Valleyview did not employ female COs at the time of our interviews, but the data drawn from an institution with characteristics similar to Valleyview typify the responses of female officers. If this officer is correct in her assessment of the contributions that women bring to supervising inmates, implications for change in training and education might be significant.

> The presence of male officers in a female institution very often comes across to the female inmate as a physical threat; whereas a female officer in a male institution often becomes an emotional lift for inmates and introduces a more human aspect to the institutional setting of all-male surrounding. Concerning a female doing a "male" job—a female not just in corrections, but in any predominantly male occupation must or *is expected* to do sometimes two or three times as much [work], both in quantity and quality, than the best male on the job to be given half the credit that is extended to the poorest male performer in that particular institution. In plain English, a man can really "screw up" the particular assignment: eyes will roll toward the heavens, but then it is overlooked. (Note to R. Blair from a female correction officer; emphasis added)

Another variable that is pushing the education factor to the fore of officer training is the growing diversity in the inmate population. Officers in all institutions shared their reservations about the need for communication skills and supervisory techniques that would equip them to more effectively work with special-need inmates. At the time of the interviews, inmates with mental disabilities were becoming more visible. A correction officer offered this view of the situation:

> Six years ago we didn't have as many insane people, and Christ, today, we're polluted with them. When you deal with them, they can't listen like other inmates; they're out in left field; you can't talk with them. Like down here in RHU [Restricted Housing Unit], they're throwing stuff at you all the time. What can you do? About the only option is to move them to B block; once they're there we get them declared insane and from there they are sent to an insane asylum. But it's frustrating because they only keep them at _____ for a few months and we get them right back again. In relation to them you have to change your strategy. They're different from the regular type. You can't use the same talking technique; you have to try cigarettes, humor; some guys just forget it. (Interview by R. Blair with anonymous correction officer; emphasis added)

Some officers, as this one suggested, "just forget it." Others do not, and we frequently were informed that supervisors were careful to assign officers with the requisite communication skills (or natural talents) to supervise inmates with mental disabilities. Other inmate groups are receiving specialized attention as well, including those with AIDS and the elderly. One institutional training coordinator reflected on the relevance of CO education for the growing diversity in the inmate population and on the need for officers to have an enriched repertoire of skills:

> The lower the level of education you have, the less likely you are to do the job, and the less objective you are about the work. I definitely see a need for education of officers. You need education to be a professional in here. Education helps you make a decision quickly and objectively. Also, it helps if you have lived in a lot of different neighborhoods, because you're getting all different kinds of offenders, and you're getting more difficult types of offenders who resist supervision.
>
> The all-male society is at the heart of it. Among the officers, there is competition for promotions; inside the fence there is competition for survival, both physical and psychological. You need the proper tools in your own mind, and if you don't have them, you tend to fall back on basic force. (Interview by R. Blair with an anonymous training coordinator)

Even the older officers are beginning to see the need for upgrading educational requisites for an increasingly complex role. An officer with 25 years of experience shared the following assessment of changes he observed.

> Fifteen years ago there was a line between the officers and inmates, and each knew where he stood. In the '70s, the inmates

got court appointed rights. At the time we were considered guards, and that's what we did; now we have to evaluate a man, and we have to put this evaluation on paper, and the evaluation can be taken to court. If you blow the evaluation in court, the state won't back you up. And when you do this evaluating of inmates, you can't just give orders like in the service.

Things have really changed. Inmates now know their civil liberties; we have younger and younger drug users, and we have middle-class people too. We're not just dealing with the lower classes, and our roles are not clearly defined like they used to be. You have a different inmate now, and the education standards for officers have gone up. In the past, only a few officers had an education, but it wasn't needed then. (Interview by R. Blair with a correction officer)

The increasing diversity in both the inmate population and the officer force is paving the way for a variety of changes, many of which have implications for education that is relevant for the officer role. The final test of the efficacy of education, however, is in the behavior of officers. How does education influence interaction between officers and inmates?

One of the dozen female officers discussed the importance of education for the correction officer role. Education involves more than just being able to identify with the culture and "rap" with inmates. She traces the sources of her professionalism to her college education in the areas of law enforcement and corrections.

I see the job as a profession and a career. I see the need for a sharp uniform, professional conduct, training, a particular way of relating to inmates. I have become more relaxed, use more slang in my speech, talk more, but I still only speak with inmates if it's a necessity, and I am careful not to rap with them. Instead of doing their job, a lot of officers are into rapping and in doing that, they just aren't paying attention all the time; they walk around with a slouch, talk at inappropriate times, and so forth. (Interview by R. Blair with a correction officer)

An officer who had been viciously attacked by an inmate had returned to duty after a prolonged period of recovery. He was a liberal arts college graduate. With some reluctance he agreed to discuss the unfortunate incident. His analysis was not unlike that of an athlete who blew an assignment and lost the big game. He seemed to be blaming himself, not the inmate, for his misfortune.

It was a hard lesson. All the cues were right there, but I didn't read them. Instead of picking them up I misread them, because, for one thing, it was a sunny day and I was feeling good. Another thing, it was Sunday, and I was a little too relaxed. But when I look back on the attack, I can feel the signals: the number of

> guys on the block; there were no people in the divide at the time when it's usually crowded. A few guys were milling around watching me. I just wasn't paying attention to the environment. I pay attention to a lot more things now, and even when I'm making my rounds, I listen more and try to look around more. My senses have developed. . . . (Interview by R. Blair with a correction officer)

There is no suggestion in the quote that a liberal arts education made any difference at all in the incident that occurred. When we probed for perceived connections with his background, the officer repeated a familiar refrain: education helps, but it needs to be combined with a set of skills that include being able to "communicate with inmates" and, he added, "the officer has to know himself." Officers are less reticent to discuss the implications of training for on-the-job functioning. Those who do not dismiss outright their Academy training, tend to cite specific tools and techniques that they learned at the Academy, or they give a generally unqualified endorsement to training. The following quote, however, is reflective of views shared by many officers that suggest possibly new thinking about the relevance of education:

> For the past years, a new breed of officers has entered this prison. They are younger and have lived in the atmosphere of our society and know more about criminals. Guys who went through the basic training class with me come to the institution with a different kind of knowledge than the old timers. We have, as our goal, to make things better in here. I don't mean we're soft hearted, but trying to encourage decency and respect. Our goal is to treat men as humans. The older breed didn't attend training school and learn this, and they did not live in the environment where there was a mixture of races. (Interview by R. Blair with a correction officer)

Perhaps inmates are the best source for documenting the effects of education on the correction officer role. A routine part of our fieldwork was to interview inmates. We followed a procedure of randomly selecting a ward or block and then selecting every other cell for interviewees. The education factor was not our usual topic of conversation in the interviews, but a number of inmates cited the importance of education when we asked them to reflect on the characteristics of a good or poor officer. The following quote is typical of comments of inmates in the institutions we studied.

> Usually the more adept guards have more education. But the good guards are street-smart too. They have seen the hard times and can identify with us. They are consistent in application of

the rules. They have common sense and can tell the difference between types of people. They know the types and take the time to discern the differences between them. They allow privacy and know when to bend. They use good common sense in situations. (Interview by R. Blair with an inmate)

Discussion

Our question on higher education was not specific enough to tap the type of education that may be applicable to being effective as a correction officer. For example, we did not establish whether the correction officer who had completed college had a degree in criminal justice, corrections, sociology, business, or another field. Our findings also suggest that the education factor is very closely intertwined with other factors such as experience, rank, age, the security level of the institution, and even the characteristics of the community in which the facility is housed. Our findings suggest that the college educated correction officer is likely to adhere to a professional standard regardless of the institution in which the person is employed. We expected that those college educated officers working in maximum security facilities would experience more alienation and dissatisfaction than those working in minimum security facilities. This did not turn out to be the fact. Perhaps the knowledge gained from attending college is useful to the correction officer who must be flexible, resourceful, and adaptable to various settings and situations. This may explain the similarity in their responses, even though the college educated officers were working in drastically different settings. On the other hand, many officers working in the minimum security facilities complained of the "hardcore offenders" being sent to the minimum security institutions. In fact, they contended that the only difference between working in a maximum and minimum security facility is the structure of the building, with the inmates and programs being the same for both types of facilities. Correction officers with a college education are often isolated in an institution because many inmates, correction officers, and administrators are not sure what to expect from college educated officers. They are usually coming from the outside and bringing in "foreign notions and ideas." Thus the staff is not always eager to accept those with a college education. Once the college educated officer becomes aware that he or she is not being accepted, alienation can result.

From our qualitative analysis we found that the meanings and interpretations the prison staff placed on the role of education are many and varied, and they reflect attitudes and rationalizations that result from a combination of variables working together: cultural background, individual traits of officers, role situations, and the unique qualities and history of a given institution.

Additional research would have to be completed to determine if a generalized or a more specialized educational program best serves the interests of the correction officer. In addition, the responses of the supervisors who commented on the importance of education to the role of correction officer must be interpreted with some caution, because their comments may in fact be in regard to training, not general education. As noted, many of the supervisors indicated that the college educated correction officer brings to the job a more professional orientation than the typical non-college educated correction officer. While the supervisors may also concede that college educated correction officers tend to be more adept at understanding the behavior of different ethnic and racial groups and overall more skilled in interpersonal communication and human relations, nevertheless, they hold fast to the belief that the job cannot be learned in a classroom. They are the first to admit that even the technical type of training which is received in the correction officer training academy falls short in preparing the officer for the experiences he or she will face in a correctional institution.

We tend to be in complete agreement with this view. Correctional work in the final analysis is no different from that of most other professions. Just as a doctor, nurse, or teacher completes an internship, residency, or student teaching assignment, the correction officer learns the subtleties of the correction officer role while on the job, and no amount of formal education is an adequate substitute. Unfortunately, too often this on-the-job training is completed in a trial-and-error manner without appropriate guidance and instructions.

References

Benton, Ned. 1988. "Personal Management: Strategies for Staff Development," *Corrections Today,* 50(5) (August): 102–106

Blair, Robert and Peter C. Kratcoski. 1992. "Professionalism Among Correctional Officers: A Longitudinal Analysis of Individual and Structural Determinants," in Peter J. Benekos and Alida V. Merlo (eds.) *Corrections: Dilemmas and Directions.* Cincinnati, OH: Anderson Publishing Co.

_____. 1992. "The Education Factor in the State Correction Officer Role," Paper presented at the annual meeting of the American Society of Criminology, New Orleans, LA.

Clemmer, Donald. 1940. *The Prison Community.* New York: Rinehart and Co.

Crouch, Ben M. and Geoffrey P. Alpert. 1980. "Prison Guards' Attitudes Toward Components of the Criminal Justice System," *Criminology* 18(2) (August): 227–236.

Crouch, Ben M. and James W. Marquart. 1980. "On Becoming a Prison Guard," in Ben Crouch (ed.), *The Keepers*, Springfield, IL: Charles Thomas Publishers, 63–106.

Cullen, Francis, Bruce Link, Nancy Wolfe, and James Frank. 1985. "The Social Dimensions of Correctional Officer Stress." *Justice Quarterly* 2(4) (December): 505–533.

Davidson, R. Ted. 1974. *Chicano Prisoners: The Key to San Quentin.* New York: Holt, Rinehart & Winston.

Duffee, David. 1972. *Using Correctional Officers in Planned Change.* Washington, D.C.: National Institute of Law Enforcement, National Technical Information Service.

Giallombardo, Rose. 1966. *Society of Women: A Study of a Women's Prison.* New York: John Wiley & Sons.

Hepburn, John R. and Nancy Jurik. 1986. "Individual Attributes, Occupational Conditions and the Job Satisfaction of Correctional Security Officers," Paper presented at the annual meeting of the American Society of Criminology, Atlanta (October).

Jacobs, J. B. 1978. "What Prison Guards Think: A Profile of the Illinois Force." *Crime and Delinquency,* 25 (April): 185–196.

Jurik, Nancy C. 1985. "Individual and Organizational Determinants of Correctional Officer Attitudes Toward Inmates." *Criminology,* 23: 523–539.

Jurik, Nancy C., Gregory J. Halemba, Michael C. Musheno, and Bernard V. Boyle. 1987. "Educational Attainment, Job Satisfaction, and the Professionalization of Correctional Officers." *Work and Occupations,* 14: 106–125.

Jurik, Nancy C. and Russ Winn. 1986. "Describing Correctional Security Dropouts and Rejects: An Individual or Organizational Profile," Paper presented at the annual meeting of the Academy of Criminal Justice Sciences, Orlando, FL.

Kassebaum, G., D. Ward, and D. Wilner. 1964. "Some Correlates of Staff Ideology in the Prison," *Journal of Research in Crime and Delinquency,* 1: 96–109.

National Advisory Commission on Criminal Justice Standards and Goals: Corrections. 1973. Washington, D.C.: U.S. Government Printing Office.

Philliber, S. 1987. "Thy Brother's Keeper: A Review of the Literature on Correctional Officers." *Justice Quarterly,* 4 (March): 9–37.

Poole, Eric D. and Robert M. Regoli. 1980. "Examining the Impact of Professionalism on Cynicism, Role Conflict, and Work Alienation Among Prison Guards." *Criminal Justice Review,* 5: 57–65.

Rafter, Nicole H. 1992. "Criminal Anthropology in The United States." *Criminology,* 30 (November): 525–545.

Shamir, Boaz and Amos Drory. 1981. "Some Correlates of Prison Guards' Beliefs," *Criminal Justice and Behavior,* 8(2) (June): 233–249.

Silvestri, George and John Lukasiewicz. 1989. "Projections of Occupational Employment, 1988–2000," *Monthly Labor Review*, 112: 42–65.

Toch, Hans. 1978. "Is a 'Correctional Officer' by Any Other Name a 'Screw'?" *Criminal Justice Review* 3(2): 19–35.

5

A New Look at Officers' Role Ambiguity

Frances E. Cheek
Marie Di Stefano Miller

The role of the correctional officer has long been recognized as difficult. Many studies have identified a basic ambiguity, which has been attributed primarily to the double purposes of custody and treatment. These studies have documented that this dual and fluctuating orientation has created a basic confusion in the definition of policies and procedures for managing correctional facilities (Meyer, 1972; Ohlin, 1974; Conrad, 1975; and Cohn, 1979). For the correctional officer—the front-line implementer of these policies and procedures—this has been a continuous source of stressful role ambiguity (Cressey, 1959; Grusky, 1959; Priestly, 1972; and Pogrebin, 1979).

Officer/Manager Duality

Although confusing correctional goals must be acknowledged as a major source of role ambiguity for correctional officers, observational and research evidence indicates another significant source of role ambiguity. In the course of research and training activities in the area of correctional stress, conducted over the past five years, we have

Reprinted from *Correctional Officers: Power, Pressure and Responsibility.* College Park, MD: American Correctional Association, 1983: 11–16. Used with permission of the American Correctional Association, Inc., Lanham, MD, found that lack of recognition and support of correctional officers in the managerial aspect of their role generates a lot of stress. In other words, the officer/manager duality is a more significant source of role ambiguity than the custody/treatment duality.

Thus, in a 1978 pilot study (Cheek and Miller, 1978) of the experience of stress of 24 New Jersey county correctional officers, it was found that "lack of clear job guidelines for job performance" was the most significant source of stress. This was not an unexpected finding in view of the many studies describing correctional officer role ambiguity as a result of conflicting correctional goals. However, surprisingly, "conflict between the role of custodian and the role of rehabilitator" was seen as much less stressful by the officers.

To explore this finding further a more comprehensive study was conducted, examining the stress experience of 143 state and county correctional officers (Cheek and Miller, 1979). This study confirmed the earlier finding of the significance of role ambiguity, and also revealed that two additional related administrative items, lack of autonomy in decision making and lack of administrative support, were major sources of correctional stress. Statistical analysis further confirmed these findings: A measure of stress-related physical symptoms and illnesses developed from Selye's (1976) scale of stress levels was highly correlated with items in these three administrative categories.

Flexibility in Rule Enforcement

To clarify these findings, officers in stress classes from New Jersey and other states were asked why these three items were major sources of stress. This questioning uncovered an intriguing situation that cast a new light on officers' role ambiguity.

The officers reported that there were indeed guidelines for their job performance, countless rules and regulations designed to ensure that their major responsibility—the custody of inmates—was carried out successfully. However, it appeared that experienced and effective officers never went "by the book," enforcing every rule on every occasion—for several reasons. First, the many complex human situations that must be dealt with could not be adequately covered by any set of rules, so that flexibility in rule enforcement was necessary. Moreover, as Sykes (1959) and others (Carroll, 1974) have pointed out, bending correctional rules is necessary to secure compliance from inmates so that control can be maintained. Thus, when inmates behave well, the rules are bent favorably; when they behave poorly, a tightening up occurs. In this way, negotiation secures compliance, in a situation where coercive enforcement, a limited resource at best, would produce resentment and hostility and make control of this hostile captive group difficult.

However, while bending rules is a necessary tool for securing compliance, it can lead to a confusing situation in a correctional facility. The rules tend to be differentially enforced, from one officer to another and from one shift to the next. Inmates can use the situation to manipulate, and new officers face a perplexing learning situation. Little consistency in rule enforcement may be observable to new officers, and their previous training, if any, many seem irrelevant. Moreover, information about how to perform their job may be difficult to obtain because their supervisors or other officers may withhold advice.

Advice may be withheld because no one is willing to take responsibility in a situation where everyone is dangerously vulnerable. The vulnerability is a direct result of discretionary rule enforcement. As we have noted, if officers are to carry out their task of controlling inmates successfully they cannot go by the book. But if they do not go by the book, they may be subject to disciplinary action. Thus, they are caught in a double bind.

Administrative Support

Because of this double bind and officers' subsequent vulnerability, administrative support becomes critical. When officers act according to common sense to resolve situations but break a rule in so doing, they must be sure of administrative support for their actions. However, as previously mentioned, the New Jersey study showed that lack of administrative support is a major source of stress for correctional officers. For instance, a class of 25 officers undergoing basic training (three months to two years in their jobs) were asked whether their immediate supervisors would support them if something went wrong in a case where they handled a difficult situation using their best judgment but by bending a rule. Out of the class of 25, only one officer raised his hand. In a class of 18 advanced officers, only one indicated he could expect support in such a situation.

Another major source of stress for correctional officers, identified in the New Jersey stress study, was lack of participation in decision making regarding policies and regulations. Officers complain that even though they are responsible for administering the rules and regulations that govern their own work situation, and are directly responsible for supervising and managing relations with inmates, they are not seen as part of the management structure.

Rules that Don't "Fit"

Policies and rules are regularly developed at higher levels, and often by those unfamiliar with the actual work setting. Hence, officers may have to work in a context of rules that don't "fit." Moreover, officers feel they have no power to change poor or impractical policies and rules. Officers report that if they want to change a policy or rule it is best to work through inmates, who are seen in many cases as more powerful change agents in the correctional setting.

This powerlessness results from the fact that in the correctional administrative structure, officers, not inmates, are seen as the bottom level. Indeed, officers are not seen as part of the administrative structure, despite their critical front-fine managerial relationships with inmates. Thus, they are not typically involved in administrative staff meetings, and must regularly function without input into decision making and often without being informed of decisions that are made.

Cressey (1959) commented upon this situation:

> The guard, who is the lowest-level worker in a prison, is also a manager. He is managed in a system of regulations and controls from above, but he also manages, by a corresponding system of regulations, the inmates who are in his charge. Essentially because he is a worker, he cannot be given full discretion to produce a desired end product such as inmate docility or inmate rehabilitation, and essentially because he is a manager his activities cannot be bureaucratized in a set of routine procedures.

Dangerous Implications

However, the importance of this concept of the officer as manager has not been recognized in subsequent analyses of the role of the officer. Thus, in a much more recent publication (Johnson, 1977), we find the following quote, which repeats the traditionally perceived structural position of the officer without awareness of its dangerous implications for administrative ineffectiveness in corrections.

> The "prison guard" occupies a place at the bottom of the positions which collectively comprise the custodial prison's organization. Therefore, he receives instructions (role norms) from those individuals holding positions of authority in higher levels of the organization. Significantly, as the occupant of the lowest status in the official organization, the "prison guard" has the most direct and continuous relationship with the inmates who are the "material" of this system.

That the role of the officer is truly a managerial one was further confirmed in a later study of the effects of automated surveillance on control in a small county jail (Cheek and Miller, 1981). It was observed that when the officers began to interact less with the inmates, as they used the automated surveillance technology, rule enforcement became chaotic, and control was reduced. Control could not be maintained by officers watching inmates from a distance, but rather by active negotiation, within a context of relationships built in face-to-face interactions—a managerial function. Another intriguing factor in the loss of control was that supervisor-officer interaction was also reduced by the automated surveillance, and this prevented the operation of an informal structure of custody staff relationships, which had previously served to maintain a consistent system of discretionary rule enforcement.

Significantly then, officers' managerial role is maintained through the informal, rather than the formal, structure. However, lack of recognition and legitimation of their managerial role by the formal structure poses severe and stressful problems for officers. They suffer both from a lack of adequate training and preparation for the managerial role and from the lack of a formal administrative structure that operates to maintain the effectiveness of the role and supports its functioning.

The Officer as a Manager

Do the job requirements of the correctional officer fit the model of a manager as developed by authorities in the field? The classical or traditional definition of the manager (Fayol, 1916) contains four aspects: (1) planning, (2) organizing, (3) coordinating and (4) controlling. However, a more contemporary authority (Drucker, 1974) points out that managers do not necessarily perform all these functions; he describes five aspects of the role: (1) setting objectives, (2) organizing, (3) motivating, (4) communicating and evaluating and (5) developing people.

Drucker points out that it is not only direct control or command over people that makes a manager, but responsibility for their contributions to organizational purposes. Hence, responsibility for others rather than power over them is the distinctive criterion of management.

In the correctional setting, the role of the correctional officer has traditionally been seen as primarily one of direct command of the inmates in terms of enforcing the rules, which, as Drucker says, does not make him or her a manager. However, the situation is much more complex. The officer is actually responsible for the smooth running of the tier, which must be accomplished not by enforcing rules, but by negotiating them within the context of an informal network of interpersonal relations with inmates, in which they are motivated to perform appropriately. In other words, managing the interpersonal network and working with and developing people are the primary functions of the correctional officer role—a managerial role, in Drucker's terms.

Managers as Developers of People

More detail on the managerial role of correctional officers in terms of their function in developing people is offered in Mintzenberg (1975), who from his direct observational studies of a cross-cultural sample of managers tells us that the most important roles of a manager are interpersonal, informational and decisional; he/she must be a leader, a monitor, but also a resource distributor, negotiator and disturbance handler.

These observations, as well as Drucker's comments that managers must be responsible for developing people under them, convey an important message regarding officers' rehabilitative role, which is that of the manager rather than the social worker. Thus, it is important to note that the most effective managers will respect those they supervise as human beings, clarify the rules and guidelines under which they operate, allow them as much autonomy as possible, and encourage self-control and a sense of responsibility.

The self-image of those managed in either case must not be destroyed but rather supported. In this sense, a most important one, correctional officers act to rehabilitate those in their charge because they encourage self-respect, self-control and responsibility through their managerial practices. Institutions that destroy these qualities in officers can hardly hope to support them in inmates.

Implications

The implications of the concept of the officer as a manager are far-reaching. The concept clarifies officers' rehabilitative role and sets it within the context of good managerial practice. Moreover, it also suggests that recruitment practices should be sensitive to the higher-level nature of the role, and special training should be geared to officers' managerial function. (A three-day managerial training program for correctional officers has been developed in New Jersey by the authors and is being pilot tested.) Particularly in today's complex, stressful and violent prison settings, more appropriate training can reduce current alarmingly high rates of burnout and turnover in new recruits. Managerial training for more experienced staff would be helpful in reducing their stress, too.

Finally, it is important that correctional administrators and supervisors, particularly those dealing directly with officers, be given training to guide them in developing management and supervisory practices that will recognize and support officers in their critical managerial role.

References

Carroll, L. *Hacks, Blacks and Cons.* Lexington, MA: D.C. Heath, 1974.

Cheek, F. E., and M. Miller. "A Study of Correction Officer Stress," New Jersey

Department of Corrections, unpublished report, 1978.

Cheek, F. E., and M. Miller. "Stress Awareness and Coping Techniques Training for Correctional Officers." Delivered at the Annual Meeting of the American Academy of Criminal Justice Sciences, Cincinnati, OH, March 15, 1979.

Cheek, F. E., and M. D. Miller. "Serendipitous Effects of Automated Surveillance in Terms of Loss of Control of the Correctional Institution: Implications for the Role of the Correction Officer." Paper presented at the Annual Meeting of the American Academy of Criminal Justice Sciences, Philadelphia, PA, March 1981.

Cohn, A. W. "The Failure of Correctional Management—Revisited," *Federal Probation*, No. 3, 1979.

Conrad, J. P. "We Should Never Have Promised a Hospital," *Federal Probation*, December 1975.

Cressey, D. "Contradictory Directives in Complex Organizations: The Case of the Prism," *Administrative Science Quarterly*, Vol. 4, 1959, pp. 1–19.

Drucker, P. E. *Management Tasks, Responsibilities, Practices*. New York: Harper and Row, 1974.

Fayol, H. *Industrial and General Administration*. London: Pitman & Sons, 1916.

Grusky, C. "Role Conflict in Organization: A Study of Prison Camp Officials," *Administrative Science Quarterly*, Vol. 3, 1959, pp. 457–472.

Johnson, R. "Ameliorating Prison Stress: Some Helping Roles for Custodial Personnel," *International Journal of Criminology and Penology*, 1977, pp. 263–273.

Meyer, J. C., Jr. "Change and Obstacles to Change in Prison Management," *Federal Probation*, June 1972.

Mintzenberg, H. "The Manager's Job: Folklore and Fad," *Harvard Business Review*. New York: Harper and Row, July–August 1975.

Ohlin, L. E. "Organizational Reform in Correctional Agencies," in Daniel Glaser (ed.) *Handbook of Criminology*, Chicago: Rand McNally, 19174, pp. 995–1020.

Pogrebin, M. "Role Conflict Among Correctional Officers in Treatment Oriented Correctional Institutions," *International Journal of Offender Therapy and Comparative Criminology*, Vol. 1, 1979, pp. 149–155.

Priestly, P. "The Prison Welfare Officer—A Case of Role Strain," *British Journal of Sociology*, Vol. 28, 1972, pp. 221–235.

Selye, H. *The Stress of Life*. New York: McGraw-Hill, 1976.

Sykes, G. *The Society of Captives*. Princeton, NJ: University Press, 1959.

6

Burnout
Avoiding the Consequences of
On-The-Job Stress

Richard M. Morris

Stress and its presence in the workplace are undergoing close examination. Once looked upon as a factor in productivity and creativity, stress is now viewed as a debilitation factor in a worker's performance. The intention of this article is to outline the causal factors in stress and to suggest that the factors be treated as a group.

A certain amount of stress is needed for one to perform at peak ability. Stress is the agent that causes action and reaction, and certain amounts of stress are necessary for life. The same as a banjo string that if too tightly wound would snap or too loosely wound would produce no sound, the correct amount of tension that gives the desired sound can be compared to the factor of stress in daily life.

Most health care professionals know there is an enormous degree of stress engendered in law enforcement and security work. Repeated confrontations in what is perceived as impossible situations requiring a response (damned-if-you-do, damned-if-you-don't situations) create feelings of inadequacy for those who must make ambiguous decisions during constant ambiguous situations. Shift work, constant fear and anticipation of danger and death, confrontation with injury and violence, negative attitudes that prevail during the course of a workday, prejudice, and hostility and suspicion by the general public add to this, invariably causing anxiety, disillusionment, and disappointment with the job.

Source: *Corrections Today*, 48(6) (August 1988): 122–26. Reprinted with permission from the American Correctional Association, Lanham, MD.

Correctional officers and others involved in security work are prime targets for this type of stress. Working in a correctional environment can drain one's senses. Because an officer's senses must be operating continuously when on duty in a correctional facility, the drain on his/her senses is also continuous.

In the private sector, an individual who works 10 or more hours a day and gets the job done quickly is often considered a successful executive. The criterion for success is completing a project in the shortest amount of time. In this atmosphere, the strongest of survivors reaches the top. This type of environment, although successful in the short run, is very costly in its long-term effects. Absenteeism and employee turnover are two of the most immediate symptoms of this work environment. Quite simply, the pressure is too much.

Lately, the analysis of stress has moved into the public sector, with surveys being conducted to determine job burnout. People who work in social programs under government auspices (i.e., programs for the mentally handicapped, physically handicapped, or educationally deficient) often experience what is known as job burnout. Viewed as stress in its most extreme form, job burnout is simply the inability of an employee to continue performing his/her function. Many of the reasons for job stress are reasons for job burnout. Burnout occurs when stress has been so intense for such a long period that it is difficult for an employee to perform even the most basic requirements of his/her job.

Stressors in Correctional Work

There are certain stressors shared by employees in both the private and public sector. Some stressors found in correctional work are also found in other occupations, including administrative policy concerning work assignments, procedures and policy, and lack of administrative backing and support (including the relationship and rapport between correctional officer and supervisor). Stress is also caused by job conflict—a situation in which officers are caught between discrepant situations. Other common stressors in the workplace are inactivity, physical and/or mental work underload and idleness, shift work, working hours other than the normal work schedule, responsibility for the lives and welfare of others, inequities in pay or job status, and being underpaid and under-recognized for one's work.

Correctional officers are also subject to specific stressors including unfavorable attitudes held by the public toward correctional officers, daily crisis situations, daily situations posing a threat or overwhelming officers emotionally, racial situations, confrontations among officers and minority groups, and court rulings that make it seem almost impossible not to violate someone's human or civil rights.

The stressors encountered in security work affect both the organization and individual. Stress can be a prime factor in employee absenteeism, employee turnover, increased costs for overtime, and early retirements. Various studies have indicated excessive stress can lead to alcoholism, drug dependence, heart attacks or other illnesses, divorce, and other family problems.

There are two methods of identifying excessive stress in the workplace. A review of employee sick leave, absentee records, and the job-turnover rate can be used as empirical indicators, but the concerned supervisor will generally recognize that something is wrong. For example, poor or reduced performance, lack of enthusiasm for work, and sudden changes in employee work habits are all common indicators. A review of both the empirical data and the impressions of supervisors is usually the first step in developing a stress management program.

Recommendations for Stress Management

Most stress management programs share three common ingredients. First, the components of stress are defined. Second, warning signals and effects of stress are explained. Third, participants in the program are taught a method of overcoming, reducing and/or dealing with stress. This method can include relaxation techniques, self-hypnosis, and behavior modification. The general principle of stress management is that, although a particular stressful situation cannot be changed, an individual's perception of that situation and his/her subsequent actions can be.

Health maintenance is one further item that is part of most, but not all, stress management programs. Programs focusing on nutritional needs and physical exercise are included in health maintenance. For those individuals who deal in security work, health maintenance is probably an important aspect of a stress management program. An individual in good physical shape may be able to sustain long periods of stressful activity much better than an individual not physically fit.

One factor in stress often overlooked is the physical environment. A stressful environment is generally perceived in terms of an individual's relationship with his/her work and the human contacts in that workplace. The physical environment (i.e., lighting, heating, coolness, dampness, and spacial relationships) can affect individuals in ways that are not readily noticeable. This would seem entirely applicable to those involved in security work. Correctional officers are generally confined to a limited area. A poorly lit area, where the officer is unable to observe the activity of those who are confined, can easily raise the stress level of that officer. Dampness, coldness, or excessive heat can also affect that officer's performance.

Stressful Environments

Ways the organizational structure contributes to employee stress should also be examined. A stress program directed at individuals—and not at the organization—may be effective in the short run, but it will not have any long-term benefits. An employee can be taken out of the stressful environment and recharged, but the stressful environment will once again wear him/her down.

A comprehensive stress management program can also include the family in reducing the level of stress in the individual. Essentially there are two parts to daily life. The first is the relationship between self and family; the second is the relationship between self and the workplace. For the security officer, this is a severe contrast. He/she moves from a comfortable and friendly environment into one that is the complete opposite. This sudden shift undoubtedly affects the amount of stress in an officer's life, and that amount of stress, in turn, affects that officer's family.

One method of reducing stress in a correctional officer's life may be to include the family in the initial training given to that officer. For example, one or two days in the training program of an officer can be set aside so the type of work the officer will be doing can be explained to spouses and other family members. This way the family can have a greater understanding of the stress the individual officer is under. At the least, inclusion of family in the officer's training will establish a bond between the two distinct parts of that officer's daily life.

To summarize, an effective and comprehensive stress management program may include, but certainly not be limited to, the following items:

- A definition of the components of stress.
- An explanation of the warning signals and effects of stress.
- A method for overcoming, reducing, and dealing with stress.
- A health maintenance program, including physical fitness.
- An analysis of the physical environment.
- An analysis of the organizational structure.

• The inclusion of the family in a stress management program.

Individuals in the security field involved in stress management programs strongly suggest that the stress program be conducted by fellow officers. They do so for two reasons: 1) officers generally relate better to fellow officers, and 2) the cost of the stress management program can be effectively reduced by using individuals already included in the personnel budget.

As this article indicates, the study of stress in security work has not fully matured. There are people conducting studies, but the scope of the problem almost defies explanation due to over-crowded institutions, changing work forces, changing inmates, court decisions, the question of custody versus treatment, etc. Also, an important first step in a stress program is diagnosis of the seriousness of stress problems in an organization.

It is clear that stress cannot be treated in short training programs. An individual can be told what is happening to him/her, but unless something can be done about it the stress remains.

There is more to stress management than just learning how to stay calm. Personal health management is important. Breaking away from the only-those-inside-can-know attitude is also important. Peer counseling, not just peer instruction, is important. Nobody has a lock on the best method, if there is one.

Section *III*

Crime Prevention, Restorative Justice, and Diversion

The fact that the traditional methods of dealing with criminal offenders and juvenile delinquents have not always produced the desired results has generated demands for alternative approaches. The "get tough on crime" approach resulted in dramatic increases in the number of arrests, overburdening of the courts to process these cases, and overcrowding in jails and prisons. Still, crime remains a serious problem. Recently, emphases have shifted to directly involving citizens in criminal justice activities through crime prevention programs and toward finding alternatives to the traditional manners of handling offenders. One such approach is "restorative justice"—assuring that individual victims of crimes and the community in general receive recompense for the traumas, threats to safety, and additional costs of providing effective security caused by the offenders.

Clarke (1993) noted that crime prevention can be accomplished through environmental design, defensive space, and problem oriented policing. However, it should not be limited to the measures designed to combat criminal activity taken by the police and the criminal justice system, since improving citizens' quality of life is the key goal of such efforts. Leighton (1994, ii.iii) argued that "improving social conditions also reduces and prevents crime by ameliorating those underlying causes which foster motivations for engaging in criminal activities."

Crime prevention activities can be highly organized or can be very spontaneous. For example, the International Centre for the Prevention of Crime was developed to provide assistance to communities, cities, and countries in finding ways to reduce delinquency, crime, and violence. This worldwide organization has developed a wide range of strategies for crime prevention, including:

> Mobilizing agencies such as schools, housing, and social services to reduce the factors that predispose young persons to delinquency;
>
> Fostering better design of buildings, products, and communities to make it harder, more risky, or less rewarding for offenders to commit crime; [and]
>
> Facilitating partnerships between police, justice services, private sector and private citizens as well as those concerned with social development in order to solve crime problems and promote effective sanctions for offenders. (1997:1)

Many crime and delinquency prevention programs attempt to get at the root causes of the crime problem. This is particularly true in regard to delinquency prevention efforts. In selection 7, "Day Treatment: Community-Based Partnerships for Delinquent and At-Risk Youth," Wolford, Jordan, and Murphy describe the day treatment approach to juvenile delinquency prevention and rehabilitation. This community-based model for preventing delinquency and treating delinquents links the schools, courts and various other service providers in a coordinated program that provides the types of interventions at-risk and delinquent youths need in order to facilitate positive behavior change. The authors describe the day treatment programs for juvenile delinquents and at-risk youths that operate throughout the state of Kentucky. These programs combine an alternative education school, at which attendance is mandatory, with various types of counseling. The students are given close supervision in small classes and receive individual and group counseling. The administrative staff, counselors, and teachers all work as a team in assisting the youths with resolving conflict problems, developing positive peer relationships, and establishing goals. They are referred to community services and possible employment opportunities.

The concept of restorative justice is very closely related to crime prevention, since the victims of crime and the members of the community are involved in the decision making pertaining to the control, prevention, and sanctioning of criminal activities that directly affect them. In restorative justice, crime victims play a major role in the justice process. Restorative justice ensures that the community is involved in some way in the justice process and that offenders are held accountable to the victims and the community, as well as to the state.

Bazemore and Griffiths (1997) note that restorative justice applies to various models in which the community becomes involved in decision making pertaining to juvenile or criminal justice. In circle sentencing, the judge, prosecutor, defense counsel, victims, offenders, and treatment service providers all become involved in the sentencing process. In family group conferencing, victims, offenders, police, and social service agencies become involved in seeking appropriate solutions to community and family problems. In victim-offender mediation the crime victim, the offender and an impartial neutral third party try to work out a mutually acceptable solution to a conflict. The mediator does not have the power to force an agreement or to impose a decision on either party. Mediation is an alternative to formal processing, and the victim of a crime, if not satisfied with the manner in which the mediation process is handled, can always withdraw and request that the case be handled through the formal court process. However, victims have generally expressed satisfaction with this alternative dispute resolution method because they are directly involved in the process and they can state what they believe must be accomplished through mediation in order to feel satisfied that they have been treated "justly." Victim-offender mediation is predominantly used in cases in which the criminal or delinquent acts of the offenders are of a nonviolent and less serious nature. Since the process is informal, the offender is diverted out of the formal court process and avoids having a criminal or delinquent record. This diversion process is in keeping with the underlying philosophy of restorative justice, since it is in the best interest of the community to have the offender integrated into the life of the community as a functioning member, rather than be isolated from the community as a result of being sent to a correctional facility.

In summary, the restorative justice models discussed above ensure that the offender will be held accountable to the victim as well as the community. They assure the protection of the rights and the needs of individual crime victims and, to a larger extent, focus on protecting the interests and needs of the entire community. However, restorative justice should not be equated with retributive justice. Consideration of the interests and needs of the offender are encompassed in the restorative justice concept. Indeed, mediation, drug courts and other diversion approaches are endorsed because they are believed to be viable approaches to the treatment of offenders, which are conducive to producing positive changes in the offender and that in turn will be beneficial to the entire community. The only demand made by the advocates of restorative justice is that the interests of the victim and the community be balanced with the interests and attention given to the offender.

In selection 8, "What's 'New' About The Balanced Approach?" by Bazemore, the balanced approach to juvenile justice is explained. It is distinguished from the traditional individual treatment approach and from the retributive justice approach, which has gained popularity in many jurisdictions. This article illustrates how the restorative justice philosophy can be applied to juvenile justice.

In selection 9, "Communications in a Teen Court: Implications for Probation," by Beck, the teen (peer) court process is described, and research on the effectiveness of these courts as vehicles for restorative justice, delinquency prevention, and diversion is presented.

In selection 10, "The Mediation Process," Kovach gives several definitions of mediation, presents a historical overview of mediation and provides a description of its current uses in the United States. He explains the traditional mediation process and the role assumed by the mediator.

In selection 11, "A Manual For Mediators," Arthur, a juvenile court judge with more than 25 years experience, provides a detailed list of vital "do's and don'ts" for mediators and describes practices that have been shown to be effective by those involved in the mediation process.

In selection 12, "Holding Juvenile Offenders Accountable: A Restorative Justice Perspective," Umbreit differentiates the concept of restorative justice from the more traditional retributive view of justice. He notes that in the retributive justice model, "the state" is the primary victim of the crime and the individual is considered a secondary victim. In restorative justice the emphasis is reversed, with the individual becoming the primary victim. In restorative justice, the offender must acknowledge the obligation owed to the victim and agree to make amends. This obligation can often be met without invoking formal justice processes by giving restitution directly to the victim, participating in community work service projects, agreeing to the outcome of victim-offender mediation or by providing personal service to the victim.

References

Bazemore, Gordon and Curt Taylor Griffiths. 1997. "Conferences, Circles, Boards, and Mediations: The 'New Wave' of Community Justice Decision-making," *Federal Probation*, Vol. 61, No. 2:25–37.

Clarke, Ronald V. 1993. *Crime Prevention Studies*, Vol. 1. Monsey, NY: Criminal Justice Press.

International Centre for the Prevention of Crime. *Building Safety and Quality of Life Through Problem-Solving Partnerships*. Montreal, Canada: International Centre for the Prevention of Crime.

Leighton, Barry. 1994. "Foreword," *Crime Problems: Community Solutions— Environmental Criminology as a Developing Prevention Strategy*, ed. Gregg Saville. Port Moody: B.C.: AAG Inc. Publications: i–iv.

7

Day Treatment
Community-Based Partnerships for Delinquent and At-Risk Youth

Bruce I. Wolford
Forrest Jordan
Kathryn Murphy

Overview

Day treatment is a community-based nonresidential program for at-risk and delinquent youth which blends education and treatment services. In Kentucky Alabama, Pennsylvania and an increasing number of other states, these programs provide year-round education and treatment services through a collaborative delivery system that includes the social service department, local school districts and human services agencies. In the continuum of services available to at-risk youth, the day treatment model is often referred to as a half-way in/half-way out approach. Day treatment is a transitional program that can provide an alternative to a residential placement (half-way in) or a structured bridge between an out-of-home placement and the community for youth returning from a residential setting (half-way out). The goals of day treatment programs are to provide continuing education for at-risk students while assisting youth in coping with the non-cognitive barriers to learning. The ultimate aim is to effect a return to public schools and/or completion of an equivalent degree.

Source: *Juvenile and Family Court Journal,* 48(1) (Winter 1997): 35–42.

Development of Day Treatment

Kentucky currently operates eighteen day treatment programs in the communities with the highest rates of youth commitments to the juvenile justice system. In Alabama, eight Community Training Programs for Youth (CITY) enroll over 300 juveniles. Day treatment programs in Kentucky were initiated during the 1970s under federal Law Enforcement Assistance Administration (LEAA) grants (Day Treatment Programs for At-Risk and Delinquent Youth, 1995). The Commonwealth began to remove youth from its large state training school (Kentucky Village) to day treatment programs or group homes which provided significantly lower cost, community-based alternatives to the then traditional juvenile institutions (Snarr, 1989).

Despite the low levels of violent juvenile offenses (less than one-half of 1% of 10–17-year-old youths arrested [Brooks, 1996]), there is increased public concern regarding youth involvement in violent crimes (OJJDP, 1996). This concern, coupled with increasing commitments of youth from Kentucky's district courts, has placed greater demands on the limited number of residential beds available for delinquents and youthful offenders. Kentucky has responded to the increased concern over juvenile justice issues by expanding day treatment programs. Five new day treatment programs have been established in the 1990s. The 1996 session of the Kentucky General Assembly appropriated $1.5 million to establish a minimum of six additional programs by 1998. A recent report prepared for the General Assembly called for establishing day treatment programs in each of Kentucky's 59 judicial districts. Currently only 28 percent of judicial districts have a day treatment program. (Day Treatment Programs for At-Risk and Delinquent Youth, 1995.)

Alabama CITY programs have operated for over ten years. The Alabama programs have reduced the demand for residential placements and the progression of youth through the juvenile justice systems (Earnest, 1996).

The increasing importance of day treatment programming is reflected in the establishment of national standards. Seventeen of Kentucky's existing day treatment programs have been accredited by the American Correctional Association (ACA). In fact, the ACA developed its current set of day treatment standards in cooperation with the Kentucky Department of Juvenile Justice (Standards, 1993).

Expanding the Continuum of Resources

Day treatment programs provide a vital link in the continuum of resources available to the court, school and juvenile justice professionals in their efforts to provide meaningful interventions for at-risk and delinquent youth (see Table 1). Traditionally, no single agency or system approach to addressing the needs of these youth has proved effective (Kennedy et al., 1996).

Day treatment programs are significantly different from most alternative education efforts. As Table 1 indicates, day treatments are a more intensive intervention than most alternative education programs. Youth in day treatment are frequently under a court order or commitment to the state, and may have been provided day treatment as a final community option as a result of violent or disruptive behavior either in or out of school. The treatment component of these programs is generally more extensive than those available in alternative education programs.

Day treatment provides communities with a blended treatment and education program that allows youths to remain in their own homes. The placement in day treatment is often presented to the youth and his/her family as their last option prior to an out-of-home placement. For youths returning from a residential placement, day treatment participation provides a structured step down from the stricter 24-hour regiment of institutional placements. Day treatment programs can continue to reinforce the treatment programming provided in the residential setting while providing closer supervision, smaller class size and more accountability than would be offered the youths in most public schools.

Whether used as a pre- or post-residential placement experience, day

---

Table 1
Continuum of Interventions for At-Risk and Delinquent Youth

	Intervention
Least Restrictive Intervention	• Family Resource and Youth Service Centers
	• Enrollment in Alternative Schools
	• Court Designated Worker Diversions
↓	• Probated to Department of Juvenile Justice
	• Day Treatment Programs
↓	• Juvenile Detention Placements
	• Therapeutic Foster Care
↓	• Private Child Caring Program Placement
	• Psychiatric Residential Treatment Facilities
↓	• Department of Juvenile Justice Group Home or Residential Facility Placement
Most Restrictive Intervention	• Psychiatric Hospitals
	• Youthful Offender Placement in Department of Juvenile Justice Facilities

treatment programs are designed as short respites (the average length of stay is 6 months) to help youths regain self- and academic control for reentry to a more traditional public or adult education program. The youth who annually participate in day treatment programming in Kentucky, Alabama and other jurisdictions are better and more cost effectively served in the community than in a more expensive residential placement. The typical day treatment program costs 75–80% less than an out-of-home placement. Day treatment placement options in Kentucky have allowed the Commonwealth to maintain one of the nation's lowest per capita number of secure juvenile justice residential beds.

Profile of Youth in Day Treatment

Youths in day treatment have been determined to be at-risk for suspension and/or expulsion by the schools, courts, and social agencies, such as the Department of Juvenile Justice (DJJ). Most live at home or in foster care placements, although 14% are under DJJ supervision in a residential group home located near the day treatment program. The youths are approved for enrollment in day treatment programs by a community-based, multi-disciplinary team placement committee comprised of educators, treatment staff and administrators.

The average age of youths in day treatment programs has been decreasing for the past decade. The current average age of 14.5 years reflects an increasing number of admissions of middle school youth. The majority of youths (51%) enrolled in day treatment are committed to the state; however, a significant percentage (49%) are court or school referred. The typical day treatment student is a white male living in a single-parent home with a total annual household income of less that $10,000, and has been committed to the Justice Cabinet by the District Court for property crimes or status offenses. Prior to placement in day treatment, the typical youth is in the 5th, 6th, or 7th grade and has been suspended from school. The youths in day treatment are typically the communities most severely at-risk of further penetration into the juvenile justice system. These youths are typically either in their last community-based, nonresidential placement or re-entering the community for a residential placement. Less severely at-risk youths are typically in other alternative education programs. The profile of a day treatment student is very similar to youths in residential care with the exception that youths in a residential setting have a more extensive history of community and out-of-home placements. There are significantly more females in day treatment than in residential placements. The percentages of minorities in day treatment are very similar to those in

Table 2
**Profile of State Agency Children in
Department of Juvenile Justice Day Treatment Programs***

Demographic Data	
Male	69%
Age (average)	14.5 years
Race	
Caucasian	82%
African-American	15%
Other	03%
Family income under $10,000	32%
Lived with parent(s) at time of placement	86%
Lived in single parent home	50%
Legal Status	
Youth committed to Justice Cabinet	51%
Committed crimes against a person	18%
Committed property crimes	16%
Status offender	21%
Previous School Experience	
Previous special education placement	25%
Last grade completed in public school (5–7)	76%
Suspended from school	62%
High school drop out	05%
GED exam completed	04%

*This profile of state agency children in Department of Juvenile Justice Day Treatment Programs was developed based on a May 1994 census conducted by the Kentucky Educational Collaborative for State Agency Children. A total of 613 youth enrolled in day treatment programs were included in this census.

residential placements although both populations occur at a significantly greater rate than in Kentucky's general population (7%).

Collaborative Management

Site-based decision making, a hallmark of the Kentucky Education Reform Act (KERA), prevails in day treatment programs. The composition and mix of day treatment populations vary among the eighteen centers. Both middle and high school programs exist. The schools, courts and the Department for Juvenile Justice are the primary referral sources for youth placements in day treatment. Placement criteria and procedures for day treatment programs are established at the local level and vary significantly among communities. Although no ideal population profile exists, an equal blending of school referrals, court ordered and state committed youth frequently occurs.

The eighteen-day treatment programs are currently operated under one of the following three administrative models:

(1) *State Operated.* Treatment staff are employees of Kentucky Department for Juvenile Justice. Educators work for the local school district (33% of programs).

(2) *School Contracted.* All staff (treatment and education) are employees of the local school district under contract with Kentucky Department for Juvenile Justice (50% of programs).

(3) *Multi-Agency.* Treatment staff are employees of a non-profit community based agency under contract with Kentucky Department for Juvenile Justice. Educators work for local school district (17% of programs).

Very effective programs can be identified under each of the three models; however, all programs established since 1983 have been under contracts with local school districts. These school contracted programs have proved less costly to operate with a single administrator responsible for both treatment and education. Personnel include a program director, head teacher, teachers, counselors, juvenile treatment aides, teacher aides, and clerical personnel. Most staff work full time and are generally evenly distributed between treatment and education assignments. Department for Juvenile Justice and Kentucky Department of Education (KDE) regulations call for staff-to-youth ratios significantly lower than those found in public schools in the Commonwealth (Table 3).

Table 3
Day Treatment Staff/Youth Ratio

	Staff		Youth
Counselors	1	to	15
Teachers (without aide)	1	to	10
Teachers (with aide)	1	to	15

In 1994, Kentucky Educational Collaborative for State Agency Children (KECSAC) staff conducted job analyses utilizing selected focus groups of day treatment educational administrators and teachers. The educators identified the major duties which were included in their jobs. A "duty" was defined as: *a general area of competence that successful workers in the occupation must demonstrate or perform on an on-going basis. A duty includes two or more distinct tasks.*

The duties were prioritized based on the educators' determination of criticality or importance (see Table 4). "Criticality" is a measure of job tasks that panelists believed were essential and/or most important components of their role. Day treatment program administrators identified the following task as most critical: planning, developing and maintaining education programs/services. Day treatment program teachers identified the implementation of education programs as their most critical duty (Wolford, 1995).

Table 4

**Duties of Day Treatment Teachers and Education Administrators
Ranked on Basis of Criticality**

	Day Treatment Teachers	**Day Treatment Educational Administrators**
Most Critical Duty ↓ ↓ ↓ Least Critical Duty	• Implement education programs	• Plan develop and maintain education program/services
	• Monitor student behavior	• Supervise personnel
	• Develop/modify programs for special needs	• Establish and maintain education philosophy, goals, and objectives
	• Develop and perform assessments	• Manage the education office
	• Provide transitional services	• Monitor compliance with special education
	• Maintain professional competence	• Manage fiscal operations
	• Conduct classroom administrative functions	• Promote personal and professional development
	• Manage material/equipment	• Represent SAC educational program (and/or LEA)
	• Explore and acquire alternative resources	• Maintain physical plant

Kentucky Educational Collaborative for State Agency Children

The Kentucky Education Reform Act (KERA), passed by the General Assembly in 1990, called for sweeping changes in the funding and delivery of elementary and secondary education in the Commonwealth. However, KERA did not specifically address the needs of State Agency Children. In response to this deficiency, the Kentucky General Assembly passed Senate Bill 260 (SB 260) in 1992, which called for the establishment of the Kentucky Educational Collaborative for State Agency Children (KECSAC) (KRS.158.135). The Collaborative, which is administered by the Training Resource Center at Eastern Kentucky University, works with local educational agencies and treatment programs to provide quality educational experiences that meet the varying needs of youth designated as State Agency Children (SAC). These educational experiences include academic, pre-vocational, vocational, special education, social skills, and post-secondary offerings, which comply with state and federal educational laws and regulations.

Kentucky House Bill 826 (HB 826), passed by the General Assembly in March, 1994, broadened the eligibility for State Agency Children beyond those located in state operated and contracted day treatment, group homes and residential placements. Under HB 826, the definition of "State Agency Children" was expanded to include youth placed or financed through the Justice Cabinet in other residential treatment programs. The General Assembly also provided for a 50% increase in SAC funds for the estimated 1,100 newly eligible SAC. In 1996 the General Assembly provided for an 100% increase in State Agency Children's Funds to provide support and equitable funding for the daily estimated 3,000 SAC participating in educational programs. A portion of the increase was also directed toward the establishment of six new day treatment programs.

If the education of at-risk youth is to be taken seriously, evaluation is essential (Goldsmith, 1995). One of the Collaborative's major activities has been to establish baseline data from which to measure the impact of the education reform efforts on State Agency Children. Since 1994, the Collaborative has used an external evaluator to monitor KECSAC's development process and its long-term impact. Evaluation activities to date have included a census of all State Agency Children and surveys of all treatment program administrators, educational administrators, and teachers serving state agency children. The "Listen to the Children Project" included in-depth interviews with over 250 State Agency Children regarding their educational experience both prior to and during placement in a treatment program. The findings of this project are summarized in a KECSAC report.

The evaluation process focused next on the impact of day treatment programs. The current KECSAC efforts builds on an earlier study (Hobbs and Kennedy, 1992) which reported that 45% of youths who completed day treatment programs remained in school for up to two years after completion or graduated. During the 1996–97 School Year, the KECSAC external evaluator began a pilot follow-up of former day treatment participants to re-examine the post-release experiences of former day treatment students.

Funding

The primary funding for educational services is provided by the Kentucky Department of Education (KDE) and is based on average daily attendance (ADA). Funds are drawn both from the Supporting Educational Excellence in Kentucky (SEEK) Fund and from the State Agency

Children's Fund (SACF) administered by KECSAC. Other educational funding sources include federal funds provided under Title I and local school district contributions. The treatment/administration components of day treatment programs are funded by the Kentucky Department for Juvenile Justice (DJJ) either through direct provision of services in state operated programs, or by contract with local education agencies and other providers (see Figure 1).

Figure 1
Day Treatment Programs Funding Sources

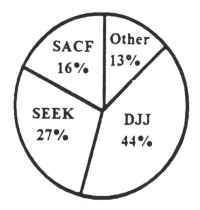

SACF = State Agency Children's Funds
SEEK = Supporting Educational Excellence in Kentucky
DJJ   = Department for Juvenile Justice
Other = Includes federal Title I, local school district contributions, community
         mental health agency accessed funds, donations, and grants

---

Treatment Components

The treatment component of the day treatment programs has been a blending of education and counseling. Individualized instruction and limited class size provide an enriched academic setting. Group, individual and family counseling are vital elements of the treatment regime. Systems of behavior management are used in every program. Students work their way through a phase system, earning increasing levels of responsibility and privileges for appropriate behavior and educational achievement. Day treatment programs are operated on an indeterminate sentencing basis with youth working their way out of the program through academic achievement and positive behavior.

The programs, which range in size from 30 to 75 students, have a limited treatment staff consisting of a program director, counselors, and juvenile treatment assistants. The treatment staff work to create a safe, secure and nurturing environment where youth can establish positive relationships with adult role models. Staff members assist youth in identifying and accessing community resources and opportunities.

A collaborative treatment team made up of program and education staff works with youth and their families to develop an individual treatment plan for each student. Collaborative treatment/education programs such as conflict resolution and InnerVisions, are provided in many centers. Positive program outcomes include re-entry in the public school, graduation, earning a GED, job placement. and pursuit of post-secondary education.

Education

Local school district personnel (currently 55 districts) provide all educational services to state agency children. Most of the day treatment centers provide services to youth from multiple school districts and counties. A host school district, which frequently provides the physical plant for the center, employs the educational staff. The composition of the student body and the distribution of the local contribution and SEEK funds are determined by the cooperating school districts. The state statute which established KECSAC and the State Agency Children's Fund (KRS 158.135), mandated a 230-day school year for all state agency children. Programs operate Monday through Friday during traditional school hours throughout the year. Academic offerings include traditional Carnegie Unit courses, GED preparation, life skills education, conflict resolution, and job seeking and retention courses. Extended evening and weekend programming are being added to many programs.

The academic and vocational offerings available to State Agency Children vary significantly among programs. The curriculum is established by the local school district and is not, in most cases, governed by either DJJ or KECSAC regulations or procedures. A significant portion of day treatment youths (38%) are enrolled in special education programs. The vast majority of State Agency Children (80%) participate in the federally funded Title I Program for Neglected or Delinquent Children. There are, however, very limited opportunities for these youth to participate in formal vocational education programs.

A recent report by KECSAC identified the most serious educational problems experienced by State Agency Children in the Division of Youth Services programs (Coffey, 1995), (see Table 5).

This report indicated that Division of Youth Services educational programs for State Agency Children (SAC) are generally traditional and reflect the curriculum in the local school system. Most SAC pro-

Table 5
Educational Problems/Deficiencies Among State Agency Children*

Degree of Seriousness	Area
More Serious	Reading Comprehension
	Social Skills
↓	Math Skills
	Thinking/Problem Solving
	Motivation/Attitudes
	Low Achievement
↓	Lack of Self-Esteem
	Study Skills
	Life Skills
	Spelling/Vocabulary
↓	Family Involvement
	Attendance
Less Serious	Writing Skills

* Ranked in descending order based on frequency of response

grams offer mathematics, Reading/Language Arts, and Title I. Two-thirds of the programs also offer Special Education, Life Skills, Social Skills, Social Sciences, Physical and Biological Sciences, Health/Physical Education, and Drug/Alcohol Education. There is a scarcity of vocational programs, and formal transition programming existed in only a few locations. The KECSAC External Evaluator reported that there seemed to be no standardized or clearly defined curriculum for SAC programs. Generally, teachers worked with children on traditional school subjects, on the theory that they must keep up with their regular school and return and graduate. "Curriculum" was listed as a high priority item by many of the State Agency Children educators surveyed (Coffey, 1995). The low student/teacher ratio and limited enrollment allowed the educational staff to focus on the individual child's needs. The day treatment experience provided many youths with new opportunities to succeed in the classroom, perhaps for the first time in many years.

Enhancing Day Treatment Programming

A select number of day treatment supervisors and head teachers participated in a focus group (June 1995). The participants were asked to identify changes which could be made to enhance day treatment programming. The group's recommendations (not listed in order of priority or importance), were:

1. Continue and expand training and administrative support that helps to unify treatment initiatives such as conflict resolution, InnerVisions, and relapse prevention with education.

2. Establish a youth-to-counselor ratio of 10:1.

3. Strive to achieve greater parity between wages and resources for education and treatment staff.

4. Consider piloting program "resource homes" to provide supplemental short-term residential programs for some day treatment participants.

5. Establish a youth-to-line worker ratio of 10:1.

6. Convene annual day treatment training/institute to include both treatment and education personnel.

7. Develop a model and provide training and support for a certified treatment team including both education and treatment staff.

8. Expand support for transitional services between day treatment and school re-entry.

9. Expand use of distance training and educational opportunities for both the youth and staff in day treatment.

10. Examine the applicability of treatment activities in the six-hour school day.

11. Examine alternative models for site-based decision making in day treatment programs.

12. Develop pilot program(s) to use day treatment as a re-entry program for youth returning from residential programs.

13. Utilize day treatment programs as focal points for other community-based interventions for at-risk and delinquent youth such as day and evening reporting and counseling centers.

14. Systematically collect, analyze, and report follow-up/outcome data on day treatment participants.

Conclusion

Over the past three decades, day treatment programs have helped to expand the continuum of services for at-risk and delinquent youth. Day treatment programs in Kentucky and Alabama have been nationally recognized as innovative juvenile justice programming options. These lower cost, community-based programs have been developed through the collaborative efforts of education, judicial, and social service professionals. The programs have provided an effective alternative to out-of-home placement and have proved (based on preliminary data) to be significant positive influences on youths' retention in and completion of a high school education.

As education, juvenile justice, mental health, and child welfare professionals along with state and local legislative bodies struggle with issues relating to youth violence and crime, day treatment programming should be given increased attention and support as an alternative to residential placements. Effective day treatment programs force collaboration across agencies/local boundaries and expand the range of community options for at-risk youth. Day treatment programs make sense for children and communities.

References

Brooks, T. R. (1996, Winter), "And Justice for All," *Children's Voice, 5.*

Coffey, O. D. (1995). *State Agency Children in Division of Youth Services Programs: An Educational Profile.* Richmond: Eastern Kentucky University, Kentucky Educational Collaborative for State Agency Children.

Day Treatment Programs for At-Risk and Delinquent Youth in Kentucky (1995). Richmond: Eastern Kentucky University, Kentucky Educational Collaborative for State Agency Children.

Earnest, E. (1996, August), "Youth Day Treatment Program Works for Alabama," *Corrections Today.*

Goldsmith, H. (1995), *Residential Education: An Option for America's Youth.* Hershey, PA: The Milton Hershey School.

Hobbs, L. & J. K. Kennedy (1992, Summer), "Community-Based Day Treatment for Troubled Youth: Kentucky Responds to the Challenges," *Perspectives* 16.

Juvenile Offenders and Victims: 1996 Update on Violence (1996). Pittsburgh, PA: National Center for Juvenile Justice, Office of Juvenile Justice and Delinquency Prevention.

Kennedy, J. et al. (1976), "A Day School Approach to Aggressive Adolescents," *Child Welfare IV.*

Snarr, R. (1989), *A History of Services for the Commonwealth's Children 1890–1989.* Richmond: Eastern Kentucky University, Training Resource Center.

Standards for Juvenile Day Treatment Programs (1993). Laurel, MD: American Correctional Association.

Wolford, B., T. McGee, & B. Barbour. (1995), *The Task of Teaching Troubled Youth: A Job Analysis.* Richmond: Eastern Kentucky University, Kentucky Educational Collaborative for State Agency Children.

8

What's "New" about the Balanced Approach?

Gordon Bazemore

In 1988, this journal and the National Council of Juvenile and Family Court Judges (NCJFCJ) broke new ground by publishing a monograph outlining a "Balanced Approach" mission for juvenile probation (Maloney, Romig and Armstrong, 1988). Since that time, interest in the Balanced Approach as a mission not only for probation, but also for the juvenile justice system as a whole, has increased exponentially. In the past three years, some fourteen states, including most recently California and Pennsylvania, have adopted Balanced Approach language in their juvenile justice codes (Klien, 1996). Other states, such as Florida, and a much larger number of local juvenile courts, probation departments and residential programs, have issued policy statements that specifically require probation staff to use Balanced Approach objectives when developing dispositional recommendations and supervision plans.[1]

Meanwhile, a worldwide movement based on *restorative justice*, now recognized by many as the underlying value or philosophical framework for the Balanced Approach (Zehr, 1990; Van Ness, 1993; Bazemore and Umbreit, 1995), has had rather dramatic practical impact on juvenile justice policy and practice in some nations. Several European countries, as well as Canada and Australia, have made significant policy changes directly influenced by restorative justice practices and values. Since 1989, New Zealand has required that all juvenile offenders over 14 (with the exception of offenders involved in

Source: *Juvenile and Family Court Journal*, 48(1) (Winter 1997): 1–19.

serious violent crimes and child welfare cases) be referred to a conference in which restorative goals are addressed in community meetings including victims, offenders, their respective support groups and/or families, and other citizens (McElrae, 1993; Morris and Maxwell, 1993).

As interest has grown, and as the amount of commentary and published literature on the Balanced Approach and restorative justice has increased, the practical meaning of the new mission and philosophical framework for the juvenile court and the juvenile justice system has been a source of some controversy and confusion. Some have viewed Balanced Approach proponents as apologists for the current system and have implied that the new mission is "nothing new." These observers seem to view the Balanced Approach as simply another effort to reaffirm the juvenile court's individual treatment mission or even to resurrect and obfuscate *parens patriae* abuses (Feld, 1995).[2] In contrast, others have argued that "balance" is effectively impossible and have implied that the new mission's advocates are simply apologists for the new retributive, just deserts, approaches to juvenile justice reform (Forst and Blomquist, 1992). Some policymakers and professionals have added to the confusion by adopting the new mission's language as "window dressing" for public relations purposes to create support for current practices that often have little to do with balanced intervention (Bazemore, 1992).

A premise of this paper is that the Balanced Approach mission has often been misunderstood and trivialized. Superficial criticisms and misinterpretations notwithstanding, however, important practical and conceptual questions and concerns about the Balanced Approach have yet to be addressed. This paper attempts to answer what is now the most frequently asked question about the new mission: "How is it different?" To do so, I will argue that the Balanced Approach can be distinguished from both the individual treatment mission and the new retributive, or just deserts, mission for juvenile justice based on six related dimensions.

What Is It? Balancing Community Needs, Achieving New Goals

- In inner-city Pittsburgh, young offenders in an intensive day treatment program solicit input from community organizations about service projects the organizations would like to see completed in the neighborhood. The offenders then work with community residents on projects that include home repair and gardening for the elderly, voter registration drives, painting homes and public buildings, and planting and cultivating community gardens.

- In Florida, youthful offenders, sponsored by the Florida Department of Juvenile Justice and supervised by The 100 Black Men of Palm Beach County, Inc., plan and execute projects that serve a shelter for caring and treating abused, abandoned, and HIV positive/AIDS infected infants and children.

- In cities and towns in Pennsylvania, Montana and Minnesota—as well as in Australia and New Zealand—family members and other citizens acquainted with an offender or victim of a juvenile crime gather to determine what should be done in response to the offense. Often held in schools, churches or other community-based facilities, these *Family Group Conferences* are facilitated by a Community Justice Coordinator or Police Officer, and are aimed at ensuring that offenders are made to hear community disapproval of their behavior, and at developing an agreement for repairing the damage to victim and community and a plan for reintegrating the offender.

- In Minnesota, Department of Corrections staff collaborate with local police and citizens groups to establish family group conferencing programs and ways to inform the community about, and to involve them in, offender monitoring and victim support. In Dakota County, a Minneapolis suburb, local retailers and senior citizens whose businesses and homes have been damaged by burglary or vandalism call a crime repair "hotline" to request a work crew of probationers to repair the damage.

- In Deschutes County, Oregon, offender work crews cut and deliver firewood to senior citizens and recently worked with a local contractor to build a homeless shelter.

- In more than 150 cities and towns throughout North America victims and offenders meet with volunteer mediators in victim-offender mediation sessions or other victim-offender meetings to allow victims to express their feelings about the crime to the offender, gain information about the offense, and develop a restitution agreement with the offender.

- In Palm Beach County, Florida, as part of an effort to assist juvenile justice administrators in their goal of creating a community and organizational culture responsive to victim needs, victims' advocates train juvenile justice staff on sensitivity in their interaction with victims and help prepare a victim awareness curriculum for youths in residential programs.

- In several Montana cities, college students and other young adult "corps members" in the Montana Conservation Corps supervise juvenile offenders on environmental restoration, trail building and other community service projects and also serve as mentors to one or more of the young offenders.

As juvenile justice systems around the country are being dismantled or dismembered (e.g., Lemov, 1993), many professionals have become demoralized. Others appear to view the current juvenile justice crisis as an opportunity for creative thought and action. Many of these professionals view the Balanced Approach as a "third alternative" for juvenile justice aimed at preserving a juvenile court with a distinctive youth justice mandate that is neither punitive nor lenient in focus (Bazemore, 1996; cf. Rosenberg, 1993; Bazemore and Umbreit, 1995).

The Balanced Approach mission is a "back-to-basics" (some say "*forward* to basics") attempt to reorient juvenile justice systems to respond more effectively to community expectations. Essentially, most citizens expect that any "justice" system will support fundamental community needs to sanction youth crime; to rehabilitate and reintegrate offenders; and to enhance public safety by assisting the community in preventing and controlling crime. Increasingly, justice systems have also been expected to address a fourth need, to attempt to restore victim loss.

To meet these needs the Balanced Approach authors advanced three overall purposes for juvenile justice intervention (Maloney, Romig and Armstrong, 1988). These purposes define three macro goals for the juvenile justice system and micro goals to be addressed in the response to each case (see Figure 1). Contrary to the assumptions of some critics of the new mission, "balance" does not mean simply attempting to provide equal or appropriate doses of punishment and treatment.[3] Rather, "balance" is achieved at a system level when administrators ensure that resources are allocated equally among efforts to ensure accountability to crime victims, to increase competency in offenders, and to enhance community safety. Balance is achieved in each case by giving equal attention to broader needs which underlie new sanctioning, safety, and rehabilitative goals as depicted in Figure 1.

Figure 1
Balanced Approach

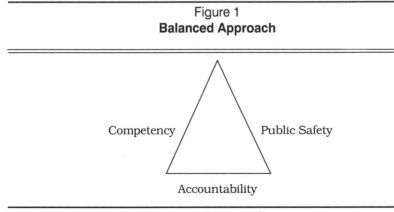

Competency / Public Safety

Accountability

What do these goals mean and how do they address these broader needs? The authors of the Balanced Approach have designated the three goals of the juvenile justice system using common terms— "accountability," "competency," and "community protection"—in a somewhat uncommon way. Defining these goals is an important first step in distinguishing what are in fact unique approaches to sanctioning, rehabilitation, and public safety enhancement under the Balanced Approach mission.

Accountability. Sanctioning needs are best met (1) when offenders assume responsibility for the crime and the harm caused to victims, (2) when they take action to make amends by restoring the loss, and (3) when communities and victims play active roles in sanctioning and feel satisfied with the process. Because an offense incurs a primary obligation to crime victims, accountability cannot be equated simply with being responsible to the court or to juvenile justice professionals such as by merely obeying curfew, complying with drug screening, or writing an essay. Nor can accountability be equated with punishment. If the sanctioning process is to allow communities to set tolerance limits, express disapproval of juvenile crime, and provide appropriate consequences for harmful behavior, the process works best when it allows crime victims and other citizens maximum involvement and input.

Competency. Rehabilitation needs are best met when young offenders make measurable and demonstrated improvements in educational, vocational, social, civic, and other competencies that improve their ability to function as capable, productive adults. When competency is defined as the capacity to do something well that others value, the standard for achieving success in competency development is ultimately measured in the community. Competency cannot be equated with the absence of bad behavior (e.g., being drug free does not provide young offenders with the support and bonds to law-abiding adults they need to avoid further delinquency). Nor can it be attained simply by completing a treatment program. While treatment and remedial services provide critical support for competency development, competencies are most likely to be increased when youth assume active rather than passive roles in service and work projects involving community members. Hence, competency development must also involve increasing the capacity of adults and community groups to allow troublesome youths opportunities to practice competent behavior.

Community Protection. Public safety needs are best met when community groups increase their ability to prevent crime, resolve conflict, and reduce community fear and when known offenders are adequately monitored and develop internal controls. Locked facilities are an important part of any public safety approach. But they are the least cost-effective component of a balanced strategy which invests heavily in citizen involvement in monitoring offenders and developing new ways to prevent youth crime. A complete strategy to decrease risk to citizens and reduce fear must be "problem-oriented" as well as case-driven. In practice, such a strategy would first ensure that the time of offenders under supervision in the community is structured around work, education, community service, victim awareness and other activities during waking hours, and that community adults, including but not limited to parents, are assigned clear roles in monitoring offenders. Finally, such a strategy would begin to cultivate and promote new partnerships with community police officers and new roles for juvenile justice professionals as resources to schools, employers, and other community groups in prevention and positive youth development (e.g., as advisors to schools in mediation and conflict resolution).

Representing jurisdictions and communities as diverse as inner-city Pittsburgh, rural Oregon, suburban Minnesota, and urban South Florida (Bazemore and Umbreit, 1995), professionals attempting to develop a balanced focus on these three goals share a commitment to "reinvent" a new juvenile justice system based on a new vision. The vision is one of a *community-oriented* response to youth crime based on the restorative justice philosophical framework (Zehr, 1990; Van Ness, 1993; Bazemore and Umbreit, 1995). Through the restorative "lens" (Zehr, 1990), crime is viewed as important because of the harm it causes victims' communities, and offenders (Van Ness, et al., 1989). Hence, rather than focus solely on treating or punishing the offender, the "justice" process and any justice system should be concerned first with repairing this harm and preventing its reoccurrence. From a restorative perspective true "balance" in juvenile justice must ultimately be gauged in terms of the system's effectiveness in meeting the needs of victims and communities, as well as offenders, and involving each as clients or co-participants in the justice process.

Core elements of this restorative vision, and much of the difference between the new system envisioned and current alternatives, are encompassed in the community-building interventions described at the beginning of this section. Juvenile justice professionals making the most significant changes consistent with the Balanced Approach mission are building on new partnerships with youth and victim advocates and with concerned citizens and civic groups, while using these interventions as small demonstrations which can point the way to more holistic changes in the organizational culture and structure of their agencies (Carey and Umbreit, 1995). In doing so, they are using the new mission as a concrete "roadmap" to guide them toward this restorative vision for changing the relationship between the juvenile justice system and the community (Bazemore and Day, 1996).

How Is It Different?
Systemic v. Programmatic Reform

What they're saying about the Balanced Approach:

"This is what we've always done. What's new? Where's the Beef?"

"We do that competency development, but we just call it treatment. Accountability? Oh yeah, that's our detention center and our jail tours."

"My caseload is 53 and I'm stuck in court 20 hours a week. Don't talk to me about working with the community."

"Now I know what my job is really about!"

"As a manager, I have a better sense of how to allocate, or reallocate, our resources. And my staff are getting a better sense of what their role is and how this fits with my vision of what the community's role should be. We know we're really 'out of balance' but now we have a strategic plan to move forward without chasing every fad and new program that comes along."

"We can also talk to the community about what we're doing in a way that they understand and want to help; our judges and prosecutors are also starting to find some common ground with us in probation. The biggest surprise is that I never expected crime victims could be our allies!"

(A Community Member) "I'm glad to see somebody is finally trying to instill some responsibility in these kids. I'm happy to help when it's obvious that we're trying to make taxpayers out of these kids, rather than tax liabilities."

(A Victim) "In the mediation session I learned that the offender was just a little kid and not the threat I thought he was. I also learned he had some needs that weren't being met but for the first time (I've been a victim before), it seemed like someone was responding to my needs and listening to me."

(An Offender) "When I first walked into the conferencing meeting and saw the victim and her friends and then saw my grandfather there, I wished I could have gone to jail instead. But once everybody had talked about the crime, I began to realize that Mrs. B was really hurt and scared by what I had done. I had to work hard to earn the money to pay her back and to do the community service hours (but the work on the crew was pretty fun) and I thought it was fair after all."

Few juvenile justice professionals claim to support an "unbalanced approach"; similarly, few favor incompetent offenders or oppose public safety and accountability. Many, if not most, initially support the model but believe, as reflected in the first comment in the box above, that the

Balanced Approach is "nothing new." Others, as reflected in the last comment in the top half of the table, remind us that staff are unlikely to refocus their efforts toward achieving balanced approach objectives unless significant changes are made in current role expectations and the current juvenile justice process.

In one sense, most components of the Balanced Approach are not new. Restorative justice is based on ancient values and practices that have been at the core of many religious and ethical traditions (Van Ness, 1993; Zehr, 1990). In addition, the balanced mission was developed based on programs and practices such as restitution, community service, work experience, and victim-offender mediation that have been proved effective over two decades of field experience and research.[4] But, while almost all juvenile courts and juvenile justice systems have used these practices at least sporadically, in most systems they receive low priority relative to other requirements.

Any justice system or agency can add new programs and many jurisdictions have adopted a wide array of specialized units. Certainly programs are available in many jurisdictions to support interventions consistent with the balanced mission. However, if only 10% of offenders are referred to a court's restitution program, and similar proportions complete meaningful community service, or meet with their victims, the jurisdiction can hardly be said to be "balanced" or "restorative." While useful, programmatic change alone does not change the focus of intervention in the system as a whole. In jurisdictions working to implement the Balanced Approach, however, managers view it as a framework for integrating and institutionalizing these practices as core, rather than secondary or tertiary, interventions and as a tool to help them plan, execute, and monitor change (Bazemore and Washington, 1995).

Currently, decisions about staff roles—what it is that juvenile justice professionals "do" in the response to youth crime—as well as resource allocation and management approaches, are based primarily on tradition and the needs of juvenile justice bureaucracies (e.g., for case workers, service providers). Too often, these decisions seem to be based on the need to be in step with the "program trend of the month." Seldom are staff roles and management imperatives reexamined to ensure that they are driven by essential community needs and expectations.

What is most "new" and different about the Balanced Approach mission, therefore, is its agenda for systemic restructuring to make juvenile justice value- and client-driven and outcome-oriented. Such reform at the level of mission seeks to alter both the content and process of intervention, and by changing the role of victims, other citizens, offenders, and staff, to also change the context of intervention. In so doing, reform based on the balanced mission is aimed at reordering the priorities of staff and the relationship between juvenile justice agencies and their clients. As a Figure 2 suggests, in juvenile justice systems and agencies using the Balanced Approach mission, managers and staff are being challenged to base decisions and actions on a different set of values or guiding principles, which in turn demand a commitment to three clients rather than one. New decision-making processes, which involve victims, citizens, and offenders actively in the justice process and which are sensitive to their needs, determine what will be done in response to the crime. In turn, new performance outcomes gauge the success of an intervention based on the extent to which measurable changes are brought about in the status of each client. Finally, these outcomes are used to establish intervention priorities and initiate new programs (or discontinue old ones) based on their ability to accomplish competency, accountability, and public safety objectives, rather than simply to punish offenders or deliver treatment in the traditional sense.

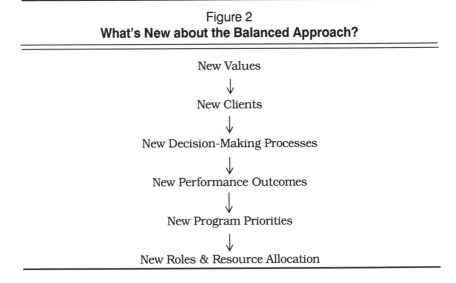

Figure 2
What's New about the Balanced Approach?

New Values
↓
New Clients
↓
New Decision-Making Processes
↓
New Performance Outcomes
↓
New Program Priorities
↓
New Roles & Resource Allocation

How Do We Know It When We See It?
Six Ways the Balanced Approach Is Different

As the remainder of this article will illustrate, the six differences shown in Figure 2 underscore the limits of both the treatment and retributive justice missions and distinguish the Balanced Approach mission as a strategy for systemic juvenile justice reform.

Different Values: Restorative Justice

As implied earlier, several practices and programs commonly associated with the Balanced Approach such as community service and restitution are currently used with some regularity in many juvenile courts. Unfortunately, however, such sanctions may be included in a dispositional order simply to fulfill statutory requirements or to accomplish punishment, diversion or other objectives that have little to do with the goals of the new mission (e.g., Bazemore and Maloney, 1994). In the absence of restorative values or principles and a commitment to address the needs of victims, offenders, and communities, such practices will do little to increase "balance" in the juvenile justice response to crime and may even further alienate these primary clients of a balanced justice system (Bazemore and Umbreit, 1995; Umbreit, 1994).

If crime is important because it damages real people and communities, the "justice" process should focus primarily on repairing this harm. The most important question to be answered in a restorative response to crime is not "what do we do to punish or treat the offender." Rather, as Howard Zehr (1990) suggests, the justice process must begin with three primary questions: 1) What is the harm? 2) What needs to be done to make it right? and 3) Who is responsible?

Questions one and two are best answered with input from victims, offender(s), and other citizens in decision-making processes that maximize their input into the disposition of the case. These questions are addressed in the sections which follow. Restorative values are also unique in their designation of responsibility. First, offenders are responsible for making it right with their victims, and a restorative juvenile justice system would ensure that offenders are, to the greatest extent possible, held accountable for the damage and suffering caused to victims and victimized communities. However, the system cannot assume sole responsibility. Rather, restorative justice affirms that not only government (i.e., the juvenile justice system), but victims, offenders, and communities (especially families) must be actively involved in the justice process (e.g., Zehr, 1990; Van Ness, 1993). As in any relationship, a community's general health is directly related to the extent to which members participate in decisions governing the community. One of the most important things a justice system can do is work to strengthen the capacity of communities to respond to crime and empower them to do so. As Canadian Judge Barry Stuart observes:

> When citizens fail to assume responsibility for decisions affecting the community, community life will be characterized by the absence of a collective sense of caring, a lack of respect for diverse values, and ultimately a lack of any sense of belonging. Conflict, if resolved through a process that constructively engages the parties involved, can be a fundamental building ingredient of any relationship. (Stuart, 1995)

From a restorative justice perspective, crime is often a symptom of community conflict and disharmony (e.g., Van Ness et al., 1989). If this is true, neither community "justice" nor community safety can be achieved by a government "war on crime." Justice and safety also cannot be achieved simply by punishing or treating individual offenders, but will instead require peacemaking efforts aimed at building, or rebuilding, "right relationships" (Pepinsky & Quinney, 1990; Van Ness, 1993). As community members learn to resolve disputes creatively, their capacity to do so also increases, as does the ability of the collective to sanction crime, habilitate and reintegrate offenders, and enhance public safety. When they facilitate or contribute to these processes, juvenile justice professionals are more likely to address the root causes of crime. They are also less likely to take on too much responsibility (Stuart, 1995).

What is perhaps most unique about the restorative justice value base, and most difficult for some juvenile justice professionals to accept, is its elevation of the role of crime victims in the justice process. While "victims' rights" has become a popular buzzword, victims' needs are addressed in the current system only after the needs of judges, prosecutors, probation, treatment providers and even offenders are considered. Restorative justice does not focus only on victims, nor does it define victim rights as the absence of offender rights. To bring balance to an offender-driven system, however, it is necessary to give immediate priority to victims' needs for physical and material reparation and for emotional healing.

For the most part, restorative justice values can exist side-by-side with most traditional goals of juvenile justice intervention such as rehabilitation, and even deterrence and incapacitation. Proponents of restorative justice, for example, recognize the need for attempts to deter and incapacitate some offenders, as secondary reinforcements when they willfully and repeatedly disregard restorative obligations, or to protect citizens from offenders who continually victimize others (e.g., Braithwaite and Mugford, 1994; Young, 1995). But restorative justice would give lowest priority to punishment for its own sake, and would in practice challenge current "easy" solutions that simply reinforce and devote additional resources to traditional punishment, treatment and unimaginative approaches to enhancing public safety. From a restorative perspective, it is easy to get offenders to "take the punishment" (Wright, 1990), but it is much more difficult—and more important—to get them to take responsibility. It is equally easy to get many offenders to submit passively to the requirements of treatment programs, but it is much more difficult—and more important—to get them to actively earn their way back into the community and involve themselves in meaningful, productive roles that can potentially change their image from liability to community asset. It is easy to routinely lock up offenders in the name of public safety. But it is more difficult and more important to promote genuine public safety by building community capacity to control and prevent crime (e.g., Barajas, 1995).[4]

The basic principle behind restorative justice is that justice is best served when victims, offenders and communities receive equal attention as clients of the justice system. Ultimately then, restorative justice requires a "three-dimensional" focus which guides the search for solutions and just responses to crime to mutual concern for the needs of each client, and toward efforts to ensure that each is actively involved in the justice process. Crime breaks social and civil bonds between victims, offenders, and communities; it injures relationships of mutual respect, understanding and support. Achieving "justice" will involve "restoring" victims, offenders and communities.

In this way, the values of restorative justice allow managers using the balanced mission to effectively integrate efforts to meet sanctioning, safety and rehabilitative needs, restore victim losses, and ultimately serve and involve the three clients. As will become clear in the discussion which follows, restorative values underlie each of the other five differences between the Balanced Approach and current mission alternatives.

Different Clients

Based on restorative values, the Balanced Approach offers a new vision for how three primary clients or co-participants will be involved in the juvenile justice process. As Table 1 suggests, this "community justice" vision (Barajas, 1995; Young, 1995; Bazemore & Day, 1996) is perhaps best understood by first examining what the model "looks like" for these co-participants.

By these standards of victim, offender and community participation, the new mission is a "work in progress"; no juvenile justice system today is completely "balanced" or fully restorative. But if most juvenile justice systems, including those most committed to the model, seem far away from the level of community and client involvement indicated in the table, it is not, as the practical examples in the previous section illustrate, because the model is utopian. Rather, it is because these systems are driven by insular, conceptually and practically incomplete, "closed system" paradigms (Byrne, 1988; Reiss, 1986).

Both the traditional individual treatment and the new retributive/punitive models are incomplete because they are exclusively offender-focused. Neither treatment nor punishment models address victims and other citizens as co-participants or "customers" in the juvenile justice process.

Table I
What Does It Look Like? Balanced and Restorative Justice

In a Balanced And Restorative Juvenile Justice System:

Crime Victims:

- Receive support, assistance, compensation, information and services.
- Receive restitution and/or other reparation from the offender.
- Are involved and are encouraged to give input at all points in the system and direct input into how the offender will repair the harm done.
- Have the opportunity to face the offenders and tell their story to offenders and others if they so desire.
- Feel satisfied with the justice process.
- Provide guidance and consultation to JJ professionals on planning and advisory groups.

Offenders:

- Complete restitution to their victims.
- Provide meaningful service to repay the debt to their communities.
- Must face the personal harm caused by their crimes by participating in victim offender mediation, if the victim is willing or through other victim awareness process.
- Complete work experience and active and productive tasks which increase skills and improve the community.
- Are monitored by community adults as well as juvenile justice providers and are supervised to the greatest extent possible in the community.
- Improve decision-making skills and have opportunities to help others.

Citizens, Families, and Community Groups:

- Are involved to the greatest extent possible in holding offenders accountable, rehabilitation, and community safety initiatives.
- Work with offenders on local community service projects.
- Provide support to victims.
- Provide support to offenders as mentors, employers, and advocates.
- Provide work for offenders to pay restitution to victims and service opportunities which provide skills and also allow offenders to make meaningful contributions to the quality of community life.
- Community groups assist families to support the offender in the obligation to repair the harm and increase competencies.
- Play an advisory role to courts and corrections and/or play an active role in disposition through one or more neighborhood sanctioning processes.

What does it mean to view someone as a client or customer? In the Total Quality Management (TQM) movement (e.g., Deming, 1986; Martin, 1993), the idea of a client or "customer" has three components: a recipient of service, a target of intervention and change, and a co-participant who must have input into the process and be involved to the greatest extent possible. Although it may seem unusual to view offenders and their families, victims, and community members as customers, some jurisdictions are beginning to provide services to each of these clients and are attempting through various interventions to improve the disempowered, damaged, and fearful status of crime victims, as well as the preventative capacity of community groups (e.g., Bazemore and Schiff, 1996; Young, 1995). Moreover, some juvenile justice professionals are finding the input and active involvement of each of the client groups to be most critical for effectiveness (e.g., Umbreit and Carey, 1995).

While some degree of participation from each client group of the type depleted in Table 1 is essential to achieve the goals of the Balanced Approach, currently few nonprofessionals are meaningfully involved in juvenile justice intervention. First, although some juvenile justice professionals work hard at "service brokerage," such efforts at collaboration seldom move beyond the usual network of professional social service "experts" to include employers, civic leaders, ministers, and other neighborhood residents. Unfortunately, even when "nonexperts" are recruited to work with the system, the experts may be given little time to nurture and support them.

Second, because juvenile justice has been unable to identify meaningful and appropriate roles that engage citizens in activities associated with tangible offender and victim outcomes, involvement is often short-term and unsatisfying. Even programs aimed at establishing more lasting and significant bonds between community members and offenders, such as mentoring, often fail to provide a context (e.g., mutual involvement in a community service project) in which such bonds are likely to form (Bazemore & Day, 1996).

Finally, what citizen participants have been asked to do frequently seems to appeal to a more abstract obligation to participate out of civic duty rather than personal commitment. As Braithwaite and Mugford (1994) have observed, citizens are generally more willing to become involved If they have a personal interest in the offender, victim, and/or the family of either. Hence, although "community" may be difficult to identify in areas where it seems that there is disorganization and/or little sense of caring or mutual support, almost every crime involves small, personal "communities of concern" for the victim, the offender, and their families, and those citizens directly impacted by the crime (Stuart, 1995). These personal communities can become a critical resource as a support network in a response to youth crime that meets the needs of victim, offender and the neighborhood, and it is around them that much citizen participation in an emerging community justice is being built (Braithwaite & Mugford, 1994).[5]

Precisely because they do not focus simply on punishing or providing expert treatment to offenders, the programs and practices given priority in the Balanced Approach assume and invite a high level of citizen participation. While mobilizing community involvement is by no means easy, it may be more meaningful and personally satisfying, for example, for citizens to support an offender who needs a job to make victim restitution, provide support for a victim, or provide a useful community service opportunity than to assist with paperwork or aid to a traditional counseling program.

The basic assumption, or theory, behind restorative justice is that harm to one community member is harm to everyone. Therefore, the needs of one client (e.g., the victim's needs for healing; the offender's needs to be held accountable and then reintegrated) cannot be met unless the needs of the other clients are also addressed. Moreover, public safety, rehabilitation, and sanctioning goals need not conflict. In a restorative system, practices, policies and processes aimed at repairing the harm to victims should therefore reinforce or "resonate" with those which are aimed at rehabilitative and public safety objectives. Specifically, a sanctioning process that holds offenders accountable to victims and the community is a first step in the rehabilitative process. Developing capacities for competent behavior in offenders increases community safety by increasing offender connectedness, skills, and ability to work with others. Strengthening community safety makes it possible to carry out meaningful sanctioning and effective reintegration of offenders into the community, while also supporting and restoring victims. And, finally, increasing citizens' ability to resolve conflict ultimately makes communities safer.[6]

Different Decision-Making Processes

Recently, in a large city a 32-year-old man entered the home of a neighbor, and walked upstairs into the bedroom of her 14-year-old daughter. For almost an hour, the man made lewd and offensive comments while sitting on the girl's bed. After the man had been arrested and charged, the young woman and her mother were asked by the court to complete a victim impact statement. Except for a brief moment when the man had lightly stroked her hair, she had not been physically molested by the intruder. Yet, the young girl had felt traumatized and "dirtied" by the fact that the man had sat on her bed. After talking at length with her mother, the two decided that what the girl most needed was a new bed. The victim impact statement submitted asked for $500 in restitution from the offender to cover the cost of the bed, an apology, and a recommendation for a year of therapy and other assistance for the offender. The judge ordered 12 months' jail time and a $500 fine, but payable to the court.

In a small town in the same state, a 14-year-old male, after pointing a loaded gun (which was actually a BB rifle) at a neighbor, was arrested, charged with second degree assault with a deadly weapon, and eventually sent to juvenile court intake in the small town where he resided. The neighbor, an adult male of about 35 who had been so frightened and upset by the incident that he insisted the case be fully prosecuted, was reluctantly persuaded to participate with the offender in a victim-offender mediation session. At the session, after venting his anger and frustration at being startled with the loaded weapon, the victim learned that the boy liked to hunt. When he asked in the mediation session whom the boy hunted with and learned that it was his grandfather, an idea emerged that he would later propose when it was time to discuss an appropriate sanction. The outcome of the mediation was that, at the victim's request, the boy would be required to tell his grandfather what he had done. After several days of reluctant hesitation, the boy told his grandfather and so informed the victim.

The experiences in each case were dramatically different for the offender, the victim, and even the community. Most who have heard the young man's story believe that he learned an important lesson (and did not get off easy) and that the victim was satisfied. Moreover, some have observed that the small community may have witnessed an important example of how disputes that might otherwise have created a serious offense record for the youth, wasted court time, provided little relief to the victim, and created fear in the community of "armed and dangerous" juveniles could be effectively resolved. In the first case, most agree that the victim was ignored and again victimized, that the offender got no treatment and might even have been more dangerous at the completion of his jail time, and that the community paid the cost of the jail term while receiving little in return.

Most are also upset with the judge in the first case for ignoring the victim's request. But while the conversion of the victim's request for restitution into a court fine seems especially insensitive, the judge was merely operating on the basis of the assumptions of the current system of justice decision making. Referred to by some as a retributive justice paradigm (Zehr, 1990; Bazemore and Umbreit, 1995), these assumptions result in the exclusion and disempowerment of victims, offenders and other citizens and, in part, are responsible for the general absence in most juvenile justice systems of the co-participant involvement depicted earlier in Table 1. Although these cases are not necessarily typical, the contrast between them provides a useful illustration of how victim, community and offender needs are not addressed effectively by an approach to dispositional decision making that is limited by rigid legalistic processes (see Table 2).

Table 2
Paradigms of Justice—OLD and NEW*

Victims and Community

Retributive Justice	Restorative Justice
Victims are peripheral to the process.	Victims are central to the process.
Community on sideline, represented abstractly by state.	Community as facilitator in restorative process.
Imposition of pain to punish and deter/prevent	Restitution as a means of restoring both parties; goal of reconciliation/restoration

Crime and Reaction

Retributive Justice	Restorative Justice
Crime is an act against state, a violation of a law, or an abstract idea.	Crime is an act against another person and the community.
Punishment is effective a. The threat of punishment deters crime b. Punishment changes behavior	Punishment alone is not effective in changing behavior and is disruptive to community relationships.
The criminal justice system controls crime	Crime control lies primarily in the community

The Offender

Retributive Justice	Restorative Justice
Offender accountability defined as taking punishment	Accountability defined as taking punish responsibility and taking action to repair harm
The offender is defined by deficits	The offender is defined by the capacity to make reparation
No encouragement for repentance and forgiveness	Possibilities for forgiveness

*Adapted from Zehr (1990)

In contrast, restorative processes, whose potential benefits to each co-participant are illustrated by the first case, are premised on the active participation of these clients and demand opportunities for such participation that are sensitive to and supportive of client needs. Crime victim needs are especially likely to be overlooked unless victims are given a direct voice in decision making. When actively engaged, victims will often have unique concerns and interests which are often unrelated to offender punishment, or even the need for material reparation:

> I can tell you that what most victims want most is quite unrelated to the law. It amounts more than anything else to three things: victims need to have people recognize how much trauma they've been through . . . they need to express that, and have it expressed to them; they want to find out what kind of person could have done such a thing, and why to them; and it really helps to hear that the offender is sorry—or that someone is sorry on his or her behalf. (Elaine Berzins, quoted in Stuart, 1995a, p. 12).

Most formal juvenile court proceedings with some flexible discretion by judges and other court decision makers could accommodate some of the changes needed to increase the active involvement of victims, offenders, and citizens in dispositions and thus make sanctions and court requirements more meaningful. But if critics of formal, legalistic processes are correct, minor changes in the court process will be insufficient to alter the current image of these insular systems that have proved themselves inadequate to the task. As Judge Stuart insists:

> Crime (control and prevention) should never be the sole, or even primary business of the State if *real differences* are sought in the well being of individuals, families and communities. The structure, procedures, and evidentiary rules of the formal criminal justice process coupled with most justice officials' lack of knowledge and connection to (the parties) effected by crime, preclude the state from acting alone to achieve transformative changes. (Stuart, 1995b, p. 1, emphasis in original)

Achieving balanced and restorative goals and the general vision of restorative justice are therefore likely to require that juvenile court judges and other court professionals exercise strong leadership to actively develop and promote expanded use of viable decision-making alternatives that allow for greater and more meaningful involvement of citizens and victims in decisions about the response to juveniles who commit crimes. New Zealand, as mentioned earlier, has gone furthest toward institutionalizing the active involvement of citizens and victims, as well as offenders and their families, in the court dispositional process through its nationwide adoption of the Family Group Conferencing model (McElrae, 1993; Maxwell & Morris, 1993). There are other processes as well which may be more appropriate for certain cases and work best in certain communities. Table 3 suggests some successful existing models for victim and citizen participation in decision making.

These alternative processes assume an offender who has admitted guilt or been found guilty and are concerned with dispositional decision making rather than fact finding. However, in most jurisdictions where cases are routinely plea bargained or resolved by consent decree

---

Table 3
Some Restorative Decision-Making Processes

1. *Victim Offender Mediation*—Trained mediators facilitate face-to-face discussion between offender and victim to allow for expression of feelings, discussion of harm and obligation, and arrive at agreement with offender to repair the harm.
2. *Family Group Conferencing*—Allows for community, victim and family input into the development of a restorative sanction for juvenile offender; in a process initiated by a trained facilitator.
3. *Circle Sentencing*—A sentencing and problem-solving process currently being implemented in Canada facilitated by a judge or community member and attended by victim, offenders and a variety of local citizens who support both and wish to develop a local resolution of the crime.
4. *Community Reparative Boards*—Currently being implemented in Vermont, these citizen sentencing panels develop agreements with nonfelony offenders that focus their probation on victim and community reparation, understanding of harm caused by their crime, avoiding future offending behavior.
5. *Reparative Court Hearings*—Though best implemented in an informal community setting, some judges hold special hearings to determine victim reparation as a separate part of the dispositional process in court.

---

or other informal negotiation prior to formal disposition, this may in fact account for a majority of cases (c.f., McElrae, 1993; Belgrave, 1995). Currently, there are precedents for restorative decision-making models being used around the world at several points in both the juvenile and criminal justice systems including pre-adjudication, pre- and post-disposition, as a requirement or option at institutional commitment, and as a part of aftercare (Belgrave, 1995; Umbreit, 1994; Bazemore & Schiff; 1996; Morris & Maxwell, 1993). While these alternative processes will not be fully developed overnight and will never replace the need for the court in some cases, or the need for a commitment to due process, restorative justice is a holistic model that seeks to maximize crime victim and community input through less formal, less adversarial processes at all possible points in and outside of the system.

Different Performance Objectives

If treatment and punishment are, as suggested earlier, insular in their exclusive focus on the needs and risks presented by the offender, they are also one-dimensional. That is, both the treatment and retributive missions fail to address the various, and multiple, justice needs of communities.

While the new punitive approach to juvenile justice may appease some of the public demand for retribution, it does nothing to address expectations that offenders be rehabilitated and reintegrated. In contrast, most citizens view treatment as solely related to the offender's needs. Treatment programs seem to require little of lawbreakers beyond participating in counseling, remedial services, or recreational programs, and they may even be viewed as providing only benefits to offenders, while failing to reinforce conventional values such as the work ethic (Bazemore & Umbreit, 1995b). Ultimately, retributive punishment addresses one small aspect of a community's need to sanction crime, while treatment addresses one small aspect of rehabilitation and reintegration. Neither addresses the community's need for safety and input into the process or the need for more meaningful approaches to sanctioning and rehabilitation that attempt to also involve victims and address their needs.

As models for developing outcomes that could be used to gauge the true effectiveness of juvenile justice agencies and systems and to guide the selection of programs to achieve these objectives, treatment and punishment approaches are flawed in two primary ways. First, while advocates of various treatment interventions remind us that some things do work (e.g., Gendreau and Ross, 1987), what "works" for offenders who happen to make it into treatment programs may make little difference to victims of juvenile crime, to citizens concerned with their neighborhoods' safety and to those who want to see young people held accountable for their actions (Braithwaite and Mugford, 1994). As offender-driven models, punishment and treatment are useful only in developing outcomes for offenders under court jurisdiction. They are of little assistance in articulating goals that address the need for positive changes in crime victims and communities. Second, while the long-range concern of both punishment and treatment is to prevent recidivism and the short-term goal is to gain enough control over the offender to do this, neither model offers good intermediate performance outcomes for offenders.

Completing a treatment program and ceasing bad behavior while under court supervision does not equip offenders with the capabilities and the desire to do something other than offending. Likewise, simply "taking the punishment" produces few measurable outcomes (other than possible anger and resentment). While many would also argue that juvenile justice should not be held solely responsible for reducing recidivism (and in any case, few juvenile justice agencies systematically track recidivism rates), systems and agencies should, however, be accountable for achieving other objectives that may be associated with reduced recidivism and ultimately with lower crime rates.

One purpose of the Balanced Approach mission is to provide juvenile justice systems with intermediate performance outcomes related to the primary expectations of the communities they serve. In systems applying the Balanced Approach, communities are working with juvenile justice professionals to develop intermediate outcomes to gauge success in achieving the sanctioning, rehabilitative and public safety goals put forward in the balanced mission and to assess positive change in the three juvenile justice clients. But the most important outcomes in the Balanced Approach are unlikely to be the same as those that have been given the primary focus in the traditional system. Rather, they are focused on making what Judge Stuart calls "real differences" in relationships that allow victims to heal, offenders to become reconnected, and families and communities to begin to take responsibility for these things to occur:

> ... communities should not measure the success of any ... community based initiative upon what happens to the offender. .. (Rather, they should measure) . . . the impact of community based initiatives upon victims, upon the self-esteem of others working (in the community justice process), on strengthening families, building connections within the community, on enforcing community values, on mobilizing community action to reduce factors causing crime, to prevent crime—and ultimately to make the community safer. . . . (Stuart, 1995:8)

Different Programs

Although there is no one Balanced Approach or restorative intervention or program, it has become clear, based on years of research and program experience, that there are several types of programs and practices that need to receive priority if systems are to achieve the goals of competency development, accountability, and community protection. Table 4 suggests several such interventions and sample performance outcome measures that may be used to assess impact in achieving each objective (Appendix I describes these programs in more detail).

In addition to articulating intermediate performance outcomes, juvenile justice agencies and systems will also need to conduct a baseline audit or inventory of current intervention practice. Specifically, to develop a fair evaluation of the extent to which they are accomplishing balanced and restorative goals, a thorough assessment should examine whether certain programs, practices, and processes designed to accomplish key objectives such as victim restoration, offender competency development and so on are available to the jurisdiction and are being used effectively. For example, if a jurisdiction has no systematic

Table 4
Outcome Measures and Priorities for Practice in the Balanced Approach

Competency Development
Intermediate Outcome Measures
- Proportion of youth on supervision completing successful work experience or employment (quality of experience?)
- Proportion of youth on supervision completing meaningful work/service project
- Extent of "bonding" between youth under supervision and community adults
- Increase in empathy and improved skills
- Demonstrated improvement in conflict resolution and anger management
- Measured increase in educational, interpersonal, citizenship and other competencies

Priorities for Practice
- Structured work experience and employment programs
- Service/active learning
- Cognitive and decision-making programs
- Dispute resolution training
- Intergenerational projects
- Cross-age tutoring
- Conservation and environmental awareness

Accountability
Intermediate Outcome Measures
- Proportion of offenders completing fair and appropriate restitution order or agreement
- Proportion of victims given input into the process
- Proportion of victims satisfied with the process
- Proportion of offenders showing measured increase in victim awareness and empathy
- Proportion of offenders and victims completing mediation or other resolution, mediation, and community service
- Proportion of offenders completing meaningful community service projects (number of such projects completed)

Priorities for Practice
- Restitution to victims
- Restorative community service
- Victim-offender mediation
- Direct service to victims or surrogate victims (e.g., crime repair crews)
- Victim awareness panels or victim-offender groups in treatment programs

Public Safety
Intermediate Outcome Measures
- Proportion of offenders reoffending while under juvenile justice supervision
- Number of citizens involved in preventive and monitoring activities
- Decrease in community *fear* and increase in understanding of juvenile justice
- Decrease in school violence and *increase* in school and community-based conflict resolution
- Increase in competency, empathy and internal controls for offenders under supervision

Priorities for Practice
- Structuring time of offenders being supervised in the community: work experience, community service, alternative education
- Effective use of "natural surveillance" and community guardians (e.g., employers, relatives, churches, mentors)
- Continuum of graduated community-based sanctions and surveillance (including EM and intensive supervision)
- Prevention and capacity building in schools and other community groups (e.g., mediation and dispute resolution, parenting skills)

procedure or program for determining restitution, monitoring payments, and ensuring that offenders have ways to earn funds to repay
victims, it can hardly be expected to achieve its accountability objectives (Schneider, 1985; Bazemore, 1991). Likewise, it may also be
victims, it can hardly be expected to achieve its accountability objectives (Schneider, 1985; Bazemore, 1991). Likewise, it may also be
important to critically examine the extent to which current assessment
and dispositional processes may limit efforts to achieve balanced performance outcomes. If a goal is to maximize the number of young
offenders who complete fair restitution obligations to their victims, this
goal cannot be accomplished if judges make unreasonable orders
without regard to whether the jurisdiction is providing earning
opportunities for the offender (Bazemore, 1991). If a goal is to ensure
that each offender will be required to complete a meaningful work
experience or provide community service that meets real community
needs, this goal will not be achieved if the standard practice in many
jurisdictions of sending youth with service hours, unsupervised to pick
up paper in local parks continues (Bazemore & Maloney, 1994). If a goal
is to ensure that each victim who wishes to have a face-to-face meeting
with the offender has an opportunity to do so, the goal is unlikely to be
achieved in the absence of a victim-offender mediation program or
other structured opportunity for victim input and victim-offender
dialogue such as family group conferencing (Morris & Maxwell, 1993).

Although I will not elaborate on operational issues of specific programs here, it is important to reiterate that simply adding programs in
the absence of change in values and client priorities is unlikely to lead
to balanced and restorative outcomes. As juvenile justice systems
become "program-driven," managers may develop what Goldstein
(1979; 1988) referred to in law enforcement as a means-over-ends
focus. Programs are not ends in themselves but simply a means to
achieve outcomes that flow from a clear understanding of community
and other client needs. Programs and practices are "restorative" to the
extent that they are consistent with the underlying values of restorative
justice and responsive to these clients. On the other hand, some programs with apparently restorative objectives are not based on restorative values and may be easily coopted to serve other ends (e.g., mediation and restitution programs used primarily to divert offenders
rather than involve victims and offenders in reaching agreements for
reparation; community service that is ordered primarily as punishment rather than community restoration).

Moreover, from a "community justice" perspective (Barajas, 1995;
Bazemore and Schiff, 1996), the value of a program and quality of its
implementation must also be gauged primarily in terms of the extent to
which it involves community members at all levels of planning, implementation, and monitoring. For example, one may ask of a community

service or victim-offender-mediation program which uses only paid staff and does not consult neighborhood residents on their priorities (e.g., for work service projects) whether such programs are simply *in* rather than *of* the community.

Different Roles for Juvenile Justice Professionals

The new, active roles for the three juvenile justice clients, or co-participants, discussed earlier (and depicted in Table 1) have obvious implications for the roles of juvenile justice professionals. Hence, perhaps the most important, and also most difficult, change in moving toward Balanced and Restorative Justice will be to begin to alter the job descriptions and professional role orientations of juvenile justice staff. For probation professionals accustomed to casework with individual offenders or residential treatment providers trained in institution-based treatment protocols, the role change implied by the need to engage victims and communities in the process may be a dramatic and difficult one. For many of these professionals, the idea of working with victims and community members, when time and resources to meet the needs of offenders alone appear inadequate, seems counterintuitive.

But making significant differences in the lives of offenders, the kind of differences that help to reintegrate them into conventional communities, is ultimately unlikely without the active involvement of victims and nonprofessional citizens (e.g., Stuart, 1995a & b).

Making amends to victims and then gaining the sponsorship of community adults (e.g., employers, ministers, family members) are the steps that open the doors to community acceptance for offenders. Hence, achieving rehabilitative objectives will require that juvenile justice no longer treat the offender in isolation. To make the shift toward viewing victim and community intervention as part of the juvenile justice role, probation and treatment staff will need to understand this restorative justice principle and ultimately also witness the transformative changes that can occur when community members and victims are involved in the response to youth crime (e.g., Braithwaite and Mugford 1994; Stuart, 1995).

The specifics of this role change are beyond the scope of this article and need to be worked out locally with staff, managers, and citizen advisers. Still, it is clear that the role of probation and other intervention staff in jurisdictions implementing a Balanced Approach mission will gradually be transformed from direct service provider, or even "service broker," to "community justice facilitator." As Table 5 suggests, this transformation will require that juvenile justice professionals begin to define their new roles and functions in relation to and in support of, the new more active role of each of the three co-participants. They will, for example, work with each of the three clients in activities focused on capacity-building for crime prevention, in ensuring that community adults provide opportunities for competency development and assist with monitoring offenders, in engaging employers and civic groups to provide meaningful work for offenders, and in meeting with victims and victim advocacy groups.

Judges, prosecutors, and other court decision makers will also be challenged by the Balanced Approach mission to reassess their current roles. There will, as previously noted, always be cases that require use of formal legal processes and determination of guilt through formal due process. However, judges in particular can play vital leadership roles in encouraging communities and citizens to resolve conflict creatively and informally and to begin to take more responsibility in the response to, and prevention of, youth crime (Stuart, 1995). If they are to empower victims and community members as co-participants, they must take on this challenge and take risks to expand the variety of alternative decision-making processes such as mediation, family group conferencing, and similar forums and allow greater numbers of cases to be heard in these settings.

Table 5
New Roles in the Balanced and Restorative Justice Model

The Co-Participants

Victim	Active participation in defining the harm of the crime and shaping the obligations placed on the offender.
Community	Responsible for supporting and assisting victims, holding offenders accountable, and ensuring opportunities for offenders to make amends.
Offender	Active participation in reparation and competency development.

Juvenile Justice Professionals

Sanctioning	Facilitate mediation; ensure that restoration occurs (by providing ways for offenders to earn funds for restitution); develop creative and or restorative community service options; engage community members in the process; educate community on its role.
Rehabilitation	Develop new roles for young offenders which allow them to practice and demonstrate competency; assess and build on youth and community strengths; develop partnerships.
Public Safety	Develop range of incentives and consequences to ensure offender compliance with supervision objectives; assist school and family in their efforts to control and maintain offenders in the community; develop prevention capacity of local organizations.

The Limits of Current Paradigms:
Toward Community Juvenile Justice

For the most part the decade-long debate about the future of the juvenile court and the justice system has been stale and unimaginative. Often couched in legalistic and procedural terms focused on which young offenders should receive juvenile and which should receive adult dispositions and how this should be decided, this debate has typically had little to do with the content and focus of juvenile court intervention—or with how those offenders who remain in the juvenile justice system, their communities, or their victims will benefit from this intervention. As a result, it has been of little interest to the public, a growing number of whom seem to sense that the important issues of community safety, juvenile crime, and youth development cannot be reduced to issues of the relative efficacy of juvenile and adult court.

Many citizens and a growing number of juvenile justice professionals also seem to be growing tired of the even older debate about the relative efficacy of treatment vs. punishment. For these observers, there is a suspicion that something is missing in an endless discussion about what feel like, as one judge put it, "bad choices between sending kids to jail or sending them to the beach." While recent research suggests that much of the public continues to support rehabilitation (e.g., Doble, 1996; Schwartz, 1992), many appear to doubt the capacity of juvenile justice systems to accomplish this objective and seem to suspect that neither "jail" nor "the beach" provides much of an answer.

Meanwhile, the system continues to expand and increase expenditures with relatively little to show in improved outcomes for offenders, families, and communities. At the same time, staff feel that they are working harder and doing more with less.[7] While advocates of reaffirming the individual treatment model may be right in arguing that the system has never been given adequate support, critics, as well as many defenders of juvenile justice, now argue that juvenile justice leaders have also failed to articulate a vision of success. If juvenile justice is underfunded, it is also underconceptualized. Increasingly reliant on professional experts, more facilities, and more programs, many, if not most, juvenile justice agencies and programs today have lost the critical ingredient needed to develop a meaningful response to juvenile crime: community support and meaningful citizen involvement in the justice process.

I have suggested here that debate about the future of juvenile justice has been limited by closed-system, offender-driven, and one-dimensional punishment and treatment paradigms. The individual treatment and the retributive/punitive models are not, however, the only options for juvenile justice. Treatment and punishment remain important components of many juvenile court dispositions, but it is possible to envision a more empowering, more holistic and more marketable, restorative community justice agenda for a future response to youth crime (Young, 1995; Bazemore and Day, 1996). Such an agenda would put victims' needs for information, reparation, validation, healing, and input at its core and would promote development of strong, crime-resistant neighborhoods where residents feel safe. It would emphasize the need for rehabilitative/reintegrative relationship-building between young people and adults and for active, experiential involvement of young offenders in work, service learning and other productive roles that provide more structured pathways to bonding with community members. Perhaps most important, a community juvenile justice would articulate new and more meaningful roles for crime victims, employers, civic groups, religious communities, teachers, families and other citizens in offender habilitation/rehabilitation; in a more meaningful, more effective and more educational nonretributive approach to sanctioning; and in carrying out a more effective public safety enhancement agenda (see earlier Table 1).

Conclusion: Moving Toward Balance

The Balanced Approach mission was originally proposed not to reaffirm the individualized treatment agenda of the juvenile court, but rather to restructure juvenile justice to move it closer to the community and its needs. A primary danger in the Balanced Approach's new popularity is that it will be misunderstood and inappropriately applied. Thus, supporters, as well as critics, should continue to raise questions about the use of this new mission, while also questioning the utility of current approaches. In the current political climate, it is especially important to remain alert to efforts to simply use the rhetoric of balance or restoration to disguise retributive policies that merely respond to what Dennis Maloney has referred to as policymaker "urges" to get tough.

In raising concerns about the Balanced Approach mission's value, two important questions are certain to be raised: 1) Is it viable, politically and practically; and 2) will it work?

Will It Fly? The Viability of the Balanced Approach

In considering viability, it is important to consider both the political environment around juvenile justice today and the practical feasibility of balanced reform.

Liberal or Conservative? The Politics of "Balance." Part of the popularity of the Balanced Approach, and part of its strength, is that it does not appeal to any one constituency. "Get tough" audiences hear (correctly) in the requirements that young offenders work, face their victims, and repay them and the community, an approach to sanctioning that is in many ways "tougher," as well as more meaningful, than sitting in a detention facility (Umbreit, 1994; Bazemore and Maloney, 1994). More liberal audiences hear (also correctly) that balance cannot mean abandoning hope of rehabilitation, humiliating and violating the rights of offenders, or giving up on the idea of preserving a distinct juvenile court (Feld, 1990; 1995).

While "balance" in a restorative framework cannot be a zero-sum proposition, choices between competing priorities must be made to effectively address the performance objectives of the new mission. If balance means that a greater share of system resources are needed to involve and meet needs of victims and other citizens, we are unlikely to achieve it by choosing to spend more on locked facilities for offenders or by increasing transfers to adult court. Similarly, if offenders develop competencies as a result of experience in productive work and service roles in their communities that help bond them to legitimate adults, the competency development goal will not be achieved if we simply choose to add more traditional treatment programs.

Are these "liberal" or "conservative" choices? Increasingly, many juvenile justice professionals, and especially those experimenting with the Balanced Approach, appear to be discovering that these labels are no longer useful. Is it "conservative" to expand government services by advocating for more, increasingly expensive, locked facilities and creating large juvenile (or adult) corrections bureaucracies? Is it conservative to support top-down, centralized juvenile justice agencies and systems which discharge communities of their responsibility in sanctioning crime, healing victims and reintegrating offenders? Is it "liberal," or in "the best interest of the child," to advocate for more treatment by professional experts without involving unpaid community adults in creating productive roles for young offenders which bond them to their communities? Is it liberal to ignore the plight of victims, and does more punishment for the offender really help victims?

As a community justice model, the Balanced Approach seeks to make citizens, community groups and victims active partners in meeting public justice needs. It seeks to put offenders in active, demanding roles—that they may personally experience as "punitive"—but which have much broader and more important objectives than punishment. Although politicians and policymakers may continue to label these things as liberal or conservative, if citizens feel that the juvenile court is thereby more effective in sanctioning youth crime, enhancing public safety. and helping to reintegrate offenders who truly have earned their way back into communities, they will probably not care.

Because some of the programs and practices that informed the Balanced Approach, such as work experience and community service, were initially associated with Dennis Maloney's environmental and entrepreneurial efforts in rural and small-town Oregon (Maloney, Romig, & Armstrong, 1988; Bazemore & Maloney, 1994), some have viewed the Balanced Approach as an intervention focused on rural and small-town "hoods in the woods." Ironically, as the Balanced Approach mission is now being implemented by African American juvenile justice managers and community leaders in parts of urban South Florida (as well as inner-city Pittsburgh), some practitioners in the rest of that state have begun to refer to the mission as "a black thing." As indicated also by the misinterpretation of the approach as an extension of either the treatment or punishment model, one of the threats to the Balanced Approach is being pigeonholed—culturally, politically, and ideologically.

Practical Steps. Practically speaking, implementing the reform agenda of the Balanced Approach will not be a smooth or easy process, and "balance" will not be achieved overnight. Although restorative justice is "on the ground" in entire countries, in state and local policy changes, and in hundreds of small demonstration efforts, Balanced and Restorative Justice is also a "work in progress." The new mission is also likely to provoke some opposition because it challenges assumptions that support the status quo and too often provide easy justifications for failure. Thus, it will be claimed that balanced and restorative interventions will not work because: "victims are angry and punitive and do not want to have anything to do with the offender;" "offenders have no empathy, are incompetent, and are incapable of restoring the loss or harm caused by their crimes;" "the community is apathetic and citizens do not wish to be involved;" or "juvenile justice workers are required to spend too much time in court or doing paperwork and have not been trained to work with the community."

Interestingly, juvenile justice managers committed to achieving the Balanced Approach's goals view these very rationales for opposing the approach as precisely the reasons the new mission is necessary if a distinct juvenile justice system is to be preserved (e.g., Carey and Umbreit, 1995; Bazemore and Day, 1996). That is, if victims are angry and offenders lack skills and empathy, a primary objective should be to develop interventions that facilitate *changes* in offender empathy and competency and attempt to meet the needs of victims and ask them for their input. If citizens seem apathetic, a primary objective should be to work toward reducing community apathy and noninvolvement and strengthening neighborhoods by changing the nature of current practices and decision-making processes. Finally, if staff do not have time or skills to perform such tasks, it may be time to reexamine and consider changing priorities and incentives.

Several managers are currently exploring different approaches to organizational change and community engagement in order to implement the balanced mission at a systems level in states such as Minnesota, Florida, Pennsylvania and Montana (Bazemore and Washington, 1995; Umbreit and Carey, 1995; Bazemore and Day, 1996). While there is no one best implementation strategy, to begin moving forward with the Balanced Approach mission, it is important to address three questions: 1) what is the current level of understanding and support for the goals of the Balanced Approach mission and the restorative justice vision among staff and the community; 2) what is the baseline status of current policy and practice already consistent with the Balanced Approach; and 3) what action steps need to be taken to begin to give priority to these policies and practices, and who is responsible for each step. What's "new" and different in jurisdictions where managers and staff are taking the Balanced Approach mission seriously is a process of critical self-examination, consensus-building about values. and small, but coordinated steps to demonstrate and then expand and institutionalize a balanced and restorative vision.

The six differences between the Balanced Approach and "business as usual" discussed in this article imply that managers and staff must move in sequence from an intensive examination of the level of commitment among themselves and community members to the core values of the mission and the restorative justice framework to a critical look at current relationships with the three juvenile justice clients. They must then examine the appropriateness of current decision-making processes, performance outcomes programmatic priorities and resource allocation and role definitions needed to support the new model.

Will It Work?

When interventions such as community service or work experience are guided by punitive values and goals rather than restorative principles, their failure cannot be viewed as a failure of the mission or the restorative framework. Second, because the Balanced Approach is not a treatment program but a mission for system reform, its impact cannot be accurately assessed using traditional program evaluation technologies, and the success of restorative justice interventions must be gauged by increases in victim satisfaction, offender accountability and competency development, and reductions in community fear, *as well as* recidivism. Finally, the success of the Balanced Approach will also depend on how well its core philosophy is understood, how well it is adapted to local conditions, the consistency and integrity of implementation (Armstrong, Maloney and Romig, 1990; Bazemore, 1992) and, ultimately, whether restorative justice is given a chance. While restorative justice and the balanced mission may not lead to immediate reductions in recidivism, or even rapid increases in victim and community satisfaction, critics of community justice should remember that the standard of comparison in assessing success or failure must be the current system. As a First Nations Community Justice Coordinator in the Yukon, Canada put it:

> So we make mistakes—can you say—you (the current system) don't make mistakes . . . if you don't think you do walk through our community, every family will have something to teach you. . . . By getting involved, by all of us taking responsibility, it is not that we won't make mistakes; we would be doing it together, as *community* instead of having it done to us. . . . We need to make real *differences* in the way people act and the way we treat others. . . . Only if we empower them and support them can they break out of this trap. (quoted in Stuart, 1995)

The failure of current paradigms has moved many policymakers toward more desperate attempts to "improve" the response to juvenile crime by abolishing the juvenile justice system. A growing number who want to preserve a separate and effective juvenile justice system, and see Balanced Approach mission and the restorative justice framework as providing hope for doing so, realize that any new system must be crafted not with the needs of professionals, but with the community in mind.

Notes

[1] There is substantial variation in the way in which the balanced mission is presented in this legislation and policy. While some statutes refer specifically to the Balanced Approach, others simply articulate the three goals of the mission—public safety, competency, and accountability. A growing number of juvenile justice managers, policymakers and funding agency administrators in states such as California, Montana, Pennsylvania, and Minnesota now speak of a Balanced and Restorative Justice model (Bazemore and Umbreit, 1994; Umbreit and Carey, 1995; Pennsylvania Council on Crime and Delinquency, 1996; Montana Board of Crime Control, 1996).

[2] In part because the authors of the NCJFCJ monograph came down squarely on the side of preserving the juvenile court, it has perhaps been easy for some critics of the Balanced Approach to simply equate the new mission with a defense of the individual treatment mission. Misunderstanding is also no doubt due to the fact that to date only a few jurisdictions have begun to make the systemic changes in policy and practice consistent with the vision of Maloney, Romig and Armstrong (1988) and to the fact that the restorative justice philosophy has only been sporadically discussed in most juvenile justice circles.

[3] For reasons that will be discussed later, treatment and punishment are actually viewed as secondary goals in the balanced approach mission. The critique of the individual treatment model presented here is not premised on the largely discredited "nothing works" perspective, nor is the need for an effective rehabilitative model for juvenile justice questioned.

[4] Restorative justice would essentially give new priority to goals such as victim and community involvement that have been neglected in the current system. Though punishment is likely to remain a central component of any juvenile justice model, it is perhaps the least effective and most expensive approach to sanctioning crime. For empirical evidence that criminal justice decision makers typically overestimate the perceived punitive effects of incarceration and commentary on other more educative and expressive approaches to setting tolerance limits for crime, providing consequences for offenders, and allowing for the expression of public disapproval of offending in ways that promote community solidarity and peaceful dispute resolution, see Braithwaite (1989), Wilkins (1995), Bazemore & Umbreit (1995), Crouch (1993) and Bishop, et al., 1996). A growing body of research and an emerging theoretical base is supportive of the view that the experience of making amends for harm done to victims and the community through monetary restitution and unpaid service may have positive rehabilitative as well as reparative effects (Eglash, 1975; Schneider, 1986; 1990; Butts and Snyder, 1991; Wright, 1991).

[5] For more detailed description of the New Zealand and Australian models of family group conferencing and related models such as Circle Sentencing, including research findings and critical concerns about implementation in some jurisdictions, see Maxwell and Morris (1993), Alder and Wundersitz (1994), Umbreit and Stacy (1995) and Stuart, 1995).

[6] "This concept of "resonance" in the Balanced Approach was first articulated by Troy Armstrong (see, Armstrong, Maloney and Romig, 1990). Some have also argued that it is possible to think and speak of a restorative approach to rehabilitation and a restorative approach to public safety (Van Ness, 1993; Bazemore, 1996).

[7] Indeed the critique of current policy and practice presented in this article is in no way a criticism of juvenile justice professionals. Rather, it is a critique of the bureaucratic systems which limit their effort to implement meaningful reform.

References

Alder, C. & J. Wundersitz, 1994, *Family Group Conferencing and Juvenile Justice: The Way Forward of Misplaced*, Canberra, ACT: Australian Institute of Criminology.

Armstrong, T., D. Maloney, & D. Romig, 1990, "The Balanced Approach to Juvenile Probation: Principles, Issues, and Application." *Perspectives*, Winter 8–13.

Barajas, Jr., E., 1995, "Moving Toward Community Justice," *Topics in Community Corrections*. National Institute of Corrections Community Division, Annual Issue 1995.

Bazemore, G., 1991, "New Concepts and Alternative Practice in Community Supervision of Juvenile Offenders: Rediscovering Work Experience and Competency Development," *Journal of Crime and Justice*, 14 (2), 27–52.

Bazemore, G., 1992, "On Mission Statements and Reform in Juvenile Justice: The Case of the 'Balanced Approach,'" *Federal Probation*, 5 6(3).

Bazemore, G., 1996, "Three Paradigms for Juvenile Justice," Chapter 2 in Joe Hudson and Burt Galaway (eds.), *The Practice of Restorative Justice*. Monsey, NY: Criminal Justice Press.

Bazemore, G., & S. Day, 1996, "Restoring The Balance: Juvenile Justice and Community Justice," *Juvenile Justice*. Volume III, No. 1 (3–14) December.

Bazemore, G., & S. Senjo, 1996, "Cops, Kids and Police Reform: An Exploratory Study of Themes and Styles in Police/Juvenile Interaction in Community Policing," paper presented at the American Society of Criminology Meetings, Boston, November.

Bazemore, G., & P. Cruise, 1994, "Reinventing Rehabilitation: Exploring a Competency Development Model for Juvenile Justice Intervention," *Perspectives* Fall, 12–21.

Bazemore, G., & D. Maloney, 1994, "Rehabilitating Community Service: Toward Restorative Service in a Balanced Justice System," *Federal Probation.* 58(1), 24–34.

Bazemore, G., & C. Terry, 1997, "Developing Delinquent Youth: A Reintegrative Model for Rehabilitation and a New Role for the Juvenile Justice System," *Child Welfare*.

Bazemore, G., & M. Schiff, 1996, "Community Justice/Restorative Justice: Prospects for a New Social Ecology for Community Corrections," *International Journal of Comparative and Applied Criminal Justice,* 20 (1), Fall, (311–335).

Bazemore, G., & M. Umbreit, 1995a, *Balanced and Restorative Justice for Juveniles.* Office of Juvenile Justice and Delinquency Prevention. U.S. Department of Justice, Washington, DC.

Bazemore, G., & M. Umbreit, 1995b, "Rethinking the Sanctioning Function in Juvenile Court: Retributive or Restorative Responses to Youth Crime," *Crime and Delinquency,* 41(3), 296–316.

Bazemore, G., & C. Washington, 1995, "Charting the Future of the Juvenile Justice System: Reinventing Mission and Management," *Spectrum: The Journal of State Government,* 68(2), 51–66.

Belgrave, J., 1995, *Restorative Justice: A Discussion Paper.* New Zealand Ministry of Justice. Wellington, New Zealand.

Bishop, D., C. Frazier, L. Lanza-Kuduce, & L. Wimmer, 1996, "The Transfer of Juveniles to Criminal Court: Does It Make a Difference?," *Crime & Delinquency,* 42(2), 171–191.

Braithwaite, J., 1989, *Crime, Shaming, and Reintegration.* New York: Cambridge University Press.

Braithwaite, J., & S. Mugford, 1994, "Conditions of Successful Reintegration Ceremonies," *British Journal of Criminology,* 34(2), 139–171. {Australia}

Butts, J., and S. Howard, 1991, *Restitution and Juvenile Recidivism.* Monograph. National Center for Juvenile Justice, Pittsburgh, PA.

Byrne, J. M., 1989, "Reintegrating the Concept of Community into Community-Based Corrections." *Crime & Delinquency,* 35, (3), 471–499.

Crouch, J., 1989, "Is Incarceration Really Worse? Analysis of Offenders' Preferences for Prison Over Probation," *Justice Quarterly* 10:67, 88.

Deming, W. E., 1986, *Out of Crisis.* Cambridge, MA: MIT Center for Advanced Engineering.

Dickey, W., 1995, "Why Neighborhood Supervision?" Pages 42–46 in E. Barajas (ed.), *Community Justice: Topics in Community Corrections,* National Institute of Corrections. U.S. Department of Justice, Washington, DC.

Eglash, A., 1975, "Beyond Restitution: Creative Restitution," pages 91–101 in J. Hudson & B. Galaway (eds.), *Restitution in Criminal Justice*. Lexington, PA: Lexington Books.

Feld, B., 1991, "The Punitive Juvenile Court and the Quality of Procedural Justice: Distinctions Between Rhetoric and Reality," *Crime & Delinquency* 36, 443–464.

Feld, B., 1995, "Violent Youth and Public Policy: A Case Study in Dismantling Juvenile Justice Law Reform," *Minnesota Law Review* 79, 965–992.

Forst, M. L., & M. Blomquist, 1992, "Punishment, Accountability, and the New Juvenile Justice," *Juvenile & Family Court Journal*, 23(2), 1–9.

Gendreau, P., & R. Ross, 1994, "Correctional Treatment: Some Recommendations for Successful Intervention," *Juvenile and Family Court Journal*, 34, 31–40.

Goldstein, H., 1978, "Improving Policing: A Problem-Oriented Approach," *Crime & Delinquency*, 25, 236–258.

Guarino-Ghezzi, S., & A. Klein, 1997, "A Public Safety Role for Juvenile Justice," in G. Bazemore & L. Walgrave (eds.), *Restoring Juvenile Justice*. Amsterdam: Kugler International.

Klien, A., 1996, *Balanced Approach Legislation in the States*. Monograph, Balanced and Restorative Justice Project, Florida Atlantic University, Ft. Lauderdale, Florida.

Lemov, P., 1994, "The Assault on Juvenile on Juvenile Justice," *Governing*, December, 26–31.

Maloney, D., D. Romig, & T. Armstrong, 1988, *Juvenile Probation: The Balanced Approach*. Reno, NV: National Council of Juvenile and Family Court Judges.

Martin, L., 1993, *Total Quality Management in Organizations*. Newbury Park: Sage.

McAllair, D., 1993, "Reaffirming Rehabilitation in Juvenile Justice," *Youth and Society*, 25, (1), 104–125.

McElrae, F. W. M., 1993, "A New Model of Justice," pages 1–14 in *The Youth Court in New Zealand. A New Model of Justice*. Legal Research Foundation, Pub. 34.

Moore, T., & T. O'Connell, 1994, "Family Conferencing in Wagga Wagga: A Communitarian Model of Justice," pp. 96–110 in C. Adler & J. Wundersitz (eds.), *Family Group Conferencing: The Way Forward or Misplaced Optimism?* Canberra, ACT: Australian Institute of Criminology.

Morris, A., & G. M. Maxwell, 1993, "Juvenile Justice in New Zealand: A New Paradigm," *Australia & New Zealand Journal of Criminology*. 26, March, 72–90. {New Zealand}

Montana Board of Crime Control, 1996, Request for Proposals. Helena, Montana.

Pennsylvania Council on Crime and Delinquency, 1996, Request for Proposals, Harrisburg, Pennsylvania.

Palmer, T., 1994, *The Re-Emergence of Correctional Intervention*. Beverly Hills: Sage.

Pepinsky, H. E., & R. Quinney, 1991, *Criminology as Peacemaking*. Bloomington: Indiana University Press.

Reiss, A., 1986, "Why Are Communities Important in Understanding Crime?" pages 1–33 in A. J Reiss and M. Tonry (eds.), *Communities and Crime.* Chicago: University of Chicago Press.

Regnery, A., 1985, "Getting Away with Murder: Why the Juvenile Justice System Needs an Overhaul," *Policy Review* 34:65–68.

Rosenberg, I., 1993, "Leaving Bad Enough Alone: A Response to the Juvenile Court Abolitionists," *Wisconsin Law Review*, 1993, 163–185.

Schneider, A. (ed.), 1985, *Guide to Juvenile Restitution.* Washington, DC: Office of Juvenile Justice and Delinquency Prevention.

Schneider, A., 1986, "Restitution and Recidivism Rates of Juvenile Offenders: Results from Four Experimental Studies," *Criminology*, 24,(3), 533–552.

Schneider, A., 1990, *Deterrence and Juvenile Crime: Results From a National Policy Experiment.* New York: Springer-Verlag.

Schwartz, I. M., 1992, "Public Attitudes Toward Juvenile Crime and Juvenile Justice: Implications for Public Policy," pages 225–250 in I. Schwartz, *Juvenile Justice Policy.* Lexington, MA: Lexington Books.

Sparrow, M., M. Moore, & D. Kennedy, 1990, *Beyond 911.* New York: Basic Books.

Stuart, B., 1995a, "Circle Sentencing: Mediation and Consensus—Turning Swords into Ploughshares," unpublished paper. *Territorial Court of the Yukon.*

Stuart, B., 1995b, "Sentencing Circles: Making Real Differences," unpublished paper. *Territorial Court of the Yukon.*

Umbreit, M., 1994, *Victim Meets Offender: The Impact of Restorative Justice in Mediation.* New York: Criminal Justice Press.

Umbreit, M., and S. Stacy, 1996, "Family Group Conferencing Comes to the U.S.: A Comparison with Victim Offender Mediation," *Juvenile and Family Court Journal*, 29–39.

Van Ness, D., 1993, "New Wine and Old Wineskins: Four Challenges of Restorative Justice," *Criminal Law Forum*, 4(2) 251–276.

Van Ness, D., D. Carlson, T. Crawford & R. Strong, 1989, *Restorative Justice Practice.* Monograph. Justice Fellowship, Washington, DC.

Wachtel, T., 1995, "Family Group Conferencing: Restorative Justice in Practice," *Juvenile Justice Update* 1(4).

Walgrave, L., 1993, "Beyond Retribution and Rehabilitation: Restoration as the Dominant Paradigm in Judicial Interpretation in Juvenile Crime," paper presented at International Congress on Criminology, Budapest, Hungary.

Wilkins, L., 1995, *Punishment, Crime and Market Forces.* Brookfield, VT: Dartmouth Publishing Co.

Wright, M., 1991, *Justice for Victims and Offenders.* Buckingham, Open University.

Young, M., 1995, *Restorative Community Justice: A Call to Action.* Washington DC: Report for National Organization for Victim Assistance.

Zehr, H., 1990, *Changing Lenses: A New Focus for Crime and Justice.* Scottsdale, PA: Herald Press.

9

Communications in a Teen Court
Implications for Probation

Robert J. Beck

The Peer Court

In teen or peer courts, youths who have committed delinquent acts, such as driving under the influence, burglary, drug possession, and destruction of property, but who are considered good candidates for rehabilitation, are diverted from juvenile courts to a jury of their peers, but one with legal standing. Peer courts mostly deal with first-time offenders, and a key component is that the offender must sit on one or more future peer juries to determine sentences for other offenders. The oldest peer court comparable to current versions is held to have been established in Odessa, Texas, in 1983. In a large national study of teen courts, Godwin (1996) reported that some 250 teen courts were active in 30 states. Two basic models were analyzed: 1) trial models in which teens play the roles of prosecutors and defense attorneys and in some versions, judges; 2) peer jury models in which jurors question the status offenders directly and an adult or professional judge presides (Godwin, 1996, pp. 11–12). This study is of a peer jury model with juvenile court judges presiding in Orange County, California.

The purpose of the Orange County Peer Court is to provide an alternative sentencing program. In this court, when teen offenders are adjudged a dependent child of the court under the California Welfare and Institutions Code, Section 362 (a), "the court may make any and all reasonable orders for the care, supervision, custody, conduct,

Source: *Federal Probation*, 61(4) (December 1997): 40–48.

maintenance, and support of the minor." These orders are used to divert the teen from the juvenile court to the peer court. Under part (c) of this code, the juvenile court may order the parent(s) or guardian(s) of the child to participate in a counseling or parenting program operated by an appropriate community agency during a 6-month probationary period.

Seyfrit, Reichel, and Stutts (1987) have analyzed peer juries as a juvenile justice "diversion technique" since they constitute informal adjustment of low-risk cases through community participation. The Orange County Peer Court is a hybrid of both diversion and conventional juvenile justice programs. It is a diversion in that offenses heard do not appear on an offender's record and the informal adjustments are given over to a peer jury. However, in the courts observed, an official, robed judge or commissioner presides, and the proceedings have legal standing. Should probation sanctions be violated, the cases may be referred back to the juvenile court. Arnold Binder, an important historian and critic of diversion programs, has questioned whether the Orange County Peer Court is a true diversion since the primary stated objective is to determine sanctions. Moreover, there is no clear separation from the formal court as in diversions, the most notable confound being the presence of a juvenile court judge who, while receiving recommendations from the peer jury, has sole authority to order sentences (Arnold Binder, personal communication, November, 1996). Nonetheless, the teen court studied here refers to itself as "a diversion program." We conclude that the court's function is rehabilitative and diversionary in practice, if not strictly adhering to the rules of a classic diversion program.

The 2-hour peer court sessions were held after school in large high school multipurpose rooms or auditoriums. Before examination of individual cases (three to four per session), a volunteer attorney-advisor explains the purpose of the peer court to an audience of high school students and encourages them to maintain proper demeanor. The advisor explains that the intent of the court is to rehabilitate, as well as to provide sanctions. Subsequently, the judges in their opening remarks state that the goals of the peer court are to be helpful to the offenders and to satisfy justice. However, the printed instructions to jurors emphasize that they are to undertake their investigations to determine "appropriate consequences for illegal behavior."

Members of the audience are requested to volunteer to serve on peer juries. In some cases high school classes get credit for participating as an audience and for sitting on juries. The charges are read by a probation officer, and the jurors are sworn in by the judge. Opening statements are made by offenders and their parents, who sit alongside them. Sample guideline questions are provided to jurors. Jurors then question offenders and parents. However, the purpose of the inquiry is not to determine guilt since this has been previously admitted. While most questions are permitted, the judge may exclude those that are too personal or that do not speak to the offense. With the help of the attorney-advisor, the jury then deliberates and returns with sentencing recommendations. These may be adopted or adjusted by the judge, who then orders the sentence and turns the enforcement over to a probation officer and the offenders' parents.

In the Orange County Peer Court sentences cannot include fines or jail time and must be completed within 6 months. Typical sentences include combinations of the following: performing community service; making restitution; participating in future peer courts; interviewing victims and writing an essay; obeying curfews; attending drug and alcohol programs; attending school regularly; seeking or maintaining employment; not associating in negative peer relationships; and participating in specialized programs exposing teens to the realities of the criminal justice system, e.g., visiting the county jail.

Letting peers serve as juries and make sentencing recommendations sends a clear message that criminal behavior does not have peer approval, and the involvement of peers in questioning provides peer courts with shrewd insights into the behavior of adolescents. While the peer court movement is still very young and has undergone little formal evaluation and no previous observational research of court processes, informal results suggest that the peer court may be an effective institution, and its use is spreading rapidly. The city of Bend, Oregon, reports that 95 percent of first-time offenders have not become second-time offenders through their 18th birthday. The first year of the Orange County Peer Court resulted in a non-recidivism rate of 85 percent (Gwen Vieau, personal communication, February 1996). In an early study, Seyfrit, Reichel, and Stutts (1987) concluded from a small number of youths involved in the programs surveyed that the peer jury probably could handle more serious offenses and second-time offenders as effectively as the traditional system. They argued that the positive findings of the initial evaluation warranted more research. Hissong (1991) conducted the only evaluation study of a teen court using a control group. The research found that 75 percent of 196 cases selected for study were successful as compared with 64 percent of the non-teen court participants. a statistically significant difference. The strongest effect was for 16-year-old white males. However, Godwin (1996, p. 150) reports other data showing that older juveniles had higher recidivism rates and that program effectiveness diminished after 1 year.

The Peer Court as a Developmental Setting

The purpose of the present study was not to conduct a formal research investigation of peer court effectiveness. Rather, its objective was to analyze interactions in the court from the perspective of ecological developmental theory (Bronfenbrenner, 1979). This theory is applicable to the study of individuals, such as youth offenders and their parents, undergoing traumatic or stressful transition, in the context of a restorative culture or community, i.e., the peer court. According to Bronfenbrenner's (1979) model of human development, "an ecological transition occurs whenever a person's position in the ecological environment is altered as the result of a change in role, setting or both" (p. 26). By committing a status offense, a young person has become an offender in the eyes of the family and community and, therefore, has undergone a change of role, albeit a role that may be shed in time. When young offenders are introduced into the peer court, they thereby participate in a new ecological setting, with the attendant potential for change. The focus of this developmental change is rehabilitation of the offender:

> [F]rom the viewpoint of research, every ecological transition constitutes, in effect, a ready-made experiment of nature with a built-in, before-after design in which each subject can serve as his own control . . . [and] sets the stage both for the occurrence and the systematic study of developmental phenomena. (p. 27)

It is assumed that the "developmental phenomena" provided by the peer court are the potential for offenders and their families to learn and morally develop from these experiences. In this theory, when adolescents are arrested, they thereby are placed in a transitional setting with a new role: offender. Under such conditions adults are moved to rhetoric aimed at affording them a transition to societal standards. In fact, it was observed that this peer court was a highly productive context for bringing to the surface a variety of issues pertinent to the rehabilitation of the offender. This was so for a variety of reasons.

To reiterate, the stated purpose of the peer court and its general atmosphere is rehabilitative, in part, and this message is communicated by the judge and the attorney-advisors at the beginning of each court session. In addition, the peer court, when compared with conventional courts, is a relatively open process with respect to communications. Unlike a court of law, peer courts have few restrictions on issues discussed by peers and judges with youth offenders and their parents. For example, an issue such as parent-child trust would not ordinarily be raised in conventional courts. Most noteworthy, it involves input from a group, peers, with few preconceptions as to standard issues to be dealt with under such conditions. Parents are permitted to make statements as well, and these may involve defending or criticizing the offenders. The fact that the peer court takes place in a school setting also makes for greater informality in asking about and giving advice on a host of personal issues involved in rehabilitation. Because of all these qualities, the various interactions in the peer court produce a rich body of communications concerning the issues implicated in rehabilitation including rhetoric that offenders ought to reflect on their wrongdoing, its effect on others, and suggestions for changes in lifestyle. But what is to be learned by offenders, and which learning theories inform the court's objectives?

The architects of the peer court probably intended that learning take place according to behavioral learning theory, in which sanctions (punishments) are employed to extinguish unwanted behaviors such as offending and, according to cognitive learning theories, in which the goals are new self-understandings that lead to personal transformations, i.e., rehabilitation. From a behavioral learning perspective, the peer court offers the potential for peer and parental sanctions to supplement societal sanctions as instruments for change. Peer sanctions are delivered through jurors' implicit or explicit disapproval as communicated through questions to the offender, as well as by their recommendations of sanctions. In their opening statements and in response to juror questioning, parents also have the opportunity to condemn their children's offenses. While, as we shall see, not all parents expressed disapproval, they often were compelled to do so by answering juror questions directed at their response to the offense; and many parents, in fact, expressed shock and disappointment at seeing their child arrested and brought before the court.

From a cognitive learning perspective, the peer court offers the potential for offenders to acquire improved moral self-awareness. Again, the principal technique is jury questioning, which gets at a range of moral, emotional, and social issues to which adequate responses are expected. When peer jurors ask whether the offenders, before committing their offenses, had considered that they might be caught and punished, the answers reveal variable levels of self-awareness and moral intent. In appraising these understandings, the peer community is better able to calculate offenders' degree of risk for committing future offenses and is in a better position to adjust its interventions accordingly. Ultimately of course, this strategy is experimental in terms of the intended positive effect on the offender. As Bronfenbrenner (1979) theorizes, "To demonstrate that human development has occurred, it is necessary to establish that a change produced in the person's conceptions and/or activities carries over to other settings and other times" (p. 35). While, as we shall see, rehabilitation strategies and some evidence of learned behaviors characterize the peer court, the probation period offers a more extended timeframe and diverse programs in which to measure behaviors predictive of non-recidivism.

Research Approach: Sample and Method

The author observed peer court sessions to analyze how offenders, parents, judges, and juries performed their roles. Participating program administrators, probation officers, and some judges were interviewed. The sample consisted of cases involving 20 teen offenders, of whom 10 were white, 8 Hispanic, and 2 African-American. Sixteen males and four females were studied. A variety of offenses was represented including tagging, burglary, driving without a license, driving under the influence, and destruction of property. Questions used by jurors and judges were taken down in written notes. A content analysis was performed on the questions. Individual offenders and parents were qualitatively assessed for responsiveness to questions in court in order to indicate levels of moral self-understanding, emotional involvement, reasoning, and verbal production. The data were analyzed both to provide criteria for the design of probation programs and to discriminate key behaviors that might serve to protect offenders from reoffending.

Questioning in the Peer Court:
A Typology of Questions and Their Implications

While the opening statements of the offenders and their parents would be a logical point of departure, these communications were too brief to be of substantial value. Therefore, the study focused primarily on the issues raised by jury questioning and the quality of the offenders' and their parents' responses. Some 300 questions were asked during the 20 cases, approximately 80 percent by jurors. The judges' questions tended to probe into the details of the offense where offenders' previous answers were unclear. Judges also posed rhetorical questions about offenders' performance in school, and these led to other questions about career direction and to lectures about developing constructive purposes for their lives. After performing a content analysis, the following classes of questions were categorized:

I. Peer Pressure and Relationships

Friends' influence leading to the offense. Questions exploring the role of friends in causing the status offense. "Why did you go out after curfew with your friends?" "Were you with anybody (when tagging)?"

Relationship with friends since the offense. Questions probing how the incident has changed relationships. "Are you still friends with the girl (over whom you got into trouble)?" "Do you still hang with the same friends?"

While questions about friends' influences were used to determine the offenders' share of responsibility relative to those peers, they also were useful in provoking the offenders to consider the negative moral influences of such friends in their past and future lives.

II. Story of the Offense

Sequence of events. Questions inquiring into the precipitating events that led up to the offense. "Were the keys to the car (which you used for joyriding) left out or did you take them from the purse?" "Why were you going so fast at that point?" "How far away was your friend (when you drove without a license to pick her up)?" "Did you see the policeman?"

Opportunity. Questions getting at the role of opportunity in committing the offense. "How did being a cashier contribute to your offense?"

Questions eliciting the story of the offense primarily seemed oriented to enabling the jury to explore the offenders' levels of involvement in, and moral responsibility for, the offense and hence provided criteria for sanctions.

III. State of Mind

Premeditation. Questions probing at plans to commit the offense. "How much did you think about what you were going to do?"

Intention. Questions addressing the intent of the offenders during commission of the offense. "Why did you buy a spray can of paint?" "Did you get a buzz off the beer (before proceeding to drive without a license)?"

Motive. Questions addressing motivation during the offense. "Did you take the clothing to impress your friends?"

These questions were posed to get at the offenders' degree of responsibility, but probably also to induce them to consider their moral intentions at various stages of the offense.

IV. Getting Caught

Not admitting the offense. Questions probing why the offenders didn't admit their offenses at first. "Why didn't you call the police (instead of going home and later denying what you did)?"

Feelings. Questions asking the offenders how they felt when they got caught. "How did you feel when the cops arrived at your house?"

These relatively therapeutically oriented questions were intended to arouse the offenders' sense of responsibility and remorse for compounding their offenses.

V. Post-Offense Moral Self-Understanding

Moral understanding. Questions oriented to determining whether the offenders understood why an offense was wrong. "What was wrong with what you did?" Effect on self. Questions asking about the effects of the experience on the offenders. "What have you learned from this experience?" "What's been the worst thing about being caught?"

These questions, while primarily intended to provoke moral self-understanding, also could have been used by jurors to determine how well the offenders had learned their lessons since their offenses.

VI. Post-Offense Feelings

Offender remorse and other feelings. Questions about feeling sorry about the offense. "Are you sorry about what you did?"

Victim forgiveness. "Did the neighbors forgive you (for stealing)?"

These relatively therapeutic questions served different purposes: to increase the offenders' feelings of remorse, if they had expressed little; to elicit apologies for what they had done; and as a factor in prescribing sentences.

VII. Sanctions

Consideration of sanctions before the offense. Questions concerning thoughts about possible sanctions during commission of the offense. "Didn't you know you'd be caught?" "Weren't you afraid you'd be punished?"

Punishments after the offense. "How were you punished by your family for what you did?" "Did you think your family's punishment was fair?" "What kind of curfew do you have?"

Questions on family sanctions for offenses probably were used by the peer jury to estimate the offenders' response to punishment. Acceptance of family sanctions generally was taken to be a positive factor.

VIII. Reoffending

Probability of reoffending. Questions asking about the likelihood of the offense being repeated. "Do you think you'd do it again if you hadn't gotten caught?" Further risks. Questions about habits that could get the offenders in trouble again. "Do you drink?"

While these questions were designed to get at the probability of reoffending, they seemed to produce only ritualistic answers in which the offenders promised not to offend again.

IX. Offender Characteristics

Credibility. Inquiries questioning the offenders' credibility. "Why should we believe you now, when you denied doing it at first?"

Track record. Questions probing the offenders' "criminal history." "Is this the first time you tagged?"

Moral Character. Questions directly or indirectly referring to the offenders' moral character. "What were you thinking of going out at 2 A.M.?" "Well, if you're a leader, how come you followed the other girl (in tagging)?"

These questions were designed to show the offenders how their moral reputations could be damaged by their offenses. The answers also might have been used to determine how likely the offenders were to have been rehabilitated since the offense.

X. Family Relationships

Effects of the offense on parental relationships. Questions getting at the effects of the offense on the parents. "What did your parents have to say about it?" "How do you think this makes your mother feel?" "How has this incident affected family life?" "What kind of relationship do you have with your parents?"

Trust. Questions concerning the families' trust of the offenders. "Do your parents trust you now?" "Do you believe your son's story?"

Sibling relationships. Questions about bad influence on siblings. "Were you concerned about how your sister would take this?"

These important juror questions about disrupted family relationships, parental trust, and bad influence on siblings were probably intended to stimulate feelings of responsibility and also to make the offenders realize the importance of family relationships. Responses concerning the effects on family relationships would have been useful to the jury in estimating the role of the family in carrying out the probation sentence.

XI. School

Performance in school. Questions asking about the offenders' commitment to school and often suggesting the offenders would have done better to spend their free time on their school work and not on violating society's laws. "How are you doing in school?" "When do you do your homework?"

Future plans. Questions about future school plans. "Are you planning on going to college?"

Judges often queried the offenders about school. The drift of these questions was twofold. If questions determined that the offenders were doing poorly in school, in more than half the cases, then this would indicate a poor prognosis going forward; if it were determined that the offenders were doing well, then followup questions encouraged them to get the most out of their education and not to let criminal behavior ruin their prospects.

XII. Employment

Work history. Questions concerning employment. "Did you lose your job because you let those girls charge all those clothes?" "Have you gotten a job since the incident?"

Future plans. Questions about future plans. "What will you do after high school?"

These questions were aimed at finding out the offenders' level of responsibility in working to pay restitution and, more generally, to determine whether they were recontributing members of their families.

XIII. Leisure

Activities. Questions about preferred activities. "What do you do for fun?" "Do you party a lot?" "Do you belong to any clubs?"

These questions asked whether the offenders liked to party, with the inference that, if so, this was irresponsible and could get them into trouble. As none admitted to partying, this didn't figure in their sentences.

Analysis of the Typology of Questions

These 13 groups of questions, with a total of 27 categories, provide an empirically derived set of issues that were interpreted as having been potentially useful to the jurors as criteria for sentencing, to estimate the offenders' levels of moral understanding of their offenses, and to estimate how well the offenders had been rehabilitated before appearing in court.

One primary objective of a relatively "legal" set of questions, including groups I, II, VII, and VIII, was to provide the jury information on the juveniles' degree of responsibility, and their previous family punishments, in order to prescribe sanctions. Besides determining the offenders' involvements in the offense, the questions also addressed what possible strengths the offenders might have going forward or what risks they might have shed since the offense (such as bad peer influences) that would inform the jury as to whether the offenders were on track. However, there is no evidence suggesting that the juries made such correlations between apparent offender reform and the severity of their sentences.

A relatively "moral" set of questions included groups III, IV, V, VI, IX, and X. These questions directly addressed issues implicated in the rehabilitation of the offenders. such as their self-understanding, remorse, and relationships. Questions in these groups also were posed to get at the offenders' self-knowledge at various stages in the offense. Other questions, such as "what have you learned about yourself since the offense?" were trying to get at the offenders' capacity for moral self-understanding as an outcome of being arrested and the peer court process. Group X questions were preoccupied with the offenders' relationship with parents as an impact of the offense. The jury members were concerned with the effects on trust between parents and offenders since the offense and the juveniles' understandings and acceptance that trust had to be rebuilt.

The other main group of questions, XI, XII, and XIII, were concerned with school, work, and leisure activities. These questions, a kind of "lifestyle" set, were used by the jury to provoke awareness that such activities, particularly school, were vital to rehabilitation. Other examples were concerned with ill-advised use of leisure time—Has the offender started to party, where he previously indicated he would not?—or work—Has the offender gotten a job to pay restitution? These questions, while theoretically of use in sentencing, seemed to focus more on what juveniles needed in their future life to make it productive. Above all, this meant working hard in school. Some judges also commented about certain offenders that "they had a lot going for them," particularly with respect to doing well in school or having good family support. One objective of diversions from the conventional court would be to provide experiences for youths that surpassed the administration of justice alone. In a review of the history of diversion programs, Binder (1988) concluded that they were most effective when juvenile needs were taken into account and where help was more important than sanction.

Analysis of these communications reveals that this diversion goal was met. Only part of the work of the peer court is strictly "legal" or oriented to the assessment of sanctions. Clearly recognizing that the peer court is rehabilitative in purpose, the jurors sought to use these sessions to induce the offenders to review a host of personal characteristics and their conduct of social relationships that should be assessed in order to make constructive changes in their lives.

Responses to Questioning

There were different levels of response to questions. Answers varied from 1) minimally responsive, "I don't know"; 2) moderately responsive, providing short answers, and 3) highly responsive, in which the offenders indicated self-awareness of the meanings of their offenses and expressed remorse meaningfully.

Offenders' Performance in the Peer Court

The offenders' verbalizations can be classified in terms of the degree of moral self-understanding, emotional involvement, reasoning, and verbal production they display. A significant percentage of young offenders (35 percent, N = 7) who appeared before the peer court displayed minimal communications in response to inquiry by the court into their offenses. Some offenders' responses were very brief, poorly vocalized, and inarticulate. Although the fact of being on public display could certainly have been an inhibiting factor, part of such offenders' problems, in fact, was their inability to communicate, reason about, or articulate their feelings about their offenses. For example, a boy who tagged a phone booth argued only that he had never done anything like that before. Or, a girl who had allowed two teens to be charged only $8.50 for $500 worth of clothes said, merely, that this was wrong because it was illegal. In contrast, other offenders (15 percent, N = 3) were able to make relatively elaborate statements about the offense including understanding that it was wrong by expressing some sort of self-criticism ("I was stupid to drive without a license"), by indicating that they had caused grief to their families, and by pledging not to do anything like that again. In other words, these offenders demonstrated moral self-awareness, expressed remorse, and made a commitment to productive behavior in the future. A more cynical perspective might appraise such responses as lies in the service of making a good impression. Half the cases (50 percent, N = 10) exhibited a moderate level of responsiveness.

However, if responses to these questions indicated that an offender was influenced by friends, but no longer had these friends, and that he now understood how peer pressure could get him in trouble, presumably he would be relatively more rehabilitated and less likely to reoffend than a teen who had kept these friends and displayed little understanding of peer pressure. Conversely, if answers indicated that the juvenile was likely to be engaged in risky behavior, had a poor relationship with parents, and had expressed little remorse, these might have indicated weaker rehabilitation and, therefore, a higher probability of reoffending.

Parents' Performance in the Peer Court

The relatively few questions asked of parents were generally of the following types: 1) "What was your reaction to your child doing this?"

2) "Do you approve of your child's friends (who were implicated in the offense)?" 3) "How did you punish your child?"

The parental responses provided information to the jury about some of the same rehabilitation issues as analyzed for the offenders. Parents' court performance varied as widely as offenders' and also might be used as diagnostic or predictive criteria. For example, five parents or other caregivers exhibited dysfunctional responses, including displays of a lack of moral understanding, and appeared to be relatively detached from their children's offenses. These parents said little and either only expressed mild disapproval or no disapproval. Neither had they punished their children before appearance in the peer court. Sometimes, these poor communications were only made in defense of the child. A common statement was that "the child doesn't give me trouble at home." One parent excused his child as simply succumbing to temptation. Expressing disappointment in her son, another parent devoted most of her responses to her own reactions. Moreover, some of these parents may have unwittingly depreciated or compromised the peer court through their needs to protect their children from a threat outside the family or due to nervousness. Some parents were observed displaying a number of inappropriate responses including laughing and joking, defending children's behavior, and protesting the jury's sentence. These kinds of parents apparently required rehabilitation themselves.

However, half of the parents expressed strong disapproval of their children's actions, had previously administered punishments, threatened future loss of freedom or fines, and spoke convincingly of the pain and suffering this problem had caused them. Such parents' performances were noted by judges as productive. One mother, whose English language skills were poor, but who expressed herself passionately about her child's need for moral reform, was told by the judge that "she was handling herself very well."

Within the group of participating parents, they were equally divided as to whether they offered a defense or condemned their children's actions. It is uncertain whether a defense is a positive or negative indicator. It could be a protective factor indicating parent-child closeness, but such defenses often seemed to preclude criticism of teens. Parents who both defended and criticized their children, indicating both closeness and taking the offense seriously, seemed to afford offenders the most protection in this investigator's perspective.

Is the Peer Court a Rehabilitation Setting?

As we have argued, in principle, all the questions satisfied the court's needs to estimate the sanctions required for different offenders. Particularly important in this respect is how much previous punishment had been administered by the family, the amount of remorse shown, and how much blame was accepted. But, to reiterate, the intent of the peer court as stated by its avowed, printed goals and instruction to jurors was also to help offenders become rehabilitated by understanding and forming appropriate emotional responses to their offenses. And it was observed that jurors took this goal as seriously as the need to determine consequences for offenders. Both the jurors' and judges' questions opened up rehabilitation and moral development issues that indicated that the peer court was being used as a rehabilitative setting.

The "moral" groups of questions are relevant to this purpose. Help for juveniles would be enhanced if during their court appearances they reflected on these questions, so as to learn from their experiences, and developed motives and attitudes for altering their lives. Most convincingly, approximately two-thirds of the questions asked, in particular the "moral" and "lifestyle" questions, stimulated young offenders to reflect on past experiences and consider lifestyle activities that either could doom them, such as dropping out of school, or diminish their risk, such as dropping their so-called friends who had gotten them into trouble. And while the responses to these kinds of questions also provided jurors with measures of the extent to which they had already learned from their offending experience, and hence offered information relevant to sentencing, they had the apparent effect of expanding some offenders' understanding and emotional response to the offense, at least as communicated to the jurors. There is no way, of course, that the sincerity of these communications can be verified. But one may surely form the hypothesis that, to the extent to which the offenders responded pointedly, appropriately, convincingly, and extensively to jurors' questions, these measures would predict future rehabilitative behavioral indicators, such as increased moral self-understanding and positively changed lifestyle.

If the peer court is a rehabilitative setting, then it should be regarded as a kind of "community screening," or triage, where the offenders' problems are assessed and advice and recommendations are given immediately. The social, emotional, moral, and lifestyle issues addressed in this rehabilitative setting provide evidence of the peer community's insights and views on the pertinent topic problems and constructive strategies for youth offenders. And while these peer constructions of the offense and the offenders' recovery from arrest and punishment can only provide some of the criteria for their rehabilitation, the issues they raise should be taken seriously. And, further, if interactions in the peer court provided useful issues along the themes formulated by the clusters of questions that have been analyzed, then these issues ought to constitute design criteria to frame the problems and suggest programs that would serve to extend the work of the peer court during probation.

Implications of the Research

Peer Court Reform

Intrinsic to the idea of questioning offenders is that the jurors acquire critical information about them that is useful to recommend sanctions. This was the expectation of judges, attorney-advisors, and probation officers. But, paradoxically, there was little or no correlation between what the jurors learned from their investigations and their ensuing recommendations for sanctions. There was little variation of sanctions, no matter which questions were asked, nor of the quality and fulsomeness of the answers. There were exceptions: heavy sanctions were given to a girl who thought she could smile her way out of anything. But some teens who were both asked good questions and answered well were given stiff sentences. While all juror questions have been interpreted as logically providing criteria for sentencing, in fact the information the jury received was not used for that purpose. Future research is needed to determine jury members' understanding of the intent of their own questions, their appraisal of offender answers, and the relationship of either questions or answers to the sanctions they recommend.

Probation Programs

Family Mediation Program. The findings provide several criteria for recommending a family mediation program for selected families, e.g., the 35 percent of this sample whose communications to the court were minimal or unproductive. Problems managed by family mediation are conflict resolution skills, communications skills, and agreements about everyday behavior and rules. Family mediation programs would be valuable for those parents and teens in the peer court who disagreed publicly about the causes and effects of the offense and for those parents who explicitly mentioned conflicts between themselves and their children over discipline, school, friends, and lifestyle. In other contexts, it is a common practice for juveniles who are diverted from the juvenile justice system to be recommended to family mediation. There is considerable evidence connecting family conflict, poor resolution skills, and children's conduct disorders (Amato & Keith, 1991). Families who admitted to having poor relationships, but which were apparently not severe enough to warrant family counseling, also would be good candidates for transformative mediation (Bush & Folger, 1994), whose objectives are to develop family relationships through moral transformation. Recently, Beck and Turk (1995) have developed "Family Peacemakers," a 10-hour program that operationalizes transformative mediation goals by developing and ensuring the performance of agreements concerning discipline and school involvement. The program seeks to promote change by transforming working relationships around everyday issues, uses video review of sessions to promote civil family discourse, and provides specialized mediation training for mothers or other female caregivers.

Moral Literacy Program. Given the moral content of many of the jurors' questions, it was concluded that the court was, effectively, a moral rehabilitative setting. It is recommended that the offenders' moral understanding of their offenses and social effects be a more specialized target program during probation as well. An interesting note is that the offenders are frequently required to write an essay demonstrating their understanding of their offenses and the victims' points of view. Informal evidence suggests that these essays are not generally successful, suffering from the same communications problems as the offenders' oral responses to questions in court. Yet the process offers great potential for *metacognitive learning.* In this regard, it is proposed that a probation program be designed that would direct offenders toward more intensive *reflection* on their offenses. This would be accomplished by requiring written answers to the full range of peer court questions that have been categorized and by encouraging offenders to organize their responses into a narrative demonstrating *autobiographic understanding* of the problem. Thus, for example, with respect to peer pressure, this causal factor should be reviewed in the offenders' essays to include events before the offense in question, and it should explore their needs for peer approval. Offenders also should review their feelings about, and compliance with, family discipline. An ideal metacognitive outcome would be to structure an autobiographic essay that spoke to many of the issues raised by the typology, of questions, placed the issues in historically grounded examples, and used language indicative of self-understanding that one needed to move beyond these high-risk, immature, social relationships. Finally, in these essays offenders also would report on their experiences of participation on peer juries (as part of their sentences) and any altered self-understandings that resulted.

Mother Mediation Training Program. As Bronfenbrenner (1979) theorizes, children's development is contingent on the ecological roles of third parties in mediating between children and important socializing institutions such as schools and the juvenile justice system. A recent study by Beck and Wood (1993) found that mothers and fathers in ordinary family socialization practices used informal mediation techniques to resolve fights between siblings and resulting conflicts between parents and children. Parents mediated disputes by telling their children stories about past conflicts involving the siblings' mutual responsibilities for fights. They also induced siblings to question their own motives in starting fights and to empathize with how they had hurt each other. Observational research has pointed more directly to the strategic role of women as family peacemakers in resolving everyday conflicts (Vuchinich, Emery, & Cassidy, 1988). Moreover, Van Slyck, Newland, and Stern (1992) found that success in mediation is predicted by a highly involved mother who perceives family conflicts as serious. These same researchers also referred to the well-known fact and intuitively satisfying proposition that adolescents prefer to discuss their problems with their mother. Mediation training is required for family members who could provide a permanent family resource to resolve conflicts. Mothers, older daughters, and grandmothers are the most well-situated figures to play the role of permanent family peacemakers to greatest advantage.

Prediction of Non-recidivism

It is suspected that offenders' performances in the peer court, and behavior during interventions such as in family mediation and moral literacy programs, could provide indicators of offenders' potential for reoffending. Consider the following protective factors that have been interpreted from court questions and responses. Each factor demonstrates that a particular form of learning has taken place and figures in a complex of factors that would potentially prevent future criminal behavior. The presence of the following indicators would constitute protective factors against recidivism:

1. Moral learning: indicated by statements communicating an understanding of why the actions were wrong, empathic understanding of those who have been hurt, and promises not to repeat offenses.

2. Social learning—parents: indicated by awareness that the parent-child relationship and trust have been negatively affected by the offense, that one needs to win back trust, and that one understands the value of the family.

3. Social learning—peers: indicated by awareness of how peer pressure worked to cause the offense and avowals to drop relationships that contributed to deviant acts.

4. Emotional learning: indicated by expressions of responsibility, remorse, and an emotionally sincere commitment not to reoffend.

5. Metacognitive learning: indicated by statements demonstrating self-understanding of how one got into trouble and self-assess-

ments that one has been changed constructively by the experience.

6. Learning through sanctions: indicated by statements expressing readiness to accept sanctions.

7. Lifestyle responsibility: indicated by commitments to work hard in school, to seek or continue employment, and to make contributions to the family.

Are offenders' behaviors demonstrating moral, social, emotional, metacognitive, and behavioral learning, as articulated above, predictive of non-recidivism? Does the presence of such behaviors during court appearances or during probation programs indicate diminished risk factors for future offenses? Age of the offender and severity of the offense also might need to be weighted. Further research is needed to determine which of these specific court and probation program indicators, or combination of indicators, is most predictive of non-recidivism.

References

Amato, P. R., & Keith, B. (1991). Parental divorce and the well-being of children: A meta-analysis. *Psychological Bulletin, 110*, 26–46.

Beck, R. J., & Turk, A. M. (1995). *Family Peacemakers: A manual for mediating youth offender and family relationships.* Unpublished manuscript.

Beck, R. J., & Wood, D. (1993). The dialogic socialization of aggression in a family's court of reason and inquiry. *Discourse Processes, 16*(3), 341–362.

Binder, A. (1988). Juvenile diversion: History and current status. In A. R. Roberts (Ed.), *Justice policies, programs, and services.* Chicago: Dorsey Press.

Bronfenbrenner, U. (1979). *The ecology of human development.* Cambridge: Harvard University Press.

Bush, R. A. B., & Folger, J. P. (1994). *The promise of mediation: Responding to conflict through empowerment and recognition.* San Francisco: Jossey-Bass.

Godwin, T. M. (1996). *Peer justice and youth empowerment: An implementation guide for teen court programs.* Washington, DC: National Highway Safety Administration, Department of Transportation, and the Office of Juvenile Justice and Delinquency Prevention, Department of Justice.

Hissong, R. (1991). Teen court: Is it an effective alternative to traditional sanctions? *Journal for Juvenile Justice and Detention Services 6*(2), 14–23.

Seyffir, C. L., Reichel, P. L., & Stutts, B. L. (1987). Peer juries as a juvenile justice diversion technique. *Youth and Society, 18*(3), 302–316.

Van Slyck, M. R., Newland, L. M., & Stern, M. (1992). Parent-child mediation: Integrating theory research, and practice. *Mediation Quarterly, 10*(2), 193–208.

Vuchinich, S., Emery, R. E., & Cassidy, J. (1988). Family members as third parties in dyadic family conflict: Strategies, alliances and outcomes. *Child Development, 59*(5), 1293–1302.

10

The Mediation Process

Kimberly K. Kovach

Overview

Mediation is facilitated negotiation. It is a process by which a neutral third party, the mediator, assists disputing parties in reaching a mutually satisfactory resolution. At first glance, the definition of mediation appears simple. Yet over the last few years, especially within the Alternate Dispute Resolution (ADR) field, very few items spark more controversy than the definition of mediation. In fact, it has been alleged that the term "mediator" is now used so loosely that no one may safely presume that a speaker intends its original meaning: helping people to reach their own settlement.[1] Of course debate about the "original" definition of mediation is also possible.

The term mediate is derived from the Latin "mediare," which means "to be in the middle."[2] Certainly the mediator finds himself in the middle of a dispute. But mediation involves much more than placement of the mediator. A variety of definitions for the term "mediation" exist. While these definitions differ, and are subject to debate, most people agree on the purpose of the process: to assist people in reaching a voluntary resolution of a dispute or conflict. Definitional debates primarily surround the specifics of how the assistance is actually provided.

Some of the more basic definitions of mediation include:

- The broad term describing the intervention of third parties in the dispute resolution process.[3]

Reprinted from *Mediation: Principles and Practice* by Kimberlee K. Kovach, pp. 16–29, copyright 1994 by West Publishing Co. with permission of the West Group.

- A process in which a third party facilitates and coordinates the negotiation of disputing parties.[4]

- The intervention into a dispute or the negotiation process by an acceptable impartial and neutral third party who has no authoritative decision-making power. This individual will assist disputing parties in voluntarily reaching their own neutral acceptable settlement of the issues in dispute.[5]

- A process where third parties not involved in the controversy assist disputing parties in their negotiations.[6]

- A private, voluntary, informal process where a party-selected neutral assists disputants to reach a mutually acceptable agreement.[7]

- Mediation is a process by which a third party neutral, whether one or more, acts as a facilitator to assist in the resolving of a dispute between two or more parties. It is a non-adversarial approach to conflict resolution where the parties communicate directly. The role of the mediator is to facilitate communication between the parties, assist them on focusing on real issues of the dispute, and generate options for settlement. The goal of this process is that the parties themselves arrive at a mutually acceptable resolution of the dispute.[8]

- A voluntary process where an impartial mediator actively assists disputants in identifying and clarifying issues of concern and in designing and agreeing to solutions.[9]

- A forum in which an impartial person, the mediator, facilitates communication between parties to promote reconciliation, settlement, or understanding among them.[10]

- A process in which a neutral third party assists the parties in developing and exploring their underlying interests (in addition to their legal positions), promotes the development of options and assists the parties toward settling the case through negotiations.[11]

- In its simplest term, mediation is trying to get two people to do that which they least want to do—talk to each other.[12]

The number and variety of definitions demonstrate that the mediation process is a flexible one. Although there is a structure to the mediation process, it is not rigid, but rather fluid in nature. Many other definitions of mediation are subject matter specific and often dictate diverse approaches. Since the mediation process deals with human behavior and motivation, it must also be adaptable to individual differences.

There is little doubt that the use of the mediation process has grown tremendously and will continue to do so. Much of this growth can be attributed to the process itself rather than the mediator.[13] The process which is our focus is not new. In fact, the process is deep rooted, having developed over a long period of time.

Historical Perspectives

When looking for a historical reference to the initial use of mediation, commentators often quote the Bible. Yet it can be argued that mediation was used long before recorded history, particularly in the broad context where a third party neutral served several functions. This brief historical perspective will primarily focus on the mediator in a role close to the term as we currently know it. It should be remembered, however, that because it is a flexible process, mediation has varied over its long history, influenced in part by the circumstances of its use.

International Sphere

Use of mediation, similar to that which we see today, can be traced back several hundreds, even thousands of years.[14] Mediation was used in China and Japan as a *primary* means of conflict resolution. The mediative approach was not an alternative to fighting or adversarial approaches to problem solving. Rather, mediation was the first choice for dispute settlement. Those cultures placed emphasis on peace-making and peace-keeping. A win or lose approach was not an acceptable means of resolution. For instance, China's principle use of mediation was a direct result of the Confucian view of natural harmony and dispute resolution by morals rather than coercion.[15] Chinese society therefore placed emphasis on the mediative or conciliatory approach to conflict. This has continued throughout history within that culture. Chinese mediation boards or committees are made up of several individuals from each local community and resolve more than 80 percent of all civil disputes. Today the mediation boards in China, termed People's Mediation Committees (PMCS) are the dominant institution for mediation and resolve over 7.2 million disputes per year.[16] They assist in maintaining peace and social control throughout both urban and rural communities.

In Japan, conciliation was historically the primary means of resolution with village leaders serving as mediators.[17] Current Japanese negotiation style still places an emphasis on the relationship and is often regarded as a purely conciliatory style.[18] In a negotiation, particularly in the business world, time is spent on building the relationship, without which a final agreement may not occur.

Informal dispute resolution was used in many other cultures as well. For example, Scandinavian fishermen, African tribes, and Israeli Kibbutzim all valued peace and harmony over conflict, litigation and victory.[19] The use of mediation in a historical perspective can also be seen in attempts at resolution of matters between disputing nations.[20] Some of the principles of informal dispute resolution, or mutual satisfaction in settlement rather than conceding power, made their way to the United States.

United States

The history of current mediation use in the United States has two distinct paths, neither of which is within the formal legal system. One course by which mediation developed was as a method of providing community justice. Disputes in the labor arena were the other area of historical development. It is only very recently that the courts have considered the use of mediation.

Often overlooked, however, is the application of mediative approaches to conflict by both Native Americans and colonists. In the Native American culture, peacemaking is the primary method of problem solving. More conciliatory than mediation, peacemaking is concerned with sacred justice. Disputes are handled in a way which deals with underlying causes of conflict, and mends relationships.[21] Native Americans continue to use peacemaking today.[22]

Upon settlement in the United States, various groups within the colonies placed a major emphasis on maintenance of peace. The very close proximity of living arrangements, along with the need for joint efforts in survival against the crown, contributed to peacekeeping endeavors.[23] The cultural priority of community consensus over an individual adversarial approach to conflict served as the basis for the use of mediation and other informal means of dispute settlement.[24] In addition, many colonists had developed a negative view of the legal profession, and consequently the use of litigation as a means of dispute settlement was explicitly discouraged. Accordingly, these settlers went about settling their own disputes.[25]

However, by the end of the seventeenth century, use of these nonlegalistic dispute resolution methods was in decline. A number of factors accounted for this. The population increased, and with growth and mobility, the sense of community dissipated. Moreover, the development of commerce and industry resulted in more complex dealings, use of documents, and the need for commercial laws. A large portion of common law, initially avoided, was then seen as practical and acceptable, though not in all respects.[26] Competitiveness replaced a cooperative approach to problem solving, and overt conflict increased. Litigation took a greater role in assisting in the resolving of disputes by providing a framework for order and authority.[27]

The other distinct area in which mediation was historically used was in the labor industry. In the early industrial United States, when disputes occurred within business, quick resolutions were imperative. This was particularly important where the conflict was between labor and management, and if left unresolved, could lead to strikes and a shut down of industry. As labor became unionized and disputes were common, Congress reacted in 1913 by creating the Department of Labor, and providing that the Secretary of Labor act as mediator.[28] Mediation was used so that disputes could be settled expeditiously, and strikes avoided. A speedy resolution promoted the ongoing relationship between the factions, which was very important to the continued economic development of the United States. As the area of labor relations developed,[29] and need for mediation increased, Congress in 1947, created the Federal Mediation and Conciliation Service (FMCS).[30] An independent federal agency, FMCS has jurisdiction over disputes in industries which engage in interstate commerce, private non-profit health facilities, and agencies of the federal government.[31] The Federal Mediation and Conciliation Service is still quite active today, primarily focused on mediating in labor disputes.[32]

For the general population, courts became the primary dispute resolvers, replacing communities and churches. Yet, dissatisfaction with the courts was expressed. This dissatisfaction primarily centered on issues of expense and time, although there was some concern with the complete legalization of disputes[33] as well as the relinquishing of decision making to outside parties. This dissatisfaction served as the catalyst for the current ADR movement. While the current use of mediation has some of the colonial and labor characteristics and philosophy, its primary focus is serving as an option, or adjunct, to the courts.

Current "Movement"

The current ADR movement is most often regarded as beginning with the Pound Conference in 1976.[34] Prior to that, however, there existed several programs, a few of which originally came about as a response to the conflict surrounding the civil rights movement. Others originated as an alternative method of community justice. For example, the American Arbitration Association (AAA)[35] was active in setting up pilot mediation projects funded by the Ford Foundation in the late sixties. These projects were an attempt to ease social tensions through the use of mediation. In the early seventies, the American Arbitration Association also established Dispute Resolution Centers in Philadelphia and Rochester. Cases were referred to the centers from the local court system.[36]

In 1971, through a grant from the United States Department of Justice, Law Enforcement Assistance Administration (LEAA), the Columbus, Ohio City Prosecutor's Office established a mediation program for citizens' disputes. This was the first court system sponsored dispute resolution program. It utilized law students who served as mediators to help resolve disputes involving minor criminal actions. In 1977, the program was designated by LEAA as exemplary, and its replication throughout the country was encouraged.[37] In 1975 the Institute for Mediation and Conflict Resolution opened in New York City, which pioneered mediation program development on the East Coast. While these programs introduced mediation to the legal system and the community, it was only in these select locations. There was no systematic development or coordination of these mediation programs until the Pound Conference.

The Pound Conference was called to commemorate the 70th anniversary of Dean Roscoe Pound's dissertation on the public's dissatisfaction with the American legal system.[38] It was at this Conference that the current "movement" was actually born. Conference attendees included federal judges, court administrators, and legal scholars in the American Bar Association who wanted to take a closer look at exactly why people were so dissatisfied with the way justice was administered in the United States. One focus was on the often criticized, overcrowded, and costly court system. The conference consisted of a series of discussions and debates, and a follow-up task force was established.

One result of the conference was a pilot project, consisting of the creation of three Neighborhood Justice Centers (NJC).[39] These centers were to be located in Kansas City, Los Angeles, and Atlanta, and were designed to determine if the mediation process could assist in resolving "minor disputes." Funding for the creation of these pilot centers and their evaluation was obtained from the Law Enforcement Assistance Administration (LEAA) Division of the Department of Justice. Each center proved to be successful in bringing about timely and inexpensive resolutions of disputes.[40] Cases were referred to the centers from local courts. Trained volunteers served as mediators, and in most instances the services were offered at no cost to the disputants. Party satisfaction with the process was high.[41] Based partially upon the results from these three centers, additional experimental centers were established. Today, there are over 400 centers throughout the country. While the centers were designed to provide a form of community justice, most were related to the legal system, by either court or local bar associations sponsorship.[42] Many centers have expanded to handle more than "minor" matters, and are not located in the neighborhoods. Hence, most have been renamed Dispute Resolution Centers. There is at least one in every state, and many states have a systemwide network of centers.[43]

The work of these centers led to the development of ADR use in the court system. There are a number of reasons which account for this transition. First, many of the centers were located in or near the courthouse. Second, since the programs were often sponsored by bar associations, many of the individuals who worked as center volunteers were attorneys and judges. These lawyers and judges observed firsthand the benefits of mediation and recognized that ADR processes were successful in resolving many problems. Those involved began to believe that if these processes work well in smaller matters, perhaps they would be helpful in larger ones as well.[44] The applicability of ADR in pending lawsuits became clear.

Simultaneously, the idea of a "multi-door" courthouse began to surface. This concept, which was first articulated by Professor Frank Sander at the Pound Conference,[45] basically consists of a process by which an individual can locate the most appropriate method of resolving a dispute. There is one building, or courthouse, where individuals can go to obtain a multitude of services. The individual seeking assistance would first see an interviewer, called an intake specialist, who would help assess the problem. Thereafter, the party would be directed to the most appropriate "door" for resolution of the problem. Behind these doors an individual could find a number of processes including mediation, arbitration, litigation and social services.

In the mid-eighties, the ABA Standing Committee on Dispute Resolution sponsored and assisted in the establishment of experimental multi-door centers in three cities: Tulsa, Houston, and Washington, D.C. Additional multi-door courthouses have been created in Burlington, New Jersey and Middlesex County, Massachusetts. The design of this experiment, with the location of these "doors" within the courthouse, led many to realize the applicability of ADR processes to disputes even after a lawsuit was filed. Judges heard about these processes, and realized that most cases settle, but do so very late in the case. Judges realized that by referring a matter to a dispute resolution process early, a settlement could occur more expeditiously—with generally more satisfied participants. By the late eighties, experimentation with ADR in pending litigation was on-going. Today, in many courts, both state and federal, ADR is an integral part of pre-trial procedure.

Dissection of the Mediation Process

Discussions about what mediation is are plentiful. Because of its inherent flexibility and wide application, mediation is an art, not a science. Debate occurs about whether, as an art, it can be learned. While many purport that mediators are born, not made, mediation training occurs every day. And although the mediator may be seen as an artist with attendant creativity, the process itself is subject to some technical analysis.

Generally: Traditional Models

Mediation has been given many definitions, the broadest being simply the facilitation of a settlement between individuals. The intermediary or mediator basically serves as a go-between for individuals or groups with different opinions, outlooks, ideas, and interests. Over the years of mediation's growth, a variety of outlines or views of the process have developed. Once individuals became familiar with the fundamentals of mediation, a number of modifications took place. However, it is important to first become familiar with the basics of each stage of the mediation process. A variety of authors and trainers have enumerated the stages or segments of mediation. These may range from a four- or five-stage model to one with ten or more stages. The majority of these set forth the same basic concepts, and recognize the inherent fluidity of the process.

For educational purposes, the process can be separated into nine stages, all of which should be present in nearly every mediation. In addition, there are four components of the process which are considered optional. While these stages are often part of the mediation process, they frequently occur as part of another stage. Resolution may also be reached without involvement of these steps. The optional stages are listed in parenthesis, close to where, if used, they would occur. Employment of these optional stages will depend upon the parties, the nature of the matter, and the mediator's style. The basic model is as follows:

Preliminary Arrangements

Mediator's Introduction

Opening Statements by Parties

(Ventilation)

Information Gathering

Issue Identification

(Agenda Setting)

(Caucus)

Option Generation

(Reality Testing)

Bargaining and Negotiation

Agreement

Closure

The following provides a brief introductory description of each.

The preliminary arrangement stage encompasses everything that happens prior to beginning the actual mediation session. This includes matters of referral, getting to the mediation table, selection of the mediator, the determination of who should attend, issues of fees, settlement authority issues, timing and court orders. Moreover, from the standpoint of the mediator, this stage also includes items such as gathering or gaining information from the parties or their attorneys, as well as dissemination of information about the mediator and mediation process to the parties. Selection of the location, the room or rooms to be used, and arrangement of furniture are also part of the preliminary arrangements stage of the process. Because it is the first stage, initial decisions about the process are made as part of preliminary arrangements. The impact on the process is considerable, and the importance of preliminary matters should not be overlooked.

The mediator's introduction is just that. The mediator introduces himself, the parties, and their representatives; describes the process; and sets out any ground rules that will be followed. By doing this, the mediator provides time for the parties to become comfortable. Goals and objectives from mediator's standpoint may be set out here, as well as any housekeeping details. This introduction sets the stage for the remainder of the mediation.

In the opening statements, the parties and/or their representatives are invited to make an uninterrupted presentation of their view of the case or dispute. It is important that each side be given this opportunity, and not be interrupted by either the other party or the mediator. The opening statement stage is the time for parties to fully express and explain to the mediator, and more importantly, to each other, in their own words, how they view the dispute. Ideally, there should be little restriction placed on the opening statements. However, in complex, multi-party cases, it may be necessary to establish time limits.

If the parties' opening statements do not provide a clear or complete picture of what the dispute is about, as often they do not, the mediator will engage the parties in an information gathering process. In most instances additional information is necessary, and the mediator should ask open-ended questions. During either the opening statements or the information-gathering process, the disputing parties may need to express their feelings. This is termed venting or ventilation. It is important to afford individuals an opportunity to ventilate their frustration, anger, and emotions. Often, if such emotions are not expressed, the dispute cannot be resolved.

Once it appears that sufficient information about the case has been exchanged, the mediator will attempt to identify exactly what issues are in dispute. This may or may not be similar to identifying the underlying interests of the parties.[46] Once the mediator has the issues identified, he will move the parties toward generating ideas, options or alternatives which might resolve the case. It is usually during these two stages (identifying issues and underlying interests and option generation) that the mediator may meet privately with each party. This is also termed caucusing. It is advisable, however, that some attempt at issue identification take place while the parties are together so that there is an agreement between the disputing parties and the mediator as to the actual issues in dispute. In complex cases, the mediator may also want to set an agenda, that is, determine which issues will be dealt with in a specific order. There are a variety of strategies with regard to agenda setting.

Once the potential options or alternatives for settlement have been identified by the parties and the mediator, the negotiation process begins. This is the "give and take" part of the mediation, where the mediator assists the parties in their bargaining. As part of this process, the mediator may also engage in "reality testing," that is, checking out with each side the realistic possibility of attaining what he or she is hoping for. If the parties are in a purely positional bargaining approach,[47] this will also help to move them off of unrealistic positions.

If the negotiations result in an agreement, the mediator will restate it and in many instances, draft either the complete agreement or a memorandum of settlement. If no agreement is reached, the mediator will restate where the parties are, noting any progress made in the process. The final stage of the process is closure, although in some models there is subsequent action on the part of the mediator.

While the process usually consists of these stages, it is designed to be flexible, and often there is a variation in the occurrence of one or more of the stages. Some of the stages may overlap; and many times the mediator must revisit one or more of the stages.

A number of mediation trainers see the stages a bit differently. Moore has described the process as including twelve stages, five of which take place prior to the actual mediation session. These pre-session events include collecting background information, designing a plan for mediation, and building trust and cooperation.[48]

One of the oldest ongoing programs, The Columbus, Ohio Night Prosecutor Program, in conjunction with the Center for Dispute Resolution at Capital University Law and Graduate Center utilizes a seven-stage model of mediation. The stages are

- Introduction
- Problem determination
- Summarizing
- Issue identification
- Generation and evaluation of alternatives
- Selection of appropriate alternatives
- Conclusion[49]

Folberg and Taylor also use a seven-stage model, which is as follows:

1. Introduction
2. Fact finding and isolation of issues
3. Creation of options and alternatives
4. Negotiation and decision making
5. Clarification and writing a plan
6. Legal review and processing
7. Implementation, review, and revision

They do acknowledge that not all stages will be completed in every case, and that other authors and practitioners may divide the stages differently or use different labels.[50] Compared with most models, this model is "bottom heavy"; the majority of models do not focus on activity after an agreement is reached.

Recent Adaptations and Modifications

It is beyond this work to belabor the discussion about the use of the more traditional model, also labeled purist or classic, versus recent adaptations and modifications. Even where the process is traditional, the mediator possesses a great amount of control in how it is conducted. The ability to adapt and modify the mediation process is a primary benefit of its use. Yet some argue whether "true" mediation exists, or whether it should be called something else. For instance, one well known critique was that once the court systems and lawyers got into mediation, it was the end of "good" mediation.[51] It is true that some of the most dramatic changes have been within the legal field. Even at this early stage of mediation use, there is great diversity in practice. Some lawyers have simplified the process and divided it into three primary segments or stages: joint session, caucus and conclusion. From a learning or descriptive standpoint, this is too simple and does not provide any indication about what is going on in terms of the problem-solving process. The focus is on where the parties and mediator meet, rather than on the phases which take place, and how those factors lead to settlement or resolution.

Other modifications have occurred as well. With the increased use of mediation in a greater variety of cases, it has become clear that the basic one-time intervention model may not work in all cases. As mediation was originally designed, particularly by those outside of the labor field, it was viewed as a single intervention. The mediator sat down with the parties and either an agreement was eventually reached that day or it was not. Only in rare instances, where another individual or additional information was needed, would the mediation session be rescheduled. However, in some cases, due to the number of parties involved, and the complexity or the nature of the dispute, modification of the single mediation session approach was appropriate.

The first and most prevalent of these areas was in family law. Mediation in family cases is quite different. However, because of the emotional issues involved and the nature of the dispute between the parties, many of the original divorce mediation practitioners felt that the mediation sessions should be broken down over a period of weeks. Time was needed for adjustment to the renegotiated relationship of the parties, as well as for thinking through these major life changes. Consequently, sessions were limited to approximately an hour, and took place once a week until all matters were settled.

Another arena in which mediation takes place over an extended period of time is that of public policy matters.[52] In cases involving public policy, there are a number of people with a variety of interests. It is often impossible to get everyone together at one time, in one place, with all issues on the table. Therefore, the mediation may take place in stages. Likewise, in some complex commercial disputes, the mediator may choose to resolve only portions of the case at a time. Fortunately, the mediation process has proven to be adaptable and has successfully been used in all of these instances.

The Role of a Mediator

We have looked at the mediation process, but just what a mediator does with it is often a key to its effectiveness. What, then, is the role of this person? How does he move the parties through these stages? Compiling a complete list of the different hats that a mediator must wear can be an extensive exercise. A mediator has sometimes been called a traffic cop, particularly in directing the communication. The simplest description of the mediator's role is that of a facilitator. But how one facilitates differs. A conductor of the negotiation is another role that the mediator plays. Throughout the process the role of the mediator changes. Sometimes the mediator will have to supervise, even parent, the parties. Other times, the mediator will be a teacher, not only in assisting the parties to learn the subject matter of their dispute, but also in teaching the process. At other times the mediator is a clarifier. The mediator can also serve in the role of an advocate. Not for the parties, but for the process and settlement. A devil's advocate may also be a role the mediator assumes. Attorney mediators seem to adopt this role. Certainly few would argue with the role of the mediator as a catalyst, moving the parties in the direction of resolution. Mediators have also been designated as orchestrators, deal makers,[53] and as translators of comments and proposals.[54]

The foregoing roles are descriptive of the many facets of the mediator's work, and usually do not meet with controversy. However, an in-depth examination provides a conceptual framework for the mediator's role which has led to much debate.[55] Specifically, what is it that should be expected of this neutral intervenor? There is concern about the degree of influence the mediator should have on the outcome of the case. For instance, the mediator's role can be viewed as promoting an agreement—at whatever cost, thereby achieving efficiency in settlement.[56] The goals of saving time and perhaps money for the parties may be actualized. Alternatively, the mediator's role may be to protect rights by assuring that the agreements reached in mediation are based upon informed consent.[57] Some even go a step or two further and expect the mediator to assure that the agreements are fair and stable.[58] Others want the mediator to ensure that the agreement is not only fair, but also is one which a court would enforce.[59]

If the mediator is a neutral, before, during and after the mediation, and must refrain from making judgments, how can he assume these roles? How can we be sure that the parties even want their rights protected or their agreements fair? If self-determination by the parties is an overriding feature of the mediation process,[60] then the mediator's role may be to empower the parties to make their own judgments. It has been claimed that the mediation process and the mediator, as conductor of that process should promote self-determination and empowerment. But what should the mediator do in assuring that the parties make their own decisions?

The most important thing to remember about the mediator's role is that the mediator is in control of the process. Mediation works in resolving disputes because of the process, not the person. That, of course, is not to say that a skillful mediator will not be more effective than one possessing less skill. But more often it is the procession through the stages of the process that leads parties to a mutually satisfactory resolution. The role of the mediator then, is to safeguard, maintain, and control the process. This must be distinguished from control of the content matter of the dispute—that is up to the parties. Regardless of the subject matter. of the dispute, the process remains the same. *The parties are responsible for the content; the mediator is responsible for the process.*

Notes

[1] Linda Singer, Settling Disputes 21 (1990).

[2] Merriam Webster's Collegiate Dictionary 722 (10th ed. 1993).

[3] John S. Murray et al., Processes of Dispute Resolution 247 (1988).

[4] Roberta S. Mitchell & Scot E. Dewhirst, The Mediator Handbook 13, The Center For Dispute Resolution, Capital University Law and Graduate Center (1990).

[5] Christopher W. Moore, The Mediation Process: Practical Strategies for Resolving Conflict 6 (1984).

[6] Nancy H. Rogers & Craig A. McEwen, Mediation: Law, Policy, Practice 1 (1990).

[7] Alternative Dispute Resolution: An ADR Primer (Standing Committee on Dispute Resolution 3d ed., 1989).

[8] Kimberlee K. Kovach, *ADR-Does It Work?*, South Texas College of Law, Advanced Civil Litigation Institute, (1989).

[9] Ill. Rev. Stat. § 852 (1993).

[10] V.T.C.A. Civ. Prac. & Rem. Code § 154.023(a) (Supp. 1993).

[11] Civ. Just. Reform Act Plan, W.D. Mo. (1992).

[12] *Comment*, J. Disp. Resol. 307, 309 (1991).

[13] In fact, mediators often refer to themselves as mere *caretakers* of the process.

[14] Use of mediation has been documented in ancient China over two thousand years ago. See, for example, Jerome Alan Cohen, *Chinese Mediation on the Eve of Modernization*, 55 Cal. L. Rev. 1201, 1205 (1966).

[15] Jay Folberg & Alison Taylor, Mediation: A Comprehensive Guide to Resolving Conflicts Without Litigation 2 (1984).

[16] Donald C. Clark, *Dispute Resolution in China*, 5 J. Chinese L. 245, 270 (1991).

[17] Folberg & Taylor, supra note 15, at 49.

[18] A number of books have been recently published on Japanese negotiation style. See, for example, Edward T. Hall, Hidden Differences: Doing Business with Japanese (1987), Chi Nakan, Japanese Society (1970); and *generally*, U.S. Department of State, National Negotiating Styles (Hans Binnendbk, ed., 1987).

[19] Jerold S. Auerbach, Justice Without Law 8 (1983).

[20] Jacob Bercovitch, *The Structure and Diversity of Mediation in International Relations*, in Mediation in International Relations 2 (Jacob Bercovitch and Jeffery Z. Rubin, eds., 1992).

[21] For more detail on Native American peacemaking, see generally *Special Issue*, 10 Mediation Q. 327 (1993).

[22] Diane LeResch, Editor's Notes, 10 Mediation Q. 321 (1993).

[23] Susan L. Donegan, *ADR in Colonial America: A Covenant For Survival*, 48 Arb. J. 14 (1993).

[24] Auerbach, supra note 19, at 20.

[25] Id. at 23.

[26] Paul S. Reinsch, English Common Law in the Early American Colonies 6 (1898).

[27] Auerbach, supra note 19, at 71.

[28] See William E. Simkin, and Nicholas A. Fidandis, Mediation and the Dynamics of Collective Bargaining 25 (2d ed. 1986).

[29] For a complete perspective of mediation in the labor area, see Id.

[30] Id. at 38.

[31] Deborah M. Kolb, The Mediators 7 (1983).

[32] Id.

[33] Auerbach, supra note 19, at 120.

[34] See Warren E. Burger, *Isn't There a Better Way*, 68 ABA Journal 268 (1982).

[35] The AAA, a not for profit corporation, is one of the oldest private providers of arbitration services in the United States.

[36] Paul Wahrhaftig, *Non-Professional Conflict Resolution* in Mediation: Contexts and Challenges 49 (Joseph E. Polenski and Harold M. Launer, eds., 1986).

[37] Id. at 50.

[38] Roscoe Pound, *The Causes of Popular Dissatisfaction with the Administration of Justice*, (1906), reprinted in 20 J. Am. Jud. Socy. 178 (1936) and as Appendix

B in The Pound Conference: Perspectives on Justice in the Future (A. Leo Levin et al. eds., 1979). It is interesting to note that in 1994 the ABA will be holding a Pound Two Conference. The role of ADR therein has yet to be determined.

[39] Griffen B. Bell, Report of Pound Conference Follow-up Task Force, August 1976.

[40] Royer F. Cook et al., Neighborhood Justice Centers Field Test: Final Evaluation Report (1980).

[41] Id.

[42] One exception is the San Francisco Community Boards Program which is *independent* of either a court or bar association.

[43] Public Services Division of the American Bar Association, Section of Dispute Resolution, 1993 Dispute Resolution Program Directory (1993).

[44] When alternatives to the courthouse were initially developed, only minor cases were to be handled. When the ABA created its first committee on this subject, it was termed the *Special Committee on the Resolution of Minor Disputes*. As the movement grew, so did the status of the committee and its work. Soon there was the *Standing Committee on Dispute Resolution*, and 1993 saw the birth of the ABA *Dispute Resolution Section*.

[45] Professor Sander of Harvard Law School initially outlined the concept in a paper he presented at the Pound Conference: Frank E. Sander, *Varieties of Dispute Processing* in The Pound Conference: Perspectives on Justice in the Future (A. Leo Levin et al., eds., 1979).

[46] Identifying the interests is at the core of *Principled Negotiation*, as set forth by Roger Fisher and William Ury, Getting to Yes (1981).

[47] The various types of negotiation are explored in Chapter 9 of *Mediation: Principles and Practice*.

[48] Moore, supra note 5, at 33-34.

[49] Mitchell and Dewhirst, supra note 4, at 15.

[50] Folberg and Taylor, supra note 15, at 22.

[51] Statement of Albie Davis, in James J. Alfini, *Styles of Mediation: Trashing, Bashing and Hashing It Out: Is this the End of "Good Mediation"?* 19 Fla. St. U. L. Rev. 47 (1991).

[52] These cases will also be examined in greater detail in Chapter 16 of *Mediation: Principles and Practice*.

[53] Kolb, supra note 31, at 23.

[54] Joseph B. Stulberg, *Training Interveners for ADR Processes*, 81 Ky. L. J. 977, 987 (1992–93).

[55] The role of the mediator in light of fairness, neutrality and ethical considerations is also examined in Chapters 7 and 14 of *Mediation: Principles and Practice*.

[56] Robert A. Baruch Bush, *Efficiency and Protection, or Empowerment and Recognition?: The Mediator's Role and Ethical Standards in Mediation* 41 Fla. L. Rev. 253, 260 (1989).

[57] Id. at 261.

[58] Lawrence Susskind, *Environmental Mediation and the Accountability Problem* 6 Vt. L. Rev. 1, 18 (1981).

[59] Leonard L. Riskin, *Toward New Standards for the Neutral Lawyer in Mediation* 26 Ariz. L. Rev. 329, 354 (1984).

[60] Bush, supra note 56 at 270.

11

A Manual for Mediators

Lindsay G. Arthur

Preface

This article speaks from the experience of a relatively new mediator, after some five hundred cases over about six years. Forty years of experience as a judge has helped in the very necessary functions of presiding and controlling the setting, gaining respect, and being neutral. The judicial experience, however, has been of little help in negotiating parties to a voluntary settlement. Judges make good arbitrators because they are used to hearing disputed evidence, finding the facts and handing down a binding order. But mediators must negotiate, they must persuade, they cannot dictate. This compendium contains methods, levers, arguments, and ideas for bringing parties together. All of them have been tried, some with greater success than others. Every case is full of human beings. No technique will ever always work.

The purpose of mediation is to bring the parties together, to achieve a settlement. It won't always happen. One of the parties may have an inflated idea of the value of its position. A party may want to play to the emotions of a jury. A party or his lawyer may be stupid or stubborn. A plaintiff may want more than the limits of the defendant's insurance policy and the defendant is unwilling to pay even the face of the policy without a jury telling it to. There are many reasons why a settlement can't be reached. But in about three-quarters of the cases, a settlement can be reached through mediation. It will usually be a settlement that neither party really likes; one of the objectives is for each party to feel that the other is equally unhappy.

Source: *Juvenile and Family Court Journal*, 46(2) (Spring 1995): 63–73.

Preparation

As with so much of litigation, preparation divides the successful from the bumblers. The participants sense quickly whether you are involved, whether you are a mediator, or whether you are an umpire. You need to decide your own appearances and attitudes and how you're going to act and what you're going to say. And you need to get acquainted with the facts and law of the case, at least enough to frame the key issues of this particular case.

Prepare Your Own Role

A mediator needs to think through in advance what she or he is going to do, what he or she will wear, what attitude she or he will take with the various participants before things start, what words he or she will say at the beginning to get the proceedings started, what ambiance to set. It is only courteous to speak to everyone in advance. Being distant doesn't usually prove much, being self-assured does. In the delays before getting started, talk to the parties but about anything except the case. So far as possible, talk to each of them with equal friendliness, particularly the lay parties. Your first and valuable impression of being neutral will probably be made then. If you know one of the participants, let the others know what your relationship is to negate any fear of possible partiality; the non-professionals are usually nervous, with antennae searching for indicia of impartiality and competence.

Know the Case

You need to know the essentials of the case to better enable you to assert control without depending on counsel to get the factual discussion going. But a difficulty may be that, on one hand, the lawyers send you in advance two or three inches or more of argument, depositions, medical reports, and such. To absorb it all may take several hours; not to absorb it all may pique the lawyers. To take the time to absorb it all may run up your fee to an amount which those who have to pay it deem unreasonable. In a usual case, in 15 or 20 minutes you can scan the various statements of the facts which have been filed, or at least the basic pleadings, and read the face of the police report and the summaries or "impressions" of the medical reports, then as much more as time and dollars permit. Make notes of which lawyer represents which party so as to show acquaintance with the case and to avoid an appearance of incompetence during the opening session.

Appear Neutral

Like Caesar's wife, it may be at least as important to appear neutral as to be neutral. The mediator must be very careful not to show even a hint of favoring either party. Comments on the law or the evidence, comments showing weaknesses in a case or strengths in the opponent's case must not show favoritism. Before making a negative comment, explain that you're looking at the case as a jury might, or that you want to bring out what appear to be negatives in order to get responses and explanations, or that these are things which the other party has, or may, mention. Negatives can be discussed empathetically, to assure that all the positives in the party's case are brought out.

Be Active

Take an active part in discussing the facts and the law and in asking for settlement numbers; do not be just a messenger of offers. The mediator cannot just ask the lawyers to go talk to their clients and make them accept unpleasant information; the lawyers have probably built up their clients' expectations and don't want to appear to suddenly be on the other side. The mediator usually can build supportively on what the lawyer says to the client, or the mediator can bring up unpleasant things first as an experienced outsider and let the lawyer agree that these are unfortunately true, lending support. A neutral appraisal of the case can be persuasive to the client. Don't be afraid to twist arms when with a party separately. Lawyers may want your pressure to help persuade their own client. Lawyers often feel that a case should be settled but can't convince their clients. "The common concern relayed to our Case Managers . . . is that judges do not take an active enough role. Every now and then, our clients perceive that the judge acted more as a messenger than a 'settler'—disputants look to us to actively assist them in reaching a settlement that is acceptable to all participants. This can only occur when you actively participate in the conference" (*Judicial Focus*, Resolute Systems, Inc., Oct/Nov 1993).

Provide a Level Playing Field

The mediator must be not only neutral but fair. Part of fairness is that the parties have equal strength. If one party does not have a lawyer, the mediator may have to explain things more carefully to him or her, may have to help extract favorable facts and law. It's possible that one lawyer may be obviously at a disadvantage of skills. One party may be afraid of the other or be dominated by the other and the mediator can make sure there is no fear or dominance in the mediation. But the mediator cannot overcome economic disparities or urgencies. If a plaintiff is willing to accept less money because of an urgent need for money, the mediator can't change the urgency but he can help him appraise whether the bird in hand is in fact worth losing the two that may be in the bush. A settlement should be like a sale: a knowing, willing buyer and a knowing, willing seller. Getting a settlement is not worth getting an unfair settlement.

Don't Mention Your Own Numbers

Do not suggest your own settlement range or support a party's number unless the parties have narrowed their range to realistic numbers or are close to settlement. If you come up with a number too early, you will probably be out of the ball park and thus lose credibility. Further, any number you might mention would probably be closer to one party than the other and might be interpreted as bias. It's usually better to let the parties talk numbers, realizing that in a personal injury case, the parties' first numbers are probably at least twice what the plaintiff expects to settle for and half what the defendant expects to pay . . . and they're still usually a long way apart.

Use Humor

Use humor when the discussion gets too hot. Use anecdotes to illustrate problems and solutions. "Humor [can be] a bridge over troubled waters. . . . Try to use humor that makes a point, but without barbs. . . . Make fun of yourself, not others" (SPIDR, Society of Professionals in Dispute Resolution, 20th Annual Conference, Oct. 8–11, 1992). Use "war stories" and anecdotes from other cases, or pertinent jokes which illustrate some point in the present dispute and may persuade a party to change position.

Wear Robes

In a courthouse setting, wear robes because they cast an aura of professionalism. To the laity, they are an indication of fairness and competence; to lawyers they are a reminder that court/lawyer demeanor is appropriate. In chambers, judicial robes may be impressive enough to get a party or lawyer to listen more closely to the mediator. The robes are probably more impressive in chambers if left open to indicate, like rolled-up shirt sleeves, a working attitude and not just a posturing.

Opening Joint Session

The opening session will set the tone for the proceeding: it will determine the ambiance, which may be quite formal if the parties are hostile. It will educate the parties as to what the proceedings are all about and what the proceeding hopes to accomplish. And it will give the parties a chance to see each other face to face, usually for the first time since the event precipitating the litigation, and to hear each other's version of the dispute, again usually for the first time. It should also set the stage for settlement.

Start with Everyone Present

Do not start the opening session until all parties, lawyers, and adjusters are either present or waiting by phones. Certainly you need the lawyers. There's little point in starting without an insurance adjuster if one is involved: he's the "deep pocket." If a party is missing he may think he's been deemed unimportant or that his viewpoint wasn't worth waiting for or that it's all being decided regardless of his position. Missing persons also miss the beginning ambiance, they may miss the mediator's summation of the issues, they miss the parties' presentation of their case and defenses. Better to start with everyone and then break into party groups.

Show Expertise and Neutrality

Introduce yourself with some background to show your expertise. Emphasize your neutrality. State that during the proceedings you may find it necessary to ask some questions of both parties that may sound almost hostile but that such is necessary to get at the facts and the legal position of the parties. identify others by name and relationship to the case. Very briefly summarize the facts of the case to show your familiarity with it.

Explain the Mediation Process

Explain that this initial session is designed to show the present posture of the dispute, getting each party's version of the situation out in the open for others to react to. After this, the mediator will meet separately with each party to explore their respective positions, going back and forth with them to try to narrow the gaps and find a settlement. Ask lay persons if they understand the procedures and what is going to happen.

Each Sees the Other's Position

If mediation achieves nothing else, each party will learn much more about the other party's claims, what the other party wants and why. The plaintiff may suddenly realize that the defense has a different set of facts and some evidence to prove it. The defense may realize that the plaintiff has a valid claim and some strong evidence to support it. Both sides may realize that the risks and costs of not settling are too great. Frequently one or more of the lay persons will suck in their breath in surprise and anger, at which point the mediator may bring up the ancient truism, "When both of you are sure you're right, one of you is wrong!" More likely both are partially wrong. "If mediation falls, the parties have at least gained some understanding of the opposing party's position and have enhanced the likelihood of settlement at a future date" (Charles M. Goldstein, *Alternate Dispute Resolution in Employment Litigation*, American Arbitration Association, Minneapolis Regional Office, Vol. 1, No. 2, April 1994).

Confidentiality

The parties, particularly the lawyers, will worry about confidentiality: whether what is said here can be used later, whether they should advise their clients to remain silent and let the lawyers do the talking. There are four problems: [a] Can a party disclose, voluntarily or involuntarily, what was said later in this proceeding; [b] Can a third party disclose, voluntarily or involuntarily, in some other litigation; [c] Can there be a later disclosure, voluntarily or involuntarily, to another party in the litigation; and [d] Can the mediator disclose, voluntarily or involuntarily, in this or another litigation? The Minnesota Rule is, hopefully, typical of what other jurisdictions have adopted or will adopt. It appears to cover [a], [b], and [d], essentially blocking disclosure without the parties' consent. Disclosure within the particular proceeding, [c], is covered in the last paragraph of the SPIDR Ethics excerpt below and would seem to place disclosures at the mediator's discretion to do what will promote discussions, but with an obligation to treat as confidential anything a party so requests. Possibly a further ethical admonition should be added requiring the mediator to warn a party when an unintended confidence comes out.

Rule 114.08 of the Minnesota "Alternative Dispute Resolution Rules," adopted in 1994, provides:

> (A) Without the consent of all parties and an order of the court . . . no evidence that there has been an ADR proceeding, or any fact concerning the proceeding may be admitted in a trial *de novo* or in any subsequent proceeding involving any of the issues or parties to the proceeding.

> (B) Statements made and documents produced in nonbinding ADR processes which are not otherwise discoverable are not subject to discovery or other disclosure and are not admissible in evidence for any purpose at trial . . .

(E) Notes, records, and recollections of the neutral are confidential, which means that they shall not be disclosed to the parties the public or anyone other than the neutral.

The "Ethical Standards of Professional Responsibility" adopted June 1986, by the Society of Professionals in Dispute Resolution [SPIDR], provide:

3. Confidentiality. Maintaining confidentiality is critical to the dispute resolution process. Confidentiality encourages candor, a full exploration of the issues, and a neutral's acceptability. There may be some types of cases, however In which confidentiality is not protected. In such cases, the neutral must advise the parties, when appropriate in the dispute process that the confidentiality of the proceedings cannot necessarily be maintained. Except in such instances, the neutral must resist all attempts to cause him or her to reveal any information outside the process.

A commitment by the neutral to hold information in confidence within the process also must be honored.

Settle or Strangers Will Decide

The parties are usually in a hostile mood, enamored with their own version of the case. To get them into a settlement mood, the mediator can describe their option: a settlement today worked out by the parties themselves or a verdict tomorrow by a jury of disinterested strangers. The mediator should explain that neither party is going to get what she or he is hoping for, either from the mediation or from a verdict, and that they'll get a fairer settlement if they decide it themselves rather than by a jury that is disinterested and not very happy at being called away from their daily pursuits to sit on a jury at practically no pay, deciding somebody else's problem.

Take the Bird in Hand

An argument to induce the parties to consider settlement is to suggest to both of them that a bird in hand may be better than two in the bush. The amount offered to the plaintiff today may be well below what was expected, but it may be well above what a jury would do. Or, that the amount the plaintiff will settle for today may be higher than the defendant or the insurance company had planned to pay, but it may be less than a jury would award. The option to today's settlement may be tomorrow's gamble.

Have Lawyers Summarize

Ask all lawyers to outline what they expect to prove at a trial as to each issue. Each client thus hears, probably for the first time, what the other party is claiming and how wide the gap is. The mediator may question the lawyers as to apparent issues in an effort to reduce the number of actually contested issues and disagreements.

With Each Side Alone

It is important to deal with the two sides separately. They can talk more freely. They can answer questions they wouldn't want the other side to hear. You can show them weaknesses in their case that the other side probably knows about but would harden their position if they hear it from the mediator. You can get down to numbers and discuss each item without the other side hearing. And, maybe most important, you can establish a rapport with them, a trust in your expertise and neutrality which will make it easier to persuade them later to accept a number that they don't like.

Neutralize Feelings and Emotions

A party may have personal feelings of animosity towards the other which is blocking a settlement. Give the party an opportunity to vent the hostility to the mediator. Let the pus run out of the boil. Similarly, a party may not want to suffer any more than the other party. The mediator can point out an equality of suffering, or strive to obtain an equality if needed. Mediation is often more complicated than just two lawyers bargaining over dollars and cents. Often hidden and complicated feelings are involved. A female may have a sense of dominance or attempted dominance by the opposing male, or the female may be asserting feminism as much as her monetary claim. A man may not want to appear submissive to a woman. A white person may not want to make concessions to a black person, an older person may feel defensive about the energies of a younger person. Persons of different cultures may give different meanings to the same words. A party may inadvertently refer to the other party by a name the other party considers derogatory. One person may feel that her or his economic or physical security is at risk. Feelings can confuse, often prevent, a settlement. They are seldom expressed, often are detectable in body language, sometimes have to be just sensed by the mediator. "An experienced mediator will assist the parties' negotiation by separating the emotional facets of the case from the legal aspects, by focusing on the economic realities of the case" (Charles M. Goldstein, *Alternate Dispute Resolution in Employment Litigation*, American Arbitration Association, Minneapolis Regional Office, Vol. 1, 42, April 1994).

Show the Weaknesses in the Case

Point out to each party the weaknesses of his or her case and the strengths of the opponent's case. Emphasize that the mediator is appearing only as a neutral trying to bring an experienced outsider's reality to the situation. " . . . the parties are looking for tangible reasons why they should put more money [into] the claim or consider accepting less than the last demand. The last thing the parties want is for the neutral to 'play a money game' by suggesting that they adjust their positions without discussing the merits of the claim" (*Judicial Focus*, Resolute Systems, Inc., Oct./Nov. 1993).

Show Witness Unreliability

When a party is relying on a witness to buttress the case, the mediator should point out that witnesses don't always come through: they may get stage fright, they may have memory failure, they have been exaggerating before, they may die or move away or just lose interest. Maybe worse, witnesses may not be credible, the jury may not believe them, even when they are telling the truth, or opposing witnesses may appear to be credible even when they are not telling the truth.

Quote Average Verdicts

Advise the parties, particularly the lay persons, of the range of recent verdicts for this type of injury. Averages can be learned from the mediator's experience, from conversations in mediations, from judges and clerks and lawyers involved in trials, and from various publications of lawyers' associations. Arbitration services may maintain a file of verdicts which can be used.

Help the Lawyer Persuade the Client

A lawyer may know the case should settle and may realize that the settlement offer is in the ball park but may need help getting the client to see reality. The mediator can bring neutrality and experience in to support the lawyer. Sometimes a party may be more impressed with the mediator's opinion of the case than with the lawyer's or may be more comfortable if the mediator, who is seen as neutral and competent, approves of the range of settlement being discussed. Talking separately with the party and the lawyer may give the mediator a chance to support the lawyer in producing a more realistic claim.

Try "If He Will, Will You?"

Ask a party, "Suppose I can get the other side to offer you $_____; would you be interested?" If the party says no, try another figure which is somewhere in the range of the possible. If the party says yes, go to the other party and ask the same question. If you have used a logical number, it is surprising how often you get a settlement. At the least you may find where the range is.

Try Creative Solutions

Where a considerable amount of money is involved, a 'structured settlement' may be appropriate. It is similar to an annuity. The defendant puts a sum of money which a life insurance company invests, paying out both principal and interest in monthly or annual payments to the plaintiff over the plaintiff's life. A rough formula for determining the annual amount is to multiply half the Sum by the interest rate, multiply the product by plaintiff's Expectancy, add the Sum, then divide by the Expectancy. [If defendant put up $50,000.00 and the plaintiff has an expectancy of 30 years, the annuity would be more than $250.00 every month for life for a total of over $90,000.00.] Many plaintiffs find a structured settlement attractive and would rather have it than try for a jury verdict of even two hundred thousand dollars. There may also be tax advantages. Many defendants' insurance carriers, particularly if they have a life insurance division, find the structured settlement cheaper and less risky than going to trial. Sometimes the plaintiff will only take two-thirds structured in order to have money for their lawyer's fee. Sometimes it can be structured on an annual basis with the plaintiff sending the lawyer a check each year.

Or listening to the parties may suggest a unique solution, such as an apology, an agreement not to disclose the settlement, an alternative benefit to money such as a new car or a season baseball ticket to which the defendant has access. Listen for ideas and possibilities that can be developed. Unless a case is a purely routine situation, it may have peculiarities which can form the basis of a settlement.

Ask the Lawyer if the Fee Can Be Reduced

A lawyer on a contingent fee basis may be willing to bridge the gap between the settlement offers by reducing his or her fee. If it is a contingent fee case, it may be in the lawyer's best interest to avoid the time and expense of going to trial. The lawyer may be more interested in getting a bird in the hand now than trying for a bigger bird in the bush. If the settlement possibility is within the range of reasonableness, the lawyer may be amenable to throwing part of the fee into the negotiations.

Settle to Avoid Delays

The mediator should point out that if the dispute isn't settled today, there will be delays, maybe months, maybe more. The lawyers will need to take more depositions which require finding times when doctors can be videotaped and when other witnesses can be brought in. The lawyers will need time to go through their large files and become familiar with them and index them for use in trial. The court will need time to reach the case on its trial calendar. And there maybe motions and appeals. Months will go by.

Settle to Avoid Fees and Costs

If the dispute goes to trial, it will cost each party about $2,000.00 per day for lawyers' fees and costs. This amount includes the lawyer's preparation time, physicians' and experts' fees, court reporters' fees, videotape costs for depositions, and time in actual trial. The plaintiff may not have any lawyer's fees if it is a contingent fee case, but the extra time required may persuade the lawyer to reduce the fee to get a settlement. In addition, complicated cases require complicated exhibits. Sometimes the exhibits are just charts and diagrams. Sometimes they may be three dimensional. Sometimes they may require complicated photography or mock-ups. All these expenses the client must pay.

Personal Stress of Trial

If a case does not settle, the parties must each use a considerable amount of their own time assisting the lawyer in preparing for trial, working with witnesses, and so forth. Such time may mean lost wages or time away from business. They will personally have the nervous strain of testimony with direct examination and cross-examination. If the case goes to trial, all the facts will come out and the press may get interested. The trial might have unpleasant consequences such as annoying a boss, giving information to a creditor, or apprising another litigant to file a similar suit.

An Appeal Could Hurt

The other party may appeal if the verdict appears grossly out of line, with loss of a year or so and possible new trial and a possibly greatly different outcome.

Avoid Possible Fines

There may be fines and costs due for delaying the mediation or requiring it to be continued, such contingencies as failure to have a necessary party or insurance adjuster present, being unprepared by reason of failure to complete discovery by the date set by the court. A mediator may be authorized to recommend that various fines and costs be imposed on one or both parties. These can be forestalled or waived by the mediator if the case is settled. A sample of fines and costs used by the Arbitration Division of the District Court in Hennepin County, Minnesota is set out below.

Failure to Have Necessary Party Present	$250.00
Failure to Appear on Time	$50.00
Failure to Complete Discovery by Scheduled Time	$250.00
Failure to Pay Filing Fee	$100.00
Reimburse Other Party for Needless Expense	Costs

As a Last Resort

Usually, if a case is going to settle, it will occur during the "shuttle diplomacy" of the mediator talking back and forth with the parties separately, carrying positions and responses and ideas and numbers from one to the other. Usually, there will be a point where settlement appears impossible. Curiously, if the mediator suggests quitting, one of the parties, maybe both will come up with another suggestion. But, if it ever does get to a point of apparent failure, various methods can be tried, as a"last resort."

Try a Joint Session

Where shuttle diplomacy has failed to produce a settlement, bring the lawyers and insurance adjusters together for suggestions and to determine whether further negotiations may be useful. They may often see the reality to a settlement better than the lay people and can propose methods for arriving at a resolution to the matter. If a party, or each party, gets frozen into a position, call everyone into a joint session. Summarize the present status of the matter and let them hear what the other party thinks of the various frozen issues. Ask for suggestions. Let the parties themselves argue directly with each other as long as the discussion is productive. Announce that, after talking and listening to everyone, it appears that the case can, in fact, be settled . . . with both parties equally unhappy.

Try the Mediator's Estimate

If the parties have stopped working toward a settlement and a reasonable figure is becoming apparent, the mediator can suggest a figure separately or jointly to both parties. " . . . [D]on't hesitate to use your expertise to move parties into realistic settlement ranges" (*Judicial Focus*, Resolute Systems, Inc., Oct./Nov. 1993). A possible method for finding a reasonable figure is to multiply the difference between plaintiff's last valid offer and defendant's last valid offer by .357 [a purely experiential number] and add that to defendant's last valid offer. It will not work every time, but it is worth trying. Of course, if the parties know the mediator will use such a method, they will probably skew their last offers.

Suggest Other ADR

Suggest to the parties that there are other methods of ADR which may be easier and cheaper and faster than a jury trial. There is arbitration, which is binding where the arbitrator or arbitrators not only do not try to bring about a settlement but actively stay away from hearing how the parties value their positions, where evidence is taken in a semiformal manner and interpreted by the arbitrator into a decision. Many lawyers refuse to submit to binding arbitration before a single arbitrator, feeling that everyone has biases and that it is better to average the biases out by having three arbitrators, or a jury. There is nonbinding arbitration, almost an oxymoron, where the arbitrator listens to such informal evidence as the parties want to present and gives a decision which is not binding but may be useful by giving the parties an experienced neutral's evaluation. There is a mini-trial, where strangers may be brought in to act as a jury; where the decision may or may not be binding according to how the parties agree in advance. Mediation is the usual form of Alternate Dispute Resolution, and the most difficult, but the parties may be more satisfied with the result, or less dissatisfied. Arbitration is probably the most expensive, particularly with multiple arbitrators.

Threaten a Walkout

State that the parties are unreasonable and intractable and that further negotiations are a waste of the mediator's time unless the parties are actually ready to give a little. Close your briefcase. Put your pen away. Wait, looking around at the parties. Ask each lawyer whether there is any point in further talk. Slam down the file and say something like, "I've had it with the BS. If you people don't cut out the . . . and start making some progress, I'm out of here. I've got better ways to waste my time!" (SPIDR, Society of Professionals in Dispute Resolution, 20th Annual Conference, Oct. 8–11, 1991). *Or* Ask the parties to go into another room so you can prepare for the next hearing in this room. The difficulty is that if this doesn't work, you have little recourse; you can't try something else.

When Settlement Is Reached

If the case settles, set the essentials of the agreement in writing. Designate one of the lawyers to draft the final agreement by an agreed date, sending you a copy as a means of keeping him to the date.

Accident Cases

Liability

If liability is at issue, ask each party, not the lawyers, for his or her oral version of property damage. Then ask the party to draw a diagram of the scene, maybe offering a rule to help, showing [a] little images as close to scale as possible where each vehicle or pedestrian was at the instant when first seen by the party, labeling them each #1, [b] each vehicle at the point of impact, labeling them #2, [c] each vehicle after they had come to rest, labeling them #3, then the same with any other events bearing on the liability or damages. Compare the diagram with police reports and repair bills as to what actually was repaired, asking for explanation of apparent inconsistencies. At a blank place on the chart, indicate speeds, weather, street conditions, and visibility, Ask what each person said and did right after the accident. Ask permission to show the chart to the other party.

Comparative Negligence

Estimate the comparative negligence, if any, and calculate its effect on the settlement offers. It may significantly change a party's money claims. Suggesting that a party's views on comparative negligence may not be acceptable to a jury may cause the party to be more willing to settle.

Property Damage

Ask each party separately for details as to the property damage. Look at police reports, repair bills, appraisals, photographs, and other objective evidence and compare them with the party's version, asking for an explanation of apparent inconsistencies. Since an owner may testify as to value before and after even though not an expert, obtain the party's valuations. If a vehicle was "totaled," obtain its junk value.

Mitigation of Damages

If the plaintiff could reasonably mitigate the damages, the amount of the mitigation can be subtracted from her or his claim. Ask about possible mitigation. One party will have several ideas of what should have been done, the other party will have several ideas of why nothing could be done.

Personal Injury

Ask each party, not the lawyer, for his or her oral version of the injuries and pain at the impact and thereafter up to today. Determine what parts of the body hit other objects and, if more than one contact, in what sequence. Determine what the injured party did after the accident. Inquire as to any objective evidence of pain or disability. Ask about wage loss, lost earning ability and any loss of physical abilities and recreational pursuits.

Consider All Reports

If the medical and hospital reports, including the adverse medical examiner's statement, are inconsistent with the party's version, ask for an explanation of the inconsistencies. Check police reports and compare with the parties' versions. Check hospital and doctor reports for initial reported symptoms and for initial diagnoses and for ongoing contacts, and the treatments ordered. Consider the frequency of visits, the adherence to appointments and treatments, the ongoing prognoses. Inquire of the party regarding any inconsistencies.

Impact of Prior Conditions

Emphasize the possible impact on a jury of prior accidents or prior disabilities. An obvious and important part of any case is prior trauma or disabilities which may be the cause of some or all of the present symptoms and injuries. If there are too many prior claims, there is the hidden element that the jury may decide the plaintiff is sue-happy or a professional claimant.

Evaluating Injuries

As a means of forcing consideration of each of the elements of the claim and facilitating easier analysis, require each party to fill in a

"Personal Injury Loss Statement." The purpose is to put a dollar value beside [a] past medical costs, [b] future medical costs, [c] property loss, [d] lost wages, [e] prospective lost wages, [f] past pain and suffering, [g] future pain and suffering, [h] lost hobbles and recreation, and [i] scars and disfigurements. Neither the party nor the lawyer has probably ever analyzed the dispute in this way. They may be reluctant and it may take some time. While they're doing it, excuse yourself and go meet with the other party. Get them to do the same. Then review each item separately with each party to find out how each dollar amount was computed, pointing out any apparent weaknesses in the computation. "A neutral mediator can respond to unrealistic settlement expectations on the part of either party" (Charles M. Goldstein, *Alternate Dispute Resolution,* American Arbitration Association, Minneapolis Regional Office, Vol. 1, No. 2, April 1994). Ask permission to show the chart to the other party.

Divorce Cases

Custody and Visitation

If custody is at issue, it may be for many reasons other than the best interests of the child. The custody request may be a power play or an unwillingness to give in. It may be a bargaining tool for visitation or property distribution. And usually the hidden reason will not be readily apparent. It may be a desire just to hurt the other party. The mediator's role is to take the emotion and the monetary bargaining out of the issue and reduce it to the basic question of what is best for the child or children, including their right to maintain contact and nurture from the noncustodial parent. Separating the siblings is seldom in their best interest. Dividing custody so that they have to change schools during the school year is seldom in their best interest. Liberal weekend visitation and extensive summer change of custody often will resolve the issue. One or both of the parties may want a custody study by a social worker which may be helpful if it is not being requested merely as a ploy and if it is apparent that the parties cannot work custody out for themselves. Custody studies usually require four to six weeks, during which time the children are in suspense and are aware that their future is being negotiated. If one party wants a continuance for a custody study by a private social worker paid by him, suggest that each party retain a private social worker and apportion the costs according to ability to pay.

Child Support

In most states, support is decided by legislative guidelines based upon the parties' incomes. Deviations are possible for particular circumstances, but support should not be increased or decreased as a bargain for alimony or property distribution. It should always be remembered that child support is a right of the children which the parents cannot bargain away! The court is in no way bound by any agreement of the parents and can and should reject any agreement which is not in the children's best interest or which attempts to bargain away support for an increase in property or spousal maintenance. If there is extreme hostility, a guardian ad litem for the children may be necessary to protect their interests.

Spousal Maintenance

Spousal maintenance, which is more or less similar to alimony, is money paid to a spouse who lacks the ability to maintain a reasonable lifestyle without help. A woman who has been a homemaker may have no marketable skills and thus require monetary help. A woman who has been used to an abundant life cannot be required to live on the wages of a low-paying job with a substantially lower standard of living. A woman who can reasonably support herself, but only after vocational education or training, must be paid enough to pay for the education plus enough to live on while she is getting it and for awhile thereafter until, with reasonable efforts, she obtains reasonable employment. While spousal maintenance is almost always granted to the woman, if the specifications fit, it may be awarded to the man. Spousal maintenance once waived is forever gone. The mediator therefore must inquire first whether the parties have made an agreement as to spousal maintenance and, if this entails a waiver, whether the waiving party understood that it was forever. Next the mediator must inquire as to the spouse's needs for both education and livelihood and for how long these are expected to last. There will be disagreements which the mediator can try to resolve. Sometimes, a spousal maintenance disagreement can be resolved by changing the property distribution. Child support cannot be used to balance, the right of support belongs to the children not to the parents, the amount depends on the children's needs, not the parents'.

Property Division

Property division is usually the key issue in a divorce dispute, more than custody, visitation, support, and spousal maintenance. There are various problems: the true value of the various items of property, including the value of unaccrued pensions, the value of stock in a privately held business, the value of heirlooms, and such. The issue is for experts except that these can be very expensive and time consuming and may require experts for each side. Often one party claims that a piece of property is 'nonmarital,' that it was acquired before marriage or with money not a part of the marriage, such as an inheritance, and in either case that the property or money was not merged into the marriage. The issue is evidentiary for the mediator to seek to balance. Often issues of property distribution can be resolved by balancing with spousal maintenance. The amount of child support cannot be used for balancing, the right of support belongs to the children.

Conclusion

Mediation can resolve most disputes. But the mediator must be prepared and must understand the tools, the arguments, the methods, and the procedures and how and when to use them. Since human beings are involved, it is not something that can be punched into a computer. It is always a problem of getting each party to see the other party's view of the dispute. It is often a problem of personalities. Frequently, self-esteem is involved, Often the parties have "street knowledge" of what they are entitled to and they rely on this knowledge more than their lawyers' advice. Often it is a problem of interpersonal relations. It is a fascinating process.

12

Holding Juvenile
Offenders Accountable
A Restorative Justice Perspective

Mark S. Umbreit

Our society's common understanding of the need for juvenile offenders to be held "accountable" is closely linked to the concepts of punishment and retribution—"when you violate the law, you incur a debt to society." In this viewpoint, offenders are held accountable when they have received or taken a sufficient amount of punishment.

In the restorative justice paradigm the meaning of accountability shifts the focus from incurring a debt to society to that of incurring a responsibility for making amends to the victimized person; from passively taking punishment to actively making things right. Rather than emphasizing punishment of past criminal behavior, accountability in the restorative justice paradigm taps into the offender's strengths and competencies to take direct and active responsibility to compensate the victim for material or emotional losses.

A punitive form of accountability, in which offenders usually remain in a passive role and have little understanding of the real impact their behavior had on other people, is de-emphasized. Instead, offenders are empowered to take direct and active responsibility to repair the damage they caused to the people they victimized, not to an abstraction called "society" or "the state."

Source: *Juvenile and Family Court Journal*, 46(2) (Spring, 1995): 31–42.

Accountability in the restorative justice paradigm does not mask the difficulty in working with certain high-risk, violence-prone offenders. The community must be protected from such continued violent behavior. A restorative justice understanding of accountability, however, is meant to suggest that even in such severe crimes as brutal assaults or attempted homicide the offender incurs a responsibility to the victimized person to make amends through some form of emotional or material compensation.

This article's purpose is to more clearly define accountability as an intervention strategy within the context of the restorative justice paradigm. It is also meant to provide juvenile justice managers and staff with an overview of the basic elements of restorative justice. As one of the three performance-based objectives for probation and community supervision of juvenile offenders in the Balance Approach mission, a restorative justice understanding of accountability is central to building a new agenda for restructuring entire juvenile justice systems (Bazemore, 1994). Before providing a more thorough definition of accountability, it is necessary to describe the restorative justice paradigm and how it differs from our current practice of juvenile justice.

Restorative Justice Paradigm

The restorative justice paradigm provides an entirely different theoretical framework for understanding and responding to crime. Rather than defining "the state" as the victim, restorative justice theory views criminal and delinquent behavior as first a conflict between individuals. The person who was violated is the primary victim, and the state is a secondary victim. The current retributive paradigm of justice focuses on the offender's actions, denies victim participation, and requires only the offender's passive participation.

Within the context of restorative justice, both victim and offender are placed in active problem-solving roles. All interventions focus upon the restoration of material and psychological losses to individuals and the community following the damage that results from criminal behavior. The Balanced Approach (Maloney, Romig and Armstrong, 1988), with its three main elements of holding the offender accountable to the victim, of ensuring community protection, and of promoting competency development in offenders, provides a particularly good framework for practical implementation of restorative justice theory. Rather than being only offender driven, the Balanced Approach views the juvenile justice system as having three clients: the offender, the victim and the community. A greater degree of balance is required in responding to the needs of these three groups.

Whenever possible, dialogue and negotiation (primarily in property crimes) are central elements of restorative justice. Problem solving for the future is seen as more important than establishing blame for past behavior. Public safety is a primary concern, yet severe punishment of the offender is less important than providing opportunities to empower victims in their search for closure and healing; to impress upon offenders the human impact of their behavior, and to strengthen accountability by emphasizing offender payment of restitution to the victim and/or community.

By far the most clear distinction between the dominant paradigm of retributive justice and the new paradigm of restorative justice has been developed by Zehr (1990).

While clearly more difficult (though not impossible) to apply when a violent crime is charged, the principles of restorative justice theory are having an increasing impact on social policy. Many of these principles can also be seen in the pioneering work of an Australian criminologist (Braithwaite, 1989) who addresses the issues of crime, shame and reintegration. Braithwaite argues for "reintegrative shaming," a type of social control based upon informal community condemnation of wrongdoing, but with opportunities provided for reintegrating the wrongdoer into the community.

> Crime is best controlled when . . . the community are the primary controllers through active participation in shaming offenders, and, having shamed them, through concerted participation in . . . integrating the offender back into the community . . . Low crime societies are societies where people do not mind their own business, where tolerance of deviance has definite limits, where communities prefer to handle their own problems. (Braithwaite, 1989)

While Braithwaite does not specifically address restorative justice or victim offender mediation, he argues for principles of justice which emphasize personal accountability of offenders to their victims, active community involvement, and a process of reaffirmation of the offender as a valued community member, despite their unacceptable criminal behavior, that directly relates to the restorative justice paradigm.

Accountability: A Definition

The definition of accountability in the restorative justice paradigm is based on recognition that when an offense occurs, the offender incurs an obligation to the victim. This definition of accountability has both a cognitive meaning (understanding impact of their behavior on the victim) and a behavioral meaning (taking action to make things right). This two-dimensional understanding of accountability is a central

Table 1
Paradigms of Justice—Old and New

Old Paradigm	**New Paradigm**
1. Crime defined as violation of the state	1. Crime defined as violation of one person by another
2. Focus on estabishing blame, on guilt, on past (did he/she do it?)	2. Focus on problem solving, on liabilities/obligations, on future (what should be done?)
3. Adversarial relationship and process normative	3. Dialogue and negotiation normative
4. Imposition of pain to punish and deter/prevent	4. Restitution as a means of restoring both parties; goal of reconciliation/restoration
5. Justice defined by intent and process: right rules	5. Justice defined as right relationships; judged by outcome
6. Interpersonal, conflictual nature of crime obscured, repressed; conflict seen as individual versus the state	6. Crime recognized as interpersonal conflict; value of conflict is recognized
7. One social injury replaced by another	7. Focus on repair of social injury
8. Community on sideline, represented abstractly by state	8. Community as facilitator in restorative process
9. Encouragement of competitive, individualistic values	9. Encouragement of mutuality
10. Action directed from state to offender: –victim ignored –offender passive	10. Victim's and offender's roles recognized in problem/solution: –victim rights/needs recognized –offender encouraged to take responsibility
11. Offender accountability defined as taking punishment	11. Offender accountability defined as understanding impact of action and helping decide how to make things right
12. Offense defined in purely legal terms, devoid of moral, social, economic, political dimensions	12. Offense understood in whole context –moral, social, economic and political
13. "Debt" owed to state and society in the abstract	13. Debt/liability to victim recognized
14. Response focused on offender's past behavior	14. Response focused on harmful consequences of offender's behavior
15. Stigma of crime unremovable	15. Stigma of crime removable through restorative action
16. No encouragement for repentance and forgiveness	16. Possibilities for repentance and forgiveness
17. Dependence upon proxy professionals	17. Direct involvement by participants

Howard Zehr, 1985

element in the restorative justice paradigm.

As Howard Zehr (1990) notes, the definition of "holding offenders accountable" changes when viewed through the lens of restorative justice,

> Instead of "paying a debt to society" by experiencing punishment, accountability would mean understanding and taking responsibility for what has been done and taking action to make things right. Instead of owing an abstract debt to society, paid in an abstract way by experiencing punishment, the offender would owe a debt to the victim, to be repaid in a concrete way.

How Is It Different?:
Restorative versus Retributive Accountability

A restorative justice understanding of accountability can involve a range of possible obligations incurred by the offender to the victim. Some of these interventions include financial restitution, community service (particularly victim selected service), victim offender mediation, personal service for the victim, and other victim services. Each of these interventions have the appearance of being restorative in nature. They could, however, also be used in the context of a very retributive juvenile justice system. It is necessary to look beyond appearances to determine whether an intervention is restorative. Enthusiastically talking about new correctional concepts, while failing to implement the substance of those concepts, has long plagued juvenile and criminal justice reform efforts.

Ultimately, the choice of restorative versus retributive accountability is driven by the underlying values related to our understanding of crime and delinquency. Without a strong grounding in restorative justice values, old forms of retributive accountability could take on a new appearance yet lack any substantive difference. As one of the leading architects of the restorative justice movement, Howard Zehr (1990) provides the following distinction between a retributive and restorative understanding of accountability.

Intervention Strategy

The role of probation officers would need some alteration to provide supervision within a restorative justice context. More emphasis would be placed on brokering services for victims and offenders. Probation staff would periodically be involved in community organizing and program development efforts, as well as continual networking with other social service staff. For example, to allow for increased access for juvenile offenders and their victims to a mediation program to talk about the offense and negotiate a restitution agreement, a probation officer or director would need to negotiate with one or more local dispute resolution programs to receive referrals from the court. If no mediation programs exist locally, probation staff could recruit, train and supervise a pool of community volunteers to serve as mediators. Or, they could help organize a local effort to establish anew community based dispute resolution/mediation program.

Table 2
Accountability: Retributive versus Restorative Paradigms

Retributive Accountability	Restorative Accountability
• Wrongs create guilt	• Wrongs create liabilities and obligations
• Guilt absolute, either/or	• Degrees of responsibility
• Guilt indelible	• Guilt removable through repentance and reparation
• Debt is abstract	• Debt is concrete
• Debt paid by taking punishment	• Debt paid by making right
• "Debt" owed to society in the abstract	• Debt owed to victim first
• Accountability as taking one's "medicine"	• Accountability as taking responsibility
• Assumes behavior chosen freely	• Recognizes differences between potential and actual realization of human freedom
• Free will or social determinism	• Recognizes role of social context of choices without denying personal responsibility

---

Because the involvement of victims and community volunteers is such an integral part of restorative justice and offender accountability, and because most activities involving victims and volunteers occur in the evening or on weekends, work scheduling would also need to be altered.

To implement the principles of restorative justice in probation supervision, each case will need to be viewed in three dimensions, not simply in the single dimension of the juvenile offender. The needs of the victims of the specific offenses, along with any need facing the community, should also be examined. The following table (Mackey, 1990) offers an abbreviated format for developing each case, as a normal part of supervision practice.

From a restorative justice perspective, the probation officer's primary task will become that of coordinating the development and implementation of what Burt Galaway (1983) has called a "reparative plan." This can be done within the current basic framework of key probation tasks—that of preparing reports to aid in sentencing and supervision of offenders. Galaway points out that the process of developing a reparative plan, or for the purposes of this article what we call a restorative plan, has three primary objectives:

1. To arrive at a plan for victim reparation acceptable to the offender and victim.
2. When indicated by guidelines, to develop a plan for community reparation.
3. To assist the offender in securing a community sponsor.

The process of victim offender mediation could be employed to maximize the involve merit of community members (as volunteer mediators) and crime victims in developing restorative plans for holding offenders accountable. Rather than only a marginal number of offenders in the process of victim offender mediation (current practice), supervision practice within a restorative justice framework would presume the use of mediation in a wide range of cases, perhaps in all property offenses, if the victim is willing. This is particularly so since mediation is the most direct way of involving the victim and community (through volunteer mediators) in the justice process and thereby achieving important objectives of the balanced approach to probation supervision.

Supervision practice related to community service would also change within a restorative justice framework. Every effort would need to be made to develop "victim selected" community service placements where the specific victim is consulted to determine a placement for the offender which is meaningful to them relative to their loss from the crime.

Table 3
Restorative Justice Case Development Plan

	Hurt	**Need**	**Response**
Victim			
Offender			
Community			

Accountability Interventions

Five specific accountability interventions are particularly consistent with the restorative justice paradigm. These are: financial restitution with victim input, victim directed community work service, personal service for the victim, victim offender groups, and victim offender mediation. Each of these requires cognitive and behavioral changes in the offender, the victim, and the community. Highlighting these five interventions is not meant, however, to suggest these are the only restorative justice programs. To the contrary, a great deal of creativity is needed in both adapting other current programs and designing entirely new interventions to maximize implementation of restorative justice principles that will increasingly benefit crime victims while also holding offenders accountable in meaningful ways.

Financial Restitution with Victim Input

Restitution is a process by which criminal offenders financially compensate their victims for part or all losses victims incur as a result of the crime. Use of restitution as a sanction within the juvenile justice system has grown substantially over the past two decades (Galaway and Hudson, 1990).

Restitution programs are typically managed by juvenile probation departments although some programs are run by private community-based agencies. Cases involving theft or damage to property are identified for a possible restitution order, either pre- or post-adjudication, depending on the specific case and the court's preference. Many courts simply order restitution and expect probation staff to see that it is collected. A growing number of courts operate highly structured restitution programs to monitor compliance. Structured restitution programs have been found more effective than nonstructured programs.

Restitution is central to the balanced approach and restorative justice. Restitution has long been recognized as a critical element of holding offenders accountable for their criminal behavior and compensating victims for their losses.

Victim Directed Community Work Service

An increasing number of juvenile courts require offenders to complete a specific number of hours of work to benefit the community (Bazemore and Maloney, 1994). Community work service orders are based on recognition that the entire community is victimized when an offense occurs and that offenders should be held accountable to the community as well as to the individual victim. In many jurisdictions, the juvenile probation department directly administers the court's community work service orders. In some jurisdictions, the court contracts with a private community based agency to administer the program. As with restitution programs, many hundreds of community work service programs operate in juvenile courts throughout the United States.

The use of restitution and community work service orders as juvenile court sanctions is not, however, always consistent with the underlying principles of the balanced approach and restorative justice. For example, it is quite possible to develop restitution and community service programs from a retributive, rather than a restorative, justice perspective. Restitution and community work service are most consistent with restorative justice when they include direct input from the victim, such as the victim's selecting a particularly meaningful charity as a site for community work service.

Personal Service to Victim

Some crime victims are most interested in having the offender perform some type of service to them directly, such as painting their garage or raking leaves or cutting wood. While community work service can provide benefits to the community at large, personal service to the specific crime victim can strongly reinforce the restorative justice concept of holding offenders directly accountable to their specific victims.

Often the request by victims for the offender to perform some type of unpaid work for them emerges from the victim offender mediation process, particularly when it becomes clear to the victim that the offender does not have the means to pay financial restitution. The specific amount of personal service for the victim is usually determined by dividing the amount of financial loss that would have been considered for restitution by an even dollar amount close to the minimum wage. It is important that any conversion of financial loss into personal service for the victim be based on the principle of fairness. Otherwise the value of the personal service could greatly exceed the actual loss.

While requests for personal service are not an unusual outcome of mediation, it is also important to make clear that many victims would not want to do this. For some victims, personal service by the offender could heighten their fear and apprehension, resulting in a feeling of revictimization. The use of personal service to the victim as an intervention should be clearly driven by the expressed needs of victims and never ordered by the court without their consent.

Victim Offender Groups

A number of jurisdictions have been experimenting with bringing together a small group of offenders, often inmates, with a small group of victims of crimes similar to those committed by the offenders. These groups are facilitated by a third party, such as a mediator or counselor.

They often meet on a weekly basis for a month or two. These victim offender groups seek to sensitize offenders to the human impact of their criminal behavior, even though the victim is not the victim of their crime. These groups are also meant to help crime victims understand that juvenile offenders are rarely as threatening as the image on the victim's mind. Knowing this can reduce the fear victims experience after the crime. An opportunity is also provided for the victim to express feelings about the offense's impact.

Understanding accountability from a restorative justice perspective requires an awareness by the offender of how criminal behavior affects other persons. Victim offender groups within correctional facilities or in the community represent an important and underused educational restorative justice intervention.

Victim Offender Mediation

While restorative justice principles can be found in a number of different programmatic interventions, the clearest expression of these values is seen in the emerging field of victim offender mediation (Umbreit, 1994). No other known program so directly and actively involves crime victims in the process of justice, with a focus upon holding offenders accountable while restoring emotional and material losses to both parties. In addition, the process itself can be used to negotiate and plan a more comprehensive restorative plan incorporating community service and other elements of accountability.

Victim offender mediation represents one of the most creative efforts to hold offenders personally accountable for their behavior, to emphasize the human impact of crime, to provide opportunities for offenders to take responsibility for their actions by facing their victim and making amends, to promote active victim and community involvement in the justice process, and to enhance the quality of justice experienced by both victims and offenders (Umbreit & Coates, 1993; Umbreit, 1994). More than 150 victim offender mediation programs operate in the United States, 26 in Canada, and an even larger number in Europe (Umbreit, 1994).

Victim offender mediation involves a face to face meeting, in the presence of a trained mediator who is often a community volunteer. At the meeting the parties are given time to address informational and emotional needs. Once questions have been answered and feelings expressed, the mediation session then turns to a discussion of losses and the possibility of developing a mutually agreeable restitution plan (for example, money, work for victim, work for victim's choice of a charity, etc.).

Voluntary participation by crime victims and offenders (although for offenders it is a choice within a highly coercive context) is a strong ethical principle of the victim offender mediation process. Crime victims are given the unusual opportunity to express their feelings directly to the person who violated them. They can get answers to questions such as "Why me?," or "How did you get into our house?," or "Were you stalking us and planning on coming back?". Upon seeing their offender, victims are often relieved. This "criminal" usually bears little resemblance to the frightening character they may have conjured up in their minds. The mediation process allows victims and offenders to deal with each other as people, oftentimes from the same neighborhood, rather than as stereotypes and objects.

A Continuum of Mediation Interventions in Juvenile Court

In addition to victim offender mediation there are also other restorative justice applications of mediation and conflict resolution in the juvenile justice system that promote accountability. In fact, a continuum of mediation and conflict resolution services is relevant to nearly all types of juvenile offenders, ranging from parent-child mediation for status offenders, to school mediation and gang mediation, to conflict resolution training for more serious juvenile offenders in correctional facilities. In addition to their impact in promoting a restorative justice understanding of accountability, mediation and conflict resolution programs promote competency development in juvenile offenders by tapping into their strengths and training them in important skills required throughout life.

Table 4 portrays the multiple applications of mediation and conflict resolution in the juvenile justice system (NIDR, 1991).

Gauging Progress: Developing Performance Benchmarks

Human service agencies are increasingly developing performance objectives and performance measures as a means of becoming more accountable to the public and their clients. While juvenile justice has lagged behind on this, the balanced approach/restorative justice paradigm should facilitate development of measurable and meaningful performance outcomes for juvenile justice interventions with offenders. Several examples of measurable performance objectives based on understanding accountability within the restorative justice paradigm include:

- number of victims receiving restitution

Table 4
**Possible Applications of Mediation and Conflict Resolution
in the Juvenile Justice System**

Type of Juvenile Justice Client	Application of Conflict Resolution and Mediation	Program Development
Status offender	• Parent/child mediation	• Train probation officers and/or community volunteers in parent/child mediation • Establish referral and case management systems
First offender	• Conflict resolution curriculum	• Train First Offender program staff in use of curriculum • Implement curriculum
Juvenile offender	• Mediation of resolution dialogue and agreements between victim and juvenile offender • Mediation of violent disputes between offenders and other disputants	• Train probation officers and/or community volunteers • Train probation officers and/or community volunteers in victim/offender mediation and generic mediation
Community corrections clients	• Mediation of restitution agreements between victim and offender • Mediation of parent/child conflict	• Train community corrections staff and volunteers in victim/offender and parent/child mediation
Residents in juvenile facilities	• Conflict resolution curriculum • Mediation in facilities • Parent/child mediation for departing residents	• Train staff in curriculum use • Train staff and residents in mediation • Train staff or volunteers in parent/child mediation

This chart is from the Community Dispute Resolution Manual (p. 27), National Institute for Dispute Resolution, Washington, DC. Reprinted with the permission of N.I.D.R.

• number of victims participating in victim offender mediation
• number of offenders participating in victim offender mediation
• number of offenders successfully completing their restitution obligation
• victim perceptions of fairness related to the offender's restitution obligation

- number of victims participating in other programs to hold offenders accountable

Development of rigorous and meaningful performance measures cannot be done in a vacuum, however, and should be specific to agency focus, programmatic variation and the community expectations. In the early stages of implementing a restorative justice understanding of accountability, a first step in developing performance objectives would be to identify "benchmarks" for gauging progress and assessing the integrity of implementation. In other words, it is important to have general guidelines for answering the question "how do we know accountability within the restorative justice paradigm when we see it?"

This will, in part, mean understanding some of the new practices and programs discussed earlier in this article. It is extremely important, however, for juvenile justice managers to avoid the "trap" of simply adding new programs without changing the underlying values and the fundamental logic of traditional casework supervision. Even worse is the "trap" of simply renaming current programs and practices, without any real change occurring, in such a way that they are "politically correct" in the context of the terminology of the balanced approach and the restorative justice paradigm. A restorative justice understanding of accountability requires a fundamental change in our assumptions about crime and delinquency, and a corresponding change in one's behavior in working with offenders, victims and the community. Depending on the assumptions, values, and behavior of the system, accountability interventions such as restitution can either be promoted in a retributive justice framework (as is the current case in most jurisdictions) or a restorative justice framework.

To ensure effective implementation of an accountability focus within the restorative justice paradigm, juvenile justice professionals should focus upon the issues identified in the following tables as the basis for developing benchmarks and ultimately for developing performance objectives and outcome measures. These tables provide a number of performance benchmarks that managers may use to gauge success in implementing a restorative justice understanding of accountability.

Embracing a restorative justice understanding of accountability requires a commitment to long-term systemic change—changes in the values that drive the juvenile justice system and changes in the manner in which cases/clients are defined and responded to. Moving toward a more balanced and restorative juvenile justice system is ultimately less a final destination and more a journey of organizational renewal and challenge. Most importantly, through a restorative justice understanding of accountability, victims of crime and community volunteers can play a far more active and satisfying role in building a more understandable, effective and fair juvenile justice system.

Table 5
Intervention Assumptions

1. Less emphasis on symbolic ways of having the juvenile offender be held accountable.

2. More emphasis on direct and personal ways for the juvenile offender to understand victims as people, not targets.

3. Interventions which maximize opportunities for offenders to make direct and personal amends to victims.

4. Providing victims of all property offenses involving restitution the opportunity to participate in the victim offender mediation process, with trained community volunteers, assuming both victim and offender agree.

5. Providing some victims of violent offenses the opportunity to participate in the victim offender mediation process to assist them in their need for closure, with specially trained professional or volunteer mediators, assuming both victim and offender agree.

Table 6
Supervision Practice

1. More opportunities for offenders to take direct responsibility for their behavior by compensating the victim in some form.

2. More opportunities for offenders to understand the real human impact of their behavior on those who were victimized.

3. More opportunities for offenders to express remorse and make things right with victims.

4. More opportunities for victims to have direct and active input into the process of holding juvenile offenders accountable.

5. More opportunities for members of the community to participate in the process of holding juvenile offenders accountable.

Table 7
Intermediate Objectives

1. Number of victims actively participating in the juvenile justice system.

2. Proportion of victim directed community service placements to total community service placements.

3. Proportion of victim offender mediation cases to total restitution cases.

4. Successful completion of restitution.

5. Successful completion of community service.

6. Victim satisfaction with how the justice system responded to their case.

7. Victim perceptions of fairness with process and outcome.

8. Offender perceptions of fairness with process and outcome.

References

Bazemore, Gordon (1994), "Developing a Victim Orientation for Community Corrections: A Restorative Justice Paradigm and a Balanced Approach," *Perspectives*, Special Issue, American Probation and Parole Association.

Bazemore, G. and Maloney, D. (1994), "Rehabilitating Community Service Sanctions in a Balanced Justice System," *Federal Probation*, 58(1), 24–35.

Braithwaite, J. (1989), *Crime, Shame and Reintegration*. Cambridge: Cambridge University Press.

Coates, Robert B. and Gehm, John (1989), "An Empirical Assessment," in Martin Wright and Burt Galaway (eds.) *Mediation and Criminal Justice*. London: Sage.

Galaway, Burt (1983), "Probation as a Reparative Sentence," *Federal Probation*, 46(3), 9–18.

Galaway, Burt and Hudson, Joe (1990), *Criminal Justice, Restitution, and Reconciliation*. Monsey, NY: Criminal Justice Press.

Mackey, Virginia (1990), *Restorative Justice Toward Nonviolence*. Louisville, KY: Presbyterian Criminal Justice Program.

Maloney, Dennis, Dennis Romig, and Troy Armstrong (1988), "Juvenile Probation: The Balanced Approach," *Juvenile and Family Court Journal*, 39 (3).

Marshall, Tony F. and Merry, Susan (1990), *Victims and Crime and Accountability*. London: Home Office.

National Institute for Dispute Resolution (1991), *Community Dispute Resolution Manual*. Washington, DC: NIDR.

Umbreit. Mark S. (1989), "Victims Seeking Fairness, Not Revenge: Toward Restorative Justice," *Federal Probation*, September.

Umbreit, Mark S. (1991), "Restorative Justice: Having Offenders Meet With Their Victims Offers Benefits for Both Parties," *Corrections Today Journal*,

(July). Laurel, MD: American Correctional Association.

Umbreit, Mark S. (1993), *Mediating Interpersonal Conflicts: A Pathway to Peace*. West Concord, NH: CPI Publishing.

Umbreit, Mark S. (1994), *Victim Meets Offender: The Impact of Restorative Justice & Mediation*. Monsey, NY: Criminal Justice Press.

Umbreit, Mark S. and Coates, Robert B. (1992), "The Impact of Mediating Victim Offender Conflict: An Analysis of Programs in Three States," *Juvenile & Family Court Journal*. Reno, NV: National Council of Juvenile and Family Court Judges.

Umbreit, Mark S. and Coates, Robert B. (1993), "Cross-Site Analysis of Victim Offender Mediation in Four States," *Crime & Delinquency*, 39 (4).

Van Ness, Daniel W. (1986), *Crime and Its Victims*. Intervarsity Press.

Van Ness, Daniel W. (1990), "Restorative Justice," in Burt Galaway and Joe Hudson (eds.) *Criminal Justice, Restitution and Reconciliation*. Monsey, NY: Criminal Justice Press, a division of Willow Tree Press.

Van Ness, Daniel W., Carlson, David R., Crawford, Thomas, and Strong, Karen (1989), *Restorative Justice Theory*. Reston, VA: Justice Fellowship.

Wright, Martin (1991), *Justice for Offenders*. Philadelphia, PA: Open University Press.

Wright, Martin and Galaway, Burt (1989), *Mediation and Criminal Justice*. London: Sage.

Zehr, Howard (1985), *Retributive Justice, Restorative Justice*. Elkhart, IN: Mennonite Central Committee, Office of Criminal Justice.

Zehr, Howard (1990), *Changing Lenses, A New Focus for Crime and Justice*. Scottsdale, PA: Herald Press.

Section *IV*

Classification for Correctional Treatment

The American Correctional Association (1968:10) defines classification as "the means by which offenders are assigned to different programs in an effort to provide the best available programs to fit the individual offender's needs." Classification of offenders, if properly executed, enables correctional agencies to maximize the use of their personnel and resources to provide treatment that will enable the offender to fulfill his or her specific needs and to assure, as well, that the concerns of other interested parties are met.

The most basic and familiar classifications of offenders are those made according to sex, age (juvenile or adult), severity of offense (misdemeanor or felony), and types of statutes violated (federal, state, or local). The classification of juvenile offenders has been complicated by rulings that require status offenders (those who have committed offenses that are not illegal for adults) to be housed in nonsecure settings and not be mixed with delinquent offenders (Public Law 93-415, 1974).

Classification may be made at a diagnostic or reception center, which receives newly sentenced adults and uses various indicators to assess the level of security at which each offender should be held and the type of treatment that may be given. After an offender is sent to a specific institution, an in-house classification may also be made. Juveniles placed in the custody of a state youth authority or youth commission are customarily remanded to a diagnostic and reception center where the type of setting in which the youth will be held is decided. However, in some jurisdictions judges have the power to sentence adults or send juveniles to specific institutions.

Classifications made under the guise of treatment are also developed for more effective management of prisoners. Correctional facilities are frequently typified as being maximum, medium, or minimum security; offenders are placed in terms of their perceived risk to the community and to each other. Maximum security facilities may be surrounded by outside walls or high electrified fences, have internal divisions into cell blocks, and use armed guards. Medium security facilities may be surrounded by walls or fences but have less intense segregation of prisoners and a lower level of internal surveillance. Minimum security institutions may have no readily visible security measures around the institution and may use cottage living or honors sections for many of the prisoners.

One of the first attempts to develop a prisoner classification system was made by Howard Gill in 1927. His plan included separation of prisoners into distinct groups, either within an institution or by housing them in separate facilities. Gill believed that new prisoners should be isolated from the others for purposes of observing their behavior and determining their potential for rehabilitation. From this point, prisoners would be classified as *tractable*—able to respond to treatment efforts and change their behavior; *intractable*—resistant to change and requiring forcible methods of control; *defective*—mentally ill, retarded, or physically handicapped; and those who could be handled best in some type of work-release or community placement facility. (Gill, 1970).

As classification systems became more refined, it was thought possible, through an elaborate diagnostic process, to match a specific offender with an exact form of treatment that would best suit his needs. Dr. Herbert C. Quay developed a system of classification termed *differential treatment*, which employed such specific matching. First used with delinquents at the National Training School for Boys in Washington, D.C., the program involved testing and then matching each new student with a counselor who had been trained to "treat" the type of problem behavior the youth was believed to manifest.

When rehabilitation became a paramount goal of corrections, it was necessary to develop treatment modalities to enhance the rehabilitative effort. It was also necessary to ascertain which offenders were likely to benefit from specific treatment programs. In selection 13, "The Functions of Classification Models in Probation and Parole: Control or Treatment-Rehabilitation?" Kratcoski notes that highly complex methods of classifying probationers, inmates, and parolees have been developed for administrative and management purposes, as well as for treatment and rehabilitation. The National Advisory Commission on Criminal Justice Standards and Goals, in its *Report on Corrections* (1973), made the point that classification made supposedly for purposes of treatment may in fact be used for control, convenience of the staff, evening out of the number in each treatment program, or cost efficiency.

The range of available correctional treatment is subject to the security level of the institution to which the offender is assigned. For example, total milieu therapy or guided group interaction would not be a likely treatment possibility in a maximum security institution, while behavior modification therapy would be readily available.

On the community level, a probation, parole, or juvenile aftercare officer often divides the caseload into maximum, medium, and minimum supervision levels after calculating the needs of each offender and the risk each presents to the community. Clients under maximum supervision might be seen rather frequently (once or twice a week), while those in minimum supervision may be required to report monthly, or only if some problem arises.

In selection 14, "The Case Management System Experience in Ohio," Crooks provides information on the step-by-step development, implementation, and revision of a classification system for offenders utilized by the Ohio Adult Parole Authority. Specific instruments illustrate how offenders are assigned to maximum, medium, or minimum supervision, using risk and need assessment scales. Adaptations of the classification system, based on evaluation findings and officer input, are described, and methods for training officers in risk and needs assessment are reported.

The U.S. Bureau of Prisons developed the functional unit management model in the early 1970s (Levinson and Gerard, 1973) as a means of dividing facilities into smaller units of offenders who are housed together and receive a specific form of treatment. The inmates were supervised by a specially trained treatment team. Functional units were developed to handle offenders with common problems, such as substance abuse or emotional problems. Other units included academic or vocational education emphases. Several states adopted the functional unit management concept, and their systems resemble that used by the U.S. Bureau of Prisons.

In selection 15, "Functional Unit Management," Toch discusses the origins of the functional unit management model, the premises on which the model rests, the types of units that have been developed in various correctional facilities, and the settings in which functional unit management is likely to be effective.

In selection 16, "Case Managing Multiproblem Offenders," by Toch, the four related functions of case management—needs assessment, referral, coordination, and brokerage—are defined and explained, and their applicability to case managing multiproblem offenders are discussed.

References

Committee on Classification and Casework, American Prison Association. 1968. *Handbook on Classification in Correctional Institutions.* Washington, DC: American Correctional Association.

Gill, Howard. 1970. "A New Prison Discipline: Implementing the Declaration of Principles of 1870," *Federal Probation*, Vol. 34, No. 3 (June): 31–38.

Levinson, Robert B. and Roy E. Gerard. 1973. "Functional Units: A Different Correctional Approach," *Federal Probation Quarterly*, Vol. 37, (December), 8–16.

National Advisory Commission on Criminal Justice Standards and Goals. 1973. *Report on Corrections.* Washington, DC: U.S. Government Printing Office, 202–203.

Public Law 93-415 (September 7, 1974), Title II, Part B. Sec. 223(a), (12).

13

The Functions of Classification Models in Probation and Parole
Control or Treatment-Rehabilitation?*

Peter C. Kratcoski

The use of classification systems in corrections is not a new development. When corrections moved from a punishment model to a rehabilitation or treatment emphasis in the early 20th century, classifications systems, such as that developed by Howard Gill, were used to separate prisoners according to their potential for treatment or training. Gradually, classification systems became more complex and multipurpose, and today they are used not only to classify offenders within institutions but also to assess the amount of supervision needed by offenders placed on probation in lieu of institutionalization or those paroled from prisons.

Classification systems now in use are complex and multipurposive. A distinction can be made between those that are used for administrative and management purposes and those designed to treat and rehabilitate the offender. Those of a management nature are designed to enhance control and to predict the likelihood that an offender will commit new criminal acts after release. The treatment-rehabilitation systems try to differentiate the offenders on the basis of their needs, attitudes, motivations, and attributes and then provide the treatment necessary to bring about the desired changes in values, attitudes, and skills that will inhibit the offenders from recidivating. The treatment-rehabilitation systems of classification are based on the concept of differential treatment,

* The research presented in this article was funded by a grant to the Ohio Department of Rehabilitation and Correction from the National Institute of Corrections, NIC E-P-6.

Source: *Federal Probation*, 49(5) (December 1985): 49–56.

which implies that the needs and problems of inmates and those in community supervision must be defined and treated on an individualized basis. The offender is matched with the specific treatment program which best addresses these problems and needs.

According to Edith Flynn, an effective classification system should meet the following criteria:

(1) There must be an explicit statement regarding the function and purpose of the classification system.

(2) The classification system should be dynamic and theoretically based so that it may serve to increase the system's predictive powers and its success in reducing recidivism.

(3) The assumption on which the classification system is based must be explicit.

(4) The critical variables of the classification typology applied must be specific so that the utility of the system can be empirically tested.

(5) The classification system should be useful and feasible and facilitate efficient management and optimum use of available resources.[1]

Classification of offenders within institutions was closely related to programming, while the use of classification for those placed on probation and parole was initially directed toward predicting recidivism, and levels of supervision were set up according to the assessed risk that the offender would become involved in criminal activity after release.

Since 1980, the Federal Probation System has used a Risk Prediction Scale (RPS 80) which classifies offenders for "high activity" or "low activity" supervision. The items used in this scale include completion of a high school education, the age of the offender, arrest-free status for 5 or more consecutive years before the previous offense, few prior arrests, a history of freedom from opiate usage, and a steady employment period of at least 4 months prior to arraignment for the present offense. Each item is weighted, and a cutoff point on the total score determines whether the offender will initially be assigned to low or high activity supervision.[2] Before initiation of this new system, survey data collected by the Probation Division of the Administrative Office of the U.S. Courts in 1974 and by the Research Division of the Federal Judicial Center in 1977 indicated that a variety of caseload classification methods were used by Federal probation officers. These methods ranged from purely subjective assessments to statistical prediction devices.[3]

When the National Institute of Corrections placed the development of statewide classification systems for probation and parole as a high priority funding project, various states developed systems of classification of those under supervision. These statewide systems considered both control and treatment in their classification procedures. One of the earliest states to receive funding for a new classification program was Wisconsin, and a statewide system was put into effect there in 1977. More than 30 other states have now adopted some form of statewide classification model, and the current emphasis in the field is for county level probation departments to incorporate some features of the state models in their supervision programs. Because of its early start in this area and the wide publicity given to its features, the Wisconsin classification system is often considered the prototype for development of new classification systems.

Classification models tend to have common features. One would be an assessment of the risk (danger to the community) presented by the offender. The risk classification device is designed to assess a client's potential for future criminal behavior. Items related to the offender's criminal history and socioeconomic-personal adjustment background are weighted, and a total score is used to place the offender at a specific level of supervision, with the intensity of supervision designed to reduce the threat of recidivism to a minimum. For example, the instrument used to assess risk in the Wisconsin system included the following:

(1) Number of address changes in the last 12 months;

(2) Percentage of time employed in the last 12 months;

(3) Alcohol usage problems;

(4) Other drug usage problems;

(5) Attitude;

(6) Age at first conviction;

(7) Number of prior periods of probation/parole supervision;

(8) Number of prior probation/parole revocations;

(9) Number of prior felony convictions;

(10) Convictions or juvenile adjudications for burglary, theft, auto theft, or robbery, worthless checks or forgery; and

(11) Conviction or juvenile adjudication for assaultive offense within the last 5 years.[4]

When the various states or local probation and parole departments developed their own risk instruments, there was acceptance of the format used in Wisconsin, but each supervising authority tended to vary somewhat in the number of items included, the specific focus of the items, and the weight given to each item in relation to the total score. For example, those responsible for developing a risk instrument for the Tennessee system reasoned that:

> Since laws vary from one state to another, law enforcement varies from one state to another, and people differ from one state to another, those individuals who find themselves in prison and then on parole will differ from one state to another. This . . . requires that the processes of determining levels of risk and need should be reflective of the clientele in the Tennessee Parole System.[5]

This approach of adjusting the instrument to the local conditions seems appropriate. It also apparently does not detract from the predictive power of the instrument. In classifying offenders supervised under the Federal system, several predictive devices used were found to have comparable predictive power, even though the specific items used in the instrument and the method of scoring and assignment to risk levels varied.[6]

Another feature of classification models is use of a needs instrument, which assesses the offender's needs in such areas as family support, employment, emotional problems, or drug or alcohol abuse treatment. As an offender's score on the needs instrument increases, it is assumed that the amount of time and the number of resources directed toward the case will also increase. The needs assessment instrument is most effective when clients are reassessed on a regular basis and determinations are made as to whether progress is occurring in meeting the offender's needs and working on his or her problems.

Both risk and needs instruments allow officers and supervisors the opportunity to categorize all those supervised in a matrix format: offenders with a high risk and low needs, and those with low risk and low needs. Management and officers get a very clear picture of the distribution of cases which are currently under supervision, and workload distributions can be made according to the intensity of supervision required for the offenders. The models move away from caseloads and incorporate a "work unit" concept, which is set up on the basis of the supervision levels of the offenders, the geographic distribution of the cases, the types of duties required of officers (preparation of presentence investigations or supervision only), and special types of cases handled (transfers or interstate compact cases). Theoretically, this approach should equalize the amount of work expected from each officer. Under past systems, caseloads were defined in terms of the number of cases supervised. Little attention was given to the intensity of supervision required or the amount of time needed for each case.

After assessments have been completed, the classification procedure takes place. Classification in the case management approach involves grounding the specific classification in an evaluation of the interacting forces of the case. The specific classifications of offenders generally include maximum, medium, and minimum supervision levels. They may also provide for cursory levels of supervision, with little or no contact between officer and offender. The specific classification of offenders may vary from jurisdiction to jurisdiction, even though these offenders may have common characteristics. A case perceived as low risk in one jurisdiction may be classified as a medium risk in another because of the small number of serious cases serviced there. The risk score cutoff points may vary significantly, depending on the number of cases supervised and the number of officers available. For example, Ohio and Wisconsin use essentially the same risk and needs instruments, but in Wisconsin the maximum supervision category begins at a score of 15 on the risk instrument, while in Ohio it begins at 26.

In addition to risk factors, other methods are used to classify offenders. Rather than basing classification on criminal activity, other behavioral and personality characteristics of the offender are taken into account. This information is obtained through an interview with the client or from case file information. In Ohio, four Case Supervision Approaches (CSA) are defined, including criminal orientation, multiproblem, socially deficient, and situational offenders. An individual is assigned to one of the CSA's on the basis of a structured interview. After placement at a risk level and a CSA, a case management plan for providing services to the client is developed. The offender is expected to provide input in developing this plan and should agree that the activities required of him or her are appropriate and achievable.

Once the supervision level is defined for a case, the supervision is conducted according to a formula set up for the number and types of contacts required at this level. The specifications of the case plan will direct the officer toward referrals to agencies, the amount of counseling needed, requiring drug presence tests, and setting of special conditions. Case monitoring involves verifying employment, place of residence, participation in required programs, and compliance with probation and parole conditions.

In California, the classification system differentiates both types of offenders and types of parole officers. Offenders are classified as "control," "service," or "minimum-supervision" cases. Those with high risk assessment scores are designated "control" and given intensive supervision by officers who handle only control cases and whose only function is surveillance. "Service" cases, classified by high needs assessment scores, are under the supervision of a service officer, who acts as a broker in obtaining referrals to appropriate community agencies. If a service category offender commits a new offense the service officer cannot arrest him—this function is reserved for control officers. Minimum supervision cases (those with low risk and needs scores) are seen only at a time of release from prison and at the end of the year parole, with monthly mailed-in reports from the offender taking the place of visits to the parole office. Minimum supervision specialists handle these cases, but perform no other functions. In 1981, 84 percent of the parolees were classified as control cases, 8 percent as service cases, and 8 percent as minimum supervision cases. The California parole officers were assigned to control as opposed to service or minimum supervision in a 6 to 1 ratio.[7]

Most classification systems provide for periodic reassessments of the cases. These may take place at specified time intervals (6 months, for example) or if there is a charge in jurisdiction from one unit to another or if the person supervised has committed a new offense. The reassessment instruments shift emphasis from past criminal behavior to overall performance or adjustment during the current probation or parole. The reassessment instrument taps the offender's adherence to the rules and special conditions, use of community services recommended, and overall adjustments in the areas of work, family, and personal functioning. At the time of reassessment the level of supervision may be reduced or increased, although there would be a tendency to reduce rather than increase supervision.

At the time of final evaluation before release a summary of the changes and progress which occurred during supervision is developed. Once the case has been terminated, the information available on all of the classification instruments is stored for future access, if needed.

The Effects of Classification Systems on Clients and Staff

Although the majority of states have developed some form of offender classification which attempts to provide a control and treatment formula within the same model, the evaluation of the effectiveness of these models has generally been rather sketchy. Each state has attempted some internal evaluation, and on occasion detailed evaluation by a neutral agent has taken place. The bases for the determination of effectiveness have varied, but recidivism reduction is the primary factor considered. The purpose of this section of the article is to draw attention to areas in which the departments might be affected regardless of the changes in criminal behavior which may occur after the classification system is put into operation. The manner in which the system affects the staff is generally not even considered in evaluations of its effectiveness. In this article we will look at effects of new systems on both clients and officers, including the degree to which administrators and officers accept and commit themselves to the new system, opinions of the new system's efficiency in comparison to prior systems, and the effects of standardization and the reduction of discretion on the officers' perceptions of their role and their job satisfaction. Does the new system remove autonomy and professional discretion, require upgrading of skill levels, vary or consolidate responsibility areas, increase tedious paperwork, improve communications with other officers and superiors, and reduce or enhance overall job satisfaction? For the clients, what is the expectation in regard to recidivism and community adjustment? The new systems are geared to efficiency and productive use of resources. Recidivism is not expected to decline at all supervision levels. Instead, those offenders who are placed in a maximum supervision category and who also have high needs are given the most intense supervision and concentration of services, and for them the model predicts that criminal behavior will significantly decline and that individual and social adjustment will increase. For offenders placed at lower intensity of supervision levels it is predicted that their present level of performance will not deteriorate and that they will not commit criminal offenses at levels greater than their prior performances.

A study conducted by the National Institute of Corrections involved 474 probation and parole officers who were working in nine states in which some new case management system had recently been introduced. In responding to questions about their new system, more than three of every four respondents viewed it as beneficial. The majority of negative comments about the systems dealt with very specific policy issues indigenous to the particular state system. Some of these comments centered on the inability to adequately perform as expected because of an extremely high caseload, the inclusion of juveniles in the system, problems in rural areas related to finding appropriate settings for conducting interviews, and lack of social-community support systems for referrals once the problems of offenders had been assessed. In this study 32 percent of the respondents rated the system as being "very helpful" in their job, 46 percent considered it "helpful," 14 percent considered it "moderately helpful," and 8 percent regarded it as "not helpful." Seventy-three percent indicated that the system increased their knowledge and understanding of the clients, 53 percent said that it helped improve their case planning, and 54 percent said it helped them improve their ability to anticipate problems on the job.[8]

The degree of satisfaction with new case management systems seems to depend on the commitment to the system by administrators, the preparation for changes, and the ease of the transition from one system to the other. The nature of change is also an important point. In New York City, the Department of Adult Supervision Services had to introduce radical changes in the manner in which it supervised clients because of the influx of more than 13,000 new cases annually and budget reductions. The system introduced, called the Differential Supervision Program (DSP), had three levels of supervision assigned according to risk. However, the minimum supervision level contacts consisted of a monthly telephone call by the offender to a data entry telephone operator. If the call did not occur, a computer-generated letter was sent to remind the probationer to make the call. If the call still was not received, the probation officer was notified and appropriate action taken. Carol Rauh, in evaluating the New York City program, found that two factors were important in determining acceptance or rejection of the model by the rank and file officers. One was whether the automated support services portion of the system performed adequately and actually fulfilled the standardized routine tasks expected of it. The assumption of the program was that the computer would relieve the officers of much of the routine paperwork which was extremely time consuming but contributed to the offenders' welfare. In actual operation, the computer frequently broke down or was in error, and the officers were required to handle a deluge of calls, which led to dissatisfaction and general disillusionment with the system. The second factor mentioned by Ms. Rauh as important in acceptance of the new system was the administration's support and direction. To assess administration and staff commitment, a number of interviews were completed. The higher levels of administrators were very enthusiastic and unanimous in their belief in the importance and effectiveness of the new system. However, satisfaction with the system decreased in the lower levels of administration, and was at its lowest point among the unit supervisors. Only one of the six supervisors interviewed spoke enthusiastically about the new system. This lack of belief in the system was reflected in the attitudes of the probation officers. Half of the officers interviewed reported that while it was a good idea in theory they saw little practical value in the new system. Rather than reducing their workloads, they felt that the new system had added to them. About two-thirds of the officers reported that they did not find the forms used to classify clients helpful, and only two of all the officers interviewed felt that the forms helped them focus on client problems.[9]

An extensive evaluation of the Ohio Case Management System was conducted in selected regions of the state one year after the new system had been in operation. I was the person selected to design and carry out this evaluation. As part of the evaluation, officers in one of the first regions to receive training in the new system were asked to complete an Attitude Assessment Questionnaire before they were trained in the new system. They completed the same questionnaire approximately one year after the training was received and the system had been in operation in that region. The questionnaire explored officers' perceptions of administrators' attitudes toward officers, administrators' effectiveness as perceived by the officers, and officers' positive attitudes toward change. Comparison of the results of the two administrations of the questionnaire revealed that in the post-test there was some change toward more positive attitudes, with the most significant change occurring with regard to officers' perceptions of the administrators' effectiveness.

A second phase of the evaluation of attitudes and opinions of personnel involved a qualitative assessment of the system by supervisors and officers in another region of the state in which the new Case Management System had been implemented. A semistructured interview format was used. The supervisors' responses ranged from total acceptance to a somewhat skeptical "wait and see" attitude. Problems identified included the need for an increase in personnel and adjustment in the number of work units allotted for each supervision level case and for emergency situations for cases which involved revocation procedures. The supervisors also saw a need for additional officer training in the development of case management plans. The officers in general accepted the new system as a useful tool, regarded the standardization in the new system as good, and felt it professionalized the officer's position, promoted efficiency and gave the officers the security of making case management decisions based on objective criteria. Some officers felt that it did involve more paperwork, but the majority felt that the new system was more efficient than the former system because it assisted in developing a case plan earlier and offered direction as to what would be appropriate referrals to social service agencies. Some indicated that it led to an improvement in communications with immediate supervisors. In the past, if there were some confusion or disagreement about how a case should be supervised, the officer would have to accept the supervisors' directions. Now, because of the standardized procedures, it was quite easy to explain to a supervisor how a decision on a case was reached.

In contrast to the New York City probation program, the Ohio case management system was given firm support at all administrative levels. The top administrators supported it through communications and personal appearances to discuss the merits of the system. Regional supervisors and unit supervisors were involved in the Case Management System Development Committee, which designed the instruments in conjunction with the Research Division of the Adult Parole Authority. This support by the administrators was reflected in the comments by the officers, who indicated that in the beginning they thought the new system was just a gimmick or even a way of increasing caseloads and reducing staff, but after its introduction they believed that the administration was committed to it, that the system was here to stay, and that they might as well work with it.[10]

Perhaps the most drastic change in the role of officers occurred in the California system. We noted earlier that the roles of the officers became quite specialized. The acceptance of the case management model in California by administrators, supervisors, and field officers varied. Administrators and supervisors appeared to accept the model because of its emphasis on the protection of the community. Given the current emphasis on "just desserts" for the offenders, and the fact that parole was actually abolished for a period of time in California, a model which emphasizes the control facet of parole work had strong appeal. Some of the field officers also appeared to be quite pleased with the system. They found the concept of the minimum supervision of some cases to be logical and efficient. Some also liked being responsible for only one facet of parole work. Many did not feel competent to handle the dual roles of control and service. On the other hand, some officers lamented the loss of discretion, the ability to use their own judgment in making decisions. This discretionary power was a factor which gave the officer a professional status. Others also felt that the process was more complex and cumbersome than the old system. Their most frequent complaint was that the new system has generated more paperwork, and this detracts from the main job of supervision.[11]

A latent product of extreme specialization by officers only vaguely recognized is a tendency for the department personnel to factionalize on the basis of their assignments. Officers tend to develop a perspective or orientation toward their job which reflects the major goal of their work. The control officers might begin to perceive themselves as law enforcement officers, while the service officers would view themselves as social service workers. The communication gaps and internal dissension between custody and treatment personnel are well recognized in institutional settings on both the juvenile and adult levels. The competition for resources and personnel, in particular when budgets become tight, leads to a general decline in interpersonal relations, morale, and common goal orientation. In most cases, when these conflicts occur the custody factors take priority over treatment.

Recidivism

Although the success or failure of case management systems should not necessarily be dependent on the reduction of recidivism produced, when the basic question, "Does it work?" is asked, reduction in criminal behavior tends to be the criterion which can justify an affirmative response.

The case management models developed by the various states do not suggest that an across the board reduction of criminal behavior will result after the system commences operation. If the model functions according to design, the significant reductions in recidivism should occur in the maximum supervision category. The minimum supervision category should not change, even with the reduction in supervision, and the medium supervision cases might show a reduction in criminal behavior because of the employment of a more individualized case management plan.

Systematic research on the effects on recidivism of new case management plans is trickling in, but the data only give hints regarding the long-term effects. Those who have considerable experience in the corrections field are knowledgeable enough to expect dramatic changes in criminal behavior for the maximum supervision cases. An offender whose deviant behavior dates back to childhood and whose life has followed a pattern of repeated offenses, supervision and/or incarceration is not going to change over night because of more intense supervision or a different approach to supervision.

In Wisconsin, a sample of offenders who were placed in the maximum supervision group were compared with a matched sample of cases who had not yet been included in the case management plan. Those in the control group were matched with those in the experimental group in age, sex, race, probation or parole status, employment, and items on the risk and needs instruments. The maximum supervision group under the new case plan had significantly lower recidivism than those in the control group. Thirty-seven percent of those in the control group had a new offense reported, compared to 18 percent of the experimental group. Twenty percent of the control group members had their probation or parole revoked, compared to 11 percent of the experimental group.[12] For the medium supervision cases a smaller percentage of those supervised under the new system recidivated when they were compared with the control group, but the differences were not large enough to be considered statistically significant. The recidivism in the minimum supervision group was quite low for both the experimental and control groups, confirming the hypothesis that this category of offenders can be given only cursory supervision and still not show an increase in their criminal behavior.

The findings that only 18 percent of the maximum supervision group committed a new offense and only 11 percent had their parole or probation revoked appears incredible when compared to the much higher recidivism rates generally considered to be normal for maximum supervision probationers and parolees. However, it should be noted that the Wisconsin Bureau of Community Corrections is responsible for the supervision of all adult probationers and both juvenile and adult parolees[13] and the overall characteristics of this offender population may not be comparable to what one would find in a more urban-industrialized state.

A study by the Wisconsin Bureau of Community Corrections after 2 years of experience with the case management system revealed that there was a strong correlation between the score the offenders obtained on the risk instrument and revocation rates. The higher the risk score, the higher was the revocation rate. For example, of 4,231 probationers and parolees who were terminated within 2 years after commitment to the program, 1,124 (27 percent) had a risk score between 4 and 7 and had a revocation rate of only 2.49 percent. However, at the other extreme 60 offenders (1.4 percent) had a risk score of 30 and above, and they had a revocation rate of 42.55 percent.[14]

In Wisconsin, both risk scores and needs scores were used to assign cases to supervision categories. The risk scores, however, appear to be more predictive of new criminal activity. In Wisconsin, a risk assessment score of 15 and above would lead to a maximum supervision classification, a score of 8 to 14 would result in medium supervision, and a score of 7 and below in minimum supervision.[15] About 50 percent of new clients were placed in maximum supervision.

The evaluation of the Ohio Case Management System I conducted involved a two-faceted research design. In one facet, an experimental region of the state, the first region where the new system was implemented, was used to develop a comparison of recidivism in the region before and after implementation of the system. Cases for the months of September, October, and November

1981, when the new system had been put into effect, were compared with those in the months of September, October, and November 1980. All cases which originated in parole and probation units selected for the experimental region were included. The 1980 sample had 276 cases, while the 1981 sample had 261 cases. The case files of all offenders in the samples were examined, and all criminal offenses which resulted in convictions, all alleged parole and probation violations which were confirmed, and all probation and parole "violator at large" statuses which occurred during a 12-month period from the date that the offender was placed on parole or probation were considered. The offenders were divided according to supervision level (maximum = risk score of 26 or higher; medium = risk score of 18 through 25; minimum = risk score of 0 through 17) and compared with regard to recidivism, as shown in Table 1.

Table 1

Recidivism of Cases in the Experimental Region by Supervision Level Before and After Implementation of the Case Management System

Supervision Level	Recidivism 1980		Recidivism 1981	
	N	% of Total[1]	N	% of Total[2]
Maximum	40	70%	50	63%
Medium	26	42%	32	47%
Minimum	27	17%	25	22%
TOTALS	93	34%	107	41%

[1] In 1980, there were 57 maximum supervision offenders, 62 medium, and 157 minimum.
[2] In 1981, there were 79 maximum supervision offenders, 68 medium, and 114 minimum.

As shown in Table 1, recidivism was lower for the 1981 maximum supervision group than for the maximum supervision group in 1980, although the decrease was not statistically significant. Although the recidivism increased from 1980 to 1981 in both the medium and minimum supervision levels, the increases were not statistically significant. This comparison, while not conclusive, gives some support for the assumptions underlying the Case Management System model. In the maximum supervision category, where the intensity of supervision was increased, there was a decline in the percentage who recidivated. At the minimum supervision level, where supervision was decreased, no substantial increase in recidivism occurred. The only group which performed contrary to the model's expectations was the medium supervision level. It was expected that recidivism here would remain constant, but it increased.

Of those parolees who committed new offenses, 58 percent of those in the 1980 sample committed felonies, compared to 49 percent of those in the 1981 sample. The percentage of parolees revoked and sent to prison was slightly higher for the 1980 sample (24 percent) than for the 1981 sample (23 percent). Of the probationers committing new offenses, 50 percent of those in the 1980 sample and 47 percent of those in the 1981 sample committed felonies, and 11 percent of the 1980 probationers in the sample were returned to prison, compared to 9 percent of the probationers in the 1981 sample.

The second facet of the research design involved a comparison of the sample of offenders in the experimental region, where the new Case Management System had been implemented (1981), with a sample in a control region of the state, where the system had not been implemented in that year. Since the offenders in the control region were not classified, the researchers classified them according to maximum, medium, or minimum supervision qualifying status, using the same instruments used by Parole Authority staff to classify the offenders in the experimental region. A comparison of the recidivism of the offenders in the experimental and control regions is given in Table 2.

As shown in Table 2, recidivism was almost three times as great at the maximum supervision level as at the minimum level for both the experimental and control group samples, and the recidivism for the medium level was more than twice that of the minimum. These patterns follow the projections made for the Case Management System model. However, it was projected that the recidivism for the maximum level experimental group would be lower than that for the maximum level control group because of the intense amount of supervision given to the maximum offenders in the experimental group, where the new Case Management System had been applied. This did not occur. The higher proportion of offenders in the maximum supervision category in the experimental group sample, when compared with the control group sample, no doubt had some bearing on the lack of recidivism reduction at this level. For the medium and minimum supervision

Table 2

A Comparison of Recidivism by Supervision Level
in the Experimental and Control Regions

Supervision level	Experimental[1] Region		Control[2] Region		Significance
	N	%	N	%	
Maximum	50	63%	28	60%	Not significant at .15 level
Medium	32	47%	34	44%	Chi Square Test
Minimum	25	22%	19	17%	

[1] In the Experimental Region, there were 79 maximum supervision offenders, 68 medium, 114 minimum.
[2] In the Control Region, there were 47 maximum supervision offenders, 77 medium, and 114 minimum.

levels, slight increases in recidivism also occurred in the experimental group sample, although it was projected that recidivism at the medium level would be reduced.

When the severity of new offenses by those who recidivated was compared by supervision level, the maximum level offenders in the control group had a greater proportion of felonies (33 percent) than did the maximum level experimental group (27 percent). In the medium level, the percentage committing felonies was the same for the two groups (25 percent). At the minimum level the experimental group (7 percent) and the control group (8 percent) had similar percentages committing felonies. This offense pattern follows the Case Management System model, with the maximum level offenders in the experimental group having a reduced percentage of serious offenses.

Table 3 compares the offenders revoked and sent to prison in the experimental and control regions.

As shown in Table 3, slightly higher percentages of the control region offenders in all supervision levels were revoked and sent to prison. Although these differences are not statistically significant, they support the projection of the Case Management System model that increased supervision of the maximum level cases will have positive results.[16]

Table 3

**A Comparison of Supervision Level of Offenders
Sent to Prison After a New Offense or Technical
Violation in the Experimental and Control Regions**

Supervision Level	Experimental[1] Region		Control[2] Region	
	N	%	N	%
Maximum	24	30%	17	36%
Medium	14	21%	18	23%
Minimum	6	5%	11	10%

[1] In the Experimental Region, there were 79 maximum supervision offenders, 68 medium, and 114 minimum.

[2] In the Control Region, there were 47 maximum supervision offenders, 77 medium and 114 minimum.

One should be cautious about generalizing findings from one state program to another, even if a comparable case management system were used. In Ohio, risk and needs classification instruments were adopted which are quite similar to those used in Wisconsin. However, the cutoff points in the risk instruments used to delineate the Ohio supervision levels were considerably higher (26 and above for maximum supervision, 18 to 25 for medium supervision, and 17 and below for minimum supervision) than those used in Wisconsin (15 and above for maximum, 8 to 14 for medium, and 7 and below for minimum). If one compared Wisconsin and Ohio by supervision level without taking into consideration the actual risk scores used to delineate the various levels, it would appear that recidivism was considerably higher for the Ohio offenders than for those in Wisconsin. However, if the cases from the two states were matched by actual risk scores, the proportion committing new offenses would not vary significantly in the two states.

In conclusion, it is apparent that the case management models should be evaluated in relationship to their utility and not necessarily in relationship to a reduction in criminal activity. The systems work if officers make better decisions on cases, make more appropriate referrals to community service agencies, are more efficient in their work, establish better communications with supervisions, and are more confident and satisfied with their own job performance. If the agency administrators can live with the programs, even though recidivism rates do not drop significantly, case management systems will continue to be refined and this should result in a significant improvement in community corrections.

Notes

[1] Edith Elisabeth Flynn, "Classification Systems," in *Handbook of Correctional Classification* (Cincinnati: Anderson Publishing Company, 1978), p. 86.

[2] Administrative Office of the U.S. Courts, *Guide to Judiciary Policies and Procedures: Probation Manual*, Vol. x–0§4004 (February 15, 1979).

[3] James B. Eaglin and Patricia A. Lombard, *A Validation and Comparative Evaluation of Four Predictive Devices for Classifying Federal Probation Caseloads* (Washington, D.C.: Federal Judicial Center, 1982), p. 1.

[4] S. Christopher Baird, Richard C. Heinz, and Brian J. Bemus, *The Wisconsin Case Classification/Staff Deployment Project* (Madison, Wisconsin: Department of Health and Social Services, 1979), p. 7.

[5] James W. Fox, Mitchell Stein, and Gary Ramussen, "Development of the Tennessee Case Management for Delivery of Parole Services." Paper delivered at the 1983 Convention of the Academy of Criminal Justice Sciences, San Antonio, Texas, 1983, p. 7.

[6] James B. Eaglin and Patricia A. Lombard, *A Validation . . . Caseloads*, pp. 99–122.

[7] Stephen Gettinger, "Separating the Cop for the Counselor," *Corrections Magazine*, Vol. 7, No. 2 (April 1981), p. 35.

[8] National Institution of Corrections, *Client Management Classification System Officer Survey* (Washington, D.C.: National Institute of Corrections, 1982).

[9] Carol Rauh, "Important Considerations in Ensuring the Success of a Case Management/Management Information System Model." Paper presented at the annual meeting of the Academy of Criminal Justice Sciences, San Antonio, Texas, 1983.

[10] Peter C. Kratcoski, *An Evaluation of the Case Management System Probation and Parole Sections: Division of Parole and Community Services, Ohio Department of Rehabilitation and Correction*, report submitted September 1983, pp. 171–173.

[11] Stephen Gettinger, "Separating the Cop from the Counselor," pp. 36–37.

[12] Baird, Heinz, and Bemus, *The Wisconsin Case Classification/Staff Development Project: A Two Year Follow-Up Report* (Madison, Wisconsin: Department of Health and Social Services, 1979), p. 26.

[13] *Ibid.*, p. 6.

[14] *Ibid.*, p. 10.

[15] *Ibid.*, p. 20.

[16] Peter C. Kratcoski, *An Evaluation of the Case Management System . . . Ohio Department of Rehabilitation and Correction*, pp. 174–178.

14

The Case Management System Experience in Ohio

Clifford W. Crooks

Introduction: The Wisconsin Contribution

The probation and parole case management systems currently in place at the state and county level in Ohio are by no means unique. They are, in fact, based upon the system developed and implemented in Wisconsin in the previous decade. Needless to say, a great deal has been written about the Wisconsin model and its total systems approach to the classification process. In order to fully understand Ohio's case management systems, it is important to summarize the major achievements in Wisconsin.

Responding to a legislative mandate to improve services for offenders and measure the workload of probation and parole agents, the Wisconsin Division of Corrections, Bureau of Community Corrections secured federal funds and formed the Case Classification/Staff Deployment Project (CC/SD Project) in 1975. During development and implementation, every effort was made to maximize staff input and support. Supervisors and line staff worked together, for example, to define standards. Staff were also encouraged to evaluate new procedures and predictive scales and to make suggestions for improvement.

This article first appeared in *Correctional Counseling and Treatment*, Second Edition. All rights reserved.

When the Wisconsin Classification System was implemented statewide in 1977, it contained the following integrated components which met the objectives of the CC/SD Project:

1. A risk assessment scale developed by multiple regression analysis to identify and weight offender characteristics and criminal history items that best predict further criminal behavior.

2. A risk reassessment scale developed to identify and weight offender items that reflect overall adjustment during the course of supervision.

3. A needs assessment scale and treatment guidelines developed by supervising agents to identify noncrisis, offender problem or need areas, and potential strategies and resources to service them.

4. A Client Management Classification (CMC) system and treatment strategies developed empirically in the form of a semistructured interview and agent impressions to assist in placing offenders in one of five differential treatment groups, and to provide information concerning appropriate treatment strategies for casework planning.

5. A standardized classification and reclassification process was developed for probationers and parolees. At admission to supervision, the risk and need assessment scales are scored and the offender is assigned to one of three supervision levels (specific agent contacts are required at each level). At six month intervals during supervision, the risk reassessment scale and needs scale are scored and an offender is reclassified if appropriate and assigned to the appropriate level.

6. A workload budgeting and deployment system developed as a result of time studies that measured the time required by agents to perform activities and meet supervision standards, and used in the budgetary process and to deploy staff.

7. A management information system generated as a product of the classification and reclassification process and used as a foundation for evaluation, planning, and operations.

In 1979, Wisconsin released a two year follow-up report and analysis of the CC/SD Project. In part, the report concluded that:

• Assignment to different levels of supervision based upon risk and needs assessment had a significant impact on probation and parole outcomes. There were fewer new convictions, rules violations, absconding and revocations with high need/high risk offenders as a result of increased contacts. Decreased contacts with low need/low risk offenders resulted in no adverse effects.

- The risk assessment scale demonstrated effectiveness in predicting success or failure in completing terms of probation or parole supervision.
- The needs assessment scale demonstrated high inter-rater reliability.

Components of the Wisconsin Model were duplicated in a number of probation and parole agencies throughout the country, including Ohio. The Wisconsin Model became, in fact, a National Institute of Corrections (NIC) Model Probation/Parole Classification System.

The Adult Parole Authority
Case Management System (CMS)

The Ohio Department of Rehabilitation and Corrections, Adult Parole Authority staff were first exposed to the Wisconsin Classification System at an NIC funded Case Management Institute in 1979. As a result, federal grant monies were secured and a Case Management Task Force (CMTF), made up of research, management and line staff was formed. It was generally understood that the completed case management product would contain components applicable to both the probation and parole populations serviced by the Adult Parole Authority.

The following is a summary of the integrated CMS components developed by the Task Force:

1. A comprehensive classification process was developed. As in Wisconsin, researchers reviewed a random sample of closed offender cases and used multiple regression analysis to identify strong predictors of future criminal behavior. The resulting risk assessment scale contains ten weighted items. (See Figure 1.)

   A risk reassessment scale, containing eight items, was constructed as well to evaluate an offender's adjustment during supervision. (See Figure 2.)

   Supervisory and line staff developed a needs assessment scale. It contains 13 problem or need areas (two more than the Wisconsin scale), and input for the officer's impressions of the offender's needs. It was designed, like the Wisconsin scale, to be used for classification and case planning. Need treatment guidelines comparable to Wisconsin's, were devised to assist officers in more accurately identifying and treating offender need areas and making appropriate community resource referrals. (See Figure 3.)

Figure 1   Assessment of Client Risk

Processor # _____

Client Name _____ Last First Mi	Client Number _____ Date _____
Officer _____ Last Social Security Number	Unit Location Code_____

Select the appropriate answer and enter the associated weight in score column. Total all scores to arrive at the risk assessment score.

Score

Number of Prior Felony Convictions: (or Juvenile Adjudications)	0 2 4	None One Two or more	_____
Arrested Within Five (5) Years Prior to Arrest for Current Offense (exclude traffic)	0 4	No Yes	_____
Age at Arrest Leading to First Felony Conviction (or Juvenile Adjudications)	0 2 4	24 and over 20 to 23 19 and under	_____
Amount of Time Employed in Last 12 Months (Prior to Incarceration for Parolees)	0 1 2 0	More than 7 months 5 to 7 months Less than 5 months Not appplicable	_____

Alcohol Usage Problems (Prior to Incarceration
for Parolees)
	0
	2
	4
		No interference
		  with functioning
		Occasional abuse; some
		  disruption of functioning
		Frequent abuse; serious
		  disruption; needs treatment
			_____

Other Drug Usage Problems (Prior to Incarceration
for Parolees)
	0
	2
	4
		No interference with
		  fuctioning
		Occasional abuse; some
		  disruption of functioning
		Frequent abuse; serious
		  disruption needs treatment
			_____

Number of Prior Adult Incarcerations in a State or Federal Institution	0 3 6	0 1-2 3 or more	_____
Age at Admission to Institution or Probation for Current Offense	0 3 6	30 or over 18 to 29 17 and under	_____
Number of Prior *Adult* Probation/Parole Supervisions	0 4	None One or more	_____
Number of Prior Probation/Parole Revocations Resulting in Imprisonment (Adult or Juvenile)	0 4	None One or more	_____

Total _____

Figure 2 Reassessment of Client Risk ☐ During Supervision

Processor # _____   ☐ At Final Discharge

Client Name _____	Client Number _____
Last First Mi	Date _____
Officer _____	Unit Location Code_____
Last Social Security Number	

Select the appropriate answer and enter the associated weight in score column. Total all scores to arrive at the risk assessment score.

Score

Number of Prior Felony Convictions	0	None
(or Juvenile Adjudications)	3	One
	6	Two
	7	Three or more _____
Age at Arrest Leading to First Felony Conviction	0	24 and over
(or Juvenile Adjudications)	2	20-23
	5	19 and under _____
Age at Admission to Probation/Parole Supervision	0	30 and older
for Current Offense	4	18-29
	7	17 and under _____

Rate the following based on period since last (re)assessment:

Type of Arrests (indicate most serious	0	None
excluding traffic)	2	Technical PV only
	4	Misdemeanor arrest(s)
	8	Felony arrest _____
Associations	0	Mainly with noncrimnally oriented individuals
	5	Mainly with negative individuals _____
Alcohol Usage Problems	0	No interference with fuctioning
	2	Occasional abuse; some disruption of functioning
	3	Frequent abuse; serious disruption needs treatment _____
Other Drug Usage Problems	0	No interference with functioning
	1	Occasional abuse: some disruption of functioning
	2	Frequent abuse: serious disruption; needs treatment _____
Attitude	0	No adverse difficulties/ motivated to change
	2	Periodic difficulties/ uncooperative/independent
	5	Frequently hostile/ negative/criminal orientation _____

Total _____

Figure 3 Assessment of Client Needs

Processor # _____

Client Name _____   Client Number _____
            Last   First   Mi
                                                Date _____

Officer _____   Unit Location Code_____
       Last   Social Security Number

Score

Emotional and Mental Stability

0 No symptoms of emotions and/or mental instability
2 Symptoms limit, but do not prohibit adequate functioning
6 Symptoms prohibit adequate functioning and/or has Court or Board imposed condition
8 Severe symptoms requiring continual attention and/or explosive, threatening and potentially dangerous to others or self   _____

Domestic Relationship

0 Stable/supportive relationships
3 Some disorganization or stress but potential for improvement
7 Major disorganization or stress   _____

Associations

0 No adverse relationships
2 Association with occasional negative results
4 Associations frequently negative
6 Associations completely negative   _____

Drug Abuse

0 No disruption of functioning
2 Occasional substance abuse: some disruption of functioning and/or has Court or Board conditions
7 Frequent abuse; serious disruption; needs treatment   _____

Alcohol Usage

0 No disruption of functioning
2 Occasional abuse; some disruption of functioning and/or has court or Board conditions
7 Frequent abuse; serious disruption; needs treatment   _____

Employment

0 Satisfactory employment, no difficulties reported; or homemaker, student, retired, or disabled
2 Underemployed
4 Unsatisfactory employment; or unemployed but has adequate job skills/motivation
5 Unemployed and virtually unemployable; needs motivation/training   _____

Academic/Vocational Skills/Training

0 Adequate skills, able to handle everyday requirements
2 Low skill level causing minor adjustment problems
6 No identifiable skills and/or minimal skill level causing serious adjustment problems   _____

Financial Management

0 No current difficulties
1 Situational or minor difficulties
5 Chronic/severe difficulties   _____

Attitudes

0 No adverse difficulties/motivated for change
2 Periodic difficulties/ uncooperative/dependent
4 Frequently hostile/negative/criminal orientation   _____

Residence

0 Suitable living arrangement
1 Adequate living, i.e., temporary shelter
4 Nomadic and/ or unacceptable   _____

Mental Ability (Intelligence)

0 Able to function independently
1 Some need for assistence; potential for adequate adjustment
3 Deficiencies severely limit independent functioning   _____

Health

0 Sound physical health; seldom ill
1 Handicap or illness; interferes with functioning on a recurring basis
2 Serious handicap or chronic illness; needs frequent medical care   _____

Sexual Behavior

0 No apparent dysfunction
2 Real or perceived situational or minor problems
6 Real or perceived chronic or severe problems   _____

Officer's Impressions of Needs

A. Low **0**   B. Medium **3**   C. Maximum **5**

Total _____

After the risk and need assessment and risk reassessment scales were developed, research staff tested the scales against offender case data to determine ranges of risk and need cut-off scores for three supervision levels:

Maximum: High failure potential or great number of problem/need areas requiring services.

Medium: Lower failure potential or problem/need areas, but requiring officer involvement.

Minimum: Least failure potential or few significant problem/need areas.

The CMTF added a fourth supervision level, Extended, to be used at reclassification. To be assigned to Extended, an offender must have been under active supervision for at least a year and at the Minimum level for the previous six months.

Classification is a straightforward process using the risk and need scales. Available information about an offender such as a Presentence or Parole Board Investigation, police reports, interviews or institutional records are reviewed by the officer and the scales are scored. The offender is placed in one of the three supervision levels based upon the higher classification of *either* scale.

The following are current risk and need cut-off scores for the three supervision levels:

Risk Score	Level of Supervision	Need Score
26 and above	Maximum	25 and above
18 to 25	Medium	15 to 24
17 and below	Minimum	14 and below

The following case summary and accompanying scales for Paul S., a 24-year-old male offender on parole supervision for burglary, illustrates the classification process:

> Three years ago, Paul and an accomplice went to the apartment of a female known to the accomplice. They forced open a door, entered and ransacked the rooms (the female was not there at the time). They took money a loaded revolver a butcher knife, and keys. They stole the female's automobile from a nearby lot.
>
> Both were arrested a short time later in the stolen vehicle. The accomplice had the loaded revolver and Paul had the money and knife. When questioned, Paul admitted his involvement, and told police that he and the accomplice had originally gone to the apartment to "punish" the female for

"leaving" the accomplice. Paul was convicted of burglary and sentenced to the Department of Rehabilitation and Corrections. He served three years before he was paroled.

As a juvenile, Paul was adjudicated and convicted at age 14 for the theft of a teacher's purse and placed on indefinite probation. At age 15, Paul threatened a school principal with a hammer was convicted of menacing and continued on probation. Paul was committed to a Department of Youth Services' institution at age 16 as a result of a burglary conviction and a probation violation finding. Following release, Paul served a juvenile parole period which terminated at age 18.

As an adult, Paul was convicted of felony theft at age 19 and placed on probation. Within months Paul was arrested while driving a stolen van. He was convicted for receiving stolen property, his probation was revoked and he was sentenced to the institution. Paul was released on Shock Parole and completed his supervision period without major problems. The current offense of burglary occurred when Paul was 21; it is only the second offense committed with an accomplice.

Paul was raised by his older brother. Paul completed high school and a number of basic auto mechanics courses. As a teen, he had a history of acting out when angered. A recent evaluation described Paul as "argumentative, criminally motivated and lacking in positive direction." Paul has an average intelligence.

Paul has worked primarily as a restaurant cook and dishwasher. In the year prior to his arrest for the current offense, Paul worked only three months. He was fired from his last job for chronic absenteeism.

Paul has been unemployed since his release on parole and has resided with his brother. The brother is employed, owns his own home and has no criminal record. The brother is willing to provide Paul with a residence and spending money until Paul is employed and able to rent an apartment. Paul is actively seeking employment according to his brother. (See Figures 4 and 5.)

As the scales indicate, Paul's risk score is 28 and his need score is 24. Thus, Paul would be classified as a Maximum level offender.

There are two classification exceptions. Sex offenders are not classified by the risk or need scale. In addition, officers can override the scales, with supervisory approval, and assign an offender to a higher or lower level of supervision.

Figure 4   Assessment of Client Risk

Processor # _____

Client Name	_Paul S._			Client Number _____
	Last	First	Mi	Date _____
Officer	_____			Unit Location Code_____
	Last	Social Security Number		

Select the appropriate answer and enter the associated weight in the score column. Total all scores to arrive at the risk assessment score.

Score

Number of Prior Felony Convictions:	0 None	
(or Juvenile Adjudications)	2 One	
	4 Two or more	_4_
Arrested Within Five (5) Years Prior to Arrest	0 No	
for Current Offense (exclude traffic)	4 Yes	_4_
Age at Arrest Leading to First Felony Conviction	0 24 and over	
(or Juvenile Adjudications)	2 20 to 23	___
	4 19 and under	_2_
Amount of Time Employed in Last 12 Months	0 More than 7 months	
(Prior to Incarceration for Parolees)	1 5 to 7 months	
	2 Less than 5 months	
	0 Not appplicable	_0_
Alcohol Usage Problems (Prior to Incarceration	0 No interference with functioning	
for Parolees)	2 Occasional abuse; some disruption of functioning	
	4 Frequent abuse; serious disruption; needs treatment	_0_
Other Drug Usage Problems (Prior to Incarceration	0 No interference with fuctioning	
for Parolees)	2 Occasional abuse; some disruption of functioning	
	4 Frequent abuse; serious disruption needs treatment	_0_
Number of Prior Adult Incarcerations in a State	0 0	
or Federal Institution	3 1-2	
	6 3 or more	_3_
Age at Admission to Institution or Probation	0 30 or over	
for Current Offense	3 18 to 29	
	6 17 and under	_3_
Number of Prior *Adult* Probation/Parole Supervisions	0 None	
	4 One or more	_4_
Number of Prior Probation/Parole Revocations	0 None	
Resulting in Imprisonment (Adult or Juvenile)	4 One or more	_4_

Total _24_

Figure 5 Assessment of Client Needs

Processor # _____

Client Name _Paul S._____ Last　　　First　　　Mi	Client Number _____ Date _____
Officer _____ Last　　Social Security Number	Unit Location Code_____

Score

Emotional and Mental Stability

0 No symptoms of emotions and/or mental instability	**2** Symptoms limit, but do not prohibit adequate functioning	**6** Symptoms prohibit adequate functioning and/or has Court or Board imposed condition	**8** Severe symptoms requiring continual attention and/or explosive, threatening and potentially dangerous to others or self	_8_

Domestic Relationship

0 Stable/supportive relationships	**3** Some disorganization or stress but potential for improvement	**7** Major disorganization or stress	_0_

Associations

0 No adverse relationships	**2** Associations with occasional negative results	**4** Associations frequently negative	**6** Associations completely negative	_2_

Drug Abuse

0 No disruption of functioning	**2** Occasional substance abuse: some disruption of functioning and/or has Court or Board conditions	**7** Frequent abuse; serious disruption; needs treatment	_0_

Alcohol Usage

0 No disruption of functioning	**2** Occasional abuse; some disruption of functioning and/or has court or Board conditions	**7** Frequent abuse; serious disruption; needs treatment	_0_

Employment

0 Satisfactory employment, no difficulties reported; or homemaker, student, retired, or disabled	**2** Underemployed	**4** Unsatisfactory employment; or unemployed but has adequate job skills/motivation	**5** Unemployed and virtually unemployable; needs motivation/training	_4_

Academic/Vocational Skills/Training

0 Adequate skills, able to handle everyday requirements	**2** Low skill level causing minor adjustment problems	**6** No identifiable skills and/or minimal skill level causing serious adjustment problems	_2_

Financial Management

0 No current difficulties	**1** Situational or minor difficulties	**5** Chronic/severe difficulties	_1_

Attitudes

0 No adverse difficulties/motivated for change	**2** Periodic difficulties/ uncooperative/dependent	**4** Frequently hostile/negative/criminal orientation	_4_

Residence

0 Suitable living arrangement	**1** Adequate living, i.e., temporary shelter	**·4** Nomadic and/ or unacceptable	_0_

Mental Ability (Intelligence)

0 Able to function independently	**1** Some need for assistence; potential for adequate adjustment	**3** Deficiencies severely limit independent functioning	_0_

Health

0 Sound physical health; seldom ill	**1** Handicap or illness; interferes with functioning on a recurring basis	**2** Serious handicap or chronic illness; needs frequent medical care	_0_

Sexual Behavior

0 No apparent dysfunction	**2** Real or perceived situational or minor problems	**6** Real or perceived chronic or severe problems	_0_

Officer's Impressions of Needs

A. Low **0**	B. Medium **3**	C. Maximum **5**	_3_

Total _24_

Reclassification occurs at six month intervals, when a significant event alters an offender's status, and at the termination of supervision. The risk reassessment and needs scale is scored based upon the offender's adjustment, and the offender is placed in the appropriate supervision level, as determined again, by the higher classification of either scale. Offenders may be placed in the Extended level at reclassification if they meet established criteria. The scales can be overridden at reclassification, as well.

2. A supervision policy was developed. The CMTF discovered that the Adult Parole Authority lacked a cohesive definition of supervision. The CMTF also discovered that the parole and probation sections of the agency had different policies for common tasks such as arrests, violations and the processing of terminations.

   A supervision mission was defined in terms of a fluid process encompassing information gathering, case assessment, classification, case planning, service delivery, monitoring and evaluation. In addition, nearly every Adult Parole Authority supervision policy was revised to correspond with case management concepts.

3. A process to help officers determine appropriate supervision strategies was selected. A variety of strategies were examined by the CMTF including negotiated contracts, behavioral objectives, force field analysis and Wisconsin's CMC system. The CMTF chose the CMC system and its accompanying treatment strategies. The CMC is administered to an offender within the first 30 days of supervision.

4. Structured levels of supervision were developed, with criteria for placement and movement between levels. The CMS was designed, like Wisconsin's system, to move offenders to lower supervision levels as problems are resolved or reduced and needs met. A negotiated case planning process was devised that focuses both officer and offender on problem identification, case plan behavioral objectives, the action plan necessary to achieve the objectives and the date when objectives are achieved. The case plan is written and completed by the officer at classification and reclassification. (See Figure 6.)

5. Standards for officer functions were defined. Required minimum standards for the four levels of supervision were developed by the CMTF in terms of face-to-face contacts with the offender and officer's verification of the offender's residence, employment, program participation and compliance with

Figure 6 Case Plan

Client Name _____ Client Number _____

             (Last)   (First)   (Middle)

Problem/Need (From Instrument)	Objective	Action Plan	Achieved

special conditions imposed by the court or Parole Board. Requirements are minimal for an extended case, but increase proportionally as the supervision level increases.

6. A workload system was developed to accommodate the investigative and supervision functions of the agency. Researchers conducted three work/time studies. In one of the studies, a representative number of officers used self-report forms to track time spent with cases in ten standard activities over a four month period. Study results were used to establish specific work units for supervision cases and for court and Parole Board investigations, and to define monthly workload standards.

7. A data system for management information purposes was devised. Supervision forms were designed to collect a variety of data, including demographics, classification, reclassification and termination information and workload statistics. Since implementation, the data has been collected and collated manually and used primarily for staff deployment and budgeting.

   A computerized, statewide supervision data base with entry and report retrieval capability is scheduled to be on line by 1989. Case management information will be more accessible to staff and can be used for a wider variety of purposes.

In 1980 and 1981, the CMS was implemented throughout the state, one region at a time. As part of the implementation process, staffs were trained in the use of the scales, classification and reclassification, the CMC system and case planning. Ongoing supportive contact was maintained between the CMTF and staff during training and implementation.

An evaluation of the CMS, based upon data generated in the initial implementation region, was conducted in 1984; it yielded mixed findings. The evaluator found, for example, that staff using the system were generally positive about it and that case planning and use of outside community resources by officers had improved. The risk scale was also found to be effective (the needs scale was not evaluated).

However, it was also concluded that officers supervised Minimum and Maximum offenders with the same contact frequency. There were, in fact, too many contacts for Minimum offenders and about half the required contacts for Maximum offenders. Because officer efforts were not concentrated in the appropriate areas, the CMS failed to impact upon the criminal behaviors of Maximum offenders.

Significant steps were taken to strengthen the effectiveness of the system. Follow-up training was provided to staff to reinforce supervision standards, and emphasis was placed on monitoring officer activities.

A follow-up study of the Case Management System, using methodology from the previous evaluation, was released in 1986. Overall, the findings were positive. The risk scale, for example continued to function as a solid predictive instrument. In addition, a marked increase in the referral of offenders to community service agencies was revealed. This suggested that the need scale and case planning process were effective in identifying with no apparent solution.

As in the 1984 evaluation, it was discovered that officers over-supervised Minimum level offenders and under-supervised Maximum level offenders. Despite these findings, the study documented some decrease in the criminal behavior of Maximum and Medium level offenders.

Transfer of CMS Technology

When fully implemented, the CMS applied to all parolees in Ohio, and probationers (primarily felons) under Adult Parole Authority supervision in 51 of Ohio's 88 counties. The majority of other counties had separate probation departments, each with its own individual organizational structure, policies and practices. In 1981, numerous probation departments expressed an interest in learning more about the CMS to NIC and the Adult Parole Authority. Ultimately, NIC agreed to fund a transfer of CMS technology from the state to the counties but stipulated that the counties and the state work together during the process.

Despite a history of inter-governmental conflict and adverse relations, the Adult Parole Authority and 15 urban and rural counties combined their efforts and expertise within a supportive environment of capacity building. Early in the process CMTF members conducted an orientation session for urban county personnel that focused on the concepts and benefits of CMS. During the technological transfer process, CMTF members collaborated with county staff to solve implementation and resistance problems. NIC acted as both a technical consultant and a catalyst during the transfer process.

County and state staff worked closely together in the training design and system development arena. CMTF members, for example, provided county participants with information about the various classification, reclassification and case planning components of the CMS. Adult Parole Authority staff trained urban county CMC trainers. They in turn, trained the rural county line staff in CMC interview techniques.

County and state staff also jointly developed a CMS Entrance Training Program. The four day session is designed to provide new county and state officers with an overview of the purpose and function of the risk reassessment and need scales, and the classification process (officers receive specifics concerning policies and procedures when they return to their county department or state unit). The Program also provides practical training in conducting the CMC interview using the recommended treatment strategies and writing case plans.

In addition to participating in training during the transfer process, the urban and rural counties came together to discuss common issues and problems as they reached the same level of implementation. The county departments also worked with NIC to refine their respective management information and workload systems. County implementation team members first explored creating a professional organization for Chief Probation Officers of Ohio during the transfer process.

By 1984, the 15 urban and rural counties had developed and implemented a CMS for their respective probation departments. Previously tested state classification components such as the risk, risk reassessment and needs scale were duplicated by the county departments (some of the counties later developed their own). A number of counties, however, added an assaultive indicator to their risk and risk reassessment scales. (See Figures 7, 8 and 9.)

The management information and workload technology were transferred from the state to the counties, as well. They too were reshaped to meet the individual needs of the county departments. Wisconsin's CMC system was transferred but not altered.

No formal evaluations of the various county systems have been conducted. However, the transfer of Case Management System technology from the state to county probation departments has undoubtedly resulted in improved inter-governmental relations. More importantly, professional probation practices throughout the State of Ohio have been enhanced significantly.

Figure 7 Assessment of Client Risk

Name: _____   Risk Level: _____

Case Number:

Date: _____   P.O.'s Name: _____

Select the appropriate answer and enter the associated weight in score column. Total all scores to arrive at the risk assessment score.

Score

1) Number of Prior Felony Convictions: 0 None
   (or Juvenile Adjudications)   2 One
                                              4 Two or more   _____

2) Arrested Within Five (5) Years Prior to Arrest   0 No
   for Current Offense (exclude traffic)   4 Yes   _____

3) Age at Arrest Leading to First Felony Conviction 0 24 and over
   (or Juvenile Adjudications)   2 20 to 23
                                                     4 19 and under   _____

4) Number of Prior Adult Incarcerations in a State   0 0
   or Federal Institution   3 1-2
                                                     6 3 or more   _____

5) Age at Admission to Institution or Probation   0 30 or over
   for Current Offense   3 18 to 29
                                                     6 17 and under   _____

6) Number of Prior *Adult* Probation/Parole   0 None
   Supervisions   4 One or more   _____

7) Number of Prior Probation/Parole Revoked   0 None
   or termination Due to Incarceration   4 One or more
   (Adult or Juvenile)   _____

8) Alcohol Usage Problems   0 No indication of alcohol
                                                        abuse
                                                     2 Occasional abuse
                                                     3 Some disruption of
                                                        functioning
                                                     4 Frequent abuse; serious
                                                        disruption; needs treatment _____

9) Other Drug Usage Problems   0 No indication of drug abuse
                                                     2 Occasional abuse
                                                     3 Some disruption of
                                                        functioning
                                                     4 Frequent abuse; serious
                                                        disruption needs treatment   _____

10) Amount of Full Time Employment in Last   0 More than 7 months
    12 months   1 5 to 7 months
                                                     2 Less than 5 months
                                                     0 Not applicable   _____

                                                                    Total _____

11) Adult Felony Conviction or Juvenile Felony Adjudi-   Yes   _____
    cation for Offense Involving Threat of Force, Posses- No   _____
    session of Weapon, Physical Force or Sexual Assault
    within the Last Five Years

If answer to item 11 is yes, then supervision level is
increased to next highest level.

Figure 8 Assessment of Client Risk

Client Name _____ CR_____ Probation
                                         Placement Date _____

Risk: L   M   H   Reassessment Date _____

Assessing P.O. _____   Date _____

Select the appropriate answer and enter the associated weight in the score column. Total all scores to arrive at the risk assessment score.

Score

Number of Prior Felony Convictions:
(or Juvenile Adjudications)
- 0 None
- 2 One
- 4 Two or more   _____

Arrested Within Five (5) Years Prior to Arrest
for Current Offense (exclude traffic)
- 0 No
- 4 Yes   _____

Age at Arrest Leading to First Felony Conviction
(or Juvenile Adjudications)
- 0 24 and over
- 2 20 to 23
- 4 19 and under   _____

Amount of Time Employed in Last 12 Months
(Prior to Incarceration for Parolees)
- 0 More than 7 months
- 1 5 to 7 months
- 2 Less than 5 months
- 0 Not appplicable   _____

Alcohol Usage Problems (Prior to Incarceration
for Parolees)
- 0 No interference with functioning
- 2 Occasional abuse; some disruption of functioning
- 4 Frequent abuse; serious disruption; needs treatment   _____

Other Drug Usage Problems (Prior to Incarceration
for Parolees)
- 0 No interference with fuctioning
- 2 Occasional abuse; some disruption of functioning
- 4 Frequent abuse; serious disruption needs treatment   _____

Number of Prior Adult Incarcerations in a State
or Federal Institution
- 0 0
- 3 1-2
- 6 3 or more   _____

Age at Admission to Institution or Probation
for Current Offense
- 0 30 or over
- 3 18 to 29
- 6 17 and under   _____

Number of Prior *Adult* Probation/Parole Supervisions
- 0 None
- 4 One or more   _____

Number of Prior Probation/Parole Revocations
Resulting in Imprisonment (Adult or Juvenile)
- 0 None
- 4 One or more   _____

Total _____

Officer Override — Alternate level of supervision felt to be appropriate (see reverse side for explanation). ☐

Assault Factor — If client has been convicted of 2 assaultive misdemeanors or 1 assaultive felony (including present offense), the level of supervision is moved up one step. ☐

Figure 9 Reassessment of Client Risk

Client Name _____ CR_____ Probation
                                        Placement Date _____

Risk: L M H   Reassessment Date _____

Assessing P.O. _____ Date _____

Select the appropriate answer and enter the associated weight in the score column. Total all scores to arrive at the risk assessment score.

Score

Number of Prior Felony Convictions	0	None
(or Juvenile Adjudications)	3	One
	6	Two
	7	Three or more _____
Age at Arrest Leading to First Felony Conviction	0	24 and over
(or Juvenile Adjudications)	2	20-23
	5	19 and under _____
Age at Admission to Probation/Parole Supervision	0	30 and older
for Current Offense	4	18-29
	7	17 and under _____

Rate the following based on period since last (re)assessment:

Type of Arrests (indicate most serious	0	None
excluding traffic)	2	Technical PV only
	4	Misdemeanor arrest(s)
	8	Felony arrest _____
Associations	0	Mainly with noncriminally oriented individuals
	5	Mainly with negative individuals _____
Alcohol Usage Problems	0	No interference with fuctioning
	2	Occasional abuse; some disruption of functioning
	3	Frequent abuse; serious disruption needs treatment _____
Other Drug Usage Problems	0	No interference with functioning
	1	Occasional abuse: some disruption of functioning
	2	Frequent abuse: serious disruption; needs treatment _____
Attitude	0	No adverse difficulties/ motivated to change
	2	Periodic difficulties/ uncooperative/dependent
	5	Frequently hostile/ negative/criminal orientation _____

Total _____

Officer Override—Alternate level of supervision felt to be appropriate (see reverse side for explanation). ☐

Assault Factor—If client has been convicted of 2 assaultive misdemeanors or 1 assaultive felony (including present offense), the level of supervision is moved up one step. ☐

References and Further Readings

Arling, G., B. Bemus and P Quigley (1983) *Workload Measures For Probation and Parole.*

Baird, C., B. Bemus and C. Heinz (1979) *The Wisconsin Case Classification/ Staff Deployment Project: A Two Year Follow-up Report.*

Farmer, G. (1978) *Final Report: National Institute of Corrections Capacity Building Grant FQ 2.*

Kratcoski, P. (1984) *An Evaluation of the Case Management System.*

Natter, G. (1986) *A Follow-Up Study on the Case Management System.*

15

Functional Unit Management
An Unsung Achievement

Hans Toch

A recent issue of this journal contains a list of "BOP First and Mosts."* It is an impressive list, but there is one entry that I miss—there is no mention of the introduction of unit management and of its dissemination through the Federal system in the mid-1970s. This development was unquestionably a "first." And it is an ongoing development: we have just begun to explore what units can achieve, and what we can do with them.

The idea of functional units was simple: take a prison and divide it into smaller groups of inmates and staff members. Each group of inmates (50–100 in 1970) would have its own staff team. The inmates would stay with their units and would be individually programmed. Each unit would become a specialized "mini-prison" within a larger prison and share the institution's facilities with other units.

The arrangement is analogous to neighborhoods in a city. Each neighborhood can be intimate, but is part of and has access to the amenities of the city. Each neighborhood receives municipal services, but has its own cultural flavor, which is different from those of other neighborhoods. Another analogy—which emphasizes programming—is between a prison and General Motors, which has disparate assembly areas for different cars, and "can continue production of Cadillacs even when the Chevy assembly line has run into some snags."[1]

Robert Levinson, a pioneer in conceptualizing unit management, created an imaginary automotive empire as another example:

*See *Federal Prisons Journal*, 1(4) (Summer 1990).

Source: *Federal Prisons Journal*, 2(4) (Winter 1992): 15–19.

> So FL [Flivvers Limited] establishes several subsidiaries, one for each model—Bearers, Seattles, and Tallyhoes. In this way some of the expensive effectuation equipment can be shared while workers specialize and develop expertise in producing exemplary automobiles of each type. Moreover, if there is trouble with the brakes on the Bearers, FL can still go on producing acceptable Seattles and Tallyhoes.[2]

The flexibility of Levinson's assembly lines does not spell anarchy: Flivvers Limited decides whether market trends favor small cars (Tallyhoes) or limousines (Bearers). It sets policies that affect what its assembly lines do. Levinson and Roy Gerard write that "one of the dangers in a decentralized facility is that the Functional Units may become totally 'out of step' with one another, so that the institution appears to be headed in all directions at the same time."[3] It follows that there must be ways of coordinating what the units do. As an example, "the Unit Program Plans can become part of a total Master Program Plan for the entire facility."[4]

On the other hand, units need some autonomy so that they can run programs that meet the unique needs of inmates and use the special skills of staff who design and run these programs. Autonomy also lets units develop their own cultures and identities. But the unit still functions as part of the whole prison. A few programs have lost sight of this, and ultimately have been abolished.[5]

What Can Units Do Best?

Levinson and Gerard distinguished between functions of units. One is *correction*, the concern with helpful and constructive experiences that are shaped by staff who are closest to the inmate. The second is *care*, which means efficient use of relevant resources to assist the inmates in doing time. The third use is *control*, which means keeping and monitoring inmates as they remain in the unit, so that staff can work with them.

I have listed three functions, though some would say that only two (care and control) are still alive, and that the third (correction) is dead. A discontinuance of correction, however, is hard to envisage. It would mean that inmate programming could no longer be of concern to staff in units, and that an inmate would receive neither sympathy nor assistance with efforts at self-improvement from staff members who know him. It is true that different functions may be emphasized over time, and from unit to unit. However, care and control and correction are inextricable aspects of functional inmate management, which is the task of unit staff.

One fact is critical for all three functions: the fostering of staff-inmate relationships that benefit from a shared environment and closer acquaintanceship. The foundation for this notion had been laid 15 years before the advent of unit management in a study of the Bureau of Prisons run under Ford Foundation sponsorship. The director of the study, Dan Glaser, had complained that

> . . . by randomizing his caseload through the last number assignment system, the caseworker in a large prison inadvertently reduces his chances of knowing the social environment in which his clients live. By scattering his caseload throughout the prison population, the caseworker minimizes the probability of his also knowing the cellmates or dormitory colleagues, coworkers, recreational partners, or other close inmate friends or associates of any specific client. . . . Also, when the caseload is scattered, it clearly becomes more difficult for the caseworker to see his client's customary behavior in the institution.[6]

In Glaser's reports to the Bureau of Prisons, he suggested attaching caseworkers to tiers or work assignments, in which each caseworker could get to know inmates in their natural environment, observing the pressures to which they were subjected and their capacity to cope with them. Glaser also talked of staff teaming and of "facilitating communication across traditional intra-staff lines."[7]

Among innovations he reviewed, for example, were "treatment teams" at the Federal Correctional Institution, El Reno, Oklahoma, that included custody officers assigned to dormitories to observe inmate behavior. Such experiments of the early 1960s anticipated current concerns about job enrichment for correctional officers.[8] With respect to El Reno, Glaser reported that "before long the line custodial staff seemed unanimous in considering the new system 'the best thing that ever happened' in the prison. They feel it gives them a chance to be heard, and it raises their prestige with the inmates."[9]

Another long-standing question was how to deal with antistaff norms of "inmate subcultures" in custodial prisons. Glaser speculated that "inmate pressure on other inmates to avoid communication with officers varies directly with the extent to which there is an impersonal and authoritarian orientation of staff to inmates."[10] The corollary is that a setting in which inmates and staff can relate to each other would be inhospitable to the advent of an antistaff prisoner culture. Such a setting might do more. Gerard and Levinson have observed that:

> Both staff and residents come to feel a sense of pride in "their" unit and its accomplishments. Rather than offenders finding a common cause to organize against staff, competition develops along more desirable lines, e.g., which Unit has the best record in achieving some positive goal.[11]

Functional units call for participation and involvement. Just as correctional officers, teachers, and clerical staff could be involved in teams, inmates could play an active role:

> Ways must be found to offer opportunities for Unit residents to take intramural roles of increasing responsibility both for their own activities, as well as for the smooth functioning of the Unit. In the area of decision making, as it relates to a particular individual, he should be viewed as a member of the Unit team and have a voice in program decisions affecting him.[12]

Putting the issue of inmate team membership aside, the point is that staff and inmates would have more control over their environment, and new means to enhance their own development. Self-development is enhanced where the personal contributions of team members are prized, and routinization is resisted.

Early Experiments

Like any invention, unit management is a tool. Units have to show that they can earn their keep as they are put to use.

In 1970, the Bureau of Prisons had two obvious needs. One was the need to reduce disruption and violence in prison and to protect weaker inmates from exploitation. Units could help because staff could use them to separate predatory prisoners from those susceptible to predation. Such sorting had occurred in the past, but the separating could now be done on a larger scale, based on observations at intake. Disciplinary incident rates could be measured before and after sorting inmates, to verify the efficacy of the sorting.[13]

The second need was to house substance-abusing offenders who were being committed to the system. The units made it possible to keep these offenders in regular prisons, as opposed to special institutions such as the Public Health Service's "narcotics farms." They also made it possible to experiment with treatment approaches to addiction. Most approaches capitalized on the fact that the offenders lived together as a residential community, which made it easy to use experiences of living and working as grist for treatment, and enabled teams to mobilize constructive peer pressure in resident groups. This combination is a treatment modality, called the therapeutic community.[14] It can be combined with other modalities—such as token economies—or used by itself. This makes definitions difficult, but the Bureau soon had 13 "official" therapeutic communities. Some had "siblings" outside, to which they sent graduates. Others thrived in places such as the

Federal Correctional Institutions at Lexington, Kentucky, and Fort Worth, Texas. One community (Asklepieion) ran for 6 years at the U.S. Penitentiary, Marion, Illinois.

Types of Units

Therapeutic communities are examples of units that provide *treatment*. Inmates are selected for such units because they have problems such as alcohol or drug addiction that can be ameliorated or remedied.

Other units provide *education*, *training*, or *work experiences*, and "an appropriately designed counseling program."[15] The inmates in such units have obvious deficits (marginal literacy, lack of employment skills, and so forth) that can be addressed by the unit. A third type, which covers most units in the Federal system, is *management-related*.

"Management-related" does not mean that the prison gets what it wants and the inmate loses out. For example, inmates can be sorted by personality type to separate "aggression-prone" from "victim-prone" inmates, which reduces rates of predation. Management obviously benefits through fewer incidents, but the real beneficiaries are the inmates who did not become victims. The same rule applies to other sortings in which prisoners are isolated to avoid trouble or conflict.

One can form groups to facilitate service delivery. A unit composed of elderly inmates, for example, can adjoin medical or pharmaceutical services. Young inmates can be assigned to teams that have expertise in adolescence (a side benefit is that older inmates get peace and quiet). Other teams can have expertise in problems of long-teamers, Cuban detainees, persons diagnosed HIV-positive, or other homogeneous groupings.

But classification and sorting—which means specialization of programs and staff—require time and attention and (as far as possible) uncrowded conditions. Where compromise is necessary, a bifurcated situation arises in which classification and specialization are reserved for high-priority programs, and the remaining units receive prisoners on a first-come, first-served basis. Thus, a few units are specialized and serve treatment, training/ vocational, or management functions for special populations. Most units receive representative intake subpopulations, and are programmed in more or less standard fashion. Teams can still introduce program variations (if they have autonomy). But they cannot apply Levinson's model and produce Bearers, Seattles, and Tallyhoes under the auspices of specialized experts.

Patterns of Unit Management

Unit management survives crises such as extreme crowding by changing the ratio of special to general units in the system. The challenge for management is to create special units that serve the needs of the system and the inmates, given available resources. Today, resources are scarce, but drug-related offenders need specialized drug-treatment units. Other programs could be inspired by intake disproportions involving long-term offenders, violent offenders, emotionally disturbed persons, non-English-speakers, or other groups that could benefit from special programs. With respect to this issue, managers must ask questions such as:

• How seriously would the inmates be handicapped if they were integrated into the general population?

• What problems would be created for others if these offenders became part of the population?

• Do these offenders require a specialized program, and are staff available who can administer the program?

• Can the program at issue be effective without dealing with the offenders as a group?

• Is there an institution in the system in which the program (say, residential drug treatment) can be set up without playing a wholesale game of musical chairs; i.e., creating serious disturbances in the rest of the system?

Should the answers to these questions favor the creation of a unit, other questions arise having to do with how units are patterned in the system. One model that may appeal involves the creation of institutions that are conglomerates of special units—perhaps different types of units, perhaps of the same kind. Another option places one or two special units in prisons that are otherwise unspecialized. The former model permits the concentration of resources, and the latter allows partial mixing of special and general populations and commonality of custody grading.

Beyond these immediate questions we face long-term questions, involving a future in which special programs can be routinely created, and we can afford to decide whether to move an illiterate drug addict from a therapeutic community to a remedial education unit, or vice versa. When that time comes I shall plan to write a sequel to this essay.

Notes

[1] Robert B. Levinson, "TC or not TC? That is the question," in Hans Toch (ed.), *Therapeutic Communities in Corrections*. New York: Praeger, 1980, p. 51.

[2] Robert B. Levinson, "Try softer," in Robert Johnson and Hans Toch (eds.), *The Pains of Imprisonment*. Beverly Hills, CA: Sage, 1982, p. 244.

[3] Robert B. Levinson and Roy E. Gerard, "Functional units: A different correctional approach," *Federal Probation*, 1973, 37, 8–18, p. 15.

[4] Ibid.

[5] See, for example, Joseph E. Hickey and Peter L. Scharf, *Toward a Just Correctional Community*, San Francisco: Jossey-Bass, 1980; also Elliot E. Studt, Sheldon L. Messinger, and Thomas P. Wilson, *C-Unit: Search for Community in Prison*. New York: Russell Sage Foundation, 1968.

[6] Daniel Glaser, *The Effectiveness of a Prison and Parole System*. Indianapolis: The Bobbs-Merrill Company, 1964, p. 193.

[7] *Op. cit.*, p. 197.

[8] Hans Toch and J. Douglas Grant, *Reforming Human Services*. Beverly Hills, CA: Sage, 1982.

[9] Glaser, p. 205.

[10] *Op. cit.*, p. 128.

[11] Levinson and Gerard, p. 9.

[12] *Op. cit.*, p. 14.

[13] Herbert C. Quay, *Managing Adult Inmates: Classification for Housing and Program Assignments*. College Park, MD: American Correctional Association, 1984. Further reduction of disciplinary incidents can be documented after disaggregating inmates through classification *within* units for programmatic separation. See Diane J. Spieker and Timothy A. Pierson, *Adult Internal Management System (AIMS): Implementation Manual*. Washington, DC: National Institute of Corrections and Human Resources, 1987.

[14] Hans Toch (ed.), *Therapeutic Communities in Corrections*. New York: Praeger, 1980.

[15] Levinson and Gerard, p. 10.

16

Case Managing
Multiproblem Offenders

Hans Toch

The newspaper-reading public has become increasingly aware of the possibility that the average offender may be an overwhelming composite of encrusted and obdurate problems which make interventions uninviting. Part of the ethos that "nothing works" is the presumption of unamenability. This presumption in turn rests on the premise that offenders have so many difficulties by the time we get to them that addressing any given problem makes at best a dent on the composite offender.

The multiproblem offender becomes the equivalent of the elephant in the classic story, with mental health and other service providers as the blind men who must function as tail or trunk specialists, as experts in legs, or (in the case of criminal justice personnel) as custodians of intransigent bodies. Not only do workers not intersect with the offender as a whole, but the view they obtain of the offender is bound to be segmented, parochial, and unrepresentative.

Typical of the Discovery of the Multiproblem Offender is a recent article in the *New York Times* (March 16, 1994), which talked of violent delinquents as "a generation of children born to teenage mothers . . . coming of age in neighborhoods already weakened by the addictive power of crack and the destructive force of drug dealers." The article noted that "in city after city, in town after town, there are nightmarish cases that make judges and prosecutors nostalgic for the truants and vandals that once filled their dockets."

Source: *Federal Probation*, 59(4) (December 1995): 41–47.

One nostalgic judge who was interviewed for the article told the reporter that "the problem . . . is mindboggling. You see the failure of the schools. You see the failure of the parents. You see the violence on the streets. You see the guns."

It is unquestionably true that the prevalence of violent delinquency in the United States has reached crisis proportions and that predelinquent children mature into delinquency (if one can call it maturing) at earlier ages than in the past. But the multiproblem nature of the delinquent—and of the offender generally—is not of recent vintage.

The sociologists Shaw and McKay, in a book that reports the experiences of the classic Chicago Area Study of the late thirties, wrote about delinquents that:

> [m]any other "problem" conditions might be listed, each representing a state of affairs considered undesirable by most citizens. These would include various forms of unemployment, dependency, misconduct, and family disorganization, as well as high rates of sickness and death. It may be asked: Do these other phenomena exhibit any correspondence among themselves and with rates of boys brought into court? (Shaw & McKay, 1972, p. 90)

Shaw and McKay found that the answer to their hypothetical question was a resounding affirmative. They found high intercorrelations among problems of delinquents who lived in disorganized areas of cities like Chicago. And once they and others had confirmed that social disadvantages can produce a panoply of handicaps, it not only followed that the same person could develop multiple problems, but that problems could reinforce each other in a variety of ways.

The point has recently been reemphasized by the project directors of the Program of Research on the Causes and Correlates of Delinquency. In a preliminary review of their findings, they write:

> Serious delinquents seldom come to us as "pure types." . . . There is a strong component of co-occurring problem behaviors in their careers. . . . Also, these behaviors tend to interact with each other over time. For example, delinquency seems to increase the likelihood of drug use and involvement in drug use tends to increase the frequency and seriousness of delinquency.

They also point out that:

> Serious chronic offenders have multiple deficits including individual, family, school, peer, and neighborhood factors, all of which put them at risk for delinquency. Moreover, these factors tend to cumulate and interact with each other over time. (Thornberry, Huizinga, & Loeber, 1995, p. 234)

The Adult Multiproblem Offender

When one studies adult offenders who have one known set of problems, one becomes inevitably aware of the fact that other problems coexist. In some of our recently republished research, for example, we reviewed careers of violent offenders with past mental health problems and described these careers as follows:

> Among the features that these individuals . . . seem to share are (a) the advent of symptoms or behavior problems at early ages, leading to (b) early institutional placement followed by (c) ad seriatim institutionalization and (d) an unproductive, marginal, migratory existence which includes (e) brushes with the law. The offenders often (f) have combinations of deficits, such as emotional problems exacerbated by substance abuse, that (g) color some of their offenses, raising questions of competence, and (h) impair their ability to manage in prison and profit from prison programs; this (i) decreases their prospects of successful community adjustment, thus (j) increasing the chances of recidivism, including (k) violent recidivism. (Toch & Adams, 1994, p. 47)

We also observed that it is difficult to find a "normal" offender if this term denotes an absence of problems other than criminal offending. Our comparison group—which comprised persons who came to prison without past contacts with the mental health system—yielded a mélange of unimpressively checkered careers, often starting at very early ages. We wrote in our book that:

> a reader might well conclude that differences between offenders who have mental health histories and those who lack such histories are not striking. . . . [What we found are] careers of deprivation, deficits and nonresilience, addiction and self-destructiveness, impulsivity and perversity, heteronomy and explosiveness. In this respect, the accounts are no different from the range of histories covered in thousands of presentence summaries the reader might peruse elsewhere.

> Few offenders we have described seem to be models of mental wellness as most of us would understand the phrase. These "nondisturbed" offenders are not sturdy professionals competently engaged in illegal occupations. They are not persons who resolutely elect unfortunate sources of income or drastic solutions to their problems. Many of these offenders have long-term "careers," but they drift, seemingly helplessly, from one career juncture to the next. Even when the offenders' crimes are substantial, the perpetrators are often limited and driven, or exude incompetence and marginality. (Toch & Adams, 1994, pp. 127–128)

The Response to Multiproblem Offenders

Any perusal of prison files raises questions about the appropriateness of sentencing to prison some of the offenders who are described in these documents. Such questions particularly arise where the offender is not a menace to the public, where the police and others conclude that the person's last offense was irrationally motivated or reflected the contribution of blatant disabilities, where the offender appears ineffectual or remains disturbed after arrest and preceding trial, and where he or she continues to be disruptive and/or disturbed after intake into the prison.

However, the reason for prison sentences in such cases is not hard to ascertain after one continues to study the files. Dispositional alternatives available to the courts are limited but become particularly limited with offenders who demonstrate a chronic incapacity to negotiate life. Our data appeared to suggest that the more alternatives the courts need for an offender, the fewer they are likely to have available because the offender will have outlived his or her welcome among existing dispositional options. Prisons become a viable alternative in such instances because they at least provide room, board, supervision, and what is euphemistically referred to as "structure."

A related fact is that service providers can play jurisdictional ping-pong with offenders and can advance plausible justifications for this practice. If a client who has two salient problems arrives at two intake points, both of two agencies can focus on a problem with which they are not equipped to deal, leaving the offender in limbo. A former commissioner of the correctional system in New York State, for example, noted that "it is abundantly clear that a person suffering from mental retardation and some form of mental illness is the bane of everyone's existence. The retardation people point to the mental illness and throw their hands up. The mental health people point to the retardation and do the same. . . . The current practice of labeling everything just reinforces this process" (Coughlin, 1987).

It is paradigmatic that agencies that deliver services can adjust their eligibility criteria to include or exclude clients to expand or reduce services for a variety of reasons. Criteria can become especially exclusionary for clients who are unprofitable and/or uncongenial or who pose risks or who are arguably dangerous, unless services for such clients are mandated. Many offenders also deny that they have problems or resist being referred to people whom they regard as unhelpful or inhospitable.

Yet, the literature on delinquency prevention suggests that invoking a range of services is the only way to interrupt chronic offense careers, particularly of violent delinquents. In a recent review of treatment effectiveness, Tate, Repucci, and Mulvey (1995) concluded that:

[W]e know that comprehensive, individualized community-based, family-oriented interventions appear to hold promise and have impressive initial findings of success. . . . Service provision should be reconceptualized as an ongoing care model that emphasizes intervention in multiple spheres of an adolescent's life. The most promise lies in a comprehensive, long-term commitment, not in the development of any singular, more powerful approach. (p. 780)

Thornberry, Huizinga, and Loeber (1995) have similarly pointed out that:

Programs that are monothematic—treating only family factors, etc.—simply do not map onto what is known about the risk factors for delinquency. While addressing the needs of the child in one area, monothematic programs ignore their need in other areas. Moreover, such programs ignore the interlocking nature of these factors. As a result, positive effects from a school-based program, for example, that ignores the importance of family factors in producing both school performance and delinquency may be undone by continued poor family relationships and continued involvement in delinquency. (p. 234)

The point applies with equal measure to any type of multiproblem offender. In all such cases, one is forced to concur with Thornberry, Huizinga, and Loeber (1995) that "programs that are narrowly focused will fail to recognize and respond to these co-occurring problems. To avoid that, programs should be comprehensive and prepared to deal simultaneously with a wide range of deviant and problem behaviors."

Case Management

The requisite for any approach that is thus described is case management.[1] Case management is a process that can be thought of as the hub of a multimodal service-delivery wheel (figure 1). The number of spokes in this wheel for multiproblem offenders may be large, depending on supports that are needed to keep the offender functioning at a reasonable level in an institution or in the community. Where services are needed by offenders but not provided, spokes would be missing, and we can get oddly shaped wheels whose capacity to rotate would be correspondingly diminished.

As conventionally defined, case management must exercise four related functions. The first is needs assessment, which is the task of specifying the spokes the offender's service wheel must contain. The second task is referral, which involves the installation of spokes. The third task—coordination—is that of shaping the configuration of services (i.e., their well-roundedness). The last task—brokerage—is that of inspiring the wheel to turn and to keep turning. Brokerage provides the engine and transmission for the system. To broker services, the case manager must have the power to bring people together, ranging from moral suasion to formal power vested in the organization to which the case manager belongs. Moral suasion and formal power must function in tandem. That is to say, clout must be invoked as a backup for skilled and sensitive diplomacy.

Needs Assessment and Service Delivery

The preamble to service delivery is needs assessment. Before one provides services, one must define areas of personal functioning for which the offender most pressingly requires support or rehabilitative assistance. Some would say that this activity calls for comprehensive, uniform inventories conducted by trained specialists with the help of validated instruments. Most needs assessment falls short of this requirement, leading to the conclusion that one must make do with a triage process which reserves closer scrutiny for more complex or serious cases (Toch, 1981). However, irrespective of the scope of coverage, one must also be concerned about the offender's role in needs assessment. It stands to reason that the more the offender is dealt into the process, the more cooperative he or she is likely to be at later stages of the game.[2] Minimally, it seems desirable for the offender to understand the rationale behind the diagnostician's conclusions; ideally, the offender's view of his or her needs ought to concur with that of the system.

Figure 1
The Role of Case Management in a Service Delivery System for Multiproblem Offenders

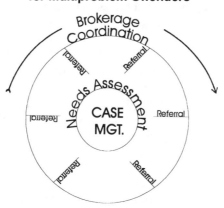

If needs assessment is the first stage of case management, an issue that immediately causes difficulties has to do with the relationship between assessment and service delivery, which may range from non-existent to incestuous. At one extreme, need specification may take no account of services that are actually available and becomes an academic (in the pejorative sense) exercise. The client emerges from such an exercise with a thick folder redolent with test results and diagnostic labels, culminating in utopian recommendations. The situation is exemplified by a memorable parole board hearing I attended in which the prisoner had been told that he wasn't being released because "you haven't participated in programs that should have been available to you."

During, the "rehabilitation" era in corrections, reception centers specialized in churning out prescriptions for rehabilitative experiences that were rarely available in prisons. Such flights of imagination were facilitated where diagnosticians were spatially and psychologically separated from institutions or agencies where the hypothetical services were delivered.

But the opposite problem arises where the specification of needs is shaped by the availability or nonavailability of funded services, which clients are coincidentally said to require or not to require. This produces a fortunate but suspicious congruence between services and candidates for service. It also produces strange variability in diagnoses among comparable populations, such that one prison system stoutly maintains that it has no emotionally disturbed inmates while another boasts an appreciable number—with no indication as to why pathology should be thus geographically clustered. The same question arises where schools with comparable populations vary in the proportion of students who are adjudged to suffer from psychological handicaps or to manifest behavioral problems.

The relationship can also obtain over time, as key problem areas are funded or unfunded or new services are instituted. The proportion of diagnosed substance abusers has historically varied more sharply than the prevalence of substance abuse. The diagnosis of posttraumatic stress disorder among female offenders has increased as programs for such offenders have proliferated. Once problems are labeled and gain salience, individuals are discovered to manifest the problems.

It is obvious that there must be correspondence between types of assessed needs and types of available services. But the challenge is to ensure that the relationship is at least reciprocal so that services are mobilized in response to assessed needs, even if this entails an expansion or modification or redeployment of the existing service spectrum. A needs assessment process must have independent integrity, but the information that one collects must be used to provide services for the process to make sense.

Coordinating Services

Assuming services are in fact available, the next task is to ensure that they are not delivered in mutual disregard and isolation, one service at a time. Case managers must be coordinators who make certain that the configuration of services corresponds to the configuration of needs. Invariably, of course, some needs are more peremptory and survival-related than others, and it stands to reason that services may have to be prioritized or sequenced. Most importantly, services have to be packaged as composites. A homeless person with mental health problems requires concurrent living arrangements and help to stay afloat. A delinquent with education and addiction problems needs schooling and specialized treatment.

A case manager would be best situated for dealing with multiproblem clients where there are agencies available that can deliver a variety of services under one roof. Next best is to have a service deliverer who specializes in hybrid customers such as forensic mental health clients or homeless alcoholics. Confluent services offer logistical advantages. They improve the chances that the offender will show up and be attended to. Hybrid services also invite conceptual coherence, such that the client is at least partly seen as a person rather than as a composite of unrelated needs. A predelinquent youth is thus best served in a school which contains persons who can take into account, and respond to, the youth's extracurricular problems.

Another combinatory concern that is important is that of supervision and support. Some offenders—such as those with low temptation resistance or those who are explosive—may have to be tightly monitored while their problems are being addressed. Disproportionately frequent contacts may be in order, both with the offender and persons in the offender's environment. Any case manager who deals with offenders thus knows that custodial and support functions are related, rather than being watertight compartments. A disturbed offender who refuses to take medication may have to be jailed, not because he has violated a condition of parole but because discontinuance of medication creates vulnerability to relapse. Surveillance also gives the case manager information about shortcomings in the support system or about unanticipated problems the offender may face.

Computers offer new options in this regard. Some information systems can detail who is delivering services to the offender. The same system tells the case manager about the availability of referral options for offenders on his or her caseload. In prisons, case managers can find out about vacancies in classrooms, shops, or mental health units and can reserve spaces where there are currently no vacancies. A proactive system can use needs assessment data to realign a spectrum of services. In Scotland, personal officers meet with prisoners to define "agreed needs" for service. Groups of such case managers can compare notes to arrive at aggregate rosters of needs. These rosters can be passed on to the prison administration, which can use the data to allocate programs to prisons (Pearce, 1994).

A key obligation of any case manager who coordinates services is that of keeping a running inventory of offender experiences over time. This inventory is crucial because offenders wend their way through a variety of systems, each of which religiously guards in-house records about its segment of the offender's career. The case manager can put such humpty dumpties together again, bridging information sources and making sure that updated cumulative histories of problems (and efforts to deal with them) are available.

This process, unfortunately, can degenerate. Many case managers have become "keepers of files." Their case-managerial function has atrophied, leaving as a residual task the job of updating folders. Files become repositories of serendipitous encounters between abandoned clients and indifferent environments. They are not a basis for case management, but a testimonial to its absence.

Brokerage

Most observers would agree that the guts of case management is brokerage. I have mentioned that brokerage involves using influence or power. Influence rests on the relationships the case manager can build. In relating to the offender, the case manager personalizes a faceless bureaucracy. This means that the case manager must show that he or she has the client's interests at heart, is physically available, is always willing to listen and to become a source of helpful advice. For those who deliver services, the case manager is a person who understands the difficulties and complexities of their job and tries to resolve crises as they arise. The case manager takes pains to supply information about those he or she refers and takes an interest in their progress. He or she serves as a link among those who deal with the offender, making service delivery less of a lonely and thankless enterprise. One option he or she could exercise is to convoke case conferences of providers who deal with the same group of offenders.

Case managers who are affiliated with organizations that lack status and resources may have to rely on the goodwill they are thus able to generate. This approach may work but limits case managers in what they can do. Case managers who lack power may have to use mostly volunteer service providers, who want new or more business. They may have to cajole resistant clients to accept assessments and consider referrals. They may have to rely on information that is voluntarily provided them.

But, fortunately, most case managers who deal with multiproblem offenders have power. The cam managers especially have power over their clients, though they may try to downplay this power. The correctional case manager is an agent who can restrict the client's freedom, can retain the client in confinement, revoke probation, rescind parole, or recommend hospital commitment. Such threats form a backdrop to benevolent transactions and are iron fists in the velvet gloves of the relationships between case managers and offenders.

Some enlightened observers may regard the punitive power vested in such case managers as a form of blackmail which contaminates their therapeutic encounters. This view ignores at least three considerations.

First, where services are provided because they address correlates of offense behavior, one is entitled to draw the offender's attention to this fact. The point being, if the offender is inclined to reject services as insufficiently subserving his desire for self-improvement, we can suggest that such involvement may be reassuring to the rest of us and that it is usually in the offender's interest to make the rest of us happy. One can reinforce this observation, moreover, by noting that support is made available to the offender as an alternative to custodial options and that the diversion that society provides, it can always take away.

On the other side of the ledger, special incentives may be needed to motivate reluctant providers to deal with offenders and to underline the point that society has a stake in getting such persons needed services.

One lastly needs authority to deal with the public. The public has a right to question the use of scarce resources on behalf of those who are undeserving while the deserving wait in line. In the United States the provision of services in criminal justice or other punitive settings creates a configuration that is attractive to the public, which favors enforced rehabilitation as a modality (Doble, 1987; Doble & Klein, 1989; Doble, Immerwahr, & Richardson, 1991). The public assigns priority to being protected from violent offenders and wants such offenders shaped up. A custodial-coercive backup for service delivery makes sense to the public and makes the case management of offenders acceptable. A system that did not include a coercive backup would not be acceptable to the public and would consequently not be viable.

This point has recently been made by Tate, Repucci, and Mulvey (1995), who note that:

> [T]he intensive, comprehensive, community-based approaches may be most acceptable only when they have a clear monitoring and sanctioning component or after some period of incarceration. Similarly, the retributive strategies may only be workable when they incorporate treatment for selected subgroups of violent offenders. Effective intervention could likely lie somewhere in the middle, where ideology could give way to reasoned program design. (p. 780)

Continuity of Case Management

In case management, there is no such thing as cradle-to-grave continuity. The best one can achieve is a relay race in which the client is passed on—like a torch—from one case manager to the next. In the process, the client undergoes chameleon-like transmutations to conform to case managers' jurisdictional boundaries. This occurs even within systems, as when a prisoner moves from prison to prison, encountering variations in institutional missions and new spectrums of program options.

This does not mean, of course, that offender careers must be disjointed, haphazardly discontinuous, or serendipitous. For one, transitions can be seamless if interface problems are attended to. Case managers can intersect by communicating with each other through case conferences or other means. A new case manager can cut into the offender's career before taking over, such as in prerelease parole programs. One can also conceive of stages in the process during which case managers work as teams, sharing concurrent jurisdiction.

In other words, sequences of case management can be anything but capricious. Some shifts are plausible reactions to changes in offender behavior. When the offender violates probation or earns a parole violation, he or she invites assignment of a new, correctional case manager. If he or she is disturbed and decompensates in the prison, he or she acquires a new hospital case manager. Any increment in problems can call for more intensive case management, where such is available.

Other sequences can be arranged to keep pace with evolving sets of needs or changes in the offender's status. Any career has an early, middle, or late segment in which offenders face different sets of problems. Transitional stages call for case managers who can assist with problems of readjustment. A disadvantaged new prisoner may need help to adjust (or readjust) to prison, a new parolee requires support to reintegrate into the community, while an about-to-be-released prisoner or parolee must be prepped for his or her impending change of status.

Some transitions can be drastic, as when offenders leave a system that supplies them with case managers, such as the juvenile or criminal justice system, and become precariously unattached. Multiproblem offenders are particularly vulnerable at such junctures because they often combine resourcelessness with obliviousness to their problems. Suspension of mandated services also places many clients at risk in a marketplace that assigns low priority to indigent, anomalous, and troublesome customers.

It becomes the responsibility of case managers at discharge points to enhance prospects of continued service delivery, if such is possible. Ideally, the case manager can look for a volunteer successor and enjoin the offender to take him or her seriously. A good strategy is to highlight some problem the offender has for which resources are available, even if it is not the offender's principal problem. This makes the organization that deals with the problem the lead agency for case management purposes, if it can be recruited to play that role.

There remains the issue of information. I have noted that an impediment to continuing case management is the zealousness with which agencies protect their files, preventing others from gaining access to them. This practice is undergirded by legal provisions designed to protect clients from ill-intentioned outsiders seeking access to embarrassing or pejorative details. And it is true that much relevant information about multiproblem offenders is unflattering and potentially stigmatizing, which makes it hard to argue that files should be promiscuously shared. By the same token, multiproblem clients are ill (and incautiously) served where those who deal with one of the client's problems must remain oblivious to his or her other problems. Tragedies have resulted, for example, where psychiatrists have treated patients who—unbeknown to them—had extensive violence involvements. Counterpart problems occur where mental health-related information is kept from other types of staff who deal with vulnerable persons, such as staff who run shelters for the homeless.

Problems are exacerbated when the offender leaves some system—such as the juvenile justice system or the school system—never to return. At such junctures, files that describe a large chunk of the offender's life tend to become inaccessible.

The problem is how to obtain information, given formal strictures and concerns about the confidentiality of records. The advent of technology does not resolve this problem because computers do not relay what is not confided to them or what the custodians of a system are unwilling to share with the next database down the line.

We are left with compromise options. One is to rest on retrospective interviews with the offender, knowing that the yield of such interviews is limited by the vagaries of memory and the selectivity of self-serving recollections. Case managers can invite service providers to share data that do not violate confidentiality such as characterizations and impressions. They can request that offenders authorize them to gain access to data sources, with the understanding that information will be deployed to improve the delivery of services. Case managers are also entitled to obtain feedback—including periodic reports—from service providers since they are sources of referrals and coordinators of services. Moreover, they can provide information to service providers in exchange for the data they obtain.

Information over time can be relayed through networking from case manager to case manager. The result of networking in the aggregate can be a cumulative database, earmarked for case management use and, possibly, for research. The rules governing such use must be specified, and it is imperative that information networks be circumscribed by ironclad understandings. Such understandings must underline the distinction between information as such, which is innocuous, and its use, which requires regulation.

Conclusion

The reader will note that I have been using the term "case manager" as if there is sufficient commonality among such functionaries as probation officers, mental health service coordinators, and prison staff members to discuss their contributions in the same breath. I am not alone in this regard, of course, since there is a presumption of shared connotations whenever case management is discussed. This is particularly so where one talks of case management as bridging the transition from one setting (such as an institution) to another (such as the community).

Case management implies systemic planning and coordination over time. Hospital discharge plans and preparole workups suggest that we expect the reintegration of clients, and one can in practice make this claim even if no follow-up activity occurs. Institutions can cite their "case management" as a testimonial to their commitment to continuity of care; if there is no continuity, they can claim that others—including clients—are dropping the ball.

Similar fictions can be played out at intake in institutional settings. Here, "case management" implies links between needs assessment and delivery of services. Unexamined correlations provide an illusion of planfulness and responsiveness to client needs. Where disjunctures occur, they can be attributed to scarce resources, offender resistance, and custody constraints, which can all be convincingly documented. A prison system that describes itself as "case managed" can thus refer to a fond but unrealized hope of coordinated programming.

The converse occurs where case management is devalued. There are professions—such as parole—that avoid the term in referring to the case managing they do to preserve a nonmushy public image. Such professions derive popularity—and budgets—from a reputation for unstinting, no-nonsense surveillance and attention to the risks that offenders pose. They receive no kudos for support they provide to individuals who are homeless, addicted, disturbed, intellectually unprepossessing, and unemployable, nor for invoking assistance to help keep such persons afloat. Case management occurs, but it becomes a sub rosa appendage to the advertised (custodial) mission. Its successes become unrecognized and its achievements unappreciated and downgraded.

Case management has retained some respectability in juvenile corrections, but occupations such as juvenile probation are accommodating their images to the demand for the control of precocious violence. Given such demands, an emphasis on the management of juveniles who combine educational deficits, membership in dysfunctional families, addiction, and mental health problems is bound to become increasingly unfashionable.

The advent of case management as I have discussed it is at times equivalent to the "discovery" by one of Molière's characters that he could speak prose. Formalizing case management substantively, however, requires systemic deployment of resources. It also draws attention to the process and to its constituent components. It especially draws attention to coordination and brokerage, which are not customarily highlighted as responsibilities of criminal justice agencies and staff.

Case management places emphasis on the continuity of service delivery and is defined as a way of achieving continuity. Case management bridges segments of the offender's career and links those who deal with the offender at different points in time. The process implies a relay network of case managers who work in tandem. And ideally, as the offender moved on, so would the information needed to case manage the offender, permitting overviews of the offender's career and his or her response (or nonresponse) to services made available to him or her over time. Such information must cross organizational borders and transcend disciplinary boundaries and provide a picture of the offender as a person reacting to his or her environment as a totality.

We are today no doubt a long way from achieving comprehensive overviews of offender careers. But we can approximate the model by tracking offenders across career segments, attending to changes in problem constellations if they occur. We can tell whether offenders mature or fail to mature with or without help from the rest of us. And we can, I hope, find some responses that help offenders solve some problems some of the time—which is the best anyone can hope to expect.

Notes

[1]The term "case management" is predominantly employed in the health care professions (see, for example, Mullahy, 1995). Historical usage, however, covers a variety of models that evolved where human services were delivered by networks of service providers (Weil, Karl, et al., 1985). The attributes of case management I discuss in this article are those that appeared uniquely applicably to multiproblem offenders, ranging from serious delinquents to adults with mental health problems.

[2]The same argument extends to those who deliver services to the offender. Assessment (and case management generally) is frequently a collaborative enterprise. At junctures where assessments are updated or reassessments occur, teams can

include program staff with whom the offender interacts. Where these persons are not members of assessment teams, their expertise can be invoked by soliciting their input.

References

Coughlin, T. A. (1987, December 29). Personal communication.

Doble, J. (1987). *Crime and punishment: The public's view.* New York: Edna McConnell Clark Foundation.

Doble, J., & Klein, J. (1989). *Punishing criminals: The public's view.* An Alabama survey. New York: Edna McConnell Clark Foundation.

Doble, J., Immerwahr, S., & Richardson, A. (1991). Punishing criminals: The people of Delaware consider the options. New York: Edna McConnell Clark Foundation.

Mullahy, C. M. (1995). *The case manager's handbook.* Gaithersburg, MD: Aspen Publishers.

New York Times. March 16, 1994.

Pearce, J. (1994). *An overview of the Scottish prison system.* Presentation to the Middle Atlantic States Correctional Association Conference, Killington, VT.

Shaw, C. R., & McKay, H. D. (1972). *Juvenile delinquency and urban areas* (Reprint edition). Chicago: University of Chicago Press.

Tate, D. C., Reppucci, N. D., & Mulvey, E. P. (1995). Violent juvenile delinquents: Treatment effectiveness and implications for future action. *American Psychologist, 50,* 777–781.

Thornberry, T. P., Huizinga, D., & Loeber, R. (1995). The prevention of serious delinquency and violence: Implications from the Program of Research on the Causes and Correlates of Delinquency. In J. C. Howell, B. Krisberg, J. D. Hawkins, and J. J. Wilson (Eds.), *Sourcebook on serious, violent and chronic juvenile offenders* (pp. 213–234). Thousand Oaks, CA: Sage Publications.

Toch, H. (1981). Inmate classification as a transaction. *Criminal Justice and Behavior, 8,* 3–14.

Toch, H., & Adams, K. (1994). *The disturbed violent offender.* Washington, DC: American Psychological Association (APA Books).

Weil, M., Karl, J. M., & Associates. (1985). *Case management in human service practice.* San Francisco: Jossey-Bass.

Section V

Casework Counseling and Crisis Intervention

Much of the effort of those involved in correctional treatment consists of attempts to discover those factors or occurrences that have some causal relationship to the offender's deviant behavior. Self-introspection helps the law violator uncover his or her motives and motivations and realize the types of reactions, urges, or views of life that have led to problem activity. The offender may also be led to be aware of or develop certain internal strengths, abilities, or qualities that can assist in his or her rehabilitation.

Casework Counseling

The treatment approach most often used in this form of correctional treatment is termed *casework counseling*. It involves a one-to-one contact between the client and the counselor. The counselor (a therapist, social worker, probation officer, parole officer, or youth worker) seeks to assist the client in becoming better adjusted to his or her current environment and also helps him or her prepare for the future. Hatcher (1978:3) describes correctional counseling as being concerned with the "application of validation techniques designed specifically for bringing about a predictable change in criminal and delinquent behavior."

The specific goals of correctional casework may involve one or more of the following:

1. Increased insight into one's problems and behavior
2. Better delineation of one's self-identity
3. Resolution of handicapping or disabling conflicts
4. Changing undesirable habits or reaction patterns
5. Improved interpersonal relationships or other competencies
6. Modification of inaccurate assumptions about oneself and one's world
7. Opening a pathway to a more meaningful and fulfilling existence (Coleman, 1964:564).

Correctional casework does not differ significantly in its goals from casework performed in any of the helping disciplines. The criminal or delinquent has many of the same problems as other individuals who seek counseling. These include facing responsibility, being able to make wise decisions, experiencing self-doubt or anxiety, and developing feelings of self-worth.

There are important differences between casework counseling in corrections and other types of counseling, however. The most profound is that correctional casework counseling is *not voluntarily sought*. The offender is not asked if he or she desires the counselor's advice and services, nor does he or she have a choice of caseworkers. This type of counseling, in which a client is required to accept counseling, is sometimes termed coercive counseling. The amenability of offenders assigned to such counseling may range on a spectrum from total rejection and refusal to cooperate to complete acceptance and cooperation. Also, the fact that the counseling is coercive increases the probability that the client will not be completely honest and open with the counselor but will try to say the kinds of things most likely to speed his or her release from the institution or from supervision. This makes it much more difficult to establish an open, honest relationship in correctional counseling than in other types of casework.

Nevertheless, the caseworker has certain advantages when counseling is coercive. He or she can require a client to enroll in an educational or job training program, submit to psychological testing, or become involved in an alcohol or drug rehabilitation program. Although the client may initially resent such direction, the positive outcomes that may result would not have been attained if the offender had been left to his or her own devices.

Although a correctional caseworker operates under general guidelines set by the courts or the institution (rules of probation or parole, institutional policies), the form of interaction between counselor and client may vary widely, and the counselor's own skills and creativity come into play in the choice of counseling style used with each client. In some instances, the counselor may involve the offender's family in the counseling process as a method of motivating the offender or helping the family change the environment that contributed to the offender's problems. In other cases, the counselor may uncover an area of interest that will open up new employment or educational opportunities for the client and help the client make a new start or turn from criminal associations.

In selection 17, "Stages of Counseling," Cavanagh describes a developmental process that must be followed if counseling is to be effective. The author lists and explains six stages of the helping process: information gathering, evaluation, feedback, the counseling agreement, changing behavior, and termination. These stages are applicable to all forms of counseling including crisis intervention. The veteran probation officer, correctional officer, or social worker who has the responsibility of providing counseling services to offenders may be thinking more in terms of getting the job done than following the developmental stages of the counseling process. Nevertheless, to be effective, the various stages mentioned must be adhered to.

In his book, *Multicultural Counseling*, Dillard (1983:3) observed that the ethnic and cultural awareness movements, which began in the 1960s and have continued to the present time, have had an important effect on counseling programs. These movements have drawn attention to the fact that "Since ethnicity plays a valid role in any pluralistic society, skilled counseling professionals also need to be able to communicate effectively with clients of diverse cultural groups." Communication is essential in any counseling situation, and good communication between the counselor and the client may never be developed if intercultural barriers exist. Not being cognizant of value differences, engaging in ethnic group or racial group stereotyping, and being insensitive to the beliefs, customs, or styles of living of others can all lead to communication barriers that make any form of counseling impossible.

In selection 18, "Recognizing and Utilizing Diversity in Counseling Approaches," Yonas and Garland provide some guidelines for correctional counselors who are working with clients of different ethnic origins. They note that not all individuals identify with their ethnic heritage to the same degree, and it is necessary for the counselor to be aware of the effect the heritage has on their daily lives.

Interviewing

The counseling process is greatly enhanced if the counselor has reliable information available pertaining to the person being counseled. This information may be obtained from many sources, including police reports, risk and needs assessments, psychological tests, talking with family, friends and other acquaintances, and through directly interviewing the person being counseled. Thus, understanding the interview process is vital in correctional counseling. Buckwalter (1983:2) defines the interview as "a controlled conversation with an investigative objective." The general purpose of the interview is for the interviewer to obtain information from the interviewee. The type of information being sought and the uses of the information obtained vary tremendously. Some interviews are conducted to investigate crime, others are completed to obtain information on a subject on which the interviewer knows very little and the person being interviewed is an expert, and others are completed for the purpose of obtaining information that can be used to develop a correctional treatment plan. Some interviews are conducted to try to persuade the interviewee to do something or to take a specific course of action, and at such times the interview can be considered a form of counseling.

In selection 19, "The Nature of Interviewing," Gorden presents the skill learning cycle as a model for interviewers to consider when preparing for interviews. This model consists of three major phases: planning, doing, and analyzing. Several skills must be developed and utilized by the interviewer during each phase of the interview process.

Selection 20, "What Do We Know about Anger Management Programs in Corrections?" by Hollenhorst, presents the underlying theory guiding anger management and the application of this theory in a variety of programs. The author notes that, while anger and violence are closely related and can often be factors precipitating criminal behavior, they nevertheless are separate behaviors. This fact must always be considered in the development and application of correctional treatment programs for the anger-prone and/or for violence-prone offenders. An analysis of the effectiveness of anger management programs is also provided.

Crisis Intervention

A special form of counseling is that termed *crisis intervention*. Any offender who has been remanded to correctional treatment has already experienced a number of personal crises, including arrest, imprisonment, court hearings and trial, sentencing, and imprisonment or assignment to correctional supervision. However, it is not likely that the offender received crisis intervention counseling during these events, except for the assistance given by a lawyer. The special, intense counseling called "crisis Intervention" is directed primarily at the crises that occur within the setting of correctional treatment. Such a need might arise when a prisoner is subjected to homosexual rape, learns that a loved one has died or is terminally ill, experiences anxiety attacks or other emotional problems as a result of imprisonment, becomes aware that his or her family is in dire financial straits or that his or her spouse is filing for divorce, experiences a drug-related episode, or attempts suicide or some other type of self-mutilation. The counseling given in such crises is necessarily more intense and of a different nature than counseling designed for long-term, less stressful interaction.

Zusman (1975:2335) defined crisis intervention in the following way:

> Crisis intervention is one term that can be used to describe a whole series of recently introduced, brief treatment techniques employing a wide variety of personnel, service organizations, auspices, and formal labels. Crisis intervention includes, for example, suicide prevention services using telephone and in-person interviews, teen-age counseling as offered through "hot line" and "drop-in centers," pastoral counseling, brief psychotherapy offered in emergency "walk-in clinics," family dispute intervention provided by specially trained policemen, window-to-window programs, and a host of similar programs.

The premise that at the time of a crisis a client may be more open to positive suggestions and more strongly motivated to change his or her life than at other times is behind much of the current emphasis on crisis intervention.

Sigafoos notes in selection 21, "Conflict Resolution: Primer for Correctional Workers," that conflict situations usually have common characteristics, and correctional workers can follow a general set of guidelines to resolve such situations. It is suggested that the correctional officers faced with a crisis situation should keep the "fight or flight" response in check, listen and assess the situation, summarize his or her initial positions, read between the lines, resolve the situation through compromise and cooperation, and implement the solution.

References

Coleman, James C. *Abnormal Psychology and Modern Life.* 1964. Glenview, IL: Scott, Foresman.

Dillard, John M. 1983. *Multicultural Counseling.* Chicago: Nelson-Hall.

Hatcher, Hayes A. 1978. *Correctional Casework and Counseling.* Englewood Cliffs, NJ: Prentice-Hall.

Zusman, Jack. 1975. "Secondary Prevention," in Alfred M. Freedman, Harold I. Kaplan, and Benjamin J. Sadock, eds., *Comprehensive Textbook of Psychiatry,* Vol. II. Baltimore: Williams & Wilkins:2335.

17

Stages of Counseling

Michael E. Cavanagh

Like any other developmental process, counseling follows a sequence. It is important for counselors to recognize a sequence so that they will have a framework within which to function and a means to evaluate where in the process they are. As in human development, these stages tend to be somewhat flexible and overlapping, and each stage must be passed through successfully if counseling is to be effective. There is more than one way to view the stages of helping. The format presented here best fits the philosophy of counseling reflected in this text.[1]

The helping process can be divided into six stages: (1) information gathering, (2) evaluation, (3) feedback, (4) the counseling agreement, (5) changing behavior, and (6) termination. Figure 1 reflects this process. It demonstrates an important concept—namely, that both the person seeking help and the counselor have two major choice points with regard to beginning the counseling relationship. The first point occurs when the person seeking help and the counselor initially meet. The person has made an uninformed decision to get help, and the counselor has made an uninformed decision to see the person; that is, the counselor does not know whether or not the person is a reasonable candidate for counseling.

The second choice point occurs after the first three stages, when both the person in counseling and the counselor have gained sufficient knowledge upon which to make an informed decision. The decision is whether to continue counseling or to seek an alternative that would be more appropriate and helpful.

Figure 1

Counseling stages.

Uninformed decision			_Informed decision_		
Stage 1	_Stage 2_	_Stage 3_	_Stage 4_	_Stage 5_	_Stage 6_
Information gathering	Evaluation	Feedback	Counseling agreement	Changing behavior	Termination

The six stages can be telescoped so that they fit both short-term and long-term counseling, just as basic surgical procedures are the same whether an operation lasts a half-hour or ten hours. Counseling meant to last only five or ten sessions would pass through each of the stages in an abbreviated manner. Long-term counseling could spend 5 sessions on the first three stages and 50 to 150 sessions on the last three. However, it is doubtful that any kind of counseling could be effective without spending at least some time in each stage. If a counselor skipped the information-gathering stage, there would be no foundation for counseling; if the evaluation stage is skipped, the counselor would not know what the person's problems are; if the feedback stage is eliminated, the person could not make an informed decision; if there is no counseling agreement, there would be no course to follow; if behaviors are not changed, there is no counseling; and if the termination stage is ignored, the person will be left with no sense of closure.

This does not imply that counseling does not actually begin until the fourth stage. Counseling begins the moment the counselor and the person in counseling meet. The first three stages can be therapeutic in themselves in that to progress through them, the person and counselor are relating on levels that deal with cognition, emotions, needs, values, and conflicts. As the counselor listens, probes, reflects, understands, and clarifies, the person can be growing in insight, confidence, and hope. The main difference between the first three stages and the last three is that the focus of the first three is on sharing important information, which can be therapeutic in itself. The focus of the last three stages is on helping the person change behavior so that he or she can live more effectively.

Stage 1: Information Gathering

The more information counselors have, the more valid their evaluations, the more accurate their feedback, and the more sound their recommendations. Therefore, it is helpful for counselors to recognize the various areas of information that must be tapped. The information index in Figure 2 represents the main sources of information for the counselor.

Continuum A-B represents the time dimension. Information about the person's past helps the counselor understand how the person got where he or she is. Information about the present indicates how well the person is functioning currently, and information about the future tells the counselor who the person wishes to become. As these pieces of information are brought together, they can give a reasonably good picture of who the person is and why the person is seeking help.

Continuum C-D reflects the importance of getting both intrapsychic and interpersonal information. Intrapsychic information consists of learning about the person's perceptions of reality; his inner conflicts and how they are handled; the relationship between who the person is, thinks he is, and wants others to think he is; as well as the person's beliefs, values, and hopes. Interpersonal information comprises the dynamics involved in how the person relates with others, whether these relationships are satisfying or dissatisfying to the person or to the people with whom he or she relates.

Continuum E-F denotes what the person thinks and feels about herself, others, and relevant events. It is not only important to know the content of the person's thoughts and feelings, but to recognize how they interact and perhaps conflict. For example, when asked how she viewed her father, a woman responds "I have nothing but the utmost respect for him." When she is asked how she *feels* about her father, she replies "I resent him more than words can say."

Figure 2

An information index.

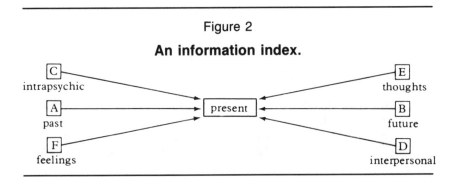

The information index highlights cautions in information gathering. Typically, people seeking help lure counselors into talking about the past, discussing interpersonal relationships, and focusing on ideas. The counselor who is successfully lured will have a fragmented and inaccurate picture upon which to make a clinical evaluation.

Questions

In addition to being aware of the various dimensions of information, it is helpful for counselors to have a clear idea of what specific information they want. The information must be relevant and gathered in a relatively short time. The following format of questions can be helpful in accomplishing this goal. Whether one asks specific questions or gathers the information indirectly depends on the counselor and the situation.

1. "Why do you feel it would be a good idea to talk with me?" This question is meant to ascertain the person's motives for seeking counseling and his or her view of the problem. A person may reply "I didn't think it would be a good idea—my mother did." A person may present the problem as feeling depressed, worried, insecure, confused, or scared. The counselor can then help the person describe the nature of his or her problem more specifically.

2. "How long have you felt this way?" The answer to this question gives the counselor some idea as to whether the problem is long-standing or of short duration. Counselors can be aware that people sometimes describe their problem as short-lived, but further probing indicates that it was present for a long time and only recently became activated.

3. "What do you think is causing these problems?" This question is meant to disclose how much insight the person has and how much responsibility he or she is taking for the problem. A person may answer "I don't have the slightest idea" or "My boss is the cause of the problem" or "I've always been insecure, and this new job is hitting every insecurity I have."

4. "How have you been dealing with the problem up to this point?" The answer to this question will give the counselor some idea of the person's defenses, adaptive responses, and use of environmental supports. The person may answer "I don't think it's a problem; my husband does" or "I've been distracting myself with work and probably eating and drinking too much" or "I have tried several alternatives that I thought a good deal about, and I've discussed it with my family, but I still need a little more help."

5. "How do you expect counseling will help you?" The question is meant to elicit the person's expectations of counseling. One person may answer "I don't have the slightest idea." Another person may respond "I think you can tell me what I should do." A third person may react "I hope you will be able to help me see what I'm doing wrong, so I can stop it."

6. "How much time and effort are you willing to invest in working on your problem?" Answers to this question will tell the counselor how accurately the person assesses the seriousness of the problem and how much personal motivation he or she has to solve it.

7. "Can you tell me some things about your past that you think may be helpful to my understanding of who you are today?" This question is meant to get a psychological snapshot of the person. A detailed case history is rarely necessary as part of the information-gathering stage and may only serve to distract from current issues and affects.

8. "What are some of your strong points?" This question is meant to give the counselor some idea of the person's strengths and also gives the person an opportunity to bolster his or her self-esteem, which may have been diminished in talking about the problem.[2]

Interaction and Reaction

In addition to having the person tell the counselor about himself or herself, the counselor must have an opportunity to see the person in action. The information the person has given is hearsay; that is, its validity depends upon the person's willingness and ability to perceive and communicate accurately. Counselors who restrict themselves to hearsay information are likely to get an inaccurate picture of the person, which will negatively affect the evaluation and feedback. Two ways counselors can become eyewitnesses to the person's dynamics are through interaction and reaction.

Interaction means two things: challenging and relating warmly with the person. *Challenging* means probing the person in a gentle, tentative way. Challenging differs from confronting, which is ordinarily inappropriate at this stage (see Stage 5 for a definition and description of confronting). When a counselor challenges the person's perceptions, motives, insights, defenses, expectations, and values, he or she invites the person to entertain the possibility that his or her way of perceiving reality and reacting to it may not be entirely accurate or helpful.

For example, a counselor may ask "Bill, you say your mom is pretty unreasonable. Is it possible that sometimes she is being reasonable but you don't want to see it that way?'' The counselor creates some natural stress to see how the person reacts to it. Does he handle the stress differently than he says he handles stress? On being challenged, does he show some behavior that he has successfully covered up until now? Does he respond by attacking, withdrawing, or deftly avoiding the challenge? Does he respond well, seeing the challenge as an opportunity to learn something about himself or to clarify a situation?

Counselors who are reluctant to challenge a person at this stage are taking the same risks as a physician who declines to thump a person's sensitive abdomen. Sometimes the best way to see where it hurts is to probe, even when it causes some pain.

Warmth is another part of interacting. Relating warmly means that the counselor naturally and genuinely communicates positive feelings toward the person by smiling, encouraging, and complimenting the person when it is appropriate. This affords the counselor a chance to see firsthand how the person responds to positive feelings, whether he or she accepts them naturally. Does she freeze and become suspicious? Does he ignore them? Does she seek them and cling to them? Does he respond well only when positive feelings are forthcoming? The answers to these questions will give the counselor some important information as to how the person handles warmth: whether the person accepts it and grows from it or rejects it and deprives himself or herself of valuable psychological fuel.

A second way to elicit firsthand information is by *reacting*. This means that the counselor is finely attuned to his or her own reactions to the person. The counselor is like a harp. When a chord is struck, the counselor knows *somebody* struck it. And, if the counselor knows he or she did not strike it, then it must have been the person. The counselor can reasonably assume that the ways the person "plays" him or her are similar to the ways the person "plays" other people. Some typical chords that are struck are feelings of threat, anger, sympathy, tenderness, affection, sexuality, frustration, confusion, distrust, repulsion, curiosity, and caution.

This information can tell the counselor how the person tends to "make" other people feel, at least under certain circumstances. This material can give the counselor otherwise unobtainable information as to how the person "gets" others to treat him or her.

The information gained from interaction and reaction affords counselors material that they could not obtain simply by asking questions and letting the person tell a consciously or unconsciously edited story.[3]

Stage 2: Evaluation

As information gathering nears an end, the counselor begins to evaluate it. This evaluation evolves around five issues.

Symptoms

Symptoms are signs indicating that a person is overloaded with stress. Academically, there are two kinds of symptoms: those included in the formal diagnostic categories—for example, those presented in the *Diagnostic and Statistical Manual* of the American Psychiatric Association (DSM III)—and those not included in any formal diagnostic classifications. Some examples of symptoms presented as diagnostic categories are depression, anxiety states, phobias, obsessions, compulsions, personality disorders (such as antisocial and passive-aggressive), sexual dysfunctioning (such as impotence and frigidity), and sexual disorders (such as child molesting and rape). Some examples of symptoms that do not fit the traditional diagnostic categories are: inordinate fear, anger, guilt, confusion, frustration, procrastination; feelings of inadequacy, hypersensitivity, fatigue, jealousy, distractibility; interpersonal conflicts; job inefficiency; and religious desolation. Many people who seek counseling refer to their symptoms as their problem. For example, a person may tell a counselor "My problem is that I'm depressed . . . or can't sleep . . . or am tense all the time."

It is important for counselors to assess the nature and severity of the symptoms. Some symptoms need immediate and direct intervention. For example, people who are deeply depressed, severely anxious, have such acute psychosomatic symptoms as severe headaches and insomnia, are currently addicted to alcohol or drugs, or are an imminent danger to themselves or others need immediate symptomatic relief because their symptoms are seriously damaging and preclude the effective use of counseling.

Other symptoms are less damaging and either do not significantly interfere with counseling or actually create sufficient distress in the person that they facilitate it. These symptoms can be monitored and may be used to gauge the progress of counseling. As the person grows in counseling, the symptoms should diminish.

Cause of Symptoms

There is one generic cause of symptoms; namely, something is significantly interfering with, or threatening to interfere with, a basic psychological need. Some of these basic needs are the need to experience a reasonable degree of security, love, esteem, accomplishment, stimulation, freedom, joy, and purpose. When an important need is interfered with, stress results. And when stress is left unmitigated, it will immediately or eventually cause symptoms, depending upon the intensity of the stress and the coping skills of the person. Basic needs can be significantly interfered with in four ways:

1. An objectively psychologically damaging event occurs (loss of a loved one, divorce, termination of a love relationship, imprisonment).

2. The person seeking help is in an important relationship with someone who is behaving in ways that significantly interfere with the person's basic needs (a woman is married to a man who treats her destructively).

3. The person seeking counseling behaves interpersonally in ways that discourage others from meeting his or her needs. For example, a man acts abrasively with women and gets rejected; a woman behaves seductively with men and gets used.

4. The person seeking counseling has intrapersonal dynamics that ultimately interfere with need fulfillment. For example, a man feels inadequate and therefore does not allow others to get close enough to meet his needs; a woman has unrealistically high expectations of herself, which she pursues to the detriment of getting her basic needs met.

These causes may not be mutually exclusive. A man may behave abrasively with women (interpersonal maladaptive behavior) because he perceives himself as inadequate and fears rejection (intrapersonal maladaptive behavior). Hence, he rejects women before they can reject him. There also may be more than one cause underlying a symptom, and two or more causes may interact. The more skilled a counselor becomes, the better he or she can see the interrelating of causes and symptoms and causes with causes. Figure 3 shows the interaction between symptoms, stress, and the causes of stress. It is important that counselors assess the cause(s) of the symptoms accurately because they will dictate the methods of resolution. If the cause is misdiagnosed, the method of resolution will be ineffective.

Relief of Symptoms

What can be done to modify the behavior that is causing the symptoms depends upon the nature of the cause. If the cause is an objectively stressful event, then cognitive restructuring, ventilation, and reassurance may gradually allow the person to feel more secure, loved, or competent. This in turn reduces the stress, which diminishes the symptoms. If the cause is a significant other interfering with the person's need fulfillment, then the person can be helped to perceive and handle the situation more constructively or to withdraw from it. If the person's maladaptive behavior in interpersonal situations is causing the symptoms, then the counselor can help the person develop better social competencies or a better sense of self, depending on the basic problem. If the cause is the person's intrapsychic conflicts, they can be isolated and the person can be taught how to deal with them more creatively. The specific steps taken and the time they require depend upon the nature of the behavior, its duration and severity.

Figure 3

Interaction between symptoms, stress, and causes of stress.

SYMPTOM

↑

OVERLOADING OF STRESS

↑

SIGNIFICANT INTERFERENCE WITH NEEDS

- Psychologically damaging event
- Significant other interferes with needs
- Person relates maladaptively with others
- Person relates maladaptively with self

Readiness for Counseling

Not everyone who seeks counseling is a reasonable candidate; that is, not all people will be able to use counseling to their advantage. The following are some factors counselors may consider when assessing the person's readiness for counseling. Each of these factors is on a long continuum. Obviously, if a person were to be at the positive end of the continuum on all these factors, it is likely that he or she would not need counseling.

1. People who accept responsibility for their problems are likely to be better candidates than those who blame others. People who express some variation of "I need to learn how to handle things better" are likely to be better candidates than those who say "If only my husband . . . wife . . . boss . . . friends . . . treated me better, everything would be all right."

2. People who are willing to work to earn feeling better are likely to be better candidates than those who want to feel better without changing their maladaptive behavior. Perls said "Very few people go in therapy to be cured, but rather to improve their neurosis."[4] Although Perls may be overgeneralizing, there is sufficient truth in his sentiment to evoke caution.

3. People with strong, intrinsic motivation to change are likely to be better candidates than those with weak intrinsic or primarily extrinsic motivation.

4. People who are psychologically minded are more likely to be good candidates than those who are not. Psychologically minded people are insightful and able and willing to appreciate the cause and effect dynamics of their behavior. For example, a person who can recognize that when she gets angry at a person she denies it but later subtly punishes the person who made her angry is likely to be a better candidate than someone who absolutely denies anger and can see no connection between her anger and her passive-aggressive behavior.

5. People who have good environmental supports that reward growth are likely to be better candidates that those who lack such supports.

6. People whose fears cause significant distress will likely be better candidates than those whose symptomatic behavior greatly reduces anxiety or provides pleasure. People who are addicted to alcohol, drugs, or food; those who compulsively gamble, steal, or sexually act out; and those whose symptoms act as effective tools to get much needed attention or as weapons with which to punish others are less promising candidates for counseling.

7. People who are capable of communicating in ways that can be understood and of listening in ways that allow them to assimilate information are likely to be better candidates than those whose symptoms significantly interfere with their ability to communicate. For example, people with severe depression, agitation, withdrawal; those with cognitive disturbances such as hallucinations, delusions, disorientation, or memory impairment; and people with speech disorders such as mutism, verbigeration, or echolalia are not good candidates for counseling.

Great caution must be exercised in deciding who is a reasonable and who is a poor candidate for counseling. Persons who are not good candidates at present can be referred by the counselor to a more appropriate type of intervention (detoxification, chemotherapy, weight-control programs, behavior modification, hospitalization), which may enable them to become reasonable candidates in the future. It is possible for a counselor to accept a poor candidate into counseling. This can be done as long as the counselor does not give the person false hope regarding the effects of counseling.[5]

Person/Counselor Fit

Not all counselors can help all people who seek their help, and it is a destructive expectation for counselors to think otherwise. Counseling relationships are similar to marriages: when serious, ongoing problems arise, it is often a consequence of two people trying to stay together who never should have started together. Counselors who feel that they can help and should agree to help anyone who makes an appointment are deluding themselves. The main medium through which a counselor works is the therapeutic relationship. Ordinary relationships are delicate and tenuous; counseling relationships are much more so.

Counselors are human beings with weaknesses, biases, fears, angers, and values. They can learn to recognize what their delicate areas are and work to strengthen them. However, they can also recognize that once in a while a person in counseling rubs one or all of these delicate areas the wrong way. When this occurs, it is better to refer the person to someone else. One counselor may have a difficult time relating with very hostile, powerful, demanding people. Another counselor may experience inordinate stress relating with very passive, docile, clinging people. A third counselor may have difficulty accepting the person's presenting problem: homosexuality, child molesting, child beating, alcoholism, drug addiction, abortion, sexual promiscuity, rape. The more counselors are in touch with their humanity, the more sensitive they will be to the kinds of people and problems they are more likely to be able to help.

It is both a professional and ethical responsibility to screen people for counseling. Ordinarily, a counselor who agrees to see someone in counseling is communicating that he or she has *good reason* to expect that counseling will be *reasonably successful*, that the *counselor can work effectively* with the person, and that the *time, energy, hardship, and financial investment will be worthwhile*. If any one of the four italicized factors is absent, a serious professional and ethical issue arises.

One factor that greatly contributes to tarnishing the reputation of counseling is the counselor who agrees to work with people who cannot be adequately helped through counseling. This leads to the conclusion that "counseling doesn't work" instead of "counseling doesn't work with certain people," who should have been referred to a more appropriate source of intervention. Counselors who are intelligently selective are providing a positive service to people who are seeking help and to the counseling profession.[6]

It is unlikely that an evaluation will be made with absolute confidence and certainty. Human behavior is usually too complex for that. However, counselors can develop working hypotheses with a reasonable amount of confidence. When they do, they are ready for Stage 3.

Stage 3: Feedback

Feedback consists of the counselor sharing relevant information with the person seeking help. The purpose of the feedback is to provide sufficient information to enable the person to make an informed decision with regard to beginning a counseling program. Four principles can help counselors provide feedback that is meaningful and helpful.

Characteristics of the Information

The information can be given as clearly, succinctly, concretely, and prudently as possible. "Clear" means simple, jargon-free language. "Succinct" means short, without drawn-out descriptions and analogies. Feedback, even with the most psychologically disturbed people, can be given in one session. "Concretely" indicates down-to-earth, easily grasped concepts. Sometimes a simple diagram helps. "Prudently" means that the counselor instills a sense of concern (when it is appropriate) without creating a state of alarm. A helpful attitude is "You've got some problems that do need attention, but there is something you can do about each of them."

Strengths and Weaknesses

The feedback can include both strengths and weaknesses. Usually it is better to begin with strengths and finish with weaknesses. When the procedure is reversed, the person may become so defensive or demoralized that he or she may not hear some important part of the discussion of the problem. Another option is to intersperse strengths and weaknesses.

Inviting Questions

The person can be invited to ask questions both during and after the feedback. Questions can be answered in a straightforward yet supportive way. Sometimes people ask a litany of questions in order to forestall the feedback process. When this is the case, the person can be invited to hold his or her questions until the end of the session.

Recommendations

After communicating the feedback to the person, the counselor makes recommendations. The counselor can explain that recommendations are not orders but serious, well-thought-out suggestions. The following are some common recommendations:

- Continue counseling on a weekly basis or more or less frequently as the seriousness of the problem dictates.
- Continue individual counseling; or begin group, marital, or family counseling; or combine individual counseling with one of the other types.
- Continue counseling, but with another counselor. This would occur when the counselor feels that someone else would be significantly more helpful, either because of a personality conflict or because the person's problem requires help outside of the counselor's area of expertise. When this recommendation is made, it should be done prudently and without communicating to the person that he or she is being rejected.
- Recommend a more suitable type of intervention—for example, substance abuse counseling, a weight-control program, readings or a course in psychological health, a support group, or religious direction.
- Recommend no further intervention because the person's difficulties are quite normal and are simply a part of the person's development and growth.
- Recommend no further intervention because, as a result of the sessions up to this point, the person has gained sufficient insight and courage to handle the problems without further professional help.

Recommend no further intervention because, although the person has problems that merit counseling, he or she is not psychologically ready for counseling. The person may not be experiencing sufficient stress or is experiencing stress, but it is controlled by defenses that are currently impenetrable. In either case, the person's motivation and accessibility are less than those necessary for effective counseling. Counselors can exercise care not to convey that the situation is hopeless. The difference between "not being ready" and "hopeless" can be explained, accompanied by an open invitation to return at some time in the future if the person so chooses. On the other hand, these people should not be led to believe that they do not need counseling.

If the sessions preceding the feedback progressed the way they should, neither the feedback nor the recommendations will be a surprise. Counselors need not feel that the feedback should consist of dramatic insights and discoveries. Consciously and unconsciously, the counselor has been preparing the person for the feedback and recommendations as the evaluation progressed.

No matter what the recommendation, it is unhelpful for the person to make a decision on the day of the feedback. The person can be invited to think about the feedback, assimilate and discuss it with others if he or she chooses. The counselor is careful not to convey the attitude that the person would be foolish not to accept the recommendation or that the counselor does not care if the person follows the recommendation. A more helpful attitude is one that conveys "I think the recommendation is a sound one, but what is more important is that it is *your* decision."

At this point, the person in counseling has a second choice point as to whether or not to begin counseling. This time the choice is an informed one. The person understands much more about himself or herself, about the nature of counseling, and about the personality of the counselor. If the person chooses to continue counseling, he or she will be a much stronger candidate and counseling will continue with good momentum. If the person chooses not to continue counseling, this decision may save the person and the counselor a great deal of time, energy, and frustration.

Stage 4: Counseling Agreement

Although counseling has been taking place during the first three stages, both the counselor and the person in counseling possess much more information than they did when they began. Using this information as a frame of reference, the counselor and the person in counseling can come to an agreement on four issues: the practical aspects of counseling, roles, expectations, and the goals of counseling.

Practical Aspects

Practical aspects include how often the person and counselor will meet, the length of the sessions, the policy regarding canceled and failed appointments, and the billing procedures. If there is no need to modify these based on the information gained from the first three stages, it is helpful to restate them in order to underline their importance. However, sometimes the counselor has learned information that causes him or her to adjust some of the practical aspects to fit a particular person and situation. When this is the case, the counselor can explain the modifications and the reasons for them.

Roles

The second part of the agreement deals with role expectations. The specific roles depend on the counselor, the person in counseling, and the situation. For example, the counselor may explain that his or her role will be the same as it was during the first three stages or more passive, reflective, varied, confrontative, direct, ambiguous, questioning, silent, active, or listening. It is helpful for the counselor to offer a brief explanation why he or she feels the nature of the role will facilitate growth.

It is important to remember that *assuming* a role is not the same as *playing* a role. When a man returns from work, he assumes the role of father, which is helpful and appropriate. Hopefully, he does not play the role, which means that he is acting a part that is not he. A counselor may legitimately assume a role in a counseling situation that would be inappropriate to assume in other circumstances, but the role should be a part of him or her and not simply an ill-fitting cloak.

The role of the person in counseling is also discussed. A counselor may feel it is more helpful for the person to bring to each session whatever is on his or her mind or may suggest that the person's past needs more attention and should be the area of focus for a time. Another counselor may wish to concentrate mostly on the present and on feelings, or a counselor may want to focus mostly on what goes on inside the counseling room. One counselor may invite the person to relate personally as well as professionally, asking questions and getting to know the counselor, while another counselor may wish to remain more impersonal.

When both the counselor and person in counseling clearly understand and agree that their roles feel comfortable and will facilitate growth, they are in a better position to work as a synchronized team rather than stumbling over each other at every turn.

Expectations

Expectations can become more explicit than they were during the first three stages because each person has a better grasp of the situation. The counselor shares his or her expectations that involve the responsibilities of the person in counseling. These issues might deal with honesty, making concerted efforts to reach the goals of counseling, placing a high priority on counseling, doing homework assignments, discussing counseling with others, and viewing counseling as a seven-day-a-week experience rather than a 50-minute-a-week visit.

The person in counseling can also share his or her expectations of the counselor. The person can tell the counselor what he or she would find helpful and unhelpful. Often in this early stage of counseling people are not in a position to articulate clearly how the counselor can be of more help. Consequently, the counselor can help the person along these lines and invite the person to keep the counselor apprised of growing and changing expectations as counseling progresses.

Goals

As a result of the first three stages, both the person in counseling and the counselor have a clearer picture of the problems and the possible solutions. Goal setting in counseling is perhaps the most important part because it ties the whole process together. For this reason it requires a certain amount of time and care. The goals of counseling should have certain characteristics.

First, they are specific and measurable. For example, an agreed-upon goal is that a person overcome his or her fear of getting a job. This goal is specific in that it zeros in on a clear target. It is measurable because the steps toward the goal can be readily charted, and it is relatively easy to tell how much progress has been made toward accomplishing the goal.

In contrast, a person may have as a goal to be more happy, less anxious or depressed, to become a better husband or mother, or to get to know him- or herself better. These goals are so general, abstract, and difficult to measure that they are unworkable. This counselor and the person in counseling need to target in on what specifically does "more happy" mean? Why exactly does the person feel tense? Why specifically does the person think he is not a good husband? The more vague and abstract the goals, the less chance counseling has to approximate them.

Second, they are realistic. The goals of counseling are always restricted by the potential of the person in counseling and the limitations in the person's environment. For example, two 38-year-old women wish to enter law school. They seek counseling to help them make the psychological changes necessary to bring this about. For one of these women, this may be a realistic goal and for another it may not be. One woman is divorced, intelligent, and energetic. She worked as a court clerk and feels that she has the motivation, skills, and understanding of what it means to be a lawyer. She seeks counseling because she is not sure if she wants to leave the security of her present job, whether she wants to make the sacrifices that both law school and a career as an attorney demand, and whether it will deprive her two adolescent children of the parenting they still need. She knows what she wants, but she is not sure that pursuing it would be a wise choice.

The second woman is married to a man who does not want her to go to law school. He wants her home with the four school-age children, and he would have to get another job to secure a loan to finance law school. The woman is of modest intelligence and has been depressed. The thought of going to law school has served to raise her from her depression. She has no knowledge of law or law as a career but came upon the idea when she read about another woman whose life was changed when she became a lawyer. She seeks counseling because she wants to learn how she can go to law school and keep her husband happy and children healthy. It is unlikely that the second woman's goal is one that can be attained in counseling, even though it is essentially the same goal as that of the first woman.

A second aspect of realistic goals is that few of them are of an all-or-nothing nature. For example, a man seeks counseling to help him relate more effectively at work. "More effectively" for this particular man may mean increasing his effectiveness by 20, 50, or 70%. It would be unrealistic to expect counseling to allow him to function with complete effectiveness.

Third, the goals are psychologically healthy. Some people's proposed goals are consonant with psychological growth. They want to become more assertive, autonomous, and confident; less angry, fearful, and confused. Other people, however, may seek counseling to maintain equilibrium through means that are not psychologically healthy. For example, a person may want to learn to survive in a work situation that is intractably damaging, to leave a family situation in ways that would be injurious to self and others, or to begin a project for which he is not prepared and that is doomed to fail. While it is the prerogative of those in counseling to choose their own goals, it is the counselor's responsibility not to become a collaborator in destructive behavior.

Fourth, they are often hierarchical. Some people have only one goal in counseling. The previously mentioned woman who wishes to go to law school could be an example of this. Many people, however, have several goals. For example, a man may list the following goals: to be more comfortable sexually, to change jobs, to have a less conflictual relationship with his parents, to recapture religious fervor, to relate more comfortably with women on dates, and to lose 30 pounds.

The items on this list do not automatically lend themselves to a hierarchical arrangement. Once the counselor knows the man better, it may become clear that the goals cannot be arranged in alphabetical order and pursued. It may be that the inordinate pressures at work are causing ongoing damage, and until they are alleviated, the man is in no position to work on any of the other goals. Once that pressure is alleviated, the next step may be to refer the person to a medically supervised weight-control program through which he can lose weight and feel more presentable. While he is losing weight, the next step may be to explore the reasons for feeling sexually confused or uncomfortable about himself. When this issue is on its way to resolution, the next step may be to examine what makes dating an anxiety-producing experience and then to date. When the dating anxiety gets under control, the next step may be to understand and work on his conflict with his parents. When all these are reasonably under control, he may be at peace enough to be able to work on his religious doubts and conflicts.

Sometimes when the first two or three goals in the hierarchy are attained, the rest take care of themselves. For example, in the case above, the man's conflicts with his parents and his religious conflicts may be resolved as side effects of achieving the previous goals.

There are two points of caution with regard to placing counseling goals in a hierarchy. One is that the counselor must walk the middle path between excluding all material in the counseling session except that dealing directly with the current target goal and allowing the person to dabble in one target after another, which results in no consistent movement toward any goal.

The second caution is that agreed upon hierarchical goals must not be set in cement. When the counselor understands more about the person, it may become imperative to rearrange the hierarchy. In the case of the man, the counselor may discover that until his religious conflicts are resolved, there will be no movement toward any of the other goals. A shift in the hierarchy may be necessary when the person and the counselor work hard at attaining a subgoal with no meaningful results. This could indicate that another goal in the hierarchy or a hitherto unrecognized goal must be dealt with first.

Fifth, the goals belong to the person in counseling. Sometimes, especially when people bring general, abstract, or vague goals to counseling, the counselor gets trapped into making them more concrete and manageable. For example, a woman may say she is depressed but doesn't know why because she has a beautiful husband, children, and home—all any woman could ever want. After several unsuccessful attempts to help the woman articulate the cause of her distress, the counselor may decide why she is depressed: she is denying her disappointment with a marriage that has become drab; she resents the fact that her husband won't let her go back to work; she feels guilty about having recently placed her father in a convalescent hospital; and she is repressing sexual feelings because she has no place to get them met.

On the basis of these hypotheses with which the person reluctantly and tentatively agrees ("You're the doctor—I expect you know more about these things that I do"), they launch into trying to reach the counselor's goals. Of course, nothing good is likely to result from this counseling relationship because the goals are the counselor's and not those of the person in counseling. Even if the counselor is correct on all the hypotheses, the woman has never claimed the goals for herself.

It is essential that the counseling goals be clearly owned by the person and that counseling not continue until this occurs. To spend a few sessions trying to clarify goals could be appropriate. But when the goal of counseling is to discuss the goals of counseling, this usually results in unproductive expeditions in which both the counselor and the person continually meet themselves exactly where they began.

Sixth, goals are frequently evaluated. Aiming at goals in counseling is similar to aiming at any kind of target. After attempting to hit the target a few times, it is sensible to examine it to see how successful the efforts have been.

Since goals are specific and measurable, it should not be too difficult to gauge progress toward them. When the counselor and the person agree that they are progressing in the right direction and on schedule, it provides a mutual sense of confidence and accomplishment that can add momentum to their quest. If, after a reasonable time, it becomes clear that the counselor and the person have gradually strayed from the target or that they are on target but progressing too slowly, they can consider questions like the following: Is there a condition that must be met first? For example, the person may need more time to trust the counselor before becoming committed to the goal. Is there some deep ambivalence developing toward the goal as it gets closer to realization? Maybe a man is becoming less confident that divorce is the best thing for him at this point. In any case, it is much better to look at the target early and at short intervals to see the path counseling is taking than to assume counseling is squarely on track, only to discover later that it has been spiraling out of control.

Developing a counseling agreement may take one session or three or four. If the counselor and the person are still struggling and negotiating over an agreement after five sessions, it is likely that the person is not sufficiently motivated to use counseling, there is a problem in the counselor-person relationship, or else the counselor is not sufficiently skilled to develop the agreement.[7]

Stage 5: Changing Behavior

Exactly what occurs during this stage depends upon the person and his or her problem. However, there are some common experiences that occur during this stage with which counselors can be familiar. These issues may arise before this stage, but they arise more obviously and regularly at this time. The following are ten situations with which counselors frequently must deal while helping the person change behavior.

Focusing on Responsibility

This crucial issue often arises, despite the counselor's previous efforts. People in counseling frequently view counselors as psychological architects whose role is to provide a blueprint telling the person who he is, what his problem is, how he should solve his problem, and when he should take each step in the process. Even the most experienced counselor can be insidiously trapped into assuming this role. When this occurs, the counselor is taking responsibility not only for the person's changing behavior but for the person's life.

Counselors can resist the manipulations and temptations to become managers for people in counseling. If persons in counseling need someone to take the reins of their life, they likely need more intensive treatment than traditional outpatient counseling can afford. The counselor's stance toward the person in counseling should always be:

> *You* tell me who you are today.
>
> *You* tell me what your problem is today.
>
> *You* tell me how you wish to solve it.
>
> *You* tell me when you are going to try what strategies.

Obviously, a person could respond "If I could tell you all these things, I wouldn't be in counseling in the first place." And in one sense this retort is valid, but in a deeper sense it is not. The assumption underlying counseling is that the answers to these questions can lie only within the individual. The counselor's role is not to answer these questions, but to provide an environment and a relationship conducive to helping the person grow in the insight and courage necessary to answer the questions and translate the answers into practice. In other words, one of the general goals of counseling is to help a person become his or her own counselor.

Inward Searching

People who are in counseling, like most people, operate almost solely on an external level. Their approach to life is "I've got a problem here, and I have to figure out a way to solve it." The focus is almost entirely on the problem outside of them and not on the person inside. As a result, they are likely to experience the same types of problems continually.

For example, a 30-year-old woman comes to counseling because she is depressed that she cannot find a marriageable man. The more frantic and depressed she becomes, the more she sabotages her relationships with men. After several sessions of internal searching, she makes the following discoveries:

> She has a void within her that is comprised of feeling unimportant, unlovable, and purposeless, and she believes only a man can fill that void.
>
> She looks upon marriage as a psychological and social validation of herself. As long as she is unmarried, she and society look upon her as psychologically lame; as soon as

she gets married, she will be seen as psychologically healthy. A good deal of the pressure she feels is not to get married but to feel good about herself.

She thinks the best way to get a man is to be sexually active and has not realized that this is not going to get her the man that meets her qualifications. In other words, she is attracting exactly the kind of man that she dislikes.

She is very ambivalent about marriage. On one hand she wants to get married, but on the other she resents men because she needs them to make her happy. She fears her deep need for a man will enslave her just as her mother became enslaved to her father. She is fearful that if she does marry, she may find herself disillusioned, which would rule out her last hope for happiness on this earth. Her deep ambivalence is reflected in her behavior with men, causing her unnecessary conflicts.

As she works through these insights, which until now had been unconscious, she feels far less pressure to get married. She has begun to fill her void intrapsychically with a clear appreciation for her worth and goodness, to which counseling introduces her. Extrapsychically, she fills the void with new friends, a more fulfilling job, and hobbies she always enjoyed until she began her "manhunt."

When she does date, she is more selective, acts in keeping with her deeper values, and relates more comfortably. Dates are no longer examinations that she can pass or fail, but evenings to enjoy in themselves. She still would *like* to marry, but she does not *have* to marry.

People in counseling often resist inward exploration because they are fearful of what they will discover. Therefore, it is necessary for counselors to develop skills that allow them to help people work through the resistance and a sense of timing that helps them judge the right time to explore a given insight.[8]

Utilizing Insights

There are two points of view about the insights gleaned from inward searching. One is that the insights alone may bring about the psychological equilibrium necessary to reduce symptoms and create growth. The person's problem may remain, but the person has outgrown it; so it is less or no longer a nuisance.

A second point of view is that inward searching provides the blueprint for external behavioral changes and that both are necessary for maximum personality growth. This view recognizes that not all human problems are solvable, but as long as one is in counseling, one might as well try to solve the ones that are. This view combines the benefits of inward searching and problem solving into a two-part process.

The woman in the previous example did not simply rest with her inner reflections and discoveries, but used them to chart some concrete, observable changes in her daily life. She finished college, changed jobs, broadened her circle of friends and interests, changed her way of relating with men, returned to her religion, and used the psychological dividends of this change to fill her void and strengthen her being. As a result, she has not only solved the problem she brought to counseling, but has grown as a person.

Mirroring

Counselors act as mirrors in which people can see themselves. There are two ways of mirroring: intrapsychically and interpersonally. "Intrapsychically" means that counselors reflect back to people who they are so that they can make appropriate changes in their behavior. Often there is steam on the mirror that people look into daily, and it hides the parts they don't want to see. In mirroring, the counselor says, in effect, "This is the way you look to me now. If you agree that's who you are, what changes, if any, would you like to make? If you don't agree that's who you are, let's figure out why we have different perceptions." This is important because most people in counseling don't have a clear and complete picture of themselves, which leads them to behave in inappropriate and unhelpful ways. It is also important because very few, if any, people in the person's life would have the skills, concern, benevolence, and courage to reflect back to the person how he or she appears. When a person gets a clear, unbiased picture, he or she is in a position to make some meaningful changes.

Equally important is interpersonal mirroring. This means that the counselor reflects back to the person how he or she "comes on" with people and what responses this behavior elicits. The counselor might say "I'm starting to feel angry (manipulated, anxious, confused, distracted, sympathetic, bored, frightened, stupid, guilty, hurt; or warm, relaxed, comfortable, happy, empathetic, interested)." The message that the counselor is conveying is "When you act the way you are, this is the response you are likely to elicit from people. If you want that response, it's okay; but if you don't want it, let's see how and why you elicit it."

As long as counselors are affectively neutral about the issue at hand, they can trust that their reactions to the person are similar to those that other people would have. This is priceless information for people in counseling because they may be oblivious to the effects of their verbal and nonverbal communication on others. People may wonder why others "always" manipulate, reject, seduce, misunderstand, or avoid them when all they ever do is behave in friendly and reasonable ways.

Both intrapsychic and interpersonal reflection must be done as nonthreateningly as possible. It is likely to be threatening to some extent because people generally become anxious when they hear something about themselves that they didn't know, even when the feedback is positive. The only purpose of mirroring is to be helpful; it is never to put a person "in his place."

Confronting

A counselor may point out significant discrepancies in the person's behavior or lifestyle. This is different from mirroring, which simply reflects back to people who they appear to be. It also differs from challenging in that challenging is more gentle and invites people to reexamine the accuracy of their perceptions; confrontation is more assertive and focuses on people's deeper motives and contradictory behavior.

Confronting is one method of interpretation. The message in confrontation is "You say you are this, but is it possible that you are something different?" For example, a counselor may say "Bill, you keep saying you want to save your marriage, but the way you've been acting makes me wonder if there is a part of you that does not want to save it" or "Nancy, you tell me that you want to use counseling, but you consistently forget what we talk about from one session to another and seldom work on anything between sessions."

Some cautions must be exercised regarding confrontation. It is important that the relationship between the person and the counselor is strong enough to support the confrontation. In other words, although people may not enjoy confrontation, they realize it is being done in their best interests. In addition, counselors must have reasonable certitude that any confrontation has a sound basis in reality.

Timing is also important. The confrontation should take place at an appropriate time; that is, not be introduced "out of the blue" or when the person is not sufficiently strong or insightful to learn from it.

Finally, counselors can be sensitive to the nature of their motives.

Is the confrontation actually a personal attack disguised as a helpful strategy, or does it stem from a counselor whose sole interest is helping the person learn something important? If it is an attack, the tone will be "Tim, who do you think you're kidding." If it's a valid response, the tenor will be "Tim, I'd like to share some perceptions with you and see what you think about them."[9]

Giving Support

Counselors offer reassurance and positive reinforcement and reduce people's anxiety by showing them the positive and hopeful aspects of a situation and by rewarding positive behavior with genuine and spontaneous smiles, encouragement, and support. Giving support can be a very effective aid to the counseling process. On the other hand, it can also be an area for caution.

When reassuring the person, it is important that such support is justified by reality and is not a hollow pep talk that will backfire. Statements such as "I'm sure things will turn out fine" or "I have faith in you that you'll do well" are usually ill advised. A better type of reassurance is reflected in "Let's do our best, and, whatever happens, we'll work very hard together to handle it well." This communicates a more reality-based reassurance that focuses on the counseling relationship as a source of support and not on the success or failure of a particular event.

Positive reinforcement also has areas of caution. Counselors can be careful about what they reward. A man may tell a counselor that he was *finally* able to assert himself at work. He proudly relates the incident to the counselor, who congratulates him for his willingness to take a risk and for successfully asserting himself. However, if the counselor had delved more deeply into the matter, he would have seen that the "assertiveness" was a ploy to escape some rightful responsibility at work. In effect, the counselor rewarded the person for being manipulative and shirking responsibility.

It is often difficult for counselors to delve into situations that the person proudly presents as evidence of progress. There is a pressure for the counselor to allow the person to bask in the feelings of accomplishment. For the counselor to examine the situation appears distrustful and rude. However, in keeping with the axiom "All that glitters is not gold," counselors could do well to gently examine situations lest they reward a problematic behavior.

A second caution regarding positive reinforcement is that it can create a situation in which the person in counseling is growing to earn the praise of the counselor. This counseling relationship can never end because, as soon as talk of termination begins, the person regresses as he or she realizes that growth without the praise of the counselor is meaningless. Ideally, growth should be its own reward, and, as people progress in counseling, there should be less need for counselors to reward their efforts. However, in the first phases of counseling, when people's efforts are not yet sufficiently effective to merit rewarding results, it is necessary for counselors to reward their efforts. Under most circumstances, positive reinforcement should be given judiciously and probably more sparingly than it ordinarily is.

Reverse Shaping

The counselor helps shape the behavior of the person in counseling. By a judicious use of reward, expectation, insight, and confrontation, the counselor helps the person modify behavior. Reverse shaping is when the person does the same thing to the counselor. Because conscious and unconscious shaping is almost continually operative in all human beings, the shaping attempts of the person in counseling probably equal those of the counselor. People in counseling can subtly and not so subtly reward and punish counselors. Counselors who behave in ways that please people may be rewarded either by people showing new evidence of growth or by people complimenting them. When a counselor displeases a person in counseling, the person is apt to regress or attack the counselor.

When people's shaping efforts are obvious, they can be dealt with easily. But people who are "cooperative" and whose only wish is "to get strong enough to handle my own problems" can adroitly shape the counselor without the counselor being even slightly aware of it.

Some people bring a script to counseling that has a bad ending. They hire the counselor as an actor who will help them bring about the desired destructive ending in the most "officially approved" way possible. The ending of the story may be suicide, getting fired, getting rejected by loved ones, remaining in a destructive relationship, proving that one is hopeless, getting hospitalized, or making the counselor a failure. Each progressive act is an escalated attempt to shape the counselor's behavior so that he or she will help the person bring about the desired end of the story.

Counselors can react constructively to shaping behavior in two ways. The first is that, every time the person creates a situation in which the counselor feels quite pleased or quite displeased, the counselor can ask: Why is this person telling me this (doing this)?

How does he (or she) expect me to respond? Will my response be feeding into the person's strengths or weaknesses?

Second, it is helpful for counselors to focus on the agreed-upon goals of counseling, despite the person's pressures to ignore them. This will eventually either spotlight the destructive ending of the script and allow the counselor to invite the person to change the ending or cause the person to terminate when he or she sees that the counselor is not willing to be shaped. If the latter happens, it is better to have it occur early than to have the counselor continue as a co-conspirator in the person's destructive behavior.

Transference

This means that a person displaces onto a counselor feelings, attitudes, or impulses that were part of a previous relationship. The counselor who represents an authority figure likely will be reacted to in the same ways the person has reacted to authority in the past—for example, with attitudes that are defensive, hostile, or ingratiating. The person may react to the counselor's personal qualities with positive or negative transference. The way the counselor looks, speaks, sits, thinks, emotes, and values may trigger a transference reaction. A person may say "I hate it (you) when you get that god-almighty expression on your face (because you are my father when you do that)" or "I like coming here (I like you) because I feel comfortable and understood (the way my mother always made me feel)."

Sometimes the transference is direct ("I don't like you"); at other times, it is indirect—that is, directed at the counselor's profession ("I always felt people went into psychology to solve their own problems") or directed at the domain of the counselor ("Why is this room always so cold?").

Counselors can be aware that not all of a person's reactions in counseling stem from transference. People can relate to counselors directly, without transferring any residuals of past relationships. For example, the fact that a person is angry at a counselor does not mean he is manifesting negative transference. The person's anger may be present and appropriate, and to deal with it as transference would be uninsightful of the counselor and demeaning to the person in counseling. Moreover, all conflicts between the counselor and the person in counseling need not be transference. A person with a devout religious faith may not agree with some of the values of a counselor who views religion as neurotic. To label this person's value conflicts with the counselor as transference misses an important reality conflict that needs resolving.

Counselors can also be aware that all transference reactions have a quality of resistance. As long as people are spending time and energy loving or hating the counselor, they are not progressing toward the mutually agreed upon goals.

How much resistance the transference creates determines whether the counselor should interpret it or let it slide. In general, indirect expressions of mildly positive transference should receive the least attention, and direct manifestation of intensely negative transference should receive the most.

Another point of view on transference reactions is that they can be dealt with in a direct, interpersonal manner rather than in an analytical, working-through fashion. For example, a counselor may reply to a woman who challenges him on being sexist: "I agree that a sexist counselor would not be helpful to you. However, why don't we refocus on our goals, and if you see any concrete data to substantiate your concern as we go along, we can deal with it at that time." This type of response respects the woman's concern yet does not allow it to distract her and the counselor from the main purpose of counseling.

Countertransference

Countertransference consists of inappropriate reactions by the counselor to the behavior of the person in counseling. It can be positive; that is, the counselor has caring and affectionate feelings of a kind and degree that are not merited by the reality of who the person is. Countertransference also can be negative; that is, the counselor feels angry or bored with a person who has done nothing to merit these reactions. As with transference, not all pleasant or unpleasant feelings toward a person in counseling are necessarily countertransference. A counselor may have reason to like or to be upset with a person, and these reactions should not be stifled or worked through as countertransference, but dealt with appropriately.

Countertransference can be both an advantage and a hindrance to counselors. It can be an advantage when it teaches counselors something about themselves. For example, a person may have a habit of responding that angers the counselor. The counselor can then scrutinize himself or herself as to what vulnerability was tapped by the person's behavior. Countertransference can be a hindrance to counseling because strong, inappropriate feelings of liking or disliking a person can sufficiently interfere with the counselor's clinical judgment and helpful responses, causing progress in counseling to be seriously impeded. When this occurs, the counselor must assume responsibility for working through the feelings or, if necessary, refer the person to another counselor.

Interpretation

Interpretation introduces to people in counseling previously unknown information about themselves. In other words, the counselor pulls back the blinds and permits the person to see behaviors that were relegated to the subconscious or unconscious layers of personality. The goal of interpretation is increasing self-knowledge. The more self-knowledge people have, the more able they are to change their behavior.

Most interpretation centers on self-deceit. People do not wish to acknowledge parts of themselves and so repress and deny them. However, these hidden behaviors (thoughts, feelings, defenses, motives, conflicts, or values) do not disappear but influence people's actions in ways of which they are unaware. This allows people to vent these less than conscious behaviors without having to accept responsibility for them. For example, a man has unconscious, negative feelings toward his family. He thinks he comes home quite late every night because he is too busy at work. His late arrival allows him to shorten his time in an unpleasant situation and to upset the people who are upsetting him without having to face exactly what he is doing and why. In the meantime, both he and his family are unhappy, and they feel there is nothing that can be done about it.

Interpretation ordinarily poses a threat to the person in counseling because the repressed material being introduced is not pleasant or it would not have been repressed in the first place. Also, the new information that stems from interpretation means that the person will have to let go of old behaviors and adjust current behaviors to the new information. For example, once the man who gets home late discovers what he is doing and why, he will feel more anxious and have to use the anxiety to change the situation in one direction or another. Therefore, it is not unusual for people to resist interpretation.

Because interpretation in counseling is a delicate operation, counselors can be familiar with the important issues involved. Counselors need to know *what* to interpret. Generally, it is more helpful to interpret the person's defenses before the person's conflicts so that the interpretation doesn't get intercepted and defused by the defenses. It is also generally more helpful to interpret process (how and why the person is doing or not doing something in the counseling session) than content (what the person is saying).

Interpretation should be selective in that only behaviors that are significantly affecting the person need to be considered.

Counselors should also know *when* to interpret. Interpretations are more likely to fall on fertile ground when the person in counseling is close to the level of awareness required to grasp the interpretation, when the person is sufficiently relaxed and comfortable with the counselor, and when the counselor has reasonable certainty that the interpretive hypothesis is correct.

The counselor also needs to know *how* to interpret. Counselors can explain the nature of interpretation to the person and begin gradually by offering less threatening interpretations. Interpretations should be phrased tentatively ("Could it be that . . .?") and concisely since unnecessary words serve only to distract.

Interpretation plays less of a role in crisis intervention and short-term counseling than it does in counseling that is of longer duration and addresses deeper problems.[10]

Stage 6: Termination

It is helpful to remember that termination is a *stage* of counseling and not simply the last few sessions. This stage could encompass the last quarter of counseling. During it, the counselor begins preparing the person to leave counseling. The counselor increasingly points out the success the person is achieving. The message is "You seem to be doing more and more on your own and doing it well." This helps the person see that the distance traveled in counseling is a good deal longer than the distance that remains.

The counselor also begins pulling back as a source of support, feedback, and guidance. This does not mean he or she diminishes interest in the person; it only means that the counselor demonstrates the interest in a different way, much as parents show their concern for a child differently as the child matures.

Counseling becomes a place to check in. The sessions consist more of the person saying "I've got a problem that came up last week. Let me tell you what I'm going to do about it, and if you've got any thoughts you can let me know." This level of autonomy is later elevated to the final level: "Let me tell you how I solved a problem this week. I purposely didn't tell you about it because I wanted to handle it on my own. If you've got any thoughts when I'm through, I'd be glad to hear them."

Usually at about this time someone introduces the topic of termination. While it is sometimes said that it is better for people in counseling to initiate the subject of termination, this does not appear to be necessarily true. Sometimes the fact that the counselor brings it up first is supportive because people view it as a validation of their own thoughts and a compliment to their progress. Also, some people assume that bringing up termination is the rightful role of the counselor.

When initiating the topic, the counselor might say "You seem to be doing so well that I'm wondering if you have given any thought to tapering off our sessions?" Of course, the counselor would ask this question only when the person has had good momentum for a reasonable period of time. The person may respond "It's funny you ask that. We must be on the same wavelength because I have been thinking about it, too." Other responses might be "I haven't given it much thought, but I suppose it is something we should start planning for" or "No, I haven't. Why? Do *you* think I'm ready to stop?" The counselor must deal with the dynamics underlying the responses. This final response likely indicates that the person and counselor are viewing things differently or the person is dependent on counseling and resistant to even the thought of terminating.

The person in counseling who initiates the topic of termination might say "You know, I've been thinking that I may not need to come here as often because I'm handling things pretty well." The counselor may respond "Why don't you tell me what you've been thinking about it?" and react appropriately to the person's explanations.

After there is agreement that counseling has progressed to a point where terminating is an issue, the next step is usually to taper off the number of sessions. Generally, the longer the counseling relationship, the longer the tapering-off period. Tapering off usually means reducing the number of sessions from four each month to two. Sometimes that is sufficient but, with some people, it is helpful to continue tapering off to once each month and then to a "come in as the need arises" basis. Tapering off is meant to avoid the shock of autonomy that can cause separation anxiety and regressive behavior.

It is helpful to recall at this stage the nature of a goal; that is, it is something to be aimed at that may not be totally achieved. Hence, counseling does not necessarily continue until the goals are ultimately and irrevocably attained. More often, counseling helps people to approximate more closely their goals and to live more effectively with what distance remains between where they are and where they would like to be.

An adjacent concept is that a person's growth toward goals does not terminate with the end of counseling. By the time people terminate counseling, they should have built up a momentum that will continue to carry them in the direction of their goals.

The clinical judgment regarding termination considers the

relationship between how far a person has progressed in counseling and how much more counseling can or should do for the person. When people have a clear picture of their ultimate goals and good momentum in the right direction, they are ready to finish the job on their own.[11]

Finally, people do not always terminate counseling with profuse feelings of gratitude toward the counselor. Although this can be discouraging or confusing to the counselor, it is understandable. When counseling has been a difficult experience for a person and has cost a great deal of time, energy, tension, hard work, and money, the person may feel like a football player after a grueling victory. He truly enjoys the victory but he feels that he put at least as much into the victory as the coach, and the coach is getting paid. Consequently, he feels no special need to express appreciation. He's happy he's won; he feels it was worth it; he's glad it's over; and he wants to go home.

Some people still have not completely resolved the fact that they needed help or needed to depend on another person. Therefore, to thank the counselor would be admitting that they needed him or her. Obviously, it would be nice for people to resolve these feelings before the termination of counseling, but what is "nice" and what is "real" are sometimes two different things.

Some people have not been good at showing gratitude and saying goodbye for the 20 or 40 years they've been on earth; so counseling may not have changed that. It doesn't mean these people did not receive a great deal from counseling; it simply means they cannot adequately express their gratitude.

On the other hand, the fact that some people show profuse gratitude does not necessarily indicate they received a great deal from counseling. They may just be thankful that counseling is finished or that they escaped from counseling without having to face their deepest, most dreaded problem.

Counselors can take satisfaction from the fact that they helped people and that these people's lives will be better, even though some people's lives will never be more than marginally fulfilling. If a counselor expects to receive greater satisfaction than that, he or she may have to find it outside of the counseling room.

Summary

It is important that counselors recognize the developmental dimension of the counseling relationship. When counselors possess a general theoretical and practical frame of reference, it lends both direction and order to what otherwise could be a chaotic and frustrating experience.

An understanding of the stages of helping is beneficial to both counselors and people in counseling. It is helpful to counselors because the stages act as directional markers that help counselors steer a steady course toward growth. It is also helpful to people in counseling because, once the sequence of stages is explained to them, they can feel a sense of security and purpose.

Thought Questions

1. If you were limited to only *one* question in the information-gathering stage, what would you ask? Why would you ask it?

2. With regard to selecting candidates you would see in counseling, what is one type of person and one type of problem that you think would be best referred to another counselor? Why do you feel this way?

3. After a few sessions, your antagonism toward the person you are seeing reaches such a peak that it is obvious you can no longer be of help to him. When you recommend that he see another counselor, he retorts "You just don't like me. That's why you want to get rid of me." What do you respond?

4. When you experience negative countertransference toward a person in counseling, how are you likely to show it? When you experience positive countertransference toward a person, how are you likely to show it?

5. What specifically would you like to hear from a person in counseling after the successful termination of a counseling relationship? What will it mean to you if you don't hear it?

Notes

[1] Other formats can be found in Brammer (1979), Carkhuff & Anthony (1979), Weiner (1975), and Egan (1982).

[2] For self-evaluation questions that counselors can ask themselves regarding the effectiveness of their information gathering, see Benjamin (1974), pp. 20–24. He discusses questioning by the counselor on pp. 65–90.

[3] Some counselors find that psychological testing gives them an added source of information. For a summary and evaluation of tests that can be used for this purpose, see Osipow et al. (1980). For a discussion of what clients should look for in counselors, see Goldberg (1977), pp. 237–249.

[4] Perls (1969), p. 39.

[5] For further discussion of the selection of candidates for counseling, see Garfield (1980), pp. 41–68.

[6] A different discussion of evaluation can be found in Weiner (1975), pp. 51–72.

7 A thorough discussion of the importance of counseling agreements can be found in Goldberg (1977), pp. 31–61.
8 For a fuller discussion of inward searching, see Bugental (1978).
9 For a thorough discussion of confrontation, see Adler & Myerson (1973).
10 For further discussion of transference, countertransference, and interpretation, see Singer (1965).
11 Termination, like any other stage of counseling, can have its unique difficulties.

References

Adler, G., & Myerson, P. F. (Eds.). *Confrontation in psychotherapy.* New York: Science Housse, 1973.

Benjamin, A. *The helping interview* (2nd ed.). Boston: Houghton Mifflin, 1974.

Brammer, L. M. *The helping relationship process and skills* (2nd ed.). Englewood Cliffs, NJ: Prentice-Hall, 1979.

Bugental, J. F. T. *Psychotherapy and process: The fundamentals of existential-humanistic approach.* Menlo Park, CA: Addison-Wesley, 1978.

Carkhuff, R. R., & Anthony, W. A. *The skills of helping.* Amherst, MA: Human Resource Development Press, 1979.

Egan, G. *The skilled helper* (2nd ed.). Monterey, CA: Brooks/Cole, 1982.

Garfield, S. L. *Psychotherapy: An eclectic approach.* New York: Wiley, 1980.

Goldberg, C. *Therapeutic partnership: Ethical concerns in psychotherapy.* New York: Springer, 1977.

Osipow, S. H., Walsh, W. B., & Tosi, D. J. *A survey of counseling methods.* Homewood, IL: Dorsey, 1980.

Perls, F. S. *Gestalt therapy verbatim.* Lafayette, CA: Real People Press, 1969.

Singer, E. *Key concepts in psychotherapy.* New York: Random House, 1965.

Weiner, I. B. *Principles of psychotherapy.* New York: Wiley, 1975.

18

Recognizing and Utilizing Ethnic and Cultural Diversity in Counseling Approaches

David Yonas
T. Neal Garland

Introduction

The concept of *ethnicity* has been defined in numerous ways. To clarify the meaning of the term as it is used in this chapter, it should be pointed out that *ethnic group* refers to a group of people who have common ancestral origins, share certain cultural traits (including values, beliefs, and ways of doing things), have a sense of peoplehood and of belonging, are from a migrant background, and whose membership in their group is involuntary (Isajiw, 1974; Schermerhorn, 1970). *Ethnicity* refers to the extent to which individuals accept, follow, and identify with their ethnic group.

The United States is an ethnically pluralistic society. In other words, Americans can trace their ancestry to a great variety of different nations. The cultures of these ancestral nations cover virtually the entire range of variations in values, beliefs, and customs found throughout the modern world. Indeed, even within a specific ethnic group the range of variations in values and behaviors can be enormous. For example, among Italian American families there are some that are extremely traditional and follow old-world customs as closely as they can. On the other hand, others

This article first appeared in *Correctional Counseling and Treatment*, Third Edition. All rights reserved.

identify with their Italian heritage on an emotional level but practice few of the old customs. Still others have forgotten or rejected their Italian heritage to such an extent that it exerts no meaningful influence on their lives. Conflicts within ethnic families may arise when the parental or grandparental generation tries with great determination to maintain "the old ways" while the younger generation tries with equal determination to reject them. For example, an "old world" parent may use extreme corporal punishment in an attempt to force a "wayward" child to accept parental authority. The child, in turn, may use violence against the parents as a way of asserting his/her independence from such traditional authority. At times conflicts can reach a point where violence within the family brings the family members into contact with the criminal justice system.

Alba (1990) wrote that following the Second World War there was a widely held expectation in this country that ethnic Americans would be assimilated into the dominant WASP (White Anglo-Saxon Protestant) culture and that ethnicity would gradually cease to be an issue of concern to the society. An opposing point of view, however, also was quite strong. This view was that third and higher older generations of ethnic Americans were becoming increasingly comfortable with their status in the society and were therefore more likely to retain and even to emphasize their ethnic heritage (Rose, 1981).

Debates about the place of ethnicity in American society have viewed it as waxing and waning at various points in the nation's history. While it was seen as greatly decreasing in importance during the 1950s, the civil unrest of the 1960s and early 1970s is credited with creating a resurgence of interest in "roots" and, therefore, in ethnic backgrounds. Some writers argue that while the influence of ethnicity in today's America is sometimes subtle, it is nevertheless quite powerful (Greeley, 1971).

This history of the United States is essentially the history of immigrant groups, both voluntary and involuntary. The influence of the distinct beliefs, values, and practices of this multitude of ethnic backgrounds upon the identities of individual Americans and upon the society as a whole is potentially very large. When people identify themselves as members of ethnic subcultures, they may develop values and expectations related to this identity which are different from the values and expectations of members of other subcultures and of the mainstream society. This likelihood often has been ignored or minimized in analyses of American social life because of the American tendency to emphasize the individual more than the collective. A consequence of this emphasis is the assumption that all Americans share basically the same values as all other Americans. This would appear to be an unrealistic assumption, given the ethnic, social class, racial, religious, and other sources of diversity which are undeniable facts of American society.

Consistency in values and expectations allows people to assume that they know themselves and others, and it allows for behavior (of one's self and others) to be predictable. When such consistency is lacking, interaction among members of the society can become highly problematic (Gordon, 1978).

It can be said that it is commonly believed that identification with an ethnic background is widespread among Americans and that this identification has important implications for the individual's self-concept, for interactions among individuals from different ethnic backgrounds, and for the cohesiveness of the society in general. At the same time, debates have continued over the past decades—at least since the 1950s—regarding the actual importance of ethnicity in American society. It therefore is important for criminal justice professionals to take into consideration differences among people which are due to ethnic backgrounds and to understand the dynamics of their own backgrounds. Differences in behavior sometimes should be viewed as adaptive means for ethnic group members and must not be confused with individual weaknesses or automatically labeled as deviance.

Individuals learn their basic value systems within the families in which they grew up. If we assume that the United States is composed of a myriad of different ethnic groups, each of which has a value system that is somewhat different in important ways from the value system of the dominant society and from the value systems of other ethnic groups, an important question arises. This question is that of how the individual, as a member of an ethnic group, is able to learn to be a member of the larger society and to form a stable self-identity in the face of such diversity. In order to provide at least a partial answer to this question, the focus of this chapter is on the degree to which the value systems of various ethnic groups in America are similar to or different from each other and from "mainstream" American values, and on the degree to which individual members of various ethnic groups identify with their ethnic subcultures.

Dominant American Values

In order to compare the values of any ethnic group with those of the dominant or "mainstream" society, it is necessary to examine those dominant values. A *value* can be defined as ". . . an enduring belief that a specific mode of conduct or end-state of existence is personally or socially preferable to an opposite or converse mode of conduct or end-state of existence" (Rokeach, 1973, p. 14).

American institutions, including the criminal justice system, have values that are consistent with the dominant American value system. There have been numerous attempts to identify the values which characterize the dominant (White Anglo-Saxon Protestant) segment of American society. Ruesch (1967), for example, has cited the following as the dominant value orientations in American society: individualism, achievement orientation, mastery over nature, and a future orientation.

Robin Williams (1970) also has identified a number of value orientations as characteristic of the dominant culture in the United States. These value orientations include achievement and success, work, humanitarianism, efficiency and practicality, progress, material comfort, equality, freedom, external conformity, science and rationality, nationalism-patriotism, democracy, individualism, and the superiority of certain racial, ethnic, and religious groups. Williams pointed out that some of these values contradict others.

J. Katz (1985) has identified cultural values of the dominant group in the United States that are similar to those discussed by Williams. The list prepared by Katz includes rugged individualism, competition, an action orientation (including mastery and control of nature), hierarchical structure of decision making, direct communication but controlled emotions, adherence to time schedules, a Western orientation in history, the Protestant work ethic, planning for the future, emphasis on the scientific method, status and power based on economic position and material possessions, the nuclear family structure, acceptance of religion, celebration of holidays, and aesthetics based on Western beliefs. She also implied that the dominant white culture can be seen simply as one more subculture existing among a myriad of other subcultures.

Do Different Ethnic Groups Hold Different Values?

There are many popular stereotypes about the supposed characteristics of various ethnic groups. People from Scotland, for example, are said to be "thrifty." The British keep a "stiff upper lip" in the face of adversity, while "mainstream" Americans are "assertive" in nearly every situation. McGoldrick and Rohrbaugh (1987) note that a review of relevant literature reveals the following list of characteristics that are assumed to be associated with particular ethnic groups.

- Jewish American families are claimed to value such things as education, success, encouragement of children, democratic principles, verbal expression, shared suffering, guilt, and eating (Herz and Rosen, 1982; Papajohn and Spiegel, 1971; Zborowski and Herzog, 1952).

- British Americans generally place a high value on control, personal responsibility, independence, individuality, stoicism, keeping up appearances, and moderation in everything (McGill and Pearce, 1982).

- Italian Americans are described as placing a high value on the family rather than on the individual. Food is viewed not only in terms of physical nourishment, but as a major source of emotional nourishment as well. Male and female roles are clearly specified along traditional patriarchal lines. Loyalty in personal relationships is very important (Rotunno and McGoldrick, 1982).

- The stereotypes of Irish American families has included the view that strong mothers and weak or distant fathers are typical. Instead of consumption of food, drinking is the central social activity. Children are taught to behave well and to "not make a scene." They are seldom praised for doing well. Anger is not to be expressed, except against outsiders. Religious rules play a major role in the determination of family values. Suffering is a normal and expected part of life and is to be born in silence or "offered up" in atonement for one's sins (McGoldrick, 1982).

- Black Americans are seen by some as constituting a single homogeneous group, but subgroups within racial categories vary too much to allow for a meaningful single characterization of race in any particular way, although societal forces impose perceived characteristics on certain racial groups. For black families, subcultural differences with the dominant society have been exaggerated by American culture's history of institutionalized racism. The church plays an extremely important role in black culture. Family members' ability to survive under any and all conditions is an important value. Families often must make heroic efforts in order to help their children achieve a better life (Hill, 1972). In part because of the effects of the legacy of racism on males, women disproportionately have become the heads of families. Relationships between men and women exhibit a greater flexibility in roles than is the case in the dominant culture. The extended family is very important (Hines and Boyd-Franklin, 1982; Pinderhughes, 1982).

- Asian subculture in the United States also is represented by a complex mixture of different groups, including Chinese, Japanese, Laotian, Vietnamese, Cambodian, and others. In general, most Asian groups are said to place high value on the family and to emphasize the importance of respect and obligation toward older family members. Sex roles are clearly divided, with men handling the outside world and women maintaining the inner world of the family. Great emphasis is placed on children's education as an avenue to success (Shon and Ja, 1982). Form— that is, the manner in which things are said and done—is very important, as is not "losing face" (McGoldrick and Rohrbaugh, 1987). Despite these commonalities, each Asian subculture has its own differences from the others.

McGoldrick and Rohrbaugh (1987) note that while the ethnic characteristics described in the family therapy literature are basically consistent with popular stereotypes, there was little empirical research to support the existence of these descriptions. They therefore conducted an empirical study to test the extent to which the stereotypes actually described certain ethnic groups. A sample of 220 mental health professionals who identified themselves as having three out of four grandparents belonging to a single ethnic group answered questionnaires that asked about the extent to which certain values and behaviors were characteristic of the homes in which they grew up. The authors concluded that the actual life styles of the ethnic groups tested were basically consistent with popular stereotypes.

Strength of Ethnicity

Criminal justice professionals must not automatically assume that ethnicity makes people different or even assume that when a client identifies himself or herself as a member of an ethnic group that this is an important characteristic for that person. Instead, it is important for professionals to have an effective means by which to explore whether ethnicity is in fact an important part of that person's identity.

The content of an ethnic subculture is the result, among other things, of historical migration patterns, social class factors, religious beliefs, political conditions, and geography. While it is widely held that ethnic subcultures have their own unique features, there has been a tendency for ethnic Americans to move closer to the dominant American value system over time, especially as they improve their socioeconomic status. However, this assimilation process is sometimes limited by various social barriers as well as by the individual members' needs for a sense of belonging and identity (McGoldrick and Preto, 1984).

When a client identifies himself or herself as a member of an ethnic group, the ethnic identity may or may not be a truly important factor in that person's life. An important question for the criminal justice professional to explore is "To what extent does identification with an ethnic background reflect particular experiences in the individual's life?" These experiences are likely to influence the individual's values, beliefs, and actions.

McGoldrick (1982) has identified a number of factors which are likely to be indicators of the strength of an individual's ethnic identity. These factors are:

1. Place of birth of the client;
2. Place of birth of the client's mother;
3. Place of birth of the client's father;
4. Presence of relatives other than the immediate family in the client's household;
5. Most recent time (by generation) that someone in the client's family immigrated to the United States;
6. Population size of the client's area of residence;
7. Whether or not members of the client's extended family live nearby;
8. Upward socioeconomic mobility of the client;
9. Perceived importance which the client places on teaching an ethnic heritage to his or her children;
10. Whether the client's ancestors moved to the United States alone or with other family members;
11. Knowing why the client's family moved to the United States;
12. Whether or not the client wishes to visit the country of origin;
13. Whether a language other than English was spoken in the parental home;
14. Having experienced prejudice and/or discrimination because of ethnic group membership;
15. Whether or not the client lives in an ethnic neighborhood;
16. Degree of the client's participation in ethnic cultural events;
17. Having a desire to raise children with the same values as the client's parents taught him or her;
18. Whether or not the client's political preferences are based on ethnic influences;
19. Degree to which the client participates in ethnic rituals.

Nine of the questions (feeling it is important to teach one's children about their ethnic heritage, knowing why one's family migrated to the United States, wishing to visit one's country of origin, having spoken a language other than English in the parental home, having experienced discrimination because of one's ethnic membership, participating in ethnic cultural events, wanting to teach ethnic values to one's children, basing political preferences on ethnic value, and participating in ethnic rituals) have been found to be strongly related to the strength of ethnic identity (Yonas, 1992). These nine questions would be especially helpful for criminal justice professionals to ask clients, since ethnicity appears to be a "voluntary" identity for many individuals whose families have lived in the United States for many generations.

Conflicting Values of Professionals and Clients

Criminal justice services are embedded in the larger society, and, as a result, they reflect the dominant values, perceptions, and assumptions of the larger society. However, many who rely on these services do not share the dominant perspectives. Covert differences may result in conflict, friction, and misunderstandings.

Professionals, as others, are often not aware of cultural conflicts. Differences in values, goals, knowledge, and resulting expectations are further complicated by other social and economic differences.

When a client's ethnic background differs from that of a service provider, a resulting difference in values may be a significant source of friction. Communication may be impaired, and expectations may go unmet on both sides of the interaction. Conflicting perspectives imposed on members of subordinate groups have caused harm to individuals (Sue and Sue 1990). If a professional is not aware of subcultural differences in values, behavior of the members of some groups may be labeled as a "problem"or found to be lacking in some respect, while in reality such behavior may be entirely appropriate and understandable in terms of the values of those groups. A professional who can maintain an objective stance in terms of values will be better able to detect his or her own assumptions about how the client views his or her problem. Thus, in an accepting fashion, the professional can improve the quality of care and allow for a more cooperative relationship.

Utility of the Study of Ethnicity

The knowledge to be gained from a study of differences in values of different ethnic subcultures can be applied in a wide variety of settings within the criminal justice system. One such setting is that of counseling. In the field of counseling, it is the dominant culture which provides the primary values and norms for counseling theory, research, and application (Katz, 1985). As a result, many clients of counseling tend to view counselors as professionals who attempt to help others adapt or adjust to the dominant society's values (Szasz, 1974). On the other hand, professionals in a heterogeneous society like the United States find it "important to become aware of the world views of the culturally different client and how the client views the definition, roles, and function of the family" (Sue and Sue, 1990, p. 125).

Many potential problems in counseling can be eliminated or reduced in significance by the application of knowledge of ethnic differences and ethnic identities of clients. Such knowledge, for example, can reduce the tendency of some practitioners to impose their own values, standards, and solutions (derived most often from the dominant culture) upon others. A criminal justice system practitioner's sensitivity to the variations in values and beliefs between cultures and subcultures—and even within ethnic subcultures—may decrease this tendency. An "ethnically aware" practitioner will be better able to explore the important ethnic subcultural aspects of a client and the degree to which the ethnic traditions are observed. Problems between generations, intercultural relationships, perceived personal inadequacies, needs, goals, and values can be seen more clearly through an exploration of the place ethnicity and the client's culture occupy for that client. By exploring the ethnic context of the client's presenting problem and including this in the assessment and treatment plan, the practitioner may be able to address more readily the treatment needs of the client.

Sensitizing Against Stereotyping

Some criminal justice professionals (as well as others in society) may have a tendency to stereotype people of various ethnic subgroups because it is easy to see similarities among the members and therefore assume they are all alike. An appreciation of ethnic diversity will affect this tendency to generalize or to stereotype members of these groups. The differences and the related behaviors of members of the groups must be considered, and the strengths and adaptive nature of each value system should be examined in a respectful manner. In addition, each individual must be seen as unique, with characteristics that stem from factors that are stronger than ethnicity.

Future Considerations

The following are ways in which the consideration of ethnic variation may be utilized by criminal justice professionals:

1. To sensitize practitioners to ethnic variations in approaches to problem solving;
2. To provide a greater understanding of the general perspectives, common problems, and specific needs of people from specific ethnic group backgrounds;
3. To clarify the likely sources and probable nature of conflicts between service providers and clients from specific ethnic groups;
4. To suggest ways in which the organization structure and operating procedures of the criminal justice system complement or come into conflict with the value orientations and life styles of people from specific ethnic backgrounds.

Counseling the Offender Who Identifies with an Ethnic Group

Criminal justice professionals need to be aware of the cultural variations which exist within ethnic groups as well as those between ethnic groups. For example, there are variations in what is considered "family," ranging from the isolated nuclear family to the extended family or even to people who are not relatives. Approaches to problem solving vary, also, from an individual orientation to a group orientation. Varying degrees of sharing of feelings also exist. Professionals might do well to consider the following questions:

1. How are "outsiders" perceived by members of this ethnic subculture?
2. What expectations are members likely to have when involved in the criminal justice system?
3. How is authority perceived?
4. Is fate an important factor?
5. If unique values exist for an ethnic subculture, how do these values influence the lives of the members of the group?

This list of questions is not an exhaustive one. One of the best ways to learn about ethnic subcultures is to ask clients to teach service providers about their backgrounds.

References

Alba, Richard. 1990. *Ethnic Identity: The Transformation of White America*. New Haven: Yale University Press.

Gordon, M. 1978. *Human Nature, Class, and Ethnicity*. New York: Oxford University Press.

Greeley, Andrew. 1971. *Why Can't They Be Like Us?* New York: Dutton.

Herz, F., and E. Rosen. 1982. "Jewish Families," in *Ethnicity and Family Therapy*, edited by McGoldrick et al., 364–392. New York: Guilford Press.

Hill, Robert B. 1972. *The Strengths of Black Families*. New York: National Urban League.

Hines, Paulette, and Nancy Boyd-Franklin. 1982. "Black Families," in *Ethnicity and Family Therapy*, edited by McGoldrick et al., 84–107. New York: Guilford Press.

Isajiw, Wssvolod W. 1974. "Definitions of Ethnicity," *Ethnicity*, 1: 111–124.

Katz, Judith. 1985. "The Sociopolitical Nature of Counseling," *The Counseling Psychologist*, 13(October): 615–624.

McGill, D. and J. Pearce. 1982. "British Families," in *Ethnicity and Family Therapy*, edited by McGoldrick et al., 457–482. New York: Guilford Press.

McGoldrick, Monica. 1982. "Irish Families," in *Ethnicity and Family Therapy*, edited by McGoldrick, J. Pearce, and J. Giordano, 310–339. New York: Guilford Press.

McGoldrick, Monica and Nydia Preto. 1984. "Ethnic Intermarriage: Implications for Therapy." *Family Process*, 23: 347–364.

McGoldrick, Monica and M. Rohrbaugh. 1987. "Researching Ethnic Family Stereotypes," *Family Process, 26: 89–*99.

Papjohn, J. C. and J. P. Spiegel. 1971. "The Relationship of Culture, Value Orientation, and Rorschach Indices of Psychological Development," *Journal of Cross-Cultural Psychology*, 2: 257–272.

Pinderhughes, E. 1982. "Afro-American Families and the Victim System," in *Ethnicity and Family Therapy*, edited by McGoldrick et al., 108–122. New York: Guilford Press.

Rokeach, Milton. 1973. *The Nature of Human Values*. New York: The Free Press.

Rose, Peter. 1981. *They and We: Racial and Ethnic Relations in the United States*. New York: Random House.

Rotunno, Marie and Monica McGoldrick. 1982. "Italian Families," in *Ethnicity and Family Therapy*, edited by McGoldrick et al., 340–361. New York: Guilford Press.

Ruesch, Jugen. 1967. "Sociological Techniques, Social Status, and Social Control," in *Personality in Nature, Society, and Culture*, edited by Kluckhohn and Murray, 117–131. New York: Alfred A. Knopf.

Schermerhorn R. 1970. *Comparative Ethnic Relations: A Framework for Theory and Research*. New York: Random House.

Shon, S. and D. Ja. 1982. "Asian Families," in *Ethnicity and Family Therapy*, edited by McGoldrick et al., 208–228. New York: Guilford Press.

Sue, D. W. 1990. "Evaluating Process Variables in Cross-Cultural Counseling and Psychotherapy," in *Cross-Cultural Counseling and*

Psychotherapy: Foundations, Evaluations, Cultural Consideration, edited by A. Marsella and P. Pedersen. Elmsford, NJ: Pedgamon Press.

Sue, David and Derald Sue. 1990. *Counseling the Culturally Different,* 2nd ed. New York: Wiley & Sons.

Szasz, T. 1974. *The Myth of Mental Illness.* New York: Harper and Row.

Williams, Robin. 1970. *American Society,* 3rd ed. New York: Alfred Knopf.

Yonas, David. 1992. *A Study of Variations in Ethnic Value Orientation.* Dissertation, Kent State University.

Zborowski, M. and E. Herzog. 1952. *Life Is With People.* New York: Schocken Books.

19

The Nature of Interviewing

Raymond L. Gorden

Interviewing—A Pervasive Activity

Many people have such a narrow conception of interviewing that they do not recognize the pervasiveness of interviewing in their everyday lives. The parent who tries to discover why the four-year-old is crying, the student who tries to get a professor to clarify a concept, and the voter who tries to determine a political candidate's opinion on a specific issue are all interviewing whether they realize it or not. Yet such interviews often fail to obtain the information desired. The voter, for example, faced with a political candidate's evasive tactics may end the interview more exasperated than enlightened.

Similarly, in their professional roles people frequently have to conduct interviews, but they rarely have the skills needed for a high rate of success. Consider the police officer talking to a motorist for an accident report, the business manager questioning an employee to discover the cause of a dispute, and the nurse taking a medical history from a patient. Rarely do such people think of themselves as interviewers, and usually they lack adequate training in the basic skills involved. Nevertheless, a high order of skill is needed for success in these and many similar situations.[1]

Interviewing Defined

For the purposes of this book, interviewing is defined broadly to include a wide variety of situations:

Interviewing is conversation between two people in which one person tries to direct the conversation to obtain information for some specific purpose.

This definition focuses on the information-gathering function of the conversation, even though there are additional functions in various interview settings such as persuasion, instruction, or emotional support. Without the information-gathering function we may have a lecture or a sales pitch but not an interview.

This definition, though broad, excludes many forms of normal sociable conversation. For a number of reasons the word *conversation* is central to the definition and is more appropriate than a technical term such as *dyadic verbal interaction*. First, much of the relevant interaction in any interview is nonverbal. Second, a more technical phrase may suggest that an interview is an artificial form of communication that lacks the ordinary sound of conversation or that possesses the qualities of acting. Also, interviewing is intentionally defined as a form of conversation rather than a form of questioning, because many situations require the interviewer to use statements designed to provide a context for a question, to summarize a question, or to challenge the respondent.

Although the definition focuses on information gathering, other forms of conversation are often permitted within the interview for the sake of maintaining a good relationship with the respondent. These other forms should not, however, interfere with the information-gathering function.

If we want to concentrate on the most basic interviewing skills, we must focus on information gathering—the function common to all interviews.

Interviewing Learned

Several decades ago even many social scientists thought that good interviewers were born not made. Therefore, they believed, there was no value in trying to teach someone to interview. At that time researchers focused on how to *select* good interviewers, and very little literature was devoted to experiments in training people to interview. In support of this point of view, numerous attempts to improve interviewing ability through formal training proved unsuccessful. In recent decades, however, many experiments have demonstrated that a person's interviewing effectiveness can be greatly improved by guided learning experiences. A few of these studies are cited later in this chapter.

The Skill Learning Cycle

The Skill Learning Cycle as shown in Figure 1 involves twelve skills. Three are used in planning the interview, six in doing the interview, and three in analyzing the interview. Then the learner reflects on all three phases of the experience before going on to plan, do, and analyze another interview. Such thoughtful, disciplined activity covering all three phases of the Skill Learning Cycle is more productive than spending dozens of hours in mindless interviewing activity.

The effectiveness of including the whole cycle in the learning process has been shown in several studies. For example, Parker and Meeks have found that in learning guidance interviewing it is important for the learner not only to do interviews but also to analyze them.[2] Studies have also shown that an important part of analyzing one's own interview is hearing a recording of the interview. A pioneering study demonstrated this when the tape recorder first became popular.[3] Some studies have even demonstrated that in learning certain types of interviewing it is more effective for the learner to analyze other people's interviews than to practice interviewing with no analysis.[4] In one case he analysis took the form of coding the relevant information from a tape recorded interview. *Probably the most effective learning technique is to combine performance with analysis of one's own interview.*

Figure 1
Skill Learning Cycle

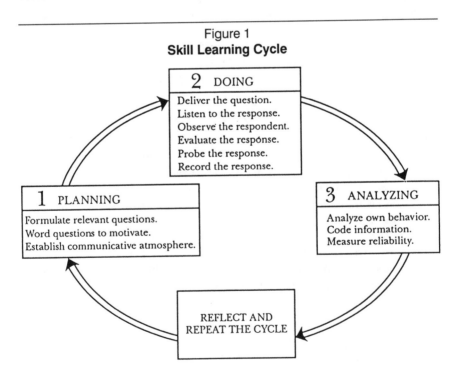

The planning phase of the cycle is important because of its vital relationship to the doing and analyzing phases. For example, formulating relevant questions in the *planning* phase is clearly related to the mental process of evaluating the relevance of the response in the *doing* phase. It is also strongly related to the process of coding the relevant information in the *analyzing* phase. As the learner experiences the complete Skill Learning Cycle, other vital connections among the three phases of the experience will become apparent.

Even the more subtle skill of observing nonverbal cues can be learned. Studies have shown that younger people are less sensitive than older people to such cues, which suggests that the ability to read nonverbal cues comes with life experience and can be learned.[5] The same research also found that people who are more sensitive to nonverbal cues generally function better both socially and intellectually.

Overall, research suggests that mere repetitive performance without planning, critical analysis, and replanning may not result in improvement. Furthermore, uncritical repetition can fix bad habits into an inflexible pattern that requires serious remedial action to change.

This chapter presents a method of practice in which thoughtful planning, sensitive interviewing, and critical self-analysis are systematically blended into a vital learning experience.

Planning

The planning phase assumes that the interviewer starts with nothing more than a problem or set of objectives; the interviewer does not depend on someone else to formulate the questions or set up the interview situation.

Formulating Relevant Questions. For a question to be useful in an interview it must first be relevant to the objectives of the interview. To arrive at relevant questions the interviewer must (1) clearly define the objectives of the interview, (2) translate each objective into specific points of information needed, and (3) translate those points into questions to be asked. The inexperienced interviewer tends to simply hand the objectives to the respondent in the guise of questions rather than breaking the objectives down into more concrete questions.

Formulating Motivating Questions. It is not enough for a question to be logically relevant to the objectives of the interview. The second quality of a useful question is that it helps to motivate by making the respondent either more willing or more able to answer the question.

Establishing a Communicative Atmosphere. Before the first question is asked the interviewer can increase the chances of obtaining the needed information by establishing a physical and verbal setting that helps the process. A poor setting can counteract the effects of the best questioning techniques.

Doing

The most frequently used interviewing skills are those in the *doing* phase of the Skill Learning Cycle, because in some interviewing situations someone other than the interviewer defines the problem and decides what questions are to be asked. However, for the purposes of learning interviewing skills, the planning and interviewing should be done by the same person. Defining the problem and formulating the questions in the planning phase will help sensitize the interviewer to what to listen for, to whether a response is relevant, to the need for further probing, and to what should be recorded. For these reasons, all of the doing skills described next assume that interviewer was also the planner.

Delivering the Question. If we assume that the exact wording of a question has been established in the planning phase, then the delivery of the question depends on nonverbal factors accompanying the question. These factors include the interviewer's body position, eye contact, facial expression, tone of voice, and pacing. All of these factors affect the respondent's ability or willingness to answer.

Listening to the Respondent. Listening is not something everyone does well, even in normal conversation. Listening is the active, intellectual process of seeking meaning in what another person says; it is hearing with a purpose. The good interviewer tries to understand what the words mean to the speaker as well as how this meaning is related to the objectives of the interview. The good interviewer listens to both the verbal and the audible nonverbal communication of the respondent. Audible nonverbal cues include the respondent's tone of voice, silences, intonation patterns, pacing, and so forth. They provide a context that completes the meaning of the verbal message.

Observing the Respondent. Just as the interviewer listens for the audible nonverbal cues, he or she *observes* the visual nonverbal cues or body language of the respondent. Cues such as body posture, movements of hands and feet, facial expression, and eye movement all constitute a nonverbal context that provides clues to the meaning and validity of the verbal message as well as to the energy level, mood, and attitude of the respondent. The interviewer should be aware of any discrepancies between the verbal and the nonverbal messages as clues to the meaning and validity of the response. The interviewer should also note *changes* in the predominant mood or attitude of the respondent as clues to the meaning of the response and to the respondent's changing need for encouragement, support, or challenge.

Evaluating the Response. After ascertaining the meaning of the response by careful listening and observation, the interviewer is ready to evaluate the response. There are three evaluative questions the interviewer must constantly keep in mind: Is the response relevant to the objective of the question? Is the information valid (true)? Is the information complete?

Probing the Response. If the interviewer's evaluation finds the response inadequate to meet the objectives of the question, then the interviewer must probe the response to improve its relevance, validity, or completeness. To probe effectively the interviewer needs to have command of a variety of probe forms that will encourage the respondent to elaborate and clarify without biasing the response with subtle suggestions or assumptions.

Recording the Response. Recording the response may be considered as part of the *doing* phase in the Skill Learning Cycle or as part of the *analysis* phase, depending on the particular method of recording that is used. For example, if the interviewer records a response by simply checking a predetermined category in order to classify a response into some analytical scheme, then recording and analyzing are being done simultaneously. On the other hand, if the interviewer writes verbatim quotes from a response or tape-records the interview, then recording the information is separate from the *analysis* phase of the Skill Learning Cycle.

Analyzing

The analyzing phase is crucial to the process of learning those performance skills needed in the doing phase. By inserting the critical analysis phase into the Skill Learning Cycle we avoid mindless repetition of the interviewing process. Before conducting a second interview on a topic, the interviewer should critically analyze the results obtained in the first interview. This critical analysis has two main aspects: objectively analyzing one's own interviewing behavior and evaluating the total amount of relevant information obtained.

Without critical analysis the interviewer may remain unaware of mistakes and may optimistically assume that the information obtained was relevant, complete, and valid. Often interviewers are shocked the first time they hear their own interviewing on tape. This may be their first realization that they loaded the questions, accepted irrelevant answers, or failed to probe for relevance, completeness, and validity.

Recording and Coding Information. The interviewer needs to know how to select the most appropriate mode for recording information. Information may be recorded for two purposes: to help the interviewer remember points that need to be probed later and to store the responses.

Once the responses have been stored, the interviewer needs to know how to winnow out the relevant from the irrelevant and then how to classify (code) this relevant information into categories meaningful to the purposes of the interview. Classifying information into categories can make one acutely aware of missing information, of responses that are too vague to classify reliably, and of one's failure to persist in the pursuit of relevant, complete, and valid information. Often, after finishing the coding, an interviewer would like to have another opportunity to interview the same respondent.

Summary

Interviewing is defined in this book as focusing on the most essential function common to the broadest range of interview situations: the information-gathering function. To learn basic information-gathering skills is to learn those skills that are useful for all types of interviews regardless of any additional functions they might have.

Interviewing skills are not simple motor skills like riding a bicycle; rather, they involve a high-order combination of observation, empathic sensitivity, and intellectual judgment. These skills can be learned by disciplined practice, particularly when learners assume responsibility for planning, doing, and analyzing their own interviews.

The Skill Learning Cycle provides an initial, guided experience for the complete interview-learning process. It also stands as a model for the learner to use in the future on a path of independent self-improvement. The potential rewards are considerable and the path can be exciting.

Notes

[1]For a more detailed analysis of interview dialogues in eight different professional settings, see Raymond L. Gorden, "Professional Settings of the Interview," in *Interviewing: Strategy, Techniques and Tactics,* 4th ed. (Chicago: Dorsey Press, 1987).

[2]Aileen Parker and Clinton Meeks, "Problems in Learning to Interview," *Counselor Education and Supervision* 7 (1967): 54–59.

[3]S. Womer and H. W. Boyd, Jr., "The Use of Voice Recorder in the Selection and Training of Interviewers," *Public Opinion Quarterly* 15 (Summer 1951): 358–63.

[4]Lester Guest, "A New Training Method for Opinion Interviewers," *Public Opinion Quarterly* 18 (Fall 1954): 287–99.

[5]Robert Rosenthal et al., "Body Talk and Tone of Voice—The Language without Words," *Psychology Today* (September 1974): 64–68.

20

What Do We Know about Anger Management Programs in Corrections?

Pamela Stiebs Hollenhorst

Introduction

Assaultive or violent behavior leading to arrest often is associated with anger. Anger management thus has earned face validity as a reasonable treatment alternative for domestic abusers, child abusers, animal abusers, substance abusers, aggressive juveniles, vandals, perpetrators of hate crimes or road rage, and other violent offenders. Such programs have been implemented in prisons, as a condition of probation or parole, and in conjunction with deferred prosecution programs and non-jail sentences. Although public awareness of anger management has increased substantially,[1] little is known about the program's effectiveness or its appropriate application. This article explores the content, application, effectiveness, and propriety of anger management programs and concludes that anger management merits additional study in order to maximize its effectiveness as an educational tool for preventing violence.

This article provides a historical context to anger control theory and documents the recent trend toward broad application of anger management programs. It explains the nature of this misunderstood emo-

Source: *Federal Probation*, 62(2) (December 1998): 52–64.

tion and the relationship of skewed perceptions and distorted thinking to the commission of crime. It also examines the content of anger management programs used in correctional settings in Madison, Wisconsin. The article distinguishes anger management from domestic violence prevention programs and notes the risks of inappropriate treatment. It describes the evaluation of anger management programs and acknowledges the challenges faced in researching program effectiveness. The article summarizes the key findings and recommends further research to determine the most appropriate and effective use of anger management.

Background

History and Theory of Anger Management

According to researchers Kemp and Strongman at the University of Canterbury, New Zealand, concern about controlling anger dates back to ancient and medieval times. The beliefs we hold today about anger control are rooted in ancient philosophy but remain important lessons for living in today's society. Some members of society who fail to learn to control their response to anger-provoking situations act aggressively and end up in courtrooms, jails, and prisons. A portion of Kemp and Strongman's research is summarized as follows:

Although Stoics valued discipline and regarded anger as useless in both war and sporting events, Aristotle believed that anger that arises from perceived injustice had value in preventing injustice. However, there was agreement among philosophers on the desirability of controlling this emotion and in the belief that self-control can be learned by training in rational thought. Seneca advised that to avoid becoming angry, one should be aware of sources of personal irritation, attempt to understand the other person's motives and extenuating circumstances, not respond to anger with anger, and not serve too much wine. It also was believed that anger can be defused with wit and that children should receive early training in self-control.[2]

Despite these long-held beliefs, the interest in studying negative emotions has primarily focused on anxiety and depression rather than on anger.[3] In the last few decades greater attention has been paid to gender differences in expressing anger and to distinguishing anger from aggression, but Kemp and Strongman note that in 2,000 years our understanding of anger has not changed significantly.

Current Applications Outside of Correctional Settings

What has changed is the widespread application of anger management programs, which have become ubiquitous. The significance of such widespread application is that there is a perceived need for such training[4] and that shared knowledge about anger control establishes and reinforces behavioral norms.

Programs labeled "Anger Management" vary in content and methods, but share the goal of teaching people how to control their responses to anger-provoking situations. Anger management is included as part of conflict resolution and violence prevention skills taught in day care[5] and elementary schools,[6] in vocational schools to promote safety,[7] in "Parenting in the '90s" classes,[8] for building productivity in the workplace,[9] for career development,[10] in management training,[11] for conquering road rage,[12] for treating alcoholism in Malaysia,[13] as a condition of participation in Midnight Basketball Leagues,[14] and as part of sports psychology training provided to athletes such as Tiger Woods.[15] The list of applications continues, including diversity training for police officers,[16] job retention training for homeless men,[17] coping skills for postal workers[18] and for disaster victims,[19] for physicians dealing with colleagues and with changes in health care delivery systems,[20] and for patients who have been diagnosed with a host of health problems.

Such widespread application across age categories, employment circumstances, and socioeconomic class strongly suggests a belief that anger management programs have value for nearly everyone. It also suggests that anger management is considered to be a necessary social skill that can be taught in a training seminar in addition to being a therapeutic treatment for violence-prone individuals. Learning to cope with emotions and to control behavior ideally may occur in childhood, but this widespread acceptance implies that people can benefit from training at any age in order to cope better with whatever stressors are present in their lives.

Training in emotional control and information-processing is part of the process of socialization—the reinforcement, punishment, or extinction of behaviors by peers, parents, teachers, and others[21]—that is deficient or absent in some criminals. Studies show that aggressive children have distorted or deficient information-processing mechanisms that lead them to experience anger when nonaggressive children do not.[22] Crimes often are committed impulsively, without rational regard for the consequences of the behavior. Anger management can address some of these impulsive acts because it is premised on cognitive restructuring—learning how to think rationally, interpret events, anticipate consequences, and distinguish the normal emotion (anger) from the resultant undesirable behavior (violence or aggression).

Changing perceptions and thoughts affects behavior. The importance of learning these skills is reflected in recent innovative application of anger management programs within the criminal justice system.

Recent Developments in Legal or Correctional Settings

The following examples illustrate how anger management programs are developing wider applications in legal proceedings and correctional settings:

- In January 1997, in response to chronic jail overcrowding, Los Angeles County developed an alternative sentencing plan, Community Based Alternatives to Custody, which includes a special lockup for domestic violence inmates, where inmates will take classes in parenting skills and anger management.[23]

- In February 1997, Multnomah County in Oregon began requiring divorcing parents to take classes on addressing their children's needs. In high-conflict divorces, the training includes anger management classes.[24]

- A Colorado law that took effect July 1, 1997, provides that a person convicted of cruelty to animals can be forced to enter an anger management training course. Proponents of the law pointed out that killers Manson, Bundy, and Dahmer had histories of torturing animals.[25]

- The Connecticut Department of Corrections includes anger management as one component of an innovative 12-step gang-busting program that doesn't shorten sentences but earns inmates privileges. A July 1997 report credits the program for reducing gang-related disturbances and assaults on staff members and inmates.[26]

- In response to increased incidents of road rage in the past year, Portland's Driver Improvement Program permits counselors for teenagers convicted of at least two moving violations before age 18 to impose limits on driving privileges or require the teen to take a course in defensive driving or anger management.[27]

- In October 1997, Idaho received a 3-year, $600,000 federal grant to finance a program to lower the recidivism rate at the North Idaho Correctional Institution by improving life skills and employability of inmates. The program includes 25 hours of anger management instruction as well as follow-up and coordination between probation and parole officers and counselors involved in the program.[28]

Learning Through Cognitive-Behavioral Therapy

Violence as a response to anger is a learned behavior that can be unlearned. One corrections official observed that there were three common variables in the background of participants in his anger management class: a family history of violence, including beatings, fights, and other abuse; disorganization in family structure and inadequate role models; and alcohol and drug problems.[29] Most participants had never been taught to respond to anger with anything other than aggression.

Anger management often is a form of cognitive-behavioral therapy,[30] a program designed to change offenders' perceptions, attitudes, and expectations that maintain their antisocial behavior. Participants first analyze their thinking patterns and question the underlying assumptions that led to the undesirable behavior. Then, through group discussion and role playing, they are introduced to alternative beliefs and behaviors. Anger management training is a complex method for developing thinking processes that leads to changes in behavior. Effective behavioral intervention programs usually employ a combination of methods to reinforce what is learned and to model desirable behavior with offenders.[31] Within an anger management curriculum, role-playing, discussion, and an effective counselor all serve to model rational thinking and social skills. Reading assignments, anger journals, and writing exercises help develop more self-awareness and self-control and increase understanding of emotions and behavior. Effective programs usually include relapse prevention in the community—a treatment component absent from the anger management programs reviewed but recommended by several counselors. Although programs have a variety of components, they generally begin with a lesson in understanding the nature of anger.

The Nature of Anger and Its Relationship to Crime

Understanding Anger

Anger is a frequently experienced, normal emotion of varying duration and intensity, ranging from mild frustration to intense rage, which is accompanied by physiological and biological changes. These changes may include increased heart rate and blood pressure; increased muscle tension manifested by clenched teeth and fists; rapid breathing, trembling, reddening of the skin, agitation, and stomach pain, as well as an increase in the level of adrenaline and noradrenaline, which are energy hormones associated with fight or flight. However normal the emotion, anger has been described as "the chief enemy of public happiness and private peace."[32] When people are angry they assume "some of the worst characteristics of the people they hate, including bullying, prejudice, violence, and arrogance."[33] Anger can be very disruptive, and it sometimes leads to aggression.

Anger is a feeling state, correlated with but independent from aggression, which is a motor behavior with intent to harm another person or object. Anger and aggression are related and may overlap, but correlation and causation are sometimes confused—experts do not agree that anger directly causes aggression.[34] One expert likens anger to an architect's blueprint; just as a blueprint makes it easier to build a house, anger makes it easier to be aggressive.[35] Anger management focuses on provocation and physical response to that provocation and on the appropriate expression of anger.

Linking Anger to Crime

Criminal behavior often involves both anger and aggression. Research shows that violent men are more angry and hostile more often than nonviolent men,[36] but the exact relationship between anger and aggression is not so clear. Whether an angry person will be aggressive depends on "situational cues, cognitive attributions and appraisals, or prior learning and the evaluation of the outcome of actions."[37] Other studies have suggested that there may be a biologic component to being predisposed to anger.[38] Whether anger leads to aggression depends on the circumstances as well as on a person's beliefs, perceptions, anticipated results, and perhaps also on the person's biologic makeup.

According to the 1991 *Uniform Crime Reports*, aggressive acts typically occur between people who know each other and frequently occur during some kind of disagreement. For example, more than 50 percent of murder victims know their assailants and 34 percent of all murders committed in 1990 followed some type of disagreement, suggesting that murder often occurs in a social context and is not random.[39] A study conducted in the early '70s showed that felonies involving personal violence were found to occur most often where a prior relationship existed between the victim and defendant. For example, for felony arrests in New York City, in 83 percent of rape arrests and 69 percent of assault arrests, the victim knew the defendant.[40]

Similarly, anger is more often experienced between acquaintances.[41] The same New York study concluded that "criminal conduct is often the explosive spillover from ruptured personal relations among neighbors, friends, and former spouses."[42] Incidents giving rise to arrest were rooted in anger between people who knew each other.[43] But anger only sometimes leads to aggression, some aggression is calm and calculated, and not all aggressive behavior is criminal. Anger management programs may be wasted on non-angry violent offenders who could be better served by other treatment, and more research is needed.

Although relatively little is known about the relationship of anger and aggression, researchers report some insights on the circumstances and thinking patterns that lead to angry aggression. Surveys of college students and community residents in 1982 and 1983 showed that 83 percent of those surveyed reported becoming angry at least once or twice per week, 88 percent of self-reported anger-causing events involved at least one other person, 50 percent of anger episodes involved someone well known, although only 10 percent of episodes reportedly led to physical aggression.[44] However, 85 percent reported the cause of anger was "a perceived injustice by another person that was preventable and voluntary."[45]

Some researchers who have attempted to discern what final event triggers violence have focused on criminal thinking patterns. A study by Deffenbacher in 1993 generated a model relevant to criminal aggression which noted that anger arises in response to an act that is judged to be intentional, preventable, unjustified, and blameworthy—thus the angry person develops a sense of righteousness that the source of anger-causing behavior should be punished.[46]

Criminal thinking follows a pattern based on skewed perceptions. The pattern of distorted thinking displayed by the angry individual includes overestimating the probability of negative outcomes, assuming that others are engaging in intentional, personal attacks, exaggerating the sense of unfairness, and failure to perceive ambiguities.[47] Following this pattern of thinking provides a moral imperative for an aggressive response, which can result in criminal aggression.[48] Alcohol, drugs, or fatigue may magnify the response. For example, alcohol use is related to impulsivity, reduced inhibition, and impaired judgment, which may aggravate relationships and predispose an individual toward violence.[49]

When angry aggression is successful in satisfying needs, violent behavior can become what psychologists term a "process addiction"[50]—a learned behavior that is reinforced by habit and by subculture. For example, in gangs, where violence is an accepted way of resolving conflict and angry expressions are valued and respected, the subculture provides motivation for criminal behavior. Whether anger management intervention will have impact depends in part on the circumstances under which anger arises.

In summary, negative thinking predisposes some people to be provoked by interpersonal interactions and to respond in an uncontrolled manner. Understanding the circumstances under which anger arises, the underlying warped perceptions, the effects of alcohol and drug abuse, and the relationship of thinking patterns to aggression is essential to anger intervention programs. Anger management training can help to prevent criminally aggressive behavior by cognitive restructuring. Changing the way people think includes developing skills in generating alternative solutions to problems and projecting the consequences of angry responses. Because a causal relationship between anger and aggression is not assumed, principles of anger management work to reduce and prevent both anger and aggression.

Anger Management Programs

Principles of Anger Management

Anger management involves learning to control one's reactions to anger-provoking situations, including the emotional feelings of anger, the physiological arousal associated with anger, and the resulting angry behavior. Anger control techniques are based on assumptions of cognitive psychology, which places emphasis on the purpose, understanding, and reasoning in behavior.[51] By making an individual more aware of the underlying thought process that leads to provocation and physiological arousal, anger control enables the individual to avoid aggressive behavior.

Strategies for managing anger include: (1) learning relaxation methods such as deep breathing and relaxing imagery; (2) cognitive restructuring, using logic to understand one's frustrations or sources of anger; (3) problem solving and recognizing that sometimes no solution may exist; (4) better communication skills by listening to underlying messages when being criticized and contemplating the best response; (5) using humor to defuse rage; and (6) changing one's environment to reduce or eliminate the source of anger.[52]

Anger management programs develop both cognitive and behavioral skills needed to employ these strategies. Cognitive skills are those related to paying attention and restructuring thoughts, whereas behavioral skills involve arousal reduction, communication enhancement, and problem solving.[53] Attentional skills increase the ability to recognize provocation cues and physical signs of arousal and are promoted by having program participants maintain an anger log to increase their self-awareness. Restructuring skills assess the anger-provoking circumstances and expectations and are developed by engaging in role-playing exercises with group discussion. Behavioral skills also are developed in an anger management curriculum in several ways: arousal reduction is achieved through positive imagery and relaxation exercises; communication is enhanced by practicing assertiveness in role-playing; and problem solving includes considering alternative responses to the events causing arousal through group discussion of hypothetical situations. The ability to learn is affected by the motivational level and intellectual ability of the participants and by the teaching style of the instructor or counselor.

According to Richard Althouse, Ph.D., anger-related behaviors are "shaped by social learning and maintained in a gender-based familial, social, and cultural context by individuals of varying levels of motivation and intellectual ability."[54] Althouse believes that an effective anger management program must address these dynamic, interrelated variables. Participants in prison programs vary in their motivation, resistance, and readiness to change. A program presenter's nonjudgmental attitude and respectful interactions with participants reduce that resistance and increase motivation, supporting the long-term goals of changing thinking patterns and modifying behavior.[55]

Dr. Althouse's anger management program addresses four considerations: the surrounding environment, one's thinking, the emotion itself, and one's behavior. It helps offenders develop the skills necessary to recognize their angry feelings, to learn the causes of anger, and to deal with it in a responsible way that will facilitate their transition to productive community life.[56]

Anger Management for Prisoners

The anger management program at Oakhill Correctional Institution[57] in Oregon, Wisconsin, is a didactic/experiential/interactive 8- to 10-week module led by Dr. Althouse in 90-minute sessions. The program is designed to facilitate an inmate's ability to avoid self-defeating, victimizing behavior when angry and to promote positive self-management and conflict resolution.[58] The ultimate goals of the program are to make the institution and the community safer.

Admittance is predicated on inmate needs as identified by Assessment and Evaluation, or an inmate may be self-referred or referred by staff members based on demonstrable need. As a condition of admission, inmates must agree to attend all sessions, to participate actively in these sessions, and to complete all assignments. In order to get credit for completing the program, participants must pass a final examination consisting of multiple-choice questions on the materials covered in the course.

The program begins with an explanation and discussion of the importance of understanding what anger is and why its management is desirable. Participants examine what triggers anger and what problems arise from anger mismanagement; they explore male socialization, including values, beliefs, behavioral alternatives, and consequences; and they rehearse interventions.

Materials distributed to participants include a list of myths and facts about anger, magazine and newspaper articles addressing the impact of anger on health, the underlying fears from which anger arises, statistics on homicide, a journal article about anger and criminality, and cartoons that illustrate and reinforce various points covered in the program. The handouts are intended to deepen participants' understanding of anger. Participants are asked to maintain an anger journal to note what triggers their anger and what symptoms indicate they are angry and to consider alternative behaviors for discussion with the group. By combining readings, discussions, and journal reflection, the program strives to be both philosophical and practical.

Dr. Althouse employs the technique of "motivational interviewing" in leading the participants to recognize their potential problems with anger management and to reduce their defensiveness. In using this technique, the counselor does not assume authority but instead expresses empathy and leaves responsibility for change with the participants, who are free to accept or reject advice. Dr. Althouse does not attempt to convince the participants of the value of the anger management program and meets their resistance with reflection. It is a deliberate, nonjudgmental technique that is designed to overcome resistance to change.

Dr. Althouse asks for verbal feedback during the sessions and written comments at the end of his sessions. Typically, although a few of the group members initially are hostile and sarcastic and participate with reluctance, most appear to be at least mildly interested at the first session. Program graduates most often rank the program as either "helpful" or "very helpful."[59] Despite the program being well received by participants, only about 15 percent of the 175 to 200 offenders who are referred to the anger management program at Oakhill each year actually receive the training.[60] The remainder are released without having received the training because Oakhill lacks sufficient staff to meet this demand.

Evaluation sheets summarizing the participants' opinions indicate that they found the presentation to be useful and informative, and they approved of the personable and respectful style in which it is taught.[61] Some participants suggested expanding the program to cover more material, while one noted that more time could be spent on discussing anger within the family. Interestingly, another comment implied that society also must learn to deal with its anger toward offenders.[62]

Aggression Replacement Therapy

Attic Correctional Services is a private, nonprofit agency under contract with the Wisconsin Department of Corrections (DOC) to provide programs for anger management, domestic violence prevention, and sex offender treatment as well as providing halfway houses in Dane County and the surrounding area. According to a field supervisor who manages the purchase of service contracts for three counties, the demand for anger management programs arose about 3 years ago when corrections agents perceived a need for a treatment program for clients on probation or in Intensive Sanctions who displayed violent tendencies but did not qualify as domestic abusers or sex offenders.[63] The program entitled Aggression Replacement Therapy (ART) initially was designed for young, assaultive, quick-tempered males who demonstrated a lack of impulse control. Attic currently is contracted to conduct sessions for 8 to 12 people who meet once per week for 90 minutes for 12 weeks at a cost of $124 per group per session. Attic conducts separate programs for men and women.

Participants in ART are referred to the program by their probation or parole officers and are required to sign an agreement stating that they will attend, take the pre- and post-tests, maintain a daily log tracking moments of anger, complete all other homework assignments, respectfully participate in group discussions and role-playing, and keep all information discussed in the group confidential. Lessons include learning constructive interpersonal skills such as expressing a complaint, responding to anger, and dealing with group pressures. Participants learn to recognize physical signs of becoming angry and to employ anger-reducing techniques such as deep breathing, backward counting, pleasant imagery, taking time-outs, and thinking ahead. Participants also learn new problem-solving styles through self-speech, a method of changing thought patterns.

The facilitator models each skill in hypothetical situations and then involves the group in role-playing to help in transferring the skills to real life situations. The final phase of the program involves dilemma discussion groups to acquire and practice the skills necessary for rational decision-making. The group is asked to solve hypothetical conflicts in order to learn how to think, reason, and resolve conflicts in real life.[64]

One case manager and group leader admitted that most participants in ART do not want to be there. In a recent introductory session, in which much time was spent on completing paperwork and explaining the structure of the program, participants were quiet and generally maintained expressions of veiled contempt. When the paperwork was completed and discussion began, a few members willingly contributed comments but most sat in silence. (As with the Oakhill session, the presence of an observer may have stifled discussion.)

The group leader later explained that group dynamics vary, and some groups are more willing to participate and share experiences. (In one instance, women in one group formed such strong bonds of friendship that a participant invited the others to her wedding, passing out invitations at the sessions.) Based on her experience as a social worker and her observations teaching classes for several years, the leader believes the program is beneficial, despite a lack of data to support that conclusion. She cited anecdotal reports from prison staff who have observed the application of anger management principles by program participants who had long-standing reputations for violent behavior but when provoked demonstrated new skills in self-control.

Anger Management in a Deferred Prosecution Program

In Dane County, Wisconsin, approximately 1,000 defendants each year are diverted from the formal criminal justice process and are referred by the district attorney's office to the Deferred Prosecution Program, a county-funded program for treatment and supervision of certain offenders. Eligible defendants are often first-time offenders who are given an opportunity to plea bargain but then have adjudication withheld pending completion of a domestic violence or general aggression counseling program and fulfillment of other conditions such as restitution. Participants sign a contract to enter the program, and when they successfully fulfill their obligations, charges are dismissed, resulting in a criminal history but no record of conviction.

Program Director Nancy Gustaf estimates that program participants are split between two general categories of violent behavior: approximately 40 percent involve domestic violence, which by definition involves a spouse or significant other in a spouse-like arrangement, and about 60 percent have displayed general aggression, which may involve roommates but not with a pattern of power and control demonstrated by those categorized as incidents of domestic violence.[65] Gustaf reports the program's clients range from ages 17 to 45 but are generally at the younger end of the spectrum and include both men and women. Participants are supervised by social workers in a manner similar to probation, with monthly meetings and follow-up checks on program participation at 6-week intervals to determine noncompliance. Participants can be assigned to one or more of several programs provided by local counseling services. Although insurance may cover the costs, participants must pay for the programs (which may be priced on a sliding scale) and contribute $10 per month to the Deferred Prosecution Program. Failure to comply with the contract terms results in being sentenced, often to probation but sometimes with jail time imposed.

The programs to which these violence-prone individuals are sentenced focus on a specific need as determined by a professional evaluation. In Madison, Wisconsin, for example, Family Services, H & S Counseling, and Attic Correctional Services offer evaluation and treatment programs for sex offenders, domestic violence offenders, and individuals referred because of angry or aggressive behavior not meeting the criteria of domestic violence. H & S offers a 15-week general aggression program and a 24- to 36-week domestic violence program; each group meets for 2 hours per week. Individuals pay for their own treatment programs. Uninsured participants pay on a sliding scale, and rates are confidential.[66]

Family Services, a nonprofit organization supported in part by United Way, conducts similar programs paid on a sliding scale by the clients, many of whom qualify for medical assistance. Clients first are evaluated to determine if underlying needs would require individual treatment before or instead of group therapy. The initial assessment costs $110, individual treatment costs $84 per session, and group sessions such as the general aggression program (which includes two facilitators) cost $64 per session.[67] Sessions are 2 hours long and meet once per week; currently, the general aggression program runs 12 weeks and domestic violence intervention runs 24 weeks. Based on evaluations from exit interviews, recidivism reports, and comments from people returning to the program, the 12-week model for general aggression is being evaluated for possible expansion to 24 weeks.[68]

Gustaf reports that out of the 1,000 annual referrals, 20 to 25 percent decline to enter the Deferred Prosecution Program, reoffend, or disappear before entering. Of the 750 who enter and sign a contract, about 70 percent complete the programs overall; for those involved in domestic violence, the success rate drops to about 60 percent.[69] Gustaf also agrees that it is important to distinguish anger management or general aggression programs from those designed to prevent domestic violence.

While some judges leave the determination of offender treatment programs to experts trained in evaluating needs and providing counseling, others assign offenders to specific treatment as a condition of sentence or probation. Those judges need to be aware of the differences between anger management and domestic violence and the danger in assigning an offender to inappropriate treatment.

Distinguishing Anger Management from Domestic Violence Programs

Content Differences

Anger management is a segment of domestic violence treatment programs, which are broader in scope and have more components, including addressing personal and psychological factors and political issues that are not addressed in an anger management curriculum. Studies show that the most aggressive and violent batterers tend to focus their attention and hostility in the control of their partners, and because this hostility is methodically planned and controlled for maximum effect, it is different from the impulsive anger addressed in anger management programs.[70] Psychologist Darald Hanusa, a private practitioner and consultant to Attic Correctional Services, believes that some judges may not be aware of the distinction between these programs. Hanusa is concerned that assigning a batterer to anger management instead of to a program for batterers may be inappropriate and damaging.[71]

Mark Seymour, co-director of H & S Counseling in Madison, agrees with Hanusa that differences in issues and in treatment styles are important. Seymour explains that in contrast to domestic violence, general aggression occurs between two adults who are not in an intimate relationship. (If a child is involved, the treatment is for child abuse.) Examples include aggression against family members, bar fights, or altercations with bosses or coworkers. In domestic violence treatment the primary issue is power and control. A main component of treatment involves challenging belief systems that support the abusive relationship, including perceptions about sexism and inequality in a relationship. Participants in a domestic violence class are taught to replace the need for power and control with new skills in healthy assertiveness and improved communication. Teaching assertiveness includes a component of anger management, but the focus is on changing the underlying power and control orientation.[72]

H & S Counseling offers a Domestic Violence Intervention Program (DVIP), which is distinguishable from the Generalized Aggression Program (GAP). DVIP is a 24-week program designed for men to eliminate power and control, oppression, sexism, intimidation, and violence in a domestic relationship. Men are taught new skills in order to interrupt the pattern of psychological, physical, or sexual abuse and to develop a healthy domestic relationship.[73] In contrast, GAP is a 15-week program available to both men and women in separate groups to work on aggression issues with adults outside of intimate relationships. This program is designed to teach new skills in order to change behavior, including skills in problem solving, appropriate expression of anger, and interpersonal communication for an aggression-free lifestyle.[74]

The clinical experience of some experts has led to the conclusion that anger management programming is not likely to be effective or properly implemented by batterers for two reasons. First, domestic abuse is not necessarily driven by anger, but by a socially learned need to control women; and, second, batterers use anger control mechanisms to get their way while continuing to abuse.[75] To prevent batterers from abusing their partners, a process of change must occur that goes well beyond the scope of anger management.[76] The fact that batterers may not lack the ability to manage anger in relationships and environments outside their home supports the conclusion that their behavior is rooted in other issues.

The Dangers of Assigning Anger Management for Batterers

Gondolf and Russell have identified the following shortcomings in using anger management programming with batterers: (1) Anger management implies that the victim provoked the anger with annoying behavior and precipitated the abuse; (2) anger management does not address other undesirable premeditated controlling behavior such as manipulating and isolating; for example, a man taking a "time out" also serves as a ploy to stop a woman from speaking up or challenging him; (3) batterers use anger as an excuse for accepting responsibility for their behavior, which in turn delays the necessary personal change by encouraging self-justification and victim-blaming; (4) anger management can be misconstrued as a "quick-fix" that enables men to use the program to manipulate their wives into returning to a still dangerous environment; (5) anger management is less threatening to the community and easier to accept than changing established sexist social conditions that give rise to domestic abuse; (6) anger management does not address the economic, social, and political injustices and patriarchal social structure that perpetuates domestic abuse and violence toward women.[77] They conclude that anger management alone might do more harm than good for batterers and their victims, and they believe that it diverts attention from societal responsibility.

"Anger management" for batterers raises some doubts because it suggests that men who are already controlling need to learn to be more controlling. But programs for batterers encompass cognitive-behavioral treatment, which is far more inclusive. Anger management, as noted earlier by Hanusa and Seymour, is only one part of the treatment provided for batterers. A national survey of programs for men who batter conducted in 1984 shows that more than 75 percent of those programs include anger management, problem-solving skill training, and communication training; and more than 50 percent include stress management and behavioral contracting.[78] To discuss all components of treatment for batterers is beyond the scope of this article, but sentencing judges should be aware of the distinctions between programs and avoid the possible risks in inappropriate sentencing.

It appears there is agreement that anger management may be useful if presented in conjunction with other training for batterers, but alone it is insufficient and potentially risky. In some instances of animal abuse, the same concerns should exist. For example, a man who kills his girlfriend's kitten or beats a dog to death in the presence of his children is a violent abuser whose behavior should raise a red flag with judges. He likely needs more than anger management—or other treatment entirely—when such behavior obviously also serves to intimidate and control others. Sentencing judges would be prudent to require a psychological evaluation to determine whether anger management is appropriate or whether some other treatment is better suited for a particular offender. Anger may be a manifestation of other problems because it is common to depression, paranoia, psychotic reactions, hormonal imbalances, and neurologic conditions.[79] Anger management may be useful training for some people lacking the awareness and cognitive skills to cope with anger, but it is not a panacea for all forms of violence.

Evaluation of Program Effectiveness

Sample Studies of Anger/Aggression Control Programs

A number of studies in prisons conclude that anger management has some value in helping prisoners cope with being incarcerated and in changing thinking patterns. Following are some examples of such studies:

Evaluation of EQUIP: "Equipping Youth to Help One Another." A study of 200 male offenders age 15 to 18 serving an average of 6 months for either parole violations or for less serious felonies (breaking and entering, receiving stolen property, burglary) at a medium-security facility in a midwestern state showed a reduction in recidivism and improvement in institutional behavior. The group received training in a multicomponent program that combines the social skills training, anger management, and moral education components of Aggression Replacement Training with "guided group interaction." The program length was not stated. The treatment group showed a recidivism rate of one-half that of the control groups after 6 months and about one-third at 12 months. Although the EQUIP group showed no gains in moral judgment, test scores for the group showed improved social skills and significant gains in institutional conduct in terms of self-reported misconduct, staff-filed incident reports, and unexcused absences from school. Informally, the staff reported that the study group was easier to manage than other groups in that there were fewer incidents of fighting, verbal abuse, staff defiance, and AWOL attempts.[80]

Anger Management Workshop for Women. A 2-hour workshop conducted on three consecutive weeks provided anger management training to a random sample of 11 medium-security women inmates at the Utah State Prison. Inmates' ages ranged from 28 to 45 with a mean of 35.4, time served ranged from 1 to 7 years with a mean of 2.2 years, and the crimes for which they were serving time included drug convictions, felony theft, forgery, and murder. The components of the training included identifying symptoms of anger, learning why people get angry, and understanding how anger can be effectively managed. Test scores revealed that the inmates felt significantly less angry at the end of the workshop, and the women reported feeling better able to cope with the frustrations of being incarcerated. The main focus was to think before acting when they became angry. Learning coping skills such as walking away from conflict and cooling down gave the women time to think and thus avoid destructive behavior. The authors acknowledge that the test sample was small, which reduces generalizability, but they selected a small group because group education and treatment is believed to be more effective in samples of 15 or fewer inmates.[81]

Canadian Study of Assaultive and Nonassaultive Offenders. A 5-week program for anger management taught to 57 male assaultive and property offenders in a maximum security jail reduced aggression and anxiety while increasing self-esteem in some of the participants. The program included explanation of the causation, symptoms, and techniques for coping with anger. Of the participants, assaultive offenders showed increased feelings of guilt but no decrease in the measure of anxiety or aggression. The authors note that increased guilt may be significant if offenders begin to consider the impact of their behavior on others.[82]

Although the prison studies suggest that anger management treatment has some value, insufficient research has been done to determine the scope of its usefulness and the duration of its effects.

An Internal Wisconsin DOC Report

A report prepared in 1995 by Michael Hammer, Ph.D., former staff psychologist at the Columbia Correctional Institution in Portage, Wisconsin, concluded that it is unknown how effective anger management programs are in helping participants, which programs are most effective, how many participants benefit, to what extent they benefit, and whether mandatory participation versus voluntary participation affects program outcome.[83] Hammer reported that much of the research on this subject has occurred since 1990, targeting incarcerated adult males with anger or aggression problems. The studies showed that the programs usually help participants reduce their anger and aggressiveness and also improve understanding of the anger process, decrease their number of conduct reports, improve ability to cope with anger-provoking situations, improve social skills, and increase guilt about their behavior.[84] Studies conducted on adolescent males reported similar results.

Although Hammer's report was not focused on domestic violence programs, he included a review of studies related to such programs because they often contain an anger management component. Anger management programs were effective in understanding and reducing domestic violence and aided in reducing passive-aggressiveness, reducing depressive symptoms, increasing relationship adjustment and satisfaction, and decreasing irrational or extreme beliefs about how relationships ought to function.[85] A study by Scales in 1995 showed that batterers' recidivism rate dropped by 50 percent after treatment. When both parties received programming, it reduced the number of arguments, improved relationships and the understanding of anger arousal, and eliminated further domestic violence for 6 to 8 months.[86] Other studies concluded that long-term violence is not abated and that although some treatment might be effective, sociopathic batterers and other individuals with personality disorders are generally resistant to such treatment.[87]

Hammer's report directed the Department's attention to several other issues. During the Assessment and Evaluation process the Department should be aware that researchers have noted a link between anger and alcoholism, with alcoholics showing the greatest degree of anger and risk for continuing anger problems.[88] Furthermore, differences exist between angry and nonangry but nonetheless aggressive inmates. Chronically angry prisoners perceive and interpret events differently based on irrational beliefs, which may have implications for assessment of treatment program needs.[89] Hammer concluded that although anger management programs have demonstrated positive results, additional research is necessary to evaluate these programs.

Although anger management programs are not a panacea, uncertainty about the programs' success does not mean that it is not useful in reducing violence. The widespread use of anger management programs in a variety of settings reinforces the message that acting in rage is not an excuse for violent behavior. As with programs for batterers, anger management programs provide a laboratory for developing an ideal treatment model. Learning the limitations of existing programs is a significant step toward improving them.

Challenges and Caveats

Challenges to Program Evaluation

In 1996 the Wisconsin Department of Corrections (DOC) created an office to conduct internal auditing of programs to evaluate implementation of programs to determine if a program is being carried out as planned and is meeting its objectives. No process audit or effectiveness evaluation is planned for the anger management programs at this time.[90] Even if there were plans to evaluate anger management programming in DOC, any evaluation of programs is problematic in several ways. Offenders move within and then out of the state's prison system, and thus they can be either difficult or impossible to track. For example, Dr. Althouse explained that he would not automatically be informed if one of his program participants reoffended and were incarcerated at another institution outside of Oakhill and Columbia, the two locations where he works. Offenders also may move out of the state and have no further contact with the Wisconsin prison system. Program graduates who are released from prison may continue to engage in violent behavior but not be reincarcerated.

It would be challenging to measure the impact of an anger management program because of the difficulty of isolating it from other factors that may influence behavior. Other influences include the shock of being incarcerated or the exposure to the court system and threat of incarceration; the impact of other treatment programs; and the influence of changes in age, physical and mental health, finances, family circumstances, and employment status.

However, some corrections officials believe that viewing an anger management program in isolation from other factors affecting behavior may be the wrong approach. Joe Lehman, secretary of corrections in Washington State, believes a better approach would be to evaluate anger management programs in terms of how their success relates to other influences and to other programs.[91] This represents systems thinking, which focuses on interrelationships rather than on the individual program. Because no program operates in a vacuum, and a program's effectiveness may be positively or adversely affected by other factors, it may be more reasonable to study these interrelationships in order to maximize whatever positive potential exists for anger management.

Caveats to Prison Research

Confronted with pandemic prison overcrowding and limited resources, policymakers should evaluate the research conducted in correctional settings in order to best allocate those resources to programs that are most effective. However, decisionmakers must exercise caution in interpreting and generalizing the results of studies and remain mindful of the limits inherent in studying prison populations. Edwin Megargee of Florida State University articulated these concerns as follows:

> Prisoners represent only a small portion of all those who commit criminal offenses, and an even smaller fraction of the overall population. Those of us who do assessment research in correctional settings must continually remember that we are dealing with atypical, highly biased samples of people exposed to massive situational influences specifically designed to alter their attitudes, personality, and behavior. Incarceration is a massive intervention that affects every aspect of a person's life for extended periods of time. We must be extremely cautious in generalizing the findings we obtain among prisoners to people in free-world settings, just as we must be careful to replicate free-world findings before applying them in correctional settings.[92]

He also cautions that offenders have different approaches to tests administered during initial assessment compared to later tests taken voluntarily for research purposes, noting that offenders who volunteer differ dramatically from those who do not.[93] For example, a report on the Anger Management Program at the Colorado State Penitentiary showed that inmates who refused to participate in the program differed in important ways from those who did participate; the most important difference was that non-participants had been significantly more aggressive in their recent behavior.[94] The efficacy and validity study noted:

> . . . the qualities which result in the greatest recent history of aggressive behavior also serve to reduce the likelihood of participation in a voluntary Anger Management Program. If confirmed in subsequent studies, this may well justify the involuntary imposition of such programs on that portion of the population which most needs it. It may also be found that this group properly avoided such a program because it would have no remarkable effect on their behavior.[95]

Conclusion

In summary, long-established principles and methods of controlling anger and aggression are being broadly used in innovative applications both outside and within legal and correctional settings as one method to reduce violence. The use of anger management as a facet of conflict resolution in schools holds promise for reducing violence in the future. However, not all of these applications may be appropriate and some may be harmful.

Widespread program application suggests that anger management is a useful social skill that can be learned and applied by people facing stress in all walks of life, including persons under supervision in the criminal justice system. Studies show that anger management programs have significant utility in reducing conduct reports in prison and have impact on reducing short-term recidivism for some juveniles. If anger management skills are useful in maintaining family and work relationships, they will be of value in integrating offenders back into the community.

Anger management training alone may be insufficient for certain offenders and potentially harmful to their victims. Domestic batterers, some animal abusers, and non-angry violent aggressors may be more appropriately served by other treatment. Alcoholism and psychiatric disorders affect behavior and impair the success of learning or implementing anger management skills. Professional assessment to determine program needs before assignment may be more costly, but also may help avoid the danger of inappropriate sentencing and reduce the waste of treatment resources.

Although formal studies, anecdotal reporting, and self-evaluation conclude that anger management counseling is of value, we do not know to what extent anger management programs have helped people, for whom the programs are most effective, or how long the programs' effects last. We have not yet learned how to maximize the potential beneficial effects of anger management by coordinating treatment with other programs which also affect behavior. Some experts believe that participation in follow-up support groups would reinforce the learning that occurs in an anger management program, just as it does for alcohol and drug abuse programs.

Learning about anger and its relationship to undesirable behavior is an important social skill that some people lack but are capable of learning. However, if we are not studying and measuring the results of anger management counseling, we don't know how effective the program is, and we may be failing to consider other alternatives that may work more effectively. Without additional research, limits on our existing knowledge complicate comparisons between programs and inhibit analysis of how best to allocate resources in the correctional system.

Anger is often involved in the commission of crime, but is anger management of use in preventing crime? The short answer is, for certain offenders, no; for some offenders, possibly; but there is much we do not know. Anger management focuses on preventing negative behavior that arises from impulsive hostile aggression by teaching self-awareness, self-control, and alternative thinking and behaviors. It is not designed to address, and likely will have no impact on, predatory or nonemotional calculated acts of aggression.

Anger management is premised on the ability to learn new skills and the willingness to implement those skills. Persons with mental illness or impaired intellectual functioning from drug abuse or alcoholism may be unable to learn the requisite skills or may be incapacitated from implementing those skills. Others may remain more influenced by community norms that call for an aggressive response to a perceived insult. We can measure what has been learned by program post-testing and by observing skill demonstration in role-playing and discussion, but we cannot accurately predict behavior.

We do not know if a program's impact depends on whether the program is voluntary or mandatory. When a program is assigned within the realm of the criminal justice system, it carries an element of coercion. Some offenders are required to complete a program before release whereas others volunteer, although we do not know their reasons for volunteering. Those reasons may include a genuine interest in self-improvement, to avoid behavior that led to contact with the criminal justice system, to favorably impress others, to avoid boredom while incarcerated, or, in the case of some batterers, to convince domestic partners to stay with them. Instructors have observed that the most initially reluctant participants express the greatest satisfaction with what they have learned.

We know that alcoholism, drug abuse, and psychiatric disorders impair thinking ability and undermine anger management skills, but we do not know what other factors may enhance or detract from what is learned in these programs. The program goals include fostering insight, increasing the ability to predict and appreciate the consequences of behavior, and restructuring a person's environment to prevent violence. While participants are in a discussion group in a controlled environment with an incentive to conform, they may be able and willing to recognize what makes them angry, to express their feelings, and to calm themselves. However, what happens outside the program is guaranteed to be different from role-playing in a therapy group. Upon release, returning to an environment that provokes frustration and provides pressure to resume negative behavior may undermine any positive change. In contrast, having a job, economic stability, and family and friends who function well in society are factors all likely to reinforce anger management skills by providing motivation and support.

If program participants feel more in control, empowered with communication skills, and better able to cope with stress and frustration, the program may have served its purpose. If participation develops social skills and improves relationships with family, friends, and coworkers, factors known to contribute to a stable and law-abiding lifestyle, the program has value. We can measure treatment outcome by testing, by observation of demonstrated skills, by conduct reports, by recidivism rates, and by evaluation of the overall differences in the quality of life such as the ability to sustain relationships and employment. But research on the results of anger management training outside of a prison environment is very limited.

Anger management can be taught in a variety of settings in a few months' time. It may improve the functioning ability of some persons and may prevent some violence, but we need to learn how to mine the program's potential for preventing crime. We already know that crime is not always prevented by the imposition of harsher criminal penalties. Our reputation as a violent society speaks for the need to learn about controlling anger. If we believe that social controls and individual self-control play a more significant role in preventing crime, then anger management programs to develop and enhance those controls merit further study.

Notes

[1] A search of Westlaw newspaper databases reveals that the term "anger management" was used in 67 documents in 1991, 372 documents in 1993, 749 documents in 1995, and 1,245 documents in 1997.

[2] Simon Kemp and K. T. Strongman, "Anger Theory and Management: A Historical Analysis," *History of Psychology*, Rand B. Evans, Ed., reprinted in *108 American Journal of Psychology 397* (Fall 1995).

[3] Howard Kassinove and Denis G. Sukhodolsky, "Anger Disorders: Basic Science and Practice Issues," *Anger Disorders: Definition, Diagnosis, and Treatment* (hereinafter *Anger Disorders)* Taylor & Francis (1995) at 3.

[4] Kassinove and Sukhodolsky in *Anger Disorders, supra*, report that in the 5-year period from 1986 to 1990, in anger-correlated or anger-caused events, more than 300 people were killed or seriously wounded in American schools and another 242 were held hostage at gunpoint.

[5] Frank J. Mifsud, "TV or Day Care?" *Maclean's* (Sept. 9, 1996) at 5.

[6] Christopher Elser, "Juvenile Crime Rate Rises—Students Caught With Weapons in School Set Record in Upper, Central Bucks Areas," *Allentown (PA) Morning Call* (July 24, 1997) at B1.

[7] Sandra Biloon and Marilyn Quinn, "Labor and Management Work Together in Connecticut's Vocational Technical Schools to Create a Safer School Environment," *Public Personnel Management* (Dec. 1, 1996) at 439.

[8] "Lifelines Health Calendar," *Florida Today* (Sept. 3, 1996) at 4D.

[9] Elaine McShulskis, "Workplace Anger, A Growing Problem," *HRMagazine* (Dec. 1, 1996) at 16.

[10] "Be an Explosives Expert—Managing Your Anger on the Job," *Men's Health* (Dec. 1, 1995) at 44.

[11] J. Carol Stuecker, "Employers Can Act to Check Workers' Anger," *Business First of Louisville* (May 26, 1997) at 36.

[12] Heesun Wee, "Conquering Road Rage; From Exercise Tapes to Anger Management, Experts Offer Tips on Beating Freeway Stress," *Los Angeles Daily News* (Nov. 17, 1997) at L3.

[13] Yong Tam Kui, "Alcoholism, A Hidden Problem in Malaysia," *The New Straits Times* (Nov. 23, 1997) at 12.

[14] Jill Hudson, "Summer Basketball Courts Young Men; Night Practice, Games Provide Energy Outlet and Food for Thought," *The Baltimore Sun* (July 17, 1997) at 1B.

[15] John McCormick and Sharon Begley, "How to Raise a Tiger," *Newsweek* (Dec. 9, 1996) at 52.

[16] A. D. Abernathy and C. Cox, "Anger Management Training for Law Enforcement Personnel," *Journal of Criminal Justice* (1994) at 459.

[17] Virginia Mullery, "Township's Heart Kept Beating: Patricia Jones Carries on a Tradition of Helping Those in Need," *Chicago Tribune* (July 20, 1997) at 1.

[18] Cynthia Eagles, "Violence at Work Plagues Couple for the Second Time: Husband Attacked 4 Years After Wife Shot," *Courier-Journal* (Louisville, KY) (July 3, 1997) at 3B.

[19] Dan Gunderson, "Weekend Edition," *Minnesota Public Radio* (Nov. 9, 1997), reporting on the emotional aftermath of North Dakota floods.

[20] Wayne M. Sotile and Mary Owen Sotile, "Managing Yourself While Managing Others," *Physician Executive* (Sept. 1, 1996) at 39.

[21] Kassinove and Sukhodolsky, *Anger Disorders, supra,* at 19.

[22] *Id.*

[23] Tina Daunt, "A Look Ahead: By Sending Home Less Risky Inmates and Tracking Them With Electronic Bracelets, the County Plans on Easing Jail Crowding and . . . Keeping the Dangerous Behind Bars," *Los Angeles Times* (July 28, 1997) at B1.

[24] Maya Blackmun, "Domestic Disputes Can Unleash Frightening Rage, Experts Say," *Portland Oregonian* (July 18, 1997) at A21.

[25] "Colorado's New Laws," *The Gazette* (Colorado Springs) (July 1, 1997) at A9.

[26] Brigitte Greenberg, "Novel Prison Program Tries to Cut Inmates' Gang Ties: A 12-Step Approach That Treats Affiliations Like an Addiction Appears to Find Success in Connecticut—Other States Watch Closely," *Los Angeles Times* (June 29, 1997) at A25.

[27] Michael J. Berlin, "Portland-Area Traffic Officials See Rise in Local Road Rage," *Portland Oregonian* (July 23, 1997) at A13.

[28] "Idaho Gets $600,000 to Assist Prisoners," *Portland Oregonian,* October 19, 1997.

[29] James Miller, assistant regional chief, Region 4, Wisconsin Department of Corrections, telephone interview, October 27, 1997.

[30] Cognitive behavioral therapy assumes that a person's thoughts, interpretations, and self-statements about external events strongly influence emotional and behavioral functioning. The goal in treatment is to identify and challenge irrational and distorted thinking patterns and to develop more adaptive beliefs. See,

e.g., *Anger Disorders, supra*, at 113.

31 Paul Gendreau, *The Principles of Effective Intervention With Offenders*, paper presented for the International Association of Residential and Community Alternatives "What Works in Community Corrections: A Consensus Conference," Philadelphia, PA, November 3–6, 1993.

32 Kassinove and Eckhardt, "An Anger Model and a Look to the Future,"*Anger Disorders, supra*, at 203.

33 A. Ellis, foreword to *Anger Disorders, supra*, at xii.

34 Kassinove and Sukhodolsky, *Anger Disorders, supra*, at 12.

35 *Id.*

36 Eric T. Gortner et al., "Psychological Aspects of Perpetrators of Domestic Violence and Their Relationships With the Victims," *The Psychiatric Clinics of North America: Anger Aggression, and Violence*, Maurizio Fava, ed., 337 at 341 (June 1997).

37 Angela Scarpa and Adrian Raine, *supra*, at 383–384.

38 *Id.* at 384–386. The authors note that possible biologic pathways to antisocial or aggressive behavior involve areas of the brain associated with inhibiting response to punishment that are mediated by the septo-hippocampal region and with activating behavior in response to reward or to escape punishment that is mediated by the limbic system. Levels of the stress hormone cortisol (used to measure emotional arousal) were found to be lower in habitually violent offenders and aggressive children, yet higher in violent alcoholics. Results are inconclusive as to the role of cortisol in emotional aggression.

39 Sergei V. Tsytsarev and Gustavo R. Grodnitsky, "Anger and Criminality," *Anger Disorders, supra*, at 93.

40 *Felony Arrests: Their Prosecution and Disposition in New York City's Courts* (Vera Institute of Justice), Longman (1981) at 135.

41 Tsytsarev and Grodnitsky, *supra*, citing Averill, 1983.

42 Malcolm Feeley, foreword to *Felony Arrests: Their Prosecution and Disposition in New York City's Courts* (Vera Institute of Justice), Longman (1981) at xii.

43 *Id.*

44 *Id.* at 93, citing a series of surveys by Averill, and *Anger Disorders, supra*, at 83.

45 *Id.*

46 *Id.*

47 *Id.* at 95.

48 *Id.*

49 Eric T. Gortner, *supra*, at 343.

50 Tsytsarev and Grodnitzky, *supra*, at 100.

51 Edward W. Gondolf and David Russell, "The Case Against Anger Control Treatment Programs for Batterers," *Response*, vol. 9, no. 3 (1986) at 1.

52 *Controlling Anger—Before It Controls You*, American Psychological Association.

53 Gondolf and Russell, *supra*, at 2.

54 Richard Althouse, *Anger Management Program*, Oakhill Correctional Institution Psychological Services program materials (August 1997).

55 *Id.*

56 James A. Gondles, Jr., executive director, American Correctional Association, foreword to *Cage Your Rage: An Inmate's Guide to Anger Control*, American Correctional Association (1992).

57 Oakhill is a minimum security correctional facility located a few miles from Madison.

58 Richard Althouse, *Oakhill Psychological Services Anger Management Program*

Outline (undated).

[59] Richard Althouse, interview at Oakhill Correctional Institution, July 24, 1997, and telephone interview, August 13, 1997.

[60] Richard Althouse, telephone interview, November 18, 1997.

[61] Richard Althouse, *Anger Management Program Summary Evaluation Sheet, OCI Clinical Services* (June/July 1996).

[62] Comments from summary of evaluation sheets, July–September 1997, on file with Dr. Althouse.

[63] Telephone interview with Michelle Rose, DOC field supervisor (July 9, 1997).

[64] *Twelve-Week Program Agenda and Introduction to ART*, Attic Correctional Services, Inc. (undated, copy on file with author).

[65] Nancy Gustaf, director, Deferred Prosecution Program, telephone interview, August 25, 1997.

[66] Mark Seymour, co-director, H & S Counseling, telephone interview, August 26, 1997.

[67] Lyndell Rubin, intake coordinator, Family Services, telephone interview, August 26, 1997.

[68] *Id.*

[69] Nancy Gustaf, *supra.*

[70] Eric T. Gortner, *supra*, at 341.

[71] Darald Hanusa, Ph.D., telephone interview, July 17, 1997. Dr. Hanusa has developed a model treatment plan for abusive men, Alternative Treatment for Abusive Men (ATAM). He also is concerned that some programs for batterers are deficient because they are too short, asserting that to be effective, programs should span a minimum of 24 weeks.

[72] Mark Seymour, telephone interview, August 26, 1997.

[73] *Do You Have a Healthy Lifestyle?*, H & S Domestic Violence Counseling, undated informational brochure.

[74] *Id.*

[75] Gondolf and Russell, *supra*, at 3.

[76] *Id.*, citing a study by Gondolf and Hanneken.

[77] Gondolf and Russell, *supra*, at 3, 4. Gondolf and Russell suggest that resocialization programs such as RAVEN and theme-centered discussion programs such as Second Step and accountability workshops are better alternatives that help batterers end abuse while avoiding the shortcomings of anger management treatment.

[78] Eddy and Myers, 1984.

[79] Jerry L. Deffenbacher, "Ideal Treatment Package for Adults with Anger Disorders," *Anger Disorders, supra*, at 152.

[80] Leonard W. Leeman et al., "Evaluation of a Multi-Component Group Treatment Program for Juvenile Delinquents," *19 Aggressive Behavior 281* (Nov. 1993).

[81] Larry L. Smith et al., "Research Note: An Anger-Management Workshop for Women Inmates," *75 Families in Society 172* (March 1994).

[82] Paul M. Valliant and Lynne M. Raven, "Management of Anger and Its Effect on Incarcerated Assaultive and Nonassaultive Offenders," *75 Psychological Reports 275* (August 1994).

[83] Michael L. Hammer, *Research on the Effectiveness of Anger Management Programs /Interventions*, paper prepared for Wisconsin DOC (1995).

[84] Hammer cites studies by Gaertner (1984); Macphearson (1986); McDougall & Boddis (1991); Napolitano & Brown (1991); Napolitano (1992); Kennedy (1992); Hunter (1993); Smith & Beckner (1993); and Valiant & Raven (1994).

[85] Studies cited include Cahn (1989); Faulkner et al. (1992); Flournoy (1993); Gelb (1994); Larsen (1988); and Scales (1995).

[86] Hammer cites studies by Deschner & McNeil 11986); Bridge (1988); Deschner, McNeil, & Moore (1986).

[87] Hammer cites studies by Lindquist, Telch, & Taylor (1983); Gondolf & Russell (1986); Gondolf (1988a, 1988b); Serin & Kuriychuk (1994).

[88] Hammer cites Potter-Efron (1991).

[89] Hammer cites Gembora (1986); McDougall & Boddis (1991).

[90] Gloria Thomas, attorney and auditor, Office of Audits, Investigations and Evaluation, Wisconsin Department of Corrections, telephone interview, August 20, 1997.

[91] Joseph D. Lehman, secretary, Washington State Department of Corrections, interview, September 12, 1997, Madison, Wisconsin.

[92] Edwin I. Megargee, "Assessment Research in Correctional Settings: Methodological Issues and Practical Problems," *7 Psychological Assessment 359* (1995).

[93] *Id.* at 365, citing studies by Dahlstrom, Panton, Bain, & Dahlstrom (1986).

[94] *Program Plan: Anger Management Program*, Colorado Department of Corrections (September 12, 1994), updated packet of materials marked "Property of NIC Information Center," dated January 17, 1996.

[95] *Anger Management Research Project*, Colorado State Penitentiary, Department of Corrections (September 16, 1994).

21

Conflict Resolution
A Primer for Correctional Workers

Chester E. Sigafoos

Resolution of potentially volatile situations is a primary ingredient in the successful management of inmates. Often, correctional staff are faced with verbally assaultive, intimidating inmates. These inmates may be directing their assaults at each other, or at staff. It is not always necessary for staff to resolve less severe conflicts by writing incident reports, or by physically overpowering the inmate. If such tactics are used, they serve to undermine the relationship staff have with inmates in three ways:

- They establish a pattern of interaction between staff and inmates that heightens tension.

- They provide examples of behavior that other inmates may then decide to use on staff.

- They reinforce the self-fulfilling prophecy some staff may have about inmates—that the only way one can handle them is with force.

Conflict resolution is a method of dealing with anyone whose behavioral and verbal actions indicate he or she is in a state of belligerence. It can be a particularly useful strategy for correctional officers to use in their daily contact with inmates. For example, each day prison staff may encounter inmates whose physical behavior may show them to be agitated, excited, or nervous. Other conflictive inmates may stand firmly, defying staff to come close to them. Their verbal actions may include talking more loudly than normal. They

Source: *Federal Prisons Journal*, 3(2) (Fall 1992): 17–23.

may shout and speak more quickly, running their words together in an unintelligible jumble of syllables.

Imagine this situation: an inmate stands firm, leaning slightly towards you; he points his finger at you while he places his other hand on his hip. He talks louder and faster than normal, slurring his speech at times, possibly even hitting you with saliva as he barks out his thoughts. What would you do in this case? What would you say? There are no textbook answers to how you should respond or what you should say when confronted with this or any other conflict situation. Each situation is different. What upsets one inmate may not upset another. People sometimes "wake up on the wrong side of bed," and are irritated by normal daily routines of life. Even though the contents of the inmate's "message" are different, what is the same about conflict situations is their context.

Most conflict situations share common elements: a heightened state of agitation, a changed facial expression, and a charged mode of speech. By examining these common elements, we can establish some basic guidelines by which conflictive inmates can be handled.

Keep "Fight or Flight" Response in Check

Let's examine the conflict situation more closely. For every action there is a reaction, and nothing could be truer than when you're faced with a conflict situation. Before you can even think of what to say, your body will react. Depending on your experience and the level of hostility directed to you, you may find yourself going to the extreme reaction of "fight or flight." In the "fight or flight" response, your body secretes hormones that prepare it to defend itself. This is a natural response when the body feels threatened, but it doesn't help solve the conflict and will probably make it worse. Although it's difficult, we need to try and temper our bodies' immediate reactions to a conflict situation. Put the response in a holding pattern. (Be happy it's there, for you may need it if the inmate goes completely "off" on you.)

Try to maintain a calm, defensive posture. If you assume a hostile, aggressive stance, this may only stimulate the already agitated inmate into a more aggressive mode. Assuming a posture that is calm (but not relaxed) and firm (but not too hard) sets the tone for conflict resolution. Your body language is just as important as your voice for sending a message.

Other inmates may be watching you. They may not be able to hear what you say, but they can see how you look. The image you project will send a message. You need to maintain a defensive posture because the inmate may try to assault you. A mentally disturbed inmate may have difficulty relating to what you say. You may think you're communicating with him when suddenly he swings at you. Standing in a good defensive posture, with your body partially to the side, will give you an edge in countering an attack. If an assault takes place, you'll be in a better position to bring the inmate under control.

So far, you've been confronted with a hostile inmate, your body has reacted, you keep the reaction in check, and you place yourself in a calm, defensive posture. You haven't said a word yet. What should you say? Should you listen or speak? Should you gain the upper hand immediately, or let the inmate "get it off his chest?" Is the inmate angry at you, or at someone or something else? Do you take this personally, or do you need to remind yourself that this particular inmate often acts this way?

Listen and Assess the Situation

In many conflict situations we find that we say something before we think about it. You are already in your calm, defensive posture. So what's your hurry? Instead of talking or yelling back at the inmate, count to five. Give yourself time to hear what he's saying. One of the most frequent complaints you'll hear from inmates is that no one listens to them. They develop a belief that what they say "falls on deaf ears." The inmate may be yelling just because he believes no one will listen. The answer to resolving this conflict, then, is to listen. Some inmates need to "unload" on someone. They vent their frustration and anger in a matter of minutes and then feel better.

Heitler (1990), in her book *From Conflict to Resolution*, presents a useful concept—the "expression of initial positions"; that is, what each side says at the beginning of the conflict resolution process. Listening is a very important component of this phase. A good listener is an active listener. Good listeners focus on what the speaker is saying. This is crucial to assessing the inmate. Is the speaker talking coherently? If not, the inmate may be under the influence of drugs or alcohol, or suffering from a serious mental disturbance. The only way you would know this is by listening. You would handle this inmate differently from one who is coherent but also agitated. If you started arguing immediately with the inmate, he might shut up, and thus deprive you of information necessary to your assessment.

Even though you may not agree with the conflictive inmate, now is not the time to argue with him. Listen to his story; don't criticize or try to demonstrate your superior knowledge. Listening doesn't mean you agree with him, it just means you've heard him.

An active listener also provides feedback to the speaker. This feedback can be both verbal and nonverbal. Nonverbal feedback includes nodding the head at appropriate times, maintaining eye contact with the speaker (not necessarily staring at him or looking through him), and, if appropriate, leaning toward the speaker (but maintaining your defensive posture).

Verbal feedback tells the speaker he's being heard and can be simple utterances like "uh huh," "yes," "I see." If the inmate says something you don't understand, perhaps because he's speaking so fast, ask him to clarify what he means. Some people are afraid to interrupt an agitated person for fear they'll "set them off." Asking the speaker for clarification shows that you are listening. Convey the message that what the speaker is saying is important, and you want to be sure you clearly understand.

In addition, when you ask someone to clarify what he's said, his reaction will usually be to talk slower and more distinctly. Have you ever heard yourself give directions to a foreign visitor? You talk much slower, make your sentences simpler, and enunciate more clearly. This is what happens when you ask a conflictive inmate to clarify what he's said. This sets a different pace of speech and tone of delivery. Instead of rambling and screaming, the inmate needs to slow down and temper his words. Many times this tactic will be sufficient to reduce the hostility level.

A second element of the assessment phase is the role of *equal time sharing*. This aspect needs to be examined more closely because of the different dynamics operating in the correctional setting. When you're dealing with a hostile inmate, he'll want to dominate the interaction by talking louder and longer. The normal staff-inmate "distribution of power"—who has control of the situation—favors the staff member. Staff become used to being in control and comfortable with a distribution of power in which the inmate is subordinate.

This "normal" asymmetry of power becomes disrupted in a conflict situation. The normally subordinate inmate acts as though he has become dominant and the staff subordinate. Staff need to be aware that power relationships frequently vary. Generally, staff dominate interactions with inmates, but that domination may be 51 percent on one occasion and 80 percent on another. The important thing to remember is that even if the inmate acquires 51 percent of the power in an interaction, eventually the power will shift back to normal levels.

Thus, if the staff member perceives that the inmate is shifting the power dimension, he or she needs to be reassured that this may only be an illusion. Just because the inmate is talking louder, faster, or longer doesn't necessarily mean the staff member has lost power in the relationship. The staff member needs to stand firm and self-confident. By doing this, the staff member holds on to the power base, which will return to its normal, asymmetrical nature once the conflict has been resolved.

In society, daily interactions between people are also characterized by fluctuations in the power dimension. Asymetrical relations (boss and subordinate, for example), if accepted by the participants, are usually satisfactory. Healthy relationships among friends and family, however, are characterized by symmetrical power dimensions. In these, friends maintain a balance of power, thereby allowing give and take in the relationship and the mutual satisfaction of each friend's needs.

When power relationships in corrections become symmetrical, a different problem arises. Allowing a relationship between staff member and inmate to become balanced may scare some staff members. They may fear that they will not be able to regain control of the situation once the inmate dominates the interaction.

We need to recognize that by giving an inmate time to yell and scream, we are not losing power. In fact, what we are doing is maintaining control over the situation, since it is "we" who are allowing the inmate to speak. All inmates do not thoroughly think through what has caused their conflicts. Letting them talk may give them the first opportunity to actually hear what they've been thinking. Sometimes, after they've heard themselves, they recognize the flaws in their thinking, and resolve the conflict themselves.

But in other instances, the inmate's logic may not be flawed. Allowing symmetry in the relationship opens the way for the exchange of information. Symmetrical relationships mean that each person has equal time to present a point of view. Some inmates don't want to allow staff equal time. The egotistical nature of the antisocial personality wants only to hear itself. These types of inmates have always had difficulties in social interactions. They don't have the ability to "decenter," or see things from another person's point of view.

Identification of the antisocial inmate can be accomplished with experience during the assessment phase of conflict resolution. If you find that the inmate yelling and screaming at you is not receptive to an even exchange of information, consider another course of action. In some situations, walking away—while saying something like "I'll come back when you're calmer"—is a possible alternative. The presence of the staff member creates a "target" or stimulus for the inmate. If that stimulus is not there, the inmate may not respond anymore. This is not to suggest that the inmate will not be dealt with. The staff member can always return to the inmate at a later time, hopefully after he has calmed down.

In most conflict situations needing resolution, however, the staff member will not have the option of walking away.

Summarize Your Initial Positions

So what do you say to the agitated inmate? Ask him if you can say something. Asking permission to speak when confronted with a hostile inmate is like throwing a curve ball when the batter expects a fast ball. Inmates are seldom asked their permission, they are usually told what do to. Some staff may balk at the idea of asking an inmate's permission to speak. But remember, this technique allows you to maintain control of the situation.

You will accomplish several things by asking permission to speak. You'll find out if he's finished talking. If he's not, he will probably tell you so. In this way you're letting him know you want to speak, but will allow him time to finish. This will set the stage for a symmetrical interaction—I'll let you speak, then you let me speak. More importantly, you will be showing respect. You'll be giving him the message that what he says is important, and you don't want to interrupt.

When the inmate indicates he is finished speaking, you're on. The delivery of your message is as important as the content. If you've just listened to a hostile, screaming inmate, you've had an excellent example of how not to talk. Speak in a clear, direct manner—loud enough to be heard, but soft enough that the inmate has to work a little to hear you. This will force him to redirect his attention from shouting and screaming to push his message out, to processing incoming information instead.

Deliver your message at a slower than normal pace. Talking rapidly to a conflictive inmate will only exacerbate his anxiety. In fact, he's liable to model your behavior and increase his talking speed. Talking slower will hopefully set a precedent.

Do not criticize, ridicule, or make fun of what the inmate said. Some staff may think the inmate's actions are a "put on." But making a joke out of what he's said will only add fuel to the fire. It's important to speak in a professional, business-like manner. Some staff successfully use humor when dealing with a conflictive inmate. This can be risky. It is wiser to use a technique you're safe with than one that could backfire.

It is important to convey that you recognize the need to listen to different points of view. You are taking the time because it is important for you to offer your thoughts in an effort to help resolve the conflict.

Feedback is a way to offer verbal information to the conflictive inmate. For example, if you respond to the inmate, saying "yes, but . . .", this does not show cooperation. The "but" is an indication that the inmate is wrong and you are right. Changing the word to "and", as in "yes, and . . .", creates a different atmosphere: "Now we can cooperate in resolving this conflict."

If we put this all together, we should end up with an atmosphere in which both participants have an equal opportunity to express their points of view. The conflictive inmate may have started out in a hostile, agitated manner, but through the use of controlled speech patterns, the staff member is able to set a tone that will promote the sharing of information.

By summarizing the initial positions, you tell the inmate you've heard what he's said. In return, and in a symmetrical fashion, the inmate has heard your point of view. This does not say that either point of view is right, just that we know where each stands. From this, a working relationship can be developed to find solutions to the conflict. Studies of interactions between people have shown how working toward a common goal enhances the relationship between enemies. This does not suggest that a staff member be "buddy-buddy" with an inmate. But it is important for staff to have positive relationships with inmates.

The goal of conflict resolution is to obtain a "win-win" situation. If one side is not allowed to present its position, we end up with "win-lose." The inmate loses by being locked up after not being allowed to talk, or the staff loses by fueling inmate animosity.

During the presentation of initial positions, each participant states what he wants. It is difficult to develop a path to a goal if neither side knows what goal is being sought. Some goals can never be attained—for example, if the inmate says his goal is to get out of prison "right now!" Other goals may be more logical.

Take the example of the inmate who is furious, upset, and "not going to take it any longer." He's been held in the reception unit, living with two other inmates, for the past 3 weeks, waiting for bedspace in the housing unit. We know what his goal is, but what about your goal? Is ensuring a safe environment for the inmates all there is to it?

Read between the Lines

The next phase involves an examination of the initial positions, and the "true" underlying reasons for those positions. One of the most difficult jobs a staff member has is being able to decipher what some inmates mean. Inmates can be experts at concealing the truth. They've been rewarded for it in the past. But one of the drawbacks of being good at deception is that sometimes you don't know what the truth is anymore. When this happens, inmates may not know why they are so upset. This makes the job of resolving the conflict more difficult.

Another source of false information could be staff members if, instead of being active listeners, they just listened to their own thoughts, focused on what they thought they heard was wrong, or began to overinterpret the inmate's position.

Exploring underlying concerns requires the participants to shift their focus. At this time, the staff member could move the discussion to other surroundings. Inmates will "front" a staff member, given the opportunity—that is, they will attempt to embarrass or upset a staff member in front of other inmates. Resolving conflict situations in front of other inmates creates additional problems. First, the inmate wants to continue to be seen as dominant. If the staff member can convince the inmate to move to another location, he or she also removes the inmate from his source of support.

Second, the onset of the conflict may have occurred in the inmate's room, or some other familiar surrounding. Removing the inmate from this surrounding creates an advantage for staff. The staff member also wants to be in familiar surroundings, thereby gaining a nonverbal edge over the inmate. Further, the initial surroundings have been linked to the onset of the conflict. Staying there may only keep the memory of the initial confrontation fresh.

Third, the staff member has reached a point with the inmate in which a mutual relationship exists. They are now in a state of cooperation rather than confrontation. It becomes easier for both to cooperate if they work in a more private setting. Some inmates may object to a staff member's suggestion of going to "their" office. This could be seen as a sign of weakness or defeat in the inmate. If that's the case, agree upon a neutral spot. When choosing the location, privacy needs to be weighed against security. You are not out of the woods yet. The inmate may have calmed down, but could be doing so in an effort to assault you when you least expect it. Sometimes walking around the compound provides all the privacy you need.

In this stage a mutual effort is undertaken with the goal of resolving the conflict. Prior to this, the atmosphere was oppositional, the perspectives were narrow, and the focus was on "I." Now the focus should be on looking at the broader picture. Change the pronoun in your sentences from "I" to "We." This establishes a new mindset in which the staff member is no longer the enemy, and the inmate is no longer the subordinate. Now you are working together to resolve the issue.

Examining underlying concerns begins with a restatement of the initial positions. Time has now passed, and the inmate may be in a clearer frame of mind. Ask the inmate to restate his position. Follow with a restatement of your position. In the example of the inmate demanding a housing unit change, the inmate now states, "I don't feel comfortable living in there." This is not the same initial position. The initial position was a demand to be moved. Now, he doesn't "feel comfortable." Why the change?

A change from the initial position may take place for several reasons. The inmate or staff member may have gained some insight into the problem, making the true reason for the conflict easier to understand. Conversely, the passage of time may create second thoughts, and the true reason may have moved farther away.

Some inmates are able to be honest with themselves and with others. For these inmates, conflict resolution will probably end up in win-win situations. For others, the ability to be honest with themselves has long been distorted and flawed. As a staff member, you may not be interested whether an inmate is being honest with himself. But at this phase of conflict resolution, your ability to accept the inmate, and show a nonjudgemental interest in his conflict, is important. Guard against the introduction of any personal bias into the relationship.

Inmates are very sensitive to being questioned. In fact, they are probably experts in the "art" of interrogation and its tactics and techniques. Just a short time ago, this inmate was yelling and screaming. The one thing we didn't want to do was antagonize him, or appear hostile or offensive. Now we are at a point at which it's necessary to obtain information. We don't want to appear offensive, because if the inmate feels he's being interrogated we're liable to end up where we started.

Here a little role playing may help. Jack Webb, in the television series "Dragnet," was famous for one expression, "just the facts." That's what we're looking for, "just the facts." And we are doing so for the purpose of achieving "our" goal, resolving the conflict.

Information is contained in the mind at various levels. Often, the surface levels do not provide the facts needed to understand underlying concerns. As you delve deeper into the reasons for the conflict, you will need both awareness and a sense of history. You'll need to be aware of how specific things affect this inmate. Why does he "feel uncomfortable"? Is it because the beds are terrible, or does he have back problems? The more you talk, the more history will be uncovered. We all have a personal history, which influences what we think about, how we think, and how we react to things.

Earlier, the role of listening was discussed. It is important in this phase too. But the listening you do now will be different. When you listen to deeper concerns, it helps if you "soften" your stance. By this, you seem more compassionate and understanding.

Here's how our hypothetical example might resolve: as you listen to the inmate talking about his problems with his housing situation, you realize something else is bothering him—family problems, perhaps. Or one of his cellmates might be trying to extort something from him. Or perhaps the other inmates in his cell are having a sexual relationship and he is upset by it. You might ask if he's ever had this problem before. There's no need to pry, and he may not want to explain fully, but the more you can talk to him on this level, the likelier you are to discover the true reason for his conflict.

During the dialogue, you have your side to present too. You'll probably want to explain the procedures for housing and the rationale behind the system. Emphasizing the aspect of fairness in placement for all inmates is important. The system isn't designed to benefit one person only. While the inmate focuses on his specific needs, the narrow perspective, the staff focuses on the needs of the institution, the broader perspective. But now you see how one inmate's problem comes in conflict with the system you represent. At this point, you would again summarize each position.

Resolve the Situation through Compromise and Cooperation

The needs of both parties have been identified. Now we must provide options that serve those needs. The generation of alternatives is a group process. Both inmate and staff member need to offer ideas. Brainstorming is most effective when it is unrestricted, free-flowing, and involves more than one person. The goal is to generate as many options as possible.

Once the possible alternatives are listed, a mutually satisfying choice can be made. Of course, the solution may not always be totally satisfactory to each person. In corrections, resolution of the conflict may not mean the inmate gets what he wants. Some needs cannot be satisfied because of policies against the proposed solution, circumstances beyond staff's control, or the irrational nature of the demands. Does this mean that conflict resolution failed? No. Just calming the inmate down, and reducing the volatility of the initial situation, is conflict resolution in itself. The goal of conflict resolution need not be the totally successful resolution of every problem.

A realistic resolution will involve compromise and cooperation. Part of picking the solution involves compromise, the give and take of negotiation. As each person presents alternatives, the pros and cons can be discussed.

Some inmates, no matter how many alternatives you look at, no matter how hard you've tried, will just not be satisfied. These rigid-thinking inmates will continue to have difficulty adjusting to prison life. With these inmates, the staff member can at least say, "I've done the best I can." Most inmates learn to adjust, but there will always be a few who seem to thrive on being miserable—that's their choice.

Implement the Solution

The final step is to review what you've both done and ensure that no unfinished business remains. In the example of the inmate seeking different housing, the staff member was able to move the inmate to a new cell within the reception unit. The inmate wasn't able to move to a housing unit like he wanted. But after the underlying reasons for his distress were revealed, the solution was easier to find.

After a conflict is successfully resolved, the relationship between inmate and staff changes. The asymmetrical nature of the relationship returns, but the quality of the relationship is now different. Inmates and staff who work together learn that with a little patience, listening, and understanding, results can be obtained— maybe not the results the inmate originally wanted, but positive results nonetheless.

Inmates come away from the experience with a different attitude. They have learned that other alternatives exist by which they can change their environment. If resolving the conflict through communication works once, perhaps it will work again. If one inmate finds it works for him, he'll probably tell others. For staff working with inmates, the little bit of time you take today may pay off tomorrow.

Section *VI*

Reality Therapy and Responsibility Training

Reality therapy is based on the principle that an individual must accept responsibility for his or her behavior, and the goal of the reality therapist is to lead the person being treated to act "responsibly."

According to Glasser (1965), the pioneer of the reality therapy concept, those in need of treatment have been unable to meet their own needs because they deny the reality of the world about them (7). Reality therapy seeks to help the one being treated to perceive the world as it really is and to behave in a reasonable, responsible manner in the light of this perception. Glasser defines two basic human needs as the key to human behavior—the need to love and be loved and the need to feel that we are worthwhile to ourselves and to others (9). He regards all irresponsible (socially unacceptable) behavior as caused by the client's inability to fulfill one or both of these needs. Glasser views a close involvement with other humans as essential to the achievement of responsible behavior and the reality therapist is called upon to become personally involved with clients.

Reality therapy differs from other types of therapy in a number of ways. It does not examine the client's past or recognize the existence of mental illness. It views all behavior as conforming to or deviating from the concept of responsible behavior. The concept of morality plays an important role in the therapy, and all acts are defined as being right or wrong. Against this background, the therapist actively instructs the client in ways to become responsible and better fulfill his or her needs.

The use of reality therapy in corrections has a strong appeal for a number of reasons. Since the therapist does not require extensive training and the therapy does not involve complicated terminology, categorizations, or treatment procedures, reality therapy can be implemented by correctional workers who operate on a paraprofessional or volunteer level, as well as by professionals in the field. It follows the basic tenets of common sense and the "golden rule" and does not involve the preparation of detailed case histories, psychological test results, or progress reports.

Critics of reality therapy maintain that it is unrealistic to deny the existence of mental illness and to maintain that any type of Individual, no matter how severe his or her problem behavior has become, can be treated in this manner. As the sole judge of the responsibility or acceptability of the client's behavior, the reality therapist is in a position to guide the behavior of the client without feedback from other professional staff, who might be critical of the manner in which the case is being handled. Finally, the therapist is seen as a strong authority figure who may alienate those whose criminal behavior is a reaction to or rebellion against authority or those who are unable to meet the expectations of authority figures.

In selection 22, "Reality Therapy: Issues and a Review of Research," Bersani reviews the success of the application of reality therapy in such settings as schools, corrections, private practice, state mental hospitals, substance abuse centers, and similar programs. Of particular interest is his finding that reality therapy is utilized in 80 percent of juvenile institutions contacted in a national survey. He also describes the issues and concerns related to the application of reality therapy, including the definition of responsible behavior and the influence of the moral convictions or preconceived notions and prejudices of the counselor in shaping the client's behavior. Acceptance of the counselor's values and judgments uncritically can lead to a client's overdependence on the counselor and inhibit the client's ability to make independent decisions.

The publication of Yochelson and Samenow's book, *The Criminal Personality: A Profile for Change,* in 1976 stimulated interest in the use of cognitive therapies for the treatment of criminal offenders. The authors contended that the one thing all criminals have in common is deviant thinking patterns. They identified fifty-two "errors in thinking" that were manifested by the criminals they studied.

The use of cognitive therapy in corrections focuses on the counselor helping the offender to think better. The application of cognitive therapies to counseling situations can take many forms. Some counseling is very confrontational. The counselor exposes the faulty thinking processes of the offender and challenges him or her to change. The direct effect that faulty thinking has in causing deviant behavior is considered in the therapy. Other forms of cognitive therapy are less confrontational and more instructive in nature.

The theoretical assumption underlying cognitive therapy is that changes in thinking patterns and the acknowledgement of one's errors in thinking will lead to behavior changes. Since many offenders have not developed the basic cognitive skills to even know what appropriate behavior is, the counseling may have to be instructive, that is, it may involve teaching the offender the types of behavior that are needed to function appropriately within society and to avoid being sanctioned. Lester and Van Voorhis (1997) suggest that most forms of cognitive therapy are directed toward cognitive restructuring, which focuses on the content of thinking and emphasizes changing beliefs, values, and attitudes or toward helping the offender improve his/her cognitive skills, with emphasis on improving the thinking process and developing logical, rational, systematic thinking patterns.

In selection 23, "Probation and Cognitive Skills," Chavaria illustrates how cognitive therapy can be applied to probation work. He contends that many offenders are cognitively impaired and thus have low critical reasoning ability. Probation officers can teach the persons they supervise techniques of cognitive skill development and also assist them with developing cognitive behavior strategies.

In selection 24, "Brief Solution-Focused Work: A Strength-Method for Juvenile Justice Practice," Clark explains the brief-solution-focused therapy model and illustrates its use in counseling juvenile offenders and their family members. This treatment model focuses on the strengths of the delinquent and family members rather than on their weaknesses and deficiencies. This approach requires that juveniles and/or parents establish meaningful goals and objectives for themselves. These goals must be achievable and time limited.

References

Glasser, William. 1985. *Reality Therapy.* New York: Harper & Row.

Lester, David and Patricia Van Voorhis. 1997. "Cognitive Therapies," in Patricia Van Voorhis et al., *Correctional Counseling and Rehabilitation*, 3rd ed. Cincinnati: Anderson.

Yochelson, Samuel and Stanton Samenow. 1976. *The Criminal Personality: A Profile For Change.* New York: Jason Aronson.

22

Reality Therapy
Issues and a Review of Research

Carl A. Bersani

Introduction

This introductory section identifies several important characteristics of reality therapy. Reality therapy in action will be discussed in the following section. The primary foci in this section are correctional settings and school settings. A subsequent section identifies a variety of issues and concerns in the application of reality therapy. The concluding section briefly reviews Glasser's recent publications.

For those who work with people with a diverse range of problems, reality therapy has increasingly become the treatment of choice. Its popularity is evident in school settings, in rehabilitation settings, among the clergy, with offenders, and in private practice. Reality therapy offers us a rather simple but clear approach for growth and behavioral change.

Although trained in psychology and psychiatry, William Glasser's disillusionment led him to devise a practical method in the treatment of clients which he labeled reality therapy. The catalysis leading to the creation of this innovative intervention strategy initially took place during his experiences with confined female delinquents. This led to the first paper dealing with reality therapy

This article first appeared in *Correctional Counseling and Treatment*, Second Edition. All rights reserved.

(1964), followed by his exceptionally well received book titled *Reality Therapy* (1965). Reality therapy is distinct from other therapies in a number of ways. We will identify several important distinctions.

Conventional therapy goals do not include client responsibility or personal actions as primary. Rather, the primary thrust of much of our therapeutic strategies is to probe into a client's past thereby gaining insight. Glasser would argue that in the process of continually examining the past in order to understand current behaviors, rationalizations for current behaviors are, unintentionally, given recognition. One of the many distinctions of reality therapy from many other therapies is the treatment focus on the here-and-now. A basic belief of reality therapy, therefore, is that clients refuse to accept responsibility for their current behaviors. Accordingly, reality therapy is designed to enable clients to develop a sense of personal responsibility for their actions and to acquire conscious control over their subsequent behaviors. This process occurs as the reality of their behaviors, their environments, and the consequences of their behavioral choices become known to them. In this therapy, dwelling on unconscious thought processes, feelings, attitudes, and the past are considered self-defeating. Attention is directed instead to the present and into the future. The client-counselor efforts are to explore which current behaviors are self-defeating and what behavioral substitutes better serve the client's needs.

All therapies encounter clients who are depressed, drug addicts, delinquents, spouse abusers and many other categories too numerous to list. However, Glasser is not concerned with the actual symptoms employed by individuals (Ososkie and Turpin, 1985). In describing the central premises of reality therapy Glasser (1965) identifies another basic belief which underlies and begins to unfold a distinction of his therapy from other therapies. He considers that all the symptomatologies expressed by clients signify they are failures because they have not grasped reality and, therefore, their need satisfactions cannot be achieved. Furthermore, they invite failure for they tend to select ineffective behaviors in their striving to meet their needs. In Glasser's (1965) own words:

> . . . all patients have a common characteristic: *they all deny the reality of the world around them.* Some break the law, denying the rules of society; some claim their neighbors are plotting against them, denying the improbability of such behavior. . . . Millions drink to blot out the inadequacy they feel but that need not exist if they could learn to be different: and far too many people choose suicide rather than face the reality that they could solve their problems by more responsible behavior. . . . therapy

will be successful when they are able to give up denying the
world and recognize that reality not only exists but that they
must fulfill their needs within its framework.

What are these needs? For Glasser, the single, most basic
psychological need required by all is the establishment of an
identity (Glasser, 1975). The identity is characterized by success
and self-esteem. Central in achieving a successful identity are the
major psychological routes of loving, being loved and in feeling
worthwhile to oneself and to other people. Most important, the shift
from a failure identity to a successful identity (and eventual changes
in attitudes and beliefs by clients and others) is contingent on
changes in the client's behaviors within meaningful interpersonal
relationships. In effect, behavioral changes by the client induces
behavioral changes in those with whom the client interacts.

Throughout his writings, Glasser continuously reminds us of
another major difference between reality therapy and conventional
therapies. This difference is the type of client-counselor involvement
desired in reality therapy. To varying degrees, conventional
therapists remain impersonal and objective. Other therapies view
involvement—the therapist becoming a separate and important
person in the client's life—as undesirable (Glasser, 1976).

For Glasser, the eventual achievement of involvement (which
reduces isolation and facilitates increased need satisfaction) begins
with a distinctive type of client-counselor relationship that goes
beyond understanding and empathizing with the client. It requires
counselors to share openly their own personal struggles with clients,
to allow their own values to be challenged by clients, and to confront
and challenge clients only when involvement evolves into a special
kind of relationship (Glasser, 1965). One earns trust and the
privilege of confronting and challenging. It is achieved through a
process of involvement where both the counselor and client convey
respect, genuineness, and acceptance of each other as unique
persons. Without this type of involvement, the underpinnings have
not been achieved for a helping process.

Reality Therapy in Action

For over 20 years the helping professions as well as society in
general were witness to the intensification of people problems.
During this period, the limitations of traditional therapeutic
approaches to treatment became apparent. The 1960s to the
present can be characterized as a persistent search for
demonstrably effective and practical models for intervention (Cohen

and Sordo, 1984). Glasser's model of reality therapy and its use in a variety of settings throughout this period is evidence of this search for a practical model of intervention which could be utilized by a wide range of contemporary practitioners.

In the years since the publication of *Reality Therapy* (1965), Glasser's counseling and therapy model has received enthusiastic support and use by highly skilled professionals as well as less skilled workers in service agencies. This popularity is in keeping with Glasser's (1984) statement that the therapy is appropriate to a wide range of behaviors and emotional problems—from mild emotional situations and maladjustments to severe anxieties, perversions and psychoses. Numerous accounts of the successful application of reality therapy with a variety of clientele in diverse settings is evident in the literature (Banmen, 1982a).

Its popularity and application have been reported in settings such as schools, corrections, private practice, state mental hospitals, substance-abuse centers, etc. Two major works convey the successful application of reality therapy by counselors working with a variety of clientele in diverse settings. *The Reality Therapy Reader* (Bassin, Bratter, and Rachin, 1976) brings together accounts of the application of reality therapy in private practice, in education, and in corrections. An edited work by Naomi Glasser (1980) includes two dozen accounts of how reality therapists have worked with a variety of clients. The range of clients helped with reality therapy include: divorced parents, self-destructive adolescents, depressed clients, psychotics who learn to acquire more responsible behavior, clients with severe handicaps, alcoholics, principals helping teachers, and teachers and school counselors helping children (Glasser, N., 1980).

Despite the numerous illustrations mentioned above of the successful application of reality therapy, Banmen (1982b) states that very little formal research evaluating the effectiveness of reality therapy exists. He further states that Glasser and many other reality therapists are increasingly concerned by this lack of formal research. Although reality therapy has not been formally researched in all possible settings and with the full range of potential clients, an examination of the existing limited research could increase our insight regarding the circumstances under which reality therapy appears successful, thereby suggesting promising endeavors and avenues for future research.

In practice, the use of reality therapy is evident in numerous and diverse types of settings. Additionally, general descriptions and testimonies of success by those practitioners utilizing reality therapy are quite apparent in the literature and in conversations with practitioners.

The limited efforts to measure the effects of reality therapy have primarily focused on the correctional and school settings. However, one can offer examples of scattered pieces of research in other settings. Browne and Ritter (1972) selected reality therapy for 16 of the most regressed patients at a V.A. hospital containing 190 psychiatric, medically infirm patients in geriatric wards as a pilot effort. Patients in these wards were diagnosed as long-term, chronic schizophrenics. With the exception of one patient, all achieved personal pride and improved sufficiently in self-care, social abilities, and personal relations making them eligible to be placed in facilities outside the hospital. One study (Zaph, 1974) researched the effects of the use of reality therapy in the community to enhance the personal growth of retarded adult women. Indications of personal growth were measured by improvements in minimum behavioral standards and in goal achievements. Success was achieved on some of these measures.

Another study used reality therapy in efforts to free 65 addicts who were in a methadone dependence program (Raubolt and Bratter, 1976). After one year, significant results in detoxification (remaining drug free, being employed, and no arrests) were achieved.

Correctional Settings

Reality therapy has many supporters among counselors. Its greatest impact appears to be in correctional settings. Vinter (1976) indicates that reality therapy is utilized in 80 percent of the juvenile institutions which were studied in a national survey. It is not known whether the use of this therapy is widespread because it fits the reality as staff understand it or because of the assumption that highly trained professionals are unnecessary in the use of this therapy. Despite its popularity and extensive use in corrections, only a small amount of formal research has been done on reality therapy.

Practitioners have frequently stated that offenders who are alienated by conventional treatment methods respond positively to reality therapy. Using reality therapy in a prison with a group of 43 inmates for 15 weeks, Williams (1976) supports this general impression. All participants found reality therapy to be at least somewhat helpful with 80 percent rating the program as very helpful to them. Many of these inmates felt that reality therapy helped them to take a more realistic and responsible outlook on life in general and prison in particular. Furthermore, none of these inmates received a disciplinary report during the 15 weeks of the program. Williams concludes that reality therapy works because its strengths coincide with many of the weaknesses of incarcerated offenders. One such connection identified by Williams is: "Where many inmates tend to live in a fantasy world of—'if onlys,' reality therapy focuses on the way life is."

One serious problem facing staff is the unrealistic vocational goals of inmates. Prior to release, many inmates avoid facing reality or pursuing a responsible course of action. A main ingredient of the Maryland Comprehensive Offender Model Program was testing and assessing in order to evaluate training or employment possibilities. Since one goal of this program was to get inmates to face reality and assume responsibility in being available for work possibilities, individual and group counseling were based on the reality therapy model. Within a one-year period 2,795 inmates were in the program; 2,170 of them were released from institutions and available for work. At the time of this report, half of those placed in jobs were self-placements. Bennight (1975) concludes that overall placement of these males exceeded normal placement by applicants who did not have the multiple barriers to employment characteristic of these males.

The research by Falker (1982), German (1975) and Molstad (1981) studied behavioral change. The Magdala Halfway House in St. Louis changed to reality therapy as its primary treatment modality. This facility handles 70 young, adult male offenders per year. Falker (1982) states that previous attempts by staff to control and change the behaviors of residents through positive and negative reinforcements were futile. The reality therapy approach was used to allow both staff and residents an opportunity to examine and evaluate their behaviors.

Among the principles of reality therapy stressed was teaching residents to plan better behaviors when their current behaviors were not fulfilling. Unable to control residents by use of punishment, staff opened new lines of communication leading to cooperative behaviors that fulfilled needs of both workers and residents. For example, "can do—let's try" atmosphere of conciliation along with rules generated by the common group to benefit both staff and clients almost eliminated negativism and various forms of hostile behaviors. Such problems at one time were the norm. Falker found that within a three-year period dramatic reductions by residents in absconding and in terminations occurred, and a significant increase occurred in residents who were successfully released. Successful release meant release to the community with a job, in training, or in school.

Glasser (1965) initially established reality therapy principles within the Ventura School for Girls in California. Considering their prior juvenile history, the Ventura School was the last stop prior to being committed to an adult prison. Of the 370 girls released on parole, only 43 violated parole. German (1975) investigated the effects of group reality therapy on juvenile inmates and staff leaders of the therapy groups. As a consequence of systematic exposure to the principles of reality therapy during group therapy sessions, it was expected that changes in certain behaviors, self-esteem, etc. would occur. German found that the experimental group viewed themselves and were viewed by their teachers as more responsible, more mature, and more acceptable persons. However, self-esteem did not increase. They did exhibit significantly fewer behaviors in the dormitory which required disciplinary action compared to the control group. It was also hypothesized that since staff leaders of the group therapy sessions were exposed to the inmates within a transactional environment, they would change their perceptions of people in general. German's findings indicated that staff leaders changed by viewing people as more positive, complex, and changeable.

Molstad (1981) assumed a position with a residential treatment facility for emotionally disturbed adolescents which had experienced close to total staff turnover. Runaways occurred almost daily; vandalism, theft, fist fights, and other aggressive behaviors were common. Treatment intervention had been based on the Transactional Analysis model. Molstad indicates the new staff felt that TA was too cognitive for these adolescents to understand.

Social workers were given intensive training in reality therapy, and the entire staff (cooks, janitors, etc.) was given a working knowledge of the approach (Molstad, 1981). For the inmates, individual, group, and family therapy were also based on the principles of reality therapy. As long as they remained in keeping with reality therapy principles, policies for each treatment unit were formulated with input from residents. Such involvement (i.e., deciding on rules, tasks, and consequences) increased the likelihood of adhering to the rules. The weekly individual sessions centered on the present, evaluating behavior, developing problem-solving techniques, developing relationships, formalizing resident plans, and developing increased resident responsibility. Daily group reality therapy sessions dealt with school problems, peer problems, family difficulties, problems in the facility, future planning, etc. Each family also experienced group reality therapy sessions. Changes in family relationships, activities, and types of interaction were common areas for discussion. Actual discharge was based on increased level of responsibility in the institution, within the family, within the school setting, and the local community.

Molstad found that behavior in the facility improved greatly when discharge responsibility was turned over to the residents. These adolescents viewed the program more seriously and worked harder toward the goal of discharge. Since accountability was stressed at both the individual and group levels, disruptive behavior and vandalism decreased quickly and drastically.

For the effects of reality therapy on the self-concept of alienated, unmotivated, drug abusing adolescents, see Brown and Kingley (1973). See Thatcher (1983) for a before and after design and a within-group comparison of the effects (for group home delinquents trained in the concepts and practices of reality therapy) on self-concept and locus of control.

There does exist a literature on the use of restitution which we will not review here. Although restitution is clearly grounded on the ideas of reality therapy, the research is not formally structured to examine reality therapy. For a discussion of how reality therapy ideas can be operationalized in traditional restitution programs, see Matthews (1979). Therapists may be especially interested in Lackman's (1986) proposal and operationalization of the behavior equivalent (undoing) to traditional restitution using the steps of reality therapy.

School Settings

The ideas of reality therapy have direct implications in school settings. Glasser first became concerned not only about behavior but also learning, since virtually all the girls at the Ventura School for Girls experienced a history of school failure (Corey, 1977). In his book *Schools Without Failure* (Glasser, 1969), he proposed a program to eliminate failure and other school related problems.

A major problem expressed by teachers in achieving an atmosphere for learning is the issue of serious behavioral problems in the classroom. Several studies have examined the application of reality therapy to classroom discipline problems. Gang (1976) selected two 4th and 5th grade teachers for training in the principles and methods of reality therapy. Each teacher selected three male students whom they considered to be serious behavior problems. Each teacher was trained in reality therapy by the researcher and through participation in a system-wide training program conducted by an associate from Glasser's Educator Training Center. Each teacher met with the researcher at least two times a week and the researcher observed each teacher at least three times a week and provided feedback. Also, trained observers monitored each student in the classroom environment, three times a week, with observations recorded in ten-second intervals.

Gang's study was divided into four phases:

Baseline: In this phase, teachers continued their natural teaching practices in the classroom. This determined where each of the six target students were in relation to the rated behaviors before the beginning of the intervention strategy.

Initial Involvement Intervention: In this phase, teachers were instructed to give each student 15 to 20 seconds of special, personal attention. This was to occur at least three times during each class period. The purpose of this was to develop an ongoing, personal relationship between teacher and student.

Varied Intervention: The teacher continued to give personal attention during this phase, but three modified reality therapy conditions were also used. In the first condition, the teacher responded only to the student's undesirable behavior by following those steps of reality therapy which ask four questions. During the second condition, the teacher responded only to desirable behavior and would follow the steps of reality therapy. In the third condition, the teacher responded to both desirable and undesirable behaviors and followed the steps of reality therapy.

Follow-up: At the conclusion of the intervention phase, trained observers continued recording classroom behavior to determine the durability of any student behavior changes that had occurred as a result of the intervention treatments.

Gang reports that the results clearly supported reality therapy as a solution for those identified as serious behavior problems. For all the target students, a highly significant decrease in the frequency of undesirable behavior occurred; a highly significant increase in the frequency of desirable behavior occurred over baseline conditions during the treatment and follow-up phases of the study. Both teachers felt the establishment of an ongoing, genuine relationship—an outcome of the plan—accounted for the successful outcomes.

The Thompson and Cates (1976) study is similar in goal and method to the Gang (1976) study. Six female elementary teachers each selected the student representing the most difficult discipline problem—a student they would most like to have absent from the school setting. Each teacher received training in a ten-step plan developed by Glasser for teaching discipline to students. The ten-step plan can be divided into three categories. First is the involvement stage. Among other things, it required teachers to stop using unhelpful behaviors and to reinforce helpful behaviors. The counseling stage required teachers to counsel students using the reality therapy process including a written contract with students that outlines a plan for changing behavior. The time-out stage includes logical consequences for misbehavior as well as written plans for correcting misbehaviors. The phases of this study and the method of monitoring/analysis were very similar to the Gang (1976) study. As in the previous study, all six students achieved significant increases in appropriate behavior and decreases in inappropriate behavior during the treatment stage compared to the baseline stage. The two studies taken together appear to support reality therapy as a tool for behavior change. Large gains in appropriate student behavior were achieved through a modest amount of positive behavioral changes on the part of teachers. For the effectiveness of reality therapy on discipline and behavior problems using an experimental and control design, see Matthews (1973).

The primary purpose of the study by Dakoske (1977) was to explore not only the short-term but also the long-term effects of reality therapy on both discipline and self-concept. Thirty selected fifth graders were randomly assigned to either a reality therapy session group or a group which received the Open Language Arts Program. Self-concept and problem behaviors were measured before and after the reality therapy sessions.

Dakoske (1977) indicates reality therapy sessions were led by a classroom teacher with assistance by the elementary school counselor. On a weekly basis, fifteen sessions were held for one hour each week. Classroom topics as recommended by Glasser (1965, 1969) were discussed by the students. The teacher provided encouragement to students to explore their ideas, feelings, and values. The principles of Glasser's approach were followed in the classroom discussions and included efforts to build interpersonal relationships and provide mutual support.

Dakoske found significant differences in favor of the group exposed to reality therapy sessions on post-test versus pre-test measures of problem behaviors and self-concept. However, post-test one year later which included no treatment for either group revealed no significant difference between the groups on self-concept. For additional studies using experimental/control groups with a pre- and post-testing design reporting favorable effects of the reality therapy process on self-concept, see Omizo and Cubberly's (1983) study of learning disabled children and Slowick, Omizo and Hammet's (1984) study of Mexican-American adolescents. Other studies which have measured the effects of the reality therapy process on school achievement, locus of control, and self-concept are: Hawes (1971), Thatcher (1983), Matthews (1973), and Shearn and Randolph (1978).

Banmen (1982b) has commented on the issue of the practitioners' skills in using reality therapy. He offers this as a possible explanation for some of the inconsistencies in some of the findings on reality therapy. In reviewing reality therapy studies, Banmen (1982b) found that positive results were more likely for behavioral changes. This review also finds increasing positive results for changes in self-concept but mixed results on locus of control. Thus, we can identify areas where reality therapy appears promising. We should also recall that in many settings and populations reality therapy is the primary treatment mode despite the lack of research validation. Thus, more research is needed in those settings and populations virtually ignored by formal research.

Issues and Concerns in the Application of Reality Therapy

When one views edited works (Bassin, et al., 1976; Glasser N., 1980), volumes by William Glasser, and diverse monographs, the numerous virtues of reality therapy appear to be common knowledge. Yet, like other therapies, reality therapy in practice is only as good as the individual counselor using it (Trojanowicz and Morash, 1983). Considering the particular mode of intervention used in reality therapy, it is one of the methods especially subject to misuse and misunderstanding, despite the fact other therapies may encounter similar problems (Ivery, 1980).

In the application of reality therapy, therefore, issues and concerns have been expressed. A number of writers raise a variety of concerns. For example, what constitutes responsible behavior? If behavior does not harm others, who decides? What is moral and correct? In practice, who really decides? Is the counselor expected to function as a value catalyst and as a model for responsible behavior? Do the principles of reality therapy contain ingredients both for involvement and for rejection? In his more recent works (see references), Glasser increases the emphasis on a nonjudgmental, noncritical, and supportive therapeutic relationship (Corey, 1986). Nevertheless in the applying of principles of reality therapy, a number of writers continue to express the concerns just mentioned. (For example, see Corey, 1986; Peterson, 1976; May, 1967; Ivery, 1980; and Arbuckle, 1975.) Ivery (1980) also cautions that reality therapy must achieve a balance in working with clients which includes environmental circumstances. What follows are some of the major problem areas with reality therapy and its application.

All counselors adhere to moral standards particular to them. Clients are confronted with the disparity between a variety of behaviors which the counselor deems conventional and acceptable versus the specific behavior of the client. Distinct from some therapies, Glasser's (1965, 1972) position is that people are failures not because their standards are too high, but because their performances (irresponsibilities) are too low. Accordingly, there is the need to enhance greater maturity to reduce irresponsible behavior. (As an aside, reality therapy is appropriate for over-socialized clients, but the statement above does not appear appropriate to this category of client.)

We should be concerned with moral standards because therapy counselors are free to incorporate their own values into the interaction process. At times counselors unconsciously incorporate their values because they assume these are the preferred ones. Clients can be especially victimized when they do not have firm convictions with regard to the allocation of responsibilities within their family, aspirations for their children, or attitudes toward homosexuality. The client may be victimized for being involved in a lifestyle not consistent with the counselor's preferred values. Reality therapy counselors continually evaluate the current behaviors of clients and may unduly assist in suggesting options for future behavior—based more on personal value sets than on those which could emerge from clients. To the extent this occurs, it is the preconceived notions and prejudices of these counselors which shape future planning. Thus far, Glasser's writings do not provide a systematic methodology for clearly separating the moral standards of the counselor from that of the client. Those who should be best able to cope with this dilemma are reality therapists who are experienced and certified.

This apparent lack of reasonable amount of uniformity by diverse counselors in the application of reality therapy creates other concerns troublesome to many adherents of reality therapy. Attention will be given to a selected number of those concerns which are central when one attempts to implement reality therapy. Beyond moral standards, another concern deals with the issue of involvement. Essentially, the problem involves the importance of the uncritical acceptance of the client as the central feature in establishing involvement. Sometimes, a subsequent shift occurs toward critically evaluating a client's future behavior. Because of this shift, the possibility does exist that the underpinnings for the relationship and for changing behavior may have changed. The mandate to accept or at least to give recognition to much of what the client has to say initially offers a solid foundation for establishing a firm emotional and cognitive relationship. After the counselor determines that the special type of involvement desirable in reality therapy has been achieved, the counselor revises the relationship in the eyes of the client by also becoming a person whose acceptance of the client appears, now, to be highly conditional on successfully achieving agreed upon behavioral changes. The counselor becomes a judge, and, perhaps, unconsciously conveys that love comes as a result of good behavior.

Thus, the concern here is the potential for the client to perceive the counselor's behavior and statements as rejection. For a client with a history of failures in relationships, this relationship is then like all others. Worse, because it may not be as apparent, in order to sustain acceptance from the counselor, the client makes behavioral changes to please the counselor. But this occurs at the expense of enhancing the client's self-determination which is the reason for the therapy and the relationship. These scenarios also bring into question whether the client is developing involvements with others beyond the therapist. The whole purpose of planning responsible behavioral changes is to become involved with others, not to expend one's energies on rescuing the involvement with the therapist.

The question of dependency as well as the termination of therapy are issues for many therapies. For reality therapy, these are serious concerns when we consider its ideas and that it is short-term therapy. Central to reality therapy is that self-worth can only be achieved by becoming involved with others in the client's real world. Despite the successes of the therapy in helping clients become more behaviorally responsible, (as the earlier research review suggests) not all clients achieve independence. Some practicing reality therapists were aware early on that some clients concluded that the counselor's evaluation and guides for behavioral changes had greater validity than their own judgments. Yochelson and Samenow (1977) state that a shortcoming of reality therapy is the lack of specifics in teaching processes of decision making that would apply beyond the immediate situation. We need to acknowledge the problem of dependency and include as part of reality therapy a strategy for learning that enables what is learned to transfer beyond the immediate behavioral change. If the counselor is perceived as the expert and concrete behavior changes are not generalized to other aspects of life, then clients are likely to sustain a dependency relationship. They are also likely to experience a crumbling of the degree of self-confidence they have attained when therapy does end.

Szasz, like Glasser, feels strongly that mental illness is not an illness. Immediately upon publication of *Reality Therapy* (1965), Szasz (1966) expressed concern that Glasser had merely relabeled everything called mental illness as irresponsibility. It is clear even in Glasser's recent writings that he continues to view all behaviors as the sole creation of the inner workings of the individual. Further, if the behavior is disruptive to elements of conventional society, one is behaving irresponsibly.

It is not difficult to concur with Glasser's major thrust. However, behavioral expressions stem from greater complexities than choosing to be irresponsible. We will identify only a few issues here. At times what others are doing is vastly more important than the irresponsible behavior of the client. The labeling processes directed toward an individual may be so pervasive that the irresponsible behavior of the client is but a symptom of a larger problem. This issue is not adequately dealt with by the principles of reality therapy.

Also, given insufficient recognition are subcultures. Indeed, some people do behave irresponsibly toward others. Yet, they may believe they possess successful identities, not failure identities. Some persons are simply happy not conforming. Some pimps may illustrate this point. Drug trafficking provides another example. Can we really assume that they consider themselves to be failures or concur with our standards of responsible behavior? Glasser does not adequately deal with this issue except to say that if the client does not critically assess existing behavior, therapy can be of no help.

Another principle of reality therapy is: "Accept no excuses." Many practitioners have difficulty following this in practice. The principle is critical since many clients have histories of using excuses as rationalizations so as not to conform. In effect, excuses are used to sanction irresponsible behavior. Yet, who does not need self-esteem defenses to preserve credibility—to smooth over interactional encounters? Those who don't are few in number. Eliminate the use of excuses for a month from the thousands of interactions experienced during that period. Now what is the status of your informal and formal relations? How are you perceived? It is apparent that valid and even invalid excuses are vehicles for orderly social interaction and relationships. In fact—at least in our society—a major feature among members is to use excuses when expectations are not fulfilled. Therefore, literally permitting no excuses can affect relationships. No excuses permitted in the "problem" area is absolutely crucial. On the other hand, permitting *normal* usage of excuses in marginal areas around the core problem is realistic and is in keeping with how people normally behave.

There is the question of whether reality therapy should explicitly include a principle dealing with the client's social relations. It would be helpful if a principle existed which emphasized and provided guidelines for the counselor to monitor what others, in addition to the client, are doing in the relationship. Explication here is critical if the counselor is to be effective in helping the client plan strategy.

One walks a precarious path when the plan for action is based mainly on what ability the client possesses in grasping and in conveying what others are like in the relationship. For this reason, some counselors have contacts with others in the relationship.

The negative influences of environmental circumstances is not directly dealt with in the steps of reality therapy. This is a major concern to therapists who incorporate this therapy in their actual practice. Reality therapy does attempt to help the client to accept and to meet the circumstances which actually surround the client. For emotional stability and to establish a successful identity, one must learn to cope with certain environmental circumstances which cannot easily be changed. Nevertheless, for many ex-cons the actual adjustments to the neighborhood can be overwhelming. Despite the plan for behavioral change, there are basic questions about the availability of appropriate associates, available employment, and the holistic exposure to an environment kindly described as negative.

The above suggests that reality therapy lacks a guide for addressing the all-embracing roles and positions within which clients are physically and mentally entrapped. What should be done after one grasps the client's relationships? At the very least we should attempt revisions, after client consensus evolves, in the fabric of the client's social web. However, once the counselor does grasp the reality of our multiple worlds, realistically achieving a successful identity should not be equated to living a conventional lifestyle.

What constitutes some of the elements of a comprehensive approach? There are some elements which are immediately apparent. But these hardly exhaust all possible elements. First, reality therapy at the individual level is primary. All other elements are supportive players for achieving the goals of the therapy. Environmental "manipulation" is a necessary tool for therapists. After client consensus evolves, the client is assisted in gradually securing appropriate relationships through groups/associates, work, and residential placement. There comes a time when group counseling serves well clients with similar problems, and those to whom the client must relate. In our society many may be striving for identity first, then goals as Glasser (1975) states. Eventually, the core of who we can be is supported and reinforced by job satisfaction. Therefore, it is the responsibility of the therapist that the maximum vocational and educational potential of the client is understood and acted upon. Lastly, any good therapist would grasp the disabilities (including social skills) and potentials of clients and routinely take advantage of the extensive network of social services actually available. Far too many therapists are not really aware of all the types of services which are available to their clients. On this point, Bratter (1976) similarly argues that the counselor's role should be one of advocate to help the client obtain needed services. Glasser (1972) has proposed a Community Involvement Center to serve failing people. Although the CIC is restricted in vision, many of the elements proposed in this comprehensive approach can easily be included in an expanded version of Glasser's center.

Recent Works

Recent works by Glasser are consistent with his discussions in his earliest writings about the principles of reality therapy. Thus, the basic beliefs conveyed in earlier writings such as *Reality Therapy* (1965); *Schools Without Failure* (1969); and *Identity Society* (1975) have not been subject to profound revisions. It does appear that Glasser's recent writings give more emphasis on particular points. For example, Corey (1986) concludes that these writings encourage the counselor to be less critical, less judgmental, and to be more accepting, less confrontational in the therapeutic milieu. This shift addresses a few concerns mentioned previously. But these concerns are not fully resolved by Glasser's recent statements. Certainly, they are unresolved in the actual practice of reality therapy.

Some of Glasser's recent writings are consistent with his earliest writings, others complement or expand reality therapy. In *Positive Addiction* (1976), Glasser appears to enrich reality therapy by recognizing the difficulties of developing one's potential including the entrapment of self-involvement which leads to *negative* addiction (drugs, overeating, etc.). Glasser's solution is addiction. The addiction to which he refers is *positive* addiction. Glasser recognizes the needs of clients to cultivate strength if reality therapy plans for behavioral change are to be successful. Positive addictions to Glasser are unlimited and very regular: running, studying, meditating, volunteering, and so on. Glasser states this lets the client's "brain spin free" (the brain becomes free from the undesirable consequences of negative addiction). Heavy involvement with positive addiction is fruitful because this mental achievement generalizes to the individual's overall pleasure and competence in other areas of life. Accordingly, Glasser would encourage the counselor to use this approach as a means for the client to acquire the needed strength to accomplish the goals of reality therapy.

Other recent works by Glasser which extend beyond reality therapy but are useful as a resource for reality therapists are

Stations of the Mind (1981), and *Control Theory* (1984). Control theory and elements of brain functioning are combined to involve theory of perception. Stated very briefly, the heart of the theory is the relation between our inner world perceptions which are internally motivated and external happenings which have no meaning until we internally interpret external happenings. It is not external forces which cause us to behave in a certain way. Instead, it's what our inner behavior makes of external behavior. In effect, we choose our emotions. For example, others are reacting to us. Others may view us as short or ugly. We may have been deceived. Reactions of being depressed or being hostile are not the only outcome. Why? Because we ought to satisfy our inner needs and therefore it is we who should control how we desire to perceive the external. It is we who choose how we perceive and that determines our view of external reality. In short, Glasser feels we cannot let the external world shape the personal world within us. We take control, interpret and interact with the external; we thereby, in turn, influence external elements in the course of satisfying our inner needs.

For reality therapists these two recent works appear to be far more practical and useful than is traditional behavioral psychology. These writings complement Glasser's reality therapy and are worth the attention of those counselors committed to this therapy.

References

Arbuckle, D. S. 1975. *Counseling and psychotherapy—an existential-humanistic view*, 3rd ed. Boston: Allyn and Bacon.

Banmen, J. 1982a. *Reality therapy bibliography*. Los Angeles: Institute for Reality Therapy.

_____. 1982b. "Reality therapy research view." *Journal of Reality Therapy*, 2(1): 28–33.

Bassin, A., Bratter, T. E., and Rachin, R. L., eds. 1976. *The Reality Therapy Reader*. New York: Harper and Row.

Bennight, K. C. 1975. "A model program for counseling and placement of offenders." *Journal of Employment Counseling*, 12(4): 168–173.

Bratter, T. E. and Raubolt, R. R., 1976. "Treating the methadone addict." In *The Reality Therapy Reader*, Bassin, A., Bratter T. E., and Rachin, R. L. (eds.). New York: Harper and Row.

Brown, L. J. and Ritter, J. I. 1972. "Reality therapy for the geriatric psychiatric patient." *Perspective in Psychiatric Care*, 10(3): 135–139.

Brown, W. and Kingley 1973. "Treating alienated, unmotivated, drug abusing adolescents." *American Journal of Psychotherapy*, 27(4): 585–598.

Cohen, B. Z. and Sordo, I. 1984. "Using reality therapy with adult offenders." *Journal of Counseling Services and Rehabilitation*, 8(3): 25–39.

Corey, G. 1986. *Theory and practice of counseling and psychotherapy*, 3rd ed. Monterey, CA: Brooks/Cole Publishing Company.

Dakoske, T. J. 1977. "Short- and long-term effects of reality therapy on self-concept and discipline of selected fifth grade students." Ph.D. diss., University of Cincinnati. *Dissertation Abstracts International*, 1977, 2338.

Falker F. (1982). "Reality therapy: a systems level approach to treatment in a halfway house." *Journal of Reality Therapy* 1(2): 3–7.

Gang, M. J. 1976. "Enhancing student-teacher relationships." *Elementary School Guidance and Counseling*, 11(2): 131–137.

German, M. L. 1975. "The effects of group reality therapy on institutionalized adolescents and group leaders." Ph.D. diss., George Peabody College for Teachers, 1975. *Dissertation Abstracts International*, 1975, 1916b.

Glasser N., ed. 1980. *What are you doing? How people are helped through reality therapy*. New York: Harper & Row.

Glasser, W., 1964. "Reality therapy: A realistic approach to the young offender." *Crime and Delinquency* 10, 135–144.

———.1965. *Reality therapy: A new approach to psychiatry*. New York: Harper & Row.

———. 1969. *Schools without failure*. New York: Harper & Row.

———. 1975. *The identity society*. Rev. ed. New York: Harper & Row.

———.1976a. "Notes on reality therapy." In *The reality therapy reader*. Bassin, A., Bratter, T. E., Rachin, R. L., (eds.) New York: Harper & Row.

———. 1976b. *Positive addiction*. New York: Harper & Row.

———. 1981. *Stations of the mind*. New York: Harper & Row.

———. 1984a. *Control theory*. New York: Harper & Row.

———. 1984b. "Reality therapy." In *Current psychotherapies*. Corsini, R. (ed.). Itasca, IL: Peacock.

Hawes, R. M. 1971. "Reality therapy in the classroom." Ph.D. diss., University of the Pacific, 1971. *Dissertation Abstracts International*, 1971, 2483.

Ivery, A. E. 1980. *Counseling and psychotherapy: Skills, theories and practice*. Englewood Cliffs, NJ: Prentice-Hall.

Lachman, S. J. 1986. "Restitution: A behavioral analog for undoing." *Journal of Reality Therapy*, 5(2): 3–10.

Matthews, D. B. 1972. "The Effects of reality therapy on reported self-concept, social adjustment, reading achievement, and discipline of fourth and fifth graders in two elementary schools." Ph.D. diss., University of South Carolina,1972, *Dissertation Abstracts International*, 1973, 4342–4843.

Matthews, W. G. 1979. "Restitution programming: Reality therapy operationalized." *Offender Rehabilitation*, 3: 319–324.

May, R. 1967. *Psychology and the human dilemma*. Princeton, NJ: D. Van Nostrand Company.

Molstad, L. P. 1981. "Reality therapy in residential treatment" In *Journal of Reality Therapy* 1(1): 8–13.

Omizo, M. M. and Cubberly, W. F. 1983. "The effects of reality therapy meetings on self-concept and locus of control among learning disabled children." *Exceptional Child* 30(3): 201–209.

Ososkie, J. N. and Turpin, J. O. 1985. "Reality therapy in rehabilitation counseling." *Journal of Applied Rehabilitation Counseling*, 16(3): 34–37.

Peterson, J. A. 1976. *Counseling and Values—A Philosophical Examination*. Cranston, RI: Carroll Press Publishers.

Raubolt, R. R. and Bratter, T. E. 1976. "Treating the methadone addict." In *The Reality Therapy Reader*, Bassin, A., Bratter, T. E. and Rachin, R. L. (eds.), New York: Harper & Row.

Shearn, D. F. and Randolph, D. L. 1978. "Effects of reality therapy methods applied in the classroom." *Psychology in the Schools*, 15(1): 79–83.

Slowick, C. A., Omizo, M. M., and Hammett, V. L. 1984. "The effects of reality therapy process on locus of control and self-concepts among Mexican-American adolescents." *Journal of Reality Therapy* 3(2): 1–9.

Szasz, T. S. 1966. "Equation of opposites." *The New York Book Review* Feb. 6:6.

Thatcher, J. A. 1983. "The effects of reality therapy upon self-concept and locus of control for juvenile delinquents." *Journal of Reality Therapy* 3(1): 31.

Thompson, C. L. and Cates, J. T. 1976. "Teaching discipline to students." *Elementary School Guidance and Counseling*, 11(2): 131–137.

Trojanowicz, R. C. and Morash, M. 1983. *Juvenile delinquency*, 3rd ed. Englewood Cliffs, NJ: Prentice-Hall.

Vinter, R. D., ed. 1976. *Time out: A national study of juvenile correction programs*. Ann Arbor: National Assessment of Juvenile Corrections.

Williams, E. W. 1976. "Reality therapy in a correctional institution." *Corrective and Social Psychiatry and Journal of Behavior, Methods and Therapy*, 22(1): 6–11.

Yochelson, S. and Samenow, S. E. 1977. *The criminal personality—The change process*, Volume II. New York: Janson Aronson.

Zapf, R. F. 1974. Group therapy with retarded adults: A reality therapy approach. Ph.D. diss., Fordham University 1973. *Dissertation Abstracts International* 1974, 4889–4890.

23

Probation and Cognitive Skills

Frederick R. Chavaria

The young man lying on his bunk that night in Chino prison had thought vaguely of the past sixty-two months and wondered what his future would be.

He walked miles of concrete—wondering, thinking, dreaming, fearing, cursing the cheap prison shoes which were already wearing out. Three days were enough. He was ready to make some bread and there was only one thing he knew for certain he was good at.

—*The Onion Field*

The Indictment

"Does nothing work?" (Martinson, 1974). Those three words, that one phrase written by Robert Martinson over 25 years ago, continue to reverberate across the correctional landscape. In his article "What Works?—Questions and Answers About Prison Reform," Martinson shocked the criminal justice world when he exclaimed, "With few and isolated exceptions the rehabilitation efforts that have been reported so far had no appreciable effect on recidivism" (Martinson, 1974, p. 25).

Martinson's article was a predicate of a larger coauthored research report that evaluated 231 studies of treatment programs conducted between 1945 and 1967 (Cullen & Gendreau, 1992). For those who have always questioned the purpose and efficacy of the concept of correctional treatment, Martinson's denunciation was the answer to their prayers. At last the opponents of treatment had tangible and scientific

Source: *Federal Probation*, 61(2) (June 1997): 57–60.

proof of what they had always suspected—treatment did not work. It was not a valid correctional concept or practice. Martinson's pronouncements assumed the mantle of irrefutable mandate, becoming synonymous with correctional treatment intervention failure while also generating enormous influence on both popular perception and professional thinking.

On the other hand, for those criminal justice practitioners and policy makers who supported the notion of correctional treatment and rehabilitation, Martinson's essay was a profound and troubling indictment. The rejection by so many of the correctional rehabilitation ideal was indeed a bitter pill to swallow. Because of probation's unique position in the criminal justice system and the fact that probation utilizes correctional interventions to work with offenders in the community, the harshness of Martinson's scathing essay was stunning. It didn't make it any easier when several years later Martinson (1979) wrote, "Contrary to my previous position, some treatment proponents do have an appreciable effect on recidivism. . . . The evidence in our survey is simply too overwhelming to ignore" (p. 224). The damage was already done; action, not words, was needed.

Retrenchment and Support for What Works

Subsequent to Martinson's initial article and his later retrenchment, several exhaustive reviews of evaluation studies were undertaken. These reviews confirmed that a substantial body of research existed "demonstrating the effectiveness of treatment" (Gendreau, 1981; Gendreau & Ross, 1979, 1981, 1987; Greenwood & Zimring, 1985; Halleck & Witte, 1977; Palmer, 1983; Van Voorhis, 1987). Indeed, for that matter there have been five extensive reviews of rehabilitation literature covering approximately 200 studies for the period 1973 to 1987 (Gendreau & Ross, 1979, 1981, 1987; Ross & Gendreau, 1980; Ross & Fabiano, 1985).

Cullen and Gendreau (1992), in their article "The Effectiveness of Correctional Rehabilitation," noted that a substantial body of literature not only supports the notion that treatment works for a variety of offenders, but, moreover, "it would be reasonable to assume that a set of underlying principles can be derived which are predicative of successful programs" (p. 235). Vern Fogg (1992) observed that when Ross and Gendreau were studying effective treatment programs they reported that:

> Nearly every notable program shared one common characteristic: some technique had an impact on the offender's thinking. Effective programs not only targeted the offender's environment, behavioral responses and skill development, they also sought to increase the

offender's reasoning skills, problem solving abilities and expand the offender's empathy toward others. (p. 24)

Support for this conclusion was derived from outcome data of two statistically sophisticated research meta-analyses conducted by Garrett (1985) and Izzo and Ross (1987).

Cullen and Gendreau (1992) detailed that effective programs tend to be characterized by specific theories such as "social learning; cognitive models; skills training, differential association and behavioral-systems family therapy" (p. 236), which in turn were linked to specific intervention strategies. Consequently, for an intervention paradigm to be effective, it is necessary for the correctional counselor/probation officer to

promote, as frequently as possible, the acquisition of pro-social attitudes and behavior on the part of the offender, to problem solve those behaviors that will aid and reward the offender for noncriminal pursuits, and to utilize community resources that provide services suitable and relevant to the offender's needs. (Cullen & Gendreau, 1992, p. 236)

Moreover, although the services provided the offender must be given in a dignified, honest, and empathetic manner, nonetheless, the offender must be keenly aware "that he or she must abide by reasonable program contingencies," which are clearly defined "by the probation order or requirement of the therapeutic contract" (Cullen & Gendreau, 1992, p. 236).

Probation and "Cog"

Probation is a subsystem of the criminal justice system. Its effectiveness is measured by the number of individuals who successfully complete their supervision and are mainstreamed back into society as functioning, productive people. Constructive and positive change in its clients is a tangible demonstration that the system is working effectively. As its overall goal, probation has a specific outcome, i.e., the modification or change of behavior through a structured program of community supervision. Inherent to the mission of probation is its responsibility to adopt correctional interventions that lead to and/or promote offender change.

It has been noted that many offenders fail to "acquire critical reasoning skills" (Ross et al., 1988, p. 45). While they may be able to rationalize their behavior, their reasoning process is flawed. Because they have developed set patterns of thinking that tend to support their criminal behavior, they are able to justify their conduct. Edward Humes (1996), in his stunning book about the juvenile justice system, provides a startling illustration of this type of thinking:

> When I was growing up, I learned how to take another person's car
> without a key, how to drive it and sell it, or just leave it somewhere.
> I learned how to sit down low and look out the windows for the
> enemy, to see them before they saw me. And finally, when I was grow-
> ing up, I learned how to load bullets into a gun. I learned how to
> carry it and aim it, and I learned how to shoot the enemy, to be there
> for my homeboys, no matter what. These are the things I learned
> when I was growing up. (pp. 16–17)

Many offenders lack interpersonal problem-solving skills and manifest egocentricity. Nathan McCall (1994), in his autobiographical
account *Makes Me Wanna Holler*, observed that "most of the guys in
prison couldn't be rehabilitated because they had never been habilitated
in the first place" (p. 214). Essentially, offenders "evidence shortcomings in any or all of the following cognitive functions: the ability to recognize the potential for problems when people interact; the ability to
conceptualize the step-by-step means needed to reach their goals; and
the ability to see the cause-and-effect relationship between their action
and other people's behavior" (Ross et al., 1988, p. 45). This point is
powerfully demonstrated by McCall's (1994) response to his girlfriend
when she announced her pregnancy:

> At first, I assumed she was pregnant by her old boyfriend, but then
> I realized that he was away and that she hadn't been with him in a
> while. . . . It was a wonder that I was surprised. In all those years
> of throwing down in bed with girls, I never took precautions. For the
> longest time, I thought the only way a woman could get pregnant was
> if she and the guy had an orgasm at the same time.

He goes on to say,

> I willingly owned up to my responsibility. I told her, "I'll do what I
> have to do to help out." But I had no idea what that meant. (p. 111)

When an offender's behavior and attitude is characterized by impulsive-
ness, a sense of powerlessness, conceptual rigidity, lack of interpersonal
problem-solving skills, egocentricity, and low critical reasoning ability, you
can reasonably assume that to some degree the offender is cognitively
impaired. "Advice, warnings or punishments often seem to leave little
impact on them because they fail to reflect back on their behavior and its
effects" (Ross et al., 1988, p. 45). Cognitively impaired offenders do not recognize the possibility that their behavior, attitudes, and thinking are linked
to and contribute to the problems they are experiencing.

While it cannot be stated unequivocally that cognitive deficits are a
cause of crime, there is sufficient evidence to suggest that those individuals who are cognitively impaired are more susceptible to developing
and maintaining criminal lifestyles.

Gendreau, Cullen, and Bonta (1994) listed seven program strategies
that lead to significant reductions in recidivism in the supervision of

offenders. One of the principal program components was cognitive social learning strategies that employ modeling, cognitive restructuring, and explicit reinforcement of and alternatives to antisocial styles of thinking, feeling, and acting (Fitzsimons, 1994). Cognitive skills training/education as used in the correctional setting is not designed to effect basic personality change; rather, it is an approach which seeks to equip offenders with prosocial thinking and behavioral skills that will allow them to avoid further criminal involvement. It is an intervention protocol that is best taught by criminal justice professionals with noncriminal backgrounds, but who have been thoroughly trained in cognition and techniques suitable for its delivery.

It is critically important, from the onset, that it be understood by policy makers and probation personnel alike that a principal aspect of the cognitive skills protocol is the proposition that antisocial behavior is not a reflection of underlying psychopathology. Instead, a basic assumption is that most offenders tend to be unsocialized and lack the prosocial skills to effect a prosocial adjustment. The cognitive skills paradigm stresses education, not therapy.

Basic Principles of Cognitive Intervention

Over the past decade there has been a proliferation of cognitive skills programs both in the United States and abroad. Most of the programs share some common principles and to some degree are connected to the seminal work concerning thinking errors researched by Yochelson and Samenow and described in their book *The Criminal Personality* (1976) while also drawing on the scholarly work and research insights of Piaget and Edward de Bono. Cognition, as a field of study, "is the study of the knowledge we possess, the organization of this knowledge, and the processes we have available to us for using this information in the everyday activities of attention, learning, memory, comprehension and problem solving" (Small, 1990, p. 1). It is an approach which proposes that goal-directed behavior is a predicate of that process. Inherent to this approach is the notion that "humans process environmental information in a series of stages between the occurrence of the stimulus and the production of a response" (Small, 1990, p. 8). Consequently, when working with offenders, an essential supposition of the cognitive model is that thinking determines behavior. Changing thinking, therefore, is a precursor to changing behavior. The change from unknown to known is understanding, and the mechanism that conveys change is the thought processes. The ability to think is a skill and the process involved can be taught. Thinking is that ellipse of time between experiencing a situation and knowing what to do about it. Implicit to teaching offenders cognitive skills techniques is recognizing that there is something practical that offenders can do to change the course of their life. Offenders are taught that they have the ability to:

- recognize their own patterns of thinking, feeling, and perception;
- recognize how these patterns result in and support their dysfunctional/criminal behavior;
- make the personal decision to change their lives by changing these patterns; and
- follow the decision to change with a practical program of cognitive skills self-change.

Some common objectives of the cognitive skills program are for offenders to develop social competence and social skills. Social competence is a broad term that can be defined as including learning the socially accepted performance of a variety of social skills in a manner that is effective and efficient (University of Kansas Institute for Research in Learning Disabilities, 1988). With respect to the development of social skills, a social skill strategy allows the offender to employ learning guidelines and rules related to selecting the best procedure and how to make decisions about their use. A social skill is a set of procedures relative to meeting a social demand (University of Kansas Institute for Research in Learning Disabilities, 1988).

How an offender approaches a task is called a strategy. A strategy includes how the offender thinks and acts when planning, executing, and evaluating performance of a task and its outcome. A cognitive strategy consists of the following.

- Stop and think before acting.
- Consider the consequences of actions.
- Conceptualize alternative ways of responding.
- Consider impact of your own behavior on others.
- Implement a process (series of steps or questions) to engage in prosocial behavior.

Some Outcomes and Final Thoughts

A cognitive skills education program, when coupled with a structured and focused supervision protocol, can work to dramatically reduce recidivism and increase offender success. Several state probation systems, such as those in Colorado, Texas, Iowa, Oregon, and Georgia, are already engaged in providing offenders with the opportunity to participate in cognitive skill-building programs as are several federal probation jurisdictions. "Colorado has been using cognitive programming for several years and their initial outcome study in 1992 showed a 41.7% revocation rate for regular probation, 29.4% for intensive supervision with treatment, and 25.4% when the correctional intervention included cognitive skills training" (Fitzsimons, 1994, p. 4). In one study researchers found that 60 percent of substance abusers in regular caseloads recidivated as compared to 18 percent in an intensive probation program that included cognitive skills training (Johnson & Hunter, 1992). During a symposium given at the federal system's Probation and Pretrial Services Academy in 1994, Professor Don Andrews of Carlton University presented research findings which indicated that when offenders are engaged in correctional interventions that include drug and alcohol treatment, employment assistance, and a structured program of cognitive skills building, recidivism is reduced by as much as 29 percent. Two of Mark Lipsey's principal conclusions, in his 1990 meta-analysis of treatment effectiveness (Andrews, 1994, p. 14), were that the best treatments were structured and focused and that the best treatments reduced recidivism rates by about 30 percent on average. Moreover, Professor Andrews observed that "there now is a human science of criminal conduct. There are theories of criminal conduct that are empirically defensible and that may be helpful in designing and delivering effective service" (1994, p. 3).

While cognitive skill deficits cannot conclusively be linked to crime, there is ample evidence to suggest that it increases the likelihood of a criminal lifestyle. Therefore, given developments in the knowledge base concerning criminal behavior and effective correctional supervision interventions, it would seem that a supervision protocol emphasizing cognitive skills training would be a prudent and useful investment of probation officer time and perhaps in the process provide an answer to probing questions posed by a young offender:

> Who is going to teach me how to be a father? How to take care of my family? How to live a life—a normal life? These are the things I never learned growing up. Who will teach me now? (Humes, 1996, p. 17)

This is probation's challenge and its future. Only time will tell if it can meet that challenge. To do so, probation may have to change some of its thinking, and as any offender will tell you—change is tough!

References

Andrews, D. A. (1994, January). *An overview of treatment effectiveness: Research and treatment principles.* Draft paper presented to chief United States probation and pretrial services officers, Linthicum, MD.

Cullen, F., & Gendreau, P. (1992). *The effectiveness of correctional rehabilitation and treatment.* In D. Lester, M. Braswell, & P. Van Voorhis

(Eds.), *Correctional counseling* (2nd ed.). Cincinnati, OH: Anderson Publishing Company.

Fogg, V. (1992). Implementation of a cognitive skills development program. *Perspectives*, 24–27.

Fitzsimons, J. (1994). *The acquisition of cognitive skills.* Paper presented to chief United States probation officers, Sonoma, CA.

Garrett, C. (1985). Effects of residential treatment on adjudicated delinquents: A meta-analysis. *Journal of Research in Crime and Delinquency*, 22(4), 287–308.

Gendreau, P. (1981). Treatment in corrections: Martinson was wrong! *Canadian Psychology*, 22, 332–338.

Gendreau, R., Cullen, F. T., & Bonta, J. (1994). Intensive rehabilitation supervision: The next generation in community corrections? *Federal Probation*, 58(1), 72–78.

Gendreau, P., & Ross, R. (1979). Effective correctional treatment: Bibliotherapy for cynics. *Crime and Delinquency*, 25, 463–489.

Gendreau, P., & Ross, R. (1981). Correctional potency: Treatment and deterrence on trial. In R. Rosesch & R. Corrado (Eds.), *Evaluation in criminal justice policy.* Beverly Hills, CA: Sage Publications.

Gendreau, P., & Ross, R. (1987). Revivification of rehabilitation: Evidence from the 1980s. *Justice Quarterly*, 4(3), 349–409.

Greenwood, R., & Zimring, F. (1985). *One more chance: The pursuit of promising intervention strategies for chronic juvenile offenders.* Santa Monica, CA: RAND.

Halleck, S., & Witte, A. (1977). Is rehabilitation dead? *Crime and Delinquency*, 23, 372–382.

Humes, E. (1996). *No matter how loud I shout.* New York: Touchstone.

Izzo, R., & Ross, R. (1987). *Meta-analysis of correctional treatment programs for juvenile delinquents.* Ottawa, Canada: Department of Criminology University of Ottawa.

Johnson, G., & Hunter, L. (1992). *Evaluation of the specialized drug offender program.* Center for Action Research, University of Colorado.

Lipton, D., Martinson, R., & Wilks, J. (1975). *The effectiveness of correctional treatment: A survey of treatment evaluation studies.* New York: Praeger.

Martinson, R. (1974). What works? Questions and answers about prison reform. *The Public Interest*, 22–54.

Martinson, R. (1979). New findings, new views: A note of caution regarding sentencing reform. *Hofstra Law Review*, 7, 243–258.

McCall, N. (1994). *Makes me wanna holler.* New York: Vintage Books.

Palmer, T. (1983), The effectiveness issue today: An overview. *Federal Probation*, 51(1), 56–62.

Ross, R. et al. (1988). (Re)habilitation through education: A cognitive model for corrections. *Journal of Correctional Education*, 39(2), 44–47.

Ross, R., & Fabiano, E. (1985). *Time to think. A cognitive model delinquency prevention and offender rehabilitation.* Johnson City, TN: Institute of Social Science and Art.

Ross, R., & Gendreau, P. (1980). *Effective correctional treatment.* Toronto, Canada: Butterworth.

Small, M. Y. (1990). *Cognitive development.* Orlando, FL: Harcourt Brace

Jovanovich.

University of Kansas Institute for Research in Learning Disabilities. (1988, October). Unk. Title.

Van Voorhis, P. (1987). Correctional effectiveness: The high cost of ignoring success. *Federal Probation*, 51(1), 55–62.

Wambaugh, J. (1973). *The onion field*. New York: Dell Publishing.

Yochelson, S., & Samenow, S. (1976). *The criminal personality* (Vol 1). New York: Jason Aronson.

24

Brief Solution-Focused Work
A Strength-Based Method
for Juvenile Justice Practice

Michael D. Clark

Introduction

Across the juvenile justice field, we hear the call to focus on the strengths of the offender and family while working for behavior change. Many delinquency workers would acknowledge that using a juvenile's strengths has value for their work. In their mission statements or codes of ethics, professional associations and bureaucracies serving our field speak of strengths and of raising competencies. In the steady stream of publications that pour from our nation's universities, criminal justice scholars often mention using offender strengths as an aspect of "what works" in offender rehabilitation.

In reality, focusing on offender and family strengths does not make the leap from statement to field work. Actual methods and interventions that utilize offender strengths in the juvenile justice field appear as a desert-like mirage: They seem visible and available from afar, only to disappear as one moves closer to them for daily field work. Upon close examination, we lack practice methods that are truly strength-based. This review is necessary as Competency-Based Brief Therapy models, originating in the family therapy field, are now being applied to abuse and neglect services (Berg, 1994) and juvenile probation services (Clark, 1994). Solution-Focused work now makes alternative, strength-based interventions

Source: *Juvenile and Family Court Journal*, 47(1) (Winter 1996): 57–65.

available that may not have been readily available before. Field workers, policy makers and the judiciary need to know there may be a better way for helping a teen and family exit our system by focusing on their strengths and healthy patterns instead of by identifying and treating their deficits and failures.

Brief Solution-Focused Work

This approach for juvenile justice practice originated from the Brief Solution-Focused Therapy model as developed by Steve De Shazer, Insoo Kim Berg and colleagues at the Brief Family Therapy Center in Milwaukee, Wisconsin (De Shazer, 1985; De Shazer, et al., 1986; Berg and Miller, 1992). This model is one of the many Competency-Based Brief Therapy approaches that have become a new movement of such significance as to be called the "Third Wave" in psychotherapy (O'Hanlon, 1994). This Third Wave follows the earlier "waves" of Freudian psychology and the behavioral-based Problem Solving approaches. A discussion of several guiding principles begins a review of this Strength-Based method.

Focus on Strengths

The dramatic departure of Solution-Focused work from current interventions is its focus on strengths and mental health. All offenders and families have some resources such as skills, capabilities, interests, positive character traits, even perseverance and hope, that can be brought to bear for exiting our system. It is a simple yet profound truth that solutions are not reached through offenders' weaknesses and failures but through offenders' strengths and healthy patterns. As reports and case plans are completed across our field, the identification and listing of strengths take a "back seat." They are added to reports (if at all) as an afterthought or as a weak attempt to counterbalance the large "laundry list" of failures and problems that have been reported. With a solution-focus, they become instead the primary information and central force that drives assessments and interventions.

Focusing on strengths is not a Pollyanna approach of "looking for the good" or believing that "things will turn out for the best." it Is not the same as ignoring or condoning the problems and the pain. It is a sophisticated approach that many believe can move juveniles and families to dismissal with greater efficiency than working from their failed side (Clark, 1995).

Solving problems only returns a person to a previous balance or equilibrium, whereas promoting and enhancing strengths leads to growth that will continue long after a juvenile and family leave our court system.

We must believe that strengths are present before we can find them. The famous physicist, Albert Einstein, believed that our theories and beliefs determine what we can see. The familiar adage, "seeing is believing" could really be restated as "believing is seeing." If we believe our offenders have strengths, this will allow us to look for and find them for utilization.

Utilization

We utilize for change all that the offender and family bring with them. Their unique words and phrases to denote both the problem and solutions are noted and used rather than favoring our own. Interests, proficiencies, and talents are forwarded. Problem-solving abilities are culled from the past to be utilized in the present. Solutions in this approach are never ready-made or "canned," but are unique and personal to our families. Although teaching and skill building will always have a place in our field, consider that it is far easier to utilize what is already present or has been successful than to import vocabulary, methods, or strategies foreign to those we work with. Finding and capitalizing on what is already present is one aspect of what makes brief work brief.

Cooperation

Traditional Problem-Focused work views cooperation as a characteristic of the offender and family. We often view our responsibility to building cooperation as being limited to showing "respect" or using empathy as we approach. Solution-Focused work requires us to view cooperation as emanating from the process and interaction between worker and offender. Our attention to this interaction must be increased.

Cooperation and motivation are raised as we allow more juvenile and family involvement in our case planning process. Recent research findings in family therapy are both interesting and thought-provoking. Miller et al. (1995) studied 30 years of clinical outcome research. This study found that no theory, model, or package of techniques proved reliably better than any other. A second finding, thought provoking for our field, is reported by the researchers: The most influential contributor to change is the client, not the therapy, not the technique, not the therapist—*but the client.* The sheer impact of their contribution when compared to other factors serves as a powerful reminder that . . . no change is likely to occur without the client's involvement.

Selekman (1993) echoes this idea:

> When clients think they have even modest personal control over their destinies, they will persist at mastering tasks, do better at managing them, and become more committed to the change process.

These findings seem lost on the juvenile justice field, and many problems that beset our field begin here. We rarely incorporate and use the view of our teens and families regarding what problems need solving and how best to solve them. Saleeby (1992) notes, "an agency designed to serve social control functions . . . is likely to develop a negative atmosphere about clients who are apt to be seen as outsiders rife with problems and deficits." If we assume clients are basically flawed or "damaged goods," this assumption leads to certain ends. A negative view directly or indirectly establishes the juvenile worker as the "expert." This expert status also stems from the paternalism generated by our field's legal doctrine of *parens patriae*. This paternalism and pessimistic view give rise to workers naming the problem and then telling our offenders what should be done and how to do it. Cooperation is lost right from the start as we often force our ideas on families without consensus. We do not give credence to their understanding and definition of the problem if they differ from ours. In many cases, our delineation of the problem may be correct. However, using only our delineation of the problem raises a central question regarding change: Do we want to be right, or do we want to be successful?

If we cooperate with what the offender and family believe is urgent to start with, they are more likely to cooperate with us later. We try to "join" with the offender as much as possible. Most juveniles want something, even if it is to be left alone. Although we might hope the goals for behavioral change would be established for more appropriate reasons, "getting the court off your back" is an acceptable point to begin your work. Berg (1994) states, "in negotiating the definition of the problem to be solved with the client, it is important, wherever possible, to stay close to the client's own definition, since he is the one who will have to make the necessary changes." This author also warns, "do not argue or debate with the client. You are not likely to change her mind through reasoning. If this approach was going to work, it would have worked by now." We have more latitude to agree with their designation of the problem and their ideas for solutions than one might think.

We often end up being the only "customer" for our services. When the juvenile does not agree with our view, we assume the added task of persuading or "cheerleading" for cooperation. Failing that, we then turn to enumerate the many consequences that may befall the teen and family for further failure to follow our lead. Although we know that turning to negative sanctions and punishment is neither cost-effective nor efficient, workers have little else to employ with Problem-Focused approaches.

Task vs. Insight Orientation

Solution-Focused work is behavioral-based and is not predicated on attainment of insight or awareness into the problem. A Solution-

Focused approach does not belabor the past, nor does it need to fully understand the problem before solution work can begin. It does not develop lengthy problem assessments where we go beyond the presenting problem(s) with the shotgun inquiry of "what else is wrong?" The juvenile and family's frame of reference is used to ascertain what brought court contact. Movement quickly begins to discover the offender's answer to the problem, setting small behavioral and achievable goals for that end.

A present and future orientation is another facet of what makes brief work brief as dismissal from court jurisdiction is in mind *from the beginning*. Termination is being negotiated while the delinquency worker is still trying to get to know the teen and family. Responsibility and accountability are not sacrificed with this approach because families are expected to *do something* in relation to the mutually defined problems that brought them into court contact.

It would be a mistake to believe that greater offender participation and developing a cooperative relationship is enough to bring about behavior change. For real change to happen, the offender and family need to change the way they think about and perceive the problem(s) and to do something that is behaviorally different than before. To accomplish this shift involves a model of questions.

A Model of Questions

The all-important technique to make this shift is questioning. Miller (1994) states: "Over time, we have learned that asking the right question often has more impact on the client than having the correct answer." Nowhere is this point more applicable than with adolescents who resist lectures, "being told what to do," or any approach that puts them in a "one down" position.

Berg and Miller (1992) posit "five useful questions" for interviewing that orient our families toward solutions. I have adapted these questions for juvenile court application.

1. *Pre-Session Change Questions.* "After being arrested and petitioned, many people notice good changes have already started before their first appointment here at the court. What changes have you noticed in your situation?" "How is this different than before?" "How did you get these changes to happen?" Numerous studies (Wiener-Davis et al., 1987; Talmon, 1990; Bloom, 1981) found a majority of clients make significant changes in their problem patterns from the time of setting up of the initial appointment to actually entering treatment. In single subject research, this author found similar responses from juveniles and families newly assigned to my juvenile probation caseload. The important point is that teens and families rarely report these changes

spontaneously. Juvenile workers must ask to elicit and amplify these changes or they remain obscure. When problems are ignored by those that experience them, they are thought to move underground where they grow and fester and return even stronger. However, when solutions are ignored, they simply fade away unnoticed, and more importantly, unused.

2. *Exception Questions.* "Have there been times recently when the problem did not occur?" "When was the most recent time when you were able to (perform the desired behavior)?" "What is different about those times?" "When did this happen?" "Who was involved?" "How did this happen?" Teens and their families typically view the complaints they bring into our courts as constant in nature, and therefore any or all exceptions usually go unnoticed. This approach holds to the adage "nothing always happens" (De Shazer, 1988) to convey there are always times when the problem does not happen or is not considered a problem by the family. Experience with this model (Clark, 1994) has shown times when the truant attends school, the angry/assaultive child walks away from a fight, the follower has said "No" to the group, or the parent did not berate or harp on the negative. The idea is simple: Look for how teens and families found success in the past and get them to repeat those same strategies in the future. It is here that the contrast between Solution-Focused work and the Problem-Focused model can be found. In the latter we are asking, "when *does* the problem happen?" "When does it get *worse*?"

Problem-Focused work is based on the idea that "if we can name the problem, the treatment will follow." However, when we selectively attend to the *problem,* many difficulties arise. Insoo Berg (1994) gives a good account of what juvenile workers often experience:

> Focusing on a problem usually implies that there is a direct cause. Someone is responsible for the problem and someone is at fault. Whenever families concentrate on problems, the conversation in the family session rapidly deteriorates into arguments, defensiveness and blaming.

Solution-Focused work finds greater utility in amplifying what is occurring during times when the problem does not happen than when it does. It is very important to note that exceptions need to be *purposeful.* To find out that during a certain period of time a substance-abusing juvenile abstained from using drugs only because the local "dealer" was out of town is certainly an exception that is of no use!

3. *Miracle (Outcome) Questions.* "What if you went to sleep tonight and a miracle happens and the problem(s) that brought you into the court (detention center) are *solved.* But because you were asleep, you don't know the miracle happened. When you wake up tomorrow, what

would you notice as you go about your day that tells you a miracle has happened and things are different?" "What else?" "Imagine yourself, for a moment, that we are now six months or more in the future, after we have worked together and the problems that brought you (this family) to court jurisdiction have been solved. What will be different in your life, six months from now, that will tell you the problem is solved?" "What else?"

The miracle question is the hallmark of Solution-Focused Brief Therapy. A miracle in this context is simply the present or future without the problem. It is used to orient the juvenile and family toward their desired outcome by helping construct a different future. Contracting about offender/family goals needs to be preceded by an understanding of what they want to happen. When (if) a worker finds no past successes to build on, the family can be helped to form a different future by imagining a "miracle." As many delinquency workers have experienced, it is often difficult to stop a family from "problem talk" and start the search for solutions. This question was designed to allow the offender and family to "put down the problem" and begin to look at what will occur when the problem is not present. Furman and Ahola (1994) report, "in our view, the single most useful issue to be talked about with clients is how they view the future without the problem. . . . When people are helped to foresee a good future for themselves, they automatically begin to view their present difficulties as a transitory phase, rather than an everlasting predicament." This question is used to identify the client's goals for court jurisdiction to end. If the juvenile begins with a fantasy response of ("a new car" or "winning the lottery," the worker can return the conversation to a more productive track by using humor or normalizing these wishes. Juveniles and family members will quickly settle in to describing a more realistic miracle.

This miracle question is followed by other questions that shape the evolving description into small, specific, and behavioral goals. "What will be the smallest sign that this (outcome) is happening?" "When you are no longer (skipping school, breaking the law, etc.), what will you be doing instead?" "What will be the first sign this is happening?" "What do you know about (yourself, your family, your past) that tells you this could happen for you?"

4. *Scaling Questions.* "On a scale of 1 to 10, where 10 is the day after the miracle and 1 is when you were arrested (petitioned—problem was at its worst), where are you today?" "Numbers help me understand better, if on a scale of 1 to 10 where 10 is your problem solved and 1 is when it was at the worst, where are you now?"

Scaling questions help us establish a baseline against which future progress may be measured. They are used at the end of the initial session and all subsequent meetings. Scaling also helps us know when a client is satisfied without having to define vague terms such as "communicating better" or "feeling better."

Once a baseline is established, they can be used to identify small, specific and behavioral actions for the juvenile. "You said a moment ago you were at 3. What would have to happen for you to move to a 4?" "What will you be doing when you are at a 4?" "What will others be doing?" "What would be the smallest (first) sign if you were moving to a 4?"

Finally, scaling questions can assess a juvenile's confidence and willingness to work. "On a scale of 1 to 10, how confident are you that you can reach this goal?" "Mother/Father you gave John a 7 but John only rated himself a 6. What do you know about John that makes you more confident?" Using scaling questions and exploring the differences in the answers can give a richness of information about assets and strengths that can be used for reaching goals.

5. *Coping Questions.* "How have you managed to cope?" "Given how bad things are, how come they're not worse?" "This problem could certainly get worse—how have you (others) stopped this from getting worse?" Coping questions are used with a small percentage of persons who present a hopeless view of the situation. They often resist any comfort or reassurance that the situation will improve.

Encouraging "pep talks" of "you can do it" or "it's not that bad" to hopeless family members never seem to work. Rather, the person becomes even more entrenched in their feelings of hopelessness and the session spirals downward. Raising self-esteem can never come from pep talks. Self-esteem can only be raised by accomplishing tasks or by honest self-appraisal of past or current accomplishments. Real encouragement and hope is summoned when individuals look inward for this honest self-appraisal of accomplishments that they know to be true about themselves. Coping questions can begin this self-appraisal and amplify what is found. Coping questions are also important to use if juveniles disclose a past traumatic event that they may be sharing for the first time.

Goal Setting

There is a difference in goals that are oriented to facilitating a client's sense of success. Out of many considerations regarding the negotiation of goals, three guidelines are important for review:

1. Goals must be meaningful to the client. If we first cooperate with the family's agenda *if at all possible*, it is easier for them to cooperate with us later. Common sense must prevail. A juvenile who is a danger to self or others may need an alternative placement regardless of the juvenile's preference. However, a majority of our cases do not pose

immediate at-risk situations, and one will find it is far easier to start where the interest and energy are, rather than trying to create it where it is not. Restitution to victims, community service work, and other requirements for dismissal can be included in mutual goal setting after juveniles believe we will pay attention to what they find important to start with.

2. Goals must be small and interactional. Goals and objectives in many delinquency case plans are far too large, encompassing numerous behaviors to reach a goal for dismissal *months* in the future. If the goal cannot be accomplished within two to three weeks, it must be pared down. In case plans we enter, most importantly the subsection on goals should not be static but should remain open to negotiation and revision as we work with juveniles and families. The most important task of an assessment is to motivate the client to do something about the situation that brought court contact, so the "first step," the "smallest sign" begins behavioral changes. These small behavioral changes can begin the systemic "ripple effect" (Spiegel and Linn, 1969) that can realize even more changes from a first step.

A Solution-Focus looks to interaction with others rather than centering on the individual psyche. Goals are established in context with others. Parents usually think only in terms of how their child must change. Questions interactional in nature pull in "observers" to subtly challenge their idea that they have no influence in the change process. An example of this challenge can be found in this interchange:

Worker: What do you suppose will be a small (first) sign that your son is "stopping all this trouble?"

Mother: He will stop skipping school and bugging his younger sister and also he wouldn't 'cuss at me like he does

Worker: Let's believe for a moment that he starts doing those things. What do you think he would say you are doing different when that happens?

Mother: He would probably say I'm not "on his case" all the time, that I'm not checking up on him.

Worker: What would he say you're doing instead?

Mother: He would say I'm trusting him more and maybe listening to him. Maybe not calling his friends to check on him all the time—he hates that.

Worker: When your son notices that you are more willing to trust him and to listen to him when you both speak, what would he say about how things will be different between the two of you?

The real utility of this kind of goal negotiation is that the mother way get the idea that she can start positive beginnings, rather than waiting passively for her son to change. It is helpful for the mother to begin to believe she has some influence, even indirect influence, on improving her son's behavior.

3. Goals must be a beginning, not an end. Many goals currently used in the juvenile justice field call for an end of an illegal or unwanted behavior. Goals have more utility if they are framed as the presence or start of a positive behavior. It is hard to be consciously aware of the absence of something, or of "not doing" something as we go about our day. It is far easier to recognize "doing" that is action or effort. "I won't talk back to my teacher" is reframed to "counting to 10," "asking for a pass to see a counselor," or "writing down how angry I am at my desk." When juveniles or family members suggest goals posed with never, not, don't or won't, questions are asked, "what will you do *instead*?" Vague, future conditions also need a concrete beginning. "So what do you need to do to start feeling better about yourself?"

Post Script on Questioning

Experience with a Solution-Focused approach (Clark, 1994) has found that despite the numerous questions asked of them, offenders and family members rarely (if ever!) refuse to answer.

The inducement stems from the realization by those we work with that we are looking for solutions rather than trying to fix blame. Questions, attending to the positives, are asked with a genuine curiosity. We are met with shoulder shrugs or stony silence when we use leading questions that adolescents and family members quickly recognize will end in their being blamed. It is important to reflect on the difference between blame and responsibility. Blame involves accusations and condemnation. Responsibility entails accountability and obligation.

Berg (1994) highlights this difference with two sets of questions:

- "The record indicates that two years ago you had your child returned to you from the foster home. What did you do right that time?"

- "What do you suppose the Social Worker thinks you did to convince him that you were ready to have your child returned?"

Compare those questions with these:

- "The record indicates that the Department placed your child in a foster home. Do you remember why that happened?"

- "What do you suppose the social worker thought was wrong with your parenting that made it necessary to take your child away from you?"

It is easy to find the difference between these two sets of questions. The first set points out in a matter-of-fact way that there were past problems but also past successes. Heavy-handed blame is bypassed yet fact and responsibility are not. The conditions of "what has been" or "what is" can be posited with a less blaming tone.

Delinquency workers wed to the Problem-Focused approach may bristle at this contrast. There is a belief with this approach that assignment of blame is all-important. They follow a conventional criterion of mental health that an accurate view of reality, including knowing one's faults as well as one's virtues, is a necessary hallmark of good mental health.

Many rigorous new studies contradict this long-held idea. Research in health psychology (Wellness Paradigm) has found that optimism, even unrealistic optimism, is associated with better physical and mental health (Peterson and Bassio, 1991). More important, social scientists now indicate that human beings may actually have an innate predisposition to process information in an optimistic fashion. Taylor (1989) reported studies of human information processing that indicate the human mind appears to have an innate predisposition to attend to positive information and to screen out negative information.

These findings are surprising to say the least. Psychology has long viewed the brain as a producer of rational thought (Ornstein and Sobel, 1987). We have always thought of our brain similar to "a scientist" where it collects data, organizes it in some logical fashion, and makes decisions based on an "accurate" perception of reality. Yet, Walters and Havens (1994) state, "the actual ways in which people process information, however, do not conform to this 'brain as scientist' model. Rather, people tend to process information about themselves and their environment in ways that are not always accurate, but are consistently self-enhancing." This mild positive bias or slightly rosy filter serves as a buffer against emotional distress and is thought to be normal, inherent, and adaptive.

These findings allow us to de-emphasize the assignment of blame. Many consider it the experienced worker's hard-earned virtue to be able to "tell it like it is." Getting people to admit their faults is exhausting work. It is not difficult to see how assigning blame, and then withstanding the defensiveness and resistance that follows, must certainly contribute to the high worker turnover rate suffered by our field. Problem-Focused work can create many obstacles that must first be overcome before we can move towards solutions.

Solution-Focused work, with its emphasis on strengths and successes, can still maintain responsibility and accountability yet avoid these obstacles. We often resign ourselves to resistance and lack of cooperation, believing it "comes with the territory" due to the nature of our work. It is not, however, the nature of our work so much as the nature of a problem-focused approach to clients. We simply do not have to drag our juveniles and families "through the mud" of their own failures and defects to bring about change. With this model of questions, resistance is lowered and cooperation is raised by what we ask, how we ask it, and (very importantly) *for what purpose* the questions are asked.

Conclusion

Many believe the Strengths Perspective and Brief Competency-Based approaches could be viable alternatives for our field. In Michigan, the Department of Social Services (Office of Delinquency Services) is strongly supporting and adopting a Strength-Based Solution-Focused approach for working with juveniles and their families. This new approach is spreading across other areas of the country. In Omaha, the local office of the Nebraska Department of Social Services—Child Protective Services has recently adopted a Competency-Based Brief approach. Bob Zimmerman, Director for this local office, stated that worker and client satisfaction are up and caseload numbers are on their way down (Personal Communication, December 21, 1994).

Several advantages to this approach should be discussed. First, this new approach aids the juvenile justice worker in being culturally sensitive. Since the problems that are named and the routes to solutions come more from the offender and family, our work has more of a natural fit. This model does not ignore or trample on the offender's personal, familial, or cultural systems, but rather operates in tandem with them. Second, we do not have to suffer the loss of committed and capable workers who leave our field due to pessimism and feeling overwhelmed by the multitude of problems. When adopting this new approach, workers will quickly notice a brighter atmosphere surrounding their work. Encouragement, hope, and optimism are afforded not only to those we work with, but also to ourselves. Third, this approach is not a cure-all. Even with the advantages of Solution-Focused Brief Approach, the full continuum of sanctions and alternative (out-of-home) placements will still be necessary in our field. We must, however, never lose sight of the fact that a majority of our juveniles do not progress to the adult correctional system. Any approach that can lessen the need for elevated (and costly) services by enhancing cooperation and motivation deserves our attention. Fourth, this approach can be joined with movements currently underway in the juvenile justice field. An example detailed in past *Juvenile and Family Court Journal* publications is the Balanced and Restorative Justice (BARJ) project that is promoted by the Office of Juvenile Justice and Delinquency Prevention (OJJDP). Those familiar with this project (and many others) will find that we do not have to "recast the die" to assimilate this approach in projects currently being implemented in many jurisdictions across our country.

It is beyond the scope of this article to provide a complete review of this Strength-Based method, but I hope this exercise will spark interest and further inquiry into an approach that many believe holds great promise for our field. I also hope that both policy makers and field workers will come to know that a real choice now exists in how best to move a juvenile and family toward court dismissal. To begin to operate from a Strengths Perspective using Solution-Focused Briefwork requires a "top down—bottom up" effort by policy makers and direct service staff. Organizations such as the National Council of Juvenile and Family Court Judges (NCJFCJ) and the Office of Juvenile Justice and Delinquency Prevention (OJJDP) can render assistance by disseminating information about this new approach to aid our field in the process of choice.

References

Berg, I. K. (1994), *Family-Based Services: A Solution-Focused Approach*. New York: W. W. Norton.

Berg, I. K., Miller, Scott (1992), *Working with the Problem Drinker: A Solution-Focused Approach*. New York: W. W Norton.

Bloom, B. L. (1981), "Focused Single-Session Therapy: Initial Development and Evaluation," in S. H. Budman (ed.), *Forms of Brief Therapy*. New York: Guilford Press.

Clark, M. (1994, October), *Solution-Focused Brief Therapy: Juvenile Justice Application*. Workshop Address presented at the 26th Annual National Juvenile Detention Association Conference, Lansing, MI.

Clark, M. (1995), "The Problem with Problem Solving: A Critical Review," *Journal for Juvenile Justice and Detention Services*, 10(1), 30–35.

de Shazer, S. (1985), *Keys to Solution in Brief Therapy*. New York: W. W. Norton.

de Shazer, S., Berg, I. K., Lipchik, E., Nunnally, E., Molnar, A., Gingerich, W., & Weiner-Davis, M. (1986), "Brief Therapy: Focused Solution Development," *Family Process*, 25, 207–222.

de Shazer, S. (1988), *Clues: Investigating Solutions in Brief Therapy*. New York: W. W. Norton.

Furman, Ahola. (1994), "Solution Talk: The Solution-Oriented Way of Talking about Problems," in M. Hoyt (ed.), *Constructive Therapies*. New York: Guilford Press.

Miller, S. (1994), "Some Questions (Not Answers) for the Brief Treatment of People with Drug and Alcohol Problems," in Sm. H. Hoyt (ed.), *Constructive Therapies*. New York: Guilford Press.

Miller, S., Huble, M., & Duncan, B. (1995), "No More Bells and Whistles," *Family Therapy Networker*, 19(2), 53–63.

O'Hanlon, W. (1994), "The Third Wave," *Family Therapy Networker*, 18(6), 19–29.

Ornstien, R., and Sobel, D. (1987), *The Healing Brain*. New York: Simon and Schuster.

Peterson, C., and Bassio, L. M. (1991), *Health and Optimism*. New York: Macmillan.

Saleeby, D. (ed.) (1992), *The Strengths Perspective in Social Work Practice*. New York: Longman.

Selekman, M. (1993), *Pathways to Change: Brief Therapy Solutions with Difficult Adolescents*. New York: Guilford Press.

Spiegel, H. and Linn, L. (1969), "The 'Ripple Effect' Following Adjunct Hypnosis in Analytic Psychotherapy," *American Journal of Psychiatry*, 126, 53–58.

Talmon, M. (1990), *Single Session Therapy: Maximizing the Effect of the First (and Often Only) Therapeutic Encounter*. San Francisco: Jossey-Bass.

Taylor, S. E. (1989), *Positive Illusions*. New York: Basic Books.

Walters, C. and Havens, R. (1994), "Good News for a Change: Optimism, Altruism and Hardiness as a Basis for Erickson's Approach," in J. Zieg (ed.), *Ericksonian Methods: The Essence of the Story*. New York: Brunner/Mazel.

Wiener-Davis, M., de Shazer, S., & Gingerich, W. J. (1987), "Building on Pretreatment Change to Construct the Therapeutic Solution: An Exploratory Study," *Journal of Marital and Family Therapy*, 13, (4), 359–363.

Section *VII*

Behavior Modification

Of all the treatment techniques described in this book, behavior modification holds the distinction of being the most debated. Proponents of this technique applaud its ease of implementation; clearly observable results; and applicability to a wide range of populations, ranging from autistic or hyperactive preschoolers through nursing-home residents troubled by problems of senility. Those who oppose or would severely restrict its use argue that it borders on "thought or mind control," reduces the production of acceptable human behavior to the level of training an animal, or has such a strong potential for abuse that it must be carefully monitored.

The truth about behavior modification's benefits and hazards certainly lies somewhere between these two extremes. Much of the criticism of behavior modification has arisen from public confusion about what it is and references to the use of electric shocks and drug therapy in some types of behavior modification. Selection 25, "Behavior Modification: Perspective on a Current Issue," clearly defines just what behavior modification is and is not, gives examples of the types of positive reinforcement and aversion stimuli that are common to behavior modification programs, and discusses the special considerations attendant upon the use of behavior modification programs in a correctional institution.

The use of behavior modification in an institution poses special problems. A therapist must walk the line between working to modify the inmates' behavior in a manner that will make them more law-abiding citizens *after* they leave the institution and changing their behavior to accommodate living *within* the walls—that is, making them more docile, easier to handle, or respectful of authority. The correctional setting provides opportunities for abuse of behavior modification techniques that would not be likely to occur elsewhere. For example, the "time out" method of aversion stimulus, which amounts to removing the offender to a room, alone, for a short period of time, could easily be expanded to punitive periods of solitary confinement. Denial of privileges could be misused in the same manner.

On the positive side, the institution offers the most controlled environment for behavior modification, since inmates are less open to outside influences and a wide range of privileges or desirable items can be offered as positive reinforcements or rewards to encourage or sustain good behavior.

Students and evaluators of behavior modification therapy generally conclude that the individual doing the reinforcing or applying aversion stimuli is the key factor in the program's success. A number of studies of behavior modification involving delinquents discovered that positive reinforcement is most important at the beginning of a program (Bednar et al., 1970); that the personalities of the therapists providing the reinforcement or aversion were important factors in behavioral changes (Tyler and Brown, 1968); and that the more clearly defined the expected behaviors were, the greater the chance of achieving them (McPherson and Cyrille, 1971). After reviewing and summarizing fourteen studies of behavior modification programs involving almost 2,000 delinquents in the United States, Romig (1976: 20) concluded that "Behavior modification is certainly no panacea for juvenile delinquency. Behavior modification did work to change certain behaviors, such as school attendance, test scores, promptness, and classroom behavior. However, it did not affect something as global as delinquency or arrest rate."

References

Bednar, R. L., P. F. Zelhart, L. Greathouse, and W. Weinberg. 1970. "Operant Conditioning Principles in the Treatment of Learning and Behavior Problems with Delinquent Boys," *Journal of Counseling Psychology* 17:492–497.

McPherson, S. B. and R. S. Cyrille. 1971. "Teaching Behavioral Methods to Parents," *Social Casework* 5:148–153.

Romig, Dennis A. 1978. *Justice for Our Children.* 1978. Lexington, MA: Lexington Books.

Tyler, V. and G. Brown. 1968. "Token Reinforcement of Academic Performance with Institutionalized Delinquent Boys," *Journal of Educational Psychology* 59: 164–168.

25

Behavior Modification
Perspective on a Current Issue

Bertram S. Brown
Louis A. Wienckowski
Stephanie B. Stolz

Introduction

In the history of civilization, people have continuously tried to control their environment and to find ways of teaching themselves and their children better means of acquiring new skills and capabilities. Common-sense notions of the ways that reward and punishment can change behavior have existed since time immemorial. Thus, elements of what is now referred to as behavior modification were used long before psychologists and other behavioral scientists developed systematic principles of learning.

As behavior modification procedures are used ever more widely, many different concerns have been expressed. On the one hand, the public and mental health professionals are concerned about whether behavior modification procedures are sufficiently well demonstrated through research for these procedures to be generally recommended and widely disseminated. On the other hand, behavior modification has acted as a conceptual "lightning rod" in the midst of stormy controversies over ethical problems associated with attempts at social influence, drawing to it such

Source: U.S. Department of Health, Education and Welfare, National Institute of Mental Health. Washington, D.C.: U.S. Government Printing Office (1976).

highly charged issues as fear of "mind control" or concerns about the treatment of persons institutionalized against their will. Apparent or actual infringements of rights, as well as some abuses of behavioral procedures, have led to litigation and calls for curbs on the use of behavior modification.

Everyone tries continually to influence his own and others' behavior, so that the individual using behavior modification procedures is distinctive only in that he is attempting to influence behavior more systematically. Commenting on this issue, one attorney has said that to be opposed to behavior modification is to be opposed to the law of gravity. Rather, the key issue is what sort of care, caution, and control should be exercised when behavioral principles are applied precisely and systematically.

This report is intended to provide an objective overview of the history and current methods of behavior modification and to review some critical issues, in an effort to aid the reader in differentiating between warranted and unwarranted concerns. We will also make some suggestions regarding ethical standards and practices.

What Is Behavior Modification?

To understand behavior modification, it is helpful first to clarify its relationship to a broader concept, behavior influence.

Behavior influence occurs whenever one person exerts some degree of control over another. This occurs constantly in such diverse situations as formal school education, advertising, child rearing, political campaigning, and other normal interpersonal interactions.

Behavior modification is a special form of behavior influence that involves primarily the application of principles derived from research in experimental psychology to alleviate human suffering and enhance human functioning. Behavior modification emphasizes systematic monitoring and evaluation of the effectiveness of these applications. The techniques of behavior modification are generally intended to facilitate improved self-control by expanding individuals' skills, abilities, and independence.

Most behavior modification procedures are based on the general principle that people are influenced by the consequences of their behavior. The current environment is believed to be more relevant in affecting the individual's behavior than most early life experiences or than enduring intrapsychic conflicts or personality structure. Insofar as possible, the behaviorally oriented mental health worker limits the conceptualization of the problem to observable behavior and its environmental context, rather than including references to hypothesized internal processes such as traits or feelings.

In professional use of behavior modification, a contractual agreement may be negotiated, specifying mutually agreeable goals and procedures. When the client is an adult who has sought therapy, the contract would be between him and the mental health worker. When the behavior modification program is to benefit a mentally disadvantaged group, such as the retarded, senile, or psychotic, the contract is often between the individuals' guardians or other responsible persons and the mental health worker. Parents, who usually make decisions affecting their young children, generally are consulted by the mental health worker regarding treatment for their children. Who the appropriate person is to make the contractual agreement for a prisoner is a complex and unsettled issue, taken up later in this report in connection with the discussion of the use of behavior modification procedures with prisoners.

Behavior therapy is a term that is sometimes used synonymously with behavior modification. In general, behavior modification is considered to be the broader term, while behavior therapy refers mainly to clinical interventions, usually applied in a one-to-one therapist-patient relationship. That is, behavior therapy is a special form of behavior modification.

Behavior modification typically tries to influence behavior by changing the environment and the way people interact, rather than by intervening directly through medical procedures (such as drugs) or surgical procedures (such as psychosurgery). Thus, behavior modification methods can be used in a broad range of situations, including the child-rearing efforts of parents and the instructional activities of teachers, as well as the therapeutic efforts of mental health workers in treating more serious psychological and behavioral problems. The effects of behavior modification, unlike the results of most surgical procedures, are relatively changeable and impermanent.

Behavior modification procedures require that the problem behavior be clearly specified. That is, the mental health worker must be able to define objectively the response that the service recipient wants to learn or to have reduced. Thus, certain kinds of problems treated by dynamic psychotherapy are simply not appropriate candidates for behavior modification. In particular, the patient who seeks therapy because of an existential crisis—"Who am I? Where am I going?"—is not an appropriate candidate for behavior modification. This quasi-philosophical problem does not lend itself to an approach that deals with specific identifiable behavior in particular environmental contexts. It is possible that a patient who describes his problem in this way actually has some specific behavioral deficits that may underlie his existential difficulties or occur alongside them. Whether a careful behavioral analysis of the patient's difficulties would reveal such deficits is not now known, however.

While it has been alleged that secret, powerful psychotechnological tools are being or would be used to control the masses, researchers in behavior modification point out that they have encouraged the dissemination of information about behavior processes. In fact, workers in this area believe that increased knowledge will help people to understand social influence processes in general and actually would enable them to counteract many attempts at control, if such attempts occurred. Many persons using behavior modification methods not only evaluate the effectiveness of their procedures, but also measure the consumers' satisfaction with the behavior modification program used.

Is Behavior Modification Merely Common Sense?

Many persons who learn about the general procedures of behavior modification say that they seem to be nothing more than common sense. To some considerable extent, this is true. For example, parents are using these techniques whenever they praise their children for good report cards in the hope of encouraging continued interest and application. On the job, promotions and incentive awards are universally accepted as ways of encouraging job performance. The very structure of our laws, with specified fines, penalties, and the like, is intended to modify behavior through aversive control.

Behavior modification, however, like other scientific approaches, imposes an organization on its subject matter. While common sense often includes contradictory advice (both "out of sight, out of mind," and "absence makes the heart grow fonder"), the principles of behavior modification codify and organize common sense, showing under what conditions, and in what circumstances, which aspect of "common sense" should be applied. The mothers and grandmothers who use what could be described as behavior modification procedures may often do so inconsistently, and then not understand why they have failed.

What Behavior Modification Is Not

As more publicity has been given to this approach, the term "behavior modification" has come to be used loosely and imprecisely in the public media, often with a negative connotation. Thus, behavior modification has sometimes been said to include psychosurgery, electroconvulsive therapy (ECT), and the noncontingent administration of drugs, that is, the administration of drugs independent of any specific behavior of the person receiving the medication. However, even though procedures such as these do modify behavior, that does not make them "behavior modification techniques," in the sense in which most professionals in the field use the term. In this report, the use of the term "behavior modification" will be consistent with its professional use; that is, behavior modification will be used to refer to procedures that are based on the explicit and systematic application of principles and technology derived from research in experimental psychology, procedures that involve some change in the social or environmental context of a person's behavior. This use of the term specifically excludes psychosurgery, electroconvulsive therapy, and the administration of drugs independent of any specific behavior of the person receiving the medication.

History of Behavior Modification

Even though behavior modification is new within the behavioral sciences, the basic experimental work designed to obtain a precise understanding of the principles of learning dates back at least 75 years. Pavlov's first book, *Work on the Digestive Glands*, was published in Russian in 1897. Since then, those initial studies have been followed up with extensive laboratory experiments on learning in both animals and humans. It is on this broad foundation of experimental research that behavior modification principles are based.

The clinical use of behavior modification has a somewhat shorter history, since reports in the scientific literature of such applications have occurred mainly within the past 15 years, although some work was done as early as the 1920s and 1930s (e.g., Jones 1924; Mowrer and Mowrer 1938). Building on animal research by Skinner and his students, the pioneering work of Lindsley (Lindsley and Skinner 1954) and Ferster and DeMyer (1961) demonstrated that the behavior of even such severely disturbed individuals as adult psychotics and autistic children actually followed the same psychological laws as that of normal persons. Wolpe (see, e.g., 1958), working from a more neurophysiologically based theory, developed the method of systematic desensitization, a technique for treating neurotic behavior patterns. Psychologists and psychiatrists in England (Shapiro 1961; Eysenck 1952) also contributed to the early growth of behavior modification.

Once these and other researchers had shown that the principles of learning applied to severely disturbed persons, the development of the field of behavior modification began to accelerate. On the whole, applied researchers have found that the principles developed in laboratory research can be applied effectively to many behavior problems in the real world.

Behavioral treatment interventions were first used with regressed psychotics and neurotic adults (Ayllon and Michael 1959; Ayllon and Azrin 1965; Wolpe and Lazarus 1966). Extensive clinical work has shown that behavior therapy techniques can be effective in eliminating many incapacitating neurotic fears, such as fear of flying in planes. Behavior therapists working with regressed psychotics have been able to develop a variety of adaptive behaviors in these patients so that the patients' lives were enriched by the availability of many new choices (e.g., Ayllon and Azrin 1968).

From these beginnings, the field of behavior modification has expanded to new clinical populations and new settings, including delinquents in halfway houses, the retarded, preschool and deaf children and drug abusers. Some autistic children, who might otherwise be continuously restrained in straightjackets because of their attempts at severe self-mutilation, have been helped by properly designed programs to control their own behavior effectively (e.g., Lovaas et al. 1973). Severely retarded children previously considered incapable of any learning other than the most basic, have, in some instances, been shown capable of acquiring some intellectual skills (e.g., Baer and Guess 1971). Delinquents who would otherwise have been incarcerated at great cost to themselves and to society have often been successfully helped in behaviorally oriented community settings, their own homes, and schools (e.g., Phillips et al. 1971). Some of the drug abusers who have chosen abstinence as a goal have been helped to attain this objective and carry on a normal life without opiates (e.g., Thomson and Rathod 1968).

A large amount of behavior modification research has been done with normal children, including research on improving classroom management, teaching methods, and parent-child relations. Children whose behavior is only mildly maladaptive can be treated by their parents or teachers, because behavior modification lends itself to use by persons not professionally trained in therapy. Most recently, behavior modification has been extended to social problems such as the facilitation of cooperative living in a public housing project, decreasing littering, encouraging the use of public transportation, and enabling unemployed persons to find jobs.

Behavior modification procedures are now used by psychologists, psychiatrists, educators, social workers, speech therapists, and members of other helping professions.

Current Practice of Behavior Modification

Behavior modification is a family of techniques. The diverse methods included under the general label have in common the goal of enhancing persons' lives by altering specific aspects of their behavior. Ideally, the mental health worker and the service recipient decide together on a mutually agreeable set of treatment goals and on the means for attaining these goals. The service recipient or his representative should be kept fully informed of the results of the treatment as it progresses, and also participate in any modification of goals or techniques.

The initial analysis of the problem typically should begin with a detailed description of the behavior that is causing distress or interfering with optimal functioning of the individual in familial, social, vocational, or other important spheres of activity. The behavioral goals are to be viewed in the context of everything the person is able to do, and also in terms of what kinds of support his usual environment is capable of providing over the long term.

This description, whenever possible, should be based on observations of the individual in the setting in which he reports that he is distressed. These observations may be careful quantitative records, or they may be statements about the relative frequency of various behaviors. The person making the observations may be the therapist or his agent, a peer of the individual receiving the service, or the individual himself. For example, a parent might be trained to tally the frequency with which a child stutters, a teacher or hospital aide might keep a record of a child's aggressive outbursts, and a well-motivated individual can count the frequency of occurrence of an unacceptable habit such as nail-biting.

In addition to obtaining this description of what the individual does and does not do, the behavioral mental health worker should try to find how the individual's behavior relates to various events and places in his current and past experiences. Relevant for behavior modification are the events that immediately precede and that immediately follow the behavior. The goal should be to determine the circumstances under which the behavior seems to occur and the environmental consequences that might be maintaining it.

Behavior modification, then, involves the systematic variation of behavioral and environmental factors thought to be associated with an individual's difficulties, with the primary goal of modifying his behavior in the direction that, ideally, he himself (or his agent) has chosen.

Transition to the Nontreatment Setting

The goal of all treatment is the maintenance of improvement after the termination of therapy. The ideal behavior modification program would include a specification of the environment in which the individual normally would be living, and a provision for establishing and strengthening behavior desired or useful in that environment. Generalization to the natural environment is helped if the behavior modification program includes a planned transition between the therapeutic program and the natural environment. The following example illustrates this principle:

> *O. Ivar Lovaas (UCLA) has been studying autistic children for a number of years.[1] He has found that when parents have been trained to carry on with a behavior modification program, children continue to improve after they have left his special treatment ward. On the other hand, the children regress if they are returned to institutions after leaving the ward, and no longer participate in a special training program.*

Examples of Behavior Modification Methods

This section briefly describes some of the most common behavior modification methods. This is a young field, and other techniques are continually being developed and evaluated by clinical researchers. Thus, the methods included here should not be considered an exhaustive list.

Methods Using Positive Reinforcement.   Positive reinforcement is a technical term that is roughly synonymous with reward. A positive reinforcer is defined as any event following a given response that increases the chances of that response recurring. Typical positive reinforcers include tangible items, such as money or food; social events such as praise or attention; and activities, such as the opportunity to engage in recreation or to watch television. However, what is reinforcing or motivating for some people—what they will work for—is not necessarily reinforcing for others. As a result, when using behavior modification procedures with any individual, the mental health worker needs to determine what particular items and activities will reinforce that person's behavior at that time.

Methods that use positive reinforcement form the major class of methods among behavior modification techniques. In general, positive reinforcement is used to develop and maintain new behavior, and the removal of positive reinforcement is used to decrease the frequency of undesired behavior. Positive reinforcement has been used in teaching social behavior, in improving classroom management, in motivating better and faster learning of academic materials, in maintaining necessary weight loss, and in teaching new skills of all sorts.

> *Positive reinforcement is being used to help disruptive underachieving children, in one research project.*[1] *Among a variety of procedures being used, teachers praise the children for appropriate behavior and send home daily reports. The children's parents reward them for good daily reports. The researcher, K. Daniel O'Leary (State University of New York, Stony Brook), reports that the children's disruptive behavior has been reduced as a result of this program.*

Although some positive reinforcers are much more effective if a person has been deprived of them for a while, others continue to be reinforcing virtually regardless of how often an individual is exposed to them. Thus, by carefully selecting reinforcers, it should not be necessary to deprive an individual beyond the natural deprivations that occur in daily life in order to be able to reinforce him positively.

One increasingly common use of positive reinforcement is in the group management procedure called a *token economy* (Ayllon and Azrin 1968). In a successful token economy program, the participants receive tokens when they engage in appropriate behavior, and, at some later time, exchange the tokens for any of a variety of positively reinforcing items and activities, just as money is used in society at large. Thus, the token economy is basically a work-payment incentive system. As such, it can be used with institutionalized persons to strengthen behavior that is compatible with that needed in the society at large, such as regular performance on a job, self-care, maintenance of one's living quarters, and exchange of currency for desired items.

One advantage of the token economy, given the limitation in professional manpower, is that nonprofessional personnel are typically the actual agents of therapeutic change. If therapeutic procedures are going to be extended to the many persons who require help, professional personnel must make increased use of those who are in direct contact with the persons requiring service. Those persons who can administer a token economy without special advanced training include nurses, aides, correctional officers, and friends and family members of the individual receiving the service. Such persons should, of course, receive appropriate professional supervision.

The early development of the token economy system took place almost exclusively in closed psychiatric wards. Token economies were found quite useful in preventing or overcoming the deterioration of normal social behavior, or what Gruenberg (1967) has called the "social breakdown syndrome," that accompanies prolonged custodial hospitalization, whatever the initial diagnosis. The token economy method is now being extended to acute psychiatric programs, to public school classrooms, and to classrooms for disadvantaged, hyperactive, retarded, and emotionally disturbed children (Anderson 1967; O'Leary and Drabman 1971). Such programs have also been used with delinquents and persons with character disorders to enhance educational achievement and to improve adjustment to military or civilian environments (Cohen and Filipczak 1971; Colman 1971). Tokens have been used to increase children's attention span and to improve self-help skills in retardates (e.g., Minge and Ball 1967).

In the behavior modification technique of *shaping*, a desired behavior is broken down into successive steps that are taught one by one. Each of the steps is reinforced until it is mastered, and then the individual is moved to the next one. In this way, the new behavior is gradually learned as what the individual does becomes a closer and closer approximation of the behavioral goal.

New behavior can also be taught by means of *modeling*. In this method, a person who already knows how to engage in some desired behavior demonstrates it for the individual who is learning. For example, if a client were learning socially appropriate ways to greet members of the opposite sex, another person might demonstrate them for the client.

> *The model demonstrating the appropriate behavior can be an actual one or an imaginary one. Alan E. Kazdin (Pennsylvania State University) is conducting a study of some facets of imaginary or covert modeling.[1] Subjects in his study are college students who have problems in assertiveness. They are taught to imagine one or several other persons engaging in the sort of assertive behavior that the subjects hope to learn, and then are tested to see how much their own assertiveness has increased.*

In *contingency contracting*, the mental health worker and the client decide together on the behavioral goals and on the reinforcement that the client will receive when the goals are achieved. For example, a parent and child might agree that it would be desirable if the home were neater, specifically, if the child's playthings were appropriately stored after a certain time in the evening. The child might request that the parent agree to take him to a favorite activity after the child had put away his playthings for a specified number of days. A contract often involves an exchange, that is, each person entering into the contract agrees both to change his own behavior and to provide reinforcement for the changes that the other person makes. Such a mutual contract is frequently used in marriage counseling.

> *The methods of contingency contracting are being studied by Henry M. Boudin (University of Florida) to see how they can be made effective for dealing with the special behavior problems characteristic of drug abusers.*[2] *The goal of this project is to reduce drug dependence in addicts who are being treated in an outpatient setting. The contracts made between the drug abusers and the therapists cover a large number of aspects of the addicts' lives. For example, an addict might agree to set up a joint bank account with his therapist, to which the addict deposits his own money. If a urine test indicates that he has broken his promise not to use illegal drugs, funds are taken from that account by the therapist and sent to some organization that the addict strongly dislikes. Contracts work both ways: If the therapist is late for an appointment with the addict or misses a therapy session, he can be required to deposit money to the addict's account. A contract involving positive reinforcement might specify that if the addict completes some amount of time on a job, he would receive a few movie passes or discounts on some number of phonograph records.*

Aversive Control.   Some types of inappropriate behavior, such as addictions and certain sexual behaviors, appear to be maintained because their immediate consequences are naturally reinforcing for the individual. In such cases, aversive control techniques are sometimes used to combat long-term consequences that may be much more detrimental to the individual than the aversive methods themselves. Aversive methods are also used for behaviors that are life-threatening, such as severe self-mutilation.

In general, an aversive stimulus, that is, something that is unpleasant to the person, is used to help the person reduce his desire to carry out the inappropriate behavior (Rachman and Teasdale 1969). After aversive therapy, for example, a man who formerly became excited sexually only when thinking of women's shoes, might report that he had lost interest in the shoes. With aversive techniques, the aversive stimulus will not occur, that is, the individual is able to avoid it, as long as he does not perform the behavior that he and the mental health worker have agreed is undesirable. When aversive therapy is appropriately conducted, it is accompanied by positive reinforcement of normal behavior.

Perhaps the most commonly used aversive stimulus in behavior modification is a brief, low-level electric shock. This type of aversive stimulus has been highly effective in ameliorating severe behavioral problems such as self-injurious behavior (see, e.g., Bucher 1969). When properly used, the shocks are very brief. Shock used this way causes no lingering pain or tissue damage and can be administered with precise control (Baer 1970). The use of shock as an aversive control procedure is entirely different from its use in electroconvulsive therapy, a procedure completely outside the scope of behavior modification.

A different type of aversive control method is the removal of positive reinforcement, such as a loss of privileges following a given behavior. This is a technique commonly used by American parents (Sears, Maccoby, and Levin 1957). One example of a technique involving the removal of positive reinforcement is the *time-out* procedure, in which an inappropriate behavior is followed by a period of brief social isolation.

The time-out procedure is one of a number of behavior modification techniques being used in a study of preschool children with poor social, language, and cognitive skills.[1] *The goal of the investigator, Donald M. Baer (University of Kansas), is to reduce these children's hyperactive and rebellious behavior. When a child engages in disruptive behavior, he is placed for a brief period in a small room adjoining the classroom. This aversive control for disruptive behavior is combined with a wide variety of positive reinforcing procedures for appropriate behavior. Positive reinforcers used in this study include attention, praise, access to preferred activities, and snacks.*

Fines are another example of aversive control; fines require the individual to give up some positive reinforcement following an instance of inappropriate behavior.

One common use of aversive stimuli is in attempts to reduce excessive drinking by associating the drinking experience with an aversive stimulus. For example, recent research on alcoholism has employed electric shock as an aversive stimulus to teach the alcoholic patient to avoid continued drinking beyond a criterion blood alcohol level. This has reportedly been successful in helping problem drinkers learn to limit their intake to moderate levels typical of social drinking (Lovibond 1970).

In research by Roger E. Vogler (Patton State Hospital and Pacific State Hospital, California), alcoholic persons being treated either in the hospital or as outpatients receive electric shock if they drink too much alcohol in a bar-like setting in the hospital.[3] Shock is also used to train the patients to discriminate when their blood alcohol concentration exceeds a specific level, and to teach them to drink slowly.

Drugs such as Anectine and Antabuse have also been used as aversive treatment for alcoholic persons (see section on Methods Using Drugs, below).

The other relatively common use of aversive stimuli is to control self-injurious and self-destructive behavior such as head-banging or tongue-biting. Such behavior can apparently be eliminated with a brief application of a strong aversive stimulus immediately after the response (Risley 1968; Bucher and Lovaas 1968).

Occasionally, infants, young children, and some mentally retarded persons "ruminate," that is, they apparently voluntarily reject food from their stomachs into their mouths where it may be reswallowed or further ejected from their mouths. When this problem is severe, it can be life-threatening and may have serious detrimental effects on the physical, emotional, and social development of the child. Thomas Sajwaj (University of Mississippi) has developed a procedure using lemon juice as a mild aversive stimulus to control the ruminative behavior: when the infant or child regurgitates, a small amount of lemon juice is immediately squirted into his mouth by an attendant.[1] Preliminary results with a few children suggest that this aversive therapy eliminates the rumination, and that no other maladaptive behavior appears.

A consistent finding from research on aversive control is that the effects of the therapeutic use of aversive stimuli seem to be restricted to the particular behavior that is associated with the aversive stimulus, in that particular situation, with that particular therapist. That is, the effects of aversive stimuli do not seem to generalize very much (Risley 1968; Bucher and Lovaas 1968).

In contrast to the somewhat limited effects of aversive stimuli in controlling undesirable behavior, the positive side effects of this treatment seem to be rather widespread. For example, it is commonly reported that once the use of aversive stimuli has eliminated a patient's self-injurious behavior, he avoids people less and is more responsive to other therapy aimed at teaching him adaptive responses.

While the effects of aversive stimuli may, in many cases, be only temporary, the individual will not make the undesirable response for at least some period of time. During that time, he is more amenable to learning new, appropriate responses. On the whole, research suggests that the most effective way of eliminating inappropriate behavior is to follow it with aversive stimuli, while at the same time positively reinforcing desired behavior. If the environment then continues to support the new, desired responses, the inappropriate behavior will soon cease to occur. Since the aversive stimuli are used only following inappropriate behavior, they will no longer be administered. The effects of the initial aversive control will, however, be lasting, because the individual will now have learned to make appropriate responses.

It is important to note, however, that in the absence of rewarded alternatives, the response that had been suppressed by an aversive technique is likely to recur. To ensure that it does not, the individual being treated should learn behavior that will be maintained by rewards that occur naturally in his environment. In some instances, simply stopping the undesirable behavior enables the individual to get natural rewards. For the "ruminating" child, for example, stopping the ejection of food in itself allows proper digestion of food, greater comfort, and normal eating, growing, and developing. In addition, the infant is now more receptive to normal learning experiences.

Overcorrection.   Overcorrection is a behavior modification method combining positive reinforcement and aversive control that is used to discourage inappropriate or disruptive behavior. In this procedure, the person who has engaged in the inappropriate behavior not only remedies the situation he has caused, but also "overcorrects" it. That is, the person is required to restore the disruptive situation to a better state than existed before the disruption. For example, a violent patient in a mental institution who overturns a bed in a dormitory might be required not only to right that bed and make it up again, but also to straighten the bedclothes on all the other beds in that dormitory. Making up the bed that was overturned corrects the situation that the violent behavior disrupted; making up all the other beds is, then, an "overcorrection."

Often an inappropriate or disruptive behavior has been receiving some sort of reinforcement. For example, stealing results in the thief acquiring goods he desires; turning over a bed might get a patient attention and concern from an otherwise busy ward staff. Thus, one function of the overcorrection procedure is to terminate any such reinforcement associated with the inappropriate behavior: the thief must return the stolen goods, for example.

Moreover, overcorrection is an aversive stimulus, because it requires effort to complete the overcorrection, and because the person cannot be engaging in other behavior while he is completing the overcorrection task. In addition, the overcorrection procedure itself may often be educative, in that the process of restoring the original situation generally requires the individual to engage in appropriate behavior.

Overcorrection has been a particularly effective technique in eliminating aggressive and disruptive behavior in institutionalized patients (Foxx and Azrin 1972; Webster and Azrin 1973). One of the advantages of overcorrection over other methods for dealing with these problems is that severe aversive stimuli may not be involved in overcorrection.

Systematic Desensitization. Gradual, progressive exposure to feared situations has long been advocated as a means of eliminating or reducing maladaptive anxiety or avoidance behavior. In systematic desensitization, the exposure is preplanned in graduated steps. In general, this procedure involves teaching the patient to relax, and then having him imagine or actually encounter increasingly disturbing situations. The patient usually does not move on to a more disturbing item until he can remain deeply relaxed with a less disturbing one. Recent research, however, has suggested that some degree of forced exposure can also be effective in reducing fears.

If a patient is afraid of heights, for example, the therapist works together with the patient to develop a list of increasingly fearful situations. For example, the patient might say he is very afraid of looking out from the top of the Empire State Building, but hardly afraid at all of climbing a small ladder. He then is trained to relax, and the therapist asks him to imagine each of the series of situations, starting with the one he is least afraid of, the one arousing little or no tension or fear. Over a series of therapy sessions, the patient will be exposed systematically to the whole list of fearful situations, and, at the end of treatment, will be able to maintain his relaxed state even while imagining scenes that were initially extremely fearful. Patients are usually encouraged to try out their newly learned ability to relax in the face of the formerly fearful situation outside of the therapy setting. Generalization of the effects of systematic desensitization from the treatment setting to real life is typically found, especially when the patient has done the "homework" of gradually facing what used to be fearful.

Systematic desensitization has been used clinically by behavior therapists to treat unreasonable fears, frigidity, insomnia, interpersonal anxiety, and other clinical problems in which anxiety is a core problem.

> *Systematic desensitization is being used with a variety of problems. For example, Thomas L. Creer (Children's Asthma Research Institute and Hospital, Denver) has demonstrated the effectiveness of systematic desensitization in the treatment of*

children's asthma.[1] *As a result of the treatment, the children learned to be less afraid of having asthma attacks and used significantly less medication. Desensitization is also being used as a treatment for insomnia (Richard R. Bootzin, Northwestern University)*[1] *and as a component of treatment for marital sexual dysfunction (Joseph LoPiccolo, State University of New York, Stony Brook).*[1]

Assertive Training.   When a person fails to stand up for his rights in an appropriately firm manner, he may not have acquired appropriate assertive behavior, or he may not be engaging in behavior that he actually knows how to do. Similarly, persons who do not express positive feelings in appropriate situations also may lack appropriate assertive skills or an appreciation of the situations in which those skills should normally be used.

Assertive training is taught by a combination of methods, including modeling of appropriate behavior by the therapist or some other person, and reinforced practice by the patient. The overall goal of this type of behavior therapy is the alteration of the patient's interpersonal interactions.

Methods Using Drugs.   On the whole, behavior modification procedures emphasize environmental manipulation. However, drugs have occasionally been used as an integral part of a behavioral treatment, either following a particular behavior, or as an adjunct to a behavioral program.

A few case studies in the literature report the use of drugs as aversive stimuli, when the therapist was attempting to reduce some inappropriate behavior. For example, succinylcholine chloride (Anectine) was given to one individual who had a severe dependency on sniffing various substances such as airplane glue. In the treatment, the patient sniffed one of these substances and was immediately injected with Anectine, which produces an extremely unpleasant sensation of drowning and suffocating. The treatment was conducted under the supervision of an anesthesiologist. After this treatment, the patient refrained from sniffing the substance that had been associated with the Anectine (Blanchard, Libet, and Young 1973).

Anectine, and emetic drugs such as Antabuse, have also been used as aversive treatment for alcoholic persons, although the evidence suggests that they are not strongly effective treatments.

When drugs are used as part of an aversive control program in behavior modification, they must take effect immediately after the occurrence of a specific inappropriate behavior. This temporal relationship between the behavior and the aversive action of the drug is considered to be an essential aspect of the therapy. As noted later in this paper, giving aversive drugs independently of a person's behavior is not behavior modification, in the sense in which we are using that term.

Drugs are also sometimes used to facilitate the progress of a behavioral program. Brevital is a drug that enhances relaxation. Some practitioners who do systematic desensitization give their patients small doses of Brevital, if the patients are otherwise having trouble learning to relax in the therapy session (Brady 1966). Usually the dosage level of the drug is gradually adjusted so that the patient soon relaxes without the assistance of the drug.

Evaluation of Behavior Modification

Collecting evidence that would show whether behavior modification is effective is not as easy as it would seem. Several conceptual issues first need to be resolved. In order to evaluate behavior modification, the types of problems for which it is appropriate must be delimited, suitable outcome measures must be selected, and appropriate comparison conditions must be chosen.

While therapists who use behavior modification feel that it is appropriate for a wide range of problems, other persons have questioned the appropriateness of a behavioral approach to many mental health problems because of their belief that the therapy for a particular problem must direct itself to the root cause of the problem. In that view, disorders of biological origin should be treated with biologically based principles, while those of psychological origin should be treated psychotherapeutically.

A substantial body of opinion insists that there need not be a relationship between the etiology of a problem and the nature of the treatment that is effective in ameliorating it (Birk et al. 1973; London 1972). A disorder with an organic or neurophysiological etiology may be responsive to a biological therapy, but it may also be markedly improved by one of the procedures based on behavior modification. Similarly, difficulties that have an environmental origin may be responsive to biological intervention, such as psychopharmacologic treatment, as well as to a behavioral treatment. Behavior modification is based on learning principles, and so is particularly suitable for those problems, whatever their etiology, where the appropriate treatment involves retraining or learning new skills.

Therapists who use behavior modification methods would choose an objective, preferably quantifiable, measure of behavior as the outcome measure for evaluating the efficacy of treatment procedures. This selection contrasts with the outcome measures preferred by classical psychodynamically oriented therapists, who feel that personality tests reflect the changes that they seek to achieve in therapy. These psychotherapists may, in fact, regard as "mere symptoms" what the behaviorally oriented therapists regard as the focus of treatment. One of the consequences of this difference in viewpoints is that it is extremely difficult to obtain general agreement on a set of outcome measures for a comparison of the effects of behavior modification and psychotherapy.

The ideal evaluation of the effectiveness of behavior modification would tell us whether behavioral procedures bring about improvement more often, more quickly, to a greater degree, longer, or at less cost than do alternative procedures, such as psychotherapy. Unfortunately, at least in part because of the difficulty in obtaining agreement among professionals on what constitutes "improvement," this sort of direct comparison has been made systematically in only a few studies.

Despite the conceptual problems in making comparisons of different kinds of treatments, however, researchers have recently begun to conduct comparative evaluations in which one group of individuals receives a standard, well-accepted treatment, conscientiously applied, while another receives some kind of behavior modification, again conscientiously applied. This kind of research is aimed at answering the important questions of relative therapeutic efficacy and cost-effectiveness. By comparing results obtained on a variety of outcome measures with existing, standard procedures and with behavior modification, researchers will begin to provide the evidence necessary for deciding whether the costs of introducing new procedures, training staff in those procedures, and making changes in supervision and recordkeeping, will be adequately repaid with a significant improvement in the functioning of the persons treated.

Although few comparisons have been made of behavior modification with other forms of treatment, large numbers of case studies and systematic evaluations of behavior modification have been reported in which the researchers have shown experimentally that the behavior modification methods were responsible for the improvements obtained. To summarize these many reports briefly, behavior therapy has been shown to be effective with some persons suffering from unjustified fears, anxiety reactions, and stuttering. Problems that have shown some improvement when individuals have been treated by behavior therapy procedures include compulsive behavior, hysteria, psychological impotence, frigidity, exhibitionism, and insomnia.

Behavior modification procedures have been used to analyze and produce significant changes in the language of institutionalized retardates who were initially deficient in language skills. Control of self-destructive and self-mutilating behavior has been achieved in a number of cases through behavior modification, as has the elimination or great reduction of milder forms of disruptive behavior, such as tantrums, whining, screaming, fighting, and destruction of property. Positive behaviors developed in institutionalized persons with behavior modification procedures include proper eating techniques and the complete range of self-care skills frequently absent in such persons. In otherwise normal preschool children, behavior modification has been used to facilitate the development of those motor, social and cognitive skills thought especially appropriate to the preschool environment, yet not appearing in the normal course of events in that setting. For example, social isolates have acquired social skills, and silent children, a readiness to speak. Hyperactive children have been taught to attend to tasks, and predelinquents have been taught friendly speech and have learned to perform skills necessary for school achievement, to take appropriate care of their living quarters, to interact cooperatively with their families, and to stop stealing and aggressive behavior (Baer 1973).

Token reinforcement systems have been shown to be effective in many classrooms for modifying behavior problems such as classroom disruption, failure to study, and low academic achievement. Chronic mental patients on wards throughout the country have learned a wide variety of appropriate social behaviors after the introduction of a token economy. The token economy has recently been introduced in a few nursing homes and wards for senile patients, and the early results appear promising. When the behavioral program is in effect, the patients come to interact more with each other and engage in more activities. Studies have shown that careful implementation of behavioral techniques can often produce improvements in the verbal and nonverbal behavior of psychotic and schizophrenic children.

Behavioral treatments have been quite successful with toilet training and most nervous habits, but somewhat less successful with alcoholism, smoking, and tics other than in a few special cases. To the extent that the symptoms of asthma are maintained by environmental consequences, the number and severity of asthmatic attacks can be reduced by behavioral programs designed to rearrange those consequences. Systematic desensitization has also been effective with some asthmatics (Price 1974).

Overall, then, much more evaluative research needs to be done with the behavioral treatments, although they do show considerable promise. With many clinical problems, behavioral procedures have been used only on a few individual cases, so that experimental evidence is lacking for the efficacy of the specific methods used. Thus, while a great range of problems appears to be responsive to behavioral treatment, for many types of problems, validating data are yet to be obtained. The existing evidence is strong enough, however, that an expert task force of the American Psychiatric Association recently concluded that behavior therapy and behavior principles employed in the analysis and treatment of clinical phenomena "have reached a stage of development where they now unquestionably have much to offer informed clinicians in the service of modern clinical and social psychiatry" (Birk et al. 1973).

Current Behavior Modification Programs: ADAMHA

The Alcohol, Drug Abuse, and Mental Health Administration (ADAMHA) is supporting behavior modification research in a wide variety of areas; the amount of that support exceeds $3 million a year, out of a total of over $121 million spent on research. Behavior modification research being conducted with ADAMHA support covers a wide range of problems and populations. Research is being done on the behavioral problems of children and adults, on persons with mild behavior problems and quite severe ones. Researchers are attempting to develop better behavioral techniques for dealing with asthma, insomnia, and hypertension, as well as evaluating new child-rearing techniques and classroom management methods. Behavioral treatments for problems of alcoholism, drug addiction, and juvenile delinquency are also being studied.

Many current projects have been described above as examples of specific behavior modification procedures. A few other projects will be described here, as further indication of the range and scope of support currently being provided.

Montrose M. Wolf, Elery L. Phillips, Dean Fixsen, and others (University of Kansas)[1] have developed a halfway house for predelinquent adolescents that uses procedures of behavior modification. This halfway house, called Achievement Place, is a community-controlled, community-based, family-style residential home for six to eight adolescents who have typically been adjudicated there by the juvenile courts. The program is designed to provide a maximum amount of motivation and instruction to the youths when they first enter, and then, as they develop skills and self-control, to reduce the amount of structure, replacing it with more natural reinforcement conditions. Behavior modification procedures include a token economy; positive reinforcement to shape appropriate social, academic, prevocational, and self-care behavior; and fines for inappropriate behavior. In addition, the adolescents' parents are trained in child management procedures so that the parents can be more successful in guiding their children toward productive lives.

Preliminary findings indicate that Achievement Place youths progress far better than do comparable youths placed on probation or sent to a State training school. This model has been copied widely, and there are now more than 30 such homes in operation in eight States, supported by State and local funds.

Nathan H. Azrin (Anna State Hospital, Illinois) has developed an extensive life-intervention scheme for alcoholic persons, based on behavior modification principles.[3] In this treatment program, vocational, family, and other social reinforcers are rearranged so that the alcoholic person learns new behavior patterns incompatible with drinking. The clients are given marital and job counseling and are introduced to alcohol-free social situations especially established for them. The effectiveness of this treatment package is being compared with that of existing hospital procedures.

A. J. Turner is receiving support for a project in which behavior modification procedures are being used in all possible service areas of the Huntsville-Madison County (Alabama) Mental Health Center.[1] The results obtained on a wide variety of measures administered to the patients in this center are being compared with results on the same measures obtained from patients in a comparable community mental health center that uses standard procedures. Thus far, the experimental community mental health center has reported a much greater decline in State hospitalizations from their catchment area than that shown by comparable counties, as well as decreases in other measures, such as average number of days in the hospital.

Critical Issues in Behavior Modification

Recently, concerns have been widely expressed over the ethical and legal aspects of behavior modification techniques.

The Fear of Control

Some people fear behavior modification and control because of prevalent contemporary attitudes of distrust and skepticism of authority in general, and "mind control" in particular; others have more specific concerns that are related to the practice of behavior modification or, often, to myths and misconceptions about the practice of behavior modification.

General Concerns About Control.   Behavior modification is most often criticized when it is used to alter the behavior of persons who are involuntary participants in therapy. Involuntary patients or subjects include those who are disadvantaged, vulnerable, or powerless because of institutionalization, age, social position, or discrimination.

Perhaps the most frequent complaints are in connection with the treatment of hospitalized mental patients and institutionalized delinquents and criminals. There has been a growing sensitivity to the ambiguity that can underlie diagnosis and choice of treatment goals for these populations. According to this view, a thin line separates social deviance from a mental illness that requires hospitalization. Society can often find it more convenient to institutionalize the deviant individual than to deal with the problem he represents. The hospitalization or incarceration thus may be more in the interest of social control than in the interest of the person's welfare.

The growing distrust of the exercise of control over the helpless and the disadvantaged even challenges the legitimacy of the authority of those who attempt to treat these persons. The authority to treat the institutionalized mentally disordered, for example, has been eroded by the growing dissemination of the notion that mental "illness" is a myth. According to this view, people should accept responsibility for their own behavior, including behavior that might otherwise be termed "mentally ill." Further, an emerging sociological model views the mentally disordered patient as a victim of stresses and strains that reside primarily within the social structure, rather than within the individual.

Credence has been increasingly given to the picture of the mental patient as a victim who is hospitalized for the convenience of society. In that view, treatment is seen as either a form of punishment or a procedure designed to make the patient conform to the requirements of an oppressive society. The mental health worker who proposes to modify the patient's behavior thus can be seen as serving the interests of the oppressor, rather than favoring the right of the person to express his individuality.

The news media, popular books, and movies have given voice to these general concerns. Also, several organizations have, in the last few years, called conferences to explore these issues. For example, the Institute of Society, Ethics, and the Life Sciences, of the Hastings Center (Hastings-on-Hudson, New York), held a series of meetings between 1971 and 1973 in which leaders in mental health research, practice, and public policy explored the problems of behavior control by drugs, the media, and physical manipulation of the brain, and discussed issues relating to the use of behavior control in education and in total institutions such as prisons and mental hospitals. The Institute has released reports summarizing these discussions.

Specific Fears of Behavior Modification. The general concerns mentioned above are relevant to all types of psychotherapy, as well as to behavior modification. In addition, people have expressed other concerns that are more specific to behavior modification procedures.

Behavior modification has been criticized with respect to its theoretical foundation, its goals, and its methods. Some mental health professionals have attacked behavior modification on the grounds that its underlying assumptions are at variance with their basic values and tend to dehumanize man (see, e.g., Carrera and Adams 1970). Contingency contracting, for example, has been said to foster a manipulative, exchange orientation to social interaction, and token economies, an emphasis on materialistic evaluation of human efforts. Mental health professionals, including persons with a behavioral orientation, have also questioned the appropriateness of accepting a patient's definition of his own problem, on the grounds that the patient's self-attribution of deviance can, like his behavior, be seen as learned behavior that is a function of consequences provided by society (Davison 1974; Begelman, 1977).

Another type of concern about the goals of behavior modification was expressed in a detailed law review critique which argued that behavior modification could be used to impose "an orthodoxy of 'appropriate conduct'" on the community (Heldman 1973), and thus to silence social and political dissent. Extremist activist organizations have described the procedures of behavior modification as "crimes against humanity."

The media and literature have incorrectly linked behavior modification with techniques such as psychosurgery, chemotherapy, electroshock, and brainwashing. The fantasied potency of imaginary or untested mind-controlling techniques, popularized in such works as *Brave New World, 1984, The Manchurian Candidate*, and *A Clockwork Orange*, has been extended to encompass standard, carefully evaluated behavior modification techniques.

Further, procedures that are encompassed within behavior modification can be misused. When this happens, critics decry behavior modification, even though the misuse is such that the procedure can no longer accurately be called "behavior modification." For example, Anectine, a drug that produces the sensation of drowning or dying, and Antabuse and other emetic drugs, have occasionally been used as components of behavior modification procedures. In aversive therapy for problems such as glue-sniffing and alcoholism, such drugs may be used as the aversive stimulus. However, these drugs have also been seriously misused, especially in prison settings, where they are given to persons in retribution for real or imagined lack of "cooperation" on their part, or as a way of keeping recalcitrant persons "in line." The noncontingent use of drugs lies outside the purview of behavior modification.

A Perspective On the Issue of Control. Like any technology, behavior modification can be used ineptly, or for ends that could be considered immoral. The technology of behavior modification, says Skinner (1971), "is ethically neutral. It can be used by villain or saint. There is nothing in a methodology which determines the values governing its use" (p. 150). When psychoanalytic therapy was first introduced, it too raised the spectre of unethical authoritarian control. It is likely that any approach to the alteration of human behavior raises these same questions.

In the view of persons working in the field of behavior modification, it is the nature of social interaction for people to influence each other. In other words, behavior is continually being influenced, and it is inevitably controlled. Therapy without manipulation is a mirage that disappears on close scrutiny (Shapiro and Birk 1967). That is, in all kinds of therapy, the therapist hopes to change the patient in some way. Bandura (1969) formulates the issue in this way: "The basic moral question is not whether man's behavior will be controlled, but rather by whom, by what means, and for what ends." Behavior modification, then, involves altering the nature of the controlling conditions, rather than imposing control where none existed before.

Behavior modification is not a one-way method that can be successfully imposed on an unwilling individual. By its very nature, behavior modification will succeed only when the individual who is receiving the consequences is responsive to them and cooperates with the program. If the environmental events following an individual's behavior are not reinforcing to him or are less reinforcing than some alternative, his behavior will not change. Similarly, if the aversive consequence that follows his behavior is less unpleasant to him than some alternative, his behavior will not change. For many persons, it is highly reinforcing to be resistant to attempts to alter their behavior and highly aversive to succumb to external control. Even though such an individual may be participating in a behavior modification program, the person conducting the program may not be able to find any consequence strong enough to compete with the individual's desire to remain unchanged. Thus, in the long run, each of us retains control over his own behavior.

This characterization is equally true, whether the persons in the behavior modification programs are voluntary, adult, clinic patients, or institutionalized individuals with senile psychotic syndrome. Even for the latter group of persons, environmental consequences will succeed in altering their behavior only if the new consequences are more reinforcing than some alternative. Because mentally disadvantaged groups, such as the senile, often are in settings lacking an array of alternative reinforcers, special care needs to be exercised in developing programs for them. Later in this paper, some procedures are suggested that might help protect disadvantaged groups from inappropriately designed programs.

Although aversive therapy procedures seem more coercive than those using positive reinforcement, the individual still must cooperate fully with the procedures in order for them to be effective. While aversive procedures may reduce the individual's motivation to engage in the undesirable behavior, the motivation probably will not be reduced to zero. Rather, the goal of the therapy generally is to reduce the motivation to the point where the individual is able to exercise self-control and avoid engaging in the undesirable behavior.

Recent fiction has dramatically portrayed individuals supposedly unable to overcome the effects of aversive therapy. This, however, is not realistic. If coercion is used in therapy—whether positive or aversive—that may indeed force the individual's cooperation for a time. But, in real life, once this coercion is removed, the individual will be able to return to his former ways if he is motivated to do so.

It is important to remember that in addition to its emphasis on environmental control, the behavioral approach also assumes that persons are able to learn behavioral principles and understand how environmental events can control their own behavior (Ulrich 1967). As behavioral principles are more widely disseminated, an increasing number of persons will have access to them. Hopefully, through the knowledge that people gain from discussions of behavioral principles in courses, workshops, articles in the public press, television "talk shows," and other such sources, they will have a better understanding of their own behavior.

As public awareness increases, the likelihood of behavior being manipulated by more knowledgeable individuals lessens. Just as a professional in behavior modification may use his understanding of behavioral principles in an attempt to alter other persons' behavior, so those other persons can make use of their own understanding and control of themselves and their environment to resist, or indeed to counterinfluence the behavior of the professional.

The behavior influence process is always a reciprocal one: The behavior manager attempts to shape the behavior of some other person through changing the consequences of that person's behavior, but, at the same time, the manager's behavior is in turn shaped by the other's response. Control always results in countercontrol.

In the ideal situation, the mental health worker using behavioral procedures would plan the goals and methods of the therapy together with the client. Persons using behavioral approaches would follow the same generally accepted ethical principles guiding other therapists, and so would strive to maintain a suitable balance between the rights of individuals and of society.

Thus, when there is controversy over the application of behavior modification, it often seems to be in instances in which these ideal conditions have not, for some reason, been met. One important benefit of the public attention to and criticism of behavior modification has been increasing sensitivity on the part of all mental health workers to issues that were formerly often neglected. For example, many therapists are only recently becoming aware of the need to involve the client or his representative more realistically in the planning of the treatment program, including the selection of both goals and methods. In the past, the mental health worker often used simply his own clinical judgment and experience as the basis for determining treatment goals and methods.

Also, the significance of the imbalance in power that is usually found between the therapist and the client is only now coming to be understood by mental health workers. Typically, the therapist comes from the more powerful classes or has a higher status within an institution, while the client is from a less powerful class or is of a lower status. In all mental health fields, including behavior modification, therapists have tended to view problems from their own perspective, so that treatment goals chosen were those that they would want for themselves or that would benefit those to whom the therapist had allegiance. In many instances, the inclusion of the client or his representative in the decision-making process is beginning to redress this imbalance. The power imbalance is a particularly serious problem, however, when the clients are involuntarily confined in an institution. Later in this report, the issues surrounding the use of behavior modification in prisons are discussed in detail.

On the whole, the goal of behavior modification, as generally practiced, is not to force people to conform or to behave in some mindless, automation-like way. Rather, the goals generally include providing new skills and individualized options and developing creativity and spontaneity.

Persons working in behavior modification have tried to be sensitive to the issue of control and to face the issue directly. Task forces on ethical issues in behavior modification have been established by each of the major professional societies whose members work in this field—the American Psychiatric Association, the American Psychological Association, and the Association for Advancement of Behavior Therapy. The first of these has published an extensive report (Birk et al. 1973).

In summary, people do fear control of their behavior, and they fear any method that seems to be effective in changing behavior. However, people need an understanding of what controls behavior and how behavior can be changed. Skinner (1971) has a thoughtful statement on this issue: "Good government is as much a matter of the control of human behavior as bad, good incentive conditions as much as exploitation, good teaching as much as punitive drill. . . . To refuse to exercise available control because in some sense all control is wrong is to withhold possibly important forms of counter-control" (pp. 180–181). Dissemination of information about behavior modification methods will make techniques of resisting oppressive control generally available, so that new methods of control can be met by new methods of countercontrol (Platt 1972).

The Use of Aversive Control

Aversive procedures can be and have been seriously misused so that they become means by which a person in power can exercise control or retribution over those in his charge. The abusive treatment may then be justified by calling it therapeutic and labeling it "behavior modification."

A Perspective on Aversive Control. While many behavior modification aversive techniques, such as shock and time-out, are effective, it is unfortunately true that they are also cheap and easy to apply, requiring little if any specialized knowledge on the part of the person using—or misusing—them. Further, aversive techniques are widely known to be included in the family of behavior modification methods. Thus legitimized, these simple aversive methods are subject to indiscriminate use and other abuses, without regard for individual rights. For example, time-out, which appropriately used should be for only short periods of time, has, in some settings, involved extraordinarily long periods of isolation in small quarters.

Aversive techniques have been used successfully to eliminate life-threatening self-destructive behavior in clinical populations.

Although the techniques themselves are unpleasant to consider, the gain from their use can be potentially great, especially when compared to the alternative, which may be long-term confinement in an institution or prolonged periods in total restraint. Thus, aversive techniques are appropriately used when the risk to the patient of continuing the self-injurious behavior is serious, alternative treatments appear to be ineffective, and potential benefits to the patient from the treatment are great. On the other hand, aversive methods should not be used to enforce compliance with institutional rules.

Suggested Procedures.   When aversive methods are used, appropriate safeguards should be included for the protection of the rights and dignity of those involved. Severe aversive methods, involving pain or discomfort, should be used only as a last resort, when the person's behavior presents immediate danger to himself or others, and when nonpainful interventions have been found to be ineffective. Aversive therapies should be conducted only under the surveillance of an appropriate review panel, preferably one including representatives of the group to which the person receiving the treatment belongs; and they should be used only with the continuing consent of the person receiving them, or of his representative. The person supervising the use of aversive methods should continually monitor the results, which should also be available to the review panel. Any method not providing significant help should be abandoned. The technique used should not violate generally accepted cultural standards and values, as determined by the review panel.

Behavior Modification in Prisons

Behavior modification has become an increasingly controversial yet important law enforcement tool. Many persons feel that the use of behavior modification in prisons conflicts with the values of individual privacy and dignity.

Persons using behavior modification procedures have been particularly criticized for their attempts to deal with rebellious and nonconformist behavior of inmates in penal institutions. Because the behavioral professional is often in the position of assisting in the management of prisoners whose antagonism to authority and rebelliousness have been the catalyst for conflict within the institution, the distinctions among his multiple functions of therapy, management, and rehabilitation can become blurred, and his allegiance confused. While the professional may quite accurately perceive his role as benefiting the individual, he may at the same time appear to have the institution, rather than the prisoner, as his primary client.

Frequently, the goal of effective modification in penal institutions has been the preservation of the institution's authoritarian control. While some prison behavior modification programs have been designed to educate the prisoners and benefit them in other ways, other programs have been directed toward making the prisoners less troublesome and easier to handle, adjusting the inmates to the needs of the institution.

A related problem is that in prisons as elsewhere, the term "behavior modification" has been misused as a label for any procedure that aims to alter behavior, including excessive isolation, sensory deprivation, and severe physical punishment. Behavior modification then becomes simply a new name for old and offensive techniques.

The question of voluntary consent is an especially difficult problem when the persons participating in a program are prison inmates (Shapiro 1974). It is not clear whether there can ever be a "real volunteer" in a prison, because inmates generally believe that they will improve their chances for early parole if they cooperate with prison officials' requests to participate in a special program. There are other pressures as well; for example, participation in a novel program may be a welcome relief from the monotony of prison life.

The use of behavior modification in the prisons came to national attention recently when the Law Enforcement Assistance Administration (LEAA) withdrew its support from some behavior modification programs. According to a spokesman for LEAA, this was done because the agency staff did not have the technical and professional skills to screen, evaluate, or monitor such programs. The termination of the programs was criticized by the American Psychological Association (APA) as an injustice to the public and to prison inmates. The APA's news release (Feb. 15, 1974) said that the LEAA decision would tend "to stifle the development of humane forms of treatment that provide the offender the opportunity to fully realize his or her potential as a contributing member of society."

A similar point of view has been expressed by Norman A. Carlson, Director of the Federal Bureau of Prisons, in discussing the difficulty of determining which programs should be described as behavior modification: "In its broadest sense, virtually every program in the Bureau of Prisons is designed to change or modify behavior. Presumably, the Federal courts commit offenders to custody because their serious criminal behavior is unacceptable to society. The assumption is that during the period of incarceration, individuals will change their patterns of behavior so that after release, they will not become involved in further criminal activity." In general, when behavior modification programs are introduced in Federal prisons, it is important that they be consistent with this philosophy.

A Perspective on the Use of Behavior Modification in Prisons.   A major problem in using behavior modification in prisons is that positive programs begun with the best of intentions may become subverted to punitive ones by the oppressive prison atmosphere. Generally, behavior modification programs are intended to give prisoners the opportunity to learn behavior that will give them a chance to lead more successful lives in the world to which they will return, to enjoy some sense of achievement, and to understand and control their own behavior better. Unfortunately, in actual practice, the programs sometimes teach submission to authority instead.

Thus, critical questions in the use of behavior modification in prisons are how goals are chosen for the program and how continued adherence to those goals is monitored. Behavior modification should not be used in an attempt to facilitate institutionalization of the inmate or to make him adjust to inhumane living conditions. Further, no therapist should accept requests for treatment that take the form "make him 'behave,'" when the intent of the request is to make the person conform to oppressive conditions.

Currently, a common position is to recommend the elimination of behavior modification programs in prisons, on the grounds that such therapy must be coercive, since consent cannot be truly voluntary. However, before this drastic step is taken, careful consideration should be given to the consequences. If constructive programs were eliminated, it would deny the opportunity of improvement for those inmates who genuinely want to participate and who might benefit from the programs. It would seem far better to build in safeguards than to discard all attempts at rehabilitation of prison inmates, whether behavior modification or any other rehabilitative method is involved.

Suggested Procedures.   The appropriate way to conduct treatment programs in prisons, and, in fact, whether such programs should even be offered, are matters by no means settled. Because of the custodial and potentially coercive nature of the prison setting and the pervasive problem of power imbalance, special procedures are needed to protect the rights and dignity of inmates when they engage in any program, not only behavior modification. Some procedures are suggested here, in an attempt to add to the dialogue about ways to give prisoners the option of participating in programs and yet not coerce them into doing so.

A review committee should be constituted to pass on both the methods and goals of proposed treatment programs, and to monitor the programs when they are put into effect. The committee should be kept continually informed of the results of the programs, including short- and long-term evaluations, and of any changes in goals or procedures. A meaningful proportion of the members of this committee should be prisoner representatives, and the committee should also include persons with appropriate legal backgrounds. The person conducting the behavior modification program should be accountable to this committee, and ultimately, to all the individuals participating in the program.

As is always the case with such review panels, conflicting philosophies and differing loyalties may make it difficult for the panel members to agree unanimously on decisions. Such a panel does, however, provide a regularized opportunity for conflicting points of view to be expressed, an opportunity generally not otherwise available. Thus, the group's discussions can, at a minimum, sensitize program administrators and prison officials to the critical issues.

When this committee, including both prisoners and staff members, has chosen the goals and methods of the program, each potential participant should have a realistic right to decline participation. If a prisoner does refuse to cooperate, he should neither lose privileges he already has, nor receive additional punishment, for so declining. The presentation of the program given to him should include a description of the benefits of participation, both in the institution and after the prisoner has left there. Ideally, the prisoner should be offered a choice among several different kinds of programs, rather than the single alternative of a behavior modification program or nothing.

Implications for Behavior Modification of Emerging Legal Rulings

In the last few years, the courts have begun to make rulings on the rights of institutionalized persons, including the mentally ill. The emerging law may have a major impact on behavior modification programs, in particular, because the recent rulings extend rights that are considered basic and that must presumably be available to all persons. While even the major decisions apply legally only in the jurisdiction where they are announced (unless they are ratified by the U.S. Supreme Court), often other areas will adopt rules or pass legislation that is consistent with the decisions, so that they often have impact far beyond a circumscribed geographic area.

The recent decisions are an important step forward in defining the rights of patients more clearly. In particular, the identification of specific items and activities to which the patients are entitled under all circumstances seems to be a major advance. Even though these legal rulings have the effect of requiring the behavioral worker to be far more ingenious in selecting reinforcers for use in institutions (as explained below), this professional inconvenience is far outweighed by the gain in human rights for the patients. No therapeutic program should have to depend for its existence on the continuation of a dehumanizing environment.

Judicial rulings are not necessary to emphasize that aversive techniques are neither legally nor ethically acceptable when they are used solely for oppressive purposes or without the consent of the person on whom they are used, or his guardian. The recent legal reinterpretations relating to human welfare have been concerned mainly with limiting possible abuses of positive reinforcement.

For example, one of the most common ways for mental hospital patients to earn money or tokens for token programs is by working in on- and off-ward jobs. Such employment is justified by mental health professionals on the grounds that it has an educational purpose: It teaches the patients skills needed in the outside world. The decision in *Wyatt v. Stickney*[4] seems to have restricted the use of hospital work as a means of earning money or tokens. In that decision, the court barred all involuntary work by mentally handicapped patients on hospital operations and maintenance, and specifically said that privileges should not be contingent on the patients' work on such jobs. A similar ruling was made in *Jobson v. Henne.*[5]

Usually when patients work on hospital jobs, they are compensated at a level far below the prevailing wage, or even below the minimum legal wage. This practice of employing institutionalized persons without normal compensation to perform productive labor associated with the maintenance of the institution has been called "institutional peonage" (Bartlett 1964). The *Wyatt* decision specified jobs that may be done by mentally handicapped patients and held that the patients must be compensated for that work at the prevailing minimum wage. Another recent case, *Souder v. Brennan,*[6] extended the principle of minimum wage compensation to all institutionalized persons in non-Federal facilities for the mentally ill and mentally retarded. While the minimum wage requirement may seem reasonable on the face of it, it may be a problem for many mental institutions and institutions for the retarded that cannot afford even the minimum wage. Under

Wyatt, apparently the only types of work exempt from minimum wage coverage are therapeutic work unrelated to hospital functioning, and tasks of a personal housekeeping nature (Wexler 1973).

Among the reinforcers used in some token economies are such basic aspects of life as food, mattresses, grounds privileges, and privacy. That is, in these programs, the patients have been able to have these items or engage in these activities only if they were able to purchase the item or activity with their tokens. According to recent legal developments, such as the *Wyatt v. Stickney* case, patients have a constitutional right to a residence unit with screens or curtains to insure privacy, a comfortable bed, a closet or locker for personal belongings, a chair, a bedside table, nutritionally adequate meals, visitors, attendance at religious services, their own clothes or a selection of suitable clothing, regular physical exercise including access to the outdoors, interaction with members of the opposite sex, and a television set in the day room. In other cases (*Inmates of Boys' Training School v. Affleck*[7] and *Morales v. Turman*[8]), similar kinds of activities and amenities were ordered to be available to juveniles in residential facilities. Thus, these legal rulings appear to have defined as basic rights many of the items and activities that have till now been employed as reinforcers in token economies.

The *Wyatt* decision was upheld on appeal by the U.S. Court of Appeals for the Fifth Circuit.[9] Even before that action, the ruling was already influential. However, because of inconsistencies among rulings, it is not clear at the moment just how much these rulings entitle the members of various institutionalized populations to have, and what sorts of items and activities can be restricted to those persons with sufficient tokens to purchase them (Wexler 1973).

Further, the new rulings do not totally prevent the inclusion in a token economy of the various items and activities named in the rulings. Rather, the result of the rulings is to permit the restriction in availability of these items and activities only with the consent of the patients or representatives of the patients. That is, these constitutional rights, like other constitutional rights, can be waived in suitable circumstances by the individuals involved. For example, a patient may consent to having his access to television restricted so that television programs might be available to him only following changes in his behavior that he desires to make.

Mental health workers who want to use the token economy procedure are now beginning to search for new types of reinforcers or new methods of reinforcement delivery that will not require special waivers of the constitutional rights of the patients. Suitable reinforcers would be those beyond which any patient would ordinarily be entitled, or to which he would normally have access. Many professionals believe that such new types of reinforcers will be developed, that behavior change can be produced without depriving patients of the basic necessities or asking them to waive their constitutional rights, and that this entire legal development is a significant step forward. The rulings, however, are recent ones, and extensive changes in practice have yet to occur.

Recent legal rulings have implications for behavior modification procedures other than the token economy. For example, *Wyatt* specified in detail the conditions under which electric shock devices could be used with mentally retarded residents. That ruling, and *New York State Association for Retarded Children v. Rockefeller*[10] also, set limits on the use of seclusion with mentally retarded and mentally ill patients.

Other legal rulings (e.g., *Rouse v. Cameron*[11] and *Donaldson v. O'Connor*[12] have held that patients have a right to treatment. Possible implications of this might be an extension of patients' rights with concomitant restrictions on the use of some behavior modification techniques. At the same time, a right to effective treatment might result in a requirement that all therapies include the sort of continual monitoring of effectiveness that is generally standard practice in behavior modification. Judicial rulings in this area have been inconsistent, however, some supporting a right to treatment (e.g., *Rouse v. Cameron* and *Wyatt v. Stickney*), and some holding that there is no legal obligation to provide treatment (e.g., *Burnham v. Department of Public Health of the State of Georgia*[13] and *New York State Association for Retarded Children v. Rockefeller*). In the 1974 appellate court decision upholding *Wyatt*, the court also overruled the lower court decision in the *Burnham* case. Thus, the Fifth Circuit Court has ruled that, for that jurisdiction, mental patients as a class have a Federal constitutional right to adequate treatment when they are committed against their will to State institutions. Inconsistencies remain, however, especially in decisions regarding voluntary hospitalization (Budd and Baer, in press). It is still too early, also, to draw clear implications for behavior modification from the appellate court decisions on right to adequate treatment.

Ethics in Behavior Modification

Recently, many persons have expressed increasing concern that those who conduct behavior modification programs should take special care that their methods are ethical and that the individuals undergoing behavior change are protected. While, on the whole, researchers and therapists using behavior modification methods have exercised normal caution, some aspects of the problem have not always received the attention that they deserve.

One difficulty in establishing ethical standards for behavior modification is that the issues and problems are different for different populations in different settings. Informed consent, for example, is clearly meaningful when a normal adult voluntarily goes to an outpatient clinic to obtain guidance in altering a specific behavior that he wants to change. However, when prisoners are offered the opportunity of participating in behavior modification, it is by no means clear that they can give truly voluntary consent.

A further difficulty in this area is that the appropriate person to determine the means and goals of treatment is different for different populations in different settings. The mental health professional must decide in each instance who his client is, that is, who the person or group is with whom he should negotiate regarding the choice of means and goals for a behavior modification program. It is often both obvious and correct that the ostensible client is the actual one. For example, a neurotic patient comes to a clinic to be relieved of his fear of flying in planes: The patient, determining for himself the goal of therapy, is the true client. Or, when a husband and wife are referred to a mental health worker to learn contingency contracting as a method of improving their marriage, it is generally clear that both partners have chosen the goal of improvement of their interpersonal relations. The mental health worker's responsibility is to assist them in achieving this goal.

On the other hand, when a behavioral consultant is asked to help a teacher keep her pupils in their seats, working quietly at all times, the ethical situation is less clear. Are these the optimum classroom conditions for learning, and are the children's best interests served by teaching them to be still, quiet, and docile (Winett and Winkler 1972; O'Leary 1972)? The mental health professional may want to suggest alternative goals, or work together with the class and the teacher in developing appropriate goals.

Similarly, when an administrator of an institution for the retarded asks a behavioral professional to establish a token economy so that the inmates will be motivated to work on jobs for the hospital, the professional may want to work together with an advisory committee to determine the relative value of that work activity for the hospital and for the retardates. While he is being asked to have the hospital as his client, he needs also to consider the rights of the patients, the potential benefits to them of the activity, and any risks that may be involved. The professional may decide, for example, that such hospital jobs have minimal benefit for the patients, and thus may feel that the institution's goal is an inappropriate one. Identifying the true client is also a critical problem when behavior modification programs are used in prisons.

Suggested Procedures.   Ethical safeguards for behavior modification programs need to take a number of factors into account: client involvement, a balance of risk and benefit, appropriate review by outside persons, the efficacy of the proposed procedures, and the plans for accountability of the program.

In discussing these complex issues, we are aware that the procedures we suggest have relevance for all types of mental health programs, not just for behavior modification. In this paper, we do not attempt to address these complex issues in that broader context. However, we recognize that the full range of concerns mentioned here applies in all mental health settings.

Ethical responsibility demands that members of the client population or their representatives be seriously consulted about both the means and the goals of programs, before the programs are introduced to change behavior. The persons planning the program need to evaluate the extent to which the members of the target population can give truly informed consent to the program. This involves (1) preparation of a description of the program and its goals so that the persons will know what is to be involved, (2) an assessment of the extent to which they are competent to understand the proposal and make an appropriate judgment about it, and (3) an evaluation of the degree to which their consent can be truly voluntary.

The client himself, or the advisory committee, together with the mental health worker, should weigh the potential benefits to the client of the change that is expected to result from the proposed behavior modification program, against an evaluation of possible risks from using the procedure. This balance can be a difficult one to reach, because the various persons involved may well each see the situation from his own point of view. Thus, the mental health worker might find a proposed technique acceptable because it produces rapid improvement in seriously maladaptive behavior, while client representatives might object to the same technique because it violates the client's rights or restricts his freedom, however briefly, and regardless of ensuing benefits. The client may disagree entirely with the goal of the program that has been chosen by the institution in which he is confined, on the grounds that he is not interested in the supposed benefits offered.

The definitions of risk and benefit will be different in different settings and will also change over time, as customs, knowledge, and values change. Thus, while all the members of an advisory committee may share the goal of helping the client, reaching consensus on how to achieve that goal may involve considerable compromise by persons representing differing points of view.

In many cases, the individual whose behavior is to be changed will be able to negotiate the proposed means and goals directly with the professional personnel. In that way, mental health worker and client can arrive at a mutual agreement or contract that would specify the rights and responsibilities of each of them. However, when the program concerns individuals who have been shown to be incapable of making their own decisions, it will be necessary for the mental health worker to deal with a representative or surrogate for the specific persons who would participate in the proposed program.

The less directly the persons are involved in the initial determination of means and goals, the more protections of those persons should be built into the system. Thus, when the mental health worker is not directly accountable to his client, an advisory committee should be established that would cooperate with the mental health professional in choosing the methods and goals of the behavior modification program. This committee should include either representatives of the persons whose behavior is to be modified, their guardians, or advocates.

The establishment of a suitably constituted review committee does not automatically guarantee that approved programs will include appropriate protections. The official guardians of the persons in the program may, for example, have a vested interest in controlling those persons in a way more convenient for the guardians than beneficial for the persons in the program. The mental health professional, too, cannot be viewed as an entirely disinterested party, especially when he is employed by the institution charged with the care of the persons in the program. In general, members of review committees need to be aware of the conflicting interests involved, and sensitive to the factors influencing their own and each other's behavior, so that subtle coercions are not used to manipulate the decision.

Effectiveness and accountability are other key elements of ethical responsibility in behavior modification. The results of the behavior modification program must be carefully monitored to ensure that the goals agreed on by the advisory committee, or by client and therapist, are being achieved. If they are not, sound practice requires a reevaluation and revision of the methods being used. In addition, the persons conducting behavior modification programs must be accountable to those whose behavior is being changed, or to their representatives. Information on the effectiveness of the program should be made available to the consumers on a regular basis.

Behavior modification programs have an additional special ethical problem because the procedures are generally simple enough to be used by persons lacking the training to evaluate them appropriately. Thus, a further safeguard that should be built into behavior modification programs is a limitation on the decision-making responsibilities of program staff to those matters in which they have expertise. Persons with appropriate professional qualifications, such as a suitable level of training and supervised clinical practice, are able to design and organize treatment programs, develop measurement systems, and evaluate the outcome of behavior modification programs. Such persons should be familiar with the ethical guidelines of their particular profession. Technicians, paraprofessionals, and other workers with only minimal training in behavior modification generally can function in the setting in which behavior is being modified, but should not initiate decisions affecting the welfare of other individuals, unless those decisions are reviewed by the professional staff (Sulzer-Azaroff, Thaw, and Thomas 1975). Given such a delegation of responsibility, review of behavior modification programs should be concerned both with the individuals who make the critical treatment decisions and with the adequacy of supervision of nonprofessional staff.

Ethical Safeguards: The Professions.   The need to adhere to sound ethical practices is accepted by all trained mental health practitioners. Practitioners using behavior modification methods are expected to adhere to existing codes of ethics formulated by their professions. In addition, the Association for Advancement of Behavior Therapy (AABT) is currently formulating a set of standards for practice. The Behavior Therapy and Research Society publishes a list of behavior therapists whose qualifications have undergone peer evaluation.

The AABT also has a system of consultative committees that are coordinated by the president of the Association. Persons who are associated with institutions or programs and who are concerned about present or proposed behavior therapy procedures can ask the AABT president to appoint a committee of persons to go to the site, investigate, and make an advisory report. These reports are compiled into a casebook of standards of practice.

Ethical Safeguards: DHEW Policy and Protections.   Much of the biological, medical, and behavioral research conducted in this country is supported by funds from the Department of Health, Education, and Welfare (DHEW). According to the current DHEW policy, which was established by the May 30, 1974, regulations (Chapter 45, Code of Federal Regulations, Subtitle A, Part 46), in activities involving human subjects, the rights and welfare of the subjects should be adequately protected; the risks to an individual from participation should be outweighed by the potential benefits to him and by the importance of the knowledge to be gained; and informed consent should be obtained by methods that are adequate and appropriate.

According to DHEW policy, risks are defined to include not only potential physical harm, but also adverse psychological reactions or social injury. The policy gives as the basic elements of informed consent: a fair explanation of the procedures to be followed and their purposes, including an identification of those that are experimental; a description of any expected discomforts and risks; a description of the benefits to be expected; a disclosure of appropriate alternative procedures that would be advantageous for the subject; an offer to answer any inquiries concerning the procedures; and an instruction that the subject is free to withdraw his consent and to discontinue participation in the project or activity at any time without prejudice to himself.

As applied to research on behavior modification, this policy means that the person receiving the service or his representative should be told that the person will be receiving behavior modification treatment, and what the treatment program will involve. He should be told what problems might arise, if any, and what the goal of the treatment is. It should be made clear to him that he should feel free to drop out of the study at any time. Not mentioned in the official regulations, but part of recommended practice in this area, is that the client or his representative should cooperate with the mental health worker in specifying the goals of the behavior modification treatment.

The DHEW regulations place primary responsibility for safeguarding the rights and welfare of subjects on the organization conducting the activities. The responsibility, however, is shared by the organization's review committee and the DHEW staff and advisory committees, each of whom determines independently the adequacy of proposed procedures for the protection of human subjects. According to the regulations, any institution conducting DHEW-funded research, development, or related activities involving human subjects must establish a committee with responsibility for reviewing any application for support of such activities, to insure that the protocol adequately fulfills the policy for the protection of the subjects.

The National Institutes of Health established a study group that is charged with reviewing various aspects of the DHEW policy on human subjects. The group drafted proposed rules dealing with protection of subjects in prisons and mental institutions, and with protection of subjects in research involving pregnant women, abortion, fetuses, and products of *in vitro* fertilization. Public comment on these proposals has been received.

Many hospitals and research institutions have used the DHEW regulations as a model for structuring their own policy for the protection of human subjects. Others have gone beyond the regulations to require, for example, the presence of the subject's personal physician, personal lawyer, and immediate kin, with specific periods of time being allocated for discussion before consent is given. This is an area that is receiving increasing attention.

The National Research Act (PL 93–348) provided for a National Commission for the Protection of Human Subjects of Biomedical and Behavioral Research, which will be in existence for 2 years, beginning in 1974. This Commission is charged with investigating a number of issues, including the problems of obtaining informed consent from children, prisoners, and the institutionalized mentally infirm when they are asked to participate in experiments. The Commission has also been asked to determine the need for a mechanism that will extend the DHEW regulations beyond DHEW-funded research activities to all activities with human subjects, including research and health services.

Summary and Conclusions

Behavior modification currently is the center of stormy controversy and debate. We have attempted to put these problems in perspective, through a discussion of what behavior modification is and what it is not, and a review of the major issues.

Many years of laboratory research provide the basis and rationale for the development of behavior modification techniques and behavioral treatments. The behavior modification methods currently being used include procedures suitable for use in the clinic, such as desensitization, and in the mental institution, such as the token economy. The procedures can be used with normal adults and children and with the mentally disadvantaged, including the retarded, the senile, and the psychotic. Behavior modification methods have been used to ameliorate a wide range of problems, including mutism, self-destructive behavior, inappropriate fears, and nervous habits. Also, behavior modification methods have been used to teach a great variety of appropriate, normal behaviors, including normal speech, appropriate social behavior, and suitable classroom skills.

The Federal Government continues to support and encourage research and demonstrations that test new behavior modification techniques, that seek to refine existing ones and apply them to new clinical populations and new settings, and that promote the dissemination of techniques that have been positively evaluated. A particularly strong need is for additional research comparing the efficacy of behavior modification methods with that of alternative treatment approaches. Research is also needed on ways to deliver behavior modification techniques to larger numbers of persons in less restrictive settings than the institutions where much of the research, until now, has been done.

Concern has been expressed that behavior modification methods may be used by those in power to control and manipulate others. Some critics have charged that the use of behavior modification methods is inconsistent with humanistic values. However, all kinds of therapies involve attempts to change the patient in some way. Behavior modification, like other therapeutic methods, requires a cooperative individual in order for it to be effective. Countercontrol, especially countercontrol based on knowledge of behavioral principles, is a major way that individuals can respond to any attempted manipulation.

The concerns that have been expressed about behavior modification have stimulated a reexamination of the assumptions and ethics of all psychosocial therapies. Ethical problems are particularly serious when therapies are used within institutions such as mental hospitals and prisons, or with the institutionalized mentally retarded and senile. In these settings, mental health workers have to be sensitive to the implications of the imbalance in power between them and their clients.

Aversive procedures, easy to abuse, have also raised serious concerns. These methods can, however, be used to benefit patients greatly, as when aversive techniques are used to eliminate life-threatening self-destructive behavior. Appropriate safeguards need to be provided, whenever aversive control techniques are proposed. Greater involvement of clients or their representatives in decisions about the means and goals of treatment programs will help protect persons participating in the programs.

Perhaps the most controversy has arisen in connection with the use of behavior modification in prisons. Behavior modification programs have, in some places, been designed to preserve authoritarian control and discipline, rather than to teach skills that would benefit the prisoners, once they are released. It is not clear whether prisoners are ever able to be true volunteers in any experimental program held in a prison. Here, too, safeguards must be built into the structure of any behavioral program.

Recent legal rulings have provided significant gains in human rights, especially for involuntarily committed patients. The rulings have called attention to possible abuses of the use of positive reinforcement and have extended the limits of institutionalized persons' basic rights.

In addition to discussing these issues, we have suggested some ways that safeguards might be designed for behavior modification programs. The issues are relevant to all types of mental health programs, and many of our proposed solutions would be applicable more generally as well. They are discussed here, however, only as they apply specifically in behavior modification.

Ethical responsibility demands that members of the client population or their representatives be consulted about both the means and goals of programs, and that these persons have an opportunity to weigh the balance of risk and benefit in any proposed program. Programs should be monitored to ensure that they are effective, and those persons conducting the programs should be accountable to those whose behavior is being changed, as long as the program is continued.

The Department of Health, Education, and Welfare is currently developing new regulations for the protection of human subjects, and the National Commission for the Protection of Human Subjects of Biochemical and Behavioral Research is also investigating related topics.

Public debate will surely continue concerning the issues that surround the use of behavior modification techniques. Professional evaluation of these techniques and public discussion of them can help prevent abuses in the use of behavior modification procedures, as well as foster public understanding and acceptance of beneficial procedures. London (1974) contends that " . . . a decent society regulates all technology that is powerful enough to affect the general welfare, at once restricting the technicians as little as possible and as much as necessary." In that context, both continued monitoring of behavior modification by the public and further research on this important technology are needed to serve society and the individuals who make it up.

Notes

[1] This project is being supported by the National Institute of Mental Health.

[2] This project is being supported by the National Institute on Drug Abuse.

[3] This project is being supported by the National Institute on Alcohol Abuse and Alcoholism.

[4] 325 F. Supp. 781 (M.D. Ala. 1971), 334 F. Supp. 1341 (M.D. Ala. 1971), 344 F. Supp. 373 (M.D. Ala. 1972), and 344 F. Supp. 387 (M.D. Ala. 1972). This case was known as *Wyatt v. Aderholt* on appeal.

[5] 335 F. 2d 129 (2d Cir., 1966).

[6] 367 F. Supp. 808 (D.D.C. 1973).

[7] 346 F. Supp. 1354 (D.R.I. 1972).

[8] 364 F. Supp. 166 (E.D. Tex. 1973).

[9] *Wyatt v. Aderholt*, No. 72–2634(5 Cir., Nov. 8, 1974).

[10] 357 F. Supp. 752 (E.D. N.Y. 1973).

[11] 373 F. 2d 451 (D.C. Cir., 1966).

[12] 493 F. 2d 507(5 Cir., 1974).

[13] 349 F. Supp. 1335 (N.D. Ga. 1972), appeal docketed, No. 72–3110, 5 Cir., Oct. 4, 1972. This case was consolidated for argument on appeal with *Wyatt*.

References

Anderson, R. C. Education psychology. *Annual Review of Psychology*, 18, 129–164, 1967.

Ayllon, T., and Azrin, N. H. The measurement and reinforcement of behavior of psychotics. *Journal of the Experimental Analysis of Behavior*, 8, 357–383, 1965.

Ayllon, T., and Azrin, N. H. *The Token Economy*. New York: Appleton-Century-Crofts, 1968.

Ayllon, T., and Michael, J. The psychiatric nurse as a behavioral engineer. *Journal of the Experimental Analysis of Behavior*, 2, 323–334, 1959.

Baer, D. M. A case for the selective reinforcement of punishment. In Neuringer, C., and Michael, J. L., eds. *Behavior Modification in Clinical Psychology*. New York: Appleton-Century-Crofts, 1970.

Baer, D. M. The control of developmental process: Why wait? In Nesselroade, J. R., and Reese, H. W., eds. *Life-span Developmental Psychology: Methodological Issues*. New York: Academic Press, 1973.

Baer, D. M., and Guess, D. Receptive training of adjectival inflections in mental retardates. *Journal of Applied Behavior Analysis*, 4, 129–139, 1971.

Bandura, A. *Principles of Behavior Modification*. New York: Holt, Rinehart and Winston, 1969.

Bartlett, F. L. Institutional peonage: Our exploitation of mental patients. *Atlantic*, 214(1), 116–119, 1964.

Begelman, D. A. Ethical and legal issues of behavior modification. In: Hersen, M.; Eisler, R.; and Miller, P., eds. *Progress in Behavior Modification*, Vol. 1. New York: Academic Press, 1977.

Birk, L. et al. *Behavior Therapy in Psychiatry*. Washington, D.C.: American Psychiatric Association, 1973.

Blanchard, E. B.; Libet, J. M.; and Young, L. D. Apneic aversion and covert sensitization in the treatment of a hydrocarbon inhalation addiction: A case study. *Journal of Behavior Therapy and Experimental Psychiatry*, 4, 383–87, 1973.

Brady, J. P. Brevital-relaxation treatment of frigidity. *Behaviour Research and Therapy*, 4, 71–77, 1966.

Bucher, B. Some ethical issues in the therapeutic use of punishment. In Rubin, R. D., and Franks, G. M., eds. *Advances in Behavior Therapy*, 1968. New York: Academic Press, 1969.

Bucher, B., and Lovaas, O. I. Use of aversive stimulation in behavior modification. In Jones, M. R., ed. *Miami Symposium on the Prediction of Behavior*, 1967. Coral Gables: University of Miami Press, 1968.

Budd, K., and Baer, D. M. Behavior modification and the law: Implications of recent judicial decisions. *Journal of Applied Behavior Analysis*, in press.

Carrera, F., III, and Adams, P. L. An ethical perspective on operant conditioning. *Journal of the American Academy of Child Psychiatry*, 9, 607–623, 1970.

Cohen, H. L., and Filipczak, J. *A New Learning Environment*. San Francisco: Jossey-Bass, 1971.

Colman, A. D. *Planned Environment in Psychiatric Treatment*. Springfield, IL: Thomas, 1971.

Davison, G. C. Homosexuality: The ethical challenge. Paper presented at the meeting of the Association for Advancement of Behavior Therapy, Chicago, November 1974.

Eysenck, N. J. Discussion on the role of the psychologist in psychoanalytic practice: The psychologist as technician. *Proceedings of the Royal Society of Medicine*, 45, 447–449, 1952.

Ferster, C. B., and DeMyer, M. K. The development of performances in autistic children in an automatically controlled environment. *Journal of Chronic Diseases*, 13, 312–345, 1961.

Foxx, R. M., and Azrin, N. H. Restitution: A method of eliminating aggressive-disruptive behavior of retarded and brain damaged patients. *Behaviour Research and Therapy*, 10, 15–27, 1972.

Gruenberg, E. M. The social breakdown syndrome—some origins. *American Journal of Psychiatry*, 123, 12–20, 1967.

Heldman, A. W. Social psychology versus the first amendment freedoms, due process liberty, and limited government. *Cumberland-Samford Law Review*, 4, 1–40, 1973.

Jones, M. C. The elimination of children's fears. *Journal of Experimental Psychology*, 7, 382–390, 1924.

Lindsley, O. R., and Skinner, B. F. A method for the experimental analysis of behavior of psychotic patients. *American Psychologist*, 9, 419–420, 1954.

London, P. The end of ideology in behavior modification. *American Psychologist*, 27, 913–920, 1972.

London, P. Behavior technology and social control—turning the tables. *APA Monitor*, April 1974, p. 2.

Lovaas, et al. Some generalization and follow-up measures on autistic children in behavior therapy. *Journal of Applied Behavior Analysis*, 6, 131–165, 1973.

Lovibond, S. H. Aversive control of behavior. *Behavior Therapy*, 1, 80–91, 1970.

Minge, M. R., and Ball, T. S. Teaching of self-help skills to profoundly retarded patients. *American Journal of Mental Deficiency*, 71, 864–868, 1967.

Mowrer, O. H., and Mowrer, W. M. Enuresis—a method for its study and treatment. *American Journal of Orthopsychiatry*, 8, 436–459, 1938.

O'Leary, K. D. Behavior modification in the classroom: A rejoinder to Winett and Winkler. *Journal of Applied Behavior Analysis*, 5, 505–511, 1972.

O'Leary, K. D., and Drabman, R. Token reinforcement programs in the classroom: A review. *Psychological Bulletin*, 75, 379–398, 1971.

Phillips, E. L., et al. Achievement Place: Modification of the behaviors of predelinquent boys within a token economy. *Journal of Applied Behavior Analysis*, 4, 45–59, 1971.

Platt, J. Beyond Freedom and Dignity: "A revolutionary manifesto." *The Center Magazine*, 5(2), 34–52, 1972.

Price, K. P. The application of behavior therapy to the treatment of psychosomatic disorders: Retrospect and prospect. *Psychotherapy: Theory, Research and Practice*, 11, 138–155, 1974.

Rachman, S., and Teasdale, J. *Aversion Therapy and Behaviour Disorders*. Coral Gables: University of Miami Press, 1969.

Risley, T. R. The effects and side effects of punishing the autistic behaviors of a deviant child. *Journal of Applied Behavior Analysis*, 1, 21–34, 1968.

Sears, R. R.; Maccoby, E.; and Levin, H. *Patterns of Child-Rearing*. Evanston, IL: Row, Peterson, 1957.

Shapiro, D., and Birk, L. Group therapy in experimental perspective. *International Journal of Group Psychotherapy*, 17, 211–224, 1967.

Shapiro, M. B. The single case in fundamental clinical psychological research. *British Journal of Medical Psychology*, 34, 255–262, 1961.

Shapiro, M. H. Legislating the control of behavior control: Autonomy and the coercive use of organic therapies. *Southern California Law Review*, 47, 237–356, 1974.

Skinner, B. F. *Beyond Freedom and Dignity*. New York: Knopf, 1971.

Sulzer-Azaroff, B.; Thaw, J.; and Thomas, C. Behavioral competencies for the evaluation of behavior modifiers. In Wood, W.S., ed. *Issues in Evaluating Behavior Modification*. Champaign, Ill.: Research Press, 1975.

Thomson, I. G., and Rathod, N. H. Aversion therapy for heroin dependence. *Lancet*, ii, 382–384, 1968.

Ulrich, R. Behavior control and public concern. *Psychological Record*, 17, 229–234, 1967.

Webster, D. R., and Azrin, N. H. Required relaxation: A method of inhibiting agitative-disruptive behavior of retardates. *Behaviour Research and Therapy*, 11, 67–78, 1973.

Wexler, D. B. Token and taboo: Behavior modification, token economies, and the law. *California Law Review*, 61, 81–109, 1973.

Winett, R. A., and Winkler, R. C. Current behavior modification in the classroom: Be still, be quiet, be docile. *Journal of Applied Behavior Analysis*, 5, 499–504, 1972.

Wolpe, J. *Psychotherapy by Reciprocal Inhibition*. Stanford, CA: Stanford University Press, 1958.

Wolpe, J., and Lazarus, A. A. *Behavior Therapy Techniques*. Oxford: Pergamon Press, 1966.

Section *VIII*

Group Counseling in Corrections

Group counseling, which involves group activity under the direction of a therapist or group leader, differs from individual, one-to-one interaction between counselor and client in a number of ways.

Hatcher (1978:152) defines it in the following manner.

> Group counseling is a planned activity in which three or more people are present for the purpose of solving personal and social problems by applying the theories and methods of counseling in a group. It can be either structured or relatively unstructured in regard to purpose or leadership. It can be an intensive emotional experience or a superficial "bull session." Its primary focus, ideally, is upon the presentation of personal and interpersonal reality in such a way that one has an opportunity to learn about self and others.

Group counseling and group treatment techniques evolved during World War II and in the postwar years. A type of group therapy termed "guided group interaction" was developed by McCorkle and Wolf as a method of treating offenders who were members of the armed forces. Following World War II, the technique was modified and adopted by civilian institutions. The most notable experiment using the guided group interaction technique was undertaken by McCorkle and Bixby in the early 1950s as part of a delinquency treatment program known as the Highfields Experiment. In this project, as in earlier group work of this type, the group members were called upon to help each other set and work toward specific goals: to lend strong peer support to efforts at positive change; and to exert sanctioning power over negative behavior. The key element of guided group interaction is the problem-solving activity that takes place in the group meetings (McCorkle, 1958).

Group counseling was introduced into the correctional system in the 1940s and 1950s for reasons of increased efficiency in handling prisoners rather than because treatment personnel had strong convictions that it would be more effective than individual counseling. Initially, group counseling had a strong educational or training emphasis and only dealt incidentally with efforts to assist offenders in solving their emotional problems. Two new types of group therapy emerged in the 1950s. Although not specifically developed for correctional treatment, they proved to be readily adaptable to correctional settings. Moreno (1957) originated "psychodrama," a type of group counseling in which the subject acts out his or her problems while other group members serve as the various "characters" for the "drama." Psychodrama episodes might include simulations of dialogues with spouses, parents, or acquaintances, with other group members acting the parts of these significant others in the subject's life. Role playing, a similar technique used by Slavson (1950), calls upon various group members to assume certain roles and simulate situations, under the guidance of a therapist or counselor.

The 1960s provided two additional forms of treatment that can be applied in a group setting: reality therapy and transactional analysis. Reality therapy involves having the correctional client gain an idea of what his or her immediate needs and behavior requirements are and accept responsibility for them. A group may be the ideal setting for a client to learn just how his or her behavior is perceived by others, realize that others care what happens to him or her, and develop a plan for better behavior in the future. Transactional analysis was originated by Berne and modified by Harris. Berne believes that behavior is directed by one of three "ego states": the "adult" ego state, characterized by rational, mature, responsible behavior; the "parent" ego state, which is judgmental of the behavior of others; or the "child" ego state, which involves emotional, self-centered responses (Berne, 1961:19). In transactional analysis, the dialogues taking place in the group situation are constantly analyzed and categorized by the group and group leader as representative of one of these ego states. The goal of TA is to help group members learn to interact at the "adult" ego level.

The 1970s witnessed another development in group counseling. Vorrath, who was involved in the earlier Highfields Experiment in guided group interaction, modified and redeveloped this technique into what he called "positive peer culture." This approach, used with juveniles, involves interaction of small groups of youths (approximately nine) under the guidance of a group leader. The influence of peers is brought to bear in identifying problems, deciding how to solve them, developing interest in and concern for all members of the group, and feeling a stake in the success of others. Those involved in positive peer culture groups define their difficulties and seek to solve them with the aid of a list of general and specific problems, which are defined when they exist and when they are solved. The list is given below.

Positive Peer Culture Problem-Solving List

1. *Low self-image*: Has a poor opinion of self, often feels put down or of little worth.

   When solved: Is self-confident and cannot easily be made to feel small or inferior. Is able to solve problems and make positive contributions to others. Doesn't feel sorry for self even though he or she may have shortcomings. Believes he or she is good enough to be accepted by anybody.

2. *Inconsiderate of others*: Does things that are damaging to others.

   When solved: Shows concern for others even if he or she does not like them or know them well. Tries to help people with problems rather than hurt them or put them down.

3. *Inconsiderate of self*: Does things that are damaging to self.

   When solved: Shows concern for self, tries to correct mistakes and improve self. Understands limitations and is willing to discuss problems. Doesn't hurt or put down self.

4. *Authority problem*: Does not want to be managed by anyone.

   When solved: Shows ability to get along with those in authority. Is able to accept advice and direction from others. Does not try to take advantage of authority figures even if they can be manipulated.

5. *Misleads others*: Draws others into negative behavior.

   When solved: Shows responsibility for the effect of his or her behavior on others who follow him or her. Does not lead others into negative behavior. Shows concern and helps rather than taking advantage of others.

6. *Easily misled*: Is drawn into negative behavior by others.

   When solved: Seeks out friends who care enough not to hurt him or her. Doesn't blindly follow others to buy friendship. Is strong enough to stand up for self and makes own decisions. Doesn't let anyone misuse him or her.

7. *Aggravates others*: Treats people in negative, hostile ways.

   When solved: Gets along well with others. Does not need to get attention by irritating or annoying others. Gets no enjoyment from hurting or harassing people. Respects others enough not to embarrass, provoke, or bully them.

8. *Easily angered*: Is often irritated or provoked or has tantrums.

   When solved: Is not easily frustrated. Knows how to control and channel anger, not letting it control him or her. Understands the put-down process and has no need to respond to challenges. Can tolerate criticism or even negative behavior from others.

9. *Stealing*: Takes things that belong to others.

   When solved: Sees stealing as hurting another person. Has no need to be sneaky or to prove self by stealing. Knows appropriate ways of getting things. Would not stoop to stealing even if he or she could get away with it.

10. *Alcohol or drug problem*: Misuses substances that could hurt self.

    When solved: Feels good about self and wouldn't hurt self. Does not need to be high to have friends or enjoy life. Can face problems without a crutch. Shows concern for others who are hurting themselves by abusing alcohol or drugs.

11. *Lying*: Cannot be trusted to tell the truth.

    When solved: Is concerned that others trust him or her. Has strength to face mistakes and failures without trying to cover up. Does not need to lie or twist the truth to impress others. Tells it like it is.

12. *Fronting*: Puts on an act rather than being real.

    When solved: Is comfortable with people and does not have to keep trying to prove self. Has no need to act superior, con people, or play the show-off role. Is not afraid of showing true feelings to others (Vorrath and Brendtro, 1974:37–38).

In addition to the obvious cost-efficiency factor of treating more than one offender at the same time, group counseling has been rated as having a number of other advantages in the correctional setting. Chief among these is the fact that it can be used to counter the influence of the inmate subculture, which makes strong demands for the prisoner's loyalty and attention. The types of openness and amenability to change that can be developed in group treatment can work to counter the strong pull of the inmate code. In addition, the brainstorming or problem-solving experience of the group as a whole may provide solutions that offenders may not have thought of or may be reluctant to accept from staff members but will try because peers who have "been there" suggest them. Another advantage of group counseling is that many members of the staff may become involved and have a stake in the treatment outcome. Although trained therapists are needed for certain types of group work, other groups can be ably directed by regular staff, student interns, or even offenders who have received training in the treatment techniques.

There are certain disadvantages to group counseling as well. These include the fact that, unless guided skillfully, sessions may become little more than occasions to air grievances. Offenders, who have the one constant goal of "getting out," may see the group setting as an appropriate spot for "conning" staff members and may display little sincerity. Deep-seated fears of revealing information that may delay release or result in physical reprisals or ostracism by other inmates can prevent candor in a group setting. Finally, personality characteristics of some offenders make it very difficult for them to feel comfortable or to participate in group sessions.

The choice of the specific treatment technique to be used in a group setting is dependent upon the leader's training, preference, assessment of the group's needs, and the goals set for the group activity. Treatment possibilities for groups designed to be primarily instructive or to attack a specific problem (alcohol or drug addiction, for example) are necessarily more limited than for groups structured for the more general purpose of improving offenders' adjustment within the correctional setting. Problem-solving group work, such as reality therapy, guided group interaction, or positive peer culture, may involve role playing or psychodrama; while group counseling geared to improving the offender's general adjustment to life would be more likely to use such techniques as transactional analysis.

In selection 26, "The Process of Group Counseling," Trotzer notes that an effective group process must involve five stages, if the knowledge gained in the group is to be transferred to activity outside it. These stages are: (1) the security stage, in which the group member is made to feel comfortable and not threatened in the group setting; (2) the acceptance stage, in which the group member comes to know that he or she is an important part of the group, that others care about him or her, and that he or she has certain problems; (3) the responsibility stage, in which the group member takes responsibility for his or her own actions and for finding solutions to problems; (4) the work stage, during which things found to be unsatisfactory in one's life must be changed; and (5) the closing stage, when the group member accepts the support and encouragement of the group as he or she gradually detaches from it (Trotzer, 1977:53–63). Romig's findings about the ineffectiveness of the majority of group counseling programs seems to indicate that many of the groups failed to get beyond the "acceptance stage" and did not plan specific procedures for the "work stage," when the problems defined by the group should be attacked.

In selection 27, "The Use of Groups," Stordeur and Stille consider the provision of treatment for violent males. Spouse-to-spouse violence has become an important concern, and innovative treatment approaches are desperately needed. The authors, who had considerable experience in counseling violent males, developed some guidelines for counseling assaultive offenders in a group setting. They note that group counseling for batterers has many advantages over individual counseling, including the reduction of the batterer's isolation from others, the opportunity to develop interpersonal skills (so that means other than violence can be used to deal with frustration), and chances to elicit aid and support from peers. The selection also focuses on the dynamics of the group, the size, structure, number and length of sessions, leadership styles, and the mix of economic and social backgrounds that appear to create the best chance for controlling or constructively channeling anger in those being treated.

References

Berne, Eric. 1961. *Transactional Analysis.* New York: Grove Press.

Hatcher, Hayes A. 1978. *Correctional Casework and Counseling.* Englewood Cliffs, NJ: Prentice-Hall.

McCorkle, Lloyd. 1958. *The Highfields Story.* New York: Holt, Rinehart and Winston.

Moreno, J. L. 1957. *The First Book on Group Psychotherapy.* New York: Beacon House.

Slavson, S. R. 1950. *An Introduction to Group Therapy.* New York: Commonwealth Fund.

Trotzer, James P. 1977. *The Counselor and the Group.* Monterey, CA: Brooks/Cole Publishing.

Vorrath, Harry H. and Larry K. Brendtro. 1974. *Positive Peer Culture.* Chicago: Aldine.

26

The Process of Group Counseling

James P. Trotzer

Background

The process of group counseling presented in this chapter has emerged from experience in a variety of settings and with a wide range of clients and age groups. Contributing to this model have been my involvement and leadership experience in schools with upper elementary, junior high, and senior high students, at the Minnesota State Prison working with inmates and staff, at the university level working with undergraduate and graduate students, in numerous human-relations workshops with a variety of educators, in church-related youth retreat groups, in interracial groups, and in other diverse settings as a consultant. This process model was developed first (Trotzer, 1972), and the rationale supplied later. In this sense the model is experience-based rather than theory-based and is rooted in observation of actual group interaction rather than in empirical assessment of hypothetical constructs.

Nature of the Process

The model described presents a developmental perspective of group counseling, which is intended for use as an aid in under-

From *The Counselor and the Group: Integrating Theory, Training, and Practice*, by J. P. Trotzer, Copyright © 1977 by Wadsworth, Inc. Reprinted by permission of the publisher, Brooks/Cole Publishing Company, Monterey, CA.

standing and directing the group process and as a framework for many different theoretical approaches and techniques. The group process itself is divided into five stages. However, the stages are not autonomous or independent of each other. Each stage has certain characteristics that distinguish it, but their meaning and impact are obtained only within the context of the total group process. The duration of each stage is dependent on the nature of the leader and group members. In some cases, the stages turn over very rapidly; in some, the stages are almost concurrent; and in others, a particular stage may continue for a long period of time and can lead to stagnation in the group process, especially if this occurs early.

Rogers' (1967) description of the group process correlates well with this idea of stages emerging and submerging in group interaction.

> The interaction is best thought of, I believe, as a varied tapestry, differing from group to group, yet with certain kinds of trends evident in most of these intensive encounters and certain patterns tending to precede and others to follow. (p. 263)

Each stage of the group is like a wave that has momentary identity as it crests but whose beginning and demise are swallowed up in the constant movement of the sea.

The Group Process and Problem-Solving

The stage cycle of the group process reflects characteristics of our basic human needs and depicts the essential qualities of good interpersonal relationships. The model also mirrors a basic pattern for successful problem-solving. The integration of the stages into a conceptualization of a method for resolving problems is readily evident. The stages of security, acceptance, responsibility, work, and closing are easily translated into a step-by-step procedure for resolving personal concerns. First of all, as we experience problems we can't solve, there is a natural tendency to hide or deny them because we don't want negative repercussions in our self-image or in reactions of others around us. Problems threaten our security as persons and our relationships with others. Therefore problems are only shared with others if an atmosphere of safety is part of our relationship with them. Feelings of trust and confidence reduce risk and facilitate our sharing of personal concerns with others. The amount of trust necessary for disclosing our problems is a product of the combined emotional seriousness of the problem and the quality of our relationships. Some problems we experience force us to use disclosure as a means of developing a trusting climate. For example, a client who has recently undergone a traumatic experience—say a close friend was injured while riding in a car the client was driving—may be motivated by intense emotional feelings to share the problem without first determining if the atmosphere is safe. Such risks are sometimes taken without a foreknowledge of trust in the relationship. However, other problems may have emotional or social overtones that demand an atmosphere of confidentiality before any self-revelations occur. In these cases the relationship must develop first and self-disclosure follows. Examples of these kinds of problems include sex problems, drug problems, and difficulties in relationships with significant others such as parents, teachers, or marriage partner. In any event, step one in resolving our problems is to find a safe place in which we can talk about them.

The second step is associated with acceptance. Although the term *acceptance* encompasses a broad range of concepts, such as acceptance of self, acceptance of others, and acceptance by others, a key point in solving a problem is to accept that problem as a part of ourselves. Until we recognize that the problems we experience are part of us, we cannot act constructively to resolve them. Denial and unwillingness to face our problems are the biggest deterrents to their resolution. In order to accept our problems, we need to know that recognition of them as our own will not be devastating to ourselves or to our relationships with others. In other words, our own acceptance of our problems is contingent to a large degree on the reactions or the perceived reactions of others. If we are accepted by others in total, if we feel we can show them all of ourselves including our problems and be received with an empathic ear, we are more willing to identify, share, and acknowledge our problems.

Taking responsibility is the third step in the problem-solving process. After we acknowledge our problems, we must also admit to our part in their cause and shoulder the responsibility to act positively to resolve them. Responsibility brings into focus the action phase of problem-solving. The realization that problem-solving is an active process and that the individual with the problem is primarily responsible for that action is a difficult but necessary step toward resolution. Clients often hope that once they have admitted to, identified, or accepted their problems something almost magical will occur and the problem will be resolved. They sometimes feel that because they have made the courageous effort to reveal themselves, their reward should be instant resolution, or at least that the counselor should take over. Therefore the process of getting clients to take responsibility for themselves is another key step in successful resolution.

The fourth step is to work out the means whereby the problem can be solved. This involves understanding the problem, identifying alternative solutions, evaluating them, planning and practicing new attitudes or behaviors, and trying them out in the real world. The helping relationship at this point is a working relationship in which all parties exert energy and intelligence toward helping the individual find and implement a successful solution.

The final step is to terminate the relationship when clients begin to experience success more than failure in their attempts to integrate changes into their lives. Terminating counseling clients should not only realize their problems are resolved but should have learned the problem-solving process and increased their confidence to use it. The following discussion will describe the life cycle of a group in which the problem-solving characteristics just detailed will be related to the group-counseling process. Each stage will be discussed separately, considering factors such as major identifying characteristics, focus, leader role, and resulting impact.

The Security Stage

The initial stage of the counseling group is characterized by tentativeness, ambiguity, anxiety, suspicion, resistance, discomfort, and other such emotional reactions on the part of both the members and the leader. The members experience these reactions because they are entering a new situation in which they cannot predict what will occur, and they are not confident of their ability to control themselves or relate well to the group. Even though orientation procedures are used, once the group comes together and interaction begins, the cognitive preparation gives way to the normal emotional reactions experienced in new social situations. Uncomfortable feelings also arise because each member is aware that he or she is in counseling and has personal concerns that are not easily shared under any circumstances.

An example of the inner turmoil a group member experiences was demonstrated by a young woman who requested admittance to a therapy group at a university counseling center. During the first session she paced and stood outside the room, struggling with the decision of whether to enter or not. The group leader, aware of her fears and misgivings about the group, left the door open and indicated to her that she could come in when she was ready. Toward the end of the session she entered the room and stood against the wall but did not join the group until the second session. So extensive was her discomfort that she did not participate until the fourth session and did not risk disclosing anything about herself until much later. Although most group members do not experience reactions to that extent, feelings of discomfort in the early sessions are always prevalent.

The security stage is a period of testing for the group members, and much of this testing takes the form of resistance, withdrawal, or hostility. Bonney (1969) points out that "resistance and hostility toward the leader and conflict among group members are . . . expected outgrowths of the basic insecurity of procedural direction and uncertainty concerning the capacity of the group to achieve its proposed aims" (p. 165). The testing takes many forms and is aimed in many directions but the most common challenges are leveled at leader competency, ground rules, and other members' actions. Rogers (1967) feels that negative expressions are a way of testing the trustworthiness and freedom of the group. All persons in the group experience some form of nervousness that generates defending types of behaviors rather than the authentic sharing of feelings.

The focus during this initial period must take into account these insecure feelings of the members. Underlying concerns that brought the members to the group should be set aside for the moment, and the here-and-now discomfort facing the group should be worked with. Some leaders like to use group warm-ups to help members express and work through these initial feelings and to establish a comfortable rapport within the group. The individual problems of the members, though they may be categorically similar, are most likely quite dissimilar in the perception of each member at this point. Thus it is important to establish a common ground so that members can make contact with each other and open lines of communication.

Since each member is preoccupied with dissatisfactions in his or her own life, an immediate focus on any one problem would lead to a rather disjointed process, which would run a high risk of losing the involvement and cooperation of all the members. This type of emphasis might also allow some members to go too deeply too quickly and scare off others. Cohn (1973) warned leaders to avoid this possibility and stressed that one essential feature of the group process is that members must be moved to deeper levels of interaction together. By initially focusing on the discomfort that all are experiencing, a common ground is established, which moves the group toward more cohesiveness. This identification with one another helps members overcome feelings of isolation and lays the foundation for the development of trust (Trotzer, 1972).

A significant aspect of the security stage is the leader's part in sharing the discomfort. Seldom will a leader enter a group without some feelings of uneasiness and hesitancy. These feelings do not reflect the skill and experience of the counselor but rather are indicative of the effort involved in working toward closeness between people and helping people with problems. If leaders do not enter groups with some of these feelings, they are probably not prepared to become involved in the very personal worlds of the members.

The leader's role in the security stage is to perform what Lifton (1966) calls "security-giving operations." Leaders must be able to gain the confidence of the members, display warmth and understanding, provide for the various needs of the members, and create and maintain a friendly and safe atmosphere in the group. Sensitivity, awareness, and an ability to communicate feelings and observations to the group without dominating it are important qualities of group leadership at this stage of the group's development.

As the group resolves the discomfort of the artificial situation, members can begin delving into the problems in their lives, and as members share their common feelings and perceptions, trust develops. Cohn (1964) emphasizes this concept of trust, suggesting that once group members trust and are trusted the groundwork is laid for making the effort needed to improve their real-life situations. Rogers (1967) states that the "individual will gradually feel safe enough to drop some of his defenses and facades" (p. 8). The members will become more willing to show their inner selves rather than just their outer selves. They will begin to direct energy toward expression—communication that allows oneself to be known to others authentically and transparently—rather than impression—communication that involves putting on a face in order to attract others (Schmuck & Schmuck, 1971).

Ohlsen (1970) also described the impact of the security stage:

> When clients come to feel reasonably secure within their counseling group, they can be themselves, discuss the problems that bother them, accept others' frank reactions to them and express their own genuine feelings toward others. (p. 91)

In other words, the development of trust provides the basis for getting down to the business of working on one's problems. Vorrath (n.d.) adds that the most dynamic experience members "gain from the group is that they learn to trust people" (p. 9). So trust has a process dimension and an outcome dimension, which give it a two-fold impact in the group process. During the security stage the development of a trusting, nonthreatening atmosphere is the primary objective. This objective is in accord with each member's basic human need for security. As trust increases, the willingness for personal involvement and commitment increases. Members are more likely to risk letting themselves and their problems, frustrations, joys, and successes be known. Because of the atmosphere created by the movement toward trust, the individual members feel freer to be themselves. When this occurs the transition into the second stage of the group-counseling process takes place.

The Acceptance Stage

The acceptance stage is directly related to our need for love and belonging and therefore has many derivatives that influence the direction of the group process. Generally this stage is characterized by a movement away from resistance and toward cooperation on the part of group members. As members begin to overcome the discomfort and threat of the group, the grounds for their fears dissipate and they become more accepting of the group situation. As they become more familiar with the group's atmosphere, procedures, leader, and members, they become more comfortable and secure in the group setting. They accept the group structure and the leader's role. This acceptance does not mean the purpose of the group is clear to members, but it does mean they are accepting the method. The meaning and purpose of the counseling group must be derived from the group members not from the group structure.

Inherent in the group members' acceptance of the group as a vehicle for their interaction is their need to belong and the need for relatedness. The members' desire to be a part of the group emerges as an important motivating factor. This desire is inwardly evident to the individual from the outset of the group. But at first it's stifled for fear of acting in a manner that might ultimately jeopardize that belonging. However, with the foundation of trust established, the members are more willing to be their real selves and risk being known for the sake of being accepted. A journal entry of a 24-year-old Vietnam veteran who chose an alcohol treatment center rather than jail effectively depicts the acceptance stage of the group process:

> At first there was no way I was going to admit to being an alcoholic or even that I had a drinking problem. But as I listened to the other guys talk about booze in their lives I began to realize they were all talking about many of the same experiences I had. The first thought that came to me was "Hey, you can't fool these cats because they've been there." I felt lots of pressure to 'fess up' but still held back because I wasn't sure

how they (the group) would take me nor was I sure I could stomach myself if I did. I finally decided to share my drinking problems when I saw the group treat another Nam vet in the group in a sensitive way, giving him support and help with a problem I thought was even worse than mine. When I did admit I had a drinking problem the group seemed to open up to me and let me in, and I also liked myself better.

As acceptance is experienced, relationships grow, and cohesiveness develops. Cohesiveness is important to the group process because it makes group members more susceptible to the influence of each other and the group. It also provides the impetus for group productivity. It is a key factor in the helping process in groups because "those who are to be changed and those who influence change must sense a strong feeling of belonging in the same group" (Ohlsen, 1970, p. 88). Thus group cohesiveness meets the members' needs to belong, provides them with a temporary protective shield from the outside world, and is a potent therapeutic factor in the change process.

The therapeutic influence of cohesiveness makes use of peer-group dynamics as its key resource in the group. As members experience genuine acceptance by fellow members, self-esteem is enhanced, ego is strengthened, self-confidence is bolstered, and they develop more courage in facing up to their problems. The impact of feeling accepted by a group of one's peers is stated succinctly by Gawrys and Brown (1963):

To be accepted and understood by the counselor is a satisfying experience: to be accepted and understood by a number of individuals is profound. (p. 106)

Within this context, then, the potential of peer-group influence can be used in a positive manner by the counselor. The group leader's role in this stage is no small factor in generating an accepting atmosphere in the group and contributing directly to the individual members' experience of feeling accepted. Leaders must be models of acceptance from the onset of the total group process. They must demonstrate a genuine caring for each of the group members. Their leadership must be characterized by acceptance of each person regardless of the behaviors he or she has exhibited outside the group. The process of acceptance is initiated by leaders who practice Rogers' (1962) concept of unconditional positive regard. As the members experience acceptance from the leader, they feel more accepting of themselves and follow the leader's model in their actions toward one another. As members feel more accepting of themselves and other members, a total atmosphere of acceptance is created.

This brings us to the primary objective of the acceptance stage from a problem-solving perspective—developing acceptance of self. For members' problems to surface in the group they must feel free to be truly themselves without fear of rejection or reprisal. As already stated, members cannot deal effectively with their problems without recognition that the problems are a part of them. Further, they must know that even though they have problems they are still persons of worth and importance. All people have the desire to like and accept themselves and to be liked and accepted by others. It is this desire that the group utilizes in helping members deal with their problems. When each member can accept feelings, thoughts, and behaviors, whether good or bad, as part of themselves and still feel accepted and respected as a person of worth, a big step has been taken in the helping process of the group.

The focus during the acceptance stage should be on the whole person and not just on isolated problem areas. In order to attain self-acceptance and acceptance of others, members must work with the total picture of themselves and others. Getting to know oneself and each other, engaging in "who am I?" and "who are you?" activities, serve to promote self-disclosure. As individuals share themselves and describe their problems, accepting problems as part of themselves occurs more naturally and is less threatening. Many leaders like to incorporate the first two stages of security and acceptance, using structured personal-sharing activities and techniques to do so. In this way sharing promotes trust, and trust encourages sharing. And members find that many of their concerns are similar to those of other members. This similarity among members leads to identification with each other and the group and facilitates openness. As members can speak more freely about their problems, they find they can embrace them without losing self-esteem or position in the group; and this experience paves the way for the more individualistic stage of responsibility.

The results of the second stage of the group-counseling process include acceptance of the group structure and the leader's role, meeting individual needs for love and belonging, acceptance of self, acceptance of others, and acceptance of problems as part of oneself. This may sound like a big order to fill, and it is. But acceptance is also a powerful force in facilitating the problem-solving process. When established, it removes many of the roadblocks in the counseling process. It enables the group to begin constructive individual help. The development of acceptance accomplishes three main objectives (Trotzer, 1972).

> 1. *It aids the group in becoming cohesive and close thus meeting Gendlin and Beebe's (1968) guideline that*

"closeness must precede unmasking."

2. *It helps each individual feel accepted as a person of worth even though life is not satisfactory at the moment. This meets Gendlin and Beebe's (1968) guideline of putting "people before purpose."*

3. *It releases the potential of peer-group influence to be used in a positive rather than negative manner.*

The Responsibility Stage

The third stage of the group-counseling process is characterized by a movement on the part of group members from acceptance of self and others to responsibility for self. There is a subtle but distinct difference between acceptance of and responsibility for self. Acceptance helps members realize and admit that problems are a part of their selves. However, acceptance alone leaves members with an avenue of retreat away from working on their problems. Members can say "yes, that's the way I am" or "that's my problem" but can disclaim any part in its cause or rectification. Acceptance allows members to claim no fault and negates any responsibility for doing anything about changing. The inclusion of responsibility, however, moves members toward resolution. The combination of acceptance and responsibility encourages members to state "yes, that's my problem, and I have to do something about it." The ground is thus made fertile for constructive change to take place.

A single mother with two children who shared her problems and frustrations in a women's counseling group at a mental-health center exemplifies the difference between acceptance and responsibility. During the fourth group meeting she talked extensively about the pain of her divorce and the subsequent difficulties of trying to raise her children alone. She became very emotional at times, and the group facilitated catharsis in a very sensitive manner. At the end of the session the group leader helped the woman put herself back together emotionally and solicited feedback from the group couched in terms of support. During the following session she was again the focus of attention, but this time members began to suggest alternatives that could possibly help her improve her life. To each alternative she responded by saying, "I already tried that" or "I don't think that would work." After several attempts to get her to consider alternatives failed, one member observed that maybe she really didn't want to do anything different in her life to overcome the problems. The woman denied that but soon afterward asked that the focus of group attention be directed elsewhere. During the following sessions this woman's problem was brought up several times by herself, other group members, or the leader, but the discussion always stalemated at the point of her taking any responsibility for the problems or for initiating changes. Eventually she told the group that she felt her problems were the result of others being unfair and insensitive to her and that she was a victim and not a cause in her situation. Soon afterward she left the group. She was willing to share her problems in the group but was not able to see herself as a contributor or take the initiative to work toward resolving them.

The issue of responsibility in the group emanates from both our needs as human beings and the nature of the problem-solving process. Members can only meet their need for esteem and respect through actions and achievements that require the person to take responsibility. If members feel causes are external they will also feel the cures must come from sources external to themselves and not from within.

Our needs are reflected in the pressure of the counseling group to move on. The social aspect of cohesiveness developed in the acceptance stage wears thin after a while, and there is a natural tendency toward getting down to the business of problems. This tendency, according to Bonney (1969), is a mark of group maturity in that group members begin to accept responsibility for the management of the group and exert their energies to the task of problem-solving. As members take increased responsibility for themselves and the therapeutic process, their chances for growth within the counseling group improve. In fact, Lindt (1958) found that only those who accepted responsibility in the helping process of the group benefited from their experience.

During the early stages of the group process the task is to develop trust and acceptance by focusing on similarities among members. This process universalizes. It helps members recognize that their problems are experienced by others (universalization), even though individual differences are apparent (Dinkmeyer and Muro, 1971). During the responsibility stage the focus changes to individualization and differentiation based on each person's uniqueness and responsibility. The atmosphere of the group provides for considerable personal freedom with the implication that members have permission to explore their weaknesses, strengths, and potentialities, to determine a way of working on problems, and to express feelings. The here-and-now emphasis is a key component in the responsibility stage, but it takes on a broader, problem-oriented perspective. During the early stages of the group the here-and-now is restricted to present feelings about the group and one's part in it and to help members focus on their here-and-now problems outside the group as well. This can be done in a step-by-step process in which expression of feelings is the starting point. The expression of personal feelings and perceptions about self and others is one basis for learning responsibility in the group. To emphasize taking responsibility for what one feels, leaders can ask members to state their own perceptions and to tack on the statement "and I take responsibility for that feeling." In this manner members learn to take responsibility for expressing hostility and caring without the threat and risk usually associated with the expression of such feelings.

As the members learn to accept responsibility for their personal feelings it becomes easier to accept responsibility for their actions and eventually their problems. These steps must be taken if the counselor and the group are to have any significant impact on the individual member's life. Mahler (1969) emphasizes the importance of responsibility for oneself:

> *Counselees must realize the importance of being responsible for their own lives, behavior, and actions, making their own decisions and learning to stand on their own perceptions. (p. 140)*

He adds that:

> *People need opportunities to learn that only by taking actions, making decisions, and accepting responsibility for their own lives can they become adults in the full sense of the word. (p. 141)*

Group counseling gives them that opportunity.

The leader's role during this stage centers around helping members realize self-responsibility. Lakin (1969) and Glasser (1965) stress the modeling nature of the leader role in which the counselor's actions must depict the proper attitude toward responsibility. Glasser feels that responsibility can only be learned through involvement with responsible people. Therefore the member's primary example to follow in the group is the leader. The leader must help members maintain a focus on themselves and their problems at this point, rather than on events, people, or situations external to the group and beyond its influence. The counseling group can only affect people and situations through its effect on the person in the immediate presence of the group. The counselor must stress an internal frame of reference rather than an external one. The question that ultimately must be faced is not "what can others do?" but "what can I do?"

The leader faces a crucial issue during the responsibility stage, and a word of caution is apropos. In our concern for our clients to "make it on their own," we often see opportunities in the group process that could be used to "teach" members responsibility. This situation must be avoided. For group members to become responsible they must experience responsibility, not be told about it. It is appropriate at times to bring up the issue of responsibility or even to confront members with it, but the choice to be responsible should be left to the members. Mahler (1969) feels that "counselors who teach in group counseling violate the concept that basic responsibility for management of one's own life is up to the individual" (p. 103). Therefore leadership should be directed toward helping members feel accepted and responsible without domination. When successful, members will feel more personal, individual responsibility and will exhibit less dependency.

The responsibility stage sets the tone for the remainder of the group-counseling process. Once members realize their responsibility for themselves and understand that neither the leader nor the group will infringe upon it, the members can direct their entire attention to problem-solving. The responsibility stage affirms the inherent worth of the members, assures them of respect as human beings, and points out the qualities necessary to enhance self-worth and resolve problems. Those qualities are self-assessment, congruence, honesty, responsibility, and commitment. When the members willingly engage in the introspective process, self-disclose, demonstrate their acceptance of others and willingness to help others, and—with very little or no help from the leader—take responsibility, the work stage of the counseling process is imminent.

The Work Stage

The character of the work stage organizes itself around the individual problems and concerns of the group members. As trust, acceptance, and responsibility are experienced and learned, it becomes increasingly evident that there are some areas in each members' life that are not satisfactory and could benefit from change. When these areas are pinpointed and discussed specifically, the work stage goes into full operation. Vorrath (n.d.) feels that the core of the group process is reached at this point, because the goal of this type of group is to work on problems and get them solved.

The work stage of group counseling is exemplified by the interaction of a human-relations group designed to improve communication and relationships between racial groups in a large urban high school. The members decided that the basic problem was not knowing how to approach students who were racially different from themselves. They tended to be hesitant, fearing overtones of prejudice might be communicated. To work on this problem, the leader first had racially similar members discuss their perceptions of racially different groups and then make suggestions that they felt would facilitate better relationships. After each subgroup had discussed their perceptions and made their suggestions, a comprehensive list of suggestions was developed in terms of skills. The leader than formed racially mixed dyads to try out the suggestions. During their work stage, partners were rotated periodically to give members the experience of trying out alternatives and building their skills and confidence with all racial groups represented.

The basic purposes of the work stage are to give group members the opportunity to (1) examine personal problems closely in an environment free of threat, (2) explore alternatives and suggestions for resolving the problems, and (3) try out new behaviors or attitudes in a safe setting prior to risking changes outside the group (Trotzer, 1972). The energy of the group is concentrated on accomplishing these three purposes through the use of feedback, clarification, and information-giving. Once in motion the productivity of the group is quite amazing and at times needs to be held in check because of the tendency to begin to solve problems before they are fully understood.

The leader role in the work stage is extremely vital from two perspectives. Leaders must be both facilitator and expert. They must be able to facilitate the discussion of problems, bringing out as many facets as possible, and create an atmosphere where alternatives can be suggested. These two processes entail mustering the total perceptual and experiential resources of the group. After a particular problem has been discussed and alternative solutions suggested, leaders must use their expertise to provide vehicles for examining the consequences of the suggestions as a means of aiding the decision-making process. These activities can take the form of role-playing, sociodramas, communication exercises, or discussion. In this way alternatives can be assessed and evaluated, thus avoiding shot-in-the-dark failures. This type of reality testing in the group provides the group member with an idea of both the feasibility of a specific alternative and the effort involved in using it to resolve the problem. It also provides the member with an opportunity to develop self-confidence before attempting to make any specific changes in the more threatening world outside the group.

Another important facet of the group process that surfaces during the work stage is the dual role of the group member as both the helper and the helped. When any one member of the group is working on a particular problem, the other members provide help through their feedback, sharing, suggestions, discussion, and participation in group activities. The experience of being in the helper role increases the members' feelings of self-worth because now they are in the position of giving rather than receiving. The giving of assistance to others also produces a more congenial attitude toward receiving assistance from others. The two-way process of helping and being helped is thus established. This process makes good use of members' altruistic tendencies, as well as allowing them to engage in "spectator therapy" where they benefit from watching others work out their problems.

During this stage the group also represents "society in microcosm" (Gazda, 1968c); that is, group members represent, as best they can, the forces, attitudes, reactions, and ideas of the world outside the group. Through the process of feedback the group helps each member develop realistic alternatives to problems that can reasonably be applied in their lives outside the group. This minisociety function is important because of its transitional value in preparing members for the task of implementing changes.

In the work stage the "healing capacity" (Rogers, 1967) of the group emerges, and the specific goals and objectives of the counseling group are dealt with. Each group has different objectives based on the diversity of the group membership and the setting in which the group is formed. However, since most counseling groups are usually organized to deal with specific problems, it is at this point in the group process where efforts are focused on resolving them. The work stage prepares members for reentry into the world where they are experiencing their problems. They are armed with a well-conceived and evaluated plan, and self-confidence has been shored up through practice and personal encouragement. However, individuals do not have to make the changes and implement their plans without some support, which brings us to the final stage of the group process, closing.

The Closing Stage

The final stage of the group-counseling process is mainly supportive in nature and is characterized by feedback, encouragement, and perseverance. Although group members may successfully work through their problems within the group, they still face the difficult task of modifying their behavior and attitudes outside the group. The expectations of significant others outside the group are still based on past experience with the group member, thus making it difficult to give encouragement or reinforcement to the member for acting in new or different ways. The group is a place where members can share their frustrations, successes, and failures and also reassess their actions for possible changes that will increase their effectiveness. Without a source of support, the chance of regression to old ways is greater.

The group also serves as a motivator. Part of this function entails rejecting excuses and confronting members with their own lack of commitment and effort if need be. Sometimes members need to be pushed out into the real world when they cannot venture forth on their own. The group has uncanny competence in assessing whether members are authentic in their efforts and whether they have performed up to their capability. During this stage the group can be both a sounding board and a control board.

Group support facilitates the integration of change into the client's life. Efforts to change and the change process itself are supported until reinforcement occurs in members' lives outside the group. As the changes become more natural parts of their life-styles, the difficulty of adapting new behaviors, feelings, and attitudes decreases. The support of the group is only necessary until the balance between ease and difficulty in implementing change swings to the ease side of the scale.

The focus of the group thus turns to members' behavior and experience outside the group and deals with progress they are making. The leader helps members discuss their experiences and feelings, offering support, understanding, and encouragement. The leader also helps members begin to take credit for their own changes instead of giving credit to the group or the counselor. In this way the individual members can integrate their new behaviors and attitudes into their everyday lives and can feel reinforcement from within themselves rather than from the group.

The closing stage for individuals may take many different forms. For example, a student who had been a member of a therapy group at a college counseling center for three years began to miss group meetings, showing up periodically but with longer time lapses between attendance. As she entered the final semester of her senior year, she relied less and less on the group for feedback and support taking more and more responsibility for herself. Her need for the group and her involvement in the group lessened, with termination coinciding with graduation.

Another example of the closing stage is the standard procedure used at an alcohol treatment center when individual patients are preparing to leave treatment. The patient's group holds a graduation ceremony for the departing member during which that person makes a commencement address reviewing and summarizing the treatment and describing goals and objectives for the future. The group then engages in a serenity prayer during which group members give support, feedback, and encouragement to the graduating member. The person is then presented with a coin that has a missing piece symbolizing the unending process involved in rehabilitation and growth. The ceremony thus serves to summarize and reinforce changes that have occurred but also prepares the person for the rigors of adjusting to life outside of the treatment center.

The point at which a group or individual member should terminate is sometimes difficult to determine. For this reason groups are often terminated on the basis of a preset time schedule, for example, after ten sessions or at the end of a quarter or semester. However, ending a group is also appropriate when group members experience more success than failure in solving their problems and feel intrinsic rather than extrinsic reinforcement for their actions in doing so. As members become more dependent on themselves, they lose their dependence on the group. As they resolve their problems and learn how to solve problems, they no longer need the group. When any of these situations occur the group has run its course and should be disbanded.

A Precautionary Note

Viewing group counseling as a developmental sequence of a set number of stages raises the possibility of unnecessary and undesirable rigidity in conceptualizing the group process. To circumvent this and maintain flexibility in this group model, it is necessary to remember that within each stage there can be many levels. Different degrees of trust, acceptance, and responsibility are reached by the group and its members at different times. Some problems discussed in the group require less trust than others. At other times it may be necessary for the process to recycle, developing deeper levels of trust, acceptance, or responsibility in order to deal with a particular problem. Bonney (1969) refers to this occurrence as the retransition stage in which the group goes back through the early phases of group development before proceeding to a deeper level. At any one time and with any one problem or person the group may have to retreat to a previous stage before it can move on to the next one. In fact, all stages may recur several times before the group has run its course.

Another consideration is that components of two or more stages may be prominent in the group at the same time. The group may be learning trust, acceptance, and responsibility while working on a particular problem. The group does not develop in a lock-step manner even though general trends can be noted and specific characteristics consistently appear at certain points in the group's development. Neither can the group process be forced to conform to an external standard or model. Rather it is a responsive and flexible process that is influenced by the leader's personality, by differences between people and their problems, and by variations in the rate at which different people develop relationships and work out individual change.

Concluding Comments

Group counseling brings into perspective the relationship between psychological needs and the socialization process, whereby human learning and problem-solving occurs through interaction. It accentuates the social learning process by focusing on the dynamics of the group itself rather than on some environmental context. Group members are given the opportunity to learn how they function individually and interpersonally. They can do this because the leader and other members have created a climate or atmosphere characterized by psychological safety and acceptance where they can take responsibility for their own lives. In such a situation members can experience the healthy attributes of individuality or uniqueness and relatedness or conformity. They learn both independence and interdependence.

Members can express themselves freely and engage in open and honest interaction with other members without the fear of rejection or reprisal that so often tempers interaction in one's environment. Within the group members can experience and learn responsibility. They can confront problems openly, knowing they will obtain support and assistance as needed. Members experience the interchanging role of being the helper and the helped as they work on their own problems and assist others with theirs. The member can discover and evaluate alternative solutions to personal concerns while at the same time building self-confidence and personal security, which serve as enabling factors in implementing change outside the group. Thus group counseling provides both a setting and a process whereby the basic objectives of a counseling program can be attained.

Learning Activities

The exercises presented here are organized in sequence to relate to the stages of group development discussed in this chapter. Although the primary characteristic and use of each activity is stage-related, there are also many other purposes for which they can be used. These activities are versatile and adaptable, depending on the leader's approach and the nature of the group.

Trust Ring[1]

Option I. This exercise is useful in demonstrating the characteristics of trust and confidentiality that are necessary for a group to work effectively. Have all group members stand in a circle in an area that is free of material objects such as chairs or tables. Members should have a strong grip on each of their partners hands or wrists. Then have the group extend out as far as possible forming a taut circle. Instruct all members to lean back exerting pressure on the circle and slowly move their feet toward the center of the circle creating a centrifugal pressure on the group. Have the group move in a clockwise direction maintaining this centrifugal pressure. After a few moments reverse the direction. Follow the exercise with a discussion of each person's reaction in terms of the amount of pressure they were personally willing to place on the group and their feelings regarding their partners and the total group. Stress the importance of the whole group going to the aid of individuals who were slipping in order to protect them and maintain solidarity in the group. Discussion can also focus on the amount of pressure the group as a whole exerted relating it to risk-taking in self-disclosure and feedback.

Option II. A variation of this exercise is to have members stand in a circle shoulder to shoulder. Instruct the members to interlock their arms around the back or waist of the persons beside them. Then have the group members lean inward and slowly move their feet away from the center of the group creating a centripetal force on the group. Have the group move alternately in a clockwise and counterclockwise manner. At the conclusion of the exercise have the group members retain their interlocking positions in the circle and discuss the reactions in the same manner as described above. An added feature of this discussion can be the impact of closeness created by the "arms around each other" dimension, relating it to the effect of warmth and closeness in developing cohesiveness and trust in the group.

Option III. This exercise is useful in working with individual members who are having difficulty developing, feeling, or understanding trust in the group. It is particularly effective in working with individuals who wish to trust the group but are having difficulty doing so. Stand one member in the center of the group and have the other members form a standing circle around him.

The initial distance between the person in the center and the circle members should be relatively small but large enough to allow freedom of movement. Instruct the member in the center to close his eyes and place his feet together. Then instruct him to fall toward the circle without moving his feet and allow the group to move him back and forth and around. The outside circle should vary the distance they allow the person to fall and the roughness they use in handling him but always be responsible for the member's safety. Follow-up discussion should center on the individual's feelings and reactions. The main thrust is to help the individual come to grips with feelings about trust and to point out the important group dynamics associated with individuals sharing problems or disclosing themselves in a group situation.

Closed Fist[2]

This activity lends itself to a consideration of the strategies used by people in negotiating trust in human relationships. It is particularly applicable to group counseling because of the risk intrinsic to the process of sharing. Break the group down into dyads. Ask the partners to exchange some material object that they value (such as a ring, a picture, or a wallet). Have each partner put the object away out of sight for the time being. Then instruct the members to think of something that is extremely valuable to them, something they would not wish to give up under any circumstances. Give the group a few minutes to choose something. Then ask one of the partners to figuratively place the thing of value in a closed fist without telling the partner what it is. Instruct the other partner to try to get it. Allow this process to proceed for a time without any intervention. Then ask for an account of what happened, noting the different strategies that were used to obtain the object and pointing out their relevance to the group process. After this discussion ask the members to try to get back the actual objects they exchanged initially.

Important factors to consider in this exercise are the type of exchange strategies that produce competitiveness, cooperation, ill will, and positive interpersonal feelings. Strategies that are conducive to positive relationships should be used in the group. Also, the value of the objects exchanged reflects the amount of commitment and trust in the relationship. Members will share more willingly and at a deeper level if there is reciprocal sharing by other members.

Life Story

Vorrath (n.d.) uses this technique to introduce new members into the group. It is especially appropriate for ongoing counseling groups that experience member turnover. New members after a brief period of time in the group are asked to tell their life stories as completely and as accurately as they possibly can. The life stories should include a description of the problems that brought the new people into the group. The other group members have the responsibility of facilitating the new member's efforts. Under no circumstances should the views of the person be challenged at this point. After the story is completed the group can begin to work with discrepancies or other factors that might relate to solving the member's problems. The main impact of this technique is that members realize their side of the story is going to be heard first. They receive guarantees that their frame of reference is important and will be considered by the group. They experience acceptance and find the group is a safe place to air their problems.

Poem of Self

This exercise helps establish a minimum level of self-acceptance for each group member and helps the group become involved in introspection and self-disclosure essential to the group process. Use the following directions in carrying out the exercise.

1. List four words (adjectives) that describe what you look like.
2. List four words (adjectives) that describe what you act like (personality).
3. List five words ending in "ing" that describe things you like to do (if you like to read, put reading).
4. List six things (nouns) that would remind people of you (for example, possessions, such as a guitar, or roles you play, such as a student).
5. List four places you would like to be.
6. On a sheet of paper draw the following diagram (you may want to hand out a mimeo form).

7. On the first line of the diagram write your full name.

8. Choose one word from list 1 (what you look like) and one word from list 2 (what you act like) and place them in the blanks in line 2.

9. Choose three words from list 3 (things you like to do) and insert them in the blanks in line 3.

10. Choose four words from list 4 (things that remind people of you) and write them in the blanks in line 4.

11. Choose two words from list 5 (places) and write them in the blanks in line 5.

12. On the bottom line write a nickname or any name by which you are called other than your given name. (This may be a derivative of your given name, such as "Toni" for Antoinette.)

On completion of the poem have each member read his or her poem to the group twice, the first time quickly with rhythm and the second time slowly so that they can catch all the words. After everyone has read and explained the meaning of the words in their poems discuss how the exercise contributed to getting to know one another.

Coat of Arms

The coat of arms has more depth to it than the poem of self and can be used in conjunction with it. This activity gets at more varied aspects of each person's life and provides a good beginning for the actual counseling process. It also combines the medium of illustration with verbal description, which makes sharing an easier process. Give each person a sheet of paper with the illustrated diagram on it or have the people draw it. Then have them fill in the numbered sections of the shield according to the following instructions.

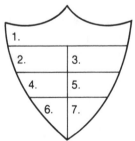

1. In the section numbered 1, write a motto or phrase that describes how you feel about life or that is a guide to your life-style. (Some people create their own; others use quotations, poems, or Bible verses.)

2. In section 2, draw a picture that represents your greatest achievement or accomplishment (no words).

3. Draw a picture that represents something other people could do to make you happy (no words).

4. Draw a picture that represents a failure or disappointment (no words).

5. Draw a picture that represents the biggest goal in your life right now (no words).

6. Draw a picture that represents a problem you would like to work on in this group (no words).

7. Write down three things you would like people to say about you if you died today.

After all the members have completed the shield, have each member describe his or hers to the group, explaining the meaning of each section. This exercise has the positive impact of acceptance since it deals with each person's strengths, weaknesses, goals, relationships with others, and problems. The instructions for the various parts can be changed to meet the demands of the situation and the needs of the members, thus making this exercise a flexible and effective tool in the hands of the group leader.

Strength Bombardment

One means of helping group members accept responsibility for themselves is to approach it from a perspective of strengths, assets, and accomplishments the member is already aware of. This exercise uses the process of self-disclosure and feedback to help members take responsibility for their behavior. First, have each group member develop a list of all positive accomplishments or achievements. Encourage the members to feel completely free about the list and not to think about the reactions of others or about the ego-related emotional connotations such a request usually conjures up. On completion of the list, have the members write a paragraph, starting with "I am," that describes their positive qualities. Assure them that no one else will see the paragraph, but indicate that they should include only positive qualities and not put in any negative ones. When the paragraph is completed have members put it away, stating that they can do what they want with it. Now have the members share their initial list of accomplishments with the group. Then place two chairs facing each other in the center of the circle. Ask one member to volunteer to take one of the chairs in order to receive positive feedback from the other members. When one person has taken a chair, each other person in turn gets up, sits in the opposite chair and gives the first person only positive feedback. There should be no "I would like you if" or "I like you but" comments, and the person receiving the feedback can only respond with expressions of appreciation, not with denials or counter remarks. This process continues until each person has received positive feedback from every other person in the group. On completion of the activity, relate the experience to the issue of responsibility and discuss how one's positive qualities can be used to help overcome one's negative qualities and problems.

Awareness and Responsibility

This technique has developed out of the Gestalt approach to group therapy and combines the concepts of personal awareness and individual responsibility. It has relevance to group counseling because it clarifies where members are personally and helps them take responsibility for their own thoughts, feelings and behavior in the group. Each group member is asked to share with the group present thoughts, feelings, and perceptions or observations using the format: "Right now I am aware . . . [members complete the statement describing what they are aware of], and I take responsibility for that." The last part of the statement is added to get individuals to affirm their own part in feeling, acting, or thinking the way they do and to prevent them from putting responsibility on others. A leader can effectively use the last part of the statement by simply asking members to add it to any statement involving a personal emotion, accusation, interpretation, or perception. In this way, the impact of the statement becomes just one person's frame of reference and allows other members the freedom to respond as they see fit without feeling threatened by the imposition of another person's point of view on them.

Gestalt Interventions

One of the ways we avoid being responsible for ourselves and in control of our own lives is through the words we use in communication (Stevens, 1971). The following intervention techniques drawn from the Gestalt approach to group therapy can be used to help group members take responsibility for their own thoughts, feelings, and behaviors and ultimately for their problems.

1. *Questions or Statements.* Many questions that group members ask are really camouflaged statements. Before responding with an answer ask the questioner to change the question into a statement that expresses personal perceptions, observations, or feelings.

2. *I Can't/I Won't Statements.* Members often use the words "I can't" in discussing problem situations, which give the impression that control is really outside of themselves. When you hear an "I can't" statement ask the member to repeat the statement using "I won't," which conveys the message that the person has a choice in the matter. "I just can't talk to my father" changes to "I just won't talk to my father."

3. *I Have to/I Choose to Statements.* Have group members make a list of "I have to" statements describing all the things in their lives that they feel they have to do. Have them share their lists in the group. Then have them change "I have to" to "I choose to" and discuss the differences between the two lists. Discussion usually pinpoints quite clearly the issue of personal responsibility and choice. As a group leader you can also ask members to substitute "I choose to" for "I have to" during group discussions. In doing this the members realize that they are responsible and that they do have a choice.

4. *I Need/I Want Statements.* Group members often express desires as needs, creating the impression that severe personal consequences will result if needs are not met. They say "I need," which depicts whatever it is as essential to their well-being. To define more accurately what really is needed and what can be done without, have members change "I need" statements to "I want" statements and discuss which is more appropriate, incorporating feedback from other members as to the accuracy of the statement.

Problem Identification and Rating

The work stage is the point in the group process at which problems should be dealt with directly. This exercise pinpoints problems that are pertinent to individual members and are relevant to other members' lives as well. Have the members anonymously write down a description of a problem they would be willing to discuss with the group. Stress the "willing to discuss" aspect. When the descriptions are finished, read them one by one to the group. After each problem is read ask members to individually rate it on a scale (5 is high and 1 is low), showing their interest in discussing the problem and their identification with it. Record each individual rating and after reading and rating all the problems, add up the totals. A hierarchy of problems develops based on the scores. Reread the highest rated problem and ask the person who wrote it to describe it in detail. The group can then work with that specific person and problem.

This procedure results in a hierarchical agenda, but if the group is particularly effective in helping the first person, other members may decide to reveal deeper problems they want help with. The problem agenda and hierarchy should be adhered to only if it is in the best interests of the group. Rigid structuring of the group focus could deter progress.

Go-Round

One of the simplest and yet most versatile and effective exercises that can be used in group counseling is the "go-round." As the name implies this technique involves going around the group person by person, giving each a specific opportunity to respond. This technique has many variations and purposes and fits at any stage of group development. For instance, a "go-round" is a good way to begin with a group to find out what everyone is thinking or feeling and to get some cues about how to proceed. A "go-round" when a group ends gives members the opportunity to say what they have not had a chance to say and is a good way to tie up loose ends. During the group sessions, go-rounds immediately following critical incidents are useful to air feelings and release tension, as well as to move the group on to the next phase of the process.

Notes

[1] The Trust Ring exercises of Options I and II were developed by Jim Ross and demonstrated in my group-counseling class at the University of Wisconsin-River Falls.

[2] This exercise was demonstrated by Dr. Dan Ficek in a Human Relations Workshop he and I led at Red Wing, Minnesota in the spring of 1974.

References

Bonney, W. C. Group counseling and developmental processes. In G. M. Gazda (Ed.), *Theories and methods of group counseling in the schools.* Springfield, IL: Charles C Thomas, 1969.

Cohn, B. Group counseling with adolescents. In B. Cohn (Ed.), *Collected articles: The adolescent and group counseling* (unpublished). Board of Cooperative Educational Services, Yorktown Heights, NY 10598, 1964.

Cohn, B. *Group counseling presentation.* Spring Group Guidance Conference, University of Wisconsin-Oshkosh, 1973.

Dinkmeyer, D. D. and Muro, J. J. *Group counseling: Theory and practice.* Itasca, IL: F. E. Peacock, 1971.

Gawrys, J., Jr., and Brown, B. O. Group counseling: More than a catalyst. *The School Counselor* 1963, 12, 206–213.

Gazda, G. M., and Larson, M. J. A comprehensive appraisal of group and multiple counseling research. *Journal of Research and Development in Education,* 1968, 1(2), 57–132.

Glasser, W. *Reality therapy.* New York: Harper & Row, 1965.

Lakin, M. Some ethical issues in sensitivity training. *American Psychologist,* 1969, 24, 923–928.

Lifton, W. *Working with groups* (2nd ed.). New York: Wiley, 1966.

Lindt, H. The nature of therapeutic interaction of patients in groups. *International Journal of Group Psychotherapy,* 1958, 8, 55–69.

Mahler, C. A. *Group counseling in the schools.* Boston: Houghton Mifflin, 1969.

Ohlsen, M. M. *Group counseling.* New York: Holt, Rinehart & Winston, 1970.

Rogers, C. R. The interpersonal relationship: The core of guidance. *Harvard Educational Review,* 1962, 32, 416-429.

Rogers, C. R. The process of the basic encounter group. In J. F. T. Bugental (Ed.), *Challenges of humanistic psychology.* New York: McGraw-Hill, 1967.

Schmuck, R. A., and Schmuck, P. A. *Group processes in the classroom.* Dubuque, IA: Brown, 1971.

Stevens, J. O. *Awareness: Exploring, experimenting, experiencing.* Moab, UT: Real People Press, 1971.

Trotzer, J. P. Group counseling: Process and perspective. *Guidelines for Pupil Services.* Madison: Wisconsin Department of Public Instruction, 1972, 10, 105–110.

Vorrath, H. H. *Positive peer culture: Content, structure and process.* Red Wing, MN: Red Wing State Training School.

27

The Use of Groups

Richard A. Stordeur
Richard Stille

Counselors have intervened in wife assault with a variety of approaches: separate individual counseling for men and women, couple counseling, couple groups, family counseling, and gender-specific groups have all been utilized in the attempt to terminate the cycle of violence. For reasons discussed in this chapter, we strongly prefer to counsel abusers in groups. Although other modes may be helpful at later stages, we believe the immediate and primary goal of stopping the violence seems best attained when a man is in a group of his peers.

Groups for assaultive men differ in several important ways from most other problem-oriented groups, general therapy groups, and personal growth groups. Counselors who have been unaware of the differences in structure, objectives, goals, counselors' roles, and facilitator styles have had difficulty when beginning these groups. Failure to tailor an approach in the planning stage to suit the characteristics and the needs of abusers and the aims of an assaultive men's counseling program can produce regrettable results; dropouts, group rebellion, therapist frustration, and marked deviation from the goal of the group can occur. In addressing many of these issues, we aim in this chapter to help counselors prepare for productive, efficiently operated groups.

From *Ending Men's Violence Agtainst Their Partners* by Richard A. Stordeur and Richard Stille, Copyright 1989 by Sage Publications, Inc. Reprinted by permission of Sage Publications, Inc.

Groups for Assaultive Men

Individual Counseling Versus Group

We have counseled batterers both individually and in groups. These contrasting experiences have led us to choose a group setting for this work whenever possible. In part, the reasons emerge from the inadequacies of individual counseling. This mode of helping an abuser is slow and arduous. The requirement to address minimization, externalization, and other problem behaviors overtly is not only difficult, it has the potential to create an adversarial atmosphere in which two roles can be highlighted—persecutor and victim. If a man regards us as persecutors we become his enemies, and it is then only natural that he strengthen his defenses. Where social and emotional isolation are problems for the man, individual meetings with a therapist are a poor remedy. Because an individual counseling relationship occurs behind closed doors, violence remains a secret and the shame associated with it remains. Furthermore, the one-to-one relationship risks reinforcing notions of psychopathology rather than the sociocultural, learned aspects of violence against women.

While the individual approach presents obstacles to change, the use of groups is based on what we believe to be the overwhelming advantages of this mode. Distinct and separate from content or counselor skill level, the group environment itself facilitates change. We can think of at least nine reasons to counsel abusers in groups:

(1) A group helps decrease a batterer's isolation. The group counseling environment requires taking risks, self-disclosure, and being vulnerable in the presence of others. It promotes trust while eroding the harmful facade of pseudoindependence demanded by the traditional male sex role. Social and emotional isolation from others is a mental health deficit, particularly when a man must deal with mounting stress levels. A group provides opportunities both to learn to rely on others and to help others.

(2) A group promotes improved interpersonal skills. A man in a group engages in discussion and role play, learns to give and receive feedback, and must do these respectfully.

(3) A group offers mutual aid among peers. The mutual aid process created by ten men multiplies the potential number of creative responses to any one man's struggle. This maximizes the self-help element while reducing the counselor's responsibility always to have an answer to a problem.

(4) As men learn to be helpful to each other, each individual's

status as a batterer makes him a special kind of expert. His credibility stems from "having been there." Additionally, because help comes from a number of individuals, men's authority issues with the counselor are deemphasized.

(5) The effect of confrontation is maximized in a group. When a therapist confronts one man on an issue, other men who struggle with the same issue are indirectly confronted. When the group observes one man struggle with an issue, each member identifies with that struggle as if he were looking in a mirror. However, because only one man is being confronted directly, defensiveness on the part of others in the group may be diluted.

(6) As a group works for change, a norm is established for attaining group objectives within a certain time. This sense of group time functions as a reference point for members who lag behind, encouraging them to keep up with the group.

(7) A group maximizes rewards for change. As each man reports a success, he is reinforced by the entire group instead of by the therapist alone.

(8) The secrecy surrounding male violence against women and children often leads both perpetrators and victims to believe they are exceptional or sick. A group helps to dispel this notion. When a batterer enters a group, he meets ordinary men who have the same problem. This event begins the consciousness-raising process whereby men learn about the prevalence of abuse and the sociocultural factors influencing ordinary people to be violent. Beyond the educational value of this revelation, we believe shame is reduced.

(9) In view of incessant funding difficulties in social services, the group approach is cost-effective.

A Psychoeducational Approach

The term *psychoeducational* has been used to describe groups for assaultive men (Ganley, 1981b). Although the implications of the term might vary according to who is using it, it seems to be one of the best available for describing a recommended overall approach in batterers' groups. When violence is viewed as learned behavior, it follows that it can be replaced by new learning. Therefore these groups are partially oriented to educating batterers. Counselors teach skills, lead discussion on various issues, facilitate role plays, and assign homework. Interestingly, the learning aspect of abuser groups is reflected by many men's tendencies to refer to the group as a "class."

Education in these groups differs from that found in most classroom situations. Classroom education is most often concerned with subject material that is external to the learner, such as facts, figures, and concepts. Although this does occur in a batterers' group, we select most material for its personal relevance to assaultive men. Members are really learning about themselves. For instance, when we teach a man that certain ways of thinking about a situation profoundly affect the way a person feels about it, he must apply this information to his struggle to be nonviolent through his participation in group exercises and self-disclosure. Therefore, there is a marked personal slant to all material.

The psychoeducational approach that we present also allows for each man to present personal issues and receive help from the counselors and other members. Although this occurs at special, predetermined points in each session, portions of these groups bear strong resemblance to ordinary therapy groups.

Counseling Duration

The duration of a man's counseling varies from one program to another. One New York program provides only 6 sessions in an "educational workshop" format (Frank & Houghton, 1982). A Minneapolis program offers 32 group sessions of assaultive men's group counseling as well as a variety of other services (Stordeur, 1983). Programs differ not only in length, but in philosophical assumptions, subjects covered, and techniques used. Hence comparing programs is complex if not unrealistic.

Our emphasis on violence as learned behavior leads us to believe that eradicating violence and replacing it with alternatives is a long process. Twenty or more years of learning cannot be altered overnight. Herein lies a problem; few agencies or communities have the resources to provide one or more years of counseling to each man. Seen in this light, most programs fall short of an ideal and simply provide what they can. Knowing that there is an ever-present discrepancy between men's needs and service availability, we chose to offer group counseling, specifically aimed at stopping the violence, that has ranged from 24 to 32 sessions. When possible, we now choose the higher figure.

Group Structure

Although we feel most comfortable with eight to ten clients in a group, we typically attempt to begin a group with ten to twelve clients. This is to account for men who drop out at some point along the way. Assuming that the majority of men are not mandated to attend, it is usually necessary to perform assessments on twenty or more men to produce the desired ten to twelve clients. Of the number of men assessed, some will not be appropriate for the group and are refused, some will openly decline an offer to enter, and some who are accepted will not show up. From our experience, we think it is advisable to have approximately fifteen men assessed and appearing to be committed to enter a group. Normally, ten to twelve will follow through and attend the first session.

Although it is possible to operate a group with more than twelve men, it makes it difficult to develop a trusting atmosphere, to give each man the attention he needs, and to finish on time. When beginning with fewer than ten men, the group may stabilize (after dropouts) at a number that decreases the program's efficiency. Sometimes it is advantageous to postpone the beginning of a group until a sufficient number of men are available.

We operate closed groups, meaning that we will not accept new members into the group after the second session. Excepting dropouts, men who begin this group finish with the same group of men 32 sessions later. Although many programs choose to operate open groups and admit new members at any point, we favor the closed group option for two reasons. The first is that it is difficult to integrate new members when considerable amounts of material have been taught prior to their entry. It would involve prohibitive amounts of group time to help new members catch up to the group. Alternatively, it could consume hours of a counselor's time in individual sessions to do the same thing. Attempting to do this would be analogous to admitting students to a course that was half finished. A second reason for running closed groups is that admitting new members after a certain point of group development destabilizes the group. The men will be familiar with each other and a bond of trust will be growing. The addition of new faces can interfere with this process by temporarily reducing spontaneity, comfort, and self-disclosure.

While closed groups have definite advantages over open ones, not all agencies are able to accomplish this. In locales where only one closed group is offered, men who miss an entry deadline could wait several months for the next group. This is no small consideration. In light of the dangerousness of battering, a shorter waiting period may better protect the battered woman. Closed groups may also be unrealistic for programs in small, rural communities, for there may never be enough men at one time to start a closed group of sufficient size. Such communities frequently use open groups and gradually build up their membership.

Our groups meet for approximately two and one-half hours each session.[1] The first two-thirds of the session consists of structured activity, such as teaching a skill, facilitating discussion, or involving the men in an exercise. After a coffee break, the last one-third of the session is Sharing Time—a period in which any man can present an issue or seek help for a problem.

While it is possible to reverse the order by beginning with Sharing Time and then proceeding to structured activity, there are two reasons not to. It can be difficult to terminate Sharing Time in favor of other tasks if many men have problems to present or if there is a man in crisis. Additionally, a man may want to discuss material from the structured portion as it relates to himself during the Sharing Time that follows.

We have also experimented with the frequency of meetings. In one of the best arrangements, the group meets twice a week for the first 16 sessions and once a week for the remainder. One reason for this is that a 32-session group that meets only once a week takes a long time to complete. A more important reason is that the portion most concerned with imparting the skills to avoid abuse needs to be completed without delay.

Confidentiality and the Group

Most counseling relationships are private affairs; the flow of information from that relationship to outsiders is strictly regulated according to "right to know" rules. Almost always it is the client who determines who has a right to know this information. The flow of information in the reverse direction is not so stringently governed. Although it is normally necessary to secure a client's permission to seek information about him (e.g., contacting previous therapists), a therapist sometimes receives information volunteered by others. In everyday therapeutic relationships, therapists often feel uncomfortable receiving unsolicited information about their clients. The ethics and the consequences of using these data in counseling can be perturbing.

Counseling offenders requires the ability to enforce accountability. To aid in this, we have made some changes in the normal flow of information. Programs in which we have worked often have men's partners attending battered women's groups, either in the same agency or in another community service. In this situation we are sometimes informed by the woman's counselor, or the woman herself, of abusive behavior between group sessions. If the woman feels safe enough to allow us to use this information in the men's group, we will confront the man if he chooses not to report it. There are other information channels we keep open. We provide probation workers of court-mandated men with general progress reports and specific reports on abuse or threats of abuse. Child protection agencies are sometimes involved in a case and may delay final disposition pending the outcome of treatment. We sometimes provide them with progress reports. The end result of this regular flow of information is that our groups are much less confidential than other counseling endeavors.

Counselors should consider the effect of these practices on the group's members prior to beginning a group. In every group we have conducted, the first time we confront a man with accounts of his abuse that he has chosen to conceal, the entire group seems shocked. The man under scrutiny may feel angry and betrayed. Similarly, a member may have strong reactions when he discovers that his probation worker knows something that he discussed only in group. For this reason, we strongly recommend that therapists discuss the confidentiality policy with each man carefully during the intake process and that each man sign a form indicating he understands the policy. Therapists should address this issue again in the first group session. If these policies are explicitly outlined and explained as nonnegotiable conditions for participation in the program, clients are more likely to accept them and less likely to feel betrayed later.

Readers may wonder if these alterations of normal confidentiality practices interfere with trust and openness in counseling. Some men become guarded and suspicious, but, in our experience, they soon regard these practices as normal. We do not see a harmful effect. Men still disclose very sensitive information under these conditions. Some men even seem motivated to disclose abuse precisely because they do not know if the therapists have knowledge of these events in advance of a group session. They prefer to take the initiative in disclosing rather than be caught trying to conceal abusive behavior. The effect is negative only when policy is explained after the fact.

The Group Counselor

Leadership Style

Assaultive men are generally not self-reflective, self-disclosing, or self-motivated. They are often highly anxious about relating to others on the level called for in a counseling group (Ganley, 1981b). They also employ defenses that are incompatible with addressing the issue of battering. If the therapist waits for anxiety to disappear and for desirable behaviors to emerge, the group will likely flounder and men will drop out. For these reasons, a nondirective counseling style is inappropriate in these groups.

We agree with Ganley's (1981 b) recommendation that counselors adopt a directive leadership style that implies certain counselor behaviors. The directive counselor is actively involved in the group process. The counselor teaches not only through words but also by modeling or demonstrating skills. Interaction among members is facilitated through structured activities. Member participation is elicited by asking questions. The counselor assigns homework, follows up on assignments, and confronts individual men and the group on their resistance to changing thoughts and behavior. When appropriate, the counselor tells members what to do and what not to do. Furthermore, the counselor sets clear limits on behavior and enforces consequences for violation of those limits.

These examples describe someone who is a very central figure in the group. The term *authoritarian* may come to mind for some readers. This pejorative term suggests a leadership style emerging from a need to wield power over others, a rigid respect for hierarchical structures, and an inability to tolerate dissent. In recommending a directive style, we are not promoting authoritarianism. While the therapist definitely assumes the position of authority in the group, the directive style is not that of a martinet. Power for its own sake is not an issue here. The therapist is always respectful of group members' feelings and rights. While also being a caregiver, the therapist maintains control over the group so that it may do its work.

We believe the directive style is most needed in the earliest stage of the group. As time passes, the therapist can relax this stance as the group gradually develops some measure of constructive autonomy. Group norms emerge, a mutual aid process is born, and members slowly learn to do with each other what the therapist modeled in the earlier sessions.

Guarding the Time

These groups use a highly structured format because the psychoeducational approach necessitates covering much material in a relatively short time. If the group is planned as having a maximum number of sessions, we guarantee that a counselor will feel pressured to keep to the schedule. Many situations will seem to conspire against accomplishing what was planned.

The reader should not underestimate the difficulty of keeping to a schedule. In any single session, a number of factors can wreak havoc. Members may arrive late. Men who have difficulty understanding material may necessitate longer periods of discussion than planned. One or more men may be in crisis while several men may be required to report abuse; a sense of urgency often develops around competing demands. It is common for novice therapists to have difficulty covering the agenda. Consequently, we advise meticulous planning of time in each session. As the therapist becomes more familiar with the material, he or she will develop the sense of timing needed to cover it all

Two and a half hours of group time can easily be consumed by attending to men's individual problems. Therapists trying to keep to a schedule are often deeply affected by the men's needfulness. There can be a temptation to postpone the educational portion of the group for that session so that men can be cared for. This is a common dilemma. Because we recognize that counselors often have to make judgment calls, we are not inflexible on this issue. However, we must caution the reader that the postponing of educational material in a batterers' group might be tempting fate. In particular, the first half of the program contains anger control skills that must be learned rapidly. A particular skill scheduled for a certain night may help prevent an assault.

Group Cofacilitation

A result of adopting a directive style in these groups is that the therapist assumes much responsibility. Attending to the resistance to change, maintaining awareness of group process, and the demands of teaching are a huge load for one person. Those who facilitate these groups alone often perceive the competing demands as an impediment to doing their best work. For this reason, having a cofacilitator, though not absolutely essential, is of tremendous value.

Cofacilitation allows one person to be engaged with the group while the other observes specific interactions and the group's process. It fends off therapist exhaustion by allowing for periodic switching of roles. Additionally, dealing with difficult clients may be easier because the differing characteristics of each therapist offer a greater variety of constructive responses. Often the best qualities in each therapist are complementary and result in effective teamwork. Furthermore, for between-session problem solving, two therapists are better than one.

Counselor's Gender

The subject of the gender of group counselors for batterers raises some interesting issues. Although there seems to be little in the professional literature concerning the gender of therapists in this specific field, most programs face this question sooner or later. The basic question is, Does it matter whether it is men or women who conduct groups for batterers? In some quarters, this is a controversial question.

In conversations with some counselors who believe men alone should do this work, we have heard a number of reasons used to support their position. There is the politically based argument according to which men have an obligation to assume the responsibility of working with other men in stopping violence against women. This frees women to work with victims. Other reasons stem from beliefs about the positive impact of male facilitators in a batterers' group. Some believe it is advantageous when two male therapists model cooperation rather than traditional male competitive behavior. Some believe that the presence of men alone will facilitate disclosures of violence in general and sexual violence in particular, while the presence of a woman would inhibit these. Also stated is the belief that an all-male group forces batterers to learn to accept nurturing from other men and thereby decreases their dependency on women.

While these are intriguing notions, we know women who have successfully conducted these groups with other women. In conversations with those who use mixed-gender teams and seem less concerned with the gender of therapists, we have been told that many North American programs seem no less successful with this approach to abuser counseling. They believe that abusers who practice traditional sex-role stereotyping may benefit from observing women demonstrating strength and equality in relationships with male co-workers. Finally, from a pragmatic perspective, many communities with scarce resources are lucky to find knowledgeable staff to run such programs. Whether these are men or women may seem a luxurious worry in many locales.

While the issue of counselor gender is certainly important in services to female victims of male abuse, we do not believe gender is a key issue in counseling male abusers. Consequently, we do not support exclusionary policies or practices based on gender as some service providers do. A therapist's personal suitability, skillfulness, and general awareness of issues surrounding violence against women seem much more relevant to working well in this area.

Women Counselors in a Batterers' Group

While it is difficult to justify claims that either gender has an advantage in counseling batterers, the presence of women counselors will affect the group in some manner. The effect is neither good nor bad; it will simply be different from groups operated solely by men. A woman entering a group should consider in advance how she will respond to a variety of special issues.

A first issue arises from batterers' curiosities and fears. The group may want to know if the woman has been battered. Beneath this question may be the hidden concern that she will be angry, harsh, and rejecting of abusers if she has been battered. We believe honesty is probably the best policy in this situation. Although she can reassure men that she is there to help, not to punish, the group will ultimately be reassured by how she behaves rather than by a statement of intent.

If she has been battered and this is revealed to the men, the group may attempt to treat her as an expert victim. They may routinely turn to her for the "battered woman's point of view." While this is not necessarily negative, it can become so if the members become preoccupied with victims and lose the focus on themselves. If she feels constrained because her role is too narrowly defined by the group, the cotherapist team should find a way to broaden her role.

A second issue stems from male sex-role conditioning. We believe this conditioning predisposes men to seek nurturing from women. Consequently, the group may attempt to relate to a woman cotherapist exclusively as the nurturer (mother). If she feels pulled in this direction, some planning with the cofacilitator may be necessary to ensure that her role is not narrowly defined for her by the group. For example, in establishing a balance that is not based on sex-role stereotypes, cofacilitators may determine that the man should consciously adopt more than his share of nurturing tasks while the woman assumes more of the directive or confrontive tasks.

Finally, and most important, a man and a woman should be conscious of how they share power between themselves in the group. Assaultive men should witness a working relationship characterized by mutual respect and equality instead of male domination. In a situation where a female trainee works with an experienced male counselor, the difference in experience and the educational aspect of the relationship should be announced to the men. This will provide an accurate interpretation for whatever degree of uncertainty and dependency she may exhibit.

Keeping Records

While there are more interesting aspects to our work, our roles also involve keeping reasonably accurate client files. Although most agencies have specific policies in this regard, we find that many counselors are irregular in making entries to client files. In extreme cases, a therapist may work with a client for months and not make entries until closing the case. We have good reasons for emphasizing this mundane activity. The first stems from our experiences in court. In our work with court-mandated abusers, we sometimes have to terminate their involvement with the program. When termination carries the threat of other penalties, some men will ask for a hearing. Whenever this has happened, we have felt relieved to have reliable, detailed records when called to testify. Second, all of our clients are more susceptible to court involvement because of assaultive behavior. Counselors may be called to court in the event of an assault, a homicide, or a suicide. Finally, detailed records are absolutely precious if the program is ever accused of negligence or malpractice.

Detailed record keeping should extend beyond assessment and individual sessions. We make file entries after every group session for every man. We record his presence or absence, his contributions to the group, and the substance of any personal issues he raises. We are particularly diligent in recording exact details of his abuse accounts or threats of violence. We also note the specifics of any intervention we make.

Communication with Men's Partners

Disclosing Information

Seeking collateral information during assessment involves interviewing the man's partner whenever possible for general information and, in particular, violence data. We believe that, once communication channels between abuser counselors and victims have been established, they should be kept open. One reason for this is that men's partners should have access to reliable information about abuser counseling. Abusers too often lie or distort information about their participation in counseling during disputes with their partners. In misrepresenting the program as supporting them in their behavior, they perpetrate a form of psychological abuse. To help reduce the impact of this tactic, the program should develop a method of imparting the following information to victims:

(1) The program views the man as entirely responsible for his behavior. His partner and children are never responsible for his actions.

(2) The man's partner is in no way responsible for his success or lack thereof in abuser counseling. He is entirely responsible for utilizing information from counseling. Additionally, the program will never attempt to intervene in her life through him. For instance, he cannot correctly claim that she must cooperate with him in some manner when he uses a particular anger control method.

(3) The abuser counseling program content is outlined for her.

(4) Counselors will never take the man's side if he describes a domestic dispute in the group (although other men often do).

(5) Abuser counseling is not a "cure" for a man's abuse. Indeed, he is not diseased. It is no more than an opportunity for him to learn how to handle himself nonabusively in relationships. Whether he learns the material and uses it in his relationships is entirely up to him. This also means the fact of finishing a group program is no guarantee that he will be nonabusive.

(6) The program unequivocally supports her and her children's rights to be free from all kinds of abuse. We will provide as much information as we can on alternatives to enduring abuse or will facilitate a referral for this purpose to an appropriate service.

(7) If the agency offers battered women's counseling, the woman is informed of this and given the opportunity to attend counseling.

This information can be given to women in two ways, each of which will depend on how the agency's abuse services are organized. The first option is that each female partner can be invited to attend an individual session with a counselor. A second, more efficient option is possible when the agency operates battered women's group counseling and a significant number of women have partners attending abuser counseling. A counselor from one of the abuser groups can be invited to a women's group session to give this information and answer questions.

Receiving Information

A second reason to maintain communication with men's partners is that counselors can periodically receive valuable information from partners. Because some men will continue to conceal their abusive behavior while enrolled in a group, we believe it advantageous to invite women to inform men's counselors of abuse. If a man decides not to report an incident of abuse to the group, counselors can confront the man with the incident and with his decision to conceal it. Counselors should never disclose a woman's report without her permission and without being confident that she has made reasonable efforts to protect herself from retaliatory abuse. To facilitate safety when women report abuse, those agencies offering group counseling for battered women should ensure that there are reliable communication channels between men's and women's counselors.

We cannot overstate the counselor's and the agency's obligation to be cautious and vigilant in attempting to ensure the safety of anyone who is a potential victim of violence. We believe this goal should always have the highest priority. As the counseling of abusers becomes more routine within an agency, and as the program proceeds, therapists may slip into complacency. We urge therapists to avoid complacency by beginning service to each abuser with the assumption that he constitutes a lethal danger to others and to himself.

Issues Related to the Use of Groups

Group Heterogeneity

Most of our groups include a broad spectrum of men. They come from a variety of socioeconomic groups, racial and cultural backgrounds, and educational levels. We have had white, upper-middle-class businessmen, teachers, and bank officials blending with the poor, the working class, new immigrants, the physically disabled, and the learning disabled. We have had educational levels ranging from fourth grade to the master's degree in a single group. In groups with a high number of court-mandated men, we have had a higher than usual number of disadvantaged clients; these groups seem to attract more frequent attention from the criminal justice system than groups made up of the more privileged elements of society. In groups containing larger numbers of voluntary clients, the privileged sectors of society have greater representation. Although each group is unique, all groups are heterogeneous.

The heterogeneity of these groups is a challenge for therapists. The program's educational facet, with its emphasis on skill development and attitude change, must be planned and conducted with foresight and care. Members differ in their abilities to read, to abstract, and to follow through with homework assignments. Written material must be selected not only for its content but also for its coherence to a range of members. Unlike a university course, in which written materials are primary learning tools, most written materials in batterers' groups should be supplementary rather than essential to the program score requirements. Because we never assume that an abuser will gain essential knowledge from handouts, we always cover core material through lecture or discussion during group. Counselors following this strategy will minimize a class bias in their approach and be more certain that all members are learning the core material.

When we discover a man having difficulty with the material, we take remedial action. For example, one of us conducted a group in which a blind man attended. His lack of sight sometimes interfered with his remembering lecture material. We remedied this in two ways. Whenever possible, we avoided overreliance on visual aids. When a chart was presented, we took pains to explain the content and assure he understood. Second, we recorded lecture and discussion portions of each group so he could review them between sessions. Programs serving the blind might consider translating written material into braille. In other instances, when we have had semiliterate men in group, we have scheduled occasional individual sessions to be certain they are learning the material. When we present material, we watch the group and look for signs of losing some men's attention. Glazed looks or staring at the walls or out the windows might suggest that therapists should change their language or strive to be more concrete.

Group Members Perpetrating Violence

Clients in batterers' counseling will experience failure from time to time. Particularly in the early portions of a group, it is common for a member to come to a session and report that he was violent. While this behavior contravenes a group rule, we expect this to happen. While a prohibition against violence is obviously necessary, it is unrealistic to expect total compliance. The learning of nonviolent alternatives is a gradual process. Initially there will be awkwardness with new skills and mistakes will abound.

Two of our colleagues began their first group by making any violent behavior automatic grounds for expulsion from the group. Very early in the group, a man was expelled. Thereafter, not a single man spoke about current violence. Instead, the group pretended everything was fine while undercurrents of hostility and suspicion made for a truly miserable experience. Although the counselors abandoned this policy, the group in question remained suspicious of the program.

Although some degree of failure is normal, readers should not infer that we indulge violence. Backsliding in a batterers' group is cause for grave concern. The counselor should feel compelled to reserve time in the group session for any man who has been violent between sessions. At the beginning of each session, we determine if this is an issue by asking the group if any man has been violent or abusive since the last meeting. If anyone has, he is directed to share this with the group and be the first to speak during Sharing Time.

We have several objectives in mind when dealing with a violence report in the group:

(1) The man should relate his version of the events.

(2) When details are lacking (as they often are), the counselor should seek more information.

(3) The therapist should respond to apparent inconsistencies, distortions, blaming of the victim, and other defenses that are obstacles to the man's accepting responsibility for his behavior and understanding his mistakes.

(4) The counselor should help the man understand as precisely as possible the points where he made mistakes.

(5) The man should be helped to see specific alternatives to abuse in that situation.

(6) Input from group members should he encouraged.

(7) If possible, those alternatives should he role-played.

Failures provide opportunities. Each man will learn some of his best lessons from a detailed analysis in group of how he and other group members went wrong. Additionally, each man will be in a better position to avoid abuse in similar future situations if mistakes and nonabusive alternatives are highlighted.

There will be situations where a member has difficulty choosing nonviolence, but counselors are reluctant to expel him from the group because he seems motivated and cooperative. Before expelling the man, counselors can try a less drastic course. For instance, they can offer the man the option of separating from his partner for the duration of the program as a condition of remaining in the group.

Toleration of mistakes, however, does have a limit. When a man is repeatedly violent and this is not remedied by counselor or group input, his continuation in the group becomes an issue. Whether it is an unwillingness to stop his abuse, inability to learn, or habitual defiance of authority, a batterer should not remain in counseling if he is not changing. Counseling may not be the appropriate response to his violence.

Contact Among Clients Outside of Counseling

To address batterers' isolation and to structure support for non-violence between sessions, group members should be encouraged to rely on each other outside the group. Usually, counselors feel reassured about the developing mutual-aid function of the group when relationships between men grow. While this is generally a positive development, it is occasionally destructive. Subgroups of men may form and coalesce around viewpoints that erode the purpose of the group. These subgroups may meet informally over coffee either before or after a group. Favorite activities include criticism of the counselors and program content, and group support for sexist and violent behavior. This may be signaled by a subgroup spokesperson seeming to speak for a number of men by using the pronoun *we*. For instance, "Last week after group we were talking about what you said and we disagreed with . . ." might be a sign that bonding is a problem instead of an asset.

We have encountered very rare, but horrific instances of subgrouping in which the subgroup's behavior was intolerable. In one case, two men formed a subgroup in which they sexually abused the partner of one of the men. While therapists might be tempted to censure the behavior and continue working with the perpetrators, this crosses all reasonable boundaries for toleration of backsliding. When a member uses the group as a recruiting ground from which he can form abusive teams, it is insufferable. As a remedy, we favor ejection of this subgroup. To keep these members in the group is more than a mockery of the program—it communicates an ambiguous message to other members about behavioral limits. We terminate members for other, less harmful transgressions than this.

Requests for Advocacy

Occasionally a member will ask a counselor to intercede on his behalf in difficulties he has with other people and systems. Most often it is a request that the therapist be his advocate. Some common requests are listed below:

(1) With an imminent court appearance on assault charges, he asks the counselor to write a positive personal reference that will help his defense.

(2) He asks the counselor to provide a positive personal reference to help in his child custody dispute.

(3) Fearing the loss of his children, he asks the counselor to intervene in a child protection investigation.

(4) Anxious about losing his partner, he asks the therapist to convince her to remain in the relationship.

Counselors would be justified in feeling discomfort about any of these requests. All of them represent a man's attempts to escape the consequences of his abuse. Counselors complying with these requests may be in an untenable position. While working in a program that ought to support protection of victims and the ability for appropriate social systems to censure abuse, they adopt a stance that undermines these goals. They compromise their own integrity and that of the program. Each of these requests also puts counselors in the position of seeming to support the promise that the batterer will not be abusive in the future. This prediction is impossible to make with any accuracy.

One way to curtail these requests is to formulate a policy outlining what kind of support can be offered to abusers. This policy can be announced to men at intake or at the first group meeting. One kind of representation we believe is appropriate is a written or verbal statement indicating that the man has enrolled in the program, and what portion of the program he has completed thus far. Additionally, an explicit, carefully worded statement concerning outcome separates the fact of completion from an assumption that the man has achieved nonviolence. For example, we commonly qualify letters confirming program participation with this statement: "Completion of this program does not guarantee that the man will not be abusive. Completion indicates that he is equipped with the skills to stop his abuse. The decision to use these skills is entirely his."

We do not mean to dismiss all forms of advocacy. There is another kind of advocacy that is both appropriate and helpful. Since many abusers come to counseling facing criminal charges, separation and divorce, the need to find new living quarters, and other serious stressors, they can benefit from help in negotiating strange systems and from receiving accurate information. This kind of assistance can reduce stress levels and indirectly help prevent abuse triggered by these stressors. Ideally, this as an adjunct service that is not part of the therapist's role. Specialized advocates operating out of a separate program within the agency or from a different social service may be helpful with these matters.

Use of Anger in the Group

The subject material in a batterers' group, the use of confrontation, and the stress associated with struggle periodically elicit powerful reactions from the men. If the arousal were labeled appropriately, it might more often be recognized and expressed as feelings of vulnerability, sadness, helplessness, or confusion. More often these are transformed into anger and there is the danger, however slight, that an angry member will be violent in the group. Interestingly, this occurrence in the group replicates his problem in his home. The same escalation mechanism is played out except that, in the group, it is less likely to result in him choosing violence.

Although violence in these groups is exceedingly rare, extreme anger can be frightening to therapists and clients. While an angry outburst can be a means of personal tension reduction, it can also have an external function; anger can be used as a conscious or unconscious attempt to control the behavior of others. People the man perceives as threatening will likely alter their behavior if they feel intimidated by his anger. A group in which one or more men frighten others will lack the safe atmosphere necessary for effective counseling. It is the counselor's job to halt such a development.

When a man becomes excessively angry in group, he should be reminded that he is capable of temporarily leaving the room to "cool down." Leaving is not an offense and it is not a sign that he is a coward fleeing confrontation. Instead, it is a sign of self-control. It demonstrates that he is able to make a choice between staying in the situation and being abusive and leaving to avoid abuse.

Concluding Remarks

In this chapter we have made a case for considering batterers' groups as a special phenomenon. While all counseling groups are similar in some ways, groups differ in other ways as a result of the focal problem, any special characteristics of clients having this problem, and the choice of interventions. We have described issues or concerns that may be peculiar to abuser groups, and in so doing, have sought to prepare readers to plan their own group programs.

For therapists beginning this work, we want to stress the need for careful, thorough preparation. Of course, clinical readiness, in terms of counseling skills and group content, is necessary, but clinical preparation is not enough. Though detailed coverage is beyond our scope, we remind the reader of another realm in which it is important to prepare for assaultive men's group counseling. That is the level of program readiness in its relationships with other community services. The professional education and networking aspect of beginning this service should not be neglected. It is important that links among services be established, that respective responsibilities be negotiated, and that other services have a general understanding of the program's approach to men who batter.

Note

[1] The group structure and many of the group rules were adapted from those employed by the Domestic Abuse Project, Minneapolis.

Section *IX*

Special Areas of
Correctional Treatment

In section three, we noted that classification models have been introduced, tested, and refined to assist probation and parole officers and
treatment personnel In supervising the client population more effectively. These models are based on the risk presented to the community
by the offender, but they also contain components which examine the
needs of the offender with regard to job opportunities, medical treatment, substance abuse counseling, mental health assessment, and
other factors. The risk element is always the overriding consideration
in determining classification as to the need for maximum, medium, or
minimum intervention of the officer and counselor in the offender's life.
The needs of the offenders, although apparent and identified, become
a secondary consideration.

In this section, we will consider counseling for various types of offenders whose needs are so paramount that they must be included in any
treatment plan. These include substance abusers, sex offenders, the
mentally ill, retarded offenders, and older inmates.

Treatment for Drug Abusers

The manner in which these offenders were involved with drugs determines to a large extent whether any form of treatment is needed. Obvi-

ously, those who were distributors of drugs, particularly the top-level dealers, may not have been abusers themselves, while many of the lower level distributors are likely to have been abusers.

A typology of drug-involved offenders was developed by Marcia R. Chaiken and Bruce D. Johnson. They described the characteristics and problems presented by occasional users, persons who sell small amounts of drugs, and those who frequently sell drugs or sell them in large amounts, as shown in Table 1.

The same authors also summarized the types of drug dealers, their level of drug use, and the types of offenses they commit, as shown In Table 2.

The Drug Court Movement

The Drug Court Movement was given considerable impetus with the passage of the Violent Crime Control and Law Enforcement Act in 1994. This federal legislation provided funding to local jurisdictions interested in establishing community-based programs which specifically focused on drug-using offenders.

Travis (1995:1) states:

> The drug court approach departed from the traditional court approach by systematically bringing drug treatment to the criminal justice population entering the court system. Traditionally, the court had referred selected offenders "out" to treatment as a condition of probation. In the drug court, treatment is anchored in the authority of the judge who holds the defendant or offender personally and publicly accountable for treatment progress.

Those offenders who are accepted for participation in the drug court program are closely monitored by the court, and they are required to complete the treatment program prescribed. The eligibility requirements and the manner in which drug courts are structured vary by jurisdiction. Some courts restrict eligibility requirements to misdemeanant offenders, while others allow both misdemeanant and felony offenders to participate. Typically, the screening will be made soon after the person is arrested for a drug-related offense. Participation in the program is voluntary. During the screening interviews, the potential participants are given information on how the program is structured, the expectations placed on those selected for the program, and the rules and regulations they must follow. They are advised that they will be expected to adhere to a treatment plan developed and administered by the court. Once admitted, they are tested and evaluated by the drug court program staff to determine the most appropriate type of treatment to be utilized. The requirements placed on each participant, as well as the treatment plan prescribed, are highly individualized, since the drug court accepts offenders with a wide variety of treatment needs.

Table 1
Types of Drug-Involved Offenders

Type of offender	Typical drug use	Typical problems	Contact with justice system
Occasional users			
Adolescents	Light to moderate or single-substance, such as alcohol, marijuana, or combination use.	Driving under influence; truancy; early sexual activity; smoking.	None to little.
Adults	Light to moderate use of single substances such as hallucinogens, tranquilizers, alcohol, marijuana, cocaine, or combination use.	Driving under influence; lowered work productivity.	None to little.
Persons who sell small amounts of drugs			
Adolescents	Moderate use of alcohol and multiple types of drugs.	Same as adolescent occasional user; also, some poor school performance; some other minor illegal activity.	Minimal juvenile justice contact.
Adults	Moderate use of alcohol and multile types of drugs including cocaine.	Same as adult occasional user.	None to little.
Persons who sell drugs frequently or in large amounts			
Adolescents	Moderate to heavy use of mutiple drugs including cocaine.	Many involved in range of illegal activities including violent crimes; depends on subtype (see Table 2).	Dependent on subtype (see Table 2).
Adults	Moderate to heavy use of multiple drugs including heroin and cocaine.	Depends on subtype (see Table 2).	Dependent on subtype (see Table 2).

Source: Marcia R. Chaiken and Bruce D. Johnson, "Characteristics of Different Types of Drug-Involved Offenders," Washington, D.C.: U.S. Department of Justice: 4–5.

Table 2
Types of Dealers Who Sell Drugs Frequently or in Large Amounts

Type of dealer	Typical drug use	Typical problems	Contact with justice system
Top-level dealers			
Adults (only)	None to heavy use of multiple types of drugs.	Major distribution of drugs; some other white-collar crime such as money laundering.	Low to minimal.
Lesser predatory			
Adolescents	Moderate to heavy drug use; some addiction; heroin and cocaine use.	Assaults; range of property crimes; poor school performance.	Low to moderate contact with juvenile or adult justice system.
Adult men	Moderate to heavy drug use; some addiction; heroin and cocaine use.	Burglary and other property crimes; many drug sales; irregular employment; moderate to high social instability.	Low to high contact with criminal justice system.
Adult women	Moderate to heavy drug use; some addiction; heroin and cocaine use.	Prostitution; theft; many drug sales; addicted babies; AIDS babies; high-risk children.	Low to moderate contact with criminal justice system.
Drug-involved violent predatory offenders:			
The "losers"			
Adolescents	Heavy use of multiple drugs; often addiction to heroin or cocaine.	Commit many crimes in periods of heaviest drug use including robberies; high rates of school dropout; problems likely to continue as adults.	High contact with both juvenile and adult criminal justice system.

(continued)

Table 2 (continued)
Types of Dealers Who Sell Drugs Frequently or in Large Amounts

Type of dealer	Typical drug use	Typical problems	Contact with justice system
The "losers"			
Adults	Heavy use of multiple drugs; often addiction to heroin or cocaine.	Commit many crimes in periods of heaviest drug use including robberies: major source of income from criminal activity: low-status roles in drug hierarchy.	High contact with criminal justice system; high incarceration.
The "winners"			
Adolescents	Frequent use of multiple drugs; less frequent addiction to heroin and cocaine	Commit many crimes; major source of income from criminal activity; take midlevel role in drug distribution to both adolescents and adults.	Minimal; low incarceration record.
Adults	Frequent use of multiple drugs; less frequent addiction to heroin and cocaine.	Commit many crimes; major source of income from criminal activity; take midlevel role in drug distribution to both adolescents and adults.	Minimal: low incarceration record.
Smugglers	None to high.	Provide pipelines of small to large quantities of drugs and money.	Variable contact.

Source: Marcia R. Chaiken and Bruce D. Johnson, "Characteristics of Different Types of Drug-Involved Offenders," Washington, D.C.: U.S. Department of Justice: 6–8.

Generally, if the person is not employed and/or seeking employment, job preparation, attending school and contributing a number of hours to community service are common requirements.

During the period of participation, the offenders are required to appear before the drug court judge at regularly assigned times, often as frequently as once a week. During this meeting, their progress is assessed. The treatment staff and the probation officers monitoring their behavior will generally make a report to the judge. Treatment services may include individual counseling, group counseling, family counseling, and mandatory attendance at meetings of alcohol and drug addiction self-help groups.

The drug court approach is appealing to criminal justice personnel because it provides for close supervision of the participants and also uses a more structured, coordinated approach to dealing with substance abuse offenders than the approach generally followed in the normal court process. In many courts, the offenders are actually diverted out of the formal process; if they successfully complete the program, they do not have a criminal conviction. These offenders move through the court quickly, reducing costs and helping to reduce the court's case load.

The number of drug courts operating throughout the United States expanded tremendously in the 1990s as a result of the millions of dollars granted by the U. S. Dept. of Justice through its Drug Courts Program Office (Belenko, 1998). In 1998, approximately 300 drug court programs were in operation in 42 states, the District of Columbia, Puerto Rico, and in federal district courts (Office of Justice Programs, 1998:3).

The treatment strategies for substance abusers involve four major modalities, according to DeLeon (1990:116). These include detoxification, methadone maintenance, drug-free outpatient settings, and residential therapeutic communities. According to DeLeon, detoxification is usually conducted in an inpatient hospital setting for a period of one to three weeks, while methadone maintenance is generally pursued on an outpatient basis, after an initial detoxification period. Those involved in treatment in drug-free outpatient settings are targets for individual and group counseling, while those treated in therapeutic communities are counseled in residential settings. The success level with a particular modality is obviously dependent upon a number of factors, including the length and level of substance abuse and the motivation of the offender to change his or her behavior.

In selection 28, "Drug Courts: Issues in Planning and Implementation," Atchue presents five models of drug court programs. These include diversion, pre-diversion plea programs, programs based on stipulation of facts, deferred sentencing, and probation with mandatory treatment as a condition. The motivation all of these models present to the offenders is the possibility of avoiding a felony conviction if they complete the drug court program and treatment successfully.

In selection 29, "Another Permanency Perspective" by McGee, a judge with many years of experience describes a "family drug court" for parents who face loss of custody of their children because of their substance abuse problems. The families enter a one-year intensive intervention program, featuring individualized case plans and referral to needed services.

Alcohol abuse treatment strategies closely parallel those used for drug abuse. Selection 30, "Counseling Alcoholic Clients," was developed as a treatment handbook for those who are involved in such counseling. It provides step-by-step guidelines and instruction on how best to conduct such interventions.

Issues in Substance Abuse Treatment

Duffee and Carlson (1996) contend that a large number of offenders in need of treatment for their substance abuse problems are not receiving treatment. This is particularly true for convicted offenders placed on probation. Resources are not available to provide treatment for all those drug abusers in need, and policy makers must make decisions as to which categories of abusers will receive the most services. Duffee and Carlson state that the decisions made by the policy makers are based on four value premises. These include providing services to the most deserving, to those most amenable to treatment, and to those most likely to cause the most harm to the community if not treated; and providing funds to the service agencies with good reputations for having well-managed drug treatment programs (p. 580). It is the position of the authors that more of the scarce resources utilized for drug abuse treatment for convicted criminals should be given to community corrections, since those on probation have the greatest potential to be treated successfully. In addition, the coordination and the communications between the probation department and the service providers needs to be improved if the drug treatment is to be effective and cost efficient.

Treating the Sex Offender

Sex offenders also present unique difficulties for correctional counseling and treatment. Many of the disorders and dysfunctions experienced by such offenders are too complex to be treated adequately by counselors who are not specifically trained to work with them. When the offender's family is closely involved, as is frequently the case, the need for family therapy may be readily apparent, but not easily accomplished. Although treatment for severe disorders, such as sexual psychopathy, is now mandated in many states. sex offenders involved in less dramatic behavior may not be offered the treatment quality or intensity needed to prevent recurrence of their offenses.

Selections 31 and 32 describe the varieties and types of treatment currently available and the roles offenders' family members can play in the treatment process. "In Treatment of the Sex Offender," DeZolt and Kratcoski note that many activities formerly defined as improper sexual behavior subject to criminal penalties are no longer liable for criminal prosecution. State codes have been revised to define specifically sexual offenses, and most of these can be categorized as sexual assaults and displays. In this article, particular attention is given to the characteristics of sexual psychopaths, rapist typologies, and typologies of sex abusers of children. The legality of treatment such as psychosurgery-castration or drug therapy is reviewed, and counseling therapies of various types are described. Institutional and community group treatment of sex offenders is discussed and evaluated, and characteristics of therapies which have been effective with sex offenders are described. Group therapy which follows the technique known as rational-emotive therapy is discussed.

In "Northwest Treatment Associates: A Comprehensive, Community-Based Evaluation and Treatment Program for Adult Sex Offenders," Knopp describes specific techniques used to retrain adult sex offenders to deal with and overcome their tendencies toward unacceptable sexual behavior and to develop appropriate sexuality. Guided group work is utilized, and behavioral treatment, geared to the specific needs of individual offenders, is included. Impulse control techniques which can be applied by the offenders themselves and stronger intrusive types of controls which may need to be applied are described. The roles that offenders' spouses and victim counselors can play in changing the behavior of adult sex offenders are given detailed consideration.

Treating the Mentally Ill and Mentally Handicapped

Another important area of correctional treatment involves mentally ill or retarded offenders. Public Law 94-142, the Education of the Handicapped Act of 1975, has important implications for both juvenile and adult correctional treatment, because it mandates free and appropriate education for all handicapped persons 21 years of age or younger. Handicapped individuals are defined in the law as mentally handicapped, hard of hearing, deaf, orthopedically impaired, visually handicapped, seriously emotionally disturbed, or learning disabled requiring special education and related services (Nelson et al., 1985:32). Because of the age range covered in the law's mandate, many offenders incarcerated in adult institutions, as well as those held in juvenile facilities, are required to receive services.

Handling mentally ill and mentally retarded offenders in institutional settings is difficult for many reasons. They must be protected from victimization by the general inmate population, and they require additional attention to help them understand the significance of what is happening to them and to reduce the traumatic effects of the incarceration experience. Community treatment, whenever possible, would seem to be the most appropriate setting for retarded or mentally ill offenders who do not pose a threat to the community.

A program at Central Prison in Raleigh, North Carolina, is designed for inmates who have been diagnosed as having serious mental disorders and are also considered dangerous and difficult to manage. According to Burkhead, Carter, and Smith (1990), the estimates of the number of inmates who have serious mental problems range from 10 to 25 percent nationwide. Generally, such inmates can function quite well, provided that they take their prescribed medication. After release, however, these same individuals are often quickly reinstitutionalized, because prison out-patient services are nonexistent or inadequate to meet their needs. Programs designed to prepare mentally ill incarcerated offenders for re-entry into the community must place strong emphasis on the importance of taking prescribed medication and developing the educational, social, and life skills needed for them to function in the community.

A model program of this type was developed in Cuyahoga County (Cleveland) Ohio, where offenders under the supervision of the county probation department were supervised at different levels, based on scores obtained from a standardized risk and needs instrument used by the department. The probation officers assigned to the mentally retarded offender unit were specifically trained to recognize the needs of these offenders and provide appropriate support, as well as individual and group counseling (Bowker and Schweid, 1992).

Nolley and his colleagues (1996) reported on a community treatment program for mentally retarded sex offenders. The mentally handicapped men were referred to the program by their case managers after they engaged in unacceptable sexual behaviors. The treatment consisted of individual therapy, education in sexuality, group therapy, and the provision of education services (p. 125). During the thirty-four months after the therapy services began, none of the men reoffended (p. 137).

In selection 33, "Treatment in Transition: The Role of Mental Health Correctional Facilities," Scott and O'Connor report on the programs at the Larned (Kansas) Correctional Mental Health Facility. This institution was created as a result of a federal court order that required the State of Kansas to create an institution that was suitable for treating mentally ill inmates. The multifaceted treatment program includes substance abuse counseling and treatment, individual and group counseling, family therapy, anger management, and treatment for those mentally ill offenders who have sexual disorders. These offenders responded well to the treatment program while they were incarcerated at the specialized facility.

Older Offenders

In selection 34, "Older Inmates: Special Programming Concerns," Kratcoski describes the needs of incarcerated older offenders and explores the question of whether elderly inmates should be housed with the general prison population or placed in separate units. It is noted that health problems are an overriding concern. In addition, special recreational or social activities may need to be developed, if the older inmates are to make satisfactory adjustments.

References

Belenko, S. 1998. *Research on Drug Courts: A Critical Review.* New York: National Center on Addiction on Substance Abuse at Columbia University.

Bowker, Arthur L. and Robert E. Schweid. 1992. "Habilitation of the Retarded Offender in Cuyahoga County," *Federal Probation*, 56 (4) (December):48–52.

Burkhead, Michael, James H. Carter and James A. Smith, III. 1990. "A Helping Hand: Reaching Out to the Mentally Ill," *Corrections Today*, Vol. 52, No. 3: 88, 90, 92.

Chaiken, Marcia R. and Bruce D. Johnson. 1994. "Characteristics of Different Types of Drug-Involved Offenders." Washington, DC: U.S. Department of Justice: 4–5, 6–8.

DeLeon, George. 1990. "Treatment Strategies," in James A. Inciardi, ed., *Handbook of Drug Control in the United States.* New York: Greenwood Press, pp. 115–138.

Duffee, David and Bonnie E. Carlson. 1996. "Competing Value Premises for the Provision of Drug Treatment to Probationers," *Crime and Delinquency*, 42 (4) (October): 574–592.

Nelson, C. Michael, Robert B. Rutherford, Jr. and Bruce I. Wolford. 1985. "Handicapped Offenders Meeting Education Needs," *Corrections Today*, 47 (5) (August):115–138.

Nolley, David, Lynne Muccigrosso, and Eric Zigman. 1996. "Treatment Successes with Mentally Retarded Sex Offenders," *Journal of Offender Rehabilitation*, 23 (1–2): 125–141.

Office of Justice Programs. 1998. *Drug Court Clearinghouse and Technical Assistance Project: Looking at a Decade of Drug Courts.* Washington, DC: National Institute of Justice.

Travis, Jeremy. 1995. *The Drug Court Movement.* Washington, DC: U.S. Department.

28

Drug Courts
Issues in Planning and Implementation

Scott H. Atchue

Introduction

Throughout the 1980s and well into the 1990s, the conservative-led "War on Drugs" has commanded a great deal of scarce criminal justice resources. As a direct result of our national drug policy's mission of eradicating drug use and reducing drug-related property and violent crime, all levels of the criminal justice system have had to reassess procedures for dealing with drug-related offenders. The large number of arrests for possession, sale, distribution, and manufacture of narcotic substance created a crisis for already strained criminal justice agencies. Law enforcement has had to shift resources away from investigating and targeting violent crimes; correctional facilities have had to deal with problems of overcrowding; and probation and parole agencies have had to supervise an exponentially increasing number of offenders. Further, the nation's judicial systems have not been immune to the problems accompanying increased enforcement activity and have undergone tremendous disruption as a result of increased criminal case filings.

As criminal caseloads increased and backlogs of drug case filings became more prevalent by the late 1980s many courts found that the potential benefits of traditional delay reduction techniques had been exhausted, existing procedures could not be streamlined further to accommodate increasing drug caseloads, operating case management

Source: *The Court Manager*, (Summer 1996): 22–24, 50.

systems were being pushed to their limits, and traditional disposition processes could not keep up with the large volume of cases generated by law enforcement strategies. In response, judicial system officials reexamined case disposition practices and adopted new mechanisms and procedures. These changes required an organizational structure amenable to change, which, in turn, required a great deal of planning by administrators and judges. The result was an innovative approach to dealing with increasing drug caseloads through Expedited Drug Case Management (EDCM) and more specifically, treatment-based drug courts.

Treatment-based drug courts, using a team approach, focusing on providing paid services, closely monitoring the progress of each defendant, and administering graduated sanctions as an alternative to additional criminal charges, differ from traditional court procedures by integrating both treatment and criminal justice resources under the leadership of the court. Whereas the traditional court processing drug cases (1) has a limited role in supervision of the defendant, (2) uses an adversarial approach seeking legal justice, and (3) regards relapse as a new violation of the criminal laws, the drug court programs form collaborative relationships among the drug court participants seeking to restore the drug-dependent defendant to a productive position within society by providing individualized, intensive, and structured treatment programs in a nonadversarial environment.

Expedited Drug Case Management (EDCM) Strategies

Expedited drug case management was developed through established differentiated case management (DCM) strategies. Drug cases present special case management and treatment intervention issues for the courts. These include (1) the need to manage large numbers of cases that vary in severity and potential sanctions, which generally predict the level of complexity of the requisite disposition process; (2) a large number of cases that involve possession of a small amount of narcotics; (3) the high level of pretrial motions and challenges to suppress evidence seized, which frequently determines the case outcome; (4) the need for laboratory analysis; (5) the importance of the court's immediate intervention for both treatment and sanctioning; and finally (6) the increasing recognition that in many cases drug use is an illness that requires treatment as well as sanctions. Managers have recognized that many drug cases can proceed through the calendar at a faster pace than other cases, if appropriate pathways exist.

DCM and EDCM are approaches used to tailor the case management process and the allocation of judicial resources to the characteristics of individual cases. These concepts are premised upon the assumption that not all cases are alike in regard to processing needs. Some may be disposed of quickly, with little or no discovery; others require extensive court interaction. The benefits of EDCM are increased productivity of judges, prosecutors, defense counsel, and staff; a reduction in the number of defendants who fail to appear and in the number of bench warrants that must be issued; reduction in pretrial jail days and costs associated with detention; and most important, more effective treatment services for offenders.

Among the common features of EDCM projects established by court systems are (1) early case screening by prosecution and defense counsel to differentiate both the adjudication requirements and treatment/supervision needs of each case, (2) redesign of the caseflow process to assure that each scheduled event meaningfully contributes to case disposition as early as possible, (3) linking of the adjudication and treatment functions, and (4) continuing collaboration among all of the various agencies that compose the criminal justice system.

The key components of an effective EDCM system begin with case differentiation criteria. Cases are commonly distinguished by the severity of the offense, whether it is a single or multi-defendant case, the severity of potential sanctions pre- and postadjudication, and whether the offense was violent or not.

The second component of an effective system is the establishment of case-processing tracks and procedures. Generally courts create three to five tracks for case placement based on complexity and disposition requirements of the caseload. Courts may limit discovery and motions activity within each track and establish variable time intervals for disposition geared to case type. Track procedures also support the court's responsibility for monitoring defendants' compliance with conditions of pretrial release and provide for immediate intervention when violations occur.

Early screening—before the first court appearance—for substance abuse dependency is necessary to evaluate treatment and the need for support services. It promotes more rapid rehabilitation. The use of alternative sanctions coupled with pretrial release has become an essential part of the EDCM process. Judges tailor the conditions for release for each defendant and monitor the needs and treatment of the offender through routine status conferences.

The EDCM process would not function without coordination and collaboration with treatment providers aimed at developing common goals and objectives for assessing the success of the defendant. It also provides communication networks for continuous reporting. Community understanding and mobilization of resources is necessary for the financial support and success of the EDCM program. Finally, the most important component is the leadership of the judicial system in coordinating among courts, treatment providers, and other agencies and assuring that program procedures are consistently applied.

Many court organizations have used DCM and EDCM principles to establish innovative ways of handling their tremendous drug caseloads. The epitome of this movement has been the establishment of special divisions or treatment-based drug courts within the existing judicial structure. These specialized courts are as varied as the jurisdictions in which they exist and have been designed to address the unique needs of the community, taking into account local resources, political realities, existing laws, and the personalities of the drug court participants. However, since these programs all have the goals of reducing caseloads and rehabilitating drug dependent offenders, they all face much the same planning and implementation issues.

Planning and Implementing a Drug Court

Courts interested in developing a treatment-based drug court program should first establish a drug court team. Although leadership for such projects has primarily been provided by judges, anyone willing to undertake the responsibility for calling meetings, identifying necessary parties, setting the agenda, and fostering participation from treatment agencies may fulfill this role. Court administrators are often called upon to play an integral part in the planning process.

Before inviting external organizations to participate in the planning phase of the project, court staff should collect preliminary materials and research on drug courts from state and local administrative offices of the courts, universities, or criminal justice agencies. Organizations such as the Center for Substance Abuse Treatment, the National Center for State Courts, and the National Association of Drug Court Professionals can help a court survey the literature and determine whether a drug court program would be feasible within the jurisdiction. The drug court team should also visit existing drug courts jurisdictions that closely resemble their own.

Once the jurisdiction decides to implement a drug court, it should assess the interest of other organizations that may be affected by or interested in the drug court program. Representatives from the legal profession should include the public defender's service, prosecutor's office, and local bar association. Law enforcement agencies, including pretrial services and probation and parole, may play an important role in screening potential program participants. Treatment providers, local health agencies, and the state alcohol or substance abuse departments may provide support for monitoring and rehabilitation. Finally, social service associations such as churches, universities, job training offices, housing providers, transit administration, and community representatives could provide important services needed in the holistic approach to transforming the drug dependent individual into a functioning member of society.

Preliminary meetings with these groups will be most productive if they provide for an open forum of ideas. Essential to the success of the program is collaboration and communication among all participants. Lacking a common understanding of the terminology and belief in the philosophy of rehabilitation, miscommunication and conflict will result in failure.

The planning team, composed of these representatives of essential resource providers, initially should develop a mission statement with clearly defined goals and objectives. Frequently, drug courts' mission statements strive to decrease recidivism, decrease caseloads, stabilize offenders suffering from addiction, or increase the number of defendants obtaining levels of literacy or employment and training. After establishing a mission and goals and conducting preliminary research, planning shifts to identifying the population to be served, defining the eligibility criteria, choosing a model, structuring the treatment program, incorporating incentives and sanctions, and securing funding. Then, finally, comes the program initiation/implementation phase, followed by monitoring and evaluation.

Five basic models of drug court programs have been designed and implemented in jurisdictions across the United States. The first is diversion. Under this model the defendant's case is postponed during participation in treatment. Speedy trial rights are waived and the case is dismissed upon successful completion of the program. Pre-diversion plea programs, the second model, require the defendant to plead guilty to participate in the program. Upon completion, however, the plea is withdrawn and the case dismissed. Under the third model, programs based on stipulation of facts, the defendant must stipulate to the facts of the case to facilitate prosecution in the event that he or she fails to successfully complete the program. If the defendant completes the program, the case is dismissed. Under the deferred sentencing model, the defendant is adjudicated guilty but sentencing is deferred pending participation in the program. If the defendant completes the program, an appropriate probationary sentence is imposed. The final model is a more traditional one, in which the defendant is placed on probation and treatment is made a condition of probation.

The emphasis of all the models is to provide defendants with an incentive of avoiding a felony conviction on their criminal record, if they are able to complete the drug court program and treatment successfully. Whichever model is chosen should reflect the existing laws, rules, and practices of the jurisdiction. In most jurisdictions, legislation will not be required to implement a treatment-based drug court program, but reviewing existing laws is advisable to determine whether modifications are needed.

Program Scope

To define the scope of the program, it is important to identify the population to be served by the drug court and the types of offenses eligible for inclusion. The criteria for acceptance may take into consideration the type of offense, severity of addiction, prior drug involvement, and prior criminal history. Many programs limit participation to low-level, nonviolent offenders with demonstrated substance abuse problems and who are charged with possession or intent to distribute. Programs have been expanded, however, to individuals who commit property or minor violent crimes as a way of dealing with the related drug addiction. Factors such as possession of a weapon, prior history of sexual offenses, defendant's release status, on probation or parole, or the defendant's lack of a drug problem may disqualify participation in drug court program. Assigning the responsibility for screening the possible participants must also be considered. Many programs use their jurisdiction's pretrial services department or the local prosecutor's office for screening. It is their responsibility to obtain the necessary background information and make recommendations for eligibility to the court.

In developing drug court programs, planners need to consider the appropriate time frame in which to intervene on behalf of the offender. Frequently, intervention occurs at the setting of bail, arraignment, or presentencing hearings. The typical philosophy behind drug court programs, however, is to intervene as early as possible after arrest so that treatment may begin at a time of crisis for the defendant. Early intervention and supervision, with continued status hearings between the judge and defendant, are necessary to support and strengthen the goals of the program. Generally today treatment is begun within one day of the initial meeting between the judge and defendant.

Treatment in the drug court program is usually offered over an extended period of time, most often one year. Supervision and treatment are broken down into multiple phases. During the initial phase the defendant may be required to meet with counseling staff and participate in urinalysis several times a week. As the defendant progresses toward detoxification, the requirements may be lessened as part of the incentive process. Relapse of the drug user, however, is seen as "the rule, not the exception" in treatment.

Therefore, drug courts have developed graduated plans of sanctions for "slipping" and noncompliance. Sanctions may include increased urinalysis, stricter supervision, curfews, electronic monitoring, shock incarceration, or termination from the program. Incentives—lessening of fees for treatment or less supervision—are also given to those who proceed well throughout the program and may end with graduation. Both systems are meant to be immediate responses to the defendant's progress.

When selecting a treatment provider, courts should be sure the provider has a full range of treatments and facilities available and is willing to share their patient's progress with regular updates to the court.

Securing funds and starting the program is one of the greatest problems the planning team faces. Funding to cover the costs of administration, testing expenses, program evaluation, treatment provider contracts, information systems, and other costs has been secured through grant programs administered by federal, state, and local agencies, such as the National Institute of Justice or state drug and alcohol agencies. Money necessary to maintain the program may come from corporations, private foundations, or program fees. Once funding is received and procedures developed, the final phase of start-up is to select the court staff and judges who will administer the program. Then training in addiction behavior and treatment is essential to help staff understand the nature of addiction and best help the program's participants to remain with the program.

Once the program is in operation, monitoring and evaluation are essential to analyze the progress of the program, its staff, treatment providers, and participants. Analysis should include awareness of the effect the program has on the overall drug program, the extent to which the program is operating efficiently, the effect of the program on the targeted population, the extent to which the goals of the program have been achieved, and finally, the cost effectiveness of the program. Documentation of program successes will help ensure its financial survival. Publication of evaluative information will help other jurisdictions determine the prospects for their own drug court programs.

Conclusion

Treatment-based drug courts provide an alternative strategy to traditional methods of handling criminal drug cases by forging partnerships between the judicial system and treatment and human services communities and by uniting the judge, prosecutor, public defender, treatment provider, and others in a team whose primary objectives are to rehabilitate the offender and relieve judicial caseloads. In essence, treatment-based drug courts are a comprehensive, systematic approach geared toward addressing the problems of drug use in a way that benefits the defendant, the community, and the criminal justice system by making efficient use of available resources and returning the offender to the community as a functioning and productive member of society.

In this way, drug courts qualify as boundary-spanning units, whereby both human resources and judicial resources are balanced with the provision of justice, so that courts may continue to survive and serve the needs of their citizens.

Sources

Cooper, C. S., "Expedited Drug Case Management," *BJA Court Bulletin* (Washington, DC., 1994).

_____ *Drug Courts: An Overview of Operational Characteristics and Implementation Issues* (Washington, DC: The American University/National Center for State Courts/National Consortium of TASC Programs, 1995).

Cooper, C. S., and S. R. Bartlett, *Drug Courts: A Profile of Operational Programs*, rev. ed. (Washington, DC: The American University/State Justice Institute, 1996).

Cooper, C. S., M. Solomon, H. Bakke, and T. Lane, BJA Expedited Drug Case Management (EDCM) Demonstration Program: Overview and Program Summaries (Washington, DC: The American University/Bureau of Justice Assistance, 1992).

Cooper, C. S., and J. A. Trotter, Jr., *Drug Case Management and Treatment Intervention Strategies in the State and Local Courts*, Vol. 1, rev. ed. (Washington, DC: The American University, 1994).

Drug Court Planning and Implementation: Selected Operational Materials (Washington, DC: The American University, 1995).

Office of State Courts Administration; Florida Supreme Court, *Treatment-Based Drug Courts: A Guide* (Tallahassee, FL: State Justice Institute, 1994).

Saari, D., *American Court Management: Theories and Practices* (Westport, CT: Quorum Books, 1982).

Scott, W. R., *Organizations: Rational, Natural, and Open Systems*, 3d ed. (Englewood Cliffs, NJ: Prentice Hall, 1992).

Weitzman, J. H., *Drug Courts: A Manual for Planning and Implementation* (Washington, DC: The American Bar Association, 1995).

29

Family Drug Court
Another Permanency Perspective

Charles M. McGee

I first learned of the drug court movement in 1993 when Judge Jack Lehman of the 8th Judicial District Court in Clark County decided to dedicate his Las Vegas area drug court as a mentor program for the U.S. Department of Justice. At that time, I was serving as a general jurisdiction District Court judge with a large criminal calendar. My main interest, however, was in family and juvenile law. I had seen the growing movement across the states to impose the stiff sentences associated with adult penology into the juvenile area, with legislators passing laws to lock more and more juveniles up. But I felt that rather than conforming to the adult court model, the Juvenile Justice system actually could give lessons to courts dealing with adults—lessons that were being ignored. In the drug court movement, at last, I found a process which took the lessons juvenile and family courts had to offer and applied them to the adult arena.

I believe that implementation of a redemptive type of justice system for drug addicts who are parents has staggering potential. Rather than looking at punishment as the goal of a criminal action, the drug court recognizes a person's ability to become a productive citizen. Any judge, warden or other person involved in the criminal justice system will tell you the primary underlying reason for the incarceration of a majority of people is involvement with drugs or alcohol. Drug courts address this problem with intensive supervision and services, applying the social

Source: *Juvenile and Family Court Journal*, 48(4) (November 1997): 65–67.

service rehabilitation mode of juvenile justice to the adult penal system. And it is working.

About four years ago. I decided to incorporate the drug court model into my dependency caseload. With the success I had seen in the general jurisdiction drug court, where the potential sanction was imprisonment, I felt there would be even greater success where the potential consequence of failure was loss of one's children. I have found this thought borne out time and time again: with appropriate support and services, most parents will do anything they can to get their children back.

In terms of regular drugs tests and frequent court appearances, the basic model for the Family Drug Court is similar to other drug courts. Participants are one or both parents who face both criminal prosecution for drug or alcohol problems and the potential for permanent loss of their children because of their chemical dependency problems. They are identified by criminal activity or by the children being removed from the home to protect them from abuse or neglect, or both. The program is voluntary. Persons nominated for the program are accepted initially on a probationary basis and given the opportunity to display their commitment to developing a responsible, drug-free lifestyle. The Family Drug Court goes even further than the general jurisdiction drug court model.

Upon acceptance, families enter into a one-year program of intensive intervention with the goal of reunifying participants and their children as a healthy, stable, productive family unit. A comprehensive assessment is conducted to identify family needs. An individualized case plan is established and services provided. And an "integrated services case manager" is assigned in most cases to make the case plan realistic and manageable for the parents.

During the year, participants are monitored by the court on a bi-weekly basis. Frequent drug tests are performed. Prior to each hearing, the judge, district attorney, defense attorney, Court Appointed Special Advocate (CASA), service providers, caseworker, and other court personnel meet to discuss the participants' progress over the previous two weeks. In this way, the court is fully aware of events and progress in each participant's life and can discuss any problems when the hearing begins. Success is reinforced, encouraged, and celebrated.

Unlike some drug courts where relapses are handled with community service or minor sanctions, relapse or failure to participate fully in the Family Drug Court program results in incarceration, normally for a short period of between one day and two weeks. Because the focus in the Family Drug Court is always on the children, the parent is made to realize full responsibility and consequences of his or her failure to perform as required.

Upon successful completion of the one-year program participants who have fulfilled the requirements and reached the established goals are allowed to graduate, although monthly follow-ups often occur for six months or longer. Program benefits include family reunification, completion of drug treatment, dismissal of charges, honorable discharge from probation, employment, housing, and a clean and sober lifestyle. Because the program has been in existence only four years, long-term statistics of its success are not yet available. Indeed, it is difficult to measure successful results. One female Drug Court participant was sentenced to a lengthy jail term because of her repeated failure to perform the requirements of the program; she is now back out and again in the program. I believe this time she will make it. What might seem a failure in a statistic is now a very probable success. Several other clients have relapsed, left the program, and have subsequently been readmitted.

Participants in the Family Drug Court are of both genders, come from many different ethnic and socioeconomic backgrounds, use every kind of drug (although the main "drug of choice" is methamphetamine), and face other complicating factors. Because of these complexities, simply addressing the chemical dependency issue is not enough for the Family Drug Court to be successful. It is essential that each case plan be individualized and that all services be provided to deal with all problems facing each family.

Often women in the program have personal histories of child and adult sexual or physical abuse. Their continued tendency to make poor choices in male companions has a direct impact on their sobriety and success in the program. Their case plans and the court monitoring must address these issues.

Many participants have dual diagnosis complications, in which they suffer not only from substance addiction, but from mental disorders. Again, both issues must be addressed with appropriate services. An often undiagnosed and untreated problem facing both parents and children in this program is fetal alcohol syndrome or fetal alcohol effect (FAS/FAE). Many children suffer from birth defects associated with prenatal alcohol exposure. Often the mother also has defects associated with her mother's alcohol abuse. Treatment of these mothers and children differs widely from many normal intervention methods. With the assistance of experts in the field, the community is beginning to establish resources for these families. The whole process must be slowed way down so the message can sink in. Often the client must be provided with a mentor who acts as her "external brain."

In almost all the cases we see, there is a need to develop a permanent external support system until the children are grown. This can be a 12-step program, a therapist, or a probation officer. Family members often are enlisted. The court continues to monitor a graduate after completion of the program for up to one year and assists in establishing the support system needed for permanent success.

Certain components of the Family Drug Court are either necessary for its success or enhance its ability to succeed:

1. No particular type of judge is necessary. However, it is essential that the judge have a real belief in the power of people to make profound changes in their lives. Ideally this judge should also be an activist in enlisting community support for the services needed for participants.

2. An integrated case manager with flexible funding resources and authority is important. Because many participants must access services from multiple agencies, the case manager must be able to oversee the delivery of services to ensure that all necessary services are provided without overlap. This case manager needs to have the ability to use funds for innovative assistance. In one case, a case manager purchased a locket for a mother suffering from FAS. She was directed to look at her child's picture in that locket each time she wanted to drink. This reminder of the consequence of her relapse has helped her to remain sober.

3. Collaboration with the criminal court and with the community is also necessary. Community support and funding may prove difficult to obtain until people start viewing and understanding what Family Drug Court offers. The community must realize that the court is not there to help drug addicts, but to help children have happy, healthy lives with their parents.

4. Services must be available on an as-needed basis. The judge must be prepared to be an advocate for the necessary services.

5. A CASA program is essential. Participants in this program need daily attention: most caseworkers and parole and probation officers have caseloads that do not allow this kind of attention. A CASA worker assigned to the participant can make the difference needed for success.

6. After-care and an external support system are required.

7. Involving families, including children, as decision makers is often the best solution for finding help for children and for establishing an ongoing support system.

8. It is helpful to involve parole and probation officers who have an orientation toward social work and caseworkers who have a strong belief in reunification. These people need to meet and work as a team to help participants toward the goal of reunification.

9. In a single word, "teamwork" is the hallmark of the Family Drug Court.

My involvement in the Family Drug Court has been the most rewarding aspect of my judicial career. Through this program, I have rediscovered the common bond that exists between a judge and those he or she judges. I have seen women come into the program with the maturity of 12-year-olds and bloom into responsible, caring, sober mothers. I have seen fathers experience a profound spiritual change, take control of their lives and end their patterns of unemployment and domestic violence. Most rewarding, I have seen children who were at risk of abuse and at risk of out-of-home placement and termination of familial bonds, happily reunited with their parents.

The juvenile justice system has always posited the existence of hope and redemption in people's lives as a force for change. By incorporating the lessons we have learned in the Juvenile Justice arena into the adult system and offering the support necessary for redemptive change through the Family Drug Court, we improve the chances for families and the lives of our children.

> *We, the undersigned, recognize your powers of transformation*
> *and empowerment as you continue your personal growth.*
> *May your journey be filled with wonderment and wellness.*

> —From the Certificate of Graduation Issued upon Successful
> Completion of Washoe County's Family Drug Court Program

30

Counseling Alcoholic Clients
A Microcounseling Approach to Basic Communication Skills

National Center for Alcohol Education

Overview of the Training Program

Counseling Alcoholic Clients: A Microcounseling Approach to Basic Communication Skills is designed to help practicing alcoholism counselors upgrade their abilities to use eight basic communication skills—attending paraphrasing, reflection of feeling, summarizing, probing, counselor self-disclosure, interpreting, and confrontation—in one-to-one interaction with a client. On completion of the program, participants will be able to:

- define each skill;
- recognize when each skill is being practiced effectively; and
- demonstrate the ability to use each skill and to integrate all skills appropriately and effectively in a simulated counseling situation.

The eight skills as defined in this program are:

Attending. Demonstration of the counselor's concern for and interest in the client by eye contact, body posture, and accurate verbal following.

Paraphrasing. A counselor statement that mirrors the client's statement in exact or similar wording.

Source: *Counseling Alcoholic Clients*. Washington, DC: U.S. Government Printing Office (1978).

Reflection of Feeling. The essence of the client's feelings, either stated or implied, as expressed by the counselor.

Summarizing. A brief review of the main points discussed in the session to insure continuity in a focused direction.

Probing. A counselor's response that directs the client's attention inward to help both parties examine the client's situation in greater depth.

Counselor Self-Disclosure. The counselor's sharing of his/her personal feelings, attitudes, opinions, and experiences for the benefit of the client.

Interpreting. Presenting the client with alternative ways of looking at his/her situation.

Confrontation. A counselor's statement or question intended to point out contradictions in the client's behavior and statements or to induce the client to face an issue the counselor feels the client is avoiding.

These skills can be classified under the broader headings of listening, processing, and feedback, three elements that comprise communication between two individuals. This program addresses communication from the counselor's perspective.

Listening is defined as receiving messages from a client by focusing attention on what the client is expressing, both verbally and nonverbally.

Processing is the complex series of events that take place within the counselor between his or her listening and responding to the client. Processing may include mentally cataloging data, categorizing, comparing, hypothesizing on significance, exploring implications, and selecting a response on the basis of the counselor's life experience, beliefs, knowledge, attitudes, feelings, self-acceptance, and other factors that influence judgment and performance.

Feedback is the verbal or nonverbal response that the counselor makes as a result of processing the information received from listening to a client.

Attending can be classified as a listening skill; the remaining seven can be classified as feedback, and as such, provide evidence of the quality of the listening and processing that precede the feedback. Processing skills are not covered explicitly in this course.

Paraphrasing, reflection of feeling, and summarizing are primarily the feedback skills that demonstrate to the client that the counselor is paying attention to what the client is expressing verbally and nonverbally. The counselor can also use these skills to help the client recognize and clarify his/her own understanding of what he/she says and the feelings related to these messages. The counselor applies the other four skills—probing, counselor self-disclosure, interpreting, and confrontation—to promote a mutual identification and understanding of the client's problems and ways to deal with those problems.

These eight skills constitute only a partial listing of skills that can be subsumed under the heading of listening, processing, and feedback. Other dimensions of processing include the counselor's knowledge about alcohol and alcoholism; specific treatment techniques (behavior shaping, modeling, goal setting, assertiveness training, relaxation training); various theories of psychological development and human behavior (Maslow, Glasser); self-awareness of feelings, values, and attitudes; and past personal and professional experiences. Other feedback skills include advising, information giving, directing, supporting, and structuring.

Mastery of all the listening, processing, and feedback skills and others such as maintaining confidentiality, record keeping, crisis intervention, and referral are necessary for effective counseling. Mastery of all these skills depends on both training and experience and requires the same focused attention that is being given to the eight basic communication skills in this program.

The eight skills covered in this training program were selected not only because of their fundamental nature but also because they represent the core of communication skills necessary for the largest number of counselor activities in one-to-one interaction. The major activities in one-to-one client interaction can be expressed in a variety of ways. In one such listing, the counselor:

1. Establishes and maintains a climate for counseling.
2. Interviews the client to gather case history information.
3. Provides safeguards for maintaining confidentiality and ethical standards.
4. Prepares and uses necessary client reports and records.
5. Seeks consultation on the client's case when needed.
6. Negotiates an individual treatment plan that is tailored to and acceptable to the client.
7. Plans strategies for intervening in the client's crisis situations outside the counseling setting.
8. Increases client understanding of the severity of the abuse by explaining the nature of alcoholism as an illness.
9. Informs and assists the client in establishing necessary contacts with community services.

10. Coordinates involvement of other resource persons in accordance with a mutually acceptable individual treatment plan for the client.

11. Increases the client's ability to recognize the possible need for counseling assistance in the future.

12. Prepares for and conducts after-care activities with the client.

13. Evaluates client progress and assists the client in doing the same so that individualized treatment plan goals can be redefined if necessary.

14. Given the client's expressed desire to discontinue participation in the treatment process, the counselor leads the client in a review of the accumulated gains of the treatment process.

By matching the eight skills and this list of activities, it is apparent that, regardless of what other skills may be required, attending, paraphrasing, reflection of feeling, and summarizing are essential to "establishing and maintaining a climate for counseling," which is fundamental to and part of all the other activities. In addition, probing, counselor self-disclosure, interpreting, and confrontation are critical to Activities 2, 6, 11, 12, 13, and 14 and are called for in certain phases of Activities 5, 7, 8, 9, and 10.

Other important aspects of the counselor/client interaction include the qualities of genuineness, warmth, empathy, immediacy, congruence, concreteness, and respect. These are not skills, but rather are conditions which the counselor can create partially through the use of the basic communication skills. These conditions are not addressed directly in the training program but will be discussed where appropriate.

In summary, this training program focuses on the presentation and practice of eight basic communication skills. These are not the only skills a counselor uses in the counseling situation; however, they are essential in establishing a foundation of client self-awareness and mutual understanding between client and counselor. Their use in a counseling session or in communicating with colleagues, family, and others will help the counselor to:

- listen effectively to find out what the other person's situation or problem is;
- let the other person know that the counselor is really hearing and understanding him/her;
- check out with the other person that the counselor's perception of the situation or problem is accurate; and
- assist the other person in his or her perception and understanding of self, situation, and possibilities for change.

The eight skills are presented one at a time. The idea is to break down the task of communicating into smaller units or skills. Participants learn and practice the individual skills separately and then practice integrating them.

The skills are presented in ten sessions, one for each of the eight skills and two integrating sessions. The first integrating session comes after the sessions presenting the first four skills and provides an opportunity to practice the integration of those four skills. The second integrating session comes after practicing the other four skills and provides the opportunity to practice the integration of all eight skills. The eight skill building sessions will follow the same basic pattern:

- an exercise illustrating one or more aspects of the skill;
- a description of the skill as it is used in this training program;
- a demonstration of each skill poorly and competently applied;
- skill practice in small groups; and
- a discussion of this skill in counseling clients with alcohol-related problems.

Feedback and Assumptions

Feedback

Feedback was described in the Overview as the verbal or non-verbal response that the counselor makes as a result of processing the information received from listening to the client. With the exception of attending, the communication skills covered in this program are classified as feedback.

Feedback used in another sense is an important aspect of this training program. During skill practice sessions, participants will take turns as counselor, client, and observer. Client and observer will give the counselor feedback dealing with his or her performance of the skill in question.

The definition of feedback as used in the context of the practice sessions is: telling the counselor what you (as observer) heard and saw as he or she practiced a particular skill, or what you (as client) felt in response to his or her practice of the skill.

The extent to which you give each other feedback and the quality of the feedback may be the critical factor in determining whether or not this workshop will be productive for you. For example, if in practice sessions neither the observers nor the clients give you significant feedback about your performance as a counselor, you might complete your training, having gone through all the prescribed activities, and have gained nothing. You may perhaps even take away a more distorted rather than a clearer picture of your capabilities. In addition being a recipient of feedback can help sharpen your perception of what constitutes useful feedback.

When giving feedback, whether positive or negative, keep these guidelines in mind. They apply to both counseling and skill practice situations.

- The purpose of feedback is to be helpful to other people by giving them useful information about what they are doing or the effect they are having on you.

- *Timing* is important. If feedback is given so long after a happening that the recipient can't remember the happening clearly, it is not likely to be helpful. Feedback is most helpful when given as soon as possible.

- *Be specific rather than general.* Generalities often raise people's defenses so that they don't get the message you are trying to give. It's much easier to hear and acknowledge "I felt annoyed when you were late for our appointment today," than it is to hear and acknowledge "You're always late and I'm sick and tired of it." (Even if the other person *is* always late and you are sick and tired of it, it's more constructive to deal with specific situations as soon as possible, rather than not give feedback and sit on your feelings until you finally explode.)

- *Being descriptive rather than judgmental* is also less likely to raise people's defenses and is more helpful."You just went through a stop light and you're driving at 40 MPH in a 20 MPH school zone, and I feel nervous," is more constructive than "You're really a lousy driver."

- The last point to remember about *feedback* is that it *Should be directed toward behavior, which is something the receiver can do something about.* While you may find you simply have to tell someone the effect that his/her height, or age, or color of eyes has on you, this is not feedback. In effect, you're not telling that person anything about himself/herself but something about yourself. Even if it's positive, such as "Darling, I just love your green eyes," you're talking about your own likes or dislikes rather than something someone else has control over and could change if he/she wanted to.

Assumptions

Despite earnest intentions to give accurate and meaningful feedback, we may sometimes unconsciously erect barriers to doing so. These barriers may derive from our own needs, beliefs, prejudices, preferences, values, or fears, and they may frequently take the form of assumptions about others. Sometimes our assumptions are on target; quite often they are far from reality. However, they are accurate often enough to encourage us to keep making assumptions.

Making assumptions often takes the form of taking observable facts about another person, developing a theory to explain those facts, and then treating the other person as if your theory is proven. In alcoholism counseling, this process might mean observing that a client's eyes are bloodshot, assuming that he/she has been drinking, and reacting to the client with anger and disappointment on the basis of your assumptions. The client, however, may actually have hay fever or may not have been able to sleep. This kind of assuming is sometimes called *pigeon-holing* or *stereotyping*.

Making assumptions can also take the form of making another person responsible for our feelings. For example, I may feel frightened; if I assume that some other person is threatening to me, then this assumption justifies or rationalizes my fear. This process could easily take place with a client who may, in reality, be dangerous only to himself/herself or not dangerous at all.

Three things to remember about assumptions are:

- Recognize that you probably have some.
- Don't take them too seriously. You can't know another person's experience, only your own perceptions of that experience. Any conclusions or theories that you may have about another may be accurate or they may be *only* your assumptions.
- Check them out. Using nonjudgmental words and tentative phrases, share your assumptions with the recipient and see whether they are accurate or not—for example, "It seems like you have been drinking today." Remember, the object in counseling another is not for the counselor to be right (and the client wrong) but rather to establish communication, build a relationship, and help the client develop the capacity to deal more effectively with his/her life.

Attending

Definition of Attending

Attending is fundamental to the use of all other counseling skills. As used here, attending implies a concern by the counselor with all aspects of the client's communication. It includes listening to the verbal content, hearing and observing the verbal and nonverbal cues to the feelings that accompany the communication, and then communicating back to the client the fact that the counselor is paying attention.

Purposes of Attending

1. It encourages the client to continue expressing his/her ideas and feelings freely.
2. It allows the client to explore ideas and feelings in his/her own way and thus provides the client with an opportunity to direct the session.
3. It can give the client a sense of responsibility for what happens in the session by enabling him/her to direct the session.
4. It helps the client relax and be comfortable in the counseling session.
5. It contributes to the client's trust of the counselor and sense of security.
6. It enables the counselor to draw more accurate inferences about the client.

Components of Attending

Effective attending has two components: (1) listening and observing and (2) communicating to the client that listening and observing is going on.

The first component of attending behavior is *listening effectively and observing* carefully. For many people, listening is a difficult task to learn. Although society does place great emphasis on spoken exchanges, many people have not learned how to listen effectively. Often, people may think they are listening when they are actually thinking about something else or are debating a subject in their head while waiting for the other person to pause so they can present some comment of their own. A client can usually sense when the counselor is listening with "half an ear."

Effective listening by itself, however, is not enough. Counseling occurs in a face-to-face situation where both participants watch, as well as listen to, each other. The difference in information gathered from seeing and hearing as opposed to hearing alone is illustrated vividly by contrasting television with radio.

The counselor learns much about the feelings of the client through observation. Frequently, nonverbal behavior that expresses feelings may appear to alter or even negate verbal messages. It is common for people to communicate much more than they intend by their body language. As a matter of fact, the nonverbal message is more likely than the spoken words to transmit the real message—for example, a facial expression showing disgust may contradict the statement, "I'm not bothered by the thought of a drunken woman."

Conversely, many of the skills, attitudes, and feelings of the counselor are conveyed to the client through nonverbal behavior such as facial expressions, posture, eye contact, and gestures. The first component of attending occurs when the counselor stays attuned to what the client is expressing verbally and nonverbally. He/she listens closely and observes carefully.

The second component of attending behavior is *letting the client know that he/she is really being heard.* The counselor communicates through his/her attentiveness to the client generally through three methods.

a. *Eye contact*—The counselor should initiate and maintain eye contact with the client. Strong impressions—favorable and unfavorable—are formed depending on the kind and amount of eye contact. In ordinary social interaction, it is considered courteous to look at the person with whom one is speaking. In counseling, this behavior is almost imperative. However, in some cases continuous eye contact might cause the client to feel uncomfortable, as could a fixed stare or an intense gaze. Varied use of eye contact is the most effective and natural behavior for the counselor and the most likely to put the client at ease.

   It is important to note that these comments on eye contact are not applicable to all cultures. For instance, maintaining direct eye contact is a hostile act to some Native Americans and may be taken as a lack of respect by some Orientals.

b. *Posture*—Body language reveals a great deal about people; posture and gestures convey distinct messages. Impressions of others are formed even from the way they sit. The counselor wants to communicate to the client by his/her body posture that he/she is interested. An upright seated position with the upper body leaning slightly forward is generally considered to convey attentiveness, but the counselor should adopt a posture in which he/she will feel relaxed and comfortable. The first position the counselor assumes won't necessarily be the only one. The counselor will undoubtedly shift positions during the counseling session, for comfort and as a reflection of his/her feelings.

   Again, a word of caution if offered regarding cultural differences in acceptable attending. In some cultures, sitting too close to a client might be considered offensive or threatening; sitting too far away might convey detachment or withdrawal, and individuals vary in the amount of distance or closeness they heed. By watching how the client uses space in relation to the counselor, the counselor will probably have an indication of what is comfortable for the client.

c. *Accurate verbal following*—The counselor communicates to the client by verbal responses that listening and observing are occurring. The most important characteristic of accurate verbal responses is that they relate directly to what the client is expressing. This means the counselor doesn't jump to new topics or interrupt the client but follows the client in what he/she is saying. The counselor takes his/her cues from the client and indicates involvement by simply nodding, using encouraging phrases such as "um-hum" or "I see," repeating key words, or posing one-word questions, such as "Oh?" or "Yes?"

Later in this training program, the counselor will practice more specific types of responses (for example, paraphrasing, reflection of feeling, and summarizing) that convey to the client that the counselor has listened and observed. At this point in the program, the counselor can demonstrate accurate verbal following by offering minimal verbal responses, making head movements, and staying with the topic.

Summary of Attending

In attending, the counselor's goal is to listen effectively, to observe the client, and to communicate his/her interest and attentiveness through direct eye contact, relaxed body posture, and accurate verbal following. The skill of attending is the foundation on which all the other skills in this program are built.

Paraphrasing

Definition of Paraphrasing

Paraphrasing is a counselor response that restates the content of the client's previous statement. Paraphrasing concentrates primarily on cognitive verbal content, that is, content which refers to events, people and things. In paraphrasing, the counselor reflects .to the client the verbal essence of his/her last comment or last few comments. Sometimes, paraphrasing may involve simply repeating the client's own words, perhaps emphasizing one word in particular.

More often, paraphrasing is using words that are similar to the client's, but fewer in number.

Paraphrasing and reflection of feeling are very similar and therefore are easy to confuse. In both skills, the counselor must identify the client's basic message, either cognitive or affective (pertaining to feeling or emotion), and give that message back to the client using his/her (the counselor's) own words.

The distinguishing feature between paraphrasing and reflection of feeling is the focus of the counselor's response. A paraphrase focuses on the words the client is speaking. Reflection of feeling focuses on the associated feeling or emotion as expressed in the client's tone of voice, rate and volume of speech, posture, and other nonverbal behavior as well as verbal content.

In actual counseling it is neither realistic nor therapeutic to perform only one skill at a time. However, for the purpose of refining the individual skills in this workshop, it is helpful to concentrate on each skill separately. Reflection of feeling will be discussed and practiced in a separate session.

Purposes of Paraphrasing

1. It communicates to the client that the counselor understands or is trying to understand what he/she is saying. Paraphrasing can thus be a good indicator of accurate verbal following.

2. It sharpens a client's meaning to have his/her words rephrased more concisely and often leads the client to expand his/her discussion of the same subject.

3. It often clarifies confusing content for both the counselor and the client. Even when paraphrasing is not accurate, it is useful because it encourages the client to clarify his/her remarks.

4. It can spotlight an issue by stating it more succinctly, thus offering a direction for the client's subsequent remarks.

5. It enables the counselor to verify his/her perceptions of the verbal content of client's statements.

Components of Paraphrasing

Paraphrasing has two components: determining the basic message and rephrasing.

The counselor uses his/her judgment to *determine the basic message* that is being expressed in the client's verbal content. Much of the time clients tend to speak in short paragraphs. They seldom state a single thought and wait for a reply. So the counselor must attend to all of the client's verbal content, but decide on the basic message being expressed in the "paragraphs."

After the counselor determines the basic message to be responded to, he/she attempts to give this content back to the client in a more precise way by *rephrasing* it. The counselor may want to combine several of the client's related comments into one response to the client.

To paraphrase effectively, then, the counselor determines the basic message from the content and rephrases it, usually in similar, but fewer words.

Checking Out

To minimize the possibility of the counselor's letting his/her assumptions distort what the client is saying, the counselor should get in the habit of checking out his/her paraphrasing. This can be done by adding phrases such as, "Is that right?" "Am I correct?" or "Have I heard you correctly?" to the paraphrase. This procedure will usually evoke a response from the client, and the counselor can then judge whether he/she is making assumptions or is accurately attending to the client. Checking out may not be necessary, however, if the client is clearly indicating agreement either verbally or nonverbally.

Assessing the Outcome of Paraphrasing

How effectively a counselor has used paraphrasing can best be judged by the client's next response after a paraphrase. If the paraphrase is effective, the client may indicate agreement by a word or gesture and may continue to talk further on the same subject.

Sometimes the counselor will not succeed in accurately distilling the client's comments, and the client may reply, "No, that's not what I meant." When this occurs, the counselor's attempt at paraphrasing has still been useful because it allows the counselor to see immediately that he/she has erred either in determining the basic message or in rephrasing the content.

In other instances the client may confirm the accuracy of the counselor's paraphrase, but, having heard his/her meaning expressed in different words, decide to modify or even reverse the meaning entirely to reflect a changed point of view.

Each of these outcomes can be regarded as evidence that the counselor's paraphrase has been effective.

Examples of Paraphrasing

Three examples of client statements and possible paraphrasing responses follow. After reading the examples, (a) indicate below each response whether it is appropriate or poor paraphrasing and why, and (b) formulate another appropriate paraphrasing response for at least one of the examples.

Client: I think I'm going to move out this weekend. All she ever does is complain about my drinking. Never does any housework, just nags me.

Counselor: Nagging and drinking don't mix.

_____

Counselor: Sounds like things are bad at home and you're trying to decide whether to leave.

_____

Counselor: It seems you've made the decision that you can't take it any more.

_____

Counselor: _____

* *

Client: I got stopped again for DWI and may lose my license.

Counselor: So your right to drive could be in jeopardy.

_____

Counselor: Sounds like this new DWI offense could mean trouble.

_____

Counselor: You just can't stop hot rodding around.

_____

Counselor: _____

* *

Client: My boss doesn't understand me at all. He doesn't realize I'm always shaky in the morning.

Counselor: I hear you saying that your boss can't see your situation the way you see it.

_____

Counselor: Your boss is firm about work starting at 9:00.

_____

Counselor: Mornings are a tough time for you.

_____

Counselor: _____

Summary of Paraphrasing

To paraphrase is to determine the basic message in the client's cognitive statements and concisely rephrase it. The rewording should capture the essence of the cognitive verbal content. Occasionally, an exact repetition of the client's remarks may be an appropriate paraphrase. More commonly, the counselor determines and rephrases the basic message of the verbal content using similar, but fewer, words.

Reflection of Feeling

Introduction

Dealing with feelings and emotions—one's own or others'—is probably the most difficult part of human relations. One cause of this difficulty is that the dominant American culture does not value open and free expression of feelings and emotions.

At an early age, we learn to control, mask, or deny our feelings. Unfortunately, with most of us, this process is learned well and reinforced continuously in our schooling. Through primary emphasis on intellectual achievement, we are conditioned to restrain, and even deny, our emotions. However, denied or suppressed feelings do not just disappear. Depending on the intensity of the feelings and how long they have been suppressed, they manifest their presence both psychologically and physically in such ways as difficulty in communicating with others, depression, fatigue, tension headaches, and psychosomatic illness. A more constructive approach is to recognize that feelings and emotions exist, accept them as part of ourselves, and learn to express them in ways that promote individual growth and mutually satisfying relationships.

In counseling, we must communicate with the client not only on the factual, or cognitive, level (meaning events, people, things), but also on the affective level (meaning feelings about events, people, and things). Frequently, we may have as clients people who have controlled, inhibited, or denied their feelings and emotions for years. One of our tasks is to help them understand that it is acceptable, even necessary, to be aware of and express their feelings in the counseling relationship. The ability of the counselor to transmit that message is based on the assumption that the counselor can get in touch with, identify, and express his/her own feelings. Our primary focus here is on helping the client to become aware of, identify, and express his/her feelings.

An important concept to understand with regard to reflection of feeling is *empathy*, which has been identified as one of the essential conditions in counseling. Empathy, in everyday language, means putting oneself in the other person's shoes. More formally, it might be defined as the counselor's attempting to perceive the world through the client's frame of reference. Thus the counselor manifests empathy through his/her ability to perceive what is happening in regard to the client's feelings and to communicate this perception to the client. Reflection of feeling is one of the ways empathy can be communicated.

Definition of Reflection of Feeling

Reflection of feeling is the counselor's expressing the essence of the client's feelings, either stated or implied. In contrast to paraphrasing, reflection of feeling focuses primarily on the emotional element of the client's communication, whether it is verbal or nonverbal. The counselor tries to perceive the emotional state or condition of the client and feed back a response that demonstrates his/her understanding of this state. Reflection of feeling, then, is an empathic response to the client's emotional state or condition.

Purposes of Reflection of Feeling

1. It conveys to the client that the counselor understands or is trying to understand what the client is experiencing and feeling. This empathy for the client usually reinforces the client's willingness to express feelings to the counselor.
2. It clarifies the client's feelings and attitudes by mirroring them in a nonjudgmental way.

3. It brings to the surface feelings of the client that may have been expressed only vaguely.

4. It gives the client the opportunity to recognize and accept his/her feelings as part of himself/herself. Sometimes the client may refer to "it" or "them" as the source of a problem, when he/she really means "I was feeling angry."

5. It verifies the counselor's perceptions of what the client is feeling. That is, it allows the counselor to check out with the client whether or not he/she is accurately reflecting what the client is experiencing.

6. It can bring out problem areas without the client feeling pushed.

7. It helps the client infer that feelings are causes of behavior.

Components of Reflection of Feeling

The reflection-of-feeling skill consists of two components: identification and formulation.

The counselor must first *identify* the basic feeling(s) being expressed verbally or nonverbally by the client. To be able to identify feelings in clients, a counselor must be able to recognize feelings in himself/herself. Although the counselor can't feel the client's feelings, he/she can infer what they might be by processing the verbal and nonverbal information the client is communicating. The counselor matches the information he/she gains with his/her experiences in order to label the feelings the client seems to be experiencing. Since the counselor has experienced feelings such as joy, anger, pain, fear, and boredom, he/she can remember how they felt.

To recognize or be aware of feelings in the client, the counselor attends to both verbal and nonverbal cues. When he/she is listening effectively to the client's statements, the counselor may perceive feelings that are either directly expressed or implied. Sometimes the verbal indications of feelings may not be as straightforward as they seem. Often "I think" and "I feel" are used interchangeably, although they have different meanings, particularly in counseling. For example, if a client says, "I felt overjoyed at the news," the counselor can infer that the client was happy. However, if the client says, "I feel he is too strict," the counselor cannot reliably infer what the client feels, but only what he/she thinks.

Distinct messages of emotional content also will come from nonverbal cues. Nonverbal indicators of feeling include such things as head and facial movements, posture, gestures, and voice tone and quality. Some examples of specific nonverbal cues are lowered head, folded arms, restlessness, crying, and slowness of speech.

Think back for a moment. When you're depressed, how does your voice sound? When you're angry, what happens to your face, mouth, eyes, jaw, and voice? When you're afraid, what happens to your eyes, your body posture, your gestures? Of course, different people will display different degrees and amounts of emotional intensity in different ways. Only after observing and interacting with a person over time can anyone begin to decide what that individual's nonverbal behavior might really be saying about how he/she is feeling.

In general, though, the counselor can be alert to such facial and body expressions as smiles, eyes widening or narrowing, worry wrinkles, drooping shoulders, or tightly clenched hands. Voice quality is an important area to attend to for signs of emotion. Loudness or softness, changes in tone or inflection, and emphasis on one word are indications of feelings. Sometimes the client may convey conflicting messages with his/her verbal and nonverbal behavior. He/she may say "I'm not upset," when his/her hands are shaking and his/her face is red.

Thus, in identifying feelings, the counselor attempts to enter the client's frame of reference by drawing on his/her own experiences with feelings. The counselor must identify the feelings the client is communicating before he/she can reflect them accurately to the client.

The second component of an effective reflection-of-feeling response is to *formulate a response* that captures the essence of the feeling expressed by the client. Although the counselor tries to understand and identify the client's feelings as well as he/she can, it is not possible to *be* the client, so any conclusions drawn should be considered tentative and presented as tentative reflections. By remaining tentative and openminded in formulating verbal responses, the counselor avoids dogmatic-sounding responses that might alienate the client if they are inaccurate.

Examples of appropriate phrases with which a counselor might begin a reflection-of-feeling response are:

> It seems that you feel. . . .
> Are you saying that you feel. . . .
> You seem to feel. . . .
> Is it possible that you feel. . . .
> I'm picking up that you feel. . . .
> You appear to be feeling. . . .
> Perhaps you're feeling. . . .
> I sense that you feel. . . .

Often, counselors find reflection of feeling one of the harder skills to master. Some common errors counselors tend to make in using this skill follow in the next section. These errors may also occur in using some of the other skills in the program.

Common Errors in Formulating Reflection-of-Feeling Responses

1. *Stereotypical language*—The counselor can fall into a pattern of always beginning reflections in the same way with a phrase such as "You feel. . . ." Some of these phrases were listed above as appropriate, but the counselor should avoid using any one of them too often. The counselor should vary his/her style of reflecting.

2. *Timing*—Sometimes the inexperienced counselor attempts to reflect feelings after every statement the client makes. This can give an impression of insincerity and may dilute the effect of the technique. At the other extreme, the counselor waits until the client has finished a long series of comments and tries to reflect many feelings in one response. Another error in timing involves pauses. Counselors often don't wait out pauses. Long pauses can mean that the client is trying to say things that are difficult for him/her to say, but the uncomfortable counselor may jump in and respond immediately, in effect interrupting and breaking off the client's struggle to express a complex or painful thought or feeling.

3. *Too-shallow or too-deep responses*—The counselor should strive to feed back to the client the essence of what he/she is expressing. The counselor should avoid either reflecting a feeling or taking away from the client's meaning by merely labeling the feeling. The goal is to communicate to the client that he/she is understood on the level where he/she is. For example, a client may say, "I feel bad. I had some drinks at the office party last night after I promised myself I wouldn't." A too-shallow response from the counselor might be, "You mean you're sorry." A too-deep response might be, "You feel *really* guilty about your drinking."

Checking Out

Checking out perceptions is as important in reflection of feeling as it is in paraphrasing, even though the reflection of feeling is phrased tentatively. The addition of a questioning phrase, usually at the end of the reflection-of-feeling statement, will insure that the counselor is not making unfounded assumptions about the client.

For example, "I sense that you feel discouraged today. Is that right?"

Assessing the Outcome of Reflection of Feeling

In reflection of feeling, as in paraphrasing, the effectiveness of the activity can be determined by the client's response. The client may confirm or disclaim the reflection. If the reflection is accurate, the client is more likely to continue discussing the feeling reflected. An inaccurate reflection will often bring a correcting response from the client, which results in clarification. In either case, the net result of reflection-of-feeling responses made by the counselor should be an increased focus on feelings by the client as he perceives that discussing feelings is acceptable in counseling.

Examples of Reflection of Feeling

Three examples of client statements and possible reflection-of-feeling responses follow. After reading the examples, (a) indicate next to each response whether it is appropriate or poor reflection of feeling and why, and (b) formulate another appropriate reflection-of-feeling response for at least one of the examples.

Client: I'm afraid that I have some influence on his drinking. Like I may be one of the reasons he drinks so much.

Counselor: You appear to be feeling guilty that you may be a part of his drinking.

_____

Counselor: You worry that you may contribute to his drinking.

_____

Counselor: You feel he drinks too much.

_____

Counselor: _____

* *

Client: I didn't want to come here. There is nothing wrong with me. I only came to see you because my wife insisted.

Counselor: You seem resentful about coming here.

_____

Counselor: You feel that you're a perfectly normal person.

_____

Counselor: I get the impression that you're annoyed.

_____

Counselor: _____

* *

Client: God, I hate my ma. She tries to run my life for me. I feel almost as strongly about my dad. He just sits back and lets her run everything. As long as he's got his booze, he's ok.

Counselor: You feel guilty because you can't accept the idea that you hate your parents.

_____

Counselor: Sounds like you resent your mother for being too strong and your father for being too weak.

_____

Counselor: I'm hearing you express two different feelings— irritation at your mother and impatience at your dad's behavior,

_____

Counselor: _____

Summary of Reflection of Feeling

Reflection of feeling involves _identifying_ the essence of the feelings the client is expressing and _formulating_ a response that indicates that the counselor understands. Usually the counselor offers fresh words that capture the basic verbal or nonverbal feeling message of the client.

Summarizing

Definition of Summarizing

Summarizing is the tying together by the counselor of the main points discussed in a counseling session. Summarizing can focus on both feelings and content and is appropriate after a discussion of a particular topic within the session or as a review at the end of the session of the principal issues discussed. In either case, a summary should be brief, to the point, and without new or added meanings.

In many respects, summarizing is similar to, or an extension of, paraphrasing and reflection of feeling in that the counselor seeks to determine the basic meanings being expressed in content or feelings and give these meanings back to the client in fresh words. Summarizing differs primarily in the span of time it is concerned with. In paraphrasing, a statement or brief paragraph occurring over a short period of time is rephrased. In summarizing verbal content, several of the client's statements, the entire session, or even several sessions are pulled together.

In reflection of feeling, the counselor responds to the last feeling or feelings expressed or displayed. In summarizing feelings, the counselor reviews numerous feelings expressed or displayed over a longer period of time.

Purposes of Summarizing

1. It can insure continuity in the direction of the session by providing a focus.
2. It can clarify a client's meaning by having his/her scattered thoughts and feelings pulled together.
3. .It often encourages the client to explore an issue further once a central theme has been identified.
4. It communicates to the client that the counselor understands or is trying to understand what the client is saying and feeling.
5. It enables the counselor to verify his/her perceptions of the content and feelings discussed or displayed by the client during the session. The counselor can check out whether he/she accurately attended and responded without changing the meanings expressed.
6. It can close discussion on a given topic, thus clearing the way for a new topic.

7. It provides a sense of movement and progress to the client by drawing several of his/her thoughts and feelings into a common theme.

8. It can terminate a session in a logical way through review of the major issues discussed in the entire session.

Components of Summarizing

Accurate summarizing has two components: selection and tying together.

The counselor uses his/her judgment to *select the key points* discussed. As the counselor picks out the highlights of content and feelings, general themes usually begin to emerge. When deciding what material to summarize, the counselor should note consistent and inconsistent patterns that have evolved in the session. For example, the client may keep coming back to one particular issue, implicitly emphasizing its importance, or the client may seem to contradict himself/herself by making conflicting statements at different times during the session.

After selecting the principal points discussed or displayed, the counselor attempts to *tie together* these points and to feed them back to the client in a more concise way. In drawing together the content and feelings, the counselor should avoid adding his/her own ideas, which could well be assumptions. The idea is to give back to the client essentially what he/she has said concisely, using fresh words.

Assessing Outcomes of Summarizing

The outcome of a summarization depends to a large extent on where in the counseling session it occurs. If the summarizing of a particular topic occurs during the session, it is likely to encourage the client to talk further. If summarizing occurs at the close of the session, it is more likely to terminate further discussion.

How effectively a counselor has summarized the essence of the verbal content and feelings the client has expressed can best be determined by the client's response to the summary. The client may affirm that the counselor has tied together points already discusses and, depending on where in the session the summary is made, continue to explore the topic, begin a related or new topic, or accept the counselor's remarks as a wrap-up of the session.

Sometimes the counselor may not have accurately pulled together the essential content and feelings of the client, or may have added assumptions of his/her own to the exchange. In that case, the client may say, "That isn't quite what I said," or "I agree with that except for. . . ." The counselor and client can then resolve areas in question before proceeding or ending the session.

As with paraphrasing and reflection of feeling, the counselor should make a practice of checking out the accuracy of a summary with the client to minimize the chances of making unwarranted assumptions.

Examples of Summarizing

To a divorced woman exploring problems that she is having with a teen-age son, who is drinking heavily:

> As I understand what you've been saying during the past few minutes, you seem to be struggling with three possible ways to handle the situation: you might continue trying to reason with your son yourself; you might ask his father to help you deal with the boy; or you might stop discussing the problem with your son and punish him by taking away his privileges.

At the end of a session with a male client:

> Let's take a look at what we've covered in today's session. It sounds like you've felt inadequate in dealing with several areas of your life—your family, your job, and now your drinking.

Summary of Summarizing

To summarize is to *select* the key points or basic meanings from the client's verbal content and feelings and succinctly *tie them together*. The summarization should accurately reflect the essence of the client's statements and feelings and should not include assumptions of the counselor. Summarizing, then, is a review of the main points already discussed in the session to insure continuity in a focused direction.

Probing

Definition of Probing

Probing is a counselor's use of a question or statement to direct the client's attention inward to explore his/her situation in more depth. A probing question, sometimes called an "open-ended question," requires more than a one-word (yes or no) answer from the client.

When phrased as a statement, the probe contains a strong

element of direction by the counselor; for example, "Tell me more about your relationship with your parents," or "Suppose we explore a little more your ideas about what an alcoholic is."

Purposes of Probing

1. It can help focus the client's attention on a feeling or content area.
2. It may help the counselor better understand what the client is describing by giving him her more information about the client's situation.
3. It may encourage the client to elaborate, clarify, or illustrate what he/she has been saying.
4. It sometimes enhances the client's awareness and understanding of his/her situation or feelings.
5. It directs the client's attention to areas the counselor thinks need attention.

Components of Probing

The two components of probing are identification and open-ended phrasing.

The counselor uses his/her judgment to *identify* a subject or feelings area touched on by the client that needs further exploration. As with the other skills practiced in this training program, it is important that the counselor use probing only after attending to the client. By listening to and observing the client, the counselor may identify matters that either seem unresolved or seem to need further development.

In probing, the counselor decides what areas might need further attention, whereas in paraphrasing, reflection of feeling, and summarizing, the counselor attempts to feed back to the client in a more concise way the same material or feelings the client presented or displayed.

After identifying the area that needs to be explored further, the counselor attempts to *phrase an open-ended question or statement* to help include such words as what, where, when, or how. For example, "When do you feel that way?" "Where does that occur for you?" It is generally best to avoid asking questions beginning with the words are, is, do, or why. The first three words tend to elicit one-word answers. "Why" frequently poses a question that the client cannot answer. As a result, the client may feel defensive and resist further exploration of the topic, or may indulge in vague speculation unrelated to the topic under discussion.

Assessing the Outcomes of Probing

As with other skills studies, how effectively a counselor has probed can best be determined by the client's response. If the probe encourages the client to talk in greater depth about his/her feelings or the content identified by the counselor, then the technique has probably been helpful. Similarly, if the probe seems to make the client more aware of a situation he/she has tended to avoid or ignore, and more apt to discuss it specifically, then the probe has been effective. In general the probe may be seen as effective when the client responds by talking further about the subject or feeling on what seems like a deeper level (as opposed to a superficial, intellectualizing level).

Sometimes, the counselor may probe an area that the client is not yet ready to discuss or deal with. In that case, the counselor might encounter extended silence or some other form of resistance on the part of the client. Or the client may simply say "I'd rather not talk about that." The probe might still be considered effective in this case, because the counselor may have succeeded in directing the client's attention to the problem area which either the client or the counselor might come back to later.

Examples of Probing

Two examples of client statements and possible probing responses follow. After reading the examples, indicate next to each response whether it is appropriate or poor probing and why.

Client: Mother and Dad were fighting and he was pounding on her and knocking her down, so I beat him up and went out and had a steak.

Counselor: How were you feeling at the point where you decided to beat your father?

_____

Counselor: Tell me more about what you were going through as that happened.

_____

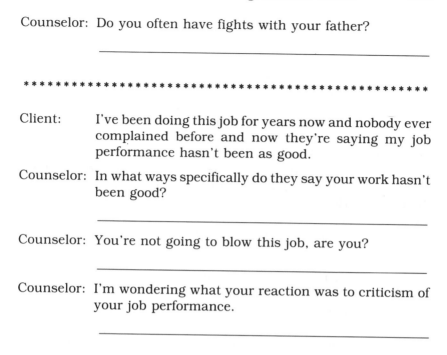

Counselor: Do you often have fights with your father?

* *

Client: I've been doing this job for years now and nobody ever complained before and now they're saying my job performance hasn't been as good.

Counselor: In what ways specifically do they say your work hasn't been good?

Counselor: You're not going to blow this job, are you?

Counselor: I'm wondering what your reaction was to criticism of your job performance.

Summary of Probing

Probing is the use of a counselor question or statement to direct the client's attention inward to explore his/her situation in depth. The counselor identifies an area which seems to need exploration and then openly phrases a response. Used effectively, probing should help both the client and counselor to better understand the client's situation.

Counselor Self-Disclosure

Introduction

The importance of identifying and responding to feelings has been stressed throughout this program. Although our focus has been on the feelings of the client, the feelings of the counselor are just as important. The counselor should be aware of his/her feelings during the counseling session, and this awareness should lead to congruency between the counselor's verbal and nonverbal behavior.

If the counselor becomes impatient with the client's evasive statements, this impatience will probably show in his/her own nonverbal behavior. Therefore, it should be constructively expressed. Showing honest and open involvement with the client by being congruent is one way the counselor can be genuine. When the counselor provides a model of genuineness, the client is more likely to perceive that being genuine is acceptable and necessary in counseling. It may also establish a pattern that the client may apply to his other social interactions.

For the counsellor to be genuine and congruent in counseling, he/she must be aware not only of feelings, but also aspects of himself/herself that others may see. In an attempt to clarify the kinds of information available about all people, Joe Luft and Harry Ingham contributed their names and ideas to the concept of Johari Window.* The Window is a visual way of describing information available about any person. The four "panes" of the Window are:

1. Information known by all about a person (open area).
2. Information known by the person, but not by others (hidden area).
3. Information known by others, but not by the person (blind area).
4. Information not known by the person or by others (unknown area).

Individual awareness, which contributes to genuineness and congruency, depends on any person's increasing the information in his/her open area while reducing the blind and hidden areas.

Definition of Self-Disclosure

Self-disclosure is a sharing by the counselor of his/her own feelings, attitudes, opinions, and experiences with a client *for the benefit of the client.* Self-disclosure should include significant content and be relevant to the client's situation. Self-disclosure *in the present* (the here and now of the counseling session) occurs when the counselor communicates his/her feelings about the client or the session, such as by saying, "I'm pleased that you can talk about these things." Self-disclosure may also include revealing experiences the counselor has had *in the past* that seem relevant to the client's current situation.

---

* For a diagram of the Johari Window and a discussion of the related concept, see:

Hanson, P. G. "The Johari Window: A Model for Soliciting and Giving Feedback," J. William Pfeiffer and John E. Jones, Editors. *The Annual Handbook for Group Facilitators.* LaJolla, CA: University Associates, 1973, pp. 114–119.

Johnson, Vernon, E. *I'll Quit Tomorrow.* New York: Harper & Row, 1973, p. 120.

Purposes of Self-Disclosure

1. It tends to build a sense of trust and rapport between the counselor and the client.

2. It helps reduce the client's feelings that he/she is unique and alone in the situation he/she is experiencing.

3. It often enables the counseling relationship to move to deeper levels.

4. It fosters a feeling of empathy in the counseling relationship when the client perceives that the counselor may indeed be able to see things from the client's point of view.

5. It tends to promote the expression of feelings by the client in the counseling relationship.

6. It may create an atmosphere in which the client feels free to express content that he/she had previously avoided.

7. It may encourage the client to explore further a particular subject or feeling by sharing the counselor's experience with a similar situation.

Guidelines for Self-Disclosure

Self-disclosure requires knowledge of *principles* to guide the appropriate timing and content of the self-disclosure.

1. *The counselor's disclosure should relate directly to the client's situation.* This principle pertains primarily to disclosures about the counselor's past experiences. To help decide whether an experience is relevant to the client's situation, the counselor may first use paraphrasing, reflection of feeling, summarizing, and probing responses to insure that he/she does understand the client's situation.

2. *The counselor should disclose only experiences that have actually happened to him/her.* Using a personal pronoun such as I, me, my, or myself in a self-disclosure can give a clear message to the client that the counselor is telling about an experience that happened to him/her and is not merely relating the hearsay experience of a third party. This principle is most appropriate to the "past" type of self-disclosure.

3. *The counselor has the option of revealing information about himself/herself on various levels of intimacy.* The counselor could reveal information that is in the open area of the Johari Window and probably known to many. Or, if the counseling relationship has

produced a deep level of mutual trust, empathy, and genuineness, the counselor might reveal to the client an aspect of himself/herself that few others know. The guiding principle as to what level of information to reveal lies in the answers to two questions: Will it benefit the client and will the counselor feel comfortable in revealing that information?

Problems of Self-Disclosure

There are also some problems associated with self-disclosure of which the counselor should be aware.

1. *Self-disclosure in the present (the here and now of the session) can have an immediate and sometimes extreme effect on the client.* When the counselor reveals a current feeling about the client (for example, that the counselor feels bored), the client may feel rejected or belittled. In deciding whether to disclose what might be perceived by the client as a negative feeling, the counselor must ask himself/herself whether he/she is disclosing for the sake of the client or out of a personal need. Positive feelings (pleasure, happiness, pride) revealed by the counselor usually do not result in as obvious reactions in the client as do negative feelings. The counselor should recall that he/she is attempting to be a genuine, honest person in the counseling relationship and therefore must consider revealing positive and negative feelings if such disclosures would benefit the client.

2. *The use of counselor self-disclosure shifts the focus of the session away from the client to the counselor.* The counselor must guard against allowing subsequent responses to leave the focus on the counselor and thus tend to deny or downgrade the experiences of the client. The counselor should keep in mind that the self-disclosure is for the benefit of the client. The client is not likely to be helped if the counselor proceeds to work through a need of his/her own.

3. *The premature use of an intimate past experience or a threatening present feeling could make the client anxious and could damage the counseling relationship.* If the counselor is quite sure that he/she understands the client's situation and that the conditions of trust, empathy, and genuineness are present in the relationship, the self-disclosure will probably be appropriate.

4. *There is a certain amount of risk to the counseling relationship any time the counselor uses self-disclosure.* The counselor reveals something personal about himself/herself that the client

may ignore, deny, or ridicule. In exposing himself/herself, the counselor stands to gain by being perceived as an honest, genuine person but runs the risk that the client's perception of him/her may change and thus change the dynamics of the counseling relationship. If the client's perception of the counselor has changed negatively because of an inappropriate self-disclosure, the counseling relationship may be disrupted.

Not all counselors may feel comfortable sharing personal experiences, but all counselors should recognize the value of the "here and now" self-disclosures that foster a climate of trust and openness. Each counselor makes his/her own decision about whether to use self-disclosure in counseling. When self-disclosure is used appropriately, the benefits, in the form of a deeper counseling relationship, can be great. The counselor will probably be using self-disclosure appropriately if he/she continually asks the question "is this disclosure for the sake of the client?"

Examples of Self-Disclosure

Below are three client statements, the first two followed by possible self-disclosure responses. After reading the examples, (a) indicate below each response whether it is appropriate or poor self-disclosure and why, and (b) formulate an appropriate self-disclosure for the third client statement. (Assume that the appropriate conditions in the relationship have been established.)

Past:

Client: You know, I feel so ashamed. All my friends are going to find out that I have a drinking problem and I don't know how I can face them.

Counselor: I think I'm aware of how you might be feeling because I can remember how ashamed I felt, at first, when I had to admit to my friends that I am an alcoholic.

_____

Counselor: I think I know how you might feel. I'm not an alcoholic, but my father is and I can remember my shame and embarrassment about the secret getting out.

_____

Counselor: I know how you feel. I felt really embarrassed when my father came to my graduation in jeans.

_____

* *

Present:

Client: Well, I did have a few drinks before coming here tonight, but it doesn't matter because I'm sticking to my treatment plan.

Counselor: I have to admit I'm feeling disappointed right now. I thought you were doing so well in staying away from alcohol.

_____

Counselor: If you think you've got problems, let me tell you how hard it is for me to go to a cocktail party and not to drink.

_____

Counselor: I'm trying very hard to control my feelings of anger toward you. I think you know that we decided you shouldn't come here if you had been drinking.

_____

* *

Client: Sometimes I feel so discouraged. It seems like nothing will ever change, no matter what I do.

Counselor: _____

Summary of Self-Disclosure

Self-disclosure involves the counselor sharing his/her own feelings, attitudes, opinions, and experiences with a client for the benefit of the client. The self-disclosure of the counselor might be revealing a present feeling or relating a relevant past experience. Both timing and appropriateness of content are central to effective self-disclosure. Used appropriately, counselor self-disclosure should increase the level of trust, genuineness, and empathy in the counseling relationship and reduce the client's feeling of being unique in his/her problems or difficulties.

Interpreting

Introduction

Most people place limits on how they will look at problems or situations. As a result of this restricted outlook, people make comments like "I could never do that." When asked why they couldn't they often don't know. They just know that they have never considered doing such a thing. This kind of thinking produces narrow vision, which hinders people from arriving at other ways of looking at problems or situations. People thus become further entrenched in the one position rather than trying to open up their vision or perspective.

The counselor, as well as the client, is subject to falling into the trap of restricted thinking. After learning the skill of interpreting, the counselor will be able to help clients broaden their perspectives. To do so, the counselor has to broaden his/her own way of viewing problems and situations.

Definition of Interpreting

Interpreting is a technique used by the counselor to present the client with alternative ways of looking at his/her situation. For example, the counselor might use a different perspective to explain events to a client so that he/she might be able to see the problem in a new light and perhaps generate his/her own fresh ways of looking at it.

Interpreting differs from reflection of feeling, paraphrasing, and summarizing in that it usually involves the addition of the counselor's ideas to the basic messages being expressed or manifested by the client. In other words, in reflection of feelings, paraphrasing, and summarizing, the counselor attempts to understand and maintain the client's frame of reference. In interpreting, the counselor offers a new frame of reference to the client. Interpreting, as defined here, is not the "in-depth" type of interpretation that psychoanalysts might do. In this training program, the emphasis in interpretation is not on digging into the client's psyche but on offering alternative points of view in regard to his/her immediate problem or situation.

Purposes of Interpreting

1. It helps the client realize that there is more than one way to look at most situations, problems, and solutions.

2. It offers the client a role model of the counselor seeking alternative ways of viewing events in life.

3. It can teach the client how to use self-interpretation to explore new points of view.

4. It can help the client understand his/her problems more clearly.

5. It often generates new and distinctive solutions to problems.

6. It may prompt the client to act more effectively when he/she sees other solutions to problems.

7. It often enables the client to gain a better understanding of his/her underlying feelings and how these might relate to verbal messages he/she has expressed.

Components of Interpreting

Effective interpreting has three components: determining and restating basic messages; adding counselor ideas for a new frame of reference; and "checking out" these ideas with the client.

The basic framework on which all of the counseling skills presented thus far have been built is the ability to listen effectively and observe carefully. It is especially important that the counselor employ the skills of attending, paraphrasing, reflection of feeling, and summarizing prior to and in conjunction with interpreting. The first step in interpreting *is to determine the basic messages* the client has expressed or displayed and restate them. The counselor seeks to determine the essence of what the client is saying or doing (the client's frame of reference) and then restates this in a paraphrase, reflection of feeling, or summary.

As the counselor is determining the basic messages and restating them, he/she probably will have some ideas or hunches about alternative ways of viewing the client's situation, or may begin to see connections, relationships, or patterns in the events the client describes. When these ideas are included in the material being restated to the client, the counselor is *adding his/her ideas* to offer the client a new frame of reference from which to view his/her situation.

Because the counselor is departing from the client's frame of reference and offering alternative viewpoints, it becomes very important to phrase any interpretation tentatively or *to check out directly* with the client his/her reaction to any new points of view. Tentative phrases such as "The way I see it . . ." or "I wonder if . . ." are appropriate ways to begin an interpretation. Sometimes the counselor might want to phrase the interpretation as a question— for example, "Do you think, then, that you might be uncomfortable

with older men because of your poor relationship with your father?"
This form of interpretation is more tentative than a statement and
thus there is a greater possibility that the client will see the offered
interpretation as a possibility rather than as a fact. Whether the
counselor is on target or completely off, the client is more likely to
react to an interpretation openly if it is offered tentatively.

Another way of checking out how the interpretation is received
by the client is to add a question onto the end of the new point of
view such as, "How does that hit you?" or "Am I really far off?"
However the counselor relays the tentativeness of his interpretation,
it is imperative that the counselor let the client know it is merely
an alternative way of looking at the situation and not necessarily
the only or right way.

Guidelines for Effective Interpreting

Interpreting is a more complex and subtle skill than others
included in this program. Because it can be a potent promoter of
behavior change, however, it is worth the effort required to learn
interpreting and use it effectively. Some general guidelines follow:

1. In formulating interpretations, the counselor should use simple
    language, close to the level at which the client is operating.
    He/she should avoid jumping too far ahead of the client,
    indulging in speculation, or stating the interpretation in such
    a way as to seem to be showing off psychological expertise. An
    example of not staying at the same level as the client's is one
    in which the counselor replies to the client's remark that he
    wishes his dad would lose some weight, with, "You're suffering
    from typical castration anxiety complicated by Oedipal
    conflicts."

2. Added ideas or explanations that the counselor offers to the
    client are often expressed to the client in terms of a particular
    theory of behavior and personality, such as Gestalt,
    behavioristic, rational emotive, or psychoanalytic. Such a
    theory will probably provide some of the labels the counselor
    will tend to put on feelings and events in the client's life. The
    counselor should, of course, be aware of what theoretical
    position he/she operates from. However, in this training
    program, no discussion of various theoretical positions is given.

3. The counselor should encourage the client to get in the habit
    of considering a range of alternative ways to view his/her
    situation. The counselor may serve as a model for this kind of
    unfettered thinking by presenting an alternative and then

asking the client to suggest others. For example, to a client who has said that feelings of loneliness have caused him to drink in the past, the counselor might say, "Let's look at some things you might do to deal with that lonely feeling, other than drink. One thing you could do is call your A.A. sponsor and talk to him for a while. What are some other things you might do?"

Outcomes Expected from Interpreting

The effectiveness of interpretation can be determined by the client's reaction to any frame of reference offered. If the alternative point of view is close to what the client has expressed, the client might immediately accept the interpretation as a useful way to rethink the problem. In fact, the client might seem to get a sudden recognition of what the problem is. A response such as "I just realized that's it," could be a typical reply.

If the interpretation varies somewhat from what the client has expressed, several reactions are possible. The client might accept a new frame of reference tentatively—"I'll have to think about that one." On the other hand, he/she might reject the interpretation completely or say "Yes, but . . ." Or the client might accept it too uncritically. The counselor should be cautious in proceeding in the direction of an interpretation that the client accepts without any hesitation, because it could mean that the client does not feel free to challenge anything the counselor says. However, if the counselor keeps in mind the procedure of checking out perceptions with the client, the counselor's interpreting and subsequent responses will be made tentatively or cautiously.

If the interpretation is too extreme, the client might become anxious or threatened and the session could be disrupted. Or the client, again, might accept the interpretation at a cautious or tentative level.

Although the client will usually make some sort of response immediately after an interpretation (as opposed to saying nothing), the actual effect of the attempt to offer an alternative point of view may not be realized by either client or counselor until later. The client may come back to the next session, after having given the new point of view some thought, and report that he/she wishes to explore that or other alternatives to the way he/she had been thinking.

Examples of Interpreting

Following are two brief client/counselor dialogues demonstrating the use of interpreting. After reading the examples, formulate an appropriate interpreting response for one of the examples.

Client: I couldn't let my son help me now that I'm down and out. I've got that shred of pride left—because, you see, I remember when he was a kid and I didn't turn my hand to help him. I traipsed around the country—his mother dies when the kid was born—and I let the relatives push him around and stick him in foster homes—and now . . .

Counselor: Your behavior in the past makes you feel embarrassed about the help your son wants to give you now, is that what you mean? (Reflection of Feeling)

Client: Yeah, yeah, I'm no good to him and then he wants to help me. I mean it felt like a knife stuck in me when we met the other day and he said, "We can make a go of it together, Dad—I've got a little money saved up." No, no, I won't let him do it. I will clear out of here. It'll be hard, but—I haven't done one thing for him, or anyone else for that matter.

Counselor: Sounds like your struggling with whether to leave or accept help from him. (Paraphrase)

Client: Yeah, I guess maybe I have always had this thing about not owing nothing to nobody and them not owing me nothing. But now I don't know—my son really seems to want to help me. I just don't know what to do.

Counselor: At this point you feel you don't deserve any help from your son, yet he seems to want to give it. Have you considered the possibility that maybe he doesn't hold the past against you and really loves you? (Interpreting)

Counselor: _____

_____

* *

Client: I keep remembering how I walked out on her and the kids. Five years ago—the law never did catch up with me—I thought I was pretty smart—but now—God, I was such a heel. I don't see how I could have done it.

Counselor: As you see it, your past behavior was pretty dreadful. (Paraphrase)

Client: Yeah, that's right. I'm so ashamed I can't look people in the eye. Now I can't find her—not a trace. Her relatives won't tell me where she is. I don't blame them—but how could I have hone it? Just because it was tough going. I tell you, I'll never have any self-respect.

Counselor: Sounds like you're feeling kind of hopeless and down now, but it also seems like you're feeling really guilty about your past. Have you thought that maybe she and the kids wouldn't want to see you after all these years and that your trying to find them is something you are doing to make you feel less guilty and not for their benefit? (Interpreting)

Counselor: _____

            _____

Summary of Interpreting

Interpreting is presenting the client with alternative ways of looking at his/her situation. It involves determining and restating the basic messages of the client, adding counselor ideas to this material for a new frame of reference, and checking out with the client the acceptability of the new point of view. Used effectively, interpreting should assist the client to realize that there is more than one way of viewing most situations and to help him/her apply this kind of unrestricted thinking to all aspects of his/her life.

Confrontation

Definition of Confrontation

Confrontation is the deliberate use of a question or statement by the counselor to induce the client to face what the counselor thinks the client is avoiding. The client's avoidance is usually revealed by a discrepancy or contradiction in his/her statements and behavior. Thus, confrontive responses point out discrepancies either within the client or in the client's interaction with the environment. In confrontation, the counselor frequently identifies contradictions that are outside the client's frame of reference, whereas paraphrasing, reflection of feeling, and summarizing involve responding within the client's frame of reference. In using confrontation, the counselor gives honest feedback about what he/she perceives is actually happening with the client. Confrontation should not include accusations, evaluations, or solutions to problems.

Purposes of Confrontation

1. It helps the client become more congruent (what he/she says corresponds with how he/she behaves) when the client sees how he/she is being perceived by the counselor.
2. It establishes the counselor as a role model in using direct, honest, and open communication.
3. It tends to focus on problems about which the client might take action or change his/her behavior.
4. It often breaks down the defenses of the client which he/she has consciously or unconsciously put up.
5. It tends to enrich the condition of empathy in the counseling relationship when the client perceives the confrontation as being done by a concerned counselor.
6. It encourages the client to acknowledge his/her feelings and behavior by bringing to the surface those he/she has denied. Once the client has accepted ownership of these feelings and behavior, he/she is more likely to accept responsibility for them.

Types of Discrepancies

A discrepancy or contradiction in the client is often a clue to the counselor that confrontation is indicated. A discrepancy or contradiction might be one of the following general types:

1. A discrepancy between how the client sees himself/herself and how others see him/her—for example, the client may describe himself as an outgoing, talkative person, but the counselor perceives the client as extremely quiet and reserved.
2. A contradiction between what the client say and how he/she behaves—for example, the client says she is not depressed, but she is talking slowly, sitting in a slumped posture, looking as if she is ready to cry.
3. A discrepancy between two statements by the client—for example, a client may say he wants to be treated for his drinking problem, but later says the only important thing to him is saving his driver's license.
4. A discrepancy between what the client says he/she is feeling and the way most people would react in a similar situation—

for example, a client may say that if his wife leaves he doesn't care if he ever gets to see his children again.

5. A contradiction between what the client is now saying he/she believes and how he/she has acted in the past—for example, a client may say she has no trouble staying away from the bottle, but she has had three slips in a month.

Using Confrontation Effectively

There are a few guidelines that the counselor should keep in mind when formulating a confrontive response. First, and perhaps more important, mutual trust and empathy must already be firmly established as part of the counseling relationship. Confrontation should come across as a positive and constructive act by a caring counselor, not as a negative and punitive act of a judgmental counselor. This attitude of empathy and caring can be transmitted not only by what the counselor says but also by his/her tone of voice and facial expression when the confrontive response is introduced into the session.

The counselor should also keep in mind that the most effective confrontive responses are those that address specific, concrete attributes of the client's behavior that the client can do something to change. It isn't very helpful to confront general behavior, for example, "You're always talking about changing your behavior, so why don't you do it?" An example of a specific confrontation would be, "You say you want to quit drinking, but what I see you doing is figuring out how to get a pint to get through the day."

Confrontation may be directed toward the client's assets (strengths) or his/her limitations (weaknesses). The counselor should be wary of always identifying contradictions that point up weaknesses in the client. Confrontive responses can be used constructively by focusing on strengths of the client. For example, to the client who expresses lack of confidence in his ability to handle stressful situations without drinking, the counselor might say, "Last time this happened you called me and did most of the work of sorting things out and deciding what to do."

In practical application, the confrontive response often takes the form of a compound statement that sets up a "you say . . ., but you do . . ." format. The second part of the statement points out the discrepancy or contradiction in the client's behavior or message. For example, "You say you don't want to see him again, but you go to places where you know he'll be." In using confrontation, then, the counselor listens to the client's feeling and content messages, observes the client's behavior, and presents evidence of a contradiction or discrepancy to the client.

Risks Involved in Confrontation

Because confrontation is an extremely powerful tool for the counselor to use, there are certain risks involved. Whenever the counselor becomes aware of a discrepancy or contradiction in the client's behavior or messages, the benefits of using confrontation must be weighed against the risks.

Risks to the Client—If trust and empathy have not been firmly established in the counseling relationship, the premature use of a confrontive response could harm the relationship. The client could become distrustful of the counselor or decide that the counselor cannot be of any help to him/her. The use of confrontation can be very threatening and anxiety-producing for the client, and if the proper conditions aren't there to begin with, it can damage or end the counseling relationship.

The use of confrontation may precipitate a crisis in the client's life. Especially if a client seems emotionally unstable about certain areas of his/her life, it might not be wise to confront him/her on those particular areas. For example, if a client has just been fired from his job and is very upset about it, the counselor should probably not confront him at that moment with his job performance.

Risks to the Counselor—Sometimes the counselor does not confront the client because the counselor is protecting himself/herself from risk. The counselor may be hesitant to point out a discrepancy for fear he/she might be wrong and would not be able to substantiate the contradiction to the client. Or the counselor might not like to deal with the extreme emotional reactions that could follow a confrontation. The counselor may not be comfortable with anger, anxiety, or tears. The counselor may pass over an appropriate confrontation situation because he/she would be uncomfortable if the usual defenses were dropped and thus wants to prevent the relationship from getting too close or intense.

In deciding whether to confront or not, the counselor must weigh the possible benefits to the client against the possible harm. In addition, if the counselor is hesitating to confront, he/she should ask himself/herself whether this reluctance is out of concern for the client or out of self-concern. If the counselor recognizes that the reluctance to confront is out of concern for himself/herself, the counselor should search himself/herself to see whether the cause of the apprehension is a legitimate concern, such as fear or physical harm from an intoxicated client, or whether it is a fear the counselor should try to resolve within himself/herself.

The Outcomes of Confrontation

If the counselor's confrontation has been effective, it could lead to exploration of previously blocked or denied feelings or behavior. In addition, an effective confrontation can often bring about a kind of breakthrough in the client's recognition that a behavior change is needed.

In practice, the counselor often may not know whether the confrontation has been effective or helpful until after several more exchanges in the session or until a later session. The client's immediate response to the confrontation sometimes does not indicate its effectiveness.

Frequently, the beginning counselor does not know what to do after he/she attempts a confrontive response. The following general guides might help:

1. If the client accepts the confrontation and agrees with the discrepancy pointed out, the counselor can use the opportunity to reinforce positive behavior. The counselor might say, "It's really a step in the right direction that you can recognize and accept this contradictory behavior so easily."

2. If the client denies the confrontation, the counselor is probably wisest to return to an empathic response, such as, "My even suggesting that seems to bother you a lot." The client may not be ready to deal with the discrepancy at that time and it would not be helpful to persist in the confrontation.

3. The client may simply act confused or ambivalent after a confrontive statement. In that case, the counselor could focus on the current feeling by saying, "You seem to feel confused by my saying that."

Examples of Confrontation

Two examples of client statements and possible confrontive responses follow. After reading the examples (a) indicate next to each response whether it is appropriate or poor confrontation and why, and (b) formulate another appropriate response for at least one example. In addition, indicate the type of discrepancy each example illustrates.

Client   (sitting with hands clenched, face muscles tight): I'm not really angry at my father for being a drunk. I mean he's been embarrassing me in front of my friends all of my life and I've gotten used to it.

Counselor: You say you're not angry, but right here as you talk about it I see you tensing up and looking upset.

_____

Counselor: You say you've gotten used to being embarrassed in front of your friends, but I don't think you really mean that.

_____

Counselor: You still seem angry about this to me and I think what you should do is go tell your father how you feel.

_____

Counselor: _____

_____

Discrepancy is between _____

and _____

* *

Client   (who has admitted past inability to abstain when "out with the boys"): I know I'm getting better. Yes sir, I'm going to be out there with the boys and it's not going to bother me at all when they're stopping for a beer.

Counselor: It's good to hear that you don't think that situation will bother you, but how does that statement fit in with the fact that you told me that you broke down and drank with them when they stopped last week?

_____

Counselor: You're not getting better at all; your past behavior shows you're a drunk and I guess you always will be.

_____

Counselor: You say that won't bother you, but from other things you've said I'm not sure you're convinced of that yourself.

_____

Counselor: _____

_____

Discrepancy is between _____

and _____

Summary of Confrontation

In confrontation, the counselor uses a question or statement to induce the client to face what the counselor thinks the client is avoiding. The counselor may, for example, point out discrepancies between the client's verbal and nonverbal behaviors, between two of the client's statements, or between the client's past behavior and his/her position or behavior in the counseling session. Used effectively, confrontation should help the client become more congruent and accept responsibility for his behavior. It can also reinforce the climate of trust, empathy, and genuineness in the counseling relationship. Because it is one of the most potent techniques the counselor can use, there are also some risks involved in using it. In deciding whether to use it or not, the counselor must determine whether the benefits of confrontation outweigh the possible harm to the client.

Bibliography

Brammer, L. *The Helping Relationship.* Englewood Cliffs, NJ: Prentice-Hall, 1973.

Crawford, J., Stancavage, F., and Jiminez, C. *Individual Counseling for Alcoholism Counselors, Participant's Manual.* Rockville, MD: National Institute on Alcoholism and Alcohol Abuse, 1975.

Gazda, G. *Human Relations Development: A Manual for Educators.* Boston: Allyn & Bacon, 1973.

Hackney, H., and Nye, S. *Counseling Strategies and Objectives.* Englewood Cliffs, NJ: Prentice-Hall, 1973.

Ivey, A., and Gluckstern, N. *Basic Attending Skills, Participant Manual.* Amherst, MA: Microtraining Associates, 1974.

_____. *Basic Attending Skills, Leader Manual.* Amherst, MA: Microtraining Associates, 1974.

_____. *Basic Influencing Skills, Participant Manual.* Amherst, MA: Microtraining Associates, 1976.

_____. *Basic Influencing Skills, Leader Manual.* Amherst, MA: Microtraining Associates, 1976.

Okun, B. *Effective Helping: Interviewing & Counseling Techniques.* N. Scituate, MA: Duxbury Press, 1987.

Shertzer, B., and Stone, S. *Fundamentals of Counseling.* Boston: Houghton-Mifflin, 1968.

Small, J. *Becoming Naturally Therapeutic: A Handbook on the Art of Counseling, with Special Application to Alcoholism Counselors.* Austin, TX: Texas Commission on Alcoholism, 1974.

31

Treatment of the Sex Offender

Ernest M. DeZolt
Peter C. Kratcoski

The concept of "sex offender" creates some difficulty in definition, because of the wide diversity of opinion and moral conviction as to what constitutes normal or acceptable sexual behavior. Researchers at the Kinsey Institute defined a sex offense as "an overt act committed by a person for his own immediate gratification which is contrary to the prevailing sexual mores of the society in which he lives, and/or is legally punishable; and results in his being legally convicted" (Gebhard, et al., 1965:8). In the past two decades, many activities which were defined as improper sexual behavior and subjected to criminal penalties became commonplace occurrences. Although premarital sexual activity, homosexual contacts, and dissemination of birth control information and devices to unmarried persons remained forbidden by statute in many jurisdictions, they were practiced with little fear of prosecution. However in a recent decision the U.S. Supreme Court upheld a Georgia law which prohibits oral or anal sexual contacts between persons (*Bowers v. Hardwick*, 1986).

In the past ten years, notable increases have occurred in the number of reported and prosecuted cases of rape and of sexual abuse of children. These increases have forced mental health professionals to reevaluate the skills and techniques applied when dealing with offenders involved in these and other sex related offenses. State criminal codes have been revised to specifically define sexual offenses and tie penalties attendant to their commis-

This article first appeared in *Correctional Counseling and Treatment*, Second Edition. All rights reserved.

sion. For example, the Ohio Revised Code (1983) classifies sexual offenses as sexual assaults and displays, prostitution offenses, and offenses related to the dissemination of obscenity and matter harmful to juveniles (§2907.02–2907.37). Prostitution and offenses related to the dissemination of obscenity and matter harmful to juveniles are generally penalized through the imposition of fines or short jail terms, and treatment is not a factor in the disposition of such cases. In contrast, the dispositions of cases involving sexual assaults and displays frequently include treatment. Such treatment may be mandated by the courts or offered as an option for the offender.

Offenses defined as sexual assaults and displays include:

Rape, broadly defined as sexual intercourse with females by force, including anal intercourse, cunnilingus, and fellatio. Included are homosexual and lesbian assaults, rape by drugging the victim, and rape as sexual conduct with a pre-puberty victim.

Sexual battery, defined as including sexual conduct by coercion, impaired judgment, or incestuous conduct between parent and child, stepparent and stepchild, a guardian and a ward, or a custodian or person "in loco parentis" with his or her charge. This category includes sexual conduct with a prisoner or hospital patient within an institution by a person with supervisory authority.

Corruption of a minor, defined as sexual conduct by an offender who is age eighteen or over who knows his or her partner is between the ages of 13 through 15.

Gross sexual imposition is analogous to rape, but involves less serious "sexual contact," including any touching of the erogenous zone of another for the purpose of sexually arousing or gratifying either person.

Sexual imposition includes sexual touching when the offender knows or has reasonable cause to believe the touching is offensive. This section of the code further forbids sexual contact when the victim is in early adolescence and the offender is age eighteen or over and four or more years older than the victim.

Importuning prohibits the soliciting of a person under thirteen years of age to engage in sexual activity, or when the solicitor is age eighteen or over and four or more years older than the person solicited.

Voyeurism prohibitions make it illegal to be involved in trespassing, invasion of privacy, and spying for the purpose of obtaining vicarious sexual thrill.

Felonious sexual penetration is the insertion of any instrument, apparatus or other object into the vaginal or anal cavity of another through compelling force, threat of force, or after impairing the other person's judgment through intoxicant, force or deception. (Ohio Criminal Code, as amended through June 30,1983 § 2907.2 through 2907.12).

While this list is not exhaustive, it represents the types of behavior which fall within the range of sexual assault and display offenses.

We noted earlier that the less serious types of sexual offenses may be ignored or punished with fines or short jail terms. However, when serious felonies of a sexual nature occur, several states have formulated laws which specifically designate the type and nature (determinate or indeterminate) of sentence which should be imposed, and even the type of facility where the offender should be housed.

While the vast majority of sexual offenders, if prosecuted and convicted, would be subject to the same types of sanctions and afforded the same treatment options as other offenders, in approximately half of the states statutes have been enacted that focus on the psychopathic sexual offender. Generally these statutes are based on the assumption that such an offender lacks the willpower to control his actions or impulses, is dangerous, and is likely to commit the same offense again if the opportunity arises. The laws are applied to offenders who are considered a serious threat to the community, notably rapists and child molesters. Although they vary in specifics, these statutes allow for commitment of the offender to a mental hospital or an institution for the criminally insane if a psychiatrist has ruled that the individual has the characteristics of a sexual psychopath. Once hospitalized or institutionalized, treatment is mandated for such an offender. The commitment can be for life, if the offender does not respond to treatment.

Washington's Sexual Psychopath Act (1975) provides for treatment in a state mental hospital for sex offenders who have been defined as sexual psychopaths. In such cases, the prosecutor files a petition alleging that the offender is a sexual psychopath who is predisposed to commit sexual offenses in a degree which constitutes a menace to the health and safety of others. After the offender is convicted, sentence is suspended while the offender undergoes a 90-day period of observation in a state mental hospital. If the diagnosis of sexual psychopathy is confirmed, the offender is committed to the hospital until the treatment staff decides that he or she should be released and the court accepts this judgment. The offender may be unconditionally discharged or placed under probation supervision for up to five years.

Sexual psychopath statutes and habitual offender statutes (which frequently are applied to sexual offenders) are grounded in the assumption that there are viable treatment programs which can change the behavior of these persons. In *Allen v. Illinois* (1986), the U.S. Supreme Court upheld an Illinois law providing for commitment to prison psychiatric wards of persons who had demonstrated propensities toward acts of sexual assault, and declared that the state is serving its purpose of treating rather than punishing such persons by committing them to institutions designed to provide psychiatric care and treatment. The fact that the prison psychiatric wards house convicted criminals as well as persons who have not been convicted of sexual offenses does not alter the fact that the state is sending them there with the intention to treat them, not to punish them (*Allen v. Illinois*, 1986).

Treatment is frequently mandated for rapists and offenders who have sexually abused children. Because such offenders present unique problems, their treatment will be the focus of this chapter. The characteristics and motivations of these offenders will be examined and programs which have been developed to treat them will be described.

Rapists—Typologies

Various typologies have been developed to examine the motivations and emotional processes of rapists. One classification, set by Groth, Burgess and Holmstrom, describes rapists in terms of four basic types:

> *The power assertive rapist* regards rape as an expression of his virility and mastery and dominance. He feels entitled to "take it" or sees sexual domination as a way of keeping women in line. The rape is a reflection of the inadequacy he experiences in terms of his sense of identity and effectiveness. . . .

> *The power reassurance rapist* commits the offense in an effort to resolve disturbing doubts about his sexual adequacy and masculinity. He wants to place a woman in a helpless, controlled position in which she cannot refuse or reject him, thereby shoring up his failing sense of worth and adequacy. . . .

> *The anger-retaliation rapist* commits rape as an expression of his hostility and rage toward women. His motive is revenge and his aim is degradation and humiliation. . . .

The anger-excitation rapist finds pleasure, thrills, and excitation in the suffering of his victim. He is sadistic and his aim is to punish, hurt, and torture his victim. His aggression is eroticized. (Groth, Burgess, and Holmstrom: 1977:1242)

In their study of 146 rape victims, these researchers concluded that approximately two-thirds of the offenses were power rape situations, and the remaining third were anger rape situations (1242).

Although a good deal of theory and research related to rapists has been developed, there is considerable confusion about the personality characteristics of the individuals who commit rapes. Some psychologists and sociologists view rape as essentially an act of violence. As a form of violent behavior, rape may be instrumental, that is, used as a means of gaining the rewards of prestige with peers, control over others, and mastery of situations. Many researchers' typologies of rapists support the notion that rape is widely used to make victims helpless, fearful, and totally under the rapists' control (Menachem, 1971; Macdonald, 1971). Such rapists may feel that their behavior will go unreported or unpunished, and this supposition is given some weight by research. In *The Crime and the Consequences of Rape* (1982), Dean and deBruyn-Kops report, on the basis of governmental and research sources, that many incidents of rape continue to be unreported and, of those reported to police, only 25% lead to arrest, while many charges are dropped or reduced to misdemeanors. They reported that only 20% of the offenders who go to trial for rape receive actual prison sentences.

Rape may also be interpreted as pathological behavior which reflects a morally defective personality. There may not be any meaning attributed to the act beyond attempting to satisfy the rapist's sexual needs. The degree of psychological abnormality attributed to the offender would determine whether treatment or punishment is in order.

For example, the *Diagnostic and Statistical Manual of Mental Disorders* (3rd ed.) lists compulsive rape under the sexual deviation category of paraphilia, and notes that sex offenses can be classified under various psychiatric conditions such as schizophrenia and manic depressive psychosis (1978:1–33). Treatment for a compulsive rapist, then, should be grounded in the assumption that this person is mentally ill.

Sex Abusers of Children—Typologies

Sexual abuse of children is regarded as a greatly underreported offense, and actual incidence may be as much as ten times the official reports (Elwell, 1979:227). Children may be abused through rape, sexual battery, gross sexual imposition, sexual imposition, or felonious sexual penetration. The female-to-male ratio of victims of sexual abuse is estimated to be 10 to 12 abused females for every male child abused, but there are indications that sexual abuse of male children is greatly underreported (Roth, 1978:3). Sexual offenses which involve family members (incest) are the least likely to be reported or fully prosecuted. There is evidence that a notable percentage of those involved in this activity were sexually abused themselves as children. Such persons tend to have been part of a disorganized lifestyle which also involved other forms of deviance and drug and/or alcohol abuse (Elwell, 1979:227–235).

The profile of an adult who sexually abuses a child is that of a young, heterosexual male, who is concerned with controlling, not injuring the young child. According to Krasner, et al., (1977:108) no force is used in 54% of all such incidents. Rosenfeld (1979) characterized the adult abuser as an individual who has experienced feelings of rejection or inadequacy and is emotionally estranged from his wife. The mother is often a key figure in the sexual abuse of female children. She may be aware that the child has assumed her sexual role and either does not protest this or even feels relieved about it. An American Humane Association study (1977:6–8) found that more than 10% of the mothers of sexually abused children had themselves been sexually abused as children. The assumption of the abused child of her mother's role may extend to taking over a good deal of the housework and care of the other children, as well as sexual contact with her father.

Gebhard and his associates at the Kinsey Institute, in a study of sexual offenders against children (1965) classified them as pedophiles (offenders who preferred sexual contact with children), sociosexually underdeveloped males (those who suffered from feelings of shyness and inferiority toward women), amoral delinquents (offenders who, when aroused, were apt to employ any convenient human or animal for gratification), mental defectives (who seek petting with children as much for attention and affection as for sexual gratification), psychotics, drunks, and senile deteriorates (characterized by deprivation, loneliness, and impotence) (216).

Issues in Treatment of Sex Offenders

Treatment modalities for rapists and other serious sexual offenders may involve three broad categories: psychosurgery-castration, drug therapy which produces "chemical castration," and counseling therapies. The use of psychosurgery-castration or drug therapy cannot be mandated without the offender's consent. An offender might agree to an operation or to use of a drug such as Depo-Provera, which reduces sexual drive and helps the offender control his sexual impulses, if a guaranteed reduction in sentence were offered as a trade-off. If an offender is diagnosed as suffering from a mental disorder, and if the offender is sentenced under a special section of the criminal code which mandates treatment, it is most likely that counseling therapies will be applied. However, even these cannot be undertaken without the offender'scooperation and consent.

Regardless of whether an offender's behavior is defined in a legal manner (by the type of act committed) or through psychological definition (emphasis placed on learned sexual deviation), once committed to an institution or hospital, the offender has the right to voluntary consent to treatment. Bohmer (1983) notes that: "Without consent from a subject, training professionals—and in some cases institutions, are technically liable for the charge of battery. At a minimum, the person to be treated should be given information about the basic nature of the treatment and the 'material risks' involved" (6). Material risks are defined by Schwitzgebel (1979) as information regarding a patient's position which a reasonable person would view as critical. He believes that information consists of six key elements: the diagnosis or purpose of the treatment, the nature and duration of the treatment, the risks involved, the prospects for success or benefits, possible disadvantages if the treatment is not undertaken, and alternative methods of treatment (6).

Mentally competent persons who have been involuntarily committed to hospitals or institutions have a right to refuse treatment. Their consent, or approval from the court, must be gained prior to beginning treatment. Although such patients have a right to treatment, they are not obliged to accept it. In contrast, mentally competent persons convicted of offenses generally do not have a legal right to refuse standard forms of treatment. However, there has been a trend toward establishing set procedures for obtaining consent from inmates prior to beginning treatment which might be termed "hazardous or exceptionally intrusive." Court decisions which have upheld a prisoner's right to refuse treatment have involved treatment which was considered "unreasonable or experimental" rather than treatment which met professionally recognized standards (Schwitzgebel, 1979:83).

Under Illinois state law, individuals may be committed to the psychiatric ward of a prison if they are proved to have a mental disorder for more than one year and had demonstrated propensities toward acts of sexual assault. Persons accused of being sexually dangerous must under law talk with state psychiatrists, who would evaluate their condition and make a determination whether these persons are mentally ill. If the determination is positive, they are housed in the psychiatric ward. In upholding the constitutionality of this law the Supreme Court noted: "The state serves its purpose of treating rather than punishing sexually dangerous persons by committing them to an institution expressly designed to provide psychiatric care and treatment." (*Allen v. Illinois*, 54 U.S. Law Week: 4966).

Another issue in the treatment of sex offenders is the return of the offender to the community. Although treatment is initiated in a hospital or institutional setting, decisions are made in many instances to gradually return sex offenders who show evidence of responding positively to treatment to the community through placement in group homes of furlough from the hospital or institution while treatment continues. Public concern about the effectiveness of treatment is sometimes coupled with a perception that offenders who have been hospitalized rather than institution-alized have escaped punishment for their misdeeds.

Avery-Clark described the trend for mental health practitioners to lobby for the placement of offenders who are suffering from psychiatric disorders directly related to their crimes in hospitals rather than in institutions. She noted that offenders who served time in hospitals usually had shorter stays than those with comparable offenses who had been institutionalized (1983:69). The concern of the local citizenry that serious sexual offenders who may still be "dangerous" are being released back into the community after a short stay in a mental hospital has resulted in movements to have legislatures establish new regulations which would require that the committing judge approve each release from a psychiatric facility. The judge's decision would be based on an evaluation of the sex offender by a psychiatrist appointed by the court.

Group Therapy for Sex Offenders in the Institutional Setting

Group therapy has been utilized as a treatment modality for rapists and sex offenders against children who have been com-mitted to institutions. Theorists (Groth, et al., 1982; Alford, et al., 1985) have suggested that these offenders commit their offenses because of personality adjustment problems. Their sexual offenses are manifestations of hostilities and anger resulting from unsolved life issues. The group therapy approach stresses the personal involvement of each offender in improving his or her interpersonal and social skills.

An institution based program which used group therapy was applied at the United States Disciplinary Barracks in Fort Leavenworth, Kansas. Twenty male inmates were divided into two groups: those who had committed sexual offenses against children, and those who had raped adults. The "sexual offenses against children" group met for one hour, once a week, for a year. The entrance guidelines for this group were based on the offender acknowledging his responsibility for the offense, understanding the inappropriate nature of the offense, having concern for the victim's response, and feeling distressed over his behavior (Groth, 1982:94).

The overall objectives of this group were reintegration of the offender's personality through the fostering of self-worth and development of interpersonal and social skills and impulse management. The actual treatment goals consisted of: keeping a written log of the issues and responses discussed in the group setting, writing an autobiography after three months in the program, developing better interpersonal skills in relating to women and forming expectation regarding women, dealing with the possibility that the offender had been a victim of sexual abuse as a child, and detecting impulses toward approaching a child with the need for sexual contact (Alford, et al., 1985).

The entrance guidelines for the rapist group were the same as those for the group of child sexual abusers. The rapist group was serviced by a male/female treatment team who "role modeled competency and self-confidence without putting each other down" (Alford, et al., 1985:84). The purpose of using the male/female team was to help break down the stereotypes of women internalized by the offenders. Therapy goals were developed through personal drawings with disclosure. Offenders were asked to draw pictures of themselves, parents, women, wives, and girlfriends, if applicable. Discussions followed in which the concepts of preference, self-image, expectations, power, control, and competition were evaluated. The offenders were asked to draw a picture of the woman they raped and compare her to the "ideal woman, wife, or mother" (Alford, 1985:84).

Both the child sex abusers and the rapists were pre- and post-tested on the Tennessee Self-Concept Scale (TSCS), which measured identity, self-satisfaction, behavior, physical self, moral-ethical self, personal self, family self, and social self (Alford: 1985). It was found that the rapists had shallow relationships with women, were possessive, lacked commitment, and had a fear of being rejected. The child molesters had a lower self-esteem of and a worse opinion of the act they committed than did the rapists. However, these opinions changed after the group therapy. Molesters were also more prone to become dependent on the therapist. Both groups relied heavily on sexual stereotypes in their relationships (Alford: 1985).

Group therapy has also been used successfully with mentally disordered sex offenders, who had been found guilty of felony sexual offenses. Not all types of mentally disordered offenders are candidates for such treatment. Excluded from participation are "psychotics, mentally retarded, legally insane, and otherwise incompetent offenders, such as those judged to stand trial by reason of insanity" (Annis, et al., 1984:428).

A program for treatment of mentally disordered sex offenders was operated at Florida State Hospital. It involved the treatment of twenty-five offenders ranging in age from 25 to 46. The group treatment involved offenders, therapists, and "victim workers," who had themselves been victims of sexual aggression. Each therapy session lasted 90 minutes, and the offenders were divided into groups of five to eight. Each "victim worker," along with one or two therapists, met with each group one to five times. The sessions involved exchange of information, culminating with the offenders detailing their sexual aggression against the victim. The group process often evolved into highly personal, often very intense, interactions with considerable disclosure by offenders and the "victim workers." (Annis, et al., 1984:430).

Approximately half of the offenders involved in this program were returned to court or prison for failure to gain from therapy, while the remaining half returned to the court or prison with a good report. The successful offenders usually received probation, reduced sentences, or assignment to a less restrictive correctional setting (Annis, et al.:428).

Evaluation of this program was accomplished through self-reports of offenders, therapists, and the "victim workers." These self-reports were administered before, during, and after the sessions, and by follow-up questionnaires. The offenders reported after completing the program that they believed they had helped educate the "victim workers" as to their human quality. They also reported that the program made them better able to share their feelings with women, improved their communication skills, gave them new perceptions of women as more than "objects," personalized their victims, and gave them a more accurate perception of society's perception of them (Annis, et al.:430–31).

The use of the "victim workers" in therapy for offenders was fairly unique. It was found that among forty-four rehabilitation programs serving incarcerated rapists, only four employed rape victims or those who work with survivors of sexual victimization in treatment roles (Annis, et al.:434). The use of victims in counseling other victims is widely applied through rape crisis centers and sexual abuse hotlines, and the possibility of their wider use in treating sexual offenders should be explored.

Behavior modification through group therapy was applied in the Missouri Sexual Offender Program. The philosophical foundation of this program was the belief that sexual offending is a learned behavior and therefore can be modified through a conscious awareness of personal behavior. The theoretical basis of the program is the supposition that when an offender assumes responsibility for his behavior and is given alternate social skills as reinforcement, socially acceptable behavior will result (Clark, 1986: 89).

The Missouri Sexual Offender Program involves two phases. During Phase I, the orientation, weekly two-hour classes were conducted to discuss the concept and the treatment with the offenders. The major possible consequence of failure to participate would be a delay in obtaining parole. After interviews, the offenders were classified as manipulative or aggressive, socially inadequate, or more average individuals who had exercised poor judgment and committed offenses as a result. A wide variety of testing instruments was also used, including the Minnesota Multiphasic Personality Inventory, the Norwicki-Strickland Personal Opinion Survey, the Rathus Assertiveness Scale, and the Anger Self-report Scale. Cognitive, affective, and behavioral disturbances specifically related to sexual concerns were evaluated with the Derogatis Sexual Functioning Inventory and the Thorne Sex Inventory (Avery-Clark, 1983). During Phase II, group therapy based on confrontative techniques, was used to heighten offender awareness regarding learned behavior. Phase II lasted 9 to 12 months with meetings held four hours each week. Evaluation of the program indicated statistically successful results.

Community Group Treatment for Sex Offenders

Community treatment of sex offenders raises the question of whether punishment or treatment should be the major purpose in dealing with sex offenders. One often overlooked benefit of community treatment of sex offenders is the possibility of educating the public regarding the existence of inappropriate sexual activity, its motivations, and the availability of treatment. State legislation in the late 1970s mandated community treatment for sex offenders. Atascadero State Hospital in California and Western State Hospital in Washington are the sites of innovative community treatment programs for sex offenders. At Atascadero State Hospital, the program begins with an orientation to educate offenders in the areas of sexual anatomy and physiology. Small group sessions are then employed to raise the offenders' level of awareness of the needs of others. Role playing is used, and college student volunteers, both heterosexual and homosexual, are brought in to assist offenders in learning to model behavior and gain assertiveness skills.

The therapy at Western State Hospital, in Washington, centers on group processing. MacDonald and Williams (1971) state the group treatment goals as awareness of problem behavior, understanding of treatment goals and expectations, acceptance of responsibility to change problem behavior, and the development of social skills to adopt new behavior patterns. In the first phase of the program, offenders' progress is measured in group living, work assignments, psychotherapy family and sexual relationships, social and recreational activities, and leadership ability. Once offenders successfully complete Phase I, they are granted work furloughs, but return to the hospital at night.

Unlike the community programs described above, which are housed in state hospitals, the Child Sexual Abuse Treatment Program (CSATP) operates in the community, funded by Santa Clara County, California. County probation officers intervene, in crisis situations involving child sexual abuse, and provide individual and family counseling. The therapy process emphasizes treatment of the involved family members separately, then as a family unit with a child, and, if necessary, marital therapy.

A group known as Parents United and a related group, Daughters United, share the counseling responsibilities with the probation officers by attending weekly meetings with the offenders similar to those held by Alcoholics Anonymous. Parents are forced to take responsibility for mistakes or oversights that led to incestuous patterns. Fathers must confront other mothers and fathers at the meetings regarding the abuse of their children. Offenders are not placed into the program until they admit and understand the seriousness of their actions. Those allowed to enter are given suspended sentences and then ordered by the judge to participate in this therapy as a condition of release to the community (Kiersh, 1980:33).

Characteristics of Effective Therapy for Sex Offenders

The counseling programs developed to treat sexual offenders, whether used in an institution, psychiatric hospital, or the community all seem to have a common theme. There is an assumption that the cause of the offense cannot totally be defined as a personality abnormality of the offender. If the offender is to change his behavior, the treatment must call for open, uninhibited communication with others who are affected by this person's behavior, including parents, spouse, other family members, or the victim. Group treatment seems to yield more positive results than individual counseling. If the group consists of offenders and counselors, the interaction may be initially characterized by dislike, distrust, aggressive behavior, insults, refusal to participate, or failure to identify with the other group members, but during the group process insights are gained. The topics and discussions during the meetings may vary tremendously, depending on the members andtheir needs.

VanNess, who supervised group therapy with violent sexual offenders over a number of years, lists the following matters as frequent topics of group discussions:

1. Being honest with yourself about the offense
2. Taking personal responsibility for your actions without blaming others
3. Understanding the laws and why you were sent to the institution
4. Understanding what happened to your victim
5. Dealing with your reputation in your community
6. Being honest with your family
7. Learning what makes you angry
8. Learning how to handle your anger
9. Learning to solve problems without using force
10. Chemical abuse and your offense
11. Building good relationships with people. (VanNess, 1983:14)

During the sessions, various techniques were used to illustrate situations which might arise with family members or institution staff. Role playing, discussions of films, and various exercises and games provided offenders opportunities for communication and learning.

VanNess identified certain patterns of behavior in the rapists' lives which have also been noted by other researchers. These included a lack of close personal relationships with other persons, particularly women, distrust of other males, a view of the world as a hostile and "dog eat dog" place, and conceptions of parents as givers or withholders rather than emotionally bonded persons. In their dealings with others, the rapists viewed power or force as the important element in relating to other persons, and had great difficulty in recognizing that men and women could treat each other as equals. In describing events which immediately preceded the rapes they committed, they invariably described some type of highly emotional incident which aroused their anger (VanNess: 1983:16).

Robinson A. Williams, who served as Assistant Director of the Treatment Center for Sexual Offenders at Western State Hospital, regarded abnormal sexual behavior as a learned method of relieving emotional stress. He maintained that sexual attacks or contacts become habitual ways of finding emotional release for offenders who feel inadequate and insecure in their relationships with women. He noted that sex offenders frequently have experienced troubled childhoods and may themselves have been victims of sexual abuse as children (Denenberg, 1974:58).

Group therapy is beneficial for sex offenders because it provides a setting in which they can relate to fellow sex offenders and feel that they will understand their problems. As the group encourages the offender to reveal his inner conflicts and fears, he becomes aware of the motivations for his offenses and begins to recognize that he must change his behavior. The group provides constant support during this awareness experience. Various steps are established, which give the offender opportunities to take more responsibility for his actions. The steps usually involve increasing degrees of physical freedom to move about the institution or the grounds and acceptance of responsibility for the activities of the group.

Most of the group therapy programs which have some demonstrated success with sex offenders appear to follow the general outlines of the technique known as rational-emotive therapy. This therapy, developed by Ellis in the 1950s, identifies irrational thinking and erroneous belief systems as the roots of problems, and involves a process of reeducation by which the person being treated acquires a more rational and tolerant view of life. The therapist functions as a teacher who leads the offender to understand how his outlook has contributed to his self-defeating behavior and how to begin to behave rationally. The group plays a key role in leading the offender to critically examine his beliefs and behavior and work to change them. The eclectic approach involved may include probing, confrontation, challenging, behavior contracts, role playing, hypnotherapy, assertiveness training, and many other techniques. Encounter groups, marriage and family therapy, and sex therapy may be used. Rational-emotive therapy is most effective with persons who are not seriously emotionally disturbed, and, because of its emphasis on the thinking process, it is unlikely to be successful for persons of limited intelligence (Corey, 1982:96–97).

References

Alford, Jane M., Gary E. Brown and James C. Kasper, 1985. "Group Treatment for Sex Offenders," *Corrective and Social Psychiatry and Journal of Behavioral Technology Methods and Treatment*, 31(3): 83–86.

Allen V. Illinois, 1986. *U.S. Law Week*: 4966

Annis, Lawrence V., Leigh G. Mathers and Christy A. Baker, 1984. "Victim Workers As Therapists for Incarcerated Sex Offenders," *Victimology: An International Journal*, 9(3–4): 426–435.

Avery-Clark, Constance A., 1983. "Sexual Offenders: Special Programatic Needs," *Corrections Today*, 45(5): 68–70.

Bohmer, Carol, 1983. "Legal and Ethical Issues in Mandatory Treatment: The Patient's Rights versus Society's Rights," In *The Sexual Aggressor*, Joanne Green and Irving R. Stuart (Eds.). New York: Van Nostrand Reinhold Company.

Bowers v. Hardwick, 1986. 54 *U.S. Law Week*: 4919.

Clark, Marie, 1986. "Missouri's Sexual Offender Program," *Corrections Today*, 48(3): 84–86.

Corey, Gerald, 1982. *Manual for Theory and Practice of Counseling and Psychotherapy*, 2nd ed., Monterey, CA: Brooks/Cole Publishing Company, 1982.

Dean, Charles and Mary deBruyn-Kops, 1982. *The Crime and the Consequences of Rape*. Springfield, IL: Charles C. Thomas.

DeFrancis, Vincent, 1977. "American Humane Association Publishes Highlights of National Study of Child Neglect and Abuse Reporting for 1975," Washington, D.C.: U.S. Department of Health, Education and Welfare, National Center on Child Abuse and Neglect, Publication OHD 77-20086:6–8.

Denenberg, R. V., 1974. "Profile/Washington State, Sex Offenders Treat Themselves," *Corrections Magazine*, 1(2): 53–64.

Diagnostic and Statistical Manual of Mental Disorders, 3rd ed., 1978. Washington, D.C.: Task Force on Nomenclature and Statistics of the American Psychiatric Association: L1–L33.

Elwell, M. E., 1979. "Sexually Assaulted Children and Their Families," *Social Casework*, 60(4): 227–235.

Gebhard, Paul H., John H. Garnon, Wardell B. Pomeroy and Cornelia V. Christenson, 1965. *Sex Offenders: An Analysis of Types*. New York: Harper & Row.

Groth, A. N., A. W. Burgess and L. L. Holmstrom, 1977. "Rape: Power, Anger, and Sexuality," *American Journal of Psychiatry*, 134: 1239–43.

Groth, A. N., W. F. Hobson and T. Gary, 1982. "The Child Molester: Clinical Observations," In *Social Work and Child Sexual Abuse*. New York: Haworth Press.

Kiersh, Edward, 1980. "Can Families Survive Incest?" *Corrections Magazine*, 6(2): 31–38.

Krasner W., Linda C. Meyer and Nancy E. Carroll, 1977. *Victims of Rape.* Washington, D.C.: U.S. Government Printing Office, 1977.

MacDonald, G. J. and R. T. Williams, 1971. "A Guided Self-help Approach to Treatment of the Habitual Sex Offender," Fort Steilacoom, Washington: Western State Hospital.

Macdonald, John M., 1971. *Rape Offenders and Their Victims.* Springfield, IL: Charles C. Thomas.

Menachem, Amir 1971. *Patterns in Forcible Rape.* Chicago: University of Chicago Press.

Ohio Criminal Law Handbook, 3rd ed., 1983. Cincinnati: Anderson Publishing Company.

Rosenfeld, Alvin A., 1979. "Endogamic Incest and the Victim-Perpetrator Model," *American Journal of Diseases of Children,* 133:406–410.

Roth, R. A., 1978. *Child Sexual Abuse—Incest Assault and Sexual Exploitation,* A Special Report from the National Center on Child Abuse and Neglect. Washington, D.C.: U.S. Department of Health and Human Services.

Schwitzgebel, R. Kirkland, 1979. *Legal Aspects of the Enforced Treatment of Offenders.* Washington: U.S. Department of Health, Education and Welfare.

Smith, Alexander B. and Louis Berlin, 1981. *Treating the Criminal Offender,* 2nd ed. Englewood Cliffs, NJ: Prentice-Hall.

VanNess, Shela R., 1983. "Rape as Instrumental Violence: A Perspective for Theory, Research and Corrections," paper presented at the annual meeting of the Academy of Criminal Justice Sciences, San Antonio, Texas.

Vetter, Harold J. and Ira J. Silverman, 1986. *Criminology and Crime.* New York: Harper & Row.

Washington Sexual Psychopath Act, 1975. Wash. Rev. Code Ann. 71.06.010 Seq. (1975).

32

Northwest Treatment Associates
A Comprehensive, Community-Based Evaluation and Treatment Program for Adult Sex Offenders

Fay Honey Knopp

Northwest Treatment Associates (NWTA) is a partnership of five practitioners[1] who collectively have 50 years of full-time experience in the treatment of sex offenders. Since 1977, in their attractive, three-story converted house, Steven Silver, Timothy A. Smith, Steven C. Wolf, Roger W. Wolfe, and Florence A. Wolfe have provided what is believed to be one of the largest and most comprehensive outpatient sex-offender evaluation and treatment programs in the United States. At any given time, approximately 200 men (and a few women) are involved actively in weekly or twice-weekly treatment in two locations.[2] Nonoffending spouses and other family members also participate in the treatment program.

More than 85 percent of NWTA's clients are attached to the criminal justice system through either court-ordered evaluations or sentences of probation with conditions of treatment.[3] Since probation provides very few treatment subsidies, NWTA's clients are mainly white and middle class.[4] "Probation views treatment as a privilege," says Roger Wolfe (1981b). "If they want community treatment, they have to work for it." The average period of time spent in treatment is 18 months, though a few stay longer. Most felony offenders are on five years' probation.

Fee schedules are on a sliding scale. They range from $40 to $70

Reprinted by permission of Safer Society Press from: *Retraining Adult Sex Offenders: Methods and Models* by Fay Honey Knopp (Orwell, VT: Safer Society Press, 1989), pp. 85–101.

for individual treatment and $13 to $23 for two-hour sessions. On each therapist's caseload, NWTA usually subsidizes at least three particularly hard-working and well-motivated clients who do not have adequate funds to purchase treatment.

Evaluation and Assessment

The majority of the people accepted into the program "graduate" or complete treatment. The reason for this comparatively low dropout rate is the selection of clients prior to treatment. Like most community-based programs, NWTA excludes individuals from treatment if they show patterns of overt physical violence, if they show an extensive history of nonsexual crimes, if they are assessed as being psychotic or suffering from severe mental illness, if they have serious substance abuse problems, if they are identified as "grossly inadequate," or if they have poor motivational levels and counterproductive attitudes that prevail despite modeling, education, and confrontation during the assessment process (R. Wolfe, 1981a, 1984).

Roger Wolfe and his colleagues, like other experienced sex-offender treatment specialists, are justifiably skeptical and often distrustful of their clients' historical perceptions of the sexually aggressive behavior that led them to their present situation. To test a client's perceptions of the behavior for which he was convicted, staff use a polygraphist with an extensive history of working with sex offenders. Staff recount, not without humor, some standard staff responses to the traditional amnesia and shadowy memories of their clients during evaluation and assessment, particularly when the polygraph has indicated that the client was involved in defensive lying:

> I have this kind of standard approach I take and it is usually effective. When a sex offender comes in and I question him about the allegations against him and his perception of them, he may say: "Well, I really don't remember if I did—but it really happened all at once and I've never thought about it before, it never entered my mind before—it was just totally spontaneous" —etcetera. I then go into my old philosopher stance, lean back in my chair, and kind of squint my eyes and say, "Y'know—I guess I believe you. If you really are the way you are representing yourself—a person who just spontaneously with no forethought raped this kid—it says to me that you are so incredibly danger-ous, you should not be on the street even this afternoon. In fact, I'm going to call the cops right now . . ." Then there's a quick

turn around. "Well . . . I suddenly remember very clearly . . ."
(S. Wolf, 1981)

Another client said he remembered his offense but "just had these brief flashes. I'm there with this kid—she's a nameless, faceless figure, and I remember trying to insert my penis, but she is only a five year old . . ." We worked on that for three or four sessions, to no avail, and then I told him we could not continue to treat him. The primary criterion for working with anybody in the community is you have to have honesty. A good client—a really honest client—is going to give us, at most, *maybe* 75 percent honesty. (R. Wolfe, 1981b)

Evaluation and assessment include psychological testing,[5] physiological monitoring via the plethysmograph (also used for monitoring treatment progress), and a period spent in one of the ongoing, guided sex-offender groups. A person under evaluation must obtain unanimous group and treatment-team sanction on four basic issues: (1) that he believes he is a sexual offender; (2) that he strongly desires specialized intervention; (3) that he will be helpful to others in their process of accomplishing similar goals; and (4) that he has demonstrated change in and outside the treatment setting.

Treatment Modalities

The NWTA treatment program consists of two major components: a confrontive, guided-group model modified for community use, and a range of behavioral treatment approaches.[6] Roger Wolfe is a strong advocate for treatment eclecticity:

Behavioral treatment is very important, but not sufficient by itself. We need both group and individual counseling to deal with the offender's characterological problems. I think a great many treatment programs exaggerate the importance of one or the other approach. I am firmly convinced you have to have both. Above all, you need individual assessment and careful, individual treatment planning for each person. It is a great deal of work. (R. Wolfe, 1981b)

Staff at NWTA are aware that one of their most important tasks is to help their clients to develop appropriate sexuality. Sexual reorientation is provided for those men who have no appropriate sexual arousal system or history. Marital counseling, sexual enhancement, and treatment for sexual dysfunction also are provided where appropriate. Says Florence Wolfe (1981), "Many of our clients have poor social skills[7] and no orientation to appropriate sexuality. We help them go through all the steps to establish their own relationships.''

Guided Sex-Offender Group

The guided sex-offender group at NWTA is a modified version of the one developed in Western State Hospital's Sex Offender Program.[8] Honesty is a program requirement, so the model is extremely confrontive. The men are expected to challenge directly any rationalization and character traits that make offending easier. The group also provides an arena for education, support for prosocial behavior, and positive role modeling.

Steven Silver, who facilitates the majority of the groups at NWTA, perceives his role as both teacher and therapist. He structures specific written and experiential situations for the men to explore. Silver, a nontraditional group therapist, is a powerful, conscious model of a nondeviant male. Though a highly skilled veteran of group process and therapy with traditional mental health patients, none of these experiences prepared him adequately for running a sex-offender group. He developed his expertise by working with offenders for 12 years and through studying the relevant literature. In describing his NWTA stance, he says,

> It is confrontive and challenging. It is insisting that behavior be totally honest and responsible. I tell our clients, "I may act like a teacher, but this is not a class. It is group therapy and every one of you has a very serious disorder." It is emphasized that the behavior has been seriously abusive and that there is certainly the potential for subsequent dangerous behavior.
>
> If you tolerate one guy minimizing what he did, four weeks later he will come back and he will have minimized it, accepted it, and be sliding backward. It is important, however, to allow the offender room to blame, rationalize, and in other ways misrepresent people and circumstances; otherwise a therapist will obtain lip service compliance without behavioral or characterological change. The offender needs to believe that his side has at least been heard.
>
> This is the hardest group therapy that has ever been structured, because the sex-offenders' therapist has to take the responsibility for ensuring that, when these men walk out of the door, they are not going to reoffend. (Silver, 1981)

In group therapy at NWTA, the offender's character pathology that facilitates sexual offending and other destructive behaviors is brought into awareness, challenged, and gradually replaced with prosocial attitudes, traits, and behaviors. Traits such as impulsivity, manipulation, dishonesty, sexual preoccupation, low frustration tolerance, denial, and deviousness are among those focused upon. The offender must take full responsibility for the harmfulness and severity of the offense. He learns preoffense warning signs (emotional, cognitive, physical, and environmental antecedents) and internal and external controls over impulses and behaviors, and he structures his life to minimize the possibility of reoffense. Learning in group occurs through confrontation, modeling of appropriate behavior, discussion, assignments, experiential exercises and lectures given by people in the field, for example, a counselor for sexually abused children. The client must complete a long series of assignments including assigned texts and pass a comprehensive written examination and a polygraph test prior to any consideration for program completion. All assignments and exercises are offender focused; the client must understand thoroughly his offending cycle and demonstrate by living a positive, prosocial lifestyle that he is willing and able to make the necessary changes (Wolfe & Wolfe, 1984).

If a person reoffends while in the group (almost always these reoffenses are misdemeanors such as exhibitionism and voyeurism), he may be taken back on a provisional basis, depending on the combined decision of probation and NWTA staff. If he does come back, Silver explains,

> I think reaccepting him depends on the level of the offense, how it came to light, and the client's attitude about it and treatment. If an exhibitionist reoffends against an adult, you are going to be considerably more tolerant than if a child molester reoffends. It also depends on how long a person has been in the program. If he has been in the group a significant length of time and reoffends, it means there is a great deal of information regarding offense-related patterns and controls that he is keeping a secret. And there must be lots of things he has not been doing, a lot of cons and scams he has been running and getting away with. It speaks to a continued pattern of deviance and to trying to "beat" treatment. (Silver, 1981)

The average length of stay in treatment groups is 18 months, during which certain tasks must be accomplished. Individuals are evaluated periodically by both their fellow group members and the treatment team. The therapist is present at all group sessions to guide, monitor, and assist the offenders in their process.

Following graduation, a client is encouraged to return to the group at any time, for any reason at no charge. If a client begins to feel himself returning to his deviant pattern or if his family notices some slipping, there is no excuse for not returning and seeking further help.

Behavioral Treatment

Sex-offender clients are given an introductory explanation of the basic principles of behavioral treatment and assigned readings to familiarize them further with the approaches. The men go to their local library, find the readings, do the prescribed work, and bring it back to NWTA.

The behavioral treatment is geared toward reducing and/or eliminating the deviant sexual arousal, which staff believe provides a major motivation for the offender's behavioral pattern. The initial step in treatment is bringing the overt behavior under control:

> Sex-offender behavior is conditioned on a very basic level—sexual arousal. The individual has a long history of carrying out that particular behavior, paired with immediate gratification. A large chunk of that is sexual gratification, but a great many other things go along with that, too. Adrenalin rush, getting away with something, escaping from discomfort or boredom—these often are overlooked. The sex offense gives the offender something to focus on as an escape from tedium, problems, anxiety, and frustration. We are talking about the immediate application of a strong, powerful package of rewards. Our theory is, if you are going to deal with the compulsive nature of that behavior, you are going to have to do some counterconditioning. (R. Wolfe, 1981b)

This procedure involves pairing the deviant behavior and its antecedents with ungratifying, negative results. It also means encouraging nondeviant behavior and pairing it with positive reinforcers.

In the case involving an incest offender, for example, Roger Wolfe might use the following scenario to pair negative imagery with the offender's deviant behavior:

> Imagine you are walking into your daughter's room. You are pulling back the covers, feeling very excited, very aroused. You are reaching down, picking up her nightie. You've touched her, your hand is covered with pus, you can smell the overwhelming stench, you brush your hand against your clothes, the pus is smeared against your clothes, the stench is really making you nauseous, you feel like you have to throw up, you taste the sweet, sickly bile in the back of your throat. . . . (and so forth).

There are many other procedures commonly used by NWTA staff. First we will describe briefly six approaches to teaching impulse control. Next we describe, in greater detail, behavioral methods aimed at reducing deviant arousal and/or increasing appropriate arousal. These include covert sensitization, covert positive reinforcement, masturbatory reconditioning, boredom aversion, and the modified aversive behavioral rehearsal technique. Last, we examine a variety of techniques used in teaching victim empathy.

Simple Impulse-Control Techniques. The methods described here are among the simplest, most concise, and least intrusive interventions taught to the offender to assist him in controlling ongoing impulses. They are considered "bandaids" in that they are short-term pragmatic attempts to preclude reoffense until more long-term modalities can have an impact.

1. *Thought-stopping*[9] is used to disrupt a deviant thinking pattern. An example is given of a heterosexual pedophile walking down the street and noticing a little girl. His eyes may wander to her buttocks. He begins to think how beautiful and little they are. "We want him to stop those thoughts, to block them out," explains Roger Wolfe. "Thought-stopping, simply stated, is to have the offender scream at the top of his lungs— 'STOP'—*inside* his head. It disrupts that thought" (R. Wolfe, 1981b).

2. *Thought-shifting* to aversive imagery is equally simple. The pedophile, for example, sees a little girl and finds himself starting to dwell on her. Immediately he must try to think of something aversive. For instance, he imagines a police officer walking up behind him, tapping him on the shoulder, and saying, "I know what you are up to," then kneeing him in the groin and calling in the neighbors to deal with "the local pervert." Realistic aversive imagery disrupts arousal and deviant thought processes and applies a punishment to those behaviors. The probability of reoffense is diminished.

3. *Impulse-charting* is a method used to help the offender to focus on what is going on in his thinking and acting patterns. NWTA gives the client little cards that list the days of the week. After the offender controls an impulse, he records a number from one to 10 that indicates the intensity of that impulse and the difficulty he had in controlling it.[10] "It gives them something to do that takes them one step further away from offending," says Roger Wolfe. "It also gives us an ongoing measure that we can quantify in terms of the strength and frequency of his impulses. We get some idea of how well the person is doing, how good our techniques are, and how well they are working. If his impulses are not decreasing, we had better go back to the drawing board and come up with a new approach" (R. Wolfe, 1981b).

For people having greater difficulty controlling their impulses, or for someone who raises suspicion that he might be on the brink of reoffending, the program utilizes stronger, more intrusive types of controls. These are most appropriate for chronic child molesters or exhibitionists, the clients who usually are the most out of control.

1. *Scheduled overmasturbation* simply places the client on an escalating masturbation schedule, timed by the clock. The frequency of masturbation is increased steadily to reduce sexual drive and thus make it easier to control. "This exercise also gives him a measure of control over his sexuality," says Roger Wolfe (1981b), "since he is used to masturbating willy-nilly. Care is taken that he is utilizing appropriate imagery."

2. *Spouse monitoring* involves asking the spouse or significant other to give the program feedback in terms of how the offender is doing,[11] by signing the checklist of tasks and homework to be completed by the client and by monitoring his behavior. Spouse monitoring is used with nearly all clients.

3. *Environmental manipulation* helps to get the offender out of situations that are high risk for him and his potential victims. For instance, with an incest or pedophile offender, one of the standard procedures is to have him move himself right out of the house, as opposed to taking the victim out of the house and doubly victimizing him/her. Other examples provided by Roger Wolfe (1981b) are practical and creative:

> These are all basic, common-sense approaches that work. Here are some examples we have used with exposers. One person had a great many impulses to expose while he was aimlessly cruising around town. We told him he can no longer cruise, but he must have a specific destination, he must call his friend and tell him to meet him at a designated place at a specific time. In group we changed the time a guy jogged, where he jogged, the way he drove to work, the way he drove home from work, and what he does on Sunday afternoons in football season. These were all situations where he had flashed. One of the most creative kinds of things we do with flashers who exhibit in their cars is to have them put their names on the front, back, and sides of the car. Also, we had one fellow who was a jogger and who flashed while he was jogging. We had him get a T-shirt with his name on it.

If these impulse-control measures are not effective, Depo-Provera may be prescribed.

Covert Sensitization.[12] Approximately 10 weeks of treatment are devoted to covert sensitization. Conditioning sessions are audio-taped, and the 40-minute tape is sent home with the client, who is instructed to listen to it daily. Monitoring by spouses or significant others and quizzing for content make compliance more likely.

Tapes also typically include covert positive reinforcement of alternatives to deviant behaviors (such as not responding to deviant stimulus situations, assertiveness, appropriate sexual behavior, and so forth). In the early sessions, the therapist constructs the tape; later, the client takes over this task, with the therapist serving as a consultant. After 10 weeks, additional elements are included in conditioning tapes.

Staff describe graphically how covert sensitization is used. First, the therapist induces a relaxed phase for about five to fifteen minutes, depending on how well trained and adept the client is in being able to drift down into a relaxed state where he can get good imagery.[13] Next he is given instructions that he is going to focus on the upcoming scenes and they are going to seem very real. The therapist then begins a description of a scene, tailor-made for the client, constructed from a fear inventory of about 175 items, from which the client has chosen those that are most fearful to him.

> We first start with a written checklist and then explore other things they are very afraid of—a bad experience where they nearly drowned, an automobile accident, a particular horror movie that really scared them—all their most relevant and immediate fears. Usually these men are fresh from their court experience, so we do all sorts of marvelous scenes about being taken down to the police station and what the judge said to them. The more impact the better, is the general rule. What you are after is finding the images that produce a strong reaction. (R. Wolfe, 1981b)

Roger Wolfe describes how one person's fear of snakes was paired with a scene reflective of his deviant pattern:

> You are restless. It is about three o'clock in the morning and you cannot sleep. You tell yourself you are going to go to the bathroom. You get up, you go to the bathroom, you urinate, and you continue to stand there. You are thinking, "Little Sally is sleeping in the room next door." You tell yourself. "Maybe I'd better check on her just to see if she kicked her covers off or something." As you are thinking that, you kind of put your hand down on your penis and you feel your excitement. You tell yourself, "She is sound asleep—she won't know if I was in there or not." You go up to her door, telling yourself she is sound asleep and you are just going to check on her, feeling sexual excitement, thinking about touching her, thinking you will just slip up her nightgown a little bit and maybe just look at her, and getting more excited. You are thinking about doing that, with your hand on the doorknob, getting really excited now, really turned on, and you gently, carefully, being really quiet, open that door, you open that door thinking about touching

her . . . and you suddenly realize there is something on the floor. There is something moving on the floor in the bedroom. My God, my God, you say—it is a snake! There is more than one. There are creepy crawly snakes all over and you can see their little forked tongues, see their beady eyes. They are moving toward you. You are just terrified standing there, you want to run, but you are just scared. A cold chill runs up and down your body. Your body gets tight. They are moving toward you. God, these cold slimy snakes are moving toward you. One of them is on your toe now . . . (R. Wolfe, 1981b)

The client, in an induced state, hears the scene for the first time at NWTA. Then he writes the scene down in his own words, monitored by his spouse or friend. A week later the client returns and guides the therapist through the scene. The therapist will check the client's memory at various points and ask for a self-report on what the impact of the tape has been.

"For instance," says Roger Wolfe, "I may ask him, at the place where his hand is on the doorknob, to tell me what he is feeling when he is home listening to the tape. Can he feel the coldness and hardness of the knob? Can he see the shadows of his own hallway? I'm trying to pick up how clear the imagery is" (R. Wolfe, 1981b). Wolfe also asks for bodily reactions to the scene. "When he says, 'That snake really scares me,' I say, 'What is your body doing?' I should hear things like 'My throat is dry, I am swallowing, my stomach flutters, and I have increased heart beat.'"

Some other measures of treatment impact are self-report of deviant impulses, plethysmograph assessment, and polygraph examination.

Covert Positive Reinforcement. The last two scenes on the tape will pair appropriate behavior with cognitive and material rewards. There are many approaches that can be used. One scene involves the offender just leaving a situation that is typical of his deviant pattern, where he would have had high impulses and temptations and could have reoffended. The scene would place him safely away from such temptations, and he would realize, "I didn't even think about it. By God, that feels really good. Hey, I'm more normal; all that work I am putting in—it is paying off." The tape would provide a material reward by having him drive home and find a letter telling him he had just been granted a job promotion.

A second approach involves an element of cognitive restructuring.[14] In this scenario, the sex offender starts repeating some of the excuses he typically has used himself. For instance, he might say, "Well it won't hurt, she's asleep, she likes it anyway, this is a good way for her to learn about sex." Then, instead of continuing this pattern, suddenly he thinks, "That's a bunch of bullshit! In fact, the reality is, it is harmful, it does hurt people, it is not okay. I don't care if she is asleep or not asleep—that is invading her privacy and that's being damaging and harmful."

Another approach, Roger Wolfe explains, is to take a range of the client's most positive behaviors and reinforce them by loading the end with rewards.

> For instance, you can walk a client through a scene where he is behaving assertively and pair that up with having him sit down in a restaurant where the waiter brings him some marvelous beefsteak. You can smell the aroma, you can see the juices kind of flowing from the steak, and there are mushrooms on top, and french fries, and so forth. The rationale for loading the end with rewards is that we want him to take the whole tape and come out of the experience feeling pretty good about himself. If he comes out of the tape feeling pretty good, it is that much easier for him to go back and do the tape again. If you do just total punishment, the client gets phobic about doing the tape. Scenes are changed with each tape to minimize adaptation and maximize generalization. (R. Wolfe, 1981b)

As mentioned earlier, the therapist makes the first few conditioning tapes and then encourages the client to construct his own. This process of gradually shifting responsibility is an integral part of NWTA's therapeutic plan:

> I think this kind of self-help approach is reflective of our total treatment philosophy. We want to train the individual to change his own behavior. We want him to become his own behavioral therapist. By the time he leaves here he should be as good as we are, if not better, in terms of dealing with his own specific problem. We learn a great deal from the types of tapes he makes. He gets into much more when he is sitting on his own with that tape recorder. The clients do an amazingly good job. We could work with them for years and years, but they know more about their patterns than we do, they know more about what turns them off than we do, and they know more about what turns them on than we do. (R. Wolfe, 1981b)

Masturbatory Reconditioning[15] *and Boredom Aversion.*[16] Staff have combined and adapted the technique of masturbatory reconditioning and boredom aversion to function within outpatient, part-time treatment. The positive masturbatory reconditioning involves having the client masturbate to an appropriate fantasy, until he has an ejaculation. Roger Wolfe points out the need for therapist monitoring:

> Their perceptions of what is an appropriate fantasy are incredible. We have had clients come in with their initial tapes

and say "I had a wonderful appropriate fantasy," and it turns out to be a tape describing what is essentially a rape! Many men in our male culture wouldn't graduate from our groups.

We have the clients focus on the antithesis of offending, that is, on warmth, caring, affectional, close, intimate human aspects of sexuality. We stress the sensual and erotic as well. When they are making their tapes, we want them to throw in lots of adjectives about warm and close, and a lot of respect for the female, what she is wanting, doing, and feeling. They focus on her feelings and responses and on their own feelings and responses. The woman should come across as a person and not a blow-up rubber doll. (R. Wolfe, 1981b)

Staff help the men develop appropriate fantasies. Their assignment at home is to verbalize the fantasy into a tape recorder while masturbating to ejaculation four to seven times a week. "The point is we want to reinforce—through the powerful mechanism of masturbatory conditioning—appropriate sexuality, and not only appropriate sexuality, but the antithesis of sexual offending where you have to make your victim a piece of meat," says Roger Wolfe (1981b).

The boredom-aversion technique is used by the offender after ejaculating to appropriate fantasies. Then he turns the tape cassette over and verbalizes 45 continual minutes of a series of his deviant sexual fantasies.[17] He must continue his fantasies for 45 minutes and cannot turn off the tape recorder until he fills up the whole side with no pauses and no blanks.

We try to have the individual repeat the full fantasy including antecedent conditions (emotional, environmental, physiological, and mental precursors). The actual sexual behavior and the immediate consequences, such as transitory feelings and his methods of resolving them (the false promise), are included. When he completes one fantasy, he begins another. (R. Wolfe, 1981b)

The Modified Aversive Behavioral Rehearsal Technique (MABRT). The MABRT, using mannequins and videotape, is a technique developed for systematically controlling deviant sexual expression in pedophiles and exhibitionists. It was adopted by NWTA's Timothy Smith and borrows many of the components of Aversive Behavioral Rehearsal (Wickramasekera, 1980). Mannequins have been used previously for assessment of sex offenders, where it was found that interacting with a "humanlike" figure elicited behavior not previously reported by the offender (Forgione, 1974).

This technique involves a client in re-enacting his sexual assault on a mannequin that is representative of the age and sex of his victims. This scene is videotaped[18] and viewed by the client, his significant other, and his treatment group. This very close simulation, including even the actual motor behaviors, is paired with powerful negative emotions that the client experiences in this situation. On a cognitive level, the client is confronted with the harmfulness, outrageousness, and absurdity of his rationalizations, feelings, and behaviors. "Sharing with others the impactful, visual depiction of his deviance is a greatly magnified mode of self-disclosure," says Roger Wolfe (Wolfe & Wolfe, 1984). "It forcefully breaks through most remnants of rationalization, justification, and minimization residual in the client."

Negative side-effects reported in the literature are almost precluded by utilizing this technique only after the client has been in treatment a minimum of six months. One unexpected side-effect of this procedure is that the emotional responses of a significant percentage of clients seem focused on the trauma they created for their victims; thus this procedure, in addition to its conditioning and cognitive impact, serves as an influential empathy training procedure (Wolfe & Wolfe, 1984).

Empathy Training. Staff use several techniques, including behavioral ones, to help the offender to come to grips with the reality of his offense and its effects on the victim. Efforts to correct the cognitive distortions in the offender's perception of the victim's feelings about sexual assault include making contact with victim counselors or advocates, as well as the techniques of cognitive restructuring, role playing, and bibliotherapy.

1. *Victim counselors* are invited to attend the group meeting, or the offender is sent to a victim advocate center, where, at his own expense, he must ask a victim counselor to tell him about victims' feelings. Wherever possible, NWTA staff try to arrange to have the counselor of his actual victim be the person to tell him of the victim's perception of the hurt and damage s/he experienced. With many clients, this process seems to have the desired level of emotional and intellectual impact.

2. *Cognitive restructuring.* The offender constructs scenes, casting himself or significant others in the role of the victim. Research such as reading and consultation with victim specialists or their spouses is assigned, to assure a thorough and accurate job. Cognitive restructuring is utilized at this point. The client focuses on his typical rationalizations; for example, an exhibitionist will say, "This will really turn her on." Scenes are constructed where he utilizes and buys the rationalizations. These scenes then are paired with aversive

imagery. Finally, alternate scenes are constructed where he catches himself in the distortion and counters with the reality message; for example, the exhibitionist will say, "That is nonsense! I have done this hundreds of times and the only responses I have ever gotten are derision, disgust, and fear." The scene continues with the client performing some operant behavior to terminate the possibility of deviant behavior. Then the client shifts to a positively reinforcing scene, a "warm pink fuzzy" (Maletsky, 1980; R. Wolfe, 1981a).

3. *Roleplaying.* The group therapist tells the client, "Okay we talked about your view of the sexual assault scene, we talked about your thoughts about what was going on in the victim's head—that she really liked what you were doing. Now we are going to give you the opportunity to do the scene and be your victim." This approach might occur on a variety of levels with the same client. He may begin with a 500-word essay on the effects of the abuse on the victim. The next step might be for him to become that victim in a role play. The offender may protest and start out by saying, "Well, I couldn't do that, because it creates all sorts of psychological trauma for me." Nevertheless, he is asked to become the victim, lying on the floor and simulating getting molested in front of 14 other group members.

   Tapes also are used. A scene is reconstructed from his victim's perspective, telling the offender, "You are 11 years old. You lie in your bed at night. You hear your dad get up. You stiffen up. You are just hoping and praying he won't come in your room tonight like he did last night." The therapist then will describe what that particular offender actually did to the victim, while the offender is imagining he is that victim. Roger Wolfe explains, "Part of the offender's rationalization in his self-defense is that the victim never resisted, so we put that into focus. One of the ways we do that is to say to the offender, 'Your victim was three feet tall and weighed about 100 pounds. You are six feet tall and weigh 200 pounds. Imagine a man who was 12 feet tall and weighed 600 pounds coming into your bedroom and saying, 'Hi, you and I are going to do it' '' (R. Wolfe, 1981b).

4. *Bibliotherapy.* Clients are asked to read books written by sexual assault victims (e.g., Brady, 1981; Morris, 1982). A report form developed by staff therapist Nancy Nissen asks clients to record arousal points, victim traits, and offender traits as they are reading. With most clients, this enhances perceptions of their victim's pain.

Reoffense Rate

The reoffense rate by graduates of NWTA's sex-offender treatment program is approximately 10 percent, according to Roger Wolfe (1981b). "Since most of the men are on probation for five years, we usually hear of any reoffense through that division. When the offender commits a new offense, it is usually the same or a lesser type for which we treated him." Rarely, the person will progress to a more serious offense.

NWTA also reports a high rate of success where the Modified Aversive Behavior Rehearsal Technique was used as a treatment component. These data show an overall success rate of 95 percent with 92 sex offenders who had engaged in a variety of, and often multiple, paraphilias. Length of follow-up ranged from one to 28 months, with a mean follow-up of 13.5 months.[19]

Northwest Treatment Associates'
Success Rates Where the MABRT is a Treatment Component

Offense Type	Number*	Reoffend	% Success	Type Reoffense
Molests female children	64	2	97	Expose, Child Molest, F. Rape
Exhibitionism	27	4	85	Expose, F. Child Molest
Voyeurism	6	1	83	Expose
Molests male children	17	0	100	_____
Rapes female children	3	1	66	Child Rape
Rapes female adults	3	0	100	_____
Grabs breasts	2	1	50	Expose
Molests boys & girls	8	0	100	_____
Cross-dresses/steals clothing	1	0	100	_____
Total Offenders & Reoffenses: Mean Success Rate	92	5	95%	

* Many of the sex offenders had multiple deviancies, so total offenses are greater then number of offenders. Sources NWTA

Wolfe reiterates the importance of continual evaluation and assessment while the offender is in treatment. He recounts the case of a person who came in as an exhibitionist and was in treatment for three or four weeks and doing very poorly. He suddenly disappeared from treatment because he was caught in a vicious rape.

Whatever your relationship to a sex offender, you should keep foremost in mind, he is an *addict*. The individual verbalization, promises, assurances, and contentions should be regarded in the same light as those of alcoholics regarding alcohol or heroin addicts regarding their drug. An approach of healthy skepticism is advised, and behavior should speak to you much louder than words. (R. Wolfe, 1981b)

Notes

1 Six additional people have an associate status, and a secretary serves as a support staff person.
2 In 1982 a branch treatment program was established in Bellingham, Washington.
3 NWTA prefers not to handle paroled sex offenders. They consider perhaps one in 20 is treatable.
4 NWTA's clientele include a small percentage of ethnic groups. Such groups are underrepresented in almost all community-based adult sex-offender treatment programs.
5 Psychological tests include the MMPI, the Abel Card-Sort of Sexual Preferences, the Clarke Sexual History Questionnaire, and a general substance abuse overview checklist.
6 As a last resort, Depo-Provera may be used to reduce sexual arousal and sexual drive.
7 See Appendix C for description of social skills training used by NWTA.
8 For a description of this program, see Chapter 9 of this book.
8 See Cautela (1969).
10 Staff report that it is not an uncommon experience for clients to falsify these records and advise programs to be cautious and to look for a plausible learning curve. Additional confusion may be caused by the fact that some clients experience a lengthy period of suppression due to the trauma of discovery.
11 See Appendix D for a sample "Partner Alert List."
12 See Cautela (1967, 1970).
13 To train the client in stress-reducing and imagery-enhancing muscle relaxation methods, Roger Wolfe spends about 20 minutes with each client explaining NWTA's systematic format for inducing deep-muscle relaxation, followed by one hour in a taped session guiding the offender through the system. The client then can play the tape at home and do the exercises on his own for one or two weeks. Hypnosis also may be used when an offender is not successful with traditional methods.
14 See Meichenbaum (1977).
15 See Abel & Blanchard (1974); Marquis (1970).
16 See Laws & O'Neil (1979); Marshall & Lippens (1977).
17 See Appendix E for sample of "Protocol for Boredom Tapes." On occasion, when boredom tapes are being reviewed in the NWTA office, the therapist will ask the client to punish any deviant arousal while listening, by inhaling the noxious odor of placenta culture.
18 See Appendix F for two release forms for clients involved in MABRT, one is for client consent and the other provides permission for NWTA to use the tapes for the purpose of training professionals in the technique.
19 Wickramasekera (1980, p. 123) reports a high MABRT success rate also, especially with 23 exhibitionists (95 percent success) followed for 22 months to nine years.

References

Abel, G., & Blanchard, E. B. "The Role of Fantasy in the Treatment of Sexual Deviancy." *Archives of General Psychiatry, 30*:4, 1974, 467–475.

Brady, K. *Father's Days*. New York: Dell, 1981.

Cautela, J. R. "Covert Sensitization."' *Psychological Record, 20*, 1967, 459–468.

Cautela, J. R. "Behavioral Therapy and Self-Control Techniques and Implications." In C. M. Franks (ed.), *Behavioral Therapy: Appraisal and Status*. New York: McGraw-Hill, 1969.

Cautela, J. R. "Covert Reinforcement." *Behavior Therapy, 1*, 1970, 35–50.

Forgione, A. G. "The Use of Mannequins in the Behavioral Assessment of Child Molesters: Two Case Reports." *Behavior Therapy, 7*, 1974, 678–685.

Laws, D. R., & O'Neil, J. A. "Variations on Masturbatory Reconditioning." Paper presented at the Second National Conference on the Evaluation and Treatment of Sexual Aggressives, New York City, May 12, 1979.

Maletsky, B. M. "Assisted Covert Sensitization." In D. J. Cox & R. J. Daitzman (eds.), *Exhibitionism: Description, Assessment & Treatment*. New York: Garland Press, 1980.

Merquis, J. "Orgasmic Reconditioning: Changing Sexual Object Choice through Controlling Masturbation Fantasies." *Journal of Behavior Therapy and Experimental Psychiatry 1*, 1970, 263–271.

Marshall, W. L., & Lippens, K. "Clinical Value of Boredom, A Procedure for Reducing Inappropriate Sexual Interest." *Journal of Nervous & Mental Disease, 165*, 1977, 283–287.

Meichenbaum, D. *Cognitive-Behavioral Modification*. New York: Plenum Press, 1977.

Morris, M. *If I Should Die Before I Wake*, Los Angeles: Tarcher, 1982.

Silver, S. Taped site-interview by F. H. Knopp, September 30, 1981.

Wickramasekera, I. "Aversive Behavioral Rehearsal." In D. J. Cox & R. J. Daitzman (eds.), *Exhibitionism: Description, Assessment & Treatment*. New York: Garland Press, 1980.

Wolf, S. Taped site-interview by F. H. Knopp, September 30, 1981.

Wolfe, F. Taped site-interview by F H. Knopp, September 30, 1981.

Wolfe, F., & Wolfe, R. Letter and notes to F. H. Knopp, May 17, 1984.

Wolfe R. "Northwest Treatment Associates: An Outpatient Approach to the Treatment of Sex Offenders." *TSA News*, August 19, 1981.(a)

Wolfe R. Taped site-interview by F. H. Knopp, September 30, 1981(b).

33

Treatment in Transition
The Role of Mental Health Correctional Facilities

Robert Scott
Thomas O'Connor

Mentally ill inmates are a challenging population. Their treatment while under correctional care is a matter of importance to policy makers, the federal courts, and the popular press. One only has to witness the fall-out from cases such as Bridgwater to see that the public will no longer tolerate notorious, high-security, mental health correctional facilities. Institutions have come a long way from when Michigan established the first hospital for the criminally insane at Ionia in 1847. Laws have also changed. Special-needs offenders appear from a variety of verdicts with or without mitigating factors just as easily as from having escaped diagnosis in the criminal justice system and the development of psychiatric symptoms while in prison. In response to criticisms of "bus therapy" (Toch, 1982), practiced by many states in shuffling mentally ill inmates back and forth between institutions with and without special units, and "chemical straitjacketing" (Sommers & Baskin, 1990), in which disturbed inmates are kept docile with psychotropic drugs, new institutions are being created for correctional mental health treatment. Larned Correctional Mental Health Facility (hereafter referred to as Larned), in Larned, Kansas, is one such institution, created 5 years ago by federal

Source: *Journal of Contemporary Criminal Justice*, 13(3) (August 1997): 264–78, copyright © 1997 by Sage Publications, Inc. Reprinted by permission of Sage Publications, Inc.

court order. Its role in the correctional system, along with those of similarly established units in other states, is examined in this article.

Special attention is paid to the analysis of programs and environment based on consideration of the treatment-specific literature regarding this type of population. Briefly, that literature includes Coulson and Nutbrown (1992), who described the properties of ideal rehabilitation programs for special-need offenders; Marshall and Pithers (1994), who found that successful rehabilitation requires comprehensiveness and relapse prevention components; Russo (1994), who found that recidivism was often a function of inmate marginality rather than the actual effects of mental illness; and both Draine (1994) and Solomon, Draine, and Meyerson (1994), who articulated how recidivism can result from poor mental health service delivery, often by overreliance on monitoring and underreliance on treatment. Thus, the need for quality, innovative treatment, and structured environment is underscored. The facility examined in this article was established to provide the ideal set of programs and environment for mentally ill inmates.

Study Description

Genesis

A federal court injunction placed on the Kansas Department of Corrections during April 1989 required the state to create an environment suitable for the treatment of mentally ill inmates. Larned was devised and opened in rural southwest central Kansas, receiving an initial group of department of corrections inmates in need of specialized mental health treatment, on January 22, 1992. Larned was subsequently accredited by the American Correctional Association.

Facility Description

The inmate population as of January 31, 1996, was 129, with a maximum capacity of 150. The population is classified into one of three security/treatment classifications. Level I inmates receive minimal privileges and freedom. Each new entrant spends at least 72 hours at this classification. Level 2 offenders enjoy heightened out-of-cell time, cafeteria privileges, and group therapy sessions. Offenders classified as Level 3 receive full facility and program access.

Outcome Measures at Larned

The ultimate goal of offenders is to evolve to Level 3 and eventually be returned to their original department of corrections unit. Larned is considered a transitional mental health facility and not a unit for final or permanent inmate placements. Within the confines of this parameter, Alexander (1992) defined successful outcome measures for correctional mental health facilities as promoting "good" or "proper" behavior.

Target Population

The Kansas Department of Corrections has, as its target population, inmates who suffer from a serious mental illness. A serious mental illness is defined as an individual who suffers from a substantial disorder of thought, perception, mood, orientation, memory, or intellectual deficit that grossly impairs judgement, behavior, or the capacity to recognize reality or function effectively in the same environment with peers.

It is emphasized that such individuals suffer from a psychological or biological dysfunction; the disturbance is not only in the relationship between the individual and society. Although social deviance may not be desirable, it does not in itself constitute a mental illness.

Typical diagnostic categories that are encompassed in such a definition include the following:

A. Organic mental disorders
   1. Dementias
   2. Drug-/alcohol-induced organic mental disorders
   3. Organic brain syndrome

B. Thought disorders
   1. Schizophrenia
   2. Delusional (paranoid) disorder
   3. Other psychotic disorders

C. Anxiety and dissociative disorders including post-traumatic stress disorder

D. Mood disorders
   1. Bipolar disorder (manic depressive illness)
   2. Major depressive disorder
   3. Dysthymic disorder (chronic depression)

E. Adjustment disorders

F. Personality disorders with a tendency to decompensate into episodes of psychotic illness such as emotional distress, suicidal tendencies, or brief psychotic episodes (i.e., paranoid personality, borderline personality, narcissistic personality, schizophrenic personality)

G. Severe eating disorders and sleep disorders

Standard definitions and diagnostic criteria for these disorders can be found in the *Diagnostic and Statistical Manual of Psychiatry (DSM-IV-R)* (American Psychiatric Association, 1994). The manual additionally provides for related physical disorders, scales for measuring the severity of stress that precipitated the disorder, and scales that measure the individual's current function and highest level of functioning in the past year.

Definition of Inmates with Behavior Disorders

It is important to differentiate those inmates with a mental illness from a second group of inmates with behavior disorders. A definition of this second group would be as follows:

> An inmate suffering from a behavior disorder is one who has a repetitive behavioral problem that causes a significant problem in conforming to societal norms of acceptable behavior; in establishing meaningful, satisfying interpersonal relations; or in maintaining a personal sense of satisfaction or well-being.

Typical diagnostic categories that would be encompassed by this definition include the following:

A. Sexual disorders
   1. Voyeurism
   2. Exhibitionism
   3. Pedophilia
   4. Frotteurism
   5. Sexual sadism

B. Impulse control disorders
   1. Intermittent explosive disorder
   2. Kleptomania
   3. Pathological gambling
   4. Pyromania

C. Psychoactive substance abuse disorders
   1. Alcohol abuse/dependence
   2. Cannabis abuse/dependence
   3. Cocaine abuse/dependence
   4. Hallucinogen abuse/dependence
   5. Inhalant abuse/dependence
   6. Phencyclidine abuse/dependence
   7. Sedative abuse/dependence
   8. Amphetamine abuse/dependence
   9. Opiate abuse/dependence

D. Personality disorders
   1. Antisocial personality disorder
   2. Other personality disorders including schizoid, histrionic, dependent, passive aggressive, obsessive compulsive personality disorders

In recent years, mental health professionals have developed programs to address the difficulties of those with behavioral disorders, which have varying degrees of effectiveness. As those with these disorders have by definition violated societal norms, there are a large number of such individuals within a correctional population.

Demographics of Larned's Inmate Population

Before one can assess the effectiveness of the environment and determine whether it is fulfilling its mission to the department of corrections, an analysis of the type of population being served and the scope of the problems faced is called for. The one thing that is clear after cursory review of the inmates as individual cases is that they are, much like their "well" department of corrections inmate counterparts, handicapped by societal marginality.

As of December 31, 1995, 62 out of 127 inmates were White, whereas 58 of the same population was Black. Hispanics, Asians, and American Indians made up the remaining 7 cases.

The mean age of Larned inmates was 35.96 years. The relatively high age of Larned inmates relative to the general department of corrections population (which averages about 27 years) is consistent with Draine (1994), who discussed advanced age as a function of recidivism among those who receive psychiatric treatment services.

A very telling indicator of social marginality of these inmates, and inmates in general, is the fact that only 20 out of 127 subjects were married. Romig (1995) indicated that a supportive spouse was a key to successful adaptation and reform. It is clear that this link to stability eludes the vast majority of the Larned population. Similarly depicting social marginality, only 4 of 103 inmates had any post-high school education. In fact, the mean grade level completed by all inmates at Larned was only 10.5.

Nearly as important as a stable and supportive family environment, Mesch and Fishman (1994) found that employment and type of employment were significant factors in the ability to "get well" and "reform." Peters, Witty, and O'Brien (1993) found that even those with jobs prior to incarceration were at risk if the employment environment was "unstructured" and lacking a disciplined atmosphere. This was particularly true among those with substance abuse problems. The population at Larned, based on these findings, is at particular risk, and in some measure, this may explain their presence at Larned in the first place. Of the inmates in the facility, only 4 out of the 116 held positions that could be considered skilled, and only 1 was a student prior to incarceration. As Table 1 indicates, job types held by Larned inmates are quite menial and marginal for the most part.

Table 1
Employment Status of Larned Inmates

Occupation	Number Skilled	Number Unskilled
Lab assistant	1	
Maintenance	1	
Manager (hotel)	1	
Welder	1	
Laborer		32
Unemployed		30
Construction		8
Food service		8
Unknown		5
Military (enlisted)		3
Janitorial		3
Cook		2
Disabled		2
Assembly line		2
Boilermaker		1
Bus driver		1
Farmhand		1
Housekeeping		1
Maid		1
Mechanic		1
Hotel work		1
Orderly		1
Plumber		1
Investigator		1
Roofer		1
Salesman		1
Student		1
Tire builder		1
Total	4	112

The one conclusion that may be drawn from this cursory review of the demographics of Larned inmates is the marginality of these individuals. In each instance, rates of risk factors are quite high, contributing to the already present psychological or biological maladies inherent to these persons. A normal extension of this review is to examine the scope of programs provided and environment sustained at Larned to facilitate the successful completion of the unit's mission.

Programs and Environment

The Larned facility provides a complete range of traditional psychiatric inpatient-type programs for inmates of the Kansas Department of Corrections. Mental health services include group and individual counseling, activity therapy, and music therapy. Specialized groups such as anger management are also offered. The facility will also provide remedial education and preparation components for the general equivalency diploma to those who desire these services. A substance abuse treatment program with specialized services tailored to the mentally ill substance abuser is also available.

Substance Abuse Counseling and Treatment

Consistent with the interpretations of Foote, Seligman, Magura, and Handelsman (1994), substance abuse treatment must be delivered within the confines of stages of recovery. Foote et al. considered the use of a drug recovery model as a component of mental health recovery favorably. Larned's population, which has a substance abuse/dependence rate of about 60 percent, receives treatment that falls somewhere in between the recommendations of Foote et al. and Van Stelle, Mauser, and Moberg (1994). Van Stelle et al. reviewed treatment options in lieu of imprisonment, instead of in consort with it.

Of course, the Larned experience has been one that melds a variety of approaches and schools of thought, including a very apparent structured component to treatment and living. The marginality of the inmates indicated the dire need for discipline and structure in their lives. The use of 12-step-type programs, with their associated rigors, is consistent with the 12-step prison delivery model forwarded by Barthwell, Bokos, Bailey, and Nisenbaum (1995).

Deters (1993) indicated the need for a structured work environment for a positive drug recovery experience. Larned has adopted this school of thought by using a rigorous classification system (Level 1 to Level 3), controlling inmate activities in a positive, not punitive, fashion. As one might receive incentive (i.e., promotion) in the civilian workplace, the Larned inmate is rewarded with classification upgrade for good work, attitude, and behavior.

Group Counseling

Counseling of both a group and individualized nature is an integral part of the Larned reformation/healing process for the mentally ill inmates it serves. Programs are tailor made to the individual, as each inmate who has a counseling component in their program is served very personally by masters and doctorally prepared and certified treatment specialists.

A consistent theme within the literature that has been adopted at Larned is the need for group counseling to be free, open, and encouraging of expression. Page (1979) first indicated the need for unstructured group counseling to openly express feelings, consistent with drug rehabilitation and other 12-step programs. Open expression is allowed and tolerated.

Further, Clow, Hutchins, and Vogler (1992) expressed concern for quality and effectiveness of group counseling processes for spouse abusers and those with uncontrolled aggression disorders. Clow et al. reiterated conventional drug treatment philosophies and the findings of Page (1979) by underscoring informality of discussion to facilitate a nonhostile and confrontational environment, whereby those with common experiences can encourage positive interpretive behavior. Fausel (1995) confirmed these opinions and practical applications by stating that Socratic discussion is required to break down stressors.

Family Therapy

The inclusion of a family therapy component of mental health treatment to criminal offenders at Larned is problematic in that just 20 of the 127 inmates were in fact married. Of this population, many do not find Larned accessible, as it is located deep in rural Kansas. Warden Nye (personal communication, 1996) indicated the fact that this particular plank of a treatment program is virtually unfeasible given the "family bond" status of the inmates; therefore, the committal of a large number of the unit's scarce resources would not be particularly prudent.

Although Carlson (1994) recommended tailor-made approaches, involving short-term treatment, geared to individual cases with emphasis on relapse prevention, Larned has been forced, much like general prison populations, to rely on informal networking through the visitation process to provide much of these support mechanisms.

This reality is unfortunate, as Daniels and Guppy (1994) reiterated that social support serves as a significant buffer to the effects of stressors on emotional well-being. Research conducted by Miller and Pylypa (1995) with the Swinomish (Washington) Tribal Mental Health Project further confirmed the importance of the family network in successful mental health treatment program delivery. In the end, however, the reality appears irreconcilable and unavoidable.

Anger Management

The procedure for counseling and/or intervention with respect to anger management is consistent with other forms of the mental health treatment regimen. Group settings for treatment and/or counseling, as outlined by Clow et al. (1992), are recommended and provided as an active part of the therapy programs of a number of the Larned inmates. Many of the inmates receiving this treatment do so in consort with substance abuse and other varied group and individual counseling.

Goldberg (1994) expressed the necessity for those with aggression and violence disorders to receive adequate structured and unstructured counseling and mental health treatment procedures. Further, Goldberg indicated that, like finding the answers to oneself through group interaction and self-awareness in drug and group counseling, rage should be explored in order to illuminate its meaning and function within the context of each individual case. Counseling and personalized case management strategies at Larned, particularly in the sexual predator unit, provide this forum for self-awareness relative to aggression. The Larned treatment staff dedicate much time and resources to this process.

Treatment of Sexual Disorders

Treatment of inmates with sexual disorders is a prime area of consideration at Larned, particularly due to the presence or the sexual predator unit and its 16 high-risk convicted sexual deviants. In all, as of December 1995, 43 of 127 inmates had been initially incarcerated within the department of corrections on a sex crime conviction.

Sex offenders are given highly personalized, rigorous, and intensive treatment programs at Larned. Larned uses a model developed by Sapp and Vaughn (1991). These researchers examined 73 sexual offender treatment programs in state correctional facilities and found that the more successful ones attempted to maximize techniques of behavior modification through psychotherapy while minimizing the use of drugs and other psychotropics.

Thornton and Hogue (1993) expressed specific concerns regarding mentally disturbed sex offenders. Thornton and Hogue articulated the need for better assessment techniques and treatment within correctional institutions. They believed that the prison experience divorces the offender from reality and ordinary life. Removed from the objects of their desire over time, sex offenders become less easily identified as problems as they appear more and more well adjusted, free from the temptations of the outside world. This is a particularly dangerous process, heightening the need for specialized treatment, recognition, and assessment, as well as the establishment of a more effective prediction model.

Little, Robinson, and Burnette (1993) suggested a process of moral recognition therapy. This technique is informal and unstructured, intertwined with the general counseling and treatment process at Larned. Identifying one's behavior as wrong or evil is a central step to self-healing and self-understanding and is a primary outcome measure of the treatment of sex offenders with mental impairment at Larned.

A final note regarding this particular treatment programming is the interesting findings of Shaw, Herkov, and Greer (1995). Shaw et al. found that a high reading level, a symbol of better education, was a function of the "best" outcome groups among treated and released sex offenders. Shaw et al.'s obvious implication is that an educational component should be worked into the treatment programs of this particular subpopulation.

Analysis and Discussion

Although Larned is still in its infancy, relatively speaking, the attempt has clearly been made to create a state-of-the-art treatment facility. At this stage, it is possible to take only a cursory review of (the successes and failures of the Larned unit.

An obvious success, due most likely to the provision of a very structured and disciplined treatment environment, is the near absence of violent incidents (See Tables 2 and 3). This is extraordinary considering each of these 127 inmates had to be a "problem child" at their assigned department of corrections home. The structure of Larned, among other factors, has caused these inmates to conform.

Table 2
Fiscal Year (FY) Incident Reports at Larned

Incident	FY 1992	FY 1993	FY 1994	FY 1995	FY 1996
Inmate-staff batteries	0	0	0	0	0
Inmate-inmate batteries	14	25	23	15	8
Required use of force	56	126	114	76	27
Disciplinary reports	277	608	586	692	327
Inmate grievances	66	220	82	132	53
Inmate property claims	10	12	3	12	4

Table 3
Safety Incident Violations by Larned Inmates

Type of Incident	Occurences
Positive urinalysis tests	0
Dangerous contraband finds	4
Inmate homicides	0
Inmate deaths due to accident	0
Work-related staff deaths	0

A total of 462 inmates have entered Larned to receive mental health treatment since it first received transfers in January 1992. Of these 462, the number who have never left the facility is 78, whereas 384 have been successfully treated and returned to their original department of corrections unit. More telling, of the 384 who left the facility, 149 returned at some point, whereas 236 have not. From these numbers, viewed as an outcome measure, a judgment of success or failure depends on a half-full or half-empty analogous type interpretation.

Sherwood Zimmerman (personal communication, 1995), former deputy director of the New York State Department of Corrections, indicated that success or failure in correctional mental health facilities is often open to such interpretations. Further, debate over "good" versus "bad" treatment and the malaise of treatment philosophies in the 50 states cloud the ability to judge success.

The average length of stay for an inmate transferred to Larned is 327 days. Equally as interesting is the fact that the average length of time away from Larned for those released and returned was only 320 days. In essence, a treated mentally ill offender who, for the most part, is compliant while housed in the rigorous treatment and structured environment of Larned can last less than 1 year back in the less disciplined and less structured general populations, free of aggressive and specialized treatment.

Conclusion

An analysis of the programs and environment at Larned reveals certain trends relative to program successes and failures. Further, as this facility develops out of adolescence, it will continue to fine-tune its delivery procedures and processes. Several conclusions may be drawn from this cursory review of the Larned experience and existing literature regarding theory and practice at other similarly established institutions:

1. Treatment programs need to be specialized and individualized to individual case needs.
2. Replication attempts of generic treatment programs do not necessarily translate successfully from one situation to another.
3. Definitional procedures of mentally ill persons in need of treatment are often imprecise, as are decisions regarding who should "cure" these persons and when these persons are "cured."
4. Persons receiving these mental health services are handicapped by social marginality, relative to family status, substance abuse, and socioeconomic status.

5. Successful mental health programs require an integrated approach to multiple counseling techniques, depending on individualized criteria.

6. Counseling in a group/shared setting with others possessing similar maladies is imperative.

7. Involvement of family in the healing process is critical. Unfortunately, most of these inmates do not possess the requisites of family therapy or even informal social bonding to a constructive family unit.

8. Anger management therapy requires structured mental health treatment procedures, in which the individual can realize the self-destructiveness inherent in aggressive and violent behavior.

9. Similar to anger management, treatment of sexual disorders requires highly personalized, rigorous, and intensive treatment options in a structured, disciplined environment.

10. A success rate of more than 50% (no return to the Larned facility) is competitive to good, relative to successes of psychiatric service recipients in other department of corrections settings and those not in department of corrections settings.

11. Given the failure rate (returned to Larned) and with respect to the low levels of incidents at Larned versus the high levels of incidents in the general population of the department of corrections, it becomes apparent that the need for structure, discipline, and continual treatment is a necessity for ongoing successful rehabilitation and treatment.

12. Removed from the rigorous and structured setting at Larned, treatment effects erode quickly.

References

Alexander, R. (1992). Determining appropriate criteria in the evaluation of correctional mental health treatment for inmates. *Journal of Offender Rehabilitation, 18*(1–2), 119–134.

American Psychiatric Association. (1994). *Diagnostic and statistical manual of mental disorders (DSM-IV)*. Washington, DC: Author.

Antonowicz, D., & Ross, R. (1994). Essential components of successful rehabilitation programs for offenders. *International Journal of Offender Therapy and Comparative Criminology, 38*(2), 97–104.

Barthwell, A., Bokos, P., Bailey, J., & Nisenbaum, M. (1995). A continuum of care for substance abusers in the criminal justice system. *Journal of Psychoactive Drugs, 27*(1), 39–47.

Blanchard, G. (1986). Male victims of child sexual abuse: A portent of things to come. Journal of Independent Social Work, 1(1), 19–27.

Blau, P. (1964). *Exchange and power in social life*. New York: John Wiley.

Carlson, J. (1994). Family and family therapy in the USA. *DISKURS*, 4(2), 44–51.

Clow, D., Hutchins, D., & Vogler, D. (1992). TFA systems: A unique group treatment of spouse abusers. *Journal of Specialists in Group Work*, 17(2), 74–83.

Coulson, G., & Nutbrown, V. (1992). Properties of an ideal rehabilitative program for high-need offenders. *International Journal of Offender Therapy and Comparative Criminology*, 36(3), 203–208.

Cox, J., McCarty, D., Landsberg, G., & Paravati, P. (1988). A model for crisis intervention services within local jails. *International Journal of Law and Psychiatry*, 11(4), 391–407.

Daniels, K., & Guppy, A. (1994). Occupational stress, social support, job control and psychological well-being. *Human Relations*, 47(12), 1523–1544.

Draine, J., & Solomon, P. (1994). Jail recidivism and the intensity of case management services among homeless persons with mental illness leaving jail. *Journal of Psychiatry and Law*, 22(2), 245–261.

Draine, J., Solomon, P., & Meyerson, A. (1994). Predictors of reincarceration among patients who receive psychiatric services in jail. *Hospital and Community Psychiatry*, 4–5(2), 163–167.

Fausel, D. (1995). Stress inoculation training for step-couples. *Marriage and Family Review*, 21(1–2), 137–155.

Foote, J., Seligman, M., Magura, S., & Handelsman, L. (1994). An enhanced positive reinforcement model for the severely impaired cocaine abuser. *Journal of Substance Abuse Treatment*, 11(6), 525–539.

Goldberg, C. (1994). The uninterpreted rage: Protecting the therapeutic alliance in the treatment of borderline patients. *Clinical Social Work Journal*, 22(3), 291–302.

Little, G., Robinson, K., & Burnette, K. (1993). Cognitive behavioral treatment of felony drug offenders: A five year recidivism report. *Psychological Reports*, 73(3, Pt. 2), 1089–1090.

Marshall, W., & Pithers, W. (1994). A reconsideration of treatment outcome with sex offenders. *Criminal Justice and Behavior*, 21(1), 10–27.

Mechanic, D. (1994). Establishing mental health priorities. *Milbank Quarterly*, 72(3), 501–514.

Mesch, G., & Fishman, G. (1994). First readmission of the mentally ill: An event history analysis. *Social Science Research*, 23(4), 295–314.

Miller, B., & Pylypa, J. (1995). The dilemma of mental health paraprofessionals at home. *American Indian and Alaska Native Mental Health Research*, 6(2),13–33.

Nye, H. (1996, February 5). *Larned Mental Health Correctional Facility*, Presentation to the House Appropriations Subcommittee for fiscal years 1996 and 1997, Washington, DC.

Page, R. (1979). Developmental stages of unstructured counseling groups with prisoners. *Small Group Behavior*, 10(2), 271–278.

Peters, R., Witty, T., & O'Brien, J. (1993). The importance of the work family with structured work and relapse prevention. *Journal of Applied Rehabilitation Counseling*, 24(3), 3–5.

Romig, C., & Gruenke, C. (1994). Aiding the parolee adjustment process: A systemic perspective on assessment. *Contemporary Family Therapy: An*

International Journal, 16(4), 301–314.

Russo, G. (1994). Follow-up of 91 mentally ill criminals discharged from the maximum security hospital in Barcelona P.G. *International Journal of Law and Psychiatry*, 17(3), 279–301.

Sapp, A., & Vaughn, M. (1991). Sex offender rehabilitation programs in state prisons: A nationwide survey. *Journal of Offender Rehabilitation*, 17(1–2), 55–75.

Shaw, D., Vondra, J., Hommerding, K., Keenan, K., & Dunn, M. (1994). Chronic family adversity and early childhood behavior: A longitudinal study of low income families. *Journal of Child Psychology and Psychiatry and Applied Disciplines*, 35(6), 1109–1122.

Shaw, T., Herkov, M., & Greer, R. (1995). Examination of treatment completion and predicted outcome among incarcerated sex offenders. *Bulletin of the Academy of Psychiatry and the Law*, 23(1), 35–41.

Smith, A., & Bassin, A. (1992). Kings County Court probation: A laboratory for offender rehabilitation. *Journal of Addictions and Offender Counseling*, 13(1), 11–22.

Solomon, P., Draine, J., & Meyerson, A. (1994). Jail recidivism and receipt of community mental health services. *Hospital and Community Psychiatry*, 45(8), 793–797.

Sommers, I., & Baskin, D. (1990). The prescription of psychiatric medication in prison. *Justice Quarterly*, 7, 739–755.

Thornton, D., & Hogue, T. (1993). The large scale provision of programs for imprisoned sex offenders: Issues, dilemmas and progress. *Criminal Behavior and Mental Health*, 3(4), 371–380.

Toch, H. (1982). The disturbed disruptive inmate: Where does the bus stop? *Journal of Psychiatry and Law*, 10, 327–349.

Van Stelle, K., Mauser, E., & Moberg, P. (1994). Recidivism to the criminal justice system of substance abusing offenders diverted into treatment. *Crime and Delinquency*, 40(2), 175–196.

Wierson, M., & Forehand, R. (1995). Predicting recidivism in juvenile delinquents: The role of mental health diagnoses and the qualification of conclusion by race. *Behaviour Research and Therapy*, 33(1), 63–67.

34

Older Inmates
Special Programming Concerns

Peter C. Kratcoski

Introduction

Those developing programming for state and federal institutions in the 1990s are faced with such concerns as overcrowding, an increasingly violent prison population, care for AIDS infected inmates and the need to prevent its spread, and pressures to direct funding toward highly visible uses. In this climate, the increasing number of older inmates in these institutions and their special problems may not receive a great deal of consideration by correction administrators. It is necessary to draw attention to the older inmates and their needs.

A report completed by the U.S. Bureau of Prisons Office of Research and Evaluation (1989) revealed that almost 12% of the U.S. Bureau of Prisons inmate population was age 50 or above at the time of the report, and it was estimated that in the year 2005 more than 16% will be age 50 or above. A survey of federal prisons and state prison systems found that there were more than 24,000 inmates age 50 and above housed in long-term institutions on January 1, 1989 (Camp and Camp, 1989).

The presence of ever increasing numbers of older inmates in federal and state institutions presents dilemmas for administrators and planners. The declining physical health of persons age 50 and older may create a need for changes in the physical plants, since a number of the prisoners may be unable to climb stairs, and ramps or wheelchair accessibility may be required. Expanded medical and mental health services and recreational, educational, and social programs for the older inmates will also be needed.

Research on the adjustment of older inmates to prison life is rather scarce. One study of imprisoned persons age 50 and above discovered that older inmates who were incarcerated for the first time were more positive in their sentiments about prison life and conditions than were older inmates who had been incarcerated on other occasions. Feelings of fear of being victimized by younger inmates were frequently expressed by older inmates housed in the geriatric unit of one correctional facility. The older inmates also complained more frequently than younger ones about lack of privacy and constant noise. In addition, most reported that they had not developed friendships within the institution (Vito and Wilson 1985).

Older inmates' adjustment is affected by the degree to which they are isolated from families and friends. Sabath and Cowles (1988) found that family contacts, education, and health had effects on the positive institutional adjustment of the inmates. The older offenders who were able to maintain contacts with their families were found to be better adjusted than those who could not do so. Those who had attained enough education to read and take part in institutional activities that required the ability to read were more likely to make a positive adjustment. Poor health contributed to the emotional isolation of the older inmates, since it limited their ability to participate in institutional activities.

A survey (Fultz, 1989) of all of the older inmates aged 60 and above incarcerated in the Maryland correctional system revealed that of the 89 inmates in the system, 20% were housed in maximum security, 72% in medium and 8% in minimum. The largest concentration was at the Maryland House of Corrections in Jessup, where the "old man's unit" consisted of 46 single cells. Fultz found that the older inmates tended to adapt to prison life by not becoming involved. More than 90% of the older inmates wanted to be housed with their own age group.

Correctional administrators and policy makers have generally responded to the older inmate situation in one of the following ways:

1. They have ignored the problem, stating that, since 85 to 90% of the inmate population is in the younger age brackets, the limited resources available for programming should be allocated to them.

2. Some states have constructed new correctional facilities or converted existing facilities for the older inmates. However, this

type of facility is still quite rare and will generally serve the dual function of providing the specific type of housing needed by older inmates and serving the needs of the physically handicapped or those with debilitating illnesses. Often, the older inmates are also those who are handicapped or seriously ill.

3. Older inmates are mixed with the general population, without any special concern for their housing needs. In these instances, provision is made for their recreational needs, work assignments, or special medical problems.

4. A special unit is established for older inmates within the larger institution. Here, the older inmates are housed separately from the others, but may have contact with them in work, recreation, or educational programs, or in the dining halls.

The fourth approach is the least commonly utilized, and is generally considered necessary only when a large proportion of the older inmates have rather severe health problems.

Research Design

To elicit responses from older inmates in regard to their institutional adjustment in the areas of educational, recreational, and security needs, physical and mental health, and social relations, a questionnaire with multiple choice items and a few open-ended questions was prepared. Permission was given to administer this questionnaire to inmates in eight U.S. Bureau of Prison facilities, three state institutions in Florida, and three state institutions in Ohio. Three of the institutions housed female offenders. One of the state facilities in which males were housed was specifically established for older inmates, and one of the federal institutions housing males was developed as a medical/geriatric facility. None of the facilities housing women had established separate units for the older inmates. The older inmates in the other correctional facilities involved in the study were dispersed randomly throughout the facility. At these institutions, age was not a factor considered by the administration when the unit assignments were made.

An interview schedule with questions related to perceived problems of older offenders, institutional responses to these problems, and plans for the future was developed for use with selected administrators, correction officers, and support staff. Several members from each category were interviewed at each of the correctional facilities included in the study.

The research was completed in the following manner. All of the older inmates were asked to report to a specific area in the institution. After an introduction, the purpose of the research was briefly explained. Inmates were told participation was voluntary and they could leave at any time. The questions were read and scored by the research team for those who could not read. It did not appear that there was any significant resistance to the research. Many of the inmates did not participate because they were on work details. Others had just finished work assignments and were sleeping; some were attending school; others just didn't want to be bothered. In several cases, the questionnaires were distributed by the support staff. A total of 482 usable inmate questionnaires and 62 interviews with correction officers, support staff, and administrators were included in the study. The older inmates' adjustment to the institutional setting was measured by a set of questions pertaining to their lives in regard to visitors, institutional activities, health problems, relations with other inmates and staff, feelings of fear, and victimization by other inmates.

Findings and Analysis

The larger portion of the older inmates included in this study were housed in correctional facilities in which an inmate's age was not given special consideration when the specific facility assignment or unit assignment within the institution was made. Most older inmates were classified on the basis of security considerations, which were determined by the nature of their offenses. For example, in the course of our study we had contact with inmates beyond the age of seventy who were living in a maximum security penitentiary.

Comparisons were made between the responses of the inmates housed in the facilities specifically developed for the older inmate and those held in institutions where the older inmates were dispersed throughout the prison population. Special attention was given to the responses of the older female inmates, since the needs of persons in this category tend to be overlooked when correctional policies and programs are designed.

One section of the questionnaire pertained to visitors. Almost half of the older inmates in both types of settings had visitors regularly, while the other half stated that they "rarely" or "never" had visitors. The most frequent types of visitors were spouses, children, and other relatives, with visits from friends, lawyers, social agency representatives, and volunteers being much less frequent.

The inmates in the older inmate institution were less likely to have definite release plans. One-third of this group stated that they would live in a shelter home or didn't know where they would live on release. Most of the older inmates in both categories participated regularly in several forms of recreational activities. There was a tendency for both groups to pick the quiet games and non-physical activities. More than half of the respondents in the older inmate institution were dissatisfied with the number and range of activities, compared to less than one-third in the other facilities who were dissatisfied. More than half of those in the older inmate institutions were involved in some type of educational program, compared to 38% of the older inmate respondents housed in the other institutions. The same held true for involvement in self-help groups such as Alcoholics Anonymous and drug abuse programs (51 to 30%). A significantly larger proportion of those housed in the older inmate institution participated in activities and programs sponsored by external groups, and the respondents housed in the older inmate correctional facility attended religious services more frequently than did the inmates housed in the other facilities included in the study. As would be expected, few of the older inmates in either type of institution were satisfied with their living quarters. Most of the inmates had common complaints such as insufficient space, lack of proper ventilation and stuffy, damp, or cold quarters. However, those living in the institution which housed all age groups were more likely to mention such things as noise, inconsiderate inmates, stale air from smokers, aggressive inmates, being placed on the top bunk, and the location of the dining rooms and toilets as major housing problems.

Approximately one-third of the older inmates in both types of settings stated that the other inmates in the institution were friendly and helpful and there was no difference in the proportion of inmates who stated that they avoided interacting with other inmates. However, a larger number of older inmates in the non-specialized institution found the other inmates, particularly the younger ones, to be aggressive and violent.

The large majority of the older inmates in both types of institutional settings claimed they were never threatened by other inmates, and only a few of the older inmates in either type of institution stated that they were ever beaten by other inmates. Several of the older inmates in both types of institutional settings stated that they were fearful for their life in the institution and afraid of the other inmates. However, they constituted a very small proportion of the respondents. Thus, the findings do not support one of the major arguments for having separate units or institutions for older inmates, that older inmates will be intimidated, exploited and abused by the younger ones if they are not housed in separate units or facilities away from the younger inmates.

It appears that the overall health of those housed in the older inmate institution was significantly worse than that of those housed in the other institutions. Sixty percent of those in the older inmate institution stated that their present health was excellent or good, compared to 92% of the older inmates housed in the other institutions. Forty percent of those in the older inmate institution stated that their health condition was below average or poor.

A large percentage of the older inmates housed in the specialized facilities claimed that their health had declined since coming to the institution. The most persistent health problems mentioned by those in the older inmate institution pertained to mental factors such as worry, depression, and anxiety. Forty-seven percent of the respondents housed in the older inmate institution were given treatment at a prison hospital, compared to 20% of the older inmates at the other facilities.

A significantly larger proportion of the older inmates in the specialized institution was incarcerated for the first time. This may help explain their greater anxiety and concern about their situation.

Older Women in Prison

As previously mentioned, three of the correctional facilities included in the study housed women. Twenty percent of the respondents in the study were female. In general, the older female inmates appeared to have more difficulty adjusting to institutional life than did the older male inmates. Female inmates were less likely to have visitors or to participate in recreational and social activities than were male inmates. Only 19% of the older women stated that they participated in some kind of structured activity on a daily basis, compared to 50% of the older men. When compared with the older male inmates, females were less likely to become friendly with other inmates. In addition, a larger proportion of the older female inmates than of the males stated that they were either occasionally, frequently, or always afraid, and a larger proportion of the older female inmates than of the males claimed that their health was "poor" or "terrible."

The older women were generally dissatisfied with their living quarters. Insufficient space, poor ventilation, noise, lack of privacy, and the hostility of other inmates were very common complaints. The larger majority of the older women would have preferred to live with other inmates who were about their own age. One study by Kratcoski and Babb (1990) revealed that one factor affecting adjustment problems of the older women inmates is the fact that most state correctional facilities for women accommodate all types of offenders, and the security level for women prisons is generally geared toward the most dangerous inmates. Thus, the programs, visiting privileges, and activities are developed in line with the need for greater security required for serious offenders.

The work opportunities available for women in prison are generally not on a par with those available for men, and it was acknowledged that the opportunities to engage in meaningful employment tended to be quite limited. In addition, the older female inmates' lack of skills, poor physical health, and the attitude expressed by many of the women that they were too old to learn new skills or to do anything useful were important factors affecting the adjustment of older women in the area of work.

One administrator noted that new institutional responsibilities have resulted from increases in the number of older female inmates, observing, "I feel that the responsibilities have increased since the influx of older inmates, due to the special problems that have occurred. For example, many are wheelchair bound, overweight, and lack initiative to be a part of the correctional system in terms of productivity."

Programs for Older Inmates in a Special Institution

One of the facilities included in this study was specifically designed to house older inmates. A three-story building originally used as a hospital was converted to a correctional institution. It is classified as medium security and has dormitory style living areas. In the yard there are benches, a miniature golf course, a walking path, volleyball and a horseshoe game. Inmates wear a variety of clothing and have identification badges instead of numbers. Rules tend to be flexible. While everyone who is capable of working is assigned a job, many of the jobs are make-shift. Inmates with physical problems are allowed to ride the elevator. Attending school is considered as full-time employment. A work release program is available to some of the inmates. The mean age of the inmates at this facility was 55 and the range was 38 to 87.

The correctional officers, social service staff, and administrators interviewed at this correctional facility were almost unanimously in agreement that it is better for older inmates to be in such an institution than to be randomly dispersed throughout the various correctional institutions in the state.

While many of the older inmates had committed serious offenses, including murder and rape, this often was their first time in an institution, and they were experiencing considerable adjustment problems. Since the older inmate facility was not specifically designed as a geriatric institution, the inmates were supposed to follow a program similar to that in other correctional facilities of a comparable level of security. All of the inmates were supposed to work. The most difficult task of the administration was to find ways to keep the inmates busy. Many, if not the majority, were incapable of completing strenuous work, and the administration had to be imaginative in its work programming.

For example, they employed elevator operators even though the elevator was self-service. The administration contracted with nearby state and county agencies to provide a letter and flyer stuffing service, a job which could be performed sitting down, allowing inmates who were lame and even in wheelchairs to participate. Attending school was defined as a form of employment, and many of the older inmates took advantage of this opportunity. It was not unusual to see 60- or 70-year-old men learning to read and write.

The staff insisted that the correctional officers and administration needed specialized training if they were to be effective. The correctional staff must be cognizant of the effects of the aging process and the needs of the older inmates. It was pointed out that institutional rules must often be relaxed. Many inmates who violate rules or appear to be disobeying orders may not have heard the orders, or may not have understood the rules. The inmates may be forgetful, misinterpret instructions, or not even be aware of the meaning of the slang terms often used by the staff and correctional officers.

Older inmates need more attention and assistance than the younger inmates, since they do not tend to become involved in the inmate subculture and are less likely to be assisted by family and friends while incarcerated. They are more fearful of being released and having to return to the community, and they are more likely to have serious physical and mental health problems than their younger counterparts. The correctional officers and other staff must be trained to deal with this. For example, some older inmates may be bed wetters, others need to make constant trips to the bathroom or take medicine at regular intervals, and the staff must be willing and trained to help accommodate them.

If given the opportunity, many of the older inmates would be satisfied to vegetate rather than become involved in recreational, social, and educational activities. Thus, it is very important to get every inmate involved in these types of programs to the extent possible. Generally, the educational programs available to the older inmates are not designed to prepare them for jobs, but rather to help raise their self-esteem. If the inmates are functional illiterates, they must participate in the Adult Basic Education Program. Others who have graduated from high school are encouraged to enroll in the college courses which were offered by a near-by college. One of the unit managers had developed a Life Skills Education program, and those inmates who had a reasonable chance of being released before they died were encouraged to complete the program. The program consists of locating housing after release, adjusting to having a criminal record, obtaining financial resources such as food stamps, medicaid, or employment, writing resumes, developing social skills, taking care of personal hygiene and becoming involved in community activities.

As mentioned, a number of the older inmates had committed types of offenses that are extremely upsetting to the community. For example, many were child molesters. This type of offender is generally disliked by both the staff and other inmates, and normally they have an extreme amount of guilt to deal with. Special group counseling sessions were available at the institutions for these offenders. The staff encouraged volunteers of various types to come into the institution. The staff was in agreement that more effort must be made to encourage volunteers to come into the prison. Some of the older inmates were able to maintain some contact with the community through town visits.

The older inmates were encouraged to participate in recreational activities to the extent of their ability. A gym, a weight room, a machine exercise room, and a small outdoor softball field were available. Games were organized to be competitive, but not extremely physical. For example, basketball tournaments were scheduled in which the players shot foul shots instead of scrimmaged. Softball was played with a soft rubber ball. Many of the inmates used the body building equipment and were in excellent physical condition. Thus, the staff in general was quite convinced that older inmates benefitted from being housed in an institution which was programmed for the needs of the older inmates. Rather than vegetate, as many believe happens in such an institution, they tend to have more opportunity to participate in the various social, recreational, work and educational activities available than they would have if they were interspersed in regular facilities. For the staff, a job in an institution for older offenders may actually be much more demanding than one in a regular correctional facility, and correction officers working in these types of facilities need special training if they are to effective.

The Fort Worth Comprehensive Health Unit

The Comprehensive Health Unit located at the Federal Correctional Institution at Fort Worth is designed to hold 147 offenders who must meet the following criteria:

1. Are appropriate for a level one, coed facility
2. Have some on-going medical/health problem which precluded conventional housing
3. Require 24-hour medical coverage
4. Have ambulatory problems
5. Have limited work ability
6. Require close proximity to both in- and outpatient services
7. Are able to attend to their own personal hygiene such as bathing, eating, dressing, and cleaning their own room, not a hospital-type inmate (Federal Bureau of Prisons, 1987, p. 6)

Administrators and support staff at Fort Worth were asked it special programs were needed for the older inmates. Some of the respondents stated that the existing programs were adequate. Others cited a "need for additional structured recreational and cultural programs," "allowances for personal TVs and radios in their rooms," and "better educational programs that directly benefit older inmates, since most of them are not interested in traditional educational programs." Many of the comments centered on the importance of obtaining the training and experience to assist those inmates with serious health problems. Comments on this matter included, "There is a need for special training in medical areas to learn to deal with severe health problems," and, "Inmates who are medical cases cannot work and need more attention." It was also mentioned that older inmates need to receive special counseling when they are near to their release dates, since "many are retired or unable to work" and these must learn how to become active in the community in ways that do not center on work.

The manager of the Comprehensive Health Unit mentioned that even inmates with rather severe health problems are not excluded from institutional activities. If able to do so, these inmates are required to do light jobs for the prisons industry, perform small janitorial services, or assist at the school.

In an interview, Ron Hixson, the unit manager of the Comprehensive Health Unit of Fort Worth, mentioned that cleanliness and access are two major concerns of the staff members who work with chronically ill or handicapped inmates in a geriatric facility such as Fort Worth. The environmental design of the facility must allow for maximum mobility, and a clean living unit is one way to prevent the spread of disease within the unit. Special health oriented programs for the inmates at Fort Worth include stress management, health wise, drug facts and positive mental attitude. A nurse/counselor is assigned to the regular unit staff for the purpose of medical monitoring and to give information in self-health care and preventative medicine (Kratcoski and Pownall, 1989: 22).

Although the older inmates had more health problems, many of the staff members at Fort Worth were convinced that the older inmates were better adjusted to prison life. It was stated that, "older inmates take advantage of every program made available to them," and "do not require the strong authority figures that the young ones do." One administrator believed that the correction officers could become more effective if they were given specialized training on how to supervise older inmates. He stated, "Custodial [workers] normally don't tune in to the understanding phase of aging. They have to do a better job of simplifying rules and go the extra mile in discussing rules and why we're applying them to aged inmates."

Programs for Older Inmates in the Non-Specialized Institutions

Even if it is shown that special facilities or units are more desirable for older offenders, there is no guarantee that they will be housed in that manner. To date, few of the states have developed specialized facilities for older inmates. The larger majority of the state correctional systems and the U.S. Bureau of Prisons distribute the inmate population on the basis of security needs and regional consideration, rather than on the basis of age.

Most of the staff and administrators of the non-specialized facilities included in this study mentioned the positive effects of having older inmates intermixed with the younger inmates. It was stated that the older inmates tend to have a calming effect on the younger inmates with whom they are housed. Usually they adjust quite well. Even though they are not physically able to protect themselves from younger more aggressive inmates, they will develop a group of friends who will look after them.

It was pointed out by one unit manager working in a federal facility that "black older men have a positive influence on the younger black males. They are seen as father figures and are generally respected and protected. On the other hand, the same relationship does not exist for the white older inmates, who tend to stay by themselves and are ignored by the young white men." However, it was conceded that when mixed in with the younger inmates, there was more resistance by older inmates to participation in educational and physical activities. Even if they were required to attend school in cases in which they tested below the 8th grade level, they would tend to be passive and "just put in the time" (personal interview with unit manager).

The administrators and staff agreed that if predictions are true and a larger proportion of the future inmate population are older offenders, there will be a need for more staff, and it will put a drain on the resources of the facilities. In addition, the staff will need specialized training to work with this segment of the population. For example, a dentist working in a federal facility which houses approximately 150 inmates could affect the quality and the variety of dental work competed, since the older inmate will tend to have more dental needs and complex problems than the typical younger offender.

The administrators and staff at these facilities conceded that the health problems for the older inmates are generally more complex than those of the general population. They will show up at sick call more often, and it is hard to find meaningful work assignments for some of them who are in poor health. In order to prevent or retard health problems, the U.S. Bureau of Prisons has developed a commitment to facilitating health consciousness throughout the system. Most of the Bureau of Prisons administrators emphasize a holistic approach to positive health. Everything that happens in the institutions, including provision of appropriate living quarters, balanced nutritious meals, and anti-smoking campaigns, is designed to promote good health. The older inmates are encouraged, along with all others, to participate in recreational activities and become health conscious. If 10 to 15% of the population of a correctional facility is composed of older inmates, it is possible to develop special recreational, social and educational programs for the older inmates even though they are housed within the general population.

It was stated by several staff members employed in U.S. Bureau of Prisons institutions that inmates' health sometimes improves after they are institutionalized, because they receive proper diet and regular exercise. While this generalization appears to hold true for the older male inmates, it does not seem to be true for the older females. Since increased involvement in institutional activities may improve or at least maintain inmates' health, older inmates, both men and women, should be encouraged to participate in activities to the extent of their ability and should be rewarded for participating.

At one federal penitentiary an "Over 40" league was organized. Several softball teams were formed, and weight lifting competitions and handball and tennis matches were organized. The competitive nature of the events, along with being able to compete at one's own age level, resulted in a much larger participation than would normally be the case before the activities were restricted to a specified age group. The staff at this facility was also able to organize a pre-release program geared specifically to the needs of the older persons who will reenter the community.

The staff in one of the women's facilities indicated that it is difficult to get older women involved in educational, recreational, or health-oriented exercise programs. This may at least partially result from cultural conditioning which emphasizes passivity in women. Moreover, many of the women in these facilities had never been employed outside the home and were not planning on employment after release. One innovative recreation director addressed the older women's reluctance to become involved in activities by starting an experiential drama program. The woman were given hypothetical problems related to aging, family, and other common concerns to which they responded through drama and dance. This program had been successful in increasing the older women's involvement.

Summary

The research presented lends support to some of the arguments for creation of special institutions for older inmates, since they tend to have more needs than those housed in the other facilities. However, most correctional administrations believe that older inmates make the best adjustments when they are housed in the general population.

As long as older inmates continue to be housed in institutions with inmates of all ages, special programs must be developed to serve their needs. Most administrators believe it is best to keep the older inmates mixed in with the other younger inmates, since it is easier to administer the prison when such a policy is followed, but other administrators suggest that it may be best to house them in separate units or even separate facilities because of the great demands they put on the staff and resources. Thus, the positive effect of control enhancement is offset by the negative effect of drawing too much on the staff and resources. Regardless of whether administrators choose to build new facilities, assign special units of prisons for older offenders, or continue to keep them in the general population, health care for older offenders will continue to be a major concern, and the administrators of prisons will have to include provisions for more extensive health care services in their long-range planning.

Since providing adequate health care as mandated by law will become more and more expensive, it would appear that this is an area in which the contracting of services with the private sector could provide a partial solution to the problem.

References

Camp, G. M., and C. Graham Camp. 1989. *The Corrections Yearbook.* South Salem, NY: Criminal Justice Institute, pp. 30–31.

Federal Bureau of Prisons. 1987. "Unit Plan for Comprehensive Health Unit, Fort Worth, Texas." Washington, DC: U.S. Government Printing Office, September.

Fultz, L. 1989. "Older inmates in Maryland." Unpublished doctoral dissertation University of Maryland, College Park, MD.

Kratcoski, Peter C. 1990. "A Study of Older Inmates In Federal Correctional Facilities." Unpublished paper presented at the Annual Meeting of the American Society of Criminology, Baltimore.

Kratcoski, Peter C. and Susan Babb. 1990. "Adjustment of Older Inmates: An Analysis by Institutional Structure and Gender," *Contemporary Criminal Justice* 6(4) (December): 264–281.

Kratcoski, Peter C. and George Pownall. 1989." "Federal Bureau of Prison Programming for Older Inmates," *Federal Probation* 53(2) (June): 28–35.

Sabath, Michael J. and Ernest L. Cowles. 1988. "Factors Affecting the Adjustment of Elderly Inmates in Prison." In Belinda McCarthy and Robert Langworth (eds.), *Older Offenders.* New York: Praeger. pp. 178–196.

Vito, Gennaro F. and Deborah G. Wilson. 1985. "Forgotten People: Elderly Inmates," *Federal Probation* 49(1) (March): 18.

Section X

Correctional Treatment
Past, Present, and Future

Does correctional treatment have a future? The corrections field does not operate in a vacuum, and the various social, economic and political factors that are of importance for the entire country eventually will be manifested in the correctional sphere. Thus the increasing crime rates of the 1970s, which may have resulted from a wide variety of factors, were interpreted by many to be a direct outcome of the failure of correctional treatment, coddling of offenders, and too little emphasis on punishment. Politicians and correctional administrators were quick to realize that they were on safe ground with the general public if they took a "hard line" approach. They could back up their position with studies which seemed to prove that rehabilitative programs, in particular those operated in institutional settings, had not achieved the expected results. Consequently, the 1980s witnessed a greatly reduced commitment to rehabilitation and correctional treatment and an increased emphasis on punishment as a deterrent, which continued through the 1990s.

A careful examination of correctional treatment programs geared toward rehabilitation reveals that it is not possible to definitively state whether most of the programs were failures, successes, or neutral aspects of the correctional process. Most of the earlier treatment programs did not have research or evaluation components built into them. Programs of an experimental nature were initiated, completed, and discontinued without any evidence being gathered as to their effectiveness. As the various federal and state agencies funding these programs began to require evaluation reports, the evaluation was generally conducted by the agency directing the program or contracted with a research consulting firm. The findings were frequently open to question.

Interagency research on the effectiveness of programs seemed at first glance to be appropriate, since staff members had access to records and information that might be difficult for outside researchers to obtain. However, those given the responsibility of evaluating programs within agencies were usually not well versed in research methodology or program design techniques and not well qualified to make recommendations for further development or program changes. Administrators who had committed themselves to a certain treatment philosophy could successfully ignore findings contrary to their expectations about the success of the programs being conducted under their direction. Evaluations conducted by outside consulting firms also had their limitations. Consulting agency staff usually did not have direct experience or expertise in correctional treatment and were oversensitive to the direction given to them. The incentive to make the programs "look good" to please the agencies and therefore receive more contracts also came to bear in this evaluation approach.

In the 1990s, correctional planners and administrators began to turn to community-based treatment as an alternative to institutionalization. Economic considerations played an important part in this emerging trend. Prison overcrowding and lack of funds for building new facilities made placement of many offenders in the community a practical necessity. Despite this revitalization of community corrections, the number of inmates incarcerated in U.S. prisons reached an all-time high in the late 1990s and the prison population is not expected to decline until well into the new century.

Institutional Treatment and Programming

The concepts of treatment and rehabilitation have not been abandoned in U.S. prisons, but, as noted earlier in this book, the inmates' participation in the various treatment programs (with a few exceptions) is no longer mandatory. In the prison setting, rehabilitation activities emphasized today often are work or education related, since such programs have been shown to be the most conducive to preparing the inmates for successful adjustment in the community after release. Those directly involved in corrections, from the institutional administrators to the corrections officers, realize that the prison experience must include elements beyond punishment. Inactivity and boredom contribute strongly to prison disruptions. Thus, involvement of the inmates in some type of productive activity, such as prison industries or education programs, has benefits for both the system and the inmates.

Seiter (1990:12) described how federal prison industries (FPI) have provided productive work programs for the Federal Bureau of Prisons. He noted that the FPI operates much like a business, but "nevertheless, it is not 'in business' to maximize profits, but to fulfill its correctional mission of employing and training inmates." There are thousands of inmates employed in federal prison industries, and more than 250 products are manufactured in the various industries housed in the federal prisons located throughout the United States. The products include textiles (mattresses, clothing, sheets, towels), wooden furniture, metal lockers and seating, and complicated electronic equipment, such as data input systems. Prison industries are also found in the state prison systems. However, they generally are not as developed as those in the federal system, and they do not offer the number and variety of jobs present in the federal prisons. The scarcity of prison industry jobs and other work programs often leads to situations in which two or three persons may be give part-time work assignments for work that one person working full time could effectively handle (Silverman and Vega, 1996:397).

Providing educational opportunities for inmates has also received increased emphasis in the 1990s. Lillis (1994f) indicates that approximately 90 percent of the inmate population could benefit from some form of educational programming. Beck et al. (1993) found that almost half of the inmates surveyed participated in some type of educational program while they were imprisoned.

In any correctional institution, it is typical to find illiterate inmates. Even within the prison setting, this creates serious handicaps for them. Their illiteracy makes it difficult for them to complete forms or even read written rules and regulations, and their opportunities for meaningful employment are minimal. Some states and the U.S. Bureau of Prisons have instituted mandatory educational programs for the functionally illiterate.

In selection 36, "Mandatory Literacy," McCollum describes the Federal Bureau of Prisons' policy of mandatory literacy for inmates, which was established in 1982, with all inmates who read below a sixth grade level required to participate. The literacy standard was increased to the eighth grade level in 1986. The Crime Control Act of 1990 made this eighth grade literacy standard for inmates housed in the U.S. Bureau of Prisons institutions a legal standard.

Treatment in a Community Setting

In the introduction of this book, it was noted that the emphasis on community corrections and community treatment has increased in recent years, stimulated by the need to reduce the number of inmates housed in already crowded institutions. Such intermediate sanctions as shock incarceration (boot camps), electronic monitoring, drug courts, intensive probation supervision, day reporting centers and community treatment centers have been developed to retain some offenders in the community who otherwise would have been institutionalized. The intensified supervision needed for such offenders and the mandatory treatment they require for specific problems have created renewed interest in and expansion of community treatment and increased funding for such programs.

The halfway house movement, which began in the 1960s under the sponsorship of religious or public service groups and initially involved providing for the basic physical needs of homeless or alcoholic individuals, enjoyed a renaissance in the 1990s. Courts began to place offenders in halfway houses as a last resort before incarceration (halfway in); parole authorities allowed certain offenders to live in such settings before they were returned to the community and independent living (halfway out). As government agencies and private foundations offered grants for the development of such facilities to local communities, residential treatment began to emerge as the new hope for correctional treatment. The small-group setting characteristic of most residential treatment centers seemed to be ideally suited to using group treatment techniques, and new hope emerged for rehabilitative treatment in community settings. The lower cost of placing offenders in community treatment, compared to institutionalization, also had an appeal, and the possibilities for job placement or educational opportunities for offenders provided an added dimension.

Boot camps, a form of shock incarceration, have received considerable positive attention from the public, correctional policy makers and politicians. The strict military-style discipline used in these facilities has been regarded as likely to produce positive changes. These programs, which are typically located in the community or in a structure attached to a prison, are designed for short-term incarceration (3 to 6 months), and geared toward nonviolent youthful offenders. After release from the boot camps, the offenders are usually placed on probation or parole, or given some other type of community supervision.

Boot camps have been established for male and female offenders, and also for juvenile offenders. Typically, the programs include a number of military-like activities, such as marching, close order drill, and calisthenics, with strict discipline and formal interaction with staff members. The participants will normally be expected to have at least twelve hours of activity each day. For juveniles, a portion of this time is dedicated to schooling. For adults, much of the day is spent in work activities, with educational instruction and various forms counseling taking place during the late afternoon or early evening hours. MacKenzie and

Souryal (1994) reported that in 1992 boot camp programs for adults were being operated by 25 states and by the U.S. Bureau of Prisons. In some instances, potential participants are given the choice of attending a boot camp or serving a prison sentence. The positive rehabilitative effects of boot camps have not been demonstrated by empirical research. MacKenzie and her colleagues (1992) did not find evidence that shock incarceration resulted in reduced recidivism, and Gransky and her associates (1993) found that boot camp programs might provide more treatment than typical prisons, but there was little evidence that the participants had enhanced their education or employment skills as a result of the short-term boot camp experience.

Another popular form of community supervision, electronic monitoring, is used in most jurisdictions in conjunction with a variety of other treatment or supervision options. The leading candidates for electronic monitoring are low-risk offenders who have been placed on home detention or probation, but in some states electronic monitoring has been used with parolees. The number of individuals being supervised in this way is expected to increase as the equipment becomes more sophisticated and the cost of supplying and monitoring the equipment decreases. Electronic monitoring has been promoted as a means for reducing the cost of supervising nonviolent probationers or parolees and providing accurate information on their daily activities. The use of monitors has been criticized because their use places the emphasis of correctional activity on controlling the behavior of the offender rather than changing his/her attitudes and values or on developing new job skills or enhancing education, which might produce long-range solutions to the offender's problems. It has also been shown that after the monitoring is removed the offender is likely to revert to former behavior patterns. Nevertheless, the use of monitoring will continue and expand because other options, such as incarceration, are more expensive and may even be unavailable because of overcrowded conditions.

Gowen (1995), a U.S. probation officer, described how monitoring is applied in a federal probation district in Southern Mississippi. For these programs, the two types of probationers who are prime candidates for home confinement and electronic monitoring are substance abusers and offenders who have failed to comply with their probation conditions by not reporting to their supervising officers, not completing their assigned community service, or committing technical violations. After the first year of electronic monitoring, the outcome was viewed as positive, the program was expanded, and some higher-risk cases were added.

In selection 37, "Home Confinement: A '90s Approach to Community Supervision," Altman and Murray describe the duties of probation officers who supervise offenders placed on home confinement who are monitored with electronic devices. The benefits derived from this community corrections innovation are also discussed.

Role of the Correctional Counselor in Community Treatment

Correctional treatment personnel continue to serve many of their traditional functions in community treatment settings, but they are also called upon to assume new roles. One such role is that of "client advocate," not in terms of taking an offender's part in struggles against those in authority, but in terms of helping the client locate needed service and finding the means to obtain such services. As Shulman (1979) stated:

> . . . the very institutions set up to solve problems became so complex themselves that new problems were generated. Social, medical, and educational systems are difficult to negotiate, even for individuals who are well equipped to deal with them, never mind those with limited education and resources. The services established for people are often so complex that it is difficult for individuals to make use of them.

The treatment counselor, in addition to having training in various treatment techniques, is called upon to act as a "service broker," that is, the person who discovers and links those in need of specific services with the exact agency in the community that can provide those services most efficiently and effectively. Such activity presupposes a great deal of knowledge and well-developed contacts on the treatment counselor's part. The types of services in which the "service broker" must have connections would include psychological testing and treatment, social welfare, vocational rehabilitation, and educational testing and placement. Telling offenders where to seek help at the exact time when they are ready or willing to accept it may be the key activity a correctional treatment counselor performs. In all this coordination, the offender's contribution and efforts toward self-help and self-motivated change cannot be overlooked. Now that the emphasis appears to be on "justice," an offender who has received and accepted a just punishment for his or her misdeeds would also be able to expect a just and compassionate response to his efforts to secure treatment or assistance which, although no longer *required* or even regarded as a *right* of an adult offender, is available when sought in a sincere manner.

Privatization in Corrections

Given the current and likely to continue emphasis on incarceration and its deterrent effects, the prison population will continue to increase, and correctional services will also grow. Privatization of correctional services has been advanced as one way of dealing with this reality.

Privatization in corrections involves the use of the private sector to perform functions and services that formerly were handled by the correctional agencies themselves. Saxton (1988) noted four ways in which privatization has occurred in recent years. These include operation or management of prison industries by private firms, private financing of correctional construction, including lease-purchase agreements, total private sector operation of correctional facilities, or contracting for services such as medical treatment, food preparation or specialized treatment for offenders (pp. 16–17).

Ethridge and Marquart (1993), who examined the involvement of the private sector in the Texas correctional system, noted that correctional facilities administered by the private sector have smaller inmate populations than those administered by state correctional agencies and that the privately administered facilities are in a better position to prepare the inmates for reentry into the community upon release. While privatization of institutional operations may increase in the future, it is not likely to lead to a solution to the problems of overcrowding and lack of funds. However, privatization through community-based service offerings and residential center management is likely to grow in significance.

In selection 38, "Privatizing Discretion: 'Rehabilitating' Treatment in Community Corrections," Lucken observes that community correctional workers, including probation and parole officers, rarely provide the counseling and other treatment services that in the past were considered to be an integral part of their roles. Now, these services are provided by "resource brokers," who are employed by private agencies. This trend toward privatizing community corrections becomes evident when the types of contracts for treatment services local, state, and federal governments make with private agencies are reviewed. These include services for treatment of substance abusers, offenders with mental health problems, sex offenders, domestic violence counseling, life skills development, and vocational and educational counseling. The author notes that with this great dependence on private service providers the potential for abuse is always present. These providers are in a position to determine when the court-ordered treatment programs for the offender can be terminated, or if additional treatment is required. The profit motive may affect such decisions.

References

Beck, A., D. Gilliard, L. Greenfeld, C. Harlow, T. Hester, L. Jankowski, T. Snell, and J. Stephan. 1992. *Survey of State Prison Inmates, 1991.* Washington, DC: U.S. Department of Justice.

Ethridge, Philip A. and James P. Marquart. 1993. "Private Prisons in Texas: The New Penology for Profit," *Justice Quarterly,* 10 (1) (March):29–48.

Gransky, Laura A., Thomas C. Castellano, and Ernest L. Cowles. 1993. "Is There A 'New Generation' of Shock Incarceration Facilities?: The Evolving Nature of Goals, Program Components, and Drug Treatment Services," paper presented at the annual meeting of the Academy of Criminal Justice Sciences, Kansas City, KS: March 16–20.

Lillis, J. 1994. "Education in U.S. Prisons: Part Two." *Corrections Compendium,* 29 (3) (March): 10–16

Mackenzie, Doris, James W. Shaw, and Claire Souryal. 1992. "Characteristics Associated with Successful Adjustment to Supervision: A Comparison of Parolees, Probationers, Shock Participants, and Shock Dropouts," *Criminal Justice and Behavior,* 19 (December): 438–454.

Mackenzie, Doris and Claire Souryal. 1994. *Multisite Evaluation of Shock Incarceration.* Washington, DC: National Institute of Justice.

Saxton, Samuel F. 1988. "Contracting for Services: Different Facilities, Different Needs," *Corrections Today,* 40 (6) (October): 16–17.

Seiter, Richard P. 1990. "Federal Prison Industries: Meeting the Challenge of Growth," *Federal Prisons Journal,* 1 (3) (Spring): 11–15.

Shulman, Lawrence. 1979. *The Skills of Helping.* Itasca, IL: F. E. Peacock.

Silverman, Ira J. and Manuel Vega. 1996. *Corrections: A Comprehensive View.* Minneapolis/St. Paul: West.

35

Mandatory Literacy
Evaluating the Bureau of Prisons' Long-Standing Commitment

Sylvia G. McCollum

While education programs for inmates have always been a priority, the Federal Bureau of Prisons established its first mandatory literacy program for Federal prisoners in 1982. The program began modestly, with the 6th grade as the literacy standard and a mandatory enrollment period of 90 days. In 1986 the standard was increased to the 8th grade; the 90-day enrollment remained unchanged. In 1991, a high school diploma or its equivalent, the General Educational Development certificate or GED, was made the new literacy standard, and the required enrollment period was raised to 120 days to accommodate the anticipated longer time necessary to achieve the higher standard.

Several program-related conditions remained constant over the years, despite the changing standard:

- All promotions in institution-based and prison industry jobs above the entry level were contingent on meeting the literacy standard.

- All institutions were required to employ a special education instructor to work with students with special needs.

- Instructional materials were multimedia and computer-based wherever possible to assist the instructors, particularly in drill and practice.

- Most important, each institution's education department was

Source: *Federal Prisons Journal*, 3(2) (Fall 1992): 33–36.

required to establish incentive programs to motivate and recognize student accomplishments. (McCollum, 1989)

The impact of the mandatory program was almost immediate. Previously empty classrooms filled up. Students who had been diverted to institution or prison industry assignments were routed to education first, to meet their education requirements. The table below tells the story.

Literacy completions rose more than 700 percent during the period 1981–1990, compared with an increase of about 123 percent in the Bureau's average daily inmate population during the same period.

Adult Basic Education Program, 1981–1990*

Fiscal year	New enrollments	Completions	BOP avr. daily pop	Increase over prev. yr. Compl.	Pop.
1981	2,653	1,441	24,933	—	—
1982	3,785	1,983	27,730	37.6%	11.2%
1983	6,004	3,774	29,718	90.3	7.2
1984	6,896	4,909	30,723	30.1	3.4
1985	8,048	5,221	33,263	6.4	8.3
1986	9,000 est.	6,161	38,402	18.0	15.4
1987	n/a	n/a	41,838	n/a	8.9
1988	10,665	8,384	43,837	n/a	4.8
1989	11,380	10,138	47,804	20.9	9.0
1990	13,204	11,872	55,542	17.1	16.2
Increase '81–'90	**10,551**	**10,431**	**30,609**	**723.9%**	**122.8%**

*In 1991 the Bureau of Prisons adopted the GED as its literacy standard and revised its education data system to merge ABE and GED data. ABE enrollments are now reported only at the GED level.
Note: The Bureau established a new Education Data System in fiscal year 1987. Data for that year are not available.
Source: BOP internal data systems: Inmate Information System, Inmate Program Reporting System, and Education Data System.

Education and Recidivism

The question of whether prison programs, especially education, have any effect on repeat offenders is a continuing concern of correctional administrators. Correctional educators have frequently responded to the question by pointing to the value of education as a positive use of time that contributes to effective prison management. They have also suggested that postrelease outcomes should not be correlated with any one prison program or situation, that it was the total prison experience (as well as the families and communities to which prisoners returned, general economic conditions at the time of release, and the prevailing community attitude toward ex-offenders) that significantly contributed to postrelease success or failure. Pownall (1976), in a pioneering study of post-release success predictors, found that preincarceration employment was the best barometer by which to forecast postrelease employment and the capacity to stay out of prison.

Notwithstanding the precautions not to tie postrelease behavior to any single prison program—and the earlier studies that did not find a direct link between participation in prison education and post-incarceration behavior—a respectable number of studies have begun to connect education and positive postimprisonment outcomes.

Ryan (1990) defined the components of effective literacy programs for adult prisoners, then described several literacy programs in State and Federal prisons that showed positive outcomes. Reports from Canada (*Forum*, 1991) of an analysis of seven basic education programs among adult male inmates, including samples ranging from 75 to 3,000 men, showed a positive effect on recidivism. A Bureau of Prisons study (Saylor and Gaes, 1991) reported that inmates who worked in prison industries and who participated in vocational training "showed better adjustment, and were less likely to be revoked at the end of their first year back in the community, were more likely to be employed in the halfway house and community, and earned slightly more money than inmates who had similar background characteristics, but who did not participate in work and vocational training programs." Although more inmates in this study participated in work programs, the 15 percent of prisoners who completed vocational training were just as likely to succeed as their counterparts who worked in industries.

Beyond the basic literacy levels, several recent studies have suggested that advanced education also contributes to reduced recidivism. A New Mexico prison study (Fairchild, 1990) reported a 15-percent recidivism rate for prisoners who had completed one or more college courses, compared with a 68 percent rate for the general population. A Folsom Prison study (Fairchild, 1990) in the early 1980s reported zero recidivism for college graduates, compared with 55 percent for the general prison population within 3 years of release from Folsom. Still another study of a State prison, this time the Indiana Reformatory (Fairchild, 1990), reported that of the more than 200 prisoners who had earned a degree in a Ball State University extension program begun in 1976, none had returned to the Reformatory.

Another recent study (Wreford, 1990) traced State Prison of Southern Michigan prisoners who participated in a college program offered by the Jackson Community College from 1976 through 1986. The study concluded, "After taking into account the differences between released graduates and the criterion groups, the recidivism rates of the graduates (907) were significantly lower than those of both the national sample and the Michigan parolees."

The New GED Literacy Standard

The Bureau of Prisons' long-standing commitment to literacy is based on many factors, not least the hoped for postrelease success of individual offenders. However, quite independent of this consideration are the additional factors of the positive use of time while incarcerated and the impact of positive programming on a prison's internal climate. The average length of sentence served by Federal prisoners is rapidly approaching 10 years. As well, the increase in the number confined has led to severe crowding, which can contribute, in the absence of positive uses of time, to heightened levels of tension. Both staff and inmates alike suffer when idleness is excessive.

The quality of the inmate workforce available to provide institution services, including maintenance, and to work in prison industries, is also an important consideration. Illiterate workers who cannot read instructions, fill in job-related forms, prepare brief reports, or perform work-related math are unnecessary strains on correctional systems that are already carrying heavy resource burdens. The longer sentences served also raise significant questions about the appropriate use of inmate time. Can any correctional administrator justify the return of an illiterate person to the community after 10 years of incarceration?

It was against this background that the Bureau of Prisons began considering increasing its literacy standard from the 8th grade to high school equivalency. An interesting phenomenon developed as discussions progressed. GED enrollments, which were not yet mandatory, began to increase significantly, and the number of inmates who completed the courses and were ready to take the GED test also rose significantly. The table below provides an insight into this trend.

GED History, 1981–1982

	Average Daily Population			GED Tests	
Year	**Number**	**% inc. over prev. yr.**		**Number**	**% inc. over prev. yr.**
1981	24,933	—		2,395	—
1982	27,730	11.2%		2,676	11.7%
1983	29,718	7.2		2,772	3.6
1984	30,723	3.4		3,607	30.1
1985	33,263	8.3		3,672	1.8
1986	38,402	15.4		3,800	3.5
1987	41,838	8.9		4,264	12.2
1988	43,837	4.8		3,897	−8.6
1989	47,804	9.0		3,980	2.1
1990	55,542	16.2		6,426	61.5
1991	61,404	10.6		7,896	22.7
1992	67,226	9.5		8,222	4.3

Source: Inmate Information System and GED Testing Service.

The number of GED tests administered in 1990 increased more than 60 percent above the figure for 1989, despite the fact that the average daily population increased only 16 percent. There was no significant increase in the percentage of the incoming population that did not have a GED credential. The percentage had been around 50 percent during recent years and did not change during the time that GED enrollments and completions surged upward. Teachers and supervisors of education shared the opinion that the pending mandatory literacy requirement spurred the increases, as inmates rushed to meet the anticipated standards so that they could be eligible for promotions.

Promotions to jobs above the entry-level labor grade in the Federal system have been contingent on meeting a literacy standard since the inception of the mandatory literacy program in 1982. However, as long as the standard peaked at the 6th or 8th grade and did not include the GED, the evidence suggests that many students stayed in class only long enough to meet the requirement standard, and not a minute longer. Originally, some Bureau educators involved in the development of the mandatory literacy program speculated that there would be a dramatic increase in voluntary GED enrollments and completions as a result of the interest in education generated by the successful achievement of the 6th- or 8th-grade standard. This did not happen. Non-paid attendance in school did not compete well with paid employment.

Fiscal-year-end figures for 1991 revealed that the increase in the number of inmates who took the GED test leveled off, but the rate of increase, 22.7 percent over the number tested in FY 1990, was higher than the rate of increase for any of the preceding 5 years. It was also significantly higher than the 10.6 percent increase in the average daily population. Increases leveled off in 1992, when GED completions increased only 4.3 percent over the preceding year. The lower increase was attributable, in part, to greater emphasis placed on raising the pass/fail rate, which had dropped to 62.5 percent in 1991.

The Bureau has established a 70 percent pass rate as a national goal in 1993. Bureau educators anticipate a continued increase in the number of GED completions, but at a lower rate than in 1990 and 1991, since a greater emphasis will be placed on raising the pass rate.

It's the Law

The mandatory education requirement for Federal prisoners has now been adopted into Federal legislation. The Crime Control Act of 1990 includes a requirement that the Bureau of Prisons establish an 8th-grade mandatory literacy standard. The law also provides that the enrollments must be "for a mandatory period sufficient to provide the inmate with an adequate opportunity to achieve functional literacy, and appropriate incentives which lead to successful completion of such programs. . . ." The new law placed into Federal legislation a concept that had been adopted, through policy requirements, by the Bureau of Prisons as early as 1982. Significantly, during the 1991 legislative session there was considerable discussion in the U.S. Congress about legislation to support mandatory literacy standards in State prisons.

Another source of support for mandatory literacy has developed within the American Bar Association. The Corrections and Sentencing Committee of the ABA reviewed the question of mandatory literacy at considerable length during 1990 and 1991. There was some opposition to the mandatory literacy concept, particularly as it applied to adults, but a vote to support the concept, and a Model Act, carried at the committee's May 30, 1991, meeting. The Model Act provides, among other things, for a high school diploma or its equivalent, the GED, as the mandatory literacy standard in all State adult correctional institutions. Subsequently, at the ABA's 1991 annual meeting, the Criminal Justice Section Council approved the "Recommendations Concerning Mandatory Literacy Program for Adult Offenders"; the recommendations were approved by the ABA House of delegates in February 1992 and became official ABA policy. The Bureau of Prisons' literacy program, which had begun as a direct spinoff of Chief Justice Warren E. Burger's well-known "factories with fences" speech at the graduation ceremonies of the George Washington University Law School in 1981, has now been validated in Federal legislation and in the actions of the American Bar Association.

References

Fairchild, B. (1990), The cost savings in educating inmates. *Insight.* Illinois Department of Corrections. July, pp. 4–6.

Forum (V 3, N 1, 1991): *Education and recidivism.* Correctional Services of Canada.

Saylor, W. G., and Gaes, G. G. (1991), *PREP study links UNICOR work experience with successful post-release outcome.* Office of Research and Evaluation, Federal Bureau of Prisons, Washington, DC.

McCollum, S. G. (1989), Mandatory literacy for prisons. In S. Duguid (ed.), *Correctional Education Yearbook* (pp. 121–128). Burnaby, British Columbia, Canada: Simon Fraser University.

Pownall, G. A. (1969), *Employment problems of released offenders* (Final Report 81–19–37). Washington, DC: Manpower Administration, U.S. Department of Labor.

Ryan, T. A. (1990), *Effects of literacy training on reintegration of offenders.* Presented at Freedom to Read: An International Conference on Literacy in Corrections, Ottawa, Ontario, Canada.

U.S. Congress. Public Law 101–647, 101st Congress—Crime Control Act of 1990.

Wreford, P. (1990), *Community college prison program graduation and recidivism.* University Microfilms International, Ann Arbor, Michigan.

36

Home Confinement
A '90s Approach to Community Supervision

Robert N. Altman
Robert E. Murray

It's three o'clock in the morning and an officer's pager is beeping. After several beeps the officer rolls over in bed and looks at the clock. Bleary eyed, she reads the screen on the little black box that has totally changed her life. She already knows without looking that it's an alert for one of the offenders on her caseload. Someone left home without permission or tampered with the ankle bracelet with transmitter that he or she is wearing. "This better be something really serious," the officer mutters to herself as she dials the monitoring center, trying not to wake her husband. But he's gotten so used to these calls that he doesn't even stir when the pager begins to beep.

The alert could be caused by something as simple as a power failure from a disconnected power cord or a telephone outage from a storm. At three in the morning the officer hopes it is something simple so she can get back to sleep. As the telephone rings in the monitoring center, for some unimaginable reason the officer remembers the movie *It's a Wonderful Life*, where Clarence the angel tells Jimmy Stewart that every time a bell rings an angel gets his wings. In her sleep-deprived daze the officer thinks that in her case every time the pager beeps another offender has tried his wings and "flown the coop!"

If you don't know why this officer was called in the middle of the night,

Source: *Federal Probation*, 61(1) (March 1997): 30–32.

you have missed the newest "innovation" in community corrections, home confinement. In a profession that has few avenues for creativity and where so-called innovations seem to be recycled every 10 or 20 years, developing technology has recently paved the way for a cost-saving alternative to detention and incarceration. In growing numbers courts are imposing terms of home confinement where a person is ordered to remain in his or her residence for any portion of the day. Home confinement may range from a simple nighttime curfew to actual "lock-down" home incarceration. The preferred approach is to use electronic equipment to monitor home confinement although other methods also are used.

Although many states use home confinement primarily as a method to reduce jail and prison overcrowding, federal courts use home confinement as a sentencing alternative to punish offenders without incarceration. For pretrial defendants home confinement is not a punishment, but a method to assure that they will make future court appearances and to reduce the risk that these individuals may pose to the community. It is an alternative to detention for those defendants who would otherwise be detained if home confinement were not available as a release alternative.

The federal courts use a single contractor who provides electronic monitoring equipment to more than 300 sites across the country including Hawaii, Guam, the Virgin Islands, and Puerto Rico. The contractor maintains a national monitoring center that receives signals from the monitoring equipment in each participant's residence. Officers are contacted each time one of the following "key events" occurs: unauthorized absences from the residence; failure to return to the residence from a scheduled absence; late arrivals; early departures from the residence; equipment malfunctions; tampering with the monitoring equipment; loss of electrical power or telephone service; location verification failure (where a participant moves the monitoring equipment from the residence without permission); and when the monitoring equipment misses a randomly scheduled call to the monitoring center.

The home confinement officer's field work centers on three main activities: selecting participants for the program, physically placing participants in home confinement ("hooking up" or installing the electronic equipment), and supervising participants following the hookup. Officers conduct selection investigations, visiting each potential participant at home to determine if the person qualifies for home confinement. They hook up participants and conduct frequent home visits to interview household members and physically check the equipment for signs of tampering. The hooking up process is an important time for educating participants and any other household members about how home confinement works. The officer explains the rules and structure of the program in detail and addresses any questions and hypothetical situations the participant raises. The officer may discuss how the electronic equipment works and its range of operation. The officer also discusses the participant's weekly schedule of activities, What the participant needs to do to comply with the program, and what is expected of the participant as far as his or her performance on home confinement.

Once the electronic equipment is installed, the next stage in home confinement supervision begins. To ensure that the participant complies with the terms of his or her release, officers must make field contacts to verify the participant's whereabouts. For every participant on the officer's caseload, there are a multitude of reasons to be away from the residence, each of which is subject to verification by the officer. Working, treatment sessions, religious services, medical appointments, urine testing, school, or meeting with attorneys constitute the majority of allowable out-of-residence activities.

To verify a participant's location away from the residence, officers often use a small, portable monitoring unit to pick up the radio signals generated by the participant's ankle bracelet. The officer merely drives to where the participant is scheduled to be and waits for the receiver to pick up the transmitter's signal. A code number appears on the receiver's screen and identifies the participant. Officers have picked up transmitter signals in high-rise buildings from as far away as 41 floors. They can verify that participants are at the jobsite, at the doctor's office, or in school without leaving their cars, entering buildings, or meeting participants. This small piece of technology protects the officer from entering dangerous areas, allows the participant to work without the intrusion of the officer's visit, and enables the officer to verify more offenders in one day than if face-to-face contact were required in each instance. Sometimes, however, meeting with the participant—or being observed by that person—is the most effective means of verification. Face-to-face encounters let participants know that their activities are being watched and that they should remain on their schedule in approved locations.

Home confinement is a demanding sentence for the participant as well as the home confinement officer. Home confinement affects not only the participant but household members as well. For some participants it is the first time that they have scheduled any portion of their lives. They must have permission to go to the doctor, see their attorney, or even go to the grocery store. Many must ask others to do their shopping, pick up the laundry, or take the children to school. Some participants are unable to attend family events or even to leave their residence to pick up the mail or wash the car.

Home confinement officers' responsibilities are different than those of their colleagues. Home confinement supervision is labor intensive. In essence, officers are "on call" 24 hours a day, 7 days a week because they must respond anytime there is a potential violation. The work is demanding: alerts average 10 per officer per day in the federal program, many after normal work hours. Nationally, this is an average of nearly 34,000 alerts per month. Officers also process an average of 12,500 routine schedule changes and install or remove an average of 1,500 monitoring units each month.

Sometimes it is not even the participant who is the cause for the middle-of-the-night phone call. Electrical storms in the southeast, wind storms in the northwest, snow storms in the winter all can wreak havoc on the electrical power system. If a participant loses electricity, the officer who supervises that individual can expect two telephone calls from the contractor's monitoring center—one call to let the officer know the power is out and another to let the officer know that it has been restored. Multiply that event times the number of participants on the officer's caseload, and the night's sleep may shorten considerably. Moreover, the officer's spouse loses sleep because of the calls.

Home confinement officers also must know more detail about the persons they supervise. While most officers have a broad knowledge of offender and defendant activities, home confinement officers must know specifically where the participant is supposed to be and when. For instance, they must know where the participant's work-site is hour by hour, the exact time and place of the participant's Alcoholics Anonymous meeting, and the route that the participant will take to and from work. They are "gatekeepers" of a sort, supervising participants who are only allowed to leave their homes to pursue activities narrowly defined by the court. Another important difference is that home confinement officers must deal with events immediately. They must investigate and resolve any deviation from the program set for the participant since the participant is, in effect, "incarcerated" at home. A good support person—one who is a stickler for details—can be an enormous help to the home confinement officer in gathering and relaying information, handling offender inquiries, contacting the monitoring center, and making the many phone calls required to keep track of offenders. Having help with these tasks allows officers to focus on verifying offender whereabouts and activities.

Home confinement is a cost-effective alternative to jail and prison for many defendants and offenders who do not need to be locked up. While it is a new tool for officers to use to control and guide behavior, it is not the solution for criminal activity. Even though preliminary statistics about the federal home confinement program from the Administrative Office of the United States Courts indicate that less than 10 percent of the persons placed in the program are terminated unsuccessfully and that less than 2 percent commit new crimes while in home confinement, home confinement will not stop someone who wants to commit a crime from doing so. Home confinement will provide the court with more information with which to tailor a sentence for the needs of the person and the community and additional supervision tools for officers.

Home confinement also provides a significant cost savings for the government. In fiscal year 1996 (according to the Administrative Office), if home confinement did not exist, more than 8,000 offenders would have been in prison or halfway houses and more than 5,000 defendants would have been detained in detention centers or halfway houses. The resulting annualized cost to the government and the savings from the use of home confinement would have been at least:

Cost of Incarceration:	$42 to $61 million (depending on the level of incarceration)
Cost of Home Confinement:	$19 million
Cost Savings:	$23 to $42 million
Cost of Detention:	$27 to $41 million (depending on the type of detention facility)
Cost of Home Confinement:	$12 million
Cost Savings:	$15 to $29 million
Total Cost Savings:	$38 to $70 million (depending on the level of incarceration or the type of detention facility)

The officer who was awakened in the middle of the night was able to go back to sleep. After an hour of calls to the participant's residence, she learned that he had been unable to sleep so he wandered out into the back yard and did not hear the monitoring center's telephone call. He wandered back in as the officer's call came in. He won't wander so far the next time.

The 3 a.m. calls almost seem worthwhile when an officer hears good things about the home confinement program. For example, one officer who was visiting a school to verify a participant's presence in class was thanked by the school administrator. The administrator said she was surprised that anyone actually cared where the participant might be after he was sentenced and allowed to remain in the community. To the officer, this was validation that home confinement, with the proper level of accountability, can satisfy the public's sense of justice. It is a program that promotes participant accountability, enhances public safety, builds tax burdens into taxpayers, and offers an alternative to costly prison confinement.

37

Privatizing Discretion
"Rehabilitating" Treatment in Community Corrections

Karol Lucken

Introduction

The private sector has maintained a long yet uneven presence in punishment that dates back to the seventeenth-century practice of transportation. Feeley (1991) characterizes the history of private sector involvement in punishment as one in which entrepreneurs have willingly responded to the needs of the state in times of crisis. Thus, it is not surprising that in the past decade this centuries-old tradition has been vigorously renewed and expanded, ultimately forming what Lilly and Knepper (1993) term a "corrections-commercial complex" (see also Lilly and Deflem 1996). Drawing parallels to the military industrial complex, Lilly and Knepper argue that an "iron triangle" or "subgovernment" has developed in the area of punishment. A major implication of this development is that the private sector has now assumed a permanent rather than an intermittent presence in punishment.

Private sector involvement in contemporary punishment extends not only to the supply of correctional goods and services (e.g., health care, food, education, technology/equipment) but also to the operation of correctional facilities and community-based programs. The most deliberated, although hardly the most widespread, form of involvement has been private sector operation of prisons. As of 1996, private prisons

Source: *Crime and Delinquency*, 43(3) (July 1997): 243–59, copyright © 1997 by Sage Publications, Inc. Reprinted by permission of Sage Publications, Inc.

housed only 2% of the nation's incarcerated (Thomas 1996), yet a vast body of literature has debated their effectiveness, morality, and constitutionality (Borna 1986; Bowditch and Everett 1987; Chambers 1993; Cikins 1986; Cody and Bennett 1987; Dunham 1986; Field 1987; Gentry 1986; Johnson and Ross 1990; Logan 1990, 1992; Logan and Rausch 1985; McDonald 1994; Mullen 1985; Porter 1990; Robbins 1987; Roberts and Powers 1985; Savas 1987; Shichor 1993; Thomas 1991; Woolley 1985). In this regard, the literature often has been critical, citing the potential of privatization to add (hidden) costs, eliminate inmate services and protections, and, most notably, unduly influence imprisonment policy (Bowditch and Everett 1987; Dunham 1986; Durham 1994; Field 1987; Gentry 1986; Mason 1994; Porter 1990; Robbins 1987). However, the judgments rendered thus far have been more speculative than empirical. Consequently, the corrections privatization debate in general has centered on normative issues related to privatized prisons (Lilly and Knepper 1993).

Noticeably missing from the privatization debate is discussion of community corrections. This omission becomes more glaring when one considers that the community alternatives movement was made possible in large part by the private sector (Cohen 1985; Curran 1988; Lerman 1984; Scull 1977). To date, only a small body of literature has been devoted exclusively to community corrections and the private sector. That literature has addressed private sector involvement in juvenile services (Curran 1988), adult probation (Lindquist 1980), and electronic monitoring (Lilly 1992; Lilly and Ball 1993). However, the morality or constitutionality of this involvement rarely is the focus of this literature. For example, Lindquist (1980) limits his argument to the effectiveness of the private sector in administering misdemeanor probation. Lilly (1992) and Lilly and Ball (1993) propose only that electronic monitoring will avoid the label of "fad" often ascribed to other penal reforms because of the private sector's intimate involvement in this particular strategy. Although Curran (1988) raises constitutional issues relevant to private operation of community-based juvenile facilities, his coverage of these issues is decidedly brief.

Indeed, von Hirsch (1990) observes that community sanctions traditionally are overlooked in the dialogue on ethics and punishment. Because of their apparent humaneness relative to incarcerative sanctions, they are not viewed as punitive or intrusive and therefore are assessed only in terms of their effectiveness. However, in a "new penology" that locates community sanctions in the context of a custodial continuum (Feeley and Simon 1992), ethics in community corrections is a topic deserving of increased attention (von Hirsch 1990). The growth of the private sector and the absence of guidelines in this sphere of punishment only reaffirm the need for greater scrutiny (see von Hirsch, Wasik, and Greene 1989; Morris and Tonry 1990; Tonry 1994).

This article responds to this need as well as to the need for more thorough understanding of the dimensions of correctional privatization. Specifically, it examines the role of the private sector in providing mandated counseling services to offenders under community supervision. This role is examined through a qualitative study of the operations of several private treatment agencies in a Florida jurisdiction. The ethical problems posed by this trend are raised through concrete examples of privatization's effects on both offenders and the control system. Consequently, the findings of this study tend empirical support to the body of literature questioning privatization efforts. The article concludes with discussion of policy recommendations to establish more principled treatment sanctioning in the community.

Studying Private Offender Treatment in Community Corrections

Unlike prison privatization, a coherent and comprehensive picture of private offender treatment in community corrections is lacking. National data on privatization in community corrections and/or the use of private sector contracts have not been compiled systematically. The collection of these data has been hampered by two factors in particular, namely the variation in the organizational structures of community corrections programs and varying reporting practices. The administration of probation programs differs across and even within states, with some agencies being highly centralized (state agency based), others localized (county agency based), and still others under the judicial or executive branches of government. This fact alone makes tracking this trend difficult. But it is also the case that detailed reporting of private sector contracts is not always mandated, and what is reported often is buried within other budgetary categories (personal correspondence with National Institute of Corrections, September 1996). Determining the scope of the offender treatment industry is equally problematic because accurate directories of offender treatment providers are not available (personal correspondence with National Resource Center for Batterers Intervention, Florida Statewide Coalition for Domestic Violence, Safer Society Foundation Clearinghouse for Sex Offender Programs, September 1996; see also Ewick 1993). Furthermore, because offender treatment programs are relatively unregulated, the number of certifications or licenses issued cannot be used to measure growth (personal correspondence with Florida Department of Business and Professional Regulation). To capture this latest privatization trend, then, the current study relies on fragments of national, state, and local information.

The information presented is derived from a variety of sources including various observational techniques, interviews, and documents. One form of observation refers to the author's tenure as a county (misdemeanor) probation officer in a major metropolitan jurisdiction in Florida between 1989 and 1991. This position involved extensive interaction with several substance abuse and domestic violence treatment agencies in the course of monitoring offender compliance with program conditions and attending treatment agency orientations and seminars. Subsequent to this position, the author continued to consult with former probation coworkers regarding the latest developments in offender treatment and attended a statewide treatment provider conference in 1994. In 1996, in this same jurisdiction, the author engaged in a more direct form of observation by volunteering to serve as a cotherapist in a sex offender treatment program. The author participated in two different risk-level classes each week for nine months. These various observational experiences provided insight into private treatment agency operations—including the vernacular, techniques, and rationales—that otherwise would be difficult to obtain.

In 1995, interviews also were conducted with a state-contracted treatment vendor, 15 state (felony) probation officers (across three major metropolitan jurisdictions), and 6 correctional officials (i.e., state director of adult program services, district and circuit managers, probation supervisors) with the Florida Department of Corrections. The interview questions were broadly based but aimed at uncovering the relationship between community corrections and private treatment agencies. The questions also served the purpose of confirming the insights obtained through the various forms of observation. Questions were asked about (1) the type of offender services provided, (2) the typical treatment conditions imposed by the penal system and private agencies, (3) the purpose of the community corrections/treatment agency alliance, and (4) the probation officer and offender perceptions of private treatment agency services.

Documents consisted of reports compiled by the Florida Department of Corrections. These reports indicated what the private agencies were, the nature of their services, the number of contracted offenders referred to these agencies, and the funds allocated to these agencies by the Department of Corrections. Documents were also obtained from 10 treatment agencies that serve offender populations in the areas of substance abuse, domestic violence, sexual deviance, anger management, impulse control, and driving (e.g., nonalcohol related such as driving on a suspended license or reckless driving). These documents outlined the structures and fee schedules of the various programs. Documents also were obtained from the Safer Society Foundation (a nonprofit clearinghouse on sex offender programs), the U.S. Department of Health and Human Services, and the American Probation and Parole Association (APPA). Together, these sources provide an incomplete but instructive look at this rapidly developing trend in community corrections.

Rehabilitating Offenders: "Punishment and Profit"

Although the involvement of private organizations with offenders predates the twentieth century, the formal rehabilitation of offenders traditionally has been viewed as the responsibility of the government sector (Curran 1988). Thus, for much of the twentieth century, the task of rehabilitating offenders officially has fallen on the state (and its probation/parole officers). As Simon (1993) argues, until the 1970s, the real work of intervention fell on parole agents. Through various social casework methods and close relationships with the offenders, it was presumed that reformation would occur. Rothman (1980) similarly notes that the function of probation/parole agents was to exert a rehabilitative influence. Using their own professional capacities, these agents were to design a supervision regimen that addressed the various individual needs of offenders. The Progressive vision of probation/parole was essentially a marriage of government and social science, above and apart from private power in the community (Simon 1993, p. 57).

Going Private

In the past decade, private treatment agencies have increasingly taken over the task of rehabilitating offenders. In an overburdened penal environment, treatment agencies can assist the state by providing intermediate sanction options, ensuring that offender needs are being met, and relieving probation officer role confusion (APPA 1994; Florida Department of Corrections 1995b). Probation officers claim they now provide commonsense counseling, monitor compliance with conditions, and leave the therapeutic function to the "experts" (interview data; see also Lovell 1985).

Given the frequency with which community-sanctioned offenders are court ordered for treatment evaluations, private treatment agencies have emerged as an essential partner in the supervision process. This partnership is becoming more formalized through a series of contracts between community corrections and private treatment agencies. The federal correctional system and the states of Texas and Florida have contracted with private substance abuse and mental health agencies for services such as sex offense, domestic violence, anger management, life skills, substance abuse, and vocational/educational counseling (Beto 1987; Jensen 1987). The APPA has called on intensive supervision programs nationwide to do the same (APPA 1994). Consequently, offender treatment services are proliferating even though rehabilitation no longer serves as the primary justification for punishment (Allen 1981; Feeley and Simon 1992).

Rehabilitation as Punishment

The renewed emphasis on treatment, however, is not inconsistent with the prevailing punitive penal norms. Compulsory treatment provides a second layer of supervision that, in effect, blurs the distinction between restriction and rehabilitation. In addition to the punishment conditions set forth by the state, treatment agencies are free to impose their own program conditions to bring about change in offenders' attitudes and behaviors. Offenders are required to attend weekly and, at times, biweekly treatment sessions and also can be ordered to attend support groups (e.g., Alcoholics Anonymous, Narcotics Anonymous). Additional conditions can include submitting to polygraph, urinalysis, and/or testosterone-level tests; completing homework assignments and paying additional fees for tardiness; failing to complete homework; and attending a weekly treatment session. At the request of a treatment agency counselor, offenders also can be referred for placement in a second treatment program. For example, a substance abuse agency can recommend a referral to an anger management program. An offender's progress or lack of progress in a program is routinely documented in reports submitted to the judge and/or probation officer, with dismissal from the program resulting in a violation of the community sanction (participant observation data). A violation, at a minimum, results in a return to court; at a maximum, it results in a return to jail or prison if convicted of the violation (Blomberg and Lucken 1994).

Rehabilitation for Profit

Offender treatment as a profitable enterprise can be illustrated in part by its growth. The National Drug and Alcohol and Treatment Unit Survey reports that the number of substance abuse providers alone has grown by 50% between 1980 and 1992 (U.S. Department of Health and Human Services 1995). Between 1992 and 1994, the number of community-based sex offender programs also has increased from an estimated 1,142 to 1,475, an increase of 23% (data from Safer Society Foundation 1996 database). The generic offender treatment program, Moral Reconation Therapy,[1] has been sold by Correctional Counseling, Inc. to correctional systems in 21 states (Bureau of Justice Assistance 1994; Little, Robinson, and Burnette 1994). As of 1996, 79 agencies were identified as providing domestic violence (batterer intervention) programs in

144 locations in Florida alone. Non-Secure Programs, Inc., formerly Keeton Corrections, operates programs throughout the southeastern portion of the United States. The Bridge, which began as a local offender treatment program in 1981, expanded to include four additional sites throughout Florida, becoming Bridges of America, Inc. by 1994. In 1996, Bridges of America expanded its operations to include Egypt, Russia, England, and France. Some offender treatment agencies have even assumed corporate images, at least in name: Correctional Counseling, Inc.; No Abuse, Inc.; Human Services Associates, Inc.; CARE, Inc.; Mental Health Services, Inc.; Non-Secure Programs, Inc.; Life Stream Behavioral Center, Inc.; Professional Therapy Center, Inc.; New Beginnings, Inc.; Colonial Counseling, Inc.; Osceola Mental Health, Inc.; Family Therapy, Inc.; Prevention Projects, Inc.; First Step, Inc.; Bridges of America, Inc.; We Care, Inc. (Florida Department of Corrections 1995b).

To understand fully the recent outbreak in offender treatment services, one must look beyond the fiscal crisis of the state and the advancement of the behavioral sciences and also include recent changes in insurance-subsidized treatment. Between 1987 and 1992, insurance benefits for drug abuse, alcoholism, and mental health increased dramatically, forcing private providers to limit reimbursements to reduce their overall costs (U.S. Department of Health and Human Services 1992). In right of research questioning the effectiveness of expensive hospital-based treatment over less expensive outpatient treatment, coverage policies have moved away from the former and toward the latter model (U.S. Department of Health and Human Services 1992). Consequently, the business of treating privately insured, middle-class, self-referred addicts has become less lucrative. As more shorter term outpatient programs have developed, public dollars for largely indigent state referred addicts serving time in the community have become a viable source of supplemental funding (interview data for treatment provider).

The benefits of public/correctional funding are illustrated by the case of Florida. In 1995, the Florida Department of Corrections dispersed approximately $25 million to 65 contracted mental health and substance abuse providers (personal correspondence with director of state programs, November 1996). In addition to monies received through state contracts, which pay for indigent offenders, private agencies also are funded through court-ordered self-paying offenders. In Florida, self-paying offenders constitute approximately 20 percent of all referred felony offenders (personal correspondence with corrections regional program administrator, November 1996) and all referred misdemeanor offenders.

The table that follows illustrates in greater detail the potential profitability of offender treatment. The table identifies the various fees associated with the most common treatment programs and the duration of these programs. The information contained in the table was derived from 10 offender treatment agencies serving county and state probation departments in a tricounty metropolitan jurisdiction in Florida. However, the fee amounts and types and program duration for substance abuse, domestic violence, and sexual offender programs are representative of programs nationally (personal correspondence with treatment providers, November 1994, December 1996).

The table also reports on the major offender programs of anger management and impulse control (for shoplifting, bad checks, or theft in general) as well as those for sex offenders, substance abusers, and domestic violence offenders. The standard program fee types include evaluation, treatment, and miscellaneous (drug/alcohol tests). Each figure listed under the "evaluation fees" heading reflects the cost of a single evaluation to determine whether an offender should be referred for treatment. Each figure listed under the "treatment fees" heading reflects the total cost of treatment per offender for the minimum amount of time that can be spent in treatment. For example, the anger management and impulse control programs employ a one-time flat-rate fee of $40 for eight hours. If extended anger management treatment is recommended, then an additional fee ranging, between $10 and $20 is imposed for 23 additional hours of programming. Based on a sliding scale, sex offender treatment costs between $780 and $2,082 for the typical minimum of two years of treatment and between $3,900 and $10,400 for the typical maximum of five years. The cost of substance abuse treatment varies with the intensity of the programming. Domestic violence treatment,

Offender Treatment Costs

Service	Evaluation Fees (dollars)	Treatment Fees (dollars)	Miscellaneous Fees (dollars)	Program Duration
Mental Health	150			
Anger management	No fee	40		8 hours
Extended anger				
management	No fee	10–20		23 hours
Impulse control	No fee	40		8 hours
Sex offense	45–75	780–2,080 (2 years)		2–5 years[a]
		3,900–10,400 (5 years)		
Polygraphs on request			100	
Substance abuse	25 / 40			
Outpatient				
Basic		300		12 weeks
Semi-intensive		900 / 940–1,272		12 weeks[a]
Intensive		1,500		16 weeks[a]
				24 weeks[a]
Drug/alcohol test				
on request			15 / 30	
Domestic violence	25	520–1,430		26 weeks[a]
Alcohol test on request			5	

a. Treatment can extend beyond this duration if deemed appropriate by the treatment provider.

also based on a sliding scale, ranges between $520 and $1,430 for the typical minimum duration of 26 weeks.

The various compensation figures associated with offender treatment (e.g., state funding for indigents, direct offender payments) leave little doubt that, for therapeutic entrepreneurs, crime pays. Operational overhead is, in the words of one treatment provider, "bare bones" or "modest at best." Office staff and expenses can be "minimal" (an agency can consist of one or two people), with the actual physical structure or meeting places frequently located in outdoor trailers, publicly funded buildings (e.g., police departments), or the office of a provider's already existing private counseling practice (e.g., private psychiatrists, psychologists) (participant observation data). Yet, the ethical question that arises with regard to compensation is not simply the legitimacy of the fee types and amounts imposed; rather, the question is the degree to which offender treatment decisions are made with profit considerations in mind. More broadly, does concern for the accumulation of profits and "customers" intrude on the administration of punishment?

Ethical Implications

Moral opposition to privatized offender treatment may well pale in comparison to that of privatized prisons. With the former, monetary gains are derived from helping in the community rather than from suffering in confinement. However, regardless of *where* punishment is administered, there is cause for concern when profit-motivated actors control definitions of who should be punished and the type or degree of punishment received. Thomas (1991), an advocate of privatization, concedes that "any such control, of course, would create the possibility for an abuse of the punishment process in the service of profit" (p. 32).

Ewick's (1993) "commodification of social control" concept provides a framework for understanding how the private sector can acquire varying levels of control in the punishment process. Although Ewick employs this concept in reference to a treatment industry targeting willing and law-abiding customers (diet centers), several analogies can be made to the treatment industry in question. The unifying theme is that commodification, in the realm of informal or formal social control, is a process that spawns new and variegated forms of power. It is in the realm of formal social control, however, that commodification must be viewed with greatest skepticism.

Commodification represents a process of exchange between profit-seeking vendors and consumers; private treatment agencies sell offender services to a state in need of offender control and discipline. Ewick (1993) notes that one of the distinguishing features of this process is its capacity to expand categories of deviance. She reasons that once control becomes commodified, the behaviors and conditions defined as deviant inevitably become broader and more inclusive. The profitability of social control breeds competition, which, in turn, influences the politics of demand. The following statement made by a treatment provider illustrates this point nicely: "Everyone is throwing their hat in the ring; it [offender treatment] is a pipeline to money."

Although not expanding categories of deviance, the commodification of offender treatment has expanded the range of illegal behaviors that presumably can be normalized through program intervention. To remain competitive, treatment agencies have diversified their services, providing exceedingly specialized offender programs. In addition to substance abuse, domestic violence, and sexual deviance, it is now possible to "treat" bad driving (e.g., offenders charged with non-alcohol-related infractions), bad money management (e.g., offenders charged with fraudulent check writing), bad parenting (e.g., any offenders deemed appropriate), bad tempers (e.g., offenders charged with assault or battery), and impulsive behavior (e.g., offenders charged with shoplifting). In one Florida district, 200 contracts were awarded to 11 agencies, with each of the contracts representing a different service provided (interview data).

To sustain and accelerate treatment demand, agencies advertise offender services through participation in criminal justice practitioner conferences, courtroom representation, and mass circulation of promotional pamphlets (participant observation data). The implicit and often explicit message is one of reducing recidivism and ensuring public safety. One driving program claims it can "break through the hard attitudes of today's youth" and produce "fast results." Data supporting this claim are not provided; however, claims of customer satisfaction (e.g., parent testimonials) are. Treatment agencies' regard for the quality and/or effectiveness of their services, however, remains in question. For example, one agency offered an overnight crash course in anger management at a "special" (higher) rate (interview data). Applications for substance abuse providers for a drug court in Georgia reveal a similar "quality control" problem, namely treatment agencies that are unable to furnish evaluation strategies, mission/goal statements or objectives, professional licenses, board of directors lists, reimbursement and audit information, and records documenting their experience (Givens 1996).

A second distinguishing feature of the commodification process is the intent of providers to prevent customers from exiting the market (Ewick 1993). Gradations of deviance and intervention, coupled with thorough and subjective screening mechanisms, ensure that no one is refused on the grounds that he or she is well or "normal." Consequently, offender treatment programs are scaled by varying degrees of need and risk to facilitate both entry and retention in the programs. Outpatient basic, semi-intensive, and intensive substance abuse tracks address all levels of addiction, both real and potential. For example, misdemeanants have been referred to substance abuse treatment because evaluations reveal they smoke too much, purportedly an indicator of addictive behavior in general (participant observation and interview data). To detect signs of abnormality, substance abuse evaluations probe all aspects of one's life, past and present, sexual practices included (Blomberg and Lucken 1994). Similarly, if a basic anger management program is deemed insufficient, then an offender can be referred to the extended anger management program. On this treatment continuum, then, an offender can move up or down but not out until judged ready by the treatment provider. Readiness can be determined by any combination of factors including tardiness in sessions, promptness in making payments, or disclosure of one's offense to a specified number of individuals (participant observation data and treatment agency documents).

Under these discretionary arrangements, even perfect compliance with all program rules, requirements, and urinalysis testing does not guarantee release. Offenders can be detained for being uncommunicative, an indicator of being "in denial," which in turn serves as an indicator of likeliness to reoffend (participant observation and interview data). One substance abuse agency counselor confided that quotas may be set to ensure a certain percentage of a treatment class will be referred for additional treatment, regardless of need. Accordingly, the specification of treatment duration in program orientation materials often is open-ended and ambiguous. Common phrasing includes "a minimum of 12 weeks," "over a period greater than three months," "over a period usually greater than 24 weeks," "extra groups may be required if progress is insufficient," and "approximately two to five years."

Data on felony offenders referred for evaluations across the state of Florida also illustrate the "trappings" of privatized treatment. Of the 36,226 state community-supervised offenders referred to contracted mental health or substance abuse service providers for evaluations in 1995, only 10 were released on the grounds that treatment was not needed (personal communication with state director of adult programs, November 1996).[2] Although it is true that many offenders have treatment needs, the number of offenders referred and then retained for treatment on admission to community supervision (36,216) appears disproportionate to the number of offenders admitted to community supervision who are generally designated as "in need" by the correctional system. For example, Florida operates a drug offender probation program for any offenders identified as problem substance abusers. In 1995, there were only 4,605 new admissions to this program. Sex offenders also represent a class of offenders uniformly referred for evaluation and treatment. Yet, in 1995, only 2,651 sex offenders were admitted to community supervision (Florida Department of Corrections 1995a). Domestic violence offenders, who also are uniformly referred for evaluations, are least likely to be included in the overall figure of 36,216 because they typically are supervised at the misdemeanant level.

To determine what constitutes acceptable levels of imposition by the private sector, privatization advocate Thomas (1991) provides guidance when he argues that the private sector should not control definitions of who is to be punished or the type or degree of punishment received. Although the precise interpretation of this statement is open, it would appear that the private sector's involvement in administering offender treatment has pushed these boundaries. As both the inventors and the administrators of screening/evaluation devices and treatment service types, treatment agencies in effect control definitions of who is to be punished or treated. Through the rights of expert opinion and discretion, they also control the frequency, intensity, and duration of program participation and, therefore, the type or degree of punishment or treatment received. Ultimately, these "controls" have the very real potential of impacting an offender's status on probation because probation officers and judges tend to defer to such expert opinions (Blomberg and Lucken 1994; Lovell 1985; interview and participant observation data).

The assumption that the private sector is more interested in "doing well" than "doing good" (Robbins 1987) is at the heart of much of the controversy surrounding privatization. The present study suggests that this assumption is not entirely without empirical foundation. Furthermore, the consequences associated with this conflict of interest often are aggravated by the justice system's interest in "doing something" rather than "doing nothing." For example, it is (politically) safer to have an offender in treatment in the event that the offender recidivates while under supervision (interview data). The simultaneous need to "do well" and "do something" places offenders in a somewhat precarious position. They must convince others of their normality to avoid treatment and of their reformation to avoid prolonged treatment, even though reasonable demonstrations of reformation may not lead to release from treatment (participant observation data).

Policy Implications

The experience of private treatment agencies in community corrections does give cause for concern and further investigation. Certain elements of this experience may even evoke images once attributed to an "authoritarian state in a white-coated therapeutic disguise" (Duff and Garland 1994, p. 281). It was such an image of rehabilitation that contributed to the adoption of "just deserts" policies nearly two decades ago. Ironically, however, it was the penal crisis resulting from these policies that gave rise to rehabilitation in its current privatized form. Consequently, the abuse of discretion that is part of the history of rehabilitation also has been resurrected by a more suspect authority.

Despite the defects of private offender treatment, however, abolishment is neither warranted nor likely. At a minimum, private treatment enhances rehabilitative opportunities, control, and intermediate sanction options. Subsequently, it may prevent or prolong rearrests and/or returns to custody. However, the potential or promise of positive outcomes should not prevent jurisdictions from being cautious when embracing the offerings of the private sector. Given the questions of efficacy that have long surrounded rehabilitation (treatment) (Gendreau and Andrews 1990; Logan and Gaes 1993; Martinson 1974) and the unfair practices that can and do occur in the name of rehabilitation, there certainly is room for reform.

In light of the findings presented here, reform in offender treatment could take a number of directions. They include regulation, evaluation, and reconceptualizing rehabilitation as a right (Rotman 1994). Given the general absence of regulation, licensing, and scientific evaluation, accountability has been lacking. Consequently, the private sector has developed an assortment of offender treatment programs whose content and outcomes have yet to be tested.

A more radical step in taming the indulgences of the private sector involves a reconceptualization of rehabilitation. To avoid the pitfalls of rehabilitation's past record, Rotman (1994) proposes that it be redefined as a right or an opportunity extended by the state. Using this definition, treatment becomes a form of help that is voluntary, not a form of help that is coercive. Interchangeable punishments (sanction exchange rates) and/or accountability levels (rewards and incentives), as proposed by Morris and Tonry (1990), provide a means by which this philosophy can be translated into practice. For example, offenders who do not participate in treatment can be given an equally punitive but different punishment condition (e.g., 200 hours of community service). To conceive of rehabilitation as an option available through a system of interchangeable punishments takes into account the needs of offenders as well as the needs of the state.

Conclusions

Logan and Rausch (1985) have argued that private contracting of some form seems assured of a future in corrections. This article has examined a lesser known but proliferating form, namely offender rehabilitation, and argued that ethics in community corrections matters. Specifically, private sector involvement in the administration of offender treatment has resulted in commodified social control and, therefore, intrusions on the punishment process. Although many of the findings provided reflect the practices of treatment agencies within a particular jurisdiction, the fact that these agencies maintain statewide and national affiliations suggests that these same practices would be replicated elsewhere. Nevertheless, it is proposed that offender treatment services not be abandoned but rather be implemented in a way that does not compromise the integrity of community-based sanctioning. Careful regulation and evaluation and optionalizing of rehabilitation are recommended as ways in which to achieve that integrity.

Notes

[1] "Reconation" is a term employed by the creators of this treatment program. It is intended to reflect the principles of both rehabilitation and reckoning.

[2] The figure of 36,216 does not include self-paid referrals. The Department of Corrections does not collect treatment referral data on non-contract-status offenders.

References

Allen, F. A. 1981. *The Decline of the Rehabilitative Ideal.* New Haven, CT: Yale University Press.

American Probation and Parole Association. 1994. *Restructuring Intensive Supervision Programs: Applying What Works.* Lexington, KY: American Probation and Parole Association.

Beto, Dan Richard. 1987. "Contracting for Services." *Texas Probation* (July).

Blomberg, Thomas and Karol Lucken. 1994. "Stacking the Deck by Piling Up Sanctions." *Howard Journal* 33:62–80.

Borna, Shaleen. 1986. "Free Enterprise Goes to Prison." *British Journal of Criminology* 26:321–34.

Bowditch, Christine and Ronald S. Everett. 1987. "Private Prisons: Problems Within the Solution." *Justice Quarterly* 4:441–53.

Bureau of Justice Assistance. 1994. *State and Local Programs: Focus on What Works.* Vol. 1. Washington, DC: U.S. Department of Justice, Office of Justice Programs.

Chambers, Marcia. 1993. "The Term Prison Industry Now Means Business." *National Law Journal* 25:17–19.

Cikins, Warren I. 1986. "Privatization of the American Prison System: An Idea Whose Time Has Come?" *Journal of Law and Ethics and Policy* 2:445–64.

Cody, W. J. Michael and Andy Bennett. 1987. "The Privatization of Correctional Institutions: The Tennessee Experiment." *Vanderbilt Law Review* 40:829–49.

Cohen, Stanley. 1985. *Visions of Social Control.* Cambridge, England: Polity.

Curran, Daniel J. 1988. "Destructuring, Privatization and the Promise of Juvenile Diversion: Compromising Community-Based Corrections." *Crime &*

Delinquency 34:363–78.

Duff, Antony and David Garland. 1994. "Preface: E. Rotman's Beyond Punishment." Pp. 281–83 in *A Reader on Punishment,* edited by A. Duff and D. Garland. New York: Oxford University Press.

Dunham, Douglas W. 1986. "Inmates' Rights and the Privatization of Prisons." *Columbia Law Review* 86:1475–504.

Durham, Alexis M. 1994. "The Future of Correctional Privatization: Lessons From the Past." Pp. 33–49 in *Privatizing Correctional Institutions,* edited by G. W. Bowman, S. Hakim, and P. Seidenstat. New Brunswick. NJ: Transaction Publishers.

Ewick, Patricia. 1993. "Corporate Cures: The Commodification of Social Control." *Studies in Law, Politics, and Society* 13:137–57.

Feeley, Malcolm. 1991. "The Privatization of Prisons in Historical Perspective." *Criminal Justice Research Bulletin* 6:1–10.

Feeley, Malcolm and Jonathan Simon. 1992. "The New Penology." *Criminology* 30:449–74.

Field, Joseph. 1987. "Making Prisons Private: An Improper Delegation of a Government Power." *Hofstra Law Review* 15:649–751.

Florida Department of Corrections. 1995a. *1994–1995 Annual Report,* Tallahassee: Florida Department of Corrections.

_____. 1995b. *Probation and Parole Services: Community-Based Treatment Programs.* Tallahassee: Florida Department of Corrections.

Gendreau, P. and D. A. Andrews. 1990. "Tertiary Prevention: What the Meta-Analysis of the Offender Treatment Literature Tells Us About 'What Works'". *Canadian Journal of Criminology* 32:173–84.

Gentry, James T. 1986. "The Panopticon Revisited: The Problem of Monitoring Private Prisons." *Yale Law Journal* 96:353–75.

Givens, Eugene. 1996. *Fulton County Diversionary Drug Court: Treatment Network Development.* Sudbury, MA: Advocates for Human Potential.

Jensen, Christy. 1987. *Contracting for Community Corrections Services.* Washington, DC: National Institute of Corrections.

Johnson, Byron R. and Paul P. Ross. 1990. "The Privatization of Correctional Management: A Review." *Journal of Criminal Justice* 18:351–58.

Lerman, Paul. 1984. "Child Welfare, the Private Sector, and Community-Based Corrections." *Crime & Delinquency* 30:5–38.

Lilly, Robert J. 1992. "Selling Justice: Electronic Monitoring and the Security Industry." *Justice Quarterly* 3:493–504.

Lilly, Robert J. and Richard A. Ball. 1993. "Selling Justice: Will Electronic Monitoring Last?" *Northern Kentucky Law Review* 20:505–30.

Lilly, Robert J. and Matthieu Deflem. 1996. "Profit and Penality: An Analysis of the Corrections Commercial Complex." *Crime & Delinquency* 42:3–20.

Lilly, Robert J. and Paul Knepper. 1993. "The Corrections-Commercial Complex." *Crime & Delinquency* 39:150–66.

Lindquist, Charles A. 1980. "The Private Sector in Corrections: Contracting Probation Services From Community Organizations." *Federal Probation* 44:58–63.

Little, Gregory, Kenneth Robinson, and Katherine Burnette. 1994. *Cognitive Behavioral Treatment Review and CCI News.* Vol. 3, Nos. 2–3. Memphis, TN: Correctional Counseling, Inc.

Logan, Charles H. 1990. *Private Prisons: Cons and Pros.* New York: Oxford University Press.

_____. 1992. "Well Kept Company: The Quality of Confinement in Private and Public Prisons." *Journal of Criminal Law and Criminology* 83:577–613.

Logan, Charles H. and Gerald G. Gaes. 1993. "Meta-Analysis and the Rehabilitation of Punishment." *Justice Quarterly* 10:245–63.

Logan, Charles and Sharla P. Rausch. 1985. "Punish and Profit: The Emergence of Private Enterprise Prisons." *Justice Quarterly* 2:303–18.

Lovell, David G. 1985. *Sentencing Reform and the Treatment of Offenders.* Olympia: Washington Council on Crime and Delinquency.

Martinson, Robert. 1974. "What Works? Questions and Answers About Prison Reform." *The Public Interest* 35:22–54.

Mason, Todd. 1994. "For Profit Jails: A Risky Business." Pp. 163–74 in *Privatizing Correctional Institutions,* edited by G. W. Bowman, S. Hakim, and P. Seidenstat. New Brunswick, NJ: Transaction Publishers.

McDonald, D. 1994. "Public Imprisonment by Private Means." *British Journal of Criminology* 34:29–48.

Morris, Norval and Michael Tonry. 1990. *Between Prison and Probation.* Oxford, England: Oxford University Press.

Mullen, J. 1985. "Corrections and the Private Sector." *The Prison Journal* 65:1–13.

Porter, Robert G. 1990. "The Privatization of Prisons in the U.S.: A Policy That Britain Should Not Emulate." *Howard Journal* 29:65–81.

Robbins, Ira. 1987. "Privatization of Corrections: Defining the Issues." *Vanderbilt Law Review* 40:813–28.

Roberts, A. R. and G. T. Powers. 1985. "The Privatization of Corrections: Methodological Issues and Dilemmas Involved in Evaluative Research." *The Prison Journal* 65:95–107.

Rothman, David, 1980. *Conscience and Convenience.* Boston: Little, Brown.

Rotman, E. 1994. "Beyond Punishment." Pp. 284–305 in *A Reader on Punishment,* edited by A. Duff and D. Garland. New York: Oxford University Press.

Savas, Emmanuel S. 1987. "Privatization and Prisons." *Vanderbilt Law Review* 40:88–89.

Scull, Andrew. 1977. *Decarceration: Community Treatment and the Deviant.* Englewood Cliffs, NJ: Prentice Hall.

Shichor, David. 1993. "The Corporate Context of Private Prisons." *Crime, Law, and Social Change* 20:113–18.

Simon, Jonathan. 1993. *Poor Discipline: Parole and the Social Control of the Underclass,* 1890–1990. Chicago: University of Chicago Press.

Thomas, Charles. 1991. "Prisoner's Rights and Corrections Privatization." *Business and Professional Ethics Journal* 10:3–45.

_____. 1996. *Private Adult Correctional Facility Census.* 9th ed. Gainesville: University of Florida, Center for Studies in Crime and Law.

Tonry, Michael. 1994. "Proportionality, Parsimony, and Interchangeability of Punishment." Pp. 136–59 in *A Reader on Punishment,* edited by A. Duff and D. Garland. New York: Oxford University Press.

U.S. Department of Health and Human Services. 1992. *Drug Abuse Research Series: Extent and Adequacy of Insurance Coverage for Substance Abuse Services-Institute of Medicine Report.* Vol. 1. Washington, DC: U.S. Department of Health and Human Services.

_____. 1995. *Overview of the National Drug and Alcoholism Treatment Unit Survey (NDATUS): 1993 and 1980–1992*. Washington, DC: U.S. Department of Health and Human Services.

von Hirsch, Andrew. 1990. "The Ethics of Community-Based Corrections." *Crime & Delinquency* 36:162–73.

von Hirsch, Andrew, Martin Wasik, and Judith Greene. 1989. "Punishments in the Community and the Principles of Desert." *Rutgers Law Journal* 20:595–618.

Woolley, Mary R. 1985. "Prisons for Profit." *Dickinson Law Review* 90:30–31.